ONLINE RESOURCES

IMPORTANT.

HERE IS YOUR REGISTRATION CODE TO ACCESS
YOUR PREMIUM McGRAW-HILL ONLINE RESOURCES.

For key premium online resources you need THIS CODE to gain access. Once the code is entered, you will be able to use the Web resources for the length of your course.

If your course is using **WebCT** or **Blackboard**, you'll be able to use this code to access the McGraw-Hill content within your instructor's online course.

Access is provided if you have purchased a new book. If the registration code is missing from this book, the registration screen on our Website, and within your WebCT or Blackboard course, will tell you how to obtain your new code.

Registering for McGraw-Hill Online Resources

TO gain access to your McGraw-Hill web resources simply follow the steps below:

1. USE YOUR WEB BROWSER TO GO TO: **www.mhhe.com/pattersonwtp5**
2. CLICK ON **FIRST TIME USER**.
3. ENTER THE REGISTRATION CODE* PRINTED ON THE TEAR-OFF BOOKMARK ON THE RIGHT.
4. AFTER YOU HAVE ENTERED YOUR REGISTRATION CODE, CLICK **REGISTER**.
5. FOLLOW THE INSTRUCTIONS TO SET-UP YOUR PERSONAL UserID AND PASSWORD.
6. WRITE YOUR UserID AND PASSWORD DOWN FOR FUTURE REFERENCE. KEEP IT IN A SAFE PLACE.

TO GAIN ACCESS to the McGraw-Hill content in your instructor's WebCT or Blackboard course simply log in to the course with the UserID and Password provided by your instructor. Enter the registration code exactly as it appears in the box to the right when prompted by the system. You will only need to use the code the first time you click on McGraw-Hill content.

Thank you, and welcome to your McGraw-Hill online Resources!

Higher Education

0-07-292353-9 T/A PATTERSON: WE THE PEOPLE, 5E

REGISTRATION CODE

2GQL-6UV2-QAZD-G3MG-6IUG

D0332108

eople

JCTION TO
OLITICS

TION

omas E. Patterson

essor of Government and the Press
Kennedy School of Government
Harvard University

ton Burr Ridge, IL Dubuque, IA Madison, WI New York
ancisco St. Louis Bangkok Bogotá Caracas Kuala Lumpur
on London Madrid Mexico City Milan Montreal New Delhi
Santiago Seoul Singapore Sydney Taipei Toronto

Higher Education

WE THE PEOPLE: A CONCISE INTRODUCTION TO AMER
FIFTH EDITION

Published by McGraw-Hill, a business unit of The McGraw-Hill Com
of the Americas, New York, NY 10020. Copyright © 2004, 2002, 2000
Companies, Inc. All rights reserved. Previous editions © 1998, 1995 by
All rights reserved. No part of this publication may be reproduced or dis
by any means, or stored in a database or retrieval system, without the pri
The McGraw-Hill Companies, Inc., including, but not limited to, in any
electronic storage or transmission, or broadcast for distance learning.

Some ancillaries, including electronic and print components, may not be a
outside the United States.

This book is printed on acid-free paper.

2 3 4 5 6 7 8 9 0 VNH/VNH 0 9 8 7 6 5 4 3

ISBN 0-07-281733-X

Vice president and editor-in-chief: *Thalia Dorwick*
Publisher: *Lyn Uhl*
Senior sponsoring editor: *Monica Eckman*
Editorial coordinator: *Angela W. Kao*
Developmental editor: *Kristen Mellitt*
Marketing manager: *Katherine Bates*
Senior project manager: *Marilyn Rothenberger*
Manager, New book production: *Sandra Hahn*
Production supervisor: *Enboge Chong*
Senior media technology producer: *Sean Crowley*
Manager, Design: *Laurie Entringer*
Cover/interior designer: *Mary Kazak*
Cover image: © *Getty Images/ Jake Rajs*
Director, Art : *Jeanne M. Schreiber*
Manager, Art: *Robin Mouat*
Manager, Photo research: *Brian J. Pecko*
Photo research coordinator: *Alexandra Ambrose*
Photo researcher: *Connie Gardner*
Senior supplement producer: *David A. Welsh*
Compositor: *GAC–Indianapolis*
Typeface: *10.5/13 Janson*
Printer: *Von Hoffmann Press*

The credits section for this book begins on page C-1 and is considered an extension of the
copyright page.

Library of Congress Cataloging-in-Publication Data

Patterson, Thomas E.
    We the people : a concise introduction to American politics / Thomas E. Patterson.--5ᵗʰ
    p. cm.
    Includes bibliographical references and index.
    ISBN 0-07-281733-X (alk. paper)
     1. United States--Politics and government.   I. Title.

JK274.P36 2004
320.473--dc21

                                                                      20030487

www.mhhe.com

To My Children,
Alex and Leigh

About the Author

Thomas E. Patterson is Benjamin Bradlee Professor of Government and the Press in the John F. Kennedy School of Government at Harvard University. He was previously Distinguished Professor of Political Science in the Maxwell School of Citizenship at Syracuse University. Raised in a small Minnesota town near the Iowa and South Dakota borders, he was educated at South Dakota State University and the University of Minnesota, where he received his Ph.D. in 1971.

He is the author of seven books and dozens of articles, which focus primarily on the media and elections. His most recent book, *The Vanishing Voter* (2002), describes and explains the long-term decline in Americans' electoral participation. An earlier book, *Out of Order* (1994), received national attention when President Clinton said every politician and journalist should be required to read it. In 2002, *Out of Order* received the American Political Science Association's Graber Award for the best book of the past decade in political communication. Another of Patterson's books, *The Mass Media Election* (1980), received a *Choice* award as Outstanding Academic Book, 1980–1981. Patterson's first book, *The Unseeing Eye* (1976), was selected by the American Association for Public Opinion Research as one of the fifty most influential books of the past half century in the field of public opinion.

His research has been funded by major grants from the National Science Foundation, the Markle Foundation, the Smith-Richardson Foundation, the Ford Foundation, and the Pew Charitable Trusts.

Contents

CHAPTER THREE

FEDERALISM: FORGING A NATION   68

CHAPTER FOUR

CIVIL LIBERTIES: PROTECTING INDIVIDUAL RIGHTS   101

CHAPTER FIVE
EQUAL RIGHTS: STRUGGLING TOWARD FAIRNESS   137

CHAPTER SIX

PUBLIC OPINION AND POLITICAL SOCIALIZATION: SHAPING THE PEOPLE'S VOICE

CHAPTER SEVEN

POLITICAL PARTICIPATION AND VOTING: EXPRESSING THE POPULAR WILL

CHAPTER EIGHT

POLITICAL PARTIES, CANDIDATES, AND CAMPAIGNS: DEFINING THE VOTER'S CHOICE   231

CHAPTER NINE

INTEREST GROUPS: ORGANIZING FOR INFLUENCE   269

CHAPTER TEN

THE NEWS MEDIA: COMMUNICATING POLITICAL IMAGES   300

CHAPTER ELEVEN

CONGRESS: BALANCING NATIONAL GOALS AND LOCAL INTERESTS   325

CHAPTER TWELVE
THE PRESIDENCY: LEADING THE NATION   365

CHAPTER THIRTEEN
THE FEDERAL BUREAUCRACY: ADMINISTERING THE GOVERNMENT   405

CHAPTER FOURTEEN
THE JUDICIARY: APPLYING THE LAW   438

CHAPTER FIFTEEN
ECONOMIC AND ENVIRONMENTAL POLICY:
CONTRIBUTING TO PROSPERITY   471

PREFACE

The late twentieth century has been a period of extraordinary change in America, which has raised new challenges to the practice of government. New people in the millions from Asia and Latin America have joined the American community, bringing with them cultural traditions that have made our society richer and fuller but also more fragmented and contentious. Traditional institutions, from political parties to families, have weakened dramatically, straining the fabric of our politics but also creating the possibility of adaptive new arrangements. Minorities and women, long denied access to political and economic power, are seeking a fairer share, and sometimes getting it. America's workers and firms have built a highly productive economy but are now facing the risks and opportunities of the global marketplace. The cold war that dominated our attention in foreign policy for decades has been replaced by international terrorism and localized conflicts that raise troubling new issues of domestic and world insecurity, as the September 11, 2001, attacks on the World Trade Center and the Pentagon so tragically revealed.

Scholars are striving to keep pace with these changes. Never before has scholarship been so closely tied to the real world. If much of what political scientists study is arcane, we have increasingly tried to connect our work and our thinking to the everyday realities of politics. The result is a fuller understanding of how American government operates. I have tried in this book to convey this advancement in knowledge in an accurate and interesting way.

REACHING OUT TO THE STUDENT

Anyone who writes an introductory American government text faces the challenge of describing and explaining a vast amount of scholarship. One way is to pile fact upon fact and list upon list. It's a common enough approach but it turns politics into a pretty dry subject. Politics doesn't have to be dry, and it certainly doesn't have to be dull. Politics has all the elements of drama and the added feature of affecting the everyday lives of real people.

This is a narrative-based text. It is the opposite of a text that piles list upon list and that divides its material into narrow compartments. A narrative text provides plenty of information, but it is always part of a larger discussion that is wrapped in "story" form.

Research indicates that the narrative style is a superior method for teaching students a "soft" science such as political science. They learn more readily because a narrative makes the subject more readable, more accessible, and more compelling. Studies also indicate that students can read attentively for a longer period of time when a text is narrative in form.

A narrative text weaves together theory, information, and examples in order to bring out key facts and ideas. The goal is to draw the students into the subject, give them a contextual understanding of major concepts and issues, and encourage them to think about the implications for themselves and society. To quicken this process, I begin each chapter by telling a story that addresses a basic issue. The chapter on civil liberties, for example, begins with the case of the Creighton family, whose home was raided in the middle of the night by gun-toting FBI agents who believed that the Creightons were harboring a relative who was suspected of bank robbery. The suspect was not found, and the Creightons, who were badly frightened by the intrusion, sued the FBI for wrongful search. Did the FBI have sufficient cause for a warrantless search? Or did the FBI violate the Creightons' constitutional rights? Where should society draw the line between its public safety needs and the rights of the individual? Such questions in the context of a real-life situation immediately plunge students into the chapter's subject and into the process of thinking about its importance.

This approach is part of a second pedagogical goal of this text: helping students to think critically. Critical thinking is, I believe, the most important skill that a student can acquire from a social science education. Students do not learn to think critically by engaging in rote memorization. They acquire the skill by reflecting on what they read, by resolving challenges to their customary ways of thinking, and by confronting difficult issues. To this end, I have attempted to structure the discussion in ways that ask students to think more deeply and systematically about politics. In the first chapter, for example, I discuss the inexact meanings, conflicting implications, and unfilled promise of Americans' most cherished ideals, including liberty and equality. The discussion includes the "Chinese Exclusion," a grotesque and not-well-known chapter in our history that should lead students to think what it means to be an American.

Finally, I have attempted in this book to present American government through the analytical lens of political science but in a way that captures the vivid world of real-life politics. I regularly reminded myself while writing this book that only a tiny percentage of introductory students are interested in an academic political science career. Most of them take the course because it is required or because they enjoy politics. I have sought to write a book that will kindle political interest in the first type of student and deepen interest in the second type, while also giving them the systematic knowledge that a science of politics can provide. I had a model in mind for the kind of book that could achieve these goals. It was V. O. Key's absorbing *Politics, Parties, and Pressure Groups,* which I had read many years earlier as an undergraduate student. The late Professor Key was a masterful scholar who had a deep love of politics and who gently chided colleagues whose interest in political science was confined to the "science" part.

Few scholars can match Key's brilliance, but most political scientists share his fascination with politics. The result of their combined efforts is a body of knowledge about American government that is both precise and politically astute. This scholarship gives the text its unifying core. Political scientists have identified several major tendencies in the American political system that are a basis for a systematic understanding of how it operates, namely:

- Enduring ideals that are the basis of Americans' political identity and culture and that are a source of many of their beliefs, aspirations, and conflicts
- Extreme fragmentation of governing authority that is based on an elaborate system of checks and balances, which serves to protect against abuses of political power but also makes it difficult for political majorities to assert power when confronting an entrenched or intense political minority
- Many competing groups, which are a result of the nation's great size, population diversity, and economic complexity and which, separately, have considerable power over narrow areas of public policy
- Strong emphasis on individual rights, which results in substantial benefits to the individual and places substantial restrictions on majorities
- Preference for the marketplace as a means of allocating resources, which has the effect of placing many economic issues beyond the reach of popular majorities

These tendencies are introduced in the first chapter and discussed frequently in subsequent chapters. If students forget many of the points made in this book, they may at least take away from the course a knowledge of the deep underpinnings of the American political system.

CHANGES FOR THIS EDITION

A noteworthy change from previous editions is a heightened emphasis on liberty, equality, and self-government as the three great principles of

American democracy. The origin and nature of these ideals are discussed in the first chapter, which also points out the tension that can exist among them. Subsequent chapters have boxes entitled "Liberty, Equality, and Self-Government" that ask students to grapple with issues related to these principles. New to this edition, these boxes help students to recognize just how thoroughly these principles are embedded in American political practice and thought.

These boxes and the other boxed features in the text are based on the same instructional philosophy that guided earlier editions. The boxes are not mere fillers or diversions. They are not meant to entertain in the way that some texts use titillating or trivial material to distract a student's attention. These boxes are part of a broad pedagogical strategy of heightening students' interest in politics. Once interest is generated, students naturally want to learn more about a subject and derive enjoyment through studying it.

In addition to the "Liberty, Equality, and Self-Government" boxes, each chapter has a "How the United States Compares" box and a "States in the Nation" box. The United States in many ways has the world's preeminent democracy, but it also has distinctive policies and practices. The American states, too, are quite different in their politics and policies, despite belonging to the same union. American students invariably gain a deeper understanding of their own communities when they recognize the ways in which their nation or state differs from others.

There is much that is new in the body of the text. The chapters have been thoroughly updated to include the latest scholarship and the most recent developments at home and abroad. The most substantial changes relate to the war on terrorism, but there are many other changes as well, including the 2002 elections and the 2003 Iraq war. The role of the Internet in American politics continues to feature prominently in the text's instructional content. Each chapter includes a World Wide Web icon (identified by a globe within which "WWW" appears). The icon refers to supplementary material (self-quizzes, simulations, and graphics) on the text's website.

I also emphasize developments that are a remembered part of students' lives. For most of them, Vietnam is ancient history, and the fall of the Berlin Wall is, at best, a distant memory. Students need to know about, and learn from, these events. But they sometimes learn more when asked to think deeply about events they believe they already thoroughly know. For example, many students have not thought carefully about how the War on Terrorism might affect the liberties they now take for granted.

A novel feature of *We the People* is its selected readings; each chapter is followed by a reading that develops a major point of the chapter. These

readings are intended to deepen the student's understanding of American
politics and to add flexibility to the instructor's use of the material. For an
instructor who prefers to supplement the course text with a book of readings, this text offers both. On the other hand, the instructor who wants to
limit reading assignments to the text itself can simply skip the end-of-
chapter readings or recommend them as optional items for students who
have the time and interest. The readings are contemporary ones. All come
from *The New York Times*, the result of an exclusive relationship between
the *Times* and McGraw-Hill.

YOUR SUGGESTIONS ARE INVITED

We the People has now been in use in college classrooms for more than a
decade. During that time, the text (including its full-length version, *The
American Democracy*) has been adopted at more than five hundred colleges
and universities. I am very grateful to all who have used it. I am particularly
indebted to the many instructors and students over the years who have sent
me suggestions or corrections. You can contact me at the John F. Kennedy
School of Government, Harvard University, Cambridge, MA 02138 or by
e-mail: thomas_patterson@harvard.edu

Thomas E. Patterson

SUPPLEMENTS PACKAGE

This text is accompanied by supplementary materials. Please contact your
local McGraw-Hill representative or McGraw-Hill Customer Service
(800-338-3987) for details concerning policies, prices, and availability, as
some restrictions may apply.

For Students and Instructors

OnLine Learning Center with PowerWeb
   Visit our website at www.mhhe.com/pattersonwtp5
This website contains separate instructor and student areas. The instructor
area contains the content of the Instructor's Resource CD-ROM, while the
student area hosts a wealth of study materials such as additional Internet
resources, concept lists, practice quizzes, essay questions, and thinking exercises. All chapter-by-chapter material has been updated for the new edition, and favorites such as the crossword puzzles, flashcards, video and
audio indexes, and simulations have been retained.

New assets at this site also include:

- Participation suggestions dealing with constitutional foundations, institutions, political behavior, and policy. These suggestions were created to encourage students to become more involved in politics, to demonstrate how they can make a difference, and to give them advice on how to get started.
- Updated simulations accompanied by abstracts and learning goals.

Political Science Supersite
For additional simulations, web links, games, puzzles, and more, visit the Political Science Supersite at www.mhhe.com/socscience/polisci

PowerWeb for American Government
Now built into the *We the People* Online Learning Center, this product offers daily news updates, weekly course updates, interactive activities, the best articles from the popular press, quizzing, instructor's manuals, student study material, and more.

For Students

Study Guide
0-07-281736-4
  by Willoughby Jarrell of Kennesaw State University
Each chapter includes the following: learning objectives, focus and main points (to help direct students' attention to key material), chapter summary, major concepts (listed and defined), annotated Internet resources, analytical thinking exercises, and test review questions—approximately 10 true/false, 15 multiple-choice, and 5 essay topics. The answers are provided at the end of each chapter.

2002 Midterm Election Update
0-07-281031-9
  by Richard Semiatin of American University
This 26-page supplement details the 2002 election in which the Republican party gained outright control of the U.S. Senate, acquired additional seats in the House, and increased their majority of governorships in the nation. Richard Semiatin analyzes the roller-coaster context of the election, the role of the Bush administration, and remarkable developments such as the last-minute withdrawal of Bob Torricelli from the New Jersey Senate race and the tragic death of Senator Paul Wellstone of Minnesota. This supplement also contains information on major election issues; on the media campaign, including some of the more controversial political ads (such as Congresswoman Anne Sumer's "sniper ad" in New Jersey);

on money and fund-raising; on voter participation; and finally, on the results and implications of the election. This booklet can be shrink-wrapped free with the fifth edition of *We the People*.

Impeachment and Trial Supplement
0-07-235127-6
   by Richard Semiatin of American University
This 16-page supplement offers an overview of the impeachment and trial processes within a historical and constitutional context. This supplement discusses the factors affecting the case of President Andrew Johnson in the 1860s and the vastly different, modern case of President Bill Clinton. This supplement also looks at alternatives to conviction and expulsion. This booklet can be shrink-wrapped free with the fifth edition of *We the People*.

For Instructors

Instructor's Manual
0-07-281734-8
   by Willoughby Jarrell of Kennesaw State University
For each chapter, the Instructor's Manual includes the following: learning objectives, focus points and main points, a chapter summary, a list of major concepts, a lecture outline, alternative lecture objectives, class discussion topics, and a list of Internet resources.

Instructor's Resource CD-ROM
0-07-281738-0
Tailored to the table of contents and format of the fifth edition, this CD integrates instructor resources available in the Instructor's Manual with multimedia components such as PowerPoint presentations, photographs, maps, and charts. Also available on this CD is a computerized test bank that consists of approximately 20 to 25 multiple-choice questions, 15 to 20 true/false questions, and 5 suggested essay topics per chapter, with answers given alongside the questions and page references provided.

McGraw-Hill American Government Video Library
This series of 10-minute video lecture-launchers was produced for McGraw-Hill by Ralph Baker and Joseph Losco of Ball State University.

   Video #1: Devolution within American Federalism: Welfare Reform
   0-07-303414-2
   Video #2: Public Opinion and Participation: American Students Speak
   0-07-229517-1

Video #3: Media and Politics in Presidential Campaigns
0-07-234442-3
Video #4: Women in Politics
0-07-242097-9
Video #5: Civil Liberties on the Internet
0-07-244205-0
Video #6: Affirmative Action and College Enrollment
0-07-244207-7
Video #7: The 2000 Campaign
0-07-250175-8

PageOut

At www.mhhe.com/pageout, instructors can create their own course web-sites. PageOut requires no prior knowledge of HTML, simply plug the course information into a template and click on one of 16 designs. The process provides instructors with a professionally designed website.

PRIMIS Online

Primis is McGraw-Hill's database of course materials that allows instructors to build custom textbooks for their courses. Instructors can use this text-book as a whole, or they can select specific chapters and customize this text to suit their specific classroom needs. The customized text can be created as a hard copy or as an e-book. For more information, visit the website www.mhhe.com/primis

ACKNOWLEDGMENTS

I am deeply thankful to the scholars whose sound advice has helped shape every page of this book. Their advice was invaluable. These scholars are:

Ralph Baker, *Ball State University*
Mike Horan, *University of Wyoming*
Stacey Hunter Hecht, *Bethel College*
Mark Jendrysik, *University of North Dakota*
Donald Lamkin, *Meramec Community College*
Nancy Marion, *University of Akron*
Siobhan Maroney, *Lake Forest College*
Robert Smith, *Clemson University*
June Speakman, *Roger Williams University*
Ken Warren, *St. Louis University*

I also want to acknowledge those at McGraw-Hill who contributed to the fifth edition. Monica Eckman, my editor, deserves a special thanks. Her enthusiasm for the book made my work much easier, and her numerous suggestions strengthened the book considerably. Kristen Mellitt, the development editor, provided steady assistance throughout, as did Karen Dorman, the copy editor. Marilyn Rothenberger also contributed substantially; she carefully guided the fifth edition through the production process. At Harvard, I had the steady support of Jamie Arterton, my faculty assistant. No one had a bigger hand in the preparation of the new material in this edition than Jamie. She did most of the research and a lot of the editing. She is enormously skilled and saved me uncounted hours of time. I am very grateful.

Thomas E. Patterson

CHAPTER 1

AMERICAN POLITICAL CULTURE: SEEKING A MORE PERFECT UNION

"One hears people say that it is inherent in the habits and nature of democracies to change feelings and thoughts at every moment. . . . But I have never seen anything like that happening in the great democracy on the other side of the ocean. What struck me most in the United States was the difficulty experienced in getting an idea, once conceived, out of the head of the majority.**"**

ALEXIS DE TOCQUEVILLE[1]

At 8:47 A.M. on September 11, 2001, a hijacked American Airlines passenger jet slammed into one of the twin towers of New York City's World Trade Center. Twenty minutes later, a second hijacked passenger jet hit the other tower. A third hijacked jet then plowed into the Pentagon building in Washington, D.C. Within two hours, the World Trade Center towers collapsed, killing all still inside, including police and firefighters who had rushed bravely into the buildings to help in the evacuation. Three thousand Americans were murdered that September morning, the highest death toll ever from an attack on American soil by a foreign adversary. The toll would have been even higher except for the bravery of passengers aboard United Airlines flight 93, who fought with its hijackers, causing the plane, which was aimed toward Washington, D.C., to crash in a barren Pennsylvania field.

Firefighters and other rescue workers stand at the site of the collapsed World Trade Center
Towers, which were attacked earlier that day by terrorists who had hijacked commercial airliners.
Nearly 3,000 Americans were murdered in the September 11, 2001, attacks.

That evening, a somber George W. Bush addressed the nation. Urging
Americans to stay calm and resolute, President Bush said: "America was targeted for an attack because we're the brightest beacon for freedom and opportunity in the world." Sprinkled throughout his speech were allusions to
time-honored American ideals: liberty, the will of the people, justice, and the
rule of law. "No one will keep that light from shining," said Bush.

The ideals that guided Bush's speech would have been familiar to any
generation of Americans. These ideals have been invoked when Americans
have gone to war, declared peace, celebrated national holidays, launched
major policy initiatives, and asserted new rights.[2] The ideals contained in

Bush's speech were the same ones that had punctuated the speeches of George Washington and Abraham Lincoln, Susan B. Anthony and Franklin D. Roosevelt, Dr. Martin Luther King Jr. and Ronald Reagan.

The ideals were also there at the nation's beginning, when they were put into words in the Declaration of Independence and the Constitution. Of course, the practical meaning of these words has changed greatly during the more than two centuries that the United States has been a sovereign nation. When the writers of the Constitution began the document with the words "We, the People," they did not have all Americans equally in mind. Black slaves, women, and men without property did not have the same rights as propertied white men.

Yet America's ideals have been remarkably enduring. Throughout their history Americans have embraced the same set of core values. They have quarreled over the meaning, practice, and fulfillment of these ideals, but they have never seriously questioned the principles themselves. As the historian Clinton Rossiter concluded, "There has been in a doctrinal sense, only one America."[3]

This book is about contemporary American politics, not U.S. history or culture. Yet American politics today cannot be understood apart from the nation's heritage. Government does not begin anew with each generation; it builds on the past. In the United States, the most significant link between past and present lies in the nation's founding ideals. The Frenchman Alexis de Tocqueville was among the first to see that the main tendencies of American politics cannot be explained without taking into account the country's core beliefs. "Habits of the heart" was Tocqueville's description of Americans' ideals.[4]

This chapter briefly examines the principles that have helped shape American politics since the country's earliest years. The chapter also explains basic concepts such as power, pluralism, and constitutionalism that are important in the study of American government and politics. The main points made in this chapter are the following:

★ *The American political culture centers on a set of core ideals—liberty, equality, self-government, individualism, diversity, and unity—that serve as the people's common bond.* These mythic principles have a substantial influence on what Americans will regard as reasonable and acceptable and on what they will try to achieve.

★ *Politics is the process that determines whose values will prevail in society.* The play of politics in the United States takes place in the context of democratic procedures, constitutionalism, and capitalism and involves elements of majority, pluralist, bureaucratic, and elite rule.

★ *Politics in the United States is characterized by a number of major patterns, including a highly fragmented governing system, a high degree of pluralism, an extraordinary emphasis on individual rights, and a pronounced separation of the political and economic spheres.*

POLITICAL CULTURE: THE CORE PRINCIPLES OF AMERICAN GOVERNMENT

The people of every nation have a few great ideals that characterize their political life, but as James Bryce observed, Americans are a special case.[5] Their ideals are the basis of their national identity. Other people take their identity from the common ancestry that led them gradually to gather under one flag. Thus, long before there was a France or a Japan, there were French and Japanese people, each a kinship group united through blood. Even today, it is kinship that links them. There is no way to become Japanese except to be born of Japanese parents. Not so for Americans. They are a multitude of peoples linked by a political tradition. The United States is a nation that was abruptly founded in 1776 on a set of principles that became its people's common bond.[6]

U.S. politics is remarkable for its historical continuity, which is celebrated here in a ceremony at the Capitol in Washington, D.C.

A strong bond of some kind was a necessity. Nationalities that warred constantly in Europe had to find a way to live together in the New World. Americans' shared ideals contributed to a oneness, however uneasy, among nationalities that had never before trusted one another. Their effort to find common ground has been replayed many times during America's history. The United States is, and always has been, a nation of immigrants and of people struggling for a greater level of acceptance and unity. Today, the United States has a population of almost 300 million people, nearly all of whom can trace their ancestry to some other place (see Figure 1–1). Native

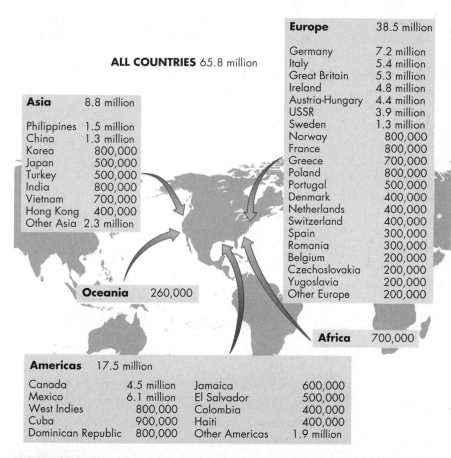

Europe	38.5 million
Germany	7.2 million
Italy	5.4 million
Great Britain	5.3 million
Ireland	4.8 million
Austria-Hungary	4.4 million
USSR	3.9 million
Sweden	1.3 million
Norway	800,000
France	800,000
Greece	700,000
Poland	800,000
Portugal	500,000
Denmark	400,000
Netherlands	400,000
Switzerland	400,000
Spain	300,000
Romania	300,000
Belgium	200,000
Czechoslovakia	200,000
Yugoslavia	200,000
Other Europe	200,000

ALL COUNTRIES 65.8 million

Asia	8.8 million
Philippines	1.5 million
China	1.3 million
Korea	800,000
Japan	500,000
Turkey	500,000
India	800,000
Vietnam	700,000
Hong Kong	400,000
Other Asia	2.3 million

Oceania	260,000

Africa	700,000

Americas	17.5 million		
Canada	4.5 million	Jamaica	600,000
Mexico	6.1 million	El Salvador	500,000
West Indies	800,000	Colombia	400,000
Cuba	900,000	Haiti	400,000
Dominican Republic	800,000	Other Americas	1.9 million

FIGURE 1-1 TOTAL IMMIGRATION TO THE UNITED STATES, 1820–2000, BY CONTINENT AND COUNTRY OF ORIGIN.

Source: U.S. Immigration and Naturalization Service.

Americans now make up about 1 percent of the population. They are out-numbered by Americans who have ancestral ties to Germany, Ireland, Africa, Poland, Mexico, or China, to name just a few.

Yet Americans are also one people, brought together through allegiance to a set of commonly held ideals such as liberty and equality. These princi-ples are habits of mind, a customary way of thinking about the world. They are part of what social scientists call **political culture,** a term that refers to the characteristic and deep-seated beliefs of a particular people about gov-ernment and politics.[7]

America's core ideals are rooted in the European heritage of the first white settlers. They arrived during the Enlightenment period, when people were awakening to the idea of human progress. These settlers wanted freedom to practice religion and hoped for a greater measure of self-government. They did not, as some Americans assume, invent an entirely new way of life. Their beliefs were shaped by European thought and practice, which in turn had been molded by Greco-Roman and Judeo-Christian traditions. As the histo-rian Paul Gagnon noted, "The first settlers did not sail into view out of a void, their minds as blank as the Atlantic Ocean. . . . Those who sailed west to America came in fact not to build a New World but to bring to life in a new setting what they had treasured most from the Old World."[8]

Colonial life expanded their vision, which then found expression in the Declaration of Independence and the Constitution. Ideals became the defin-ing feature of the American political experience. Later immigrants adopted them while also leaving a distinctive mark on the practice of these ideals. As each new generation of Americans has discovered, there is no fixed way to live out these principles, and in practice, these ideals have meant different things to different people even within the same generation. Few observers would argue, however, with the proposition that *a defining characteristic of the American political system is its enduring and powerful set of political ideals.*

AMERICA'S CORE VALUES: LIBERTY, EQUALITY, AND SELF-GOVERNMENT

An understanding of America's ideals begins with a recognition that the in-dividual comes first. Government is secondary. Its role is to serve the peo-ple as opposed to a system in which government is at the pinnacle and people are expected to glorify it. No clearer statement of this principle ex-ists than the Declaration of Independence's reference to "unalienable rights"—freedoms that belong to each and every person and that cannot lawfully be denied by government.

Liberty, equality, and self-government are widely regarded as America's core political ideals. **Liberty** is the principle that individuals should be free to act and think as they choose, provided they do not infringe unreasonably on the freedom and well-being of others. The United States, as historian Louis Hartz said, was "born free."[9] The Declaration of Independence rings with the proclamation that people are entitled to "Life, Liberty and the Pursuit of Happiness." The preamble to the Constitution declares that the U.S. government is founded to secure "the Blessings of Liberty to ourselves and our Posterity." The Statue of Liberty stands in New York harbor as the symbol of the American nation, and the "Star-Spangled Banner" rings out with the words "land of the free."

At the time of the writing of the Constitution (1787), liberty was conceived as protection against unwarranted government interference in people's lives. The First Amendment, for example, defines a set of actions that government is forbidden to take: "Congress shall make no law respecting the establishment of religion, or prohibiting the free exercise thereof; or abridging the freedom of speech, or of the press; or the right of the people to peaceably assemble, and to petition the Government for a redress of grievances."

For a long period, America's vast wilderness and great distance from the Old World granted its white settlers extraordinary freedom. Ordinary people did not have to accept second-class treatment when greater personal liberty was as close as the next area of unsettled land. With time, however, this protection diminished and a new threat to personal liberty emerged. The Industrial Revolution spawned business trusts that gouged customers and forced laborers to work long hours at low pay in unsafe factories. It became harder to think about personal liberty as simply an issue of limits on government. Americans gradually looked to government for protection

Thomas Jefferson
(1743–1826)

Thomas Jefferson was the principal author of the Declaration of Independence. It was Jefferson who coined the renowned words "Life, Liberty and the Pursuit of Happiness." A powerful advocate of personal freedom, he also wrote the state of Virginia's Bill of Rights. Elected to the presidency in 1800, his purchase of the Louisiana Territory from the French Emperor Napoleon in 1803 doubled the size of the United States. After retiring to his Monticello estate, Jefferson designed and founded the University of Virginia, which he proclaimed as his greatest achievement.

against powerful economic interests. Business regulation, social security, and minimum-wage laws were among the resulting policies.

A second American political ideal is **equality**—the notion that all individuals are equal in their moral worth and are entitled to equal treatment under the law. America provided its white settlers a new level of equality. Europe's rigid aristocratic system based on land ownership was unenforceable in frontier America. Almost any free citizen who wanted to own land could obtain it. It was this natural sense of equality that Thomas Jefferson expressed so forcefully in the writing of the Declaration of Independence: "We hold these truths to be self-evident, that all men are created equal."

Equality, however, has always been a less clearly defined concept than liberty. Even Jefferson professed not to know its exact meaning. A slave owner, Jefferson distinguished between free citizens, who were entitled to equal rights, and slaves, who were not. After slavery was abolished, Americans continued to argue over the meaning of equality, as they do today. Does it require that wealth and opportunities be widely shared? Or does it merely require that artificial barriers to advancement be removed? Despite differing opinions about such questions, the quest for equality is a distinctive feature of the American experience. Observers from Tocqueville to Bryce have seen fit to say that equality in America, as in no other country, is ingrained in people's thinking. Americans, said Bryce, reject "the very notion" that some people might be "better" than others merely because of birth or position.[10] And perhaps no ideal has so inspired Americans to political action as has their desire for fuller equality. The abolition and suffrage movements were rooted in this ideal. The more recent civil rights movements of black Americans, women, Hispanics, gays, and other groups are also testaments to the power of this ideal.

Of course, people differ in their wealth and talent, which means they are not equal in fact. Even today, for example, poor people accused of crime do not have access to the same quality of legal assistance available to the rich. In principle, however, Americans are equals, as expressed in such phrases as "equal justice under the law." These are not empty words. Although the poor have less access to legal assistance, no citizen can be tried for a felony offense without the opportunity for legal counsel, at government expense if necessary.

Self-government is America's third great political ideal. **Self-government** is the principle that people are the ultimate source of governing authority and must have a voice in how they are governed. "Governments," the Declaration of Independence proclaims, "deriv[e] their just powers from the consent of the governed." In his Gettysburg address, Lincoln extolled a government "of the people, by the people, for the people."

America's Core Political Ideals

Liberty: The belief that individuals should be free to act and think as they choose, provided they do not infringe unreasonably on the freedom and well-being of others.

Equality: The belief that all individuals are equal in their moral worth and are entitled to equal treatment under the law.

Self-government: The belief that the people are the ultimate source of governing authority and must have a voice in how they are governed.

Americans' belief in self-government originated in colonial America. The Old World was an ocean away, and European governments had no option but to allow the American colonies a degree of self-determination. Out of this experience came the dream of a self-governing nation. It was an ideal that captured the imagination even of those in the lower ranks of society. Ordinary people willingly risked their lives to the cause of self-government during the American Revolution. The ensuing federal and state constitutions were based on the idea that government is properly founded on the will of the people. "We the People," is the opening phrase of the Constitution of the United States.

At no time in the nation's history has national leadership been conferred except through the vote. At various times and places elsewhere in the world, governing power has been seized by brute force. The United States has an unbroken history of free and open elections as the legitimate means of acquiring governmental power. Etched in a corridor of the nation's Capitol building are the words Alexander Hamilton spoke when asked about the foundation of the nation's government: "Here, sir, the people govern."

Although liberty, equality, and self-government are the core American political ideals, the American creed also includes other principles. **Individualism** is a commitment to personal initiative and self-sufficiency; it asserts that people, if free to pursue their own path and if not unfairly burdened, can attain their full potential. **Unity** is the principle that Americans are one people and form an indivisible union. **Diversity** holds that individual and group differences should be respected and that these differences are themselves a source of strength. The last two principles acknowledge at once both the differences and the oneness that are part of the American experience. They are expressed in the phrase "E pluribus unum" (one out of many).

HOW THE UNITED STATES COMPARES

Capitalism, Self-Reliance, and Personal Success

The United States was labeled "the country of individualism *par excellence*" by William Watts and Lloyd Free in their book *State of the Nation*. They were referring to the emphasis that Americans place on self-reliance and the trust they have in the marketplace as a basis of economic security.

Such views also prevail in European democracies but are moderated by a greater acceptance of welfare programs. The difference between the American and European cultures reflects their differing political traditions. America was an open country ruled by a foreign power, and its revolution was fought largely over the issue of personal freedom. In European revolutions, equality was also at issue, since wealth was held by hereditary aristocracies. Europeans' concern with equality was gradually translated into a willingness to use government as a means of redistributing wealth. An example is government-paid medical care for all citizens.

Even today, Europeans are more likely to feel that their social and economic status is determined by the circumstances of birth. This outlook is evident in a Times-Mirror survey that asked respondents whether "success in life is pretty much determined by forces outside our control." The percentage of Americans and Europeans agreeing with the statement is shown in the accompanying chart.

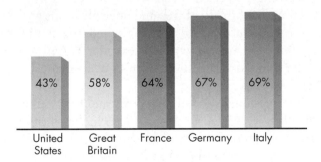

| United States | Great Britain | France | Germany | Italy |
| 43% | 58% | 64% | 67% | 69% |

The Power of Ideals

Ideals serve to define the boundaries of action. They do not determine exactly what people will do, but they affect what people will regard as reasonable and desirable. Why, for example, does the United States spend relatively less money on government programs for the poor than do other fully industrialized democracies, including Germany, France, Switzerland, the Netherlands, Spain, Britain, Sweden, Italy, and Japan? Are Americans so much better off than these other people that they have less need for welfare programs? The answer is no. Of all these countries, the United States has in both relative and absolute terms the most poverty. The United States spends less on social welfare chiefly because of its cultural emphasis on liberty and individualism. Americans have resisted giving government a larger social welfare role because of their deep-seated beliefs in self-reliance and limited government (see "How the United States Compares").

Of course, social welfare policy is not simply an issue of cultural differences. The welfare issue, like other issues, is part of the rough-and-tumble of everyday politics. There are always powerful interests aligned on both sides of important issues. In the United States, the Republican party, business groups, antitax groups, and others have resisted the expansion of the government's social welfare role, while Democrats, unions, minority groups, and others have from time to time argued for greater intervention. Nevertheless, Americans' belief in individualism, which has no exact equivalent in European society, has played a defining role in shaping U.S. welfare policy.

The distinctiveness of this cultural belief is evident in a Times-Mirror Center survey of opinions in Europe and the United States.[11] When asked whether it is the responsibility of the government "to take care of very poor people who can't take care of themselves," only 23 percent of Americans said they completely agreed. The Germans were the closest to the Americans in their response to this question, but more than twice as many of them, 50 percent, said they believed that the state should take care of the very poor. More than 60 percent of the British, French, and Italians held the same opinion. Americans do not necessarily have less sympathy for the poor; rather, they place more emphasis on personal responsibility than Europeans do.[12]

The importance of individualism to American society is also evident in the emphasis on equal opportunity. If individuals are to be entrusted with their own welfare, they must be given a fair chance to succeed on their own. Nowhere is this philosophy more evident than in the country's elaborate system of higher education, which includes nearly three thousand two-year and four-year institutions and is designed to accommodate nearly every individual who wants to pursue a college education. More than a third of the nation's young people enter college, the world's highest rate. Western Europe has nothing comparable to the American system; fewer than one in five young people in these countries go to college. The difference is reflected in the number of citizens with college degrees (see "States in the Nation"). Even the American state that ranks lowest by this indicator—West Virginia with its 15.3 percent of adults who are college graduates—has a higher percentage of residents with a bachelor's degree than does the average European country.

Of course, the idea that success is within equal reach of all Americans who strive for it is far from accurate. Young people who grow up in abject poverty and without adequate guidance know all too well the limits on opportunity. In some inner-city areas, teenage boys are more likely to spend time in jail than to spend time at college.

The Limits of Ideals

Cultural beliefs originate in a country's political and social practices, but they are not perfect representatives of these practices. They are mythic ideas—symbolic positions taken by a people to justify and give meaning to their way of life.[13] Myths contain elements of truth, but they are far from the full truth.

High ideals do not come with a guarantee that a people will live up to them. The clearest proof of this failing in the American case is the human tragedy that began nearly four centuries ago and continues today. In 1619 the first black slaves were brought in chains to America. Slavery lasted 250 years. Slaves in the field worked from dawn to dark (from "can see, 'til can't"), in both the heat of summer and the cold of winter. The Civil War brought an end to slavery but not to racial oppression. Slavery was followed by the Jim Crow era of legal segregation: black people in the South were forbidden by law to use the same schools, hospitals, restaurants, and restrooms as white people. For those who spoke out against this system, there were beatings, firebombings, castrations, rapes, and worse—hundreds of African Americans were lynched by white vigilantes in the early 1900s. Today African Americans have equal rights under the law, but in fact they are far from equal. Compared with whites, blacks are twice as likely to live in poverty, twice as likely to be unable to find a job, and twice as likely to die in infancy.[14] There have always been at least two Americas, one for whites and one for blacks.

/pattersonwtp5

Despite the lofty claim that "all men are created equal," equality has never been an American birthright. In 1882 Congress suspended Chinese immigration on the assumption that the Chinese were an inferior people. Calvin Coolidge in 1923 asked Congress for a permanent ban on Chinese immigration, saying that people "who do not want to be partakers of the American spirit ought not to settle in America."[15] Not until 1965 was discrimination

★ STATES IN THE NATION

A College Education

Reflecting their cultural beliefs of individualism and equality, Americans have developed the world's most extensive college system. Every state has at least eight colleges within its boundaries. No European democracy has as many colleges as either California (322) or New York (320).

Q: Why do the northeastern and western coastal states have a higher percentage of adults with college degrees?

A: The northeastern and western coastal states are more affluent and urbanized than most states. Thus, young people in these states can better afford the costs of college and are more likely to need a college degree for the work they intend to pursue.

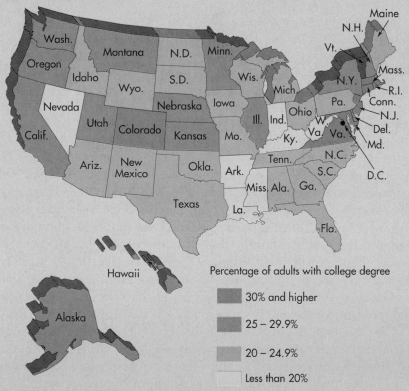

Percentage of adults with college degree

- 30% and higher
- 25 – 29.9%
- 20 – 24.9%
- Less than 20%

Source: U.S. Bureau of the Census, 2002. Based on percentage of adults twenty-five years of age or older with a college degree.

During the era of racial segregation in the South, this sign at the entrance to the Memphis public zoo meant that it was Tuesday—the only day that black people were allowed to go to the zoo. On the other six days of the week, the sign excluded black people from entering.

against the Chinese and other Asians effectively eliminated from U.S. immigration laws. The barriers to entry of Mexicans and Central and South Americans were also lowered at this time (Figure 1–2).

The claim that America is a gigantic melting pot has always been as much fable as fact. When Irish, Italian, and Eastern European immigrants reached this country's shores, they encountered nativist elements that mocked their customs and religious beliefs. In the 1800s, the Know Nothing Party sought to bar Catholics and Jews from settling in America. The Hispanic, Asian, and Middle Eastern peoples who have arrived here more recently have also been made to feel less than fully welcome. Recent polls, for example, indicate that sizable numbers of Americans would favor restricting immigration, particularly the influx of Spanish-speaking and Middle Eastern peoples. Support for restrictions rose even higher after the September 11, 2001, terrorist attacks. A Gallup poll the following month indicated that seven times as many Americans favored a decrease in immigration as favored an increase.

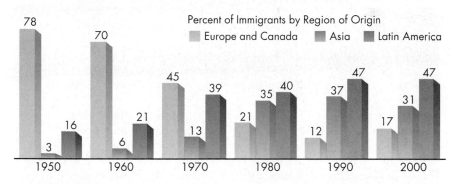

FIGURE 1-2 THE CHANGING FACE OF IMMIGRATION

Until 1965, immigration laws were biased in favor of European immigrants. The laws enacted in 1965 increased the proportion of immigrants from Asia and Latin America. *Source: U.S. Immigration and Naturalization Service. 2003. Percentages are totals for each decade, e.g., the 2000 figures are for the 1991–2000 period.*

Resistance to immigrant groups is not among the stories that Americans like to tell about themselves.[16] Such lapses of historical memory can be found among all peoples, but the tendency to rewrite history is perhaps exaggerated in the American case because Americans' beliefs are so idealistic (see Table 1–1). How could a nation that upholds the ideal of human equality have barred the Chinese, enslaved the blacks, betrayed the Indians, and subordinated women?

One reason America's ideals do not match reality is that they are general principles, not fixed rules of conduct. They derive from somewhat different experiences and philosophical traditions, and there are points at which they conflict. Equality, for instance, emphasizes fairness and an opportunity for all to partake of society's benefits, whereas liberty emphasizes personal freedom and threats posed to it by political power. Conflict between these beliefs is inevitable. Take the issue of affirmative action. Proponents say that only through aggressive affirmative action programs will women and minorities receive the equal treatment in the job market to which they are entitled. Opponents say that aggressive affirmative action infringes unreasonably on the liberty of the employer and the initiative of the work force. Each side can say that it has America's ideals on its side, and no resort to logic can persuade either side that the opposing viewpoint should prevail.

Despite their inexact meanings, conflicting implications, and unfulfilled promise, Americans' ideals have had a strong impact on their politics. If racial, gender, ethnic, and other forms of intolerance constitute the sorriest chapter in the nation's history, the centuries-old struggle of Americans to create a more equal society is among the finest chapters. Few nations have

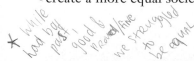

TABLE 1-1   TELLING THE AMERICAN STORY TO CHILDREN

Americans' values and myths are reflected in their preferences in teaching children about the nation's history. The stories that adults regard as least important are those that reflect unfavorably on the country's idealized image.

In teaching the American story to children, how important is the following theme . . . ?	Essential/Very important	Somewhat important	Somewhat unimportant/ Very unimportant/ Leave it out of the story
With hard work and perseverance, anyone can succeed in America.	83%	14%	4%
Our founders limited the power of government, so government would not intrude too much into the lives of its citizens.	74	19	8
America is the world's greatest melting pot in which people from different countries are united into one nation.	73	21	5
America's contribution is one of expanding freedom for more and more people.	71	22	6
Our nation betrayed its founding principles by cruel mistreatment of blacks and American Indians.	59	24	17
Our founders were part of a male-dominated culture that gave important roles to men while keeping women in the background.	38	28	35

Source: Used by permission of the Survey of the American Political Culture, James Davison Hunter and Carol Bowman, directors, University of Virginia.

battled so relentlessly against the insidious discrimination that stems from superficial human differences such as the color of one's skin. High ideals are more than mere abstractions. They are a source of human aspiration and, ultimately, of political and social change.

POLITICS: THE PROCESS OF DECIDING ON SOCIETY'S GOALS

Cultural ideals help shape what people expect from politics and how they conduct their politics. However, politics is more than the pursuit of shared ideals; it is also about getting one's own way. Commenting on the competitive nature of politics, Harold Lasswell described politics as the struggle over "who gets what, when, and how."[17]

Political conflict is rooted in two general conditions of society. One is *scarcity*. There is not enough wealth in even the richest of countries to satisfy everyone's desires. Conflict over the distribution of resources is the inevitable result. This conflict is evident, for example, in policy disputes over the financing of public schools. The quality of American schools varies widely. Affluent suburban districts have better schools and teachers than do poor inner-city districts, which reflects differences in each district's local tax base. In order to equalize quality, less affluent communities have pressed for the statewide funding of public schools, an approach that more affluent communities have resisted.

Differences in values are the other main source of political conflict. The right of abortion is freedom of choice to some and murder to others. People bring to politics a wide range of conflicting values—about abortion, about the environment, about crime and punishment, about the poor, about the economy, about almost everything imaginable.

Politics in the United States is not the life-and-death struggle between opposing groups that typifies some countries, but there are many sources of contention. Perhaps no country has more competing interests than does the United States. Its settlement by people of many lands and religions, its enormous size and geographical diversity, and its economic complexity have made the United States a pluralistic nation. *This feature—competition for power among a great many interests of all kinds—is a major characteristic of American politics.*

It is a mistake to assume, however, that competition and conflict are the sum of politics. People must find agreeable ways of living together. Politics is not only a means of settling disputes, it is also a way of promoting collective interests. Public safety and national defense are prime examples of people

Politics includes conflict and consensus. Women have had to struggle to be treated as equals in the workplace, but their efforts have been supported by public opinion and public policies.

working together for an agreed-upon purpose. Public education is another. It reflects the older generation's willingness to tax itself for the benefit of the younger generation and ultimately for the benefit of society as a whole.

In sum, politics is a process that includes conflict and consensus, competition and cooperation. Accordingly, **politics** can be defined as simply the process through which a society makes its governing decisions.

Government, Power, Authority, and Policy

What is government? What is its purpose? It might be thought that the answer to these age-old questions is that government is a means by which people work together to solve their common problems. To be sure, government can serve the collective good. But it can also serve the naked interests of a dominant faction, as in Stalin's Russia, Hitler's Germany, or Saddam Hussein's Iraq.

Government can be defined as the institutions, processes, and rules that are designed to facilitate control of a particular geographic area and its inhabitants.[18] There are only two things that all governments have in common. One is a capacity to raise revenues, usually in the form of taxation, to support governing activities. The other is coercion—the ability to force inhabitants to abide by the government's rules. Without these capacities, a government would be unable to exercise control over the territory and the inhabitants it claims to rule.

Those individuals who decide issues are said to have **power,** a term that refers to the ability of persons or institutions to control policy decisions.[19] Power is a basic concept of politics. People who have sufficient power can impose taxes, permit or prohibit abortions, protect or take private property, provide or refuse welfare benefits, impose or relax trade barriers. With so much at stake, it is perhaps not surprising that power is widely sought and tightly guarded.

When power is exercised through the laws and institutions of government, the concept of authority applies. **Authority** can be defined as the recognized right of an individual, organization, or institution to make binding decisions. By this definition, government is not the only source of authority: parents have authority over their children; professors have authority over their students; firms have authority over their employees. However, government is a special case in that its authority is more encompassing in scope and more final in nature. Government's authority extends to all people in its geographical boundaries. It can be used to redefine the authority of the parent, the professor, or the firm. Government's authority is also the most coercive. It includes the power to arrest and imprison, even to punish by death those who violate its rules.

Government needs coercive power to ensure that its laws will be obeyed. Without this power, lawlessness would prevail, as it does in Colombia, where drug lords control large areas of the country. But government power itself can be abused. In a perfect world, political power would be used in evenhanded ways for the benefit of all citizens. But the world is imperfect, and power can be used in selfish or cruel ways. "Power tends to corrupt, and absolute power tends to corrupt absolutely," was how Lord Acton described the problem.

Although no governing system can ensure that power will be applied fairly, the U.S. system strengthens this prospect through an elaborate set of *checks and balances*, including a division of authority among the executive, legislative, and judicial branches of government. Each branch acts as a check on the power of the others and balances their power by exercising power of its own. Many other democratic countries have no comparable fragmentation of power. *Extreme fragmentation of governing authority is a major characteristic of the American political system. This situation has profound implications for how politics is conducted, who wins out, and what policies result.*

Governments exercise authority through public policies. A **public policy** is a decision of government to pursue a course of action designed to produce an intended outcome. Policy can take the form of a particular program, such as Head Start, which provides disadvantaged preschool children with skills that will help them succeed once they start school. A policy can also be a set of actions that, taken together, are designed to achieve a particular objective. The war on terrorism that was launched in the aftermath of the September 11, 2001, attacks on the World Trade Center and the Pentagon, for example, is a policy that includes military, intelligence, civil defense, and law enforcement activity. A policy can also be a decision not to take action, in which case the decision has the effect of maintaining the existing policy.

The Rules of the Game of Politics

The play of politics takes place according to rules that the participants accept. The rules establish the process by which power is exercised, define the legitimate uses of power, and establish the basis for allocating costs and benefits among the participants. In America, the rules of the game of politics include democracy, constitutionalism, and capitalism.

Democracy Democracy is a set of rules designed to promote *self-government*. Democracy comes from the Greek words *demos*, which means "the people," and *kratis*, meaning "to rule." In simple terms, **democracy** is a form of government in which the people govern, either directly or through elected representatives (see Chapter 2).

Democratic government is rooted in the consent of the governed, which in practice has come to mean majority rule. The principle of majority rule, in turn, is based on the notion that the view of the many should prevail over the opinion of the few. The principle also represents a form of equality in that the vote of each citizen counts equally, a principle expressed by the phrase "one person, one vote." In practice, democracy in America works primarily through elections. There are other, more direct forms of democracy, such as the town meeting and the initiative, but the American system is mainly a representative one in which people's influence is based on their votes.

As Americans discovered during the 2000 campaign, even the one person, one vote principle is not inviolate. Al Gore received a half million more votes nationally than George W. Bush did but lost the election through the Electoral College. Each state has electoral votes equal in number to its representatives in Congress, and these votes are allocated to the candidate who wins its popular vote. The candidate with a majority of the electoral votes from all the states wins the presidency. Florida's electoral votes were decisive in the outcome of the 2000 election, and even in

Florida, the one person, one vote principle did not hold completely. Thousands of Florida's ballots went uncounted because they could not be read by machine. After a failed effort to have them counted by hand, Gore conceded the election. Polls indicated that many Americans questioned the fairness of the election, but they accepted the outcome without violent protest. Bush's peaceful accession to the presidency is an indication of just how deeply Americans are committed to a system that operates by a set of rules rather than by force or dictate.

Constitutionalism The concept of democracy implies that the will of the majority should prevail over the wishes of the minority. If taken to the extreme, however, this principle would allow a majority to ride roughshod over the minority. Such action could deprive the minority even of its liberty, a clearly unacceptable outcome. Individuals have rights and freedoms that cannot lawfully be denied by the majority.

Constitutionalism is a set of rules that restricts the lawful uses of power. In its original sense, constitutionalism in Western society referred to a government based on laws and constitutional powers.[20] **Constitutionalism** has since come to refer specifically to the idea that there are limits to the rightful power of government over citizens. In a constitutional system, officials govern according to law, and citizens have basic rights that government cannot take away or deny.[21] Free speech is an example. Government is prohibited by the First Amendment from interfering with the lawful exercise of free speech. No right is absolute, which means that some restrictions are allowed. No student, for example, has a First Amendment right to shout loudly and disrupt a classroom. Nevertheless, free speech is broadly protected by the courts. During the war with Iraq in 2003, tens of thousands of anti-war demonstrators took to the streets. There were instances where protesters were intimidated by police or were arrested for disorderly conduct, but those who opposed the government's pursuit of the war had the opportunity to express their views freely without threat of being sent to prison.

The constitutional tradition in the United States is at least as strong as the democratic tradition. In fact, a defining characteristic of the American political system is its extraordinary emphasis on individual rights. Issues that in other democracies would be resolved through elections and in legislative bodies are, in the United States, decided in courts of law as well. As Tocqueville noted, there is hardly a political issue in the United States that does not sooner or later become a judicial issue.[22] Abortion rights, nuclear power, busing, toxic waste disposal, and welfare services are among the

LIBERTY, EQUALITY, AND SELF-GOVERNMENT

What's Your Opinion?

Liberty and Security

The USA Patriot Act of 2001 was enacted less than two months after the September 11 terrorist attacks on the World Trade Center and the Pentagon. It was easily the most controversial domestic action taken by the U.S. government in the immediate aftermath of the bombings. The USA Patriot Act allows government, for example, to examine medical, financial, and educational records on the basis of a minimal standard of suspicion; to detain individuals for short periods without tangible evidence of wrongdoing; to deport noncitizens who have even minimal association with suspected terrorist groups; and to secretly search homes and offices in some instances.

According to its supporters, the legislative bill gave government the tools with which to combat terrorism and thereby protect the lives of Americans. However, opponents argued that the bill included unwarranted incursions on individual rights.

What's your view on the USA Patriot Act? Do you feel more or less secure because of it? How, primarily, do you define your security? Do you worry about becoming the victim of a terrorist attack? Or do you worry more about having your rights abused by officials engaged in the war on terrorism? Would you have the same opinion if, say, your religion or ethnicity was different than it is? How far are you willing to let government depart from normal protections of individual rights in order to combat the terrorist threat?

scores of issues that in recent years have been played out in part as questions of rights to be settled through judicial action.

Aspects of the war on terrorism are sure to follow this pattern. Opinion polls immediately after the September 11, 2001, bombings showed that most Americans were willing to grant government the authority to detain people who merely looked like they might be terrorists. Hundreds of people of Middle Eastern descent were in fact picked up and held for long periods by federal authorities. Congress responded to the terrorist attacks by granting law enforcement officials broad new powers of search

Microsoft's Bill Gates speaks to an audience about his firm's international scope. Capitalism, the organizing principle of the American economic system, emphasizes marketplace competition and self-initiative. The unequal distribution of wealth is also the foundation of elitist theory—the idea that the rich and powerful have unwarranted influence on public policy.

and surveillance. Not all provisions of the USA Patriot Act of 2001 were controversial; for example, a provision that allowed for court-approved wiretaps of specific individuals as opposed to wiretaps of specific phone numbers was widely regarded as a necessary updating of wiretap policy. However, other provisions were opposed by civil liberties groups and by some members of Congress. Among these provisions were the authority to conduct secret searches as opposed to open searches, to conduct telephone and Internet surveillance with minimal judicial supervision as opposed to close supervision, and to conduct searches of medical, financial, and educational records without demonstrating probable cause that a crime had been committed. Some or all of these provisions are sure to be tested in the courts.

Capitalism Just as democracy and constitutionalism are systems of rules for allocating costs and benefits in American society, so too is capitalism. Societies have adopted alternative ways of organizing their economies. One way is *socialism*, which assigns government a large role in the ownership of the means of production, in regulating economic decisions, and in providing for the economic security of the individual. Under the form of socialism practiced in democratic countries, such as Sweden, the government does not attempt to manage the overall economy. Under *communism*, the government does take responsibility for overall management of the economy, including production quotas, supply points, and pricing.

Capitalism is an alternative method for distributing economic costs and benefits. **Capitalism** holds that the government should interfere with the economy as little as possible. Free enterprise and self-reliance are the principles of capitalism. Firms are allowed to operate in a free and open marketplace, and individuals are expected to rely on their own initiative to establish their economic security. Firms decide what they will produce and the price they will charge for their goods and services while consumers decide on what they will buy at what price.

Like the rules of democracy and constitutionalism, the rules of capitalism are not neutral. If democracy responds to numbers and constitutionalism responds to individual rights, capitalism responds to wealth. "Money talks" in a capitalist system, which means, among other things, that wealthier people will have by far the greater say not only in economic matters but political ones as well. Most Americans see nothing wrong with this arrangement and, compared with Europeans, are more likely to accept limits on government action in the area of the economy.

For all practical purposes, this outlook places many kinds of choices, which in other countries are decided collectively, beyond the reach of

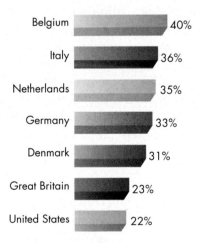

Belgium	40%
Italy	36%
Netherlands	35%
Germany	33%
Denmark	31%
Great Britain	23%
United States	22%

FIGURE 1-3 AMOUNT OF TAXES PAID BY CITIZENS

Americans pay less in taxes than Europeans do.

Source: OECD. 2003. Percentages based on income taxes (national and subnational) and employee contributions paid by a single person without dependents.

political majorities in the United States. Although Americans complain that their taxes are too high, they are taxed at substantially lower rates than Europeans are (see Figure 1–3). This situation testifies to the extent to which Americans believe that wealth is more properly allocated through the economic marketplace than through government policy. *A major characteristic of the American system is a relatively sharp distinction between what is political, and therefore to be decided in the public arena, and what is economic, and therefore to be settled in the private realm.*

Theories of Power

The rules of the political game help decide who will exercise power and to what ends. The ultimate question about any political system is the issue of who governs. Is power widely shared and used for the benefit of the many? Or is power narrowly held and used to the advantage of the few? Although this entire book is in some respects an answer to these questions, it is useful here to consider what analysts have concluded about the American political system. Four broad theories predominate (see Table 1–2). None of them describes every aspect of American politics, but each has some validity.

Government by the People: Majoritarianism A basic principle of democracy is the idea of majority rule. **Majoritarianism** is the notion that the majority prevails not only in the counting of votes but also in the determination of public policy.

TABLE 1-2 THEORIES OF POWER: WHO GOVERNS AMERICA?

There are four theories of power in America, each of which must be taken into account in any full explanation of the nation's policies.

Theory	Description
Majoritarianism	Holds that numerical majorities determine issues of policy
Pluralism	Holds that policies are effectively decided through power wielded by special interests that dominate particular policy areas
Elitism	Holds that policy is controlled by a small number of well-positioned, highly influential individuals
Bureaucratic rule	Holds that policy is controlled by well-placed administrators within the government bureaucracy

Majorities do sometimes rule in America. Their power is perhaps most evident in those states that offer voters the opportunity to decide directly on policy initiatives, which then become law if they receive a majority vote. The majority's influence is also felt indirectly through the decisions of elected representatives. When Congress in 1996 passed a welfare reform bill that included provisions requiring able-bodied welfare recipients to accept a job or job training after a two-year period or face a loss of their welfare benefits, it was acting in accord with the thinking of the majority of Americans who believe that employable individuals should be self-reliant. A more systematic assessment of the power of majorities is provided by Benjamin Page and Robert Shapiro's study of the relationship between majority opinions and more than three hundred policy issues in the period from 1935 to 1979. On major issues particularly, the researchers found that policy tended to change in the direction of change in majority opinion.[23]

Majorities do not always rule, however. In many policy areas, majority opinion is nonexistent or is ignored by policymakers. There are only a few issues at any moment that have the general public's attention and an even smaller number that it really cares about. Thus, majoritarianism cannot account for most of the policies of government. Other explanations are required.

Government by Groups: Pluralism One of these explanations is provided by the theory of **pluralism,** which focuses on group activity and holds that many policies are effectively decided through power wielded by diverse (plural) interests.

Many policies are in fact more responsive to the interests of particular groups than to majority opinion. Agricultural subsidies, broadcast regulations, and corporate tax incentives are examples. In many cases, the general public has no real knowledge or opinion of issues that concern particular groups. For pluralists, the issue of whether interest-group politics serves the public good centers on whether it serves a diverse range of interests. Pluralists contend that it is misleading to view society only in terms of majorities that may or may not form around given issues. They see society as primarily a collection of separate interests. Farmers, broadcasters, and multinational corporations have different needs and desires and, according to the pluralist view, should have a disproportionate say in policies directly affecting them. Thus, as long as many groups have influence in their own area of interest, government is responding to the interests of most Americans. Pluralists such as Robert Dahl have argued that this is in fact the way the American political system operates most of the time.[24]

Critics argue that pluralists wrongly assume that the public interest is somehow represented in a system that allows special interests, each in its own sphere, to set public policy (see Chapter 9). Any such outcome, they say, represents the triumph of minority rule over majority rule. Critics also say that many of society's interests are unable to compete effectively through group politics because of their lack of organization and money. They see a system biased in favor of a small number of powerful groups.

Government by a Few: Elitism Elite theory offers in varying degrees a pessimistic view of the U.S. political system. **Elitism** holds that power in America is held by a small number of well-positioned, highly influential individuals. A leading proponent of elite theory was the sociologist C. Wright Mills, who argued that key policies are decided by an overlapping coalition of select leaders, including corporate executives, top military officers, and centrally placed public officials.[25] Other proponents of elite theory have defined the core group somewhat differently but their contention is the same: America is essentially run not by majorities or a plurality of groups but by a small number of well-placed and privileged individuals.

Proponents of elite theory differ, however, in the extent to which they believe elites control policy for their own purposes. Some theorists, including G. William Domhoff, hold the view that elites operate behind the scenes in order to manipulate government for selfish ends.[26] Other theorists argue that some elites, at least, seek to promote the general interest. Although elites always prefer stability to disruptive change, some pursue policies intended to benefit society as a whole. One such view holds that elites compete for power through the vote and that the electorate has at least some influence on the policy choices made by the winning side.[27]

Unquestionably, certain policies are effectively controlled by a tiny circle of influential people. The nation's monetary policy, for example, is set by the decisions of the Federal Reserve Board ("The Fed"), which meets in secrecy and decides the interest rates that banks pay for the loans they receive from the Federal Reserve. These rates in turn affect the interest rates that banks charge their customers. The Fed is very responsive to the concerns of bankers. What is less clear is the Fed's responsiveness to the concerns of consumers.

Government by Administrators: Bureaucratic Rule A fourth theory holds that power resides in large government bureaucracies in the hands of career administrators. The leading proponent of the theory of **bureaucratic rule** was the German sociologist Max Weber, who argued that all large

Free speech is a familiar aspect of constitutionalism. This anti-gun control rally took place in Austin, Texas.

organizations tend toward the bureaucratic form, with the effect that decision-making power devolves to administrators whose experience and knowledge of policy issues exceeds that of elected officials.[28] Another sociologist, Roberto Michels, propounded the "iron law of oligarchy," concluding that power inevitably gravitates toward experienced administrators at the top of large-scale organizations, even in the case of organizations that aim to be governed democratically.[29]

Bureaucratic politics raises the possibility of a large, permanent government run by unaccountable administrators. Elections come and go, but the bureaucrats who staff executive agencies stay on and on. Government could not function without them, but in most cases, they are not instruments of the majority. Bureaucrats, in fact, make many key policy decisions in areas as diverse as the environment, health, and law enforcement (see Chapter 13).

Who Does Govern? The perspective of this book is that each of these theories—majoritarianism, pluralism, elitism, and bureaucratization—must be taken into account in any full explanation of politics and power in America. Some policies are decided by majority influence, whereas others reflect the influence of special interests, bureaucrats, and elites. The challenge is to distinguish the situations where each of these influence patterns predominates.

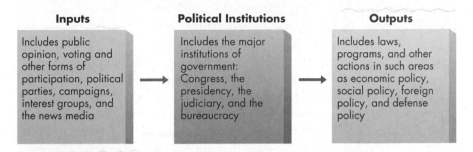

FIGURE 1-4 THE AMERICAN POLITICAL SYSTEM

This book's chapters are organized within a political system's framework.

THE CONCEPT OF A POLITICAL SYSTEM AND THIS BOOK'S ORGANIZATION

As the foregoing discussion suggests, American government is based on a great many related parts. For this reason, it is useful to regard these components as constituting a **political system.** The parts are separate but they connect with one another, affecting how each performs. The political scientist David Easton, who was a pioneer in this conception of politics, said that it makes little sense to study political relations piecemeal when they are, in reality, "interrelated."[30]

The complexity of government has kept political scientists from developing a fully explanatory model of the political system, but the concept of politics as a system is useful for instructional purposes. The concept emphasizes the actual workings of government rather than its institutional structures alone. To view politics as a system is to emphasize the connections between the parts and how change in one area affects the others. It is a dynamic conception in that the political system is constantly changing in response to new conditions and to the interplay of its various parts. And all these changes take place for a purpose. The political system is the mechanism through which society is governed.

The political-system approach characterizes this book, beginning with the organization of its chapters (see Figure 1–4). The political system operates against the backdrop of a constitutional framework that defines how power is to be obtained and exercised. This structure is the focus of the opening chapters, which examine how the Constitution defines, in theory and practice, the institutions of government and the rights of individuals. *Inputs* are another part of the political system; these are the demands that people and organizations place on government and the support they provide for institutions, leaders, and policies. These inputs are explored in chapters on public opinion, political participation, political parties, interest groups, and the news media. The functioning of governing officials is then addressed in chapters on the nation's *political institutions:* Congress, the presidency, the federal bureaucracy, and the federal courts. Some of the discussion in these chapters is devoted simply to describing these institutions, but most of the discussion explores their relationships and how their actions are affected by inputs and the constitutional system in which they operate. Throughout the book, but particularly in the closing chapters, attention is given to the political system's *outputs:* policy decisions that are binding on society. These decisions, which are made by political institutions in response to inputs, affect American life in many areas, including the economy, the environment, social welfare, education, foreign affairs, and national defense.

The chapters are collectively designed to convey a reliable body of knowledge that will enable the reader to think broadly and systematically about the nature of the American political system. To assist in this process, this chapter has identified five encompassing tendencies of American politics that will be examined more closely in later chapters. The United States has

- Enduring cultural ideals that are its people's common bond and a source of their political goals
- Extreme fragmentation of governing authority that is based on an elaborate system of checks and balances
- Many competing interests, which are the result of the nation's great size, population diversity, and economic complexity
- Strong emphasis on individual rights, which is a consequence of the nation's political traditions
- A relatively sharp separation of the political and economic spheres, which has the effect of placing many economic issues outside the reach of political majorities

Underlying this book's concern with the broad patterns of the American political system is a question that must be asked of any democracy: what is the relationship of the people to their government? The answer to this question is the foundation not only of a reasonable assessment of the state of American democracy but also of good citizenship. Responsible citizenship depends finally on an informed perspective, on a recognition of how difficult it is to govern effectively and yet how important it is to try. It cannot be said too often that the issue of governing is the most difficult issue facing any society. Nor can it be said too often that governing is a quest and a search, not a resolved issue. The Constitution's opening phrase, "We, the People," is a call to Americans to join that quest. E. E. Schattschneider said it clearly: "In the course of centuries, there has come a great deal of agreement about what democracy is, but nobody has a monopoly on it and the last word has not been spoken."[31]

SUMMARY

The United States is a nation that was formed on a set of ideals. Liberty, equality, and self-government are the foremost of these ideals, which also include the principles of individualism, diversity, and unity. These ideals became Americans' common bond and today are the basis of their political culture. Although they are mythic, inexact, and conflicting, these ideals have had a powerful effect on what generation after generation of Americans has tried to achieve politically for themselves and others.

Politics is the process by which it is determined whose values will prevail in society. The basis of politics is conflict over scarce resources and competing values. Those who have power win out in this conflict and are able to control governing authority and policy choices. In the United States, no one faction controls all power and policy. Majorities govern on some issues, while groups, elites, and bureaucrats each govern on other issues.

/pattersonwtp5

The play of politics in the United States takes place through rules of the game that include democracy, constitutionalism, and capitalism. Democracy is rule by the people, which in practice refers to a representative system of government in which the people rule through their elected officials. Constitutionalism refers to rules that limit the rightful power of government over citizens. Capitalism is an economic system based on a free-market principle that allows the government only a limited role in determining how economic costs and benefits will be allocated.

KEY TERMS

authority	government
bureaucratic rule	individualism
capitalism	liberty
constitutionalism	majoritarianism
democracy	pluralism
diversity	political culture
elitism	political system
equality	politics

power   self-government
public policy   unity

SUGGESTED READINGS

Dahl, Robert. *On Democracy*. New Haven, Conn.: Yale University Press,
    1998. A handbook on democracy by a leading advocate of pluralism.
DeLaet, Debra L. *U.S. Immigration Policy in an Age of Rights*. Westport,
    Conn.: Praeger Publishers, 2000. Analysis of the impact of civil rights
    action on the changes in U.S. immigration policy in recent decades.
Domhoff, G. William. *Who Rules America? Power and Politics in the Year
    2000*. Mountain View, Calif.: Mayfield Publishing, 1998. A critical
    assessment of American government by a leading proponent of elite
    theory.
Eck, Diana L. *A New Religious America*. San Francisco:
    HarperSanFrancisco, 2001. A look at how the 1965 change in
    immigration law has altered religion and other aspects of American life.
Lipset, Seymour Martin. *American Exceptionalism: A Double-Edged Sword*.
    New York: Norton, 1996. Argues that Americans' tendency to view
    society in idealized terms is a source of both alienation and progress.
McElroy, John Harmon. *American Beliefs: What Keeps a Big Country and a
    Diverse People United*. Chicago: I. R. Dee, 1999. An examination of the
    role of beliefs in Americans' political identity.
Schmidt, Ronald. *Language Policy and Identity Politics in the United States*.
    Philadelphia: Temple University Press, 2000. A critical assessment of
    language policy and its role in Americans' identity.

LIST OF WEBSITES

http://www.conginst.org A site that provides up-to-date survey data on
    the American political culture.

http://www.loc.gov The Library of Congress website; it provides
    access to over seventy million historical and contemporary U.S.
    documents.

http://www.stateline.org A University of Richmond/Pew Charitable
    Trusts site dedicated to providing citizens with information on major
    policy issues.

http://www.tocqueville.org Includes biographical and other references to
    Alexis de Tocqueville and his writings.

POLITICS IN THEORY AND PRACTICE

Thinking: How are Americans' beliefs about liberty, equality, and self-government related to their preference for constitutionalism? For democracy? For capitalism?

Acting: Many Americans can trace their ancestral roots to a particular ethnic group and period of time. If you can do so, consider looking into the reception your ancestors received when they arrived in America. Were they welcomed with open arms? Were they seen as a cultural threat? Did they arrive free or in chains? The Internet and your college library are among the places you can find this information. (You can check for your family's ancestors at www.nara.gov/genealogy/immigration/immigrat.html.)

The New York Times

Securing Freedom's Triumph

by George W. Bush

On the first anniversary of the terrorist attacks on the World Trade Center and the Pentagon, President George W. Bush spoke about the meaning of the war on terrorism for the country and its foreign policy. Bush's speech is a reminder that the U.S. political system was founded on ideals that are still today Americans' common bond and their vision of a more perfect world. Below is the verbatim text of Bush's speech, which appeared in The New York Times *on September 11, 2002.*

WASHINGTON—The September 11 attacks moved Americans to grief and horror and moved our nation to war. They revealed the cruelty of our enemies, clarified grave threats to our country and demonstrated the character and decency of our people. At a moment of great testing, the spirit of men and women in New York City, at the Pentagon and aboard Flight 93 became the spirit of our country. Tonight in New York, I will be speaking of what our nation has lost, what we have discovered about ourselves and what lies ahead.

The terrible illumination of these events has also brought new clarity to America's role in the world. In great tragedy, we have also seen great opportunities. We must have the wisdom and courage to seize these opportunities. America's greatest opportunity is to create a balance of world power that favors human freedom. We will use our position of unparalleled strength and influence to build an atmosphere of international order and openness in which progress and liberty can flourish in many nations. A peaceful world of growing freedom serves American long-term interests, reflects enduring American ideals and unites America's allies. We defend this peace by opposing and preventing violence by terrorists and outlaw regimes. We preserve this peace by building good relations among the world's great powers and we extend this peace by encouraging free and open societies on every continent.

The defense of peace is a difficult struggle of uncertain duration. America, along with our allies, is relentlessly pursuing terrorist networks in every part of the world to disrupt their planning, training and financing. With our allies, we must also confront the growing threat of regimes that support terror, seek chemical, biological and nuclear weapons, and build ballistic missiles. On this issue, the consequences of inaction could be catastrophic. We must deny terrorists and their allies the destructive means to match their hatred.

At the same time, we have the best opportunity in generations to build a world where great powers cooperate in peace instead of continually prepare for war. The 20th century, in particular, was dominated by a series of destructive national rivalries that left battlefields and graveyards across the earth. Competition between great nations is inevitable, but armed conflict in our world is not. September 11 revealed more clearly than ever that the world's great powers stand on the same side of a divide—united by common dangers of terrorist violence and chaos, and moving toward common values.

The United States, Japan and our Pacific friends, our NATO allies and now all of Europe share a deep commitment to human freedom. Russia is now a nation in hopeful transition, a country reaching for a better future based on democracy and the free market and an important partner in the war on terror. Chinese leaders are discovering that economic freedom is the only source of national wealth. In time, they will find that social and political freedom is the only source of national greatness. America will continue to encourage the advancement of democracy and economic openness in both Russia and China because these shared commitments bring true friendship and peace.

Common interests and values among the great powers are also the basis for promoting peace and security around the globe. In the past, great-power rivals took sides in difficult regional problems, making divisions deeper and solutions more complicated and elusive. Today, from the Middle East to South Asia, we are gathering broad international coalitions to increase the pressure for peace. America needs partners to preserve the peace, and we will work with every nation that shares this noble goal.

As we preserve the peace, America also has an opportunity to extend the benefits of freedom and progress to nations that lack them. We seek a just peace where repression, resentment and poverty are replaced with the hope of democracy, development, free markets and free trade.

More than ever, we know that weak states, like Afghanistan, can pose a great danger to the peace of the world. Poverty does not transform poor people into terrorists and murderers. Yet poverty, corruption and repression are a toxic combination in many societies, leading to weak governments that are unable to enforce order or patrol their borders and are vulnerable to terrorist networks and drug cartels.

America is confronting global poverty. Free trade and free markets have proved their ability to lift whole societies out of poverty—so the United States is working with the entire global trading community to build a world that trades in freedom and therefore grows in prosperity. Through the Millennium Challenge Account, the United States will deliver greater development assistance to poor nations that govern justly, invest in their people and encourage economic freedom. And we will continue to lead the world in efforts to reduce the terrible toll of AIDS and other infectious diseases.

America will also take the side of brave men and women who advocate human rights and democratic values, from Africa to Latin America, Asia and the Islamic world. In our diplomatic efforts, development aid, international broadcasting and educational assistance, the United States will promote moderation, tolerance and the nonnegotiable demands of human dignity   the rule of law, limits on the power of the state, and respect for women, private property, free speech and equal justice.

Terrorism has not only challenged the world, it has clarified some fundamental values. Every nation now faces a choice between lawful change and chaotic violence; between joyless conformity and an open, creative society; and between the celebration of death in suicide and murder and the defense of life and its dignity.

Many governments are being forced to reexamine their own tolerance for fanaticism and their sponsorship of hateful propaganda. Even free nations have been forced to reexamine the nature of their commitment to freedom—to determine if this commitment is a reflection of convention and culture or the universal demand of conscience and morality.

America's people and its government are responding decisively to the challenges of our changed world. We are committed to defending our society against current and emerging threats. And we are determined to stand for the values that gave our nation its birth. We believe that freedom and respect for human rights are owed to every human being, in every culture. We believe that the deliberate murder of innocent civilians and the oppression of women are everywhere and always wrong. And we refuse to ignore or appease the aggression and brutality of evil men.

Throughout history, freedom has been threatened by war and terror; it has been challenged by the clashing wills of powerful states and the designs of tyrants; and it has been tested by widespread poverty and disease. What has changed since September 11 is our nation's appreciation of the urgency of these issues—and the new opportunities we have for progress. Today, humanity holds in its hands the opportunity to further freedom's triumph over all its age-old foes. The United States welcomes its responsibility to lead in this great mission.

What's Your Opinion?

President Bush's speech envisions a world built on ideals that have characterized the American political system. Do these ideals reflect the aspirations of people everywhere? Or are the ideals culturally specific—appropriate for America but not necessarily for every country?

→ It's not a question about can we save the planet... it's a question of can we save the human race ←

CHAPTER 2

CONSTITUTIONAL DEMOCRACY: PROMOTING LIBERTY AND SELF-GOVERNMENT

❝The people must be governed by a majority, with whom all power resides. But how is the sense of this majority to be obtained?**❞**

FISHER AMES (1788)[1]

On the night of June 17, 1972, a security guard at the Watergate apartment-office complex in Washington, D.C., noticed that the latch on the door to the Democratic Party's national headquarters had been taped open. He called the police, who captured the five burglars inside. As it turned out, the men had links to Republican President Richard Nixon's Committee to Re-elect the President. Nixon called the incident "bizarre" and denied that anyone on his staff had had anything to do with the break-in.

The reality was that the Watergate break-in was part of an orchestrated campaign of "dirty tricks" designed to ensure Nixon's reelection. Funded by illegal contributions and conducted through the CIA, IRS, FBI, Secret Service, and Nixon's own operatives (called the White House "plumbers"), the dirty-tricks campaign extended to wiretaps, tax audits, and burglaries of Nixon's political opponents (the "enemies list"), who included journalists and antiwar activists in addition to Democrats.

The Senate Judiciary Committee holds hearings on allegations of illegal acts by President Richard Nixon. The congressional investigation led to Nixon's resignation.

Although the Nixon White House managed for a time to hide the truth, the facts of the dirty-tricks campaign gradually became known. In early 1974 the House Judiciary Committee began impeachment proceedings, helped along, ironically, by Nixon's own words. During Senate hearings, a White House assistant revealed that Nixon had tape-recorded all his telephone calls and personal conversations in the Oval Office. At first Nixon refused to release the tapes, but then made public what he claimed were "all the relevant" ones. The House Judiciary Committee demanded additional tapes, as did the special prosecutor who had been appointed to investigate criminal aspects of the Watergate affair. In late July the Supreme Court of the United States, which included four justices appointed by Nixon, unanimously ordered the president to supply sixty-four additional tapes. The tapes were incriminating, and two weeks later, on August 9, 1974, Richard Nixon resigned from office, the first president in U.S. history to do so.

Nixon's downfall was owed in no small measure to the handiwork, two centuries earlier, of the writers of the Constitution. They were well aware that power could never be entrusted to the goodwill of leaders. "If angels were to govern men," James Madison wrote in *Federalist* No. 51, "neither external nor internal controls on government would be necessary." Madison's point, of course, was that leaders are not angels and, as mere mortals, are subject to temptation and vice, including a lust for power—hence the Framers' insistence on constitutional checks on power, as when they gave Congress the authority to impeach and remove the president from office.

The writers of the U.S. Constitution were intent on protecting *liberty* and therefore sought to restrain the use of political power. Their system of checks and balances was designed to limit what officials can do. At the same time, however, the writers of the Constitution wanted a government that was powerful enough to act on the people's behalf. The first objective was **limited government:** a government that is subject to strict limits on its lawful uses of power. The second objective was **self-government:** a government that is subject to the will of the people as expressed through the preferences of a majority. Self-government requires that the voters' preferences find their way into public policy in a substantial and timely way. However, limited government requires restraints on the majority as a way of protecting the rights and interests of the minority. These considerations resulted in a constitution that has provision for majority rule but also has built-in restrictions on the exercise of majority power.

This chapter describes how the principles of self-government and limited government are embodied in the Constitution and explains the tension between them. The chapter also indicates how these principles have been modified in practice in the course of American history. The main points of this chapter are the following:

★ *America during the colonial period developed traditions of limited government and self-government.* These traditions were rooted in governing practices, philosophy, and cultural values.

★ *The Constitution provides for limited government mainly by defining lawful powers and by dividing those powers among competing institutions.* The Constitution, with its Bill of Rights, also prohibits government from infringing on individual rights. Judicial review is an additional safeguard of limited government.

★ *The Constitution in its original form provided for self-government mainly through indirect systems of popular election of representatives.* The Framers' theory of self-government was based on the notion that political power must be separated from immediate popular influences if sound policies are to result.

★ *The idea of popular government—in which the majority's desires have a more direct and immediate impact on governing officials—has gained strength since the nation's beginning.* Originally, the House of Representatives was the only institution subject to direct vote of the people. This mechanism has been extended to other institutions and, through primary elections, even to the nomination of candidates for public office.

Before the Constitution: The Colonial and Revolutionary Experiences

Early Americans' admiration for limited government was based partly on their English heritage. Unlike other European nations of the eighteenth century, England did not have an absolute monarchy. British courts had developed a system of precedent known as "common law," which guaranteed trial by jury and due process of law as safeguards of life, liberty, and particularly property.

This tradition was evident in the American colonies. In each colony there was a right to trial by jury. There was also freedom of expression, although of a narrow kind. Religious freedom, for example, was not granted by all the colonies. There was also a degree of self-government in all the colonies. Each had an elected assembly, and although the assemblies were usually controlled by wealthier interests, they acted as representative bodies and grew increasingly powerful as the number of settlers increased.

"The Rights of Englishmen"

The Revolutionary War was partly a rebellion against England's failure to respect its own tradition of limited government in the colonies. Many of the colonial charters had conferred upon Americans "the rights of Englishmen," but Britain showed progressively less respect for this guarantee as time went on. The period after the French and Indian War (1755–1763) was a turning point in the relationship between the colonists and Britain. Until then the colonists had viewed themselves as loyal subjects of the Crown, and although there had been occasional disputes, few voices argued for independence. In fact, colonists had fought alongside British soldiers to drive the French out of Canada and the Western territories.

At the end of the French and Indian War, however, Britain imposed burdensome taxes on the colonists. The war with France, which had also been waged in Europe, had created a severe financial crisis for the British government, which looked to the increasingly prosperous colonies for revenues. The colonies were not accustomed to paying taxes to the British. The practice was for Britain to raise its revenues from tariffs on the colonies' foreign trade while the colonists controlled and kept local taxes. But the British Parliament in 1765 levied a stamp tax on colonial newspapers and business documents. Because the colonists were not represented in the British Parliament that had imposed the tax, the colonial pamphleteer

James Otis declared that the Stamp Act violated the fundamental rights of the colonists as "British subjects and men." "No taxation without representation" became a rallying cry for the colonists.

Although Parliament backed down and repealed the Stamp Act, it then passed the Townshend Act, which imposed taxes on all paper, glass, lead, and tea. When the colonists protested, King George III sent additional British troops to America to enforce the new taxes. This action served only to further anger the colonists. Britain then tried to placate the Americans by repealing the Townshend duties except for a nominal tax on tea, which was retained in order to show the colonists that Britain was still in charge of their affairs. The colonists saw the tea tax as a petty insult, and in the "Boston Tea Party" of December 1773, a small band of patriots disguised as Native Americans boarded an English ship in Boston Harbor and dumped its cargo of tea overboard.

In 1774, the colonists met in Philadelphia at the First Continental Congress to decide what they would demand from Britain: they called for free assembly, an end to the British military occupation, their own councils for the imposition of taxes, and trial by local juries. (British authorities had resorted to shipping "troublemakers" back to London for trial.) King George III rejected their demands, and in 1775, British troops and colonial minutemen clashed at Lexington and Concord. Eight colonists died on the Lexington green in what became known as "the shot heard 'round the world." The American Revolution had begun.

The Declaration of Independence

Although grievances against Britain were the immediate cause of the American Revolution, ideas about the proper form of government were also on the colonists' minds. A century earlier, the English philosopher John Locke (1632–1704) had written that government must be restrained in its powers if it is to serve the common good. In his *Two Treatises of Government* (1690), Locke claimed that people have **inalienable rights** (or **natural rights**), including those of life, liberty, and property. In Locke's view, such rights belonged to people in their natural state before governments were created. When people agreed to come together (or, in Locke's term, entered into a "social contract") in order to have the protection that only organized government could provide, they retained their natural rights. If the government protected their natural rights, they were obliged to obey it, but if the government failed to protect these rights, they could rightfully rebel against it.[2]

Locke's ideas inspired a generation of American leaders.[3] Thomas Jefferson declared that Locke "was one of the three greatest men that ever

This is a portion of Thomas Jefferson's handwritten draft of the Declaration of Independence, a formal expression of America's governing ideals.

lived, without exception," and Jefferson paraphrased Locke's ideas in key passages of the Declaration of Independence:

> We hold these truths to be self-evident, that all men are created equal, that they are endowed by their Creator with certain unalienable rights, that among these are life, liberty and the pursuit of happiness.

That to secure these rights, governments are instituted among
men, deriving their just powers from the consent of the governed.

That whenever any form of government becomes destructive of
these ends, it is the right of the people to alter or to abolish it, and to
institute a new government.

The Declaration was a call to revolution rather than a framework for a
new form of government, but the ideas it contained—liberty, equality, individual rights, self-government, lawful powers—became the basis, eleven
years later, for the Constitution of the United States. (The Declaration of
Independence and the Constitution are reprinted in their entirety in the ap-
pendixes of this book.)

The Articles of Confederation

The first government of the United States was based not on the Constitution but on the Articles of Confederation. The Articles were adopted during the Revolutionary War and created a very weak national government
that was subordinate to the states. The colonies had always been governed
separately, and their people considered themselves Virginians, New York-
ers, or Pennsylvanians as much as they thought of themselves as Americans.
They naturally preferred a government that was constitutionally derived
from the states. Moreover, they were leery of a powerful central government. The American Revolution was sparked by grievances against the arbitrary policies of King George III, and Americans were in no mood to
replace him with a strong national authority of their own making.

Under the Articles of Confederation, each state retained its "sovereignty,
freedom and independence." There was a national Congress, but its members were appointed and paid by their respective state governments. Each
of the thirteen states had one vote in Congress, and the agreement of nine
states was required to pass legislation. Moreover, any state could block constitutional change: the Articles of Confederation could be amended only by
unanimous approval of the states.

The American union held together during the Revolutionary War out of
necessity: the states had either to cooperate or to surrender to the British.
But once the war ended, the states felt free to go their separate ways. Several states sent representatives abroad to negotiate their own separate trade
agreements with foreign nations. New Hampshire, with its eighteen-mile
coastline, even established its own navy. In a melancholy letter to Thomas
Jefferson, George Washington wondered whether the United States deserved to be called a nation.

Congress was expected to provide for the nation's defense and establish
the basis for a general economy, but the Articles of Confederation did not

give it the powers necessary to achieve these goals. The Articles prohibited Congress from interfering in the states' commerce policies, and the states were soon engaged in ruinous trade wars. The Articles also denied to Congress the power to tax; as a result, it had no money with which to build a navy and hire an army.

Shays's Rebellion: A Nation Dissolving

By 1784, the nation was unraveling. Congress was so weak that its members often did not bother to attend its sessions.[4] Finally, in late 1786, a revolt in western Massachusetts prompted leading Americans to conclude that the country's government had to be changed. A ragtag army of two thousand farmers armed with pitchforks marched on county courthouses to prevent foreclosures on their land and cattle. Many of the farmers were veterans of the Revolutionary War; their leader, Daniel Shays, had been a captain in the Revolutionary army. They had been given assurances during the Revolution that their land, which lay fallow because they were away at war, would not be confiscated for reasons of unpaid debts and taxes. They had also been told that they would get the back pay owed to them for their military service. (Congress had run out of money during the Revolution.) Instead, no back pay was received, and heavy new taxes were placed on farms. Many farmers faced loss of their property and even jail because they could not pay their creditors.

Although many Americans, including Jefferson, sympathized with the farmers, Shays's Rebellion scared propertied interests, and they called on the governor of Massachusetts to put down the revolt. He asked Congress for help, but it had no army to send.[5] The governor finally raised enough money to hire a militia that put down the rebellion, but Shays's Rebellion made it clear that Congress and the army were weak and that mob action was increasing. Fear that anarchy would overtake the country was widespread. At Virginia's urging, five states met at the Annapolis Convention in late 1786 to address the crisis. They did not reach agreement on a solution but urged Congress to authorize a constitutional convention of all the states that would be held the following spring in Philadelphia. Congress did authorize the convention but placed a restriction on it: the delegates were to meet for "the sole and express purpose of revising the Articles of Confederation."

NEGOTIATING TOWARD A CONSTITUTION

The delegates to the Philadelphia constitutional convention ignored the instructions of Congress. They drafted a plan for an entirely new form of government. Prominent delegates (among them George Washington, Benjamin Franklin, and James Madison) were determined from the outset to establish an American nation built on a strong central government.

The Constitution was written in Philadelphia during the summer of 1787 in the East Room of the Old Pennsylvania State House, where the Declaration of Independence had been signed a decade earlier. George Washington presided over the Constitutional Convention but played a less active role in the debate than many of the delegates.

The Great Compromise: A Two-Chamber Congress

Debate at the constitutional convention of 1787 began over a plan put forward by the Virginia delegation, which was dominated by strong nationalists. The **Virginia Plan** (also called the large-state plan) called for a two-chamber Congress that would have supreme authority in all areas "in which the separate states are incompetent," particularly defense and interstate trade. The Virginia Plan also provided that representation in both chambers would be based on size. Small states such as Delaware and Rhode Island would be allowed only one representative in the lower chamber, while large states such as Massachusetts and Virginia would have more than a dozen.

Not surprisingly, the Virginia Plan was roundly condemned by delegates from the smaller states. They rallied around a counterproposal made by New Jersey's William Paterson. The **New Jersey Plan** (also called the small-state plan) called for a stronger national government with the power to tax and to regulate commerce among the states; in most other respects, however, the Articles would remain in effect. Congress would have a single chamber in which each state, large or small, would have a single vote.

The debate over the New Jersey and Virginia Plans dragged on for weeks before the delegates reached what is now known as the **Great Compromise.** It provided for a bicameral (two-chamber) Congress: the House of Representatives would be apportioned among the states on the basis of population and the Senate on the basis of an equal number of votes (two) for each state.

The small states would never have agreed to join a union in which their vote was always weaker than that of large states,[6] a fact reflected in Article V of the Constitution: "No state, without its consent, shall be deprived of its equal suffrage in the Senate."

The North-South Compromise: The Issue of Slavery

The separate interests of the states were also the basis for a second major agreement: the **North-South Compromise** over economic issues. The South had a slave-based agricultural economy, and its delegates feared that the North, which had a stronger manufacturing sector, would gain a numerical majority in Congress and then proceed to enact unfair tax policies. If Congress levied high import tariffs on finished goods from foreign nations in order to protect domestic manufacturers and placed heavy export tariffs on agricultural goods, the burden of financing the new government would fall mainly on the South. Its delegates also worried that northern representatives in Congress might tax or even bar the importation of slaves.

After extended debate, a compromise was reached. Congress was to be prohibited by the Constitution from taxing exports but could tax imports. In addition, Congress would be prohibited from passing laws to end the slave trade until 1808. The South also gained a constitutional provision requiring each state to return runaway slaves to their state of origin. A final bargain was the infamous "Three-fifths Compromise": for purposes of both taxation and representation in Congress, five slaves were to be considered the equivalent of three white people; in effect, a slave was to be counted as three-fifths of a human being.

Although the Philadelphia convention has been criticized for the compromise over slavery, the southern states' dependence on slavery was a formidable obstacle to union. Northern states had no economic use for forced labor and had few slaves, whereas the southern economies were based on slavery (see Figure 2–1). John Rutledge of South Carolina asked during the convention debate whether the North regarded southerners as "fools." Southern delegates declared that they would bolt the convention and form their own union rather than join one that prohibited slavery.

A Strategy for Ratification

The compromises over slavery and the structure of the Congress took up most of the four months that the convention was in session. Some of the other issues, such as the structure and powers of the federal judiciary, were the subject of surprisingly little debate.

There remained a final issue, however: would those Americans not at the convention share the delegates' opinion of the Constitution? The delegates

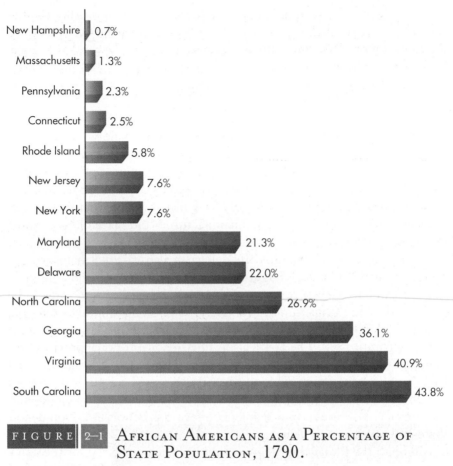

FIGURE 2-1 AFRICAN AMERICANS AS A PERCENTAGE OF STATE POPULATION, 1790.

At the writing of the Constitution, African Americans (most of whom were slaves) were concentrated in the southern states.
Source: U.S. Bureau of the Census.

realized that ratification was not a sure thing. Congress had not authorized a wholesale restructuring of the federal government and had created a barrier to any such plan. In authorizing the Philadelphia convention, Congress had stated that any proposed change in the Articles would have to be "agreed to in Congress" and then "confirmed by [all of] the states." The delegates recognized that if they followed this procedure, which required unanimity, the Constitution had no chance of ratification. Rhode Island had refused even to send a delegation to the convention. In a bold move, the delegates established their own ratifying process. They instructed Congress to submit the document directly to the states, where it would become law after being approved by at least nine states in special ratifying conventions of popularly elected delegates. It was a masterful strategy: there was little hope that all thirteen state legislatures would approve the Constitution, but nine states through conventions might be persuaded to ratify it. And indeed, North Carolina and Rhode Island were steadfastly opposed to the new union and did not ratify the Constitution until the eleven other states had ratified it and begun the process of establishing the new government.

The Ratification Debate

The debate over ratification was a contentious one. The **Anti-Federalists** (as opponents of the Constitution were labeled) raised arguments that still echo in American politics. They claimed that the national government would be too powerful and would threaten the sovereignty of the separate states and the liberty of the people. Many Americans had an innate distrust of centralized power and worried that the people's liberty could be eclipsed as easily by a distant American government as it had been by the British king. The fact that the Constitution contained no bill of rights heightened this concern. Did its absence indicate that the central government would be free to define for itself what the people's rights would be?

The presidency was also a source of concern. No such office had existed under the Articles, and some worried that it would lead to the creation of an American monarchy. Even the motives of the men who wrote the Constitution came under attack. They were men of wealth and education and had acted in response to debtors' riots. Would the Constitution become a tool by which the wealthy ruled over those with little or no money? And who would bear the burden of additional taxation? For Americans struggling with local and state tax payments, the creation of yet another tax agency was hardly an attractive proposal.

Most Anti-Federalists acknowledged a need to strengthen national commerce and defense. What they opposed was the creation of a powerful national government as the mechanism. They favored a revision of the Articles of Confederation, which in their opinion could accomplish these goals without the risk of establishing a government that could threaten their liberties, their livelihoods, and their local interests.

The **Federalists** (as the Constitution's supporters called themselves) responded with a persuasive case of their own. Their strongest arguments were set forth by James Madison and Alexander Hamilton, who along with John Jay wrote a series of essays during the New York ratification debate. The essays were published in a New York City newspaper under the pen name Publius and were entitled "The Federalist." (The essays are collectively referred to as *The Federalist Papers* and are widely acknowledged as a brilliant political treatise.) Madison and Hamilton argued that the government of the Constitution would correct the defects of the Articles; it would have the power necessary to forge a secure and prosperous union. At the same time, because

James Madison
(1751–1836)

James Madison is often called the "father of the Constitution" because he was instrumental in its writing and its ratification (through his *Federalist Papers* essays). He served as secretary of state during the Jefferson administration and was elected the fourth U.S. president in 1808. He helped lead the nation to victory over the British in the War of 1812 and, after leaving the presidency in 1817, spoke out often against the growing movement toward states' rights that led eventually to the Civil War.

of restrictions on its powers, the new government would endanger neither the states nor personal liberty. In *Federalist* Nos. 47, 48, 49, 50, and 51, for example, Madison explained how the separation of national institutions was designed to both empower and restrict the federal government. (The Federalist and Anti-Federalist arguments are discussed further in Chapter 3.)

Whether the ratification debate changed many minds is unknown. Historical evidence suggests, however, that a majority of ordinary Americans opposed the Constitution's ratification. But their voice in the state ratifying conventions was smaller than that of wealthier interests, which, in the main, supported the change. The pro-ratification forces were also bolstered by the widespread assumption that George Washington would become the first president. He was far and away the most trusted and popular American leader. In the view of most historians, the fact that Washington had presided over the Philadelphia convention and the assumption that he would become the chief executive tipped the balance in favor of ratification.

Delaware was the first state to ratify the Constitution, and Connecticut, Georgia, and New Jersey followed, an indication that the Great Compromise had satisfied several of the small states. In the early summer of 1788, New Hampshire became the ninth state to ratify. The Constitution was law. But neither Virginia nor New York had ratified, and a stable union without these two major states was almost unthinkable. They were as large in area as many European countries and conceivably could survive as independent nations. They nearly did choose a separate course. In both states, the Constitution barely passed, and then only after the Federalists promised to support a bill of rights designed to protect individual freedoms from the power of the central government.

/pattersonwtp5

TABLE 2–1   MAJOR GOALS OF THE FRAMERS OF THE CONSTITUTION

1. To establish a government strong enough to meet the nation's needs—an objective sought through substantial grants of power to the federal government in areas such as defense and commerce (see Chapter 3).

2. To establish a government that would not threaten the existence of the separate states—an objective sought through federalism (see Chapter 3) and through a Congress connected to the states through elections.

3. To establish a government that would not threaten liberty—an objective sought through an elaborate system of checks and balances.

4. To establish a government based on popular sovereignty—an objective sought through provisions for the direct and indirect election of public officials.

The Framers' Goals

A **constitution** is the fundamental law that defines how a government will legitimately operate: how its leaders will be chosen, the institutions through which these leaders will work, the procedures they must follow in making policy, and the powers they can lawfully exercise. The Constitution, which was written in Philadelphia in 1787, is exactly such a law. In theory, it is the highest law of the land: neither a popular majority nor a leader at the highest pinnacle of power stands above it. Its provisions define how power is to be acquired and can be used.

The Constitution reflected the Framers' vision of a proper government for the American people. Its provisions addressed four broad goals (see Table 2–1). One was the creation of a national government strong enough to meet the nation's needs, particularly in the areas of defense and commerce. Another goal was to preserve the states as governing entities. Accordingly, the Framers established a system of government (federalism) in which power is divided between the national government and the states. Federalism is discussed at length in Chapter 3, which will also explain how the Constitution laid the foundation for a strong national government.

The Framers' other goals were to establish a national government that was restricted in its lawful uses of power (limited government) and that gave the people a voice in their governance (self-government). These two goals and how they were written into the Constitution are the focus of the rest of this chapter.

PROTECTING LIBERTY: LIMITED GOVERNMENT

A challenge facing the Framers of the Constitution was how to control the coercive force of government. Government's unique characteristic is that it alone can legally arrest, imprison, and even kill people who break its rules.[7] Force is not the only basis of effective government, but government must be able to use force or lawless elements will take over society. The dilemma is that government itself can destroy civilized society by using its force to brutalize and intimidate its opponents. "It is a melancholy reflection," James Madison wrote to Thomas Jefferson shortly after the Constitution's ratification, "that liberty should be equally exposed to danger whether the government has too much or too little power."[8]

The men who wrote the Constitution sought to establish a government strong enough to enforce national interests, including defense and commerce among the states (see Chapter 3), but not so strong as to destroy liberty. Limited government was built into the Constitution through both grants and restrictions of political power.

Grants and Denials of Power

The Framers chose to limit the national government in part by confining its scope to constitutional **grants of power.** Congress's lawmaking powers are specifically listed in Article I, Section 8 of the Constitution. Seventeen in number, these listed powers include, for example, the powers to tax, to establish an army and navy, to declare war, to regulate commerce among the states, to create a national currency, and to borrow money. Authority *not* granted to the government by the Constitution is in theory denied to it. In a period where other governments had unrestricted powers, this limitation was remarkable.

The Framers also used **denials of power** as a means to limit government, prohibiting certain practices that European rulers had routinely used to intimidate political opponents. The French king, for example, could imprison a subject indefinitely without charge. The U.S. Constitution prohibits such action: individuals have the right to be brought before a court under a writ of habeas corpus for a judgment as to the legality of their confinement. The Constitution also forbids Congress and the states from passing ex post facto laws, under which citizens can be prosecuted for acts that were legal at the time they were committed.

As a further denial of power, the Framers made the Constitution difficult to amend, thereby making it hard for those in power to increase their lawful authority by changing the Constitution. An amendment could be proposed

LIBERTY, EQUALITY, & SELF-GOVERNMENT

What's Your Opinion?

Constitutionalism

The Englishman James Bryce ranked America's written constitution as its greatest contribution to the practice of government. The Constitution offered the world a new model of government in which a written document defining the state's lawful powers was a higher authority than the actions of any political leader or institution.

The Framers' commitment to constitutionalism grew out of their recognition that although government must have coercive power in order to carry out the actions necessary to maintain a civil society, this same power can be used by unscrupulous leaders to strip others of their liberty.

Do you think these two considerations—the coercive power of government and the corruptibility of those in whom power is invested—lead almost inevitably to a belief in limited government and to the use of constitutional measures (such as checks and balances) as a means to control the uses of power? What historical examples, other than Watergate, can you think of that illustrate the significance of constitutional limitations on the exercise of power?

only by a two-thirds majority in both chambers of Congress or by a national constitutional convention called by two-thirds of the state legislatures. Such a proposal would then become law only if ratified by three-fourths of state legislatures or state conventions. (The Constitution grants Congress the power to decide whether state legislatures or state conventions will be used in the ratifying process. The Twenty-first Amendment is the only one in which Congress specified state conventions as the ratifying mechanism; in all other cases, state legislatures have done the ratifying. The Twenty-first Amendment repealed the Eighteenth Amendment, which had prohibited the manufacture, sale, and transportation of alcoholic beverages. Congress concluded that repeal was better addressed and more likely to occur in state conventions than in state legislatures. The national constitutional convention as a means of proposing amendments has never been used. All amendments have originated with Congress.)

Using Power to Offset Power

Although the Framers believed that grants and denials of power could act as controls on government, they had no illusion that written words alone

institutions. Legislative, executive, and judicial powers in the American system are divided in such a way that they overlap; each of the three branches of government checks the others' powers and balances those powers with powers of its own. As natural as this system now might seem to Americans, most democracies are of the parliamentary type, where executive and legislative power are combined in a single institution rather than vested in separate ones. In a parliamentary system, the majority in the legislature selects the prime minister, who then serves as both the legislature leader and the chief executive (see "How the United States Compares.")

Shared Legislative Powers Under the Constitution, Congress has legislative authority, but that power is partly shared with the other branches and thus checked by them. The president can veto acts of Congress, recommend legislation, and call special sessions of Congress. The president also has the power to execute—and thereby to interpret—the laws made by Congress.

The Supreme Court has the power to interpret acts of Congress that are disputed in legal cases. The Court also has the power of judicial review; it can declare laws of Congress void when it finds that they are not in accord with the Constitution.

Within Congress, there is a further check on legislative power: for legislation to be passed, a majority in each house of Congress is required. Thus the Senate and the House of Representatives can block each other from acting.

Shared Executive Powers Executive power is vested in the president but is constrained by legislative and judicial checks. The president's power to make treaties and appoint high-ranking officials, for example, is subject to Senate approval. Congress also has the power to impeach and remove the president from office. In practical terms, Congress's greatest checks on executive action are its lawmaking and appropriations powers. The executive branch cannot act without laws that authorize its activities or without the money that pays for these programs.

The judiciary's major check on the presidency is its power to declare an action unlawful because it is not authorized by the legislation that the executive claims to be implementing.

Shared Judicial Powers Judicial power rests with the Supreme Court and with lower federal courts, which are subject to checks by the other branches of the federal government. Congress is empowered to establish the size of the federal court system, to restrict the Supreme Court's appellate jurisdiction in some circumstances, and to impeach and remove federal judges from office. More important, Congress can rewrite legislation that the

How the United States Compares

Checks and Balances

All democracies place constitutional limits on the power of government. The concept of rule by law, for example, is characteristic of democratic governments but not of authoritarian regimes. Democracies differ, however, in the extent to which political power is restrained through constitutional mechanisms. The United States is an extreme case in that its government rests on an elaborate system of constitutional checks and balances. The system employs a separation of powers among the executive, legislative, and judicial branches. It also includes judicial review, the power of the courts to invalidate actions of the legislature or executive. These constitutional restrictions on power are not part of the governing structure of all democracies.

Most democracies, for example, have parliamentary systems, which invest both executive and legislative leadership in the office of prime minister. Britain is an example of this type of system. Parliament under the leadership of the prime minister is the supreme authority in Britain. Its laws are not even subject to override by Britain's high court, which has no power to review the constitutionality of parliamentary acts.

Country	Separation of Executive & Legislative Powers?	Judicial Review?
Belgium	No	Yes
Canada	No	Yes
France	Yes	No
Germany	No	Yes
Great Britain	No	No
Italy	No	Yes
Japan	No	Yes
Mexico	Yes	Yes
United States	Yes	Yes

courts have misinterpreted and can initiate amendments when it disagrees with the courts' rulings on constitutional issues.

The president has the power to appoint federal judges with the consent of the Senate and to pardon persons convicted in the courts. The president is also responsible for executing court decisions, a function that provides opportunities to influence the way rulings are implemented.

The Bill of Rights

Although the delegates to the Philadelphia convention discussed the possibility of placing a list of individual rights (such as freedom of speech and the right to a fair trial) in the Constitution, they ultimately decided that such a list was unnecessary because of the doctrine of expressed powers: government could not lawfully engage in actions, such as the suppression of speech, that were not authorized by the Constitution. Moreover, the delegates concluded that a bill of rights was undesirable because government might feel free to disregard any right that was inadvertently left off the list or that emerged at some future time. These considerations did not allay the fears of leading Americans who believed that no possible safeguard of liberty should be omitted. "A bill of rights," Jefferson argued, "is what the people are entitled to against every government on earth, general or particular, and what no just government should refuse or rest on inference." Jefferson had included a bill of rights in the constitution he wrote for Virginia at the outbreak of the Revolutionary War, and all but four states had followed Virginia's example.

Opposition to the absence of a bill of rights led to its addition to the Constitution. Madison himself introduced a series of amendments during the First Congress, ten of which were soon ratified by the states. These amendments, traditionally called the **Bill of Rights,** include such rights as freedom of speech and religion and due process protections (such as jury trial and legal counsel) for persons accused of crimes. (These rights, termed *civil liberties*, are discussed at length in Chapter 4.)

The Bill of Rights is a precise expression of the concept of limited government. In consenting to be governed, the people agree to accept the authority of government in certain areas but not in others; the people's constitutional rights cannot lawfully be denied by governing officials.

Judicial Review

The writers of the Constitution both empowered and limited government. But who was to decide whether officials were operating within the limits of their constitutionally authorized powers? The Framers did not specifically entrust this power to a particular branch of government, although they did

Limits on Government in the U.S. Constitution

Grants of power: Powers granted to the national government by the Constitution. Powers not granted it are denied it unless they are necessary and proper to the carrying out of granted powers.

Denials of power: Powers expressly denied to the national and state governments by the Constitution.

Separated institutions sharing power: The division of the national government's power among three branches, each of which is to act as a check on the powers of the other two.

Bill of Rights: The first ten amendments to the Constitution, which specify rights of citizens that the national government must respect.

Federalism: The division of political authority between the national government and the states, enabling the people to appeal to one authority if their rights and interests are not respected by the other authority (see Chapter 3).

Judicial review: The power of the courts to declare governmental action null and void when it is found to violate the Constitution.

Elections: The power of the voters to remove officials from office.

grant the Supreme Court the authority to decide on "all cases arising under this Constitution." Moreover, at the ratifying conventions of at least eight of the thirteen states, it was claimed that the judiciary would have the power to nullify actions that violated the Constitution.[12]

Nevertheless, because the Constitution did not explicitly grant the judiciary this authority, it was a principle that had to be established in practice. The opportunity arose with an incident that occurred after the election of 1800, in which John Adams lost his bid for a second presidential term after a bitter campaign against Jefferson. Between November 1800, when Jefferson was elected, and March 1801, when he was inaugurated, the Federalist-controlled Congress created fifty-nine additional lower-court judgeships, enabling Adams to appoint loyal Federalists to those positions before he left office. However, Adams's term expired before the secretary of state could deliver the judicial commissions to all the appointees. Without this formal authorization, an appointee could not take office. Knowing this, Jefferson told his secretary of state, James Madison, not to deliver them. William Marbury was one of those who did not receive his commission, and he asked the Supreme Court to issue a writ of mandamus (a court order directing an official to perform a specific act) that would compel Madison to deliver it.

Marbury v. Madison (1803) became the foundation for judicial review by the federal courts. Chief Justice John Marshall wrote the *Marbury* opinion, which declared that Marbury had a legal right to his commission. The opinion also said, however, that the Supreme Court could not issue him a writ of mandamus because it lacked the constitutional authority to do so. Congress had passed ordinary legislation in 1789 that gave the Court this power, but Marshall noted that the Constitution prohibits Congress from expanding the Supreme Court's authority except through a constitutional amendment. That being the case, Marshall argued, the legislation that provided the authorization was constitutionally invalid.[13] In striking down this act of Congress on constitutional grounds, the Court asserted its power of **judicial review**—that is, the power of the judiciary to decide whether a government official or institution has acted within the limits of the Constitution and, if not, to declare its action null and void.

Marshall's decision was ingenious since it asserted the power of judicial review without creating the possibility of its rejection by either the executive or the legislative branch. In declaring that Marbury had a right to his commission, the Court in effect said that President Jefferson had failed in his constitutional duty to execute the laws faithfully. But since it did not order Jefferson to deliver the commission, he had no opportunity to refuse to comply with the Court's judgment. At the same time, the Court reprimanded Congress for passing legislation that exceeded its constitutional authority. Congress also had no way to retaliate. It could not force the Court to accept the power to issue writs of mandamus if the Court itself refused to do so.

PROVIDING FOR SELF-GOVERNMENT

"We the People" is the opening phrase of the Constitution. It expresses the idea that in the United States the people will have the power to govern themselves. In a sense, there is no contradiction between this idea and the Constitution's provisions for limited government, since individual *liberty* is part of the process of *self-government*. If people cannot express themselves freely, they cannot be self-governing. In another sense, however, the contradiction is clear: restrictions on the power of the majority are a denial of its right to govern society as it chooses.

The Framers believed that the people deserved and required a voice in their government, but they also feared popular government. They worried that the people would become inflamed by a passionate issue or fiery demagogue and act without due regard for the interests of the minority. To the Framers, the great risk of popular government was **tyranny of the majority:**

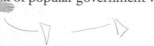

the people acting as an irrational mob that tramples on the rights of others. Their fear was not without foundation. The history of democracies was filled with examples of majority tyranny, and there were even examples from the nation's brief history. In 1786, for instance, debtors had gained control of Rhode Island's legislature and made paper money a legal means of paying debts, even though existing contracts called for payment in gold. Creditors were then hunted down and held captive in public places so that debtors could come and pay them in full with worthless paper money. A Boston newspaper wrote that Rhode Island should be renamed Rogue Island.

Democracy Versus Republic

No form of self-government could eliminate completely the threat to liberty of majority tyranny, but the Framers believed that the danger would be greatly diminished by properly structured institutions.[14] Madison summarized the Framers' intent when he said in *Federalist* No. 10 that the Constitution was "a republican remedy" for the excesses historically associated with "democratic" rule. Today the terms **democracy, republic,** and **representative democracy** are often used interchangeably to refer to a system of government in which ultimate political power rests with the majority through its capacity to choose representatives in free and open elections. To the writers of the Constitution, however, *democracy* and *republic* had different meanings. When the Framers complained about the risks of democracy, they were referring to a government subject to immediate popular influence, either because the public participated directly in policy decisions (pure or direct democracy, as in Ancient Greece or New England town meetings) or because lawmakers acted out of fear of the public (mobocracy). In their use of the term *republic*, the Framers were referring to *representative democracy* in which elected officials met in representative institutions.[15]

The Framers' concept of a proper system of representation was similar to an idea put forth by the English theorist Edmund Burke (1729–1797). In his *Letter to the Sheriffs of Bristol,* Burke argued that representatives should act as public **trustees:** they are obliged to promote the interest of those who elected them, but the nature of this interest is for the representatives, not the voters, to decide. Burke was concerned about the ease with which society could degenerate into selfishness, and he thought it imperative for representatives not to surrender their judgment to popular whim.

Limited Popular Rule

The Constitution provided that all power would be exercised through representative institutions. There was no provision for any form of direct popular participation in the making of policy decisions. In view of the fact that

TABLE 2–2 METHODS OF CHOOSING NATIONAL LEADERS		
Fearing the concentration of political power, the Framers devised alternative methods of selection and terms of service for national officials.		
Office	*Method of Selection*	*Term of Service*
President	Electoral College	4 years
U.S. senator	State legislature	6 years (1/3 of senators' terms expire every 2 years)
U.S. representative	Popular election	2 years
Federal judge	Nomination by president, approval by Senate	Indefinite (subject to "good behavior")

the United States was much too large to be governed directly by the people in popular assemblies, a representative system was necessary. Moreover, the separation of powers meant that the majority's will, again by necessity, would be filtered through an institutional structure. The Framers went beyond what was necessary, however, and placed officials at a considerable distance from the people they represented (see Table 2–2).

The House of Representatives was the only institution that would be based on direct popular election—its members would be elected for two-year terms of office through vote of the people. Frequent and direct election of House members was intended to make government sensitive to the concerns of popular majorities.

U.S. senators would be appointed by the legislatures of the states they represented. Because state legislators were popularly elected, the people would be choosing their senators indirectly. Every two years, a third of the senators would be appointed to six-year terms. The Senate was expected to check and balance the House, which, by virtue of the more frequent and direct election of its members, would presumably be more responsive to popular opinion.

Presidential selection was an issue of considerable debate at the Philadelphia convention. Direct election of the president was twice proposed and twice rejected because it linked executive power directly to popular majorities. The Framers finally chose to have the president selected by the votes of electors (the so-called **Electoral College**). Each state would have as many **electoral votes** as it had members in Congress and could select its electors by any method it chose. The president would serve four years and be eligible for reelection.

Pictured here is the Old Senate Chamber, where the U.S. Senate met until 1859, when a new and larger chamber was constructed. The Old Senate Chamber was the scene of heated debates over slavery. Daniel Webster, Henry Clay, and John C. Calhoun gained national reputations here. After the Senate vacated the chamber, it was occupied by the U.S. Supreme Court until 1935, when the Court's own building across the street from the Capitol was completed. Not until 1914 were U.S. senators chosen by direct vote of the people.

    The Framers decided that federal judges and justices would be appointed rather than elected. They would be nominated by the president and confirmed through approval by the Senate. Once confirmed, they would "hold their offices during good behavior." In effect, they would be allowed to hold office for life unless they committed a crime. Rather than a representative institution, the judiciary was a "guardian" institution that would uphold the rule of law and serve as a check on the elected branches of government.[16]

    These differing methods of selecting national officeholders would not prevent a determined majority from achieving unbridled power, but control could not be attained easily or quickly. Unlike the House of Representatives, institutions such as the Senate, presidency, and judiciary would not yield to an impassioned majority in a single election. The delay would reduce the probability that government would degenerate into mob rule driven by momentary whims.

Altering the Constitution: More Power to the People

The Constitution's provisions for limited government have stood the test of time: in its structure and formal powers, the national government today has nearly the same features as the government established in 1789. This is not true, however, of the provisions for self-government: several of the original provisions have been amended. In no other constitutional area have Americans shown a greater willingness to devise new arrangements.

A desire for change was evident nearly as soon as the Constitution was unveiled. The Framers' conception of self-government was at odds with what the average American in 1787 had come to expect. Every state but South Carolina held annual legislative elections, and several states also chose their governors through annual election. And it was not long after ratification of the Constitution that Americans sought a more substantial voice in their own governing.

Jeffersonian Democracy: A Revolution of the Spirit Thomas Jefferson, who otherwise admired the Constitution, was among the prominent Americans who questioned its provisions for self-government. And it was Jefferson who may have spared the nation a bloody conflict over the issue of popular sovereignty. Under John Adams, the second president, the national government increasingly favored the nation's wealthy interests. Adams publicly suggested that the Constitution was designed for a governing elite, while Alexander Hamilton urged him to use force if necessary to suppress popular dissent.[17] Jefferson asked whether Adams, with the aid of a strong army, planned soon to deprive ordinary Americans of their liberty. Jefferson challenged Adams in the next presidential election and, upon defeating him, hailed the victory as the "Revolution of 1800."

Although Jefferson was a champion of the common people, he had no clear vision of how a popular government might work in practice. He believed that congressional majorities were the proper expression of popular majorities and accordingly was reluctant to use his presidency as the instrument of the people.[18] Jefferson also had no illusions about a largely illiterate population's readiness for a significant governing role and feared the ruinous consequences of inciting the masses to contest the moneyed class. But Jefferson did found the nation's first political party (it was the forerunner of today's Democratic Party), which served to link like-minded leaders and thus act as a bridge across divided institutions of power. By and large, however, Jeffersonian democracy was a revolution of the spirit. Jefferson taught Americans to look upon the national government as belonging to all, not just to the privileged few.[19]

Jacksonian Democracy: Linking the People and the Presidency
Not until Andrew Jackson was elected in 1828 did the country have a powerful president who was willing and able to involve the public more fully in government. Jackson carried out the constitutional revolution that Jeffersonian democracy had foreshadowed.

Jackson recognized that the president was the only official who could legitimately claim to represent the people as a whole. Unlike the president, members of Congress were elected from separate states and districts rather than from the entire country. Yet the president's claim to popular leadership was diminished by the existence of the Electoral College. Jackson persuaded the states to choose their presidential electors on the basis of popular voting. Jackson's reform, which is still in effect today, basically places the selection of a president in the voters' hands. The winner of the popular vote in a state is awarded its electoral votes; hence the candidate who wins most of the popular votes in the states is also most likely to receive a majority of the electoral votes. Since Jackson's time, only three candidates—Rutherford B. Hayes in 1876, Benjamin Harrison in 1888, and George W. Bush in 2000—have won the presidency after losing the popular vote. (The Electoral College is discussed further in Chapter 12.)

The Progressives: Senate and Primary Elections The Progressive era of the early 1900s brought another wave of democratic reforms. The Progressives rejected the Burkean idea of representatives as trustees; they embraced instead the idea of representatives as **delegates**—officeholders who are obligated to respond directly to the expressed opinions of the people whom they represent.

The Progressives succeeded primarily in changing the way that some state and local governments operate (see "States in the Nation"). Progressive reforms at these levels included recall elections, which enable citizens through petition to require a particular officeholder to submit to election before the expiration of his or her normal term of office; the initiative, which enables citizens through petition to place legislative measures on the ballot for enactment or rejection through popular voting; and the referendum, which permits legislative bodies to submit measures to the voters for enactment or rejection.

The Progressives also brought about two changes in federal elections. One was the direct election of U.S. senators, who before the Seventeenth Amendment was ratified in 1913 had been chosen by state legislatures and were widely perceived as agents of big business (the Senate was nicknamed the "Millionaires' Club"). Senators who stood to lose their seats in a direct popular vote had blocked earlier attempts to change the

★ ‖ STATES IN THE NATION

Direct Democracy: The Initiative and Referendum

In some states, citizens can exercise their power through the initiative and the referendum. The map identifies states that have the least restrictive forms of the initiative or referendum—that is, where there is no substantial limit (except for judicial review) on what citizens through their votes can directly decide.

Q: Why are southern and northeastern states less likely to have the initiative and referendum than states elsewhere?

A: The initiative and referendum were introduced in the early 1900s by the Progressives, who sought to weaken the power of political bosses. In the Northeast, party machines had enough strength in state legislatures to block their enactment. In the South, these devices were blocked by the white establishment, which feared that blacks and poor whites would make use of them.

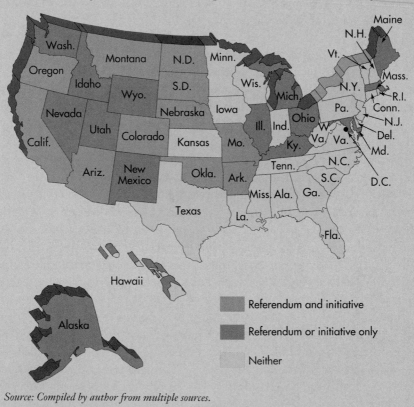

Source: Compiled by author from multiple sources.

Constitution. Eventually, however, the Senate was persuaded to support an amendment by pressure from the Progressives and by revelations that corporate bribes had influenced the selection of several senators. The second change was the **primary election,** which gives rank-and-file voters the opportunity to select party nominees. Nearly all states in the early 1900s adopted the primary election as a means of choosing nominees for at least some federal and state offices. Before this change, nominees were chosen by party leaders.

The Progressive era spawned attacks on the Framers. A prominent criticism was the historian Charles S. Beard's *Economic Interpretation of the Constitution.*[20] Arguing that the Constitution grew out of wealthy Americans' fears of the debtor rebellions, and noting that many of the Framers were themselves wealthy men, Beard claimed that the Constitution's elaborate systems of power and representation were devices for keeping power in the hands of the rich. Beard's thesis was challenged by other historians, and he later acknowledged that he had not taken the Framers' full array of motives into account. Their conception of separation of powers, for example, was a time-honored governing principle that had previously been incorporated in state constitutions. Although the Framers did not have great trust in popular rule, it would be a mistake to conclude they were foes of democracy. They were intent on balancing the demands of limited government with those of self-government and, in striking a balance, leaned toward the former, believing that the evil of unrestrained power was the greater danger to a civil society.

CONSTITUTIONAL DEMOCRACY TODAY

The type of government created in the United States in 1787 is today called a **constitutional democracy.** It is *democratic* in its provisions for majority influence through elections and *constitutional* in its requirement that power gained through elections be exercised in accordance with law and with due respect for individual rights.

By some standards, the American system of today is a model of *self-government.* The United States schedules the election of its larger legislative chamber (the House of Representatives) and its chief executive more frequently than any other democracy. In addition, it is the only major democracy that relies extensively on primary elections instead of party organizations for the selection of party nominees. The principle of popular election to office, which the writers of the Constitution regarded as a prerequisite of popular sovereignty but to be used sparingly, has been extended further in the United States than anywhere else.

By other standards, however, the U.S. system is less democratic than many others. Popular majorities must work against the barriers to influence—the elaborate system of divided powers, staggered terms of office, and separate constituencies—that were devised by the Framers. In fact, the link between an electoral majority and a governing majority is far less direct in the American system than in nearly all other democratic systems. In the European parliamentary democracies, for example, legislative and executive power are not separated, are not subject to close check by the judiciary, and are acquired through the winning of a legislative majority in national elections. The Framers' vision was a different one, dominated by a concern with *liberty* and therefore with controls on political power, a response to the experiences they brought with them to Philadelphia in the summer of 1787.

SUMMARY

The Constitution of the United States is a reflection of the colonial and revolutionary experiences of the early Americans. Freedom from abusive government was a reason for the colonies' revolt against British rule, but the English tradition also provided ideas about government, power, and freedom that were expressed in the Constitution and, earlier, in the Declaration of Independence.

SELF TEST
mhhe
✓ com
/pattersonwtp5

The Constitution was designed in part to provide for a limited government in which political power would be confined to proper uses. The Framers wanted to ensure that the government they were creating would not itself be a threat to freedom. To this end, they confined the national government to expressly granted powers and also denied it certain specific powers. Other prohibitions on government were later added to the Constitution in the form of stated guarantees of individual liberties: the Bill of Rights. The most significant constitutional provision for limited government, however, was a separation of powers among the three branches. The powers given to each branch enable it to act as a check on the exercise of power by the others, an arrangement that, during the nation's history, has in fact served as a barrier to abuses of power.

The Constitution, however, made no mention of how the powers and limits of government were to be judged in practice. In its historic ruling in *Marbury v. Madison*, the Supreme Court assumed the authority to review the constitutionality of legislative and executive actions and to declare them unconstitutional and thus invalid.

The Framers of the Constitution respected the idea of self-government but distrusted popular majorities. They designed a government that they felt would temper popular opinion and slow its momentum, so that the public's "true interest" (which includes a regard for the rights and interests of the minority) would guide public policy. Different methods were established to select the House of Representatives, the Senate, the president, and federal judges in order to keep political power out of the hands of a tyrannical majority.

Since the adoption of the Constitution, however, the public has gradually assumed more direct control of its representatives, particularly through measures affecting the way in which officeholders are chosen. Presidential voting (linked to the Electoral College), direct election of senators, and primary elections are among the devices aimed at strengthening the majority's influence. These developments are rooted in the idea, deeply held by ordinary Americans, that the people must have substantial direct control of their government if it is to serve their real interests.

KEY TERMS

Anti-Federalists
Bill of Rights
checks and balances
constitution
constitutional democracy
delegates
democracy
denials of power
Electoral College
electoral votes
Federalists
grants of power
Great Compromise
inalienable (natural) rights

judicial review
limited government
New Jersey (small-state) Plan
North-South Compromise
primary elections
representative democracy
republic
self-government
separated institutions sharing
    power
separation of powers
trustees
tyranny of the majority
Virginia (large-state) Plan

SUGGESTED READINGS

Beard, Charles S. *An Economic Interpretation of the Constitution.* New York: Macmillan, 1941. Argues that the Framers had selfish economic interests uppermost in mind when they wrote the Constitution.

Farrand, Max. *The Records of the Federal Convention of 1787.* New Haven, Conn.: Yale University Press, 1966. A four-volume work that includes all the important records of the Philadelphia convention.

Federalist Papers. Many editions, including a one-volume paperback version edited by Isaac Kramnick (New York: Penguin, 1987). A series of essays written by Alexander Hamilton, James Madison, and John Jay under the pseudonym Publius. The essays, published in a New York newspaper in 1787–88, explain the Constitution and support its ratification.

Hardin, Russell. *Liberalism, Constitutionalism, and Democracy.* New York: Oxford University Press, 1999. Analysis of the great ideas that underlie the Constitution.

Haskell, John. *Direct Democracy or Representative Government: Dispelling the Populist Myth.* Boulder, Colo.: Westview Press, 2001. Analysis of the two democratic philosophies that have affected American politics.

Sheldon, Garret Ward. *The Political Philosophy of James Madison.* Baltimore: Johns Hopkins University Press, 2000. A synthesis of James Madison's political philosophy in the context of the social and political history of his day.

Tocqueville, Alexis de. *Democracy in America,* vols. 1 and 2, ed. J. P. Mayer. New York: Doubleday/Anchor, 1969. A classic analysis (originally published 1835–1840) of American democracy by an insightful French observer.

LIST OF WEBSITES

http://www.nara.gov The National Archives site; includes an in-depth look at the history of the Declaration of Independence.

http://odur.let.rug.nl/~usa/P/aj7/about/bio/jackxx.htm A site that focuses on Andrew Jackson and his role in shaping U.S. politics.

http://www.yale.edu/lawweb/avalon/constpap.htm Includes documents on the roots of the Constitution, the American Revolution, and the Constitutional Convention.

http://www.yale.edu/lawweb/avalon/presiden/jeffpap.htm A site that includes the papers of Thomas Jefferson. His autobiography is among the available materials.

POLITICS IN THEORY AND PRACTICE

Thinking: How does the division of power in the U.S. political system contribute to limited government? How do the provisions for representative government (the various methods of choosing national officials) contribute to limited government?

Acting: In recent years, as a means of checking the power of elected officials, a number of states and localities have imposed a limit on the number of terms that representatives can serve. Although the term-limit movement has slowed in recent years, there are still opportunities to get involved on either side of the issue. If you favor term limits and want to get involved, you might start by examining the website of U.S. Term Limits (www.termlimits.org). If you oppose term limits, you could begin by looking at the Common Cause site (www.commoncause.org).

questions
pg. 56
    MARbURY vs. Madison
pg. 57
    deM vs. Rep imp?

The New York Times   reading 2

There's a Small Matter of Checks and Balances

by David E. Sanger

The U.S. Constitution establishes a system of checks and balances that is designed to control the power of government for the purpose of protecting personal freedom. In this article, which appeared on January 27, 2002, The New York Times's David Sanger raises a question that has been asked at numerous times in U.S. history. Do threats to national security upset the system of checks and balances by shifting power toward the executive?

WASHINGTON—Wartime concentrates power in the presidency. Abuses of capitalism—especially when they are Enron-sized and presided over by a president's friends—tend to swing the pendulum the other way, as Congress acts to investigate, condemn and regulate. So what happens when war and scandal, a powerful president and an ascendant Congress all take the stage at the same time?

That may well be the subtext on Tuesday night, when President Bush goes to Congress for his State of the Union address. He will be cheered wildly, from both sides of the aisle, for his conduct of the war. He will declare that the nation is strong, its economy slowly recovering. But at the same moment, he and his audience in the House chamber will be engaged in their perpetual historical struggle—not over the state of the union, but over the state of its checks and balances. George W. Bush, who was dismissed a year ago by some as an accidental president of questionable authority, has emerged as the leader of a war on terrorism with unquestioned authority to decide where the war goes next. But he has also seized the moment to assert, though not yet fully exercise, far greater powers for the executive branch at home. The most dramatic are determining who will be tried before a military tribunal rather than a civilian court, listening in on lawyer-defendant conversations in terror cases, and defining the status of prisoners at Guantanamo Bay in a way that allows the military to sidestep the Geneva Conventions.

In each case he is taking for the executive branch alone the right to rule on a question of constitutional rights or international law. But most of Congress has uttered barely a peep. Instead, Capitol Hill is abuzz with the politically safer possibilities of the Enron investigation, with its tales of document-shredding and elaborate deceptions of shareholders and employees.

Politically speaking, legislators on both sides of the aisle know that blood will be spilled on the Enron issue. Left undebated, though, is a trickier matter: Is Congress evading its critical role as a check against an accumulation of unchecked power in the presidency over domestic surveillance, liberties and security? This is wartime, the administration says. But it also says that this war will focus intensely on "homeland defense," a task that could last for decades.

Mr. Bush can claim, reasonably, that Congress gave him broad power to hunt down terrorists in the days immediately after the Sept. 11 attacks. Nonetheless, liberals and libertarians, historians and constitutional scholars, have begun to argue forcefully that his pronouncements go beyond both what Congress was thinking about in the shock of September, and what the founders envisioned before anyone conceived of skyscrapers or airplanes, much less terrorists who commit mass murder using both.

"As a matter of constitutional theory, we should be very nervous about unilateral executive pronouncements that don't rest on firm authority," said Jack Rakove, a Stanford University history professor who studies the way 210 years of politics have molded the constitutional division of power. "As a matter of politics," he adds, "it's always better for presidents to seek consent, which was the issue in the Vietnam War."

But so far the White House has shown little interest in negotiating with Senator Patrick Leahy, the Vermont Democrat and chairman of the Senate Judiciary Committee, over legislation that would define the president's powers in convening military tribunals for foreign-born terrorists—or any other legislation that may limit his freedom to act. Polls show that the American people are with Mr. Bush. They are reluctant to tie his hands in a confusing and unconventional war, in which the enemy may well be a fellow passenger in Seat 6A with plastique in his shoe. Mr. Bush's aides interpret that as carte blanche to reassert presidential authority.

Senator Leahy says that's short-sighted. "This war on terrorism is going to be going on long after George Bush is gone, and long after I am gone," he said. "So we want to make sure we do it right. Why not work out rules on military tribunals and get authorization from Congress, before it comes back to haunt the president?"

To those with a long memory, that may look like the classic battle between legislators and the executive that characterized the Vietnam war years. If it does, look again.

The lines now are a lot blurrier. Everyone involved is skittish about making political missteps in a time of high public emotion—which may explain why so few in Congress have tried to limit the president's wartime powers, and why Mr. Bush has acted with considerable restraint.

If it is true that Congress hasn't used the powers it has to rein in Attorney General John Ashcroft, it is also true that Mr. Bush has passed up two opportunities to convene military tribunals—in the case of the mysterious Al Qaeda operative Zacarias Moussaoui, and in the case of Richard Reid, who is accused of trying to blow up a plane with explosives in his soles. In both cases Mr. Bush decided to let civil trials proceed.

The White House says the cases prove Mr. Bush is not power-hungry. "The president simply needs flexibility in pursuing the war," said Ari Fleischer, the president's spokesman, who knows well that in Washington flexibility is power.

Another explanation, dismissed at the White House but alive everywhere else, is that Mr. Bush's advisers concluded that actually using his newly declared powers could set off a divisive debate, and that he should save the tribunals for really big fish like Osama bin Laden.

"I think they know that they overreached, and now they are pulling back," says Arthur M. Schlesinger Jr., the historian best known for his book "The Imperial Presidency."

In fact, Mr. Bush's political aides have spent a lot of time looking at historical precedents, and they don't always like what they've found. Karl Rove, the president's chief political adviser, is trying to determine if any post-Pearl Harbor lessons should apply as Mr. Bush navigates his way to midterm elections. It turns out that less than a year after Pearl Harbor, Franklin D. Roosevelt's Democrats lost 9 seats in the Senate and 45 in the House. And Woodrow Wilson lost both houses of Congress in 1918.

Roosevelt also faced civil liberties questions, and may not have given them enough thought. His order to intern Japanese-Americans (an order Congress did nothing to stop) has become, in history's light, the biggest blot on his presidency. And Roosevelt's speech writer, Samuel Rosenman, recalled in his memoirs that while drafting the State of the Union address for 1942, Roosevelt laughed that Attorney General Francis Biddle "has been on my neck" to declare that civil liberties would not be impaired.

Mr. Ashcroft is not suspected of losing sleep over that issue. But, in one of those wonderful oddities of history, President Bush has said his planned tribunals rest on the precedent of Roosevelt's use of a military tribunal to try Nazi saboteurs captured in America.

The citation doesn't please some libertarians. Robert A. Levy, a constitutional scholar at the Cato Institute, for example, wrote that Mr. Bush had gone so far beyond the guidelines under which the Supreme Court upheld the Roosevelt tribunal that "the order as it now stands is illegitimate." (He added, with a dig at Mr. Ashcroft: "Those of us who say so are not, in the attorney general's unfortunate and offensive words, 'giving ammunition to America's enemies.'"

Nevertheless, in an interview, Mr. Levy allowed that the rules the military has since promulgated give fairly broad protections to defendants, and "take the wind out of the sails of some of the critics."

In the end, then, the outcome of this struggle may well be decided by politics and public opinion. Mr. Bush says "Trust me," just as F.D.R. did. Congress says very little, not because it lacks the power to establish the rules, but because exercising that power risks setting off political dynamite. So, for now at least, Congress has changed the subject—with a little help from Kenneth L. Lay and Arthur Anderson.

But, as Mr. Bush never tires of saying, Sept. 11 was a new kind of attack requiring new responses. "If this is going to be a long, twilight struggle," says Professor Rakove, "then maybe we have some time to talk about how to prosecute a strategic campaign against terrorism within constitutional confines. But sooner or later, we do have to start that conversation."

What's Your Opinion?

Is the war on terrorism resulting in too large a shift of power to the executive branch?

CHAPTER 3

FEDERALISM: FORGING A NATION

❝The question of the relation of the states to the federal government is the cardinal question of our Constitutional system. It cannot be settled by the opinion of one generation, because it is a question of growth, and each successive stage of our political and economic development gives it a new aspect, makes it a new question.❞

WOODROW WILSON[1]

In late 2001, the attorney general of the United States, John Ashcroft, directed federal agents to take action against Oregon physicians who prescribed federally controlled drugs to assist terminally ill patients to commit suicide. These physicians would lose their licenses to prescribe such drugs. Ashcroft's aim was to void the Oregon law that permits physician assistance in cases where a patient, in the judgment of at least two doctors, has less than six months to live, is suffering painfully, and is mentally competent to decide whether to end his or her life. Ashcroft's action was not the first federal attempt to nullify the Oregon law. Congress had twice initiated action—in one instance, a bill actually passed the House but failed to come up for a vote in the Senate.

Oregon's voters had approved the assisted-suicide law in a statewide referendum, becoming the first state (and, as of 2003, the only state) to do so. A majority of Oregon's voters had been persuaded by the argument that no public benefit derived from requiring the dying to accept prolonged and painful suffering. Opponents had countered that society's interest in preserving life outweighs a patient's desire to die, that laws allowing doctors to assist a suicide would be abused, that doctors and relatives in some instances would persuade terminally ill patients to accept death against their will, and that depressed patients who ask to die will be granted their wish rather than be treated for their depression, after which they might choose to live. In filing suit against the Oregon law, the U.S. Department of Justice argued that "there are important medical, ethical and legal distinctions between intentionally causing a patient's death and providing sufficient dosages of pain medications to eliminate or alleviate pain."

Nevertheless, Oregon voters had twice—first in 1994 and then again in 1997—approved the state's Death With Dignity Act. They prevailed again in 2002, when a federal district court judge halted the Justice Department's effort to nullify Oregon's physician-assisted suicide law. Ashcroft immediately appealed the ruling to the U.S. Court of Appeals for the Ninth Circuit, an indication that this fight between national and state authorities could be a prolonged one.

The controversy surrounding Oregon's Death With Dignity Act is one of thousands of disagreements during American history that have hinged on whether national or state authority should prevail. Americans possess what amounts to dual citizenship: they are citizens both of the United States and of the state where they reside. The American political system is a *federal system*, one in which constitutional authority is divided between a national government and state governments: each is assumed to derive its powers directly from the people and therefore to have sovereignty (final authority) over the policy responsibilities assigned to it. The federal system consists of nation *and* states, indivisible and yet separate.[2]

This chapter on American constitutionalism focuses on federalism. The nature of the relationship between the nation and the states was the most pressing issue when the Constitution was written in 1787, and this chapter describes how that issue helped shape the Constitution. The chapter's closing sections discuss how federalism has changed during the nation's history and conclude with a brief overview of contemporary federalism. The main points presented in the chapter are the following:

★ *The power of government must be equal to its responsibilities.* The Constitution was needed because the nation's preceding system (under the Articles of Confederation) was too weak to accomplish its expected goals, particularly those of a strong defense and an integrated economy.

★ *Federalism—the Constitution's division of governing authority between two levels, nation and states—was the result of political bargaining.* Federalism was not a theoretical principle, but a compromise made necessary in 1787 by the prior existence of the states.

★ *Federalism is not a fixed principle for allocating power between the national and state governments, but a principle that has changed over the course of time in response to new political needs.* Federalism has passed through several distinct stages during the nation's history.

★ *Contemporary federalism tilts toward national authority, reflecting the increased interdependence of American society.* However, there is a current trend toward reducing the scope of federal authority.

FEDERALISM: NATIONAL AND STATE SOVEREIGNTY

Many of the nation's most prominent leaders, including George Washington and Benjamin Franklin, were delegates to the Philadelphia convention in 1787. Not all of America's top leaders were at the convention, however, and many of them were staunchly opposed to a strong national government. When rumors circulated that the delegates were planning to propose such a government, Patrick Henry, an ardent supporter of state-centered government, said that he "smelt a rat." After the convention had adjourned, he realized that his fears were justified. "Who authorized them," he asked, "to speak the language of 'We, the People,' instead of 'We, the States'?"

The question—"people versus states?"—was precipitated by the failure of the Articles of Confederation. The government of the Articles (see Chapter 2) was a union of states rather than also of people. The result was an inherently weak national government because it had no power to force the states to comply with its laws. Georgia and North Carolina, for example, contributed no money at all to the national treasury between 1781 and 1786, and the national government could do nothing more than to beg them to pay their fair share of the costs of defense, diplomacy, and other national policies.

The only realistic solution to this problem was a government based on the people. If ordered to pay taxes, individuals would either do so or face consequences—imprisonment or confiscation of property—that most of them would prefer to avoid.

Although the creation of a national government based directly on the people was therefore a goal of the writers of the Constitution, they also wanted to preserve the states as governing bodies. The states were already

Patrick Henry was a leading figure in the American Revolution ("Give me liberty or give me death!"). He later opposed ratification of the Constitution on grounds that the national government should be a union of states and not also of people.

 LIBERTY, EQUALITY, & SELF-GOVERNMENT

What's Your Opinion?

Large Versus Small Republics

During the debate over ratification of the Constitution, Americans argued over whether liberty, equality, and self-government would be better protected by the states or by the nation. The Anti-Federalists argued that a small republic was closer to the people and therefore would do more to protect their rights and interests. James Madison countered by saying that a large republic was preferable because it would have such a diversity of interests that compromise and tolerance among various groups would be required.

In your view, which side in this argument has the weight of American history behind it?

federal

National powers	Concurrent powers	State powers

National defense
Currency
Post office
Foreign affairs
Interstate commerce

Lending and borrowing of money
Taxation
Law enforcement
Chartering of banks
Transportation

Chartering of local governments
Education
Public safety
Registration and voting
Intrastate commerce

FIGURE 3–1 FEDERALISM AS A GOVERNING SYSTEM:
EXAMPLES OF NATIONAL, STATE, AND
CONCURRENT POWERS

The American federal system divides sovereignty between a national government and
the state governments. Each is constitutionally protected in its existence and authority,
although their powers overlap somewhat even in areas granted to one level (for
example, the federal government has a role in education policy).

in existence, had their own constitutions, and had popular support. When
Virginia's George Mason said he would never agree to a union that abolished the states, he was speaking for virtually all the delegates. The
Philadelphia convention thereby devised a system of government that came
to be known as **federalism.** Federalism is the division of **sovereignty,** or
ultimate governing authority, between a national government and regional
(that is, state) governments. Each directly governs the people and derives its
powers from them.

American federalism is basically a system of divided authority (see Figure
3–1). The system gives states the power to address local issues in ways of
their own choosing. At the same time, federalism gives the national government the power to decide matters of national scope. In practice, there is
some overlap between state and national action, but there is also a division
of responsibilities. The national government has primary responsibility for
national defense and the currency, among other things, while the states
have primary responsibilities for such policy areas as public education and
police protection. The national and state governments also have some concurrent powers (that is, powers exercised over the same areas of policy); for
example, each has the power to raise taxes and borrow money.

A federal system is different from a **confederacy,** which is the type of
government established by the Articles. A confederacy is a union in which

the states alone are sovereign. The authority of the central government is derived from the states, which can, at will, redefine its authority. Federalism is also different from **a unitary system,** in which sovereignty is vested solely in the national government. The people are citizens or subjects only of the national government, and the other governments derive their authority from the national government, which can, in theory at least, abolish them or redefine their authority.

In a federal system, because the national and state governments are both sovereign, the permanent existence of each is constitutionally guaranteed and each is constitutionally protected from undue interference by the other in its affairs.

Federalism was invented in America in 1787. It was different not only from a confederate or unitary system but also from any form of government the world had known. The ancient Greek city-states and the medieval Hanseatic League were confederacies. The governments of Europe were unitary in form. The United States of America would be the first nation to be governed through a true federal system.

The Argument for Federalism

Unlike many other decisions made at the Philadelphia convention, federalism had no clear basis in political theory. Federalism was a practical necessity: there was a need for a stronger national government and yet the states existed and were intent on retaining their sovereignty.

Nevertheless, the Framers developed arguments for the superiority of this type of political system. Federalism, they said, would protect liberty, moderate the power of government, and provide the foundation for an effective national government.

Protecting Liberty Theorists such as Locke and Montesquieu had not proposed a division of power between national and local authorities as a means of protecting liberty. Nevertheless, the Framers came to look upon federalism as part of the Constitution's system of checks and balances (see Chapter 2). Alexander Hamilton argued in *Federalist* No. 28 that the American people could shift their loyalties back and forth between the national and state governments in order to keep each under control. "If [the people's] rights are invaded by either," Hamilton wrote, "they can make use of the other as the instrument of redress."

Moderating the Power of Government To the Anti-Federalists (opponents of the Constitution), the sacrifice of states' power to the nation was as

How the United States Compares

Federal Versus Unitary Governments

Federalism involves the division of sovereignty between a national government and subnational (such as state) governments. It was invented in 1787 in order to maintain the preexisting American states while establishing an effective central government. Since then other countries have established *federal* governments, but most countries have *unitary* governments, in which all sovereignty is vested in a national government. In some cases, countries have developed hybrid versions. Great Britain's government is formally unitary, but Parliament has granted some autonomy to regions. Mexico's system is formally federal, but in actuality power is concentrated in the national government.

Country	Form of Government
Canada	Federal
France	Unitary
Germany	Federal
Great Britain	Modified unitary
Italy	Modified unitary
Japan	Unitary
Mexico	Modified federal
United States	Federal
Sweden	Unitary

unwise as it was unnecessary. They argued that a distant national government could never serve the people's interests as well as the states could. In support of their contention, the Anti-Federalists turned to Montesquieu, who had concluded that a small republic is more likely than a large one to respect and respond to the people it governs. When government encompasses a small area, he argued, its leaders are in closer touch with the people and have a greater concern for their interests.

James Madison took issue with this claim. In *Federalist* No. 10, Madison argued that whether a government serves the common good is a function not of its size but of the range of interests that share political power. The problem with a smaller republic, Madison claimed, is that it is likely to have a dominant faction—whether it be large landholders, financiers, an impoverished majority, or some other group—that is strong enough to take full control of government, using this power to advance its selfish interests. A large republic is less likely to have such an all-powerful faction. If financiers are strong in one area of a large republic, they are likely to be weaker elsewhere, and the same will be true of other interests. A large republic, Madison concluded, would impede the efforts of any single group to gain control and would force groups to compromise and work together. "Extend the sphere," said Madison, "and you take in a greater variety of parties and interests; you make it less probable that a majority of the whole will have a common motive to invade the rights of other citizens."

Strengthening the Union The most telling argument in 1787 for a federal system, however, was that it would overcome the deficiencies of the Articles. The Articles had numerous flaws (including a very weak executive and a judiciary subservient to the state courts), and two of them were fatal: the government had neither the power to tax nor the power to regulate commerce.

Under the Articles, Congress was given responsibility for national defense but was not granted the power to tax, and so it had to rely on the states for the money to maintain an army and navy. During the first six years under the Articles, Congress asked the states for $12 million but received only $3 million—not even enough to pay the interest on Revolutionary War debts. By 1786 the national government was so desperate for funds that it sold the navy's ships and had fewer than a thousand soldiers in uniform—this at a time when England had an army in Canada and Spain occupied Florida.

Congress was also expected to shape a national economy, yet it was powerless to do so because the Articles prohibited it from interfering with the states' commerce policies. States were free to do whatever they wanted, and they took advantage of the situation by imposing trade barriers on each other. Connecticut, for example, placed a higher tariff on manufactured goods from its trading rival Massachusetts than it did on the same goods shipped from England.

The Articles of Confederation showed the fallacy of the adage "That government is best which governs least." The consequences of an overly weak authority were abundantly clear: public disorder, economic chaos, and inadequate defense.

The Powers of the Nation

The Philadelphia convention met to decide the powers of the national government. The delegates had not been sent to determine how state government should be structured. Accordingly, the U.S. Constitution focuses on the lawful authority of the national government, which is provided through *enumerated* and *implied powers*. Authority that is not in this way granted to the national government is left—or "reserved"—to the states. Thus the states have *reserved powers*.

Enumerated Powers Article I of the Constitution grants to Congress seventeen **enumerated (expressed) powers.** These powers were intended by the Framers to be the basis for a government strong enough to forge a union that was secure in its defense and stable in its commerce. Congress's powers to regulate commerce among the states, to create a national currency, and to borrow money, for example, would provide a foundation for a sound national economy. Its power to tax, combined with its authority to declare war and establish an army and navy, would enable it to provide for the common defense. In addition, the Constitution prohibited the states from actions that would interfere with the national government's exercise of its lawful powers. Article I, Section 10 forbids the states to make treaties with other nations, raise armies, wage war, print money, or make commercial agreements with other states without the approval of Congress.

The writers of the Constitution recognized that the lawful exercise of national authority would at times conflict with the actions of the states. In such instances, national law was intended to prevail. Article VI of the Constitution grants this dominance in the so-called **supremacy clause,** which provides that "the laws of the United States . . . shall be the supreme law of the land."

Implied Powers The Framers of the Constitution also recognized that an overly narrow definition of national authority would result in a government incapable of adapting to change. Under the Articles of Confederation, Congress was strictly confined to those powers expressly granted to it, which limited its ability to respond effectively to the country's changing needs after the Revolutionary War. Concerned that the enumerated powers by themselves might be too restrictive of national authority, the Framers added the **"necessary and proper" clause,** or as it later came to be known, the **elastic clause.** Article I, Section 8 gives Congress the power "to make all laws which shall be necessary and proper for carrying into execution the foregoing [enumerated] powers." This grant gave the national government **implied powers:** the authority to take action that is not expressly authorized by the Constitution but that supports actions that are so authorized.

The Powers of the States

The Framers' preference for a sovereign national government was not shared in 1787 by all Americans. Although Anti-Federalists recognized a need to strengthen defense and interstate commerce, they feared the consequences of a strong central government. The interests of the people of New Hampshire were not identical to those of Georgians or Pennsylvanians, and the Anti-Federalists argued that only state-centered government would protect and preserve these differences.

The Federalists responded by claiming that the national government would have no interest in dominating the states.[3] The national government would take responsibility for establishing a strong defense and for promoting a sound economy, while the states would retain nearly all other governing functions, including oversight of public morals, education, and safety.

This argument did not alleviate the Anti-Federalists' fear of a powerful national government. The supremacy and "necessary and proper" clauses were particularly worrisome, because they provided a constitutional basis for future expansions of national authority. Such concerns led to demands for a constitutional amendment that would protect the states against encroachment by the national government. Ratified in 1791 as the Tenth Amendment to the Constitution, it reads: "The powers not delegated to the United States by the Constitution, nor prohibited by it to the States, are reserved to the States." The states' powers under the U.S. Constitution are thus called **reserved powers.**

FEDERALISM IN HISTORICAL PERSPECTIVE

Since ratification of the Constitution two centuries ago, no aspect of it has provoked more frequent or bitter conflict than federalism. By establishing two levels of sovereign authority, the Constitution created competing centers of power and ambition, each of which was sure to claim disputed areas as belonging within its realm of authority.

Conflict between national and state authority was also ensured by the brevity of the Constitution. The Framers deliberately avoided detailed provisions, recognizing that brief phrases would give flexibility to the government they were creating. The document does not define, for example, the difference between *inter*state commerce (which the national government is empowered to regulate) and *intra*state commerce (which is reserved for regulation by the states).

Not surprisingly, federalism has been a contentious and dynamic system, its development determined less by constitutional language than by the strength of contending interests and by the country's changing needs. Federalism can be viewed as having progressed through three historical eras, each of which has involved a different relationship between nation and states.

An Indestructible Union (1789–1865)

The issue during the first era, which lasted from the Constitution's beginnings in 1789 through the end of the Civil War in 1865, was the Union's survival. Given the state-centered history of America before the Constitution, it was inevitable that the states would dispute national policies that threatened their particular interests.

The Nationalist View: McCulloch v. Maryland A first dispute over federalism arose when President George Washington's secretary of the treasury, Alexander Hamilton, proposed that Congress establish a national bank. Thomas Jefferson, Washington's secretary of state, opposed the bank on the grounds that its activities would benefit the interests of the rich at the expense of those of ordinary people. Jefferson claimed that the bank was unlawful because the Constitution did not explicitly authorize the creation of a national bank. Hamilton and his supporters claimed that because the federal government had constitutional authority to regulate currency, it had the "implied power" to establish a national bank.

Hamilton's view prevailed when Congress in 1791 established the First Bank of the United States, granting it a twenty-year charter. When the bank's charter expired in 1811, however, Congress did not renew it. Then in 1816, Congress established the Second Bank of the United States over the objections of state and local bankers. Responding to their complaints, several states, including Maryland, attempted to drive the Second Bank of the United States out of existence by levying taxes on its operations within their borders. Edwin McCulloch, who was head cashier of the Maryland branch of the U.S. Bank, refused to pay the Maryland tax, and the resulting dispute reached the Supreme Court.

John Marshall, the chief justice of the Supreme Court, was, like Hamilton, a strong nationalist, and in *McCulloch v. Maryland* (1819) the Court ruled decisively in favor of national authority. It was reasonable, Marshall concluded, to infer that a government with powers to tax, borrow money, and regulate commerce could establish a bank in order to exercise those powers properly. Marshall's argument was a clear statement of *implied powers*—the idea that through the "necessary and proper" clause the national government's powers extend beyond a narrow reading of its enumerated powers.

Marshall also addressed the meaning of the Constitution's supremacy clause. The state of Maryland argued that it had the sovereign authority to tax the national bank even if the bank was a legal entity. The Supreme Court rejected Maryland's position, concluding that valid national law prevailed over conflicting state law. Because the national government had the

John Marshall
(1755–1835)

John Marshall forcefully expressed his nation-alist views in important Supreme Court deci-sions during his thirty-four years as chief justice. Although Marshall was a cousin to Thomas Jefferson, the two were political op-ponents. Marshall was an ardent nationalist whereas Jefferson held that national power should not unduly intrude on the states. Marshall served for a time as John Adams's secretary of state before his appointment by Adams to the post of chief justice.

power to create the bank, it could also protect the bank from actions by the states, such as taxation, that might destroy it.[4]

The *McCulloch* decision served as precedent for future assertions of na-tional authority, including a second landmark decision by the Marshall Court. In *Gibbons v. Ogden* (1824), the Court ruled on the power of Con-gress to regulate commerce. The state of New York had granted a monop-oly to Aaron Ogden to operate a ferry between New York and New Jersey. When Thomas Gibbons set up a competing ferry under a federal coastal li-censing agreement, Ogden tried to prevent Gibbons from operating it. Marshall invalidated the New York monopoly, saying it intruded on Con-gress's power to regulate commerce among the states. Going further, Mar-shall ruled that Congress's power extended *into* a state when commerce between two or more states was at issue.[5]

Marshall's opinions asserted that legitimate uses of national power took precedence over state authority and that the "necessary and proper" clause and the commerce clause were broad grants of national power. As a nation-alist, Marshall was providing the U.S. government the legal justification for expanding its power in ways that fostered the development of the nation as a nation rather than as a collection of states. This constitutional vision was of utmost significance. As Justice Oliver Wendell Holmes Jr. noted a century later, the Union could not have survived if each state had been allowed to determine for itself the extent to which it would accept national authority.[6]

The States'-Rights View: The Dred Scott Decision Although John Marshall's rulings helped strengthen national authority, the issue of slavery posed a growing threat to the Union's survival. Fearing that northern

/pattersonwtp5

members of Congress might move to abolish slavery, southern leaders did what others have done throughout American
history: they devised a constitutional argument to fit their
political desires. John C. Calhoun of South Carolina argued
that the Constitution had created "a government of states . . . not a government of individuals."[7] This line of reasoning led Calhoun to his famed
"doctrine of nullification," which declared that each state had the constitutional right to nullify a national law.

In 1832 South Carolina invoked this doctrine, declaring "null and void"
a tariff law that favored northern interests. President Andrew Jackson re-
torted that South Carolina's action was "incompatible with the existence of
the Union," a position that was strengthened when Congress authorized
Jackson to use military force against South Carolina. The state backed
down when Congress agreed to amend the tariff act slightly.

The clash foreshadowed a confrontation of far greater scope and consequence: the Civil War. War between the states would not break out for another thirty years, but in the interim, conflicts over states' rights intensified.[8]
Westward expansion and immigration into the northern states were tilting
power in Congress toward the free states, which increasingly signaled their
determination to outlaw slavery in the United States at some future time.
Attempts to find a compromise acceptable to both the North and the South
were fruitless.

The Supreme Court's infamous *Dred Scott* decision (1857) intensified the
conflict. Dred Scott, a slave, applied for his freedom when his master died,
citing a federal law—the Missouri Compromise of 1820—that made slavery
illegal in a free state or territory. Scott had lived in the North four years,
but the Supreme Court in a 7-2 decision ruled that slaves were "property"
and that persons of African descent were barred from citizenship and
thereby could not sue for their freedom in federal courts. The Court also
invalidated the Missouri Compromise, declaring that Congress had no authority to outlaw slavery in any part of the United States.[9]

The *Dred Scott* decision outraged many northerners and contributed to a
sectional split in the majority Democratic party (the northern and southern
wings nominated separate candidates) that enabled the Republican Abraham Lincoln to win the presidency in 1860 with only 40 percent of the
popular vote. Lincoln had campaigned for the gradual, compensated abolition of slavery. By the time he assumed office, seven southern states had already seceded from the Union. In justifying his decision to wage civil war
on these states, Lincoln said, "The Union is older than the states." In 1865
the superior strength of the Union army settled by force the question of
whether national authority would be binding on the states.

The American Civil War was the bloodiest conflict the world had yet known. Ten percent of fighting-age males died in the four-year war, and uncounted others were wounded. The death toll—618,000 (360,000 from the North, 258,000 from the South)—exceeded that of the American war dead in World War I, World War II, and Korean War, and the Vietnam War combined. And this death toll was in a nation with a population that was only one-ninth the size it is today.

Dual Federalism and Laissez-Faire Capitalism (1865–1937)

Although the Civil War preserved the Union, new challenges to federalism were surfacing. Constitutional doctrine held that certain policy areas, such as interstate commerce and defense, belonged exclusively to the national government, whereas other policy areas, such as public health and intrastate commerce, belonged exclusively to the states. This doctrine, known as **dual federalism,** was based on the idea that a precise separation of national and state authority was both possible and desirable. "The power which one possesses," said the Supreme Court, "the other does not."[10]

American society, however, was in the midst of changes that raised questions about the suitability of dual federalism as a governing concept. The Industrial Revolution had given rise to large business firms, which were using their economic power to dominate markets and exploit workers. Government was the logical counterforce to this economic power. Which level of government—state or national—would regulate business?

There was also the issue of the former slaves. The white South had lost the war but was hardly of a mind to share power with newly freed slaves. Would the federal government be allowed to intervene in state affairs to ensure the fair treatment of African Americans?

Dual federalism became a barrier to an effective response to these issues. From the 1860s through the 1930s, the Supreme Court held firm to the idea that there was a sharp line between national and state authority and, in both areas, a high wall of separation between government and the economy. This era of federalism was characterized by state supremacy in racial policy and by business supremacy in commerce policy.

The Fourteenth Amendment and State Discretion Ratified after the Civil War, the Fourteenth Amendment was intended to protect citizens (especially black Americans) from discriminatory actions by state governments.[11] A state was prohibited from depriving "any person of life, liberty, or property without due process of law," from denying "any person within its jurisdiction the equal protection of the laws," and from abridging "the privileges or immunities of citizens of the United States."

Supreme Court rulings during subsequent decades, however, helped to undermine the Fourteenth Amendment's promise. The Court held, for example, that the Fourteenth Amendment did not substantially limit the power of the states to determine the rights to which their residents were entitled.[12] Then, in *Plessy v. Ferguson* (1896), the Court issued its infamous "separate but equal" ruling. A black man, Adolph Plessy, had been convicted of violating a Louisiana law that required white and black citizens to ride in separate railroad cars. The Supreme Court upheld his conviction, concluding that state governments could require blacks to use separate railroad cars and other accommodations as long as those facilities were "equal" in quality to those reserved for use by whites. "If one race be inferior to the other socially," the Court concluded, "the Constitution of the United States cannot put them on the same plane." The lone dissenting justice in the case, John Marshall Harlan, had harsh words for his colleagues: "Our Constitution is color-blind and neither knows nor tolerates classes among citizens. . . . The thin disguise of 'equal' accommodations . . . will not mislead anyone nor atone for the wrong this day done."[13]

With its *Plessy* decision, the Court undercut the Fourteenth Amendment and allowed southern states to segregate the races. Black children were forced into separate schools that seldom had libraries and usually had few teachers, most of whom had no formal training. Hospitals for blacks had few doctors and nurses and almost no medical supplies and equipment. Legal challenges to these discriminatory practices were generally unsuccessful.

The *Plessy* ruling had become a justification for the separate and *unequal* treatment of black Americans.

Judicial Protection of Business Through its rulings after the Civil War, the Supreme Court also provided a constitutional basis for uncontrolled private power. The Supreme Court was dominated by adherents of the doctrine of laissez-faire capitalism (which holds that business should be "allowed to act" without interference), and they interpreted the Constitution in ways that frustrated government's attempts to regulate business activity. In 1886, for example, the Court decided that corporations were "persons" within the meaning of the Fourteenth Amendment, and thus their property rights were protected from substantial regulation by the states.[14] The irony was inescapable. A constitutional amendment that had been enacted to protect the newly freed slaves was ignored for this purpose but was used instead to protect fictitious persons—business corporations.

The Court also weakened the national government's regulatory power by narrowly interpreting its commerce power. The Constitution's **commerce clause** says that Congress shall have the power "to regulate commerce" among the states but does not spell out the economic activities included in the grant of power. When the federal government invoked the Sherman Antitrust Act (1890) in an attempt to break up a monopoly on the manufacture of sugar, the Supreme Court blocked the action, claiming that interstate

Between 1865 and 1937, the Supreme Court's rulings severely restricted national power. Narrowly interpreting Congress's constitutional power to regulate commerce, the Court forbade Congress to regulate child labor and other aspects of manufacturing.

commerce covered only the "transportation" of goods, not their "manufacture."[15] Manufacturing was deemed part of intrastate commerce and thus, according to the dual federalism doctrine, subject to state regulation only. However, because the Court had previously decided that the states' regulatory powers were restricted by the Fourteenth Amendment, the states were relatively powerless to control manufacturing activity.

Although the national government subsequently made some headway in business regulation, the Supreme Court remained an obstacle. An example is the case of *Hammer v. Dagenhart* (1918), which arose from a 1916 federal act that prohibited the interstate shipment of goods produced by child labor. The act was popular because factory owners were exploiting children, working them for long hours at low pay. Citing the Tenth Amendment, the Court invalidated the law, ruling that factory practices could be regulated only by the states.[16] However, in an earlier case, *Lochner v. New York* (1905), the Court had prevented a state from regulating labor practices, concluding that such action was a violation of firms' property rights.[17]

In effect, the Supreme Court had denied both Congress and the states the authority to decide economic issues. As the constitutional scholars Alfred Kelly, Winifred Harbison, and Herman Belz concluded, "No more complete perversion of the principles of effective federal government can be imagined."[18]

National Authority Prevails Judicial supremacy in the economic sphere ended abruptly in 1937. For nearly a decade, the United States had been mired in the Great Depression, which President Franklin D. Roosevelt's New Deal was designed to alleviate. The Supreme Court, however, had ruled much of the New Deal's economic recovery legislation to be unconstitutional. A constitutional crisis of historic proportions seemed inevitable until the Court suddenly reversed its position. In the process, American federalism was fundamentally and forever changed.

The Great Depression revealed clearly that Americans had become a national community with national economic needs. By the 1930s, more than half the population lived in cities (only 20 percent did so in 1860), and more than ten million workers were employed by industry (only one million were so employed in 1860). Urban workers were typically dependent on landlords for their housing, on farmers and grocers for their food, and on corporations for their jobs. Farmers were more independent, but they too were increasingly a part of a larger economic network. Their income depended on market prices and shipping and equipment costs.[19]

This economic interdependence meant that no area of the economy was immune if things went wrong. When the depression hit in 1929, its effects could not be contained. A decline in spending was followed by a drop in production, a loss of jobs, unpaid rents and grocery bills, and a shrinking market for foodstuffs, which led to a further decline in spending, and so on, creating a relentless downward spiral. At the depths of the Great Depression, one-fourth of the nation's work force was unemployed.

The states by tradition had responsibility for welfare, but they were nearly penniless because of declining tax revenues and the growing ranks of poor people. The New Deal programs offered a way out of the crisis; for example, the National Industry Recovery Act (NIRA) of 1933 called for a massive public works program to create jobs and for coordinated action by major industries. However, the New Deal was opposed by economic conservatives (who accused Roosevelt of leading the nation down the road to communism) and by justices of the Supreme Court. In *Schechter v. United States* (1935), the Court invalidated the Recovery Act by a 5-4 vote, ruling that it usurped powers reserved to the states.[20]

Frustrated by the Court, Roosevelt in 1937 proposed his famed Court-packing plan. Roosevelt recommended that Congress enact legislation that would permit an additional justice to be appointed to the Court whenever a seated member passed the age of seventy. The number of justices would increase, and Roosevelt's appointees would presumably be more sympathetic to his programs. Roosevelt's scheme was resisted by Congress, but the controversy ended with "the switch in time that saved nine," when, for reasons that have never become fully clear, Justice Owen Roberts abandoned his opposition to Roosevelt's policies and thus gave the president a 5-4 majority on the Court.

Within months, the Court upheld the 1935 National Labor Relations Act, which gave employees the right to organize and bargain collectively.[21] In passing the act, Congress had argued that labor-management disputes disrupt the nation's economy and therefore could be regulated through the commerce clause. In upholding the act, the Supreme Court in effect granted Congress the authority to apply its commerce powers broadly.[22] During this same period, the Court also loosened its restrictions on Congress's use of its taxing and spending powers.[23] These decisions removed the constitutional barrier to increased federal authority, a change that the Court later acknowledged when it said that Congress's commerce power is "as broad as the needs of the nation."[24]

In effect, the Supreme Court had finally recognized the obvious: that an industrial economy is not confined by state boundaries and must be subject to national regulation. It was a principle that business itself also increasingly accepted. The nation's banking industry, for example, was saved in the 1930s from almost complete collapse by the creation of a federal regulatory agency, the Federal Deposit Insurance Corporation (FDIC). By insuring depositors' savings against loss, the FDIC gave depositors the confidence to keep their money in banks, enabling many banks to remain solvent despite the depression.

Toward National Citizenship

The fundamental change in the constitutional doctrine of federalism as applied to economic issues that took place in the 1930s was paralleled by similar changes in other areas. One area is civil rights. As will be discussed in Chapter 5, federal authority has compelled states and localities to eliminate government-sponsored discrimination and, in some cases, to create compensatory opportunities for minorities and women. In 1954, for example, the Supreme Court held that racial segregation in public schools was unconstitutional on grounds that it violated the Fourteenth Amendment.[25]

The idea that Americans are equal in their rights regardless of where they reside has also been applied in other areas. As Chapter 4 will discuss, states have been required to broaden individual rights of free expression and fair trial. An example is the Supreme Court's *Miranda* ruling, which requires police officers to inform crime suspects of their rights at the time of arrest.[26]

Of course, important differences remain in the rights and privileges of the residents of the separate states, as could be expected in a federal system. The death penalty, for example, is legal in some states but not others, and states differ greatly in terms of their services, such as the quality of their public schools. Nevertheless, national citizenship—the notion that Americans should be equal in their rights and opportunities regardless of the state in which they live—is a more encompassing idea today than in the past.

FEDERALISM TODAY

Since the 1930s, the relation of the nation to the states has changed so fundamentally that dual federalism is no longer even a roughly accurate description of the American situation.[27]

An understanding of the nature of federalism today requires a recognition of two countervailing trends. The first trend is a long-term *expansion* of national authority that began in the 1930s and continued for the next half century. The national government now operates in many policy areas that were once almost exclusively within the control of states and localities. The national government does not dominate these policy areas, but it does have a significant role. Much of this influence stems from social welfare policies that were enacted in the 1960s as part of President Lyndon Johnson's Great Society program, which included initiatives in health care, public housing, nutrition, welfare, urban development, and other areas reserved previously to states and localities.

The second trend is more recent and involves a partial *contraction* of national authority. Known as *devolution* the recent trend involves the "passing down" of authority from the national government to the state and local levels. Devolution has reversed the decades-long increase in federal authority but only in some areas and then only to a moderate degree.

Stated differently, the national government's policy authority has expanded greatly since the 1930s, even though that authority has been reduced somewhat in recent years. Each of these trends will now be explained.

Interdependency and Intergovernmental Relations

Interdependency is a primary reason why national authority increased dramatically in the twentieth century. Modern systems of transportation, commerce, and communication transcend local and state boundaries. These systems are national, even international, in scope, which means that problems affecting Americans in one part of the country are likely also to affect Americans living elsewhere. This situation has required Washington to assume a larger policy role: national problems ordinarily require national solutions.

Interdependency has also encouraged national, state, and local policymakers to work together to solve policy problems. This collaborative effort has been described as **cooperative federalism.**[28] The difference between this system of federalism and the older dual federalism has been likened to the difference between a marble cake, whose levels flow together, and a layer cake, whose levels are separate.[29]

Cooperative federalism is based on shared policy responsibilities rather than sharply divided ones. An example is the Medicaid program, which was created in 1965 as part of Johnson's Great Society initiative and which provides health care for the poor. The Medicaid program is jointly funded by the national and state governments, operates within eligibility standards set by the national government, and gives states some latitude in determining the benefits that recipients receive. The Medicaid program is not an isolated example. Literally hundreds of policy programs today are run jointly by the national and state governments. In many cases, local governments are also involved. The characteristics of these programs are the following:

• Jointly funded by the national and state governments (and sometimes by local governments too)
• Jointly administered, with the states and localities providing most of the direct service to recipients and a national agency providing general administration

• Jointly determined, with both the state and national governments (and sometimes the local governments) having a say in eligibility and benefit levels, and with federal regulations, such as those prohibiting discrimination, giving an element of uniformity to the various state and local efforts

Cooperative federalism should not be interpreted to indicate that the states are now powerless and dependent. States have retained most of their traditional authority. In fact, the states have a larger influence in many policy areas than Washington does (see Figure 3–2). Nearly 95 percent of the funding for public schools, for example, is provided by states and localities, which also set most of the education standards, from teachers' qualifications to course requirements to the length of the school day. Moreover, the policy areas dominated by the states—such as education, law enforcement, and transportation—tend to be those that have the greatest impact on people's daily lives. Finally, contrary to what many Americans might think, state and

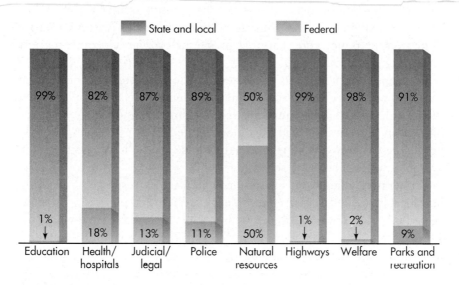

FIGURE 3–2 FEDERAL AND STATE/LOCAL GOVERNMENT EMPLOYEES, AS PERCENTAGE OF ALL GOVERNMENT EMPLOYEES WHO WORK IN SELECTED POLICY AREAS

Although federal authority has reached into areas traditionally dominated by the state governments, state and local governments still dominate many policy areas. One indicator is the high percentage of government employees in selected areas who work for state or local governments.

Source: U.S. Bureau of the Census, 2003.

local governments have nearly six times as many employees as the federal government.

Nevertheless, the federal government's involvement in policy areas traditionally reserved for the states has increased its policy influence and has diminished state-to-state policy differences.[30] Before the enactment of the federal Medicaid program in 1965, for example, poor people in many states were not entitled to government-paid health care. Now most poor people are eligible regardless of where in the United States they live.

Government Revenues and Intergovernmental Relations

The interdependency of American society—the fact that developments in one area affect what happens elsewhere—is one of the two major reasons why the federal government's policy role has expanded greatly since the early twentieth century. The other reason is the federal government's superior taxing capacity. States and localities are in an inherently competitive situation with regard to taxation. A state or locality cannot raise taxes very high without losing residents or firms to a location where taxes are lower. People and businesses are much less likely to move to another country in search of a lower tax rate. The result is that the federal government raises more tax revenues than do all fifty states and the thousands of local governments combined (see Figure 3–3).

Fiscal Federalism The federal government's revenue-raising advantage has helped make money the basis for many of the relations between the national government and the states and localities. **Fiscal federalism** refers to

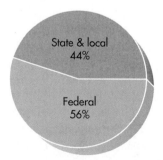

FIGURE 3–3 **Federal, State, and Local Shares of Government Tax Revenue**

The federal government raises more tax revenues than all state and local governments combined.

Source: U.S. Department of Commerce, 2003.

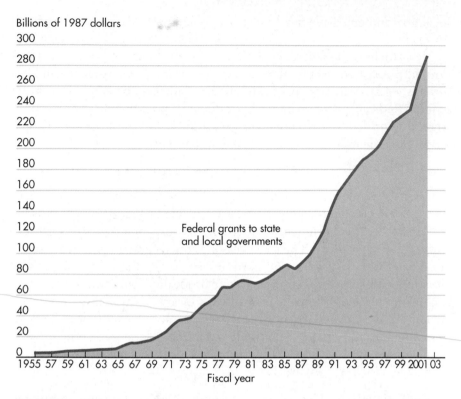

Billions of 1987 dollars

Federal grants to state
and local governments

Fiscal year

FIGURE 3-4 FEDERAL GRANTS TO STATE AND LOCAL
GOVERNMENTS

Federal aid to states and localities has increased dramatically since the 1950s, although some of the increase is attributable to inflation. One dollar in 1955 was worth the same as five dollars in 2000. In terms of 1955 dollars, federal grants totaled about $50 billion in 2000.

Source: Office of Management and Budget, 2003.

the expenditure of federal funds on programs run in part through state and local governments.[31] The federal government provides some or all the money for a program through **grants-in-aid** (cash payments) to states and localities, which then administer the program.

The pattern of federal assistance to states and localities during the last four decades is shown in Figure 3–4. Federal grants-in-aid increased manyfold during this period. A sharp rise occurred in the late 1960s and early 1970s as a result of President Johnson's Great Society programs. Roughly one in every five dollars spent by local and state governments in recent decades has been raised not by them, but by the government in Washington (see "States in the Nation").

★ | STATES IN THE NATION

Federal Grants-in-Aid to the States

Federal assistance accounts for a significant share of state revenue, but the variation is considerable. Louisiana (a third of its total revenue comes from federal grants-in-aid) is at one extreme. Nevada (a seventh of its revenue) is at the other extreme.

Q: Why do states in the South, where anti-Washington sentiment is relatively high, get more of their revenue from the federal government than most other states?

A: Many federal grant programs are designed to assist low-income people, and poverty is more widespread in the South. Moreover, southern states have traditionally provided fewer government services, and federal grants therefore constitute a larger proportion of their budgets.

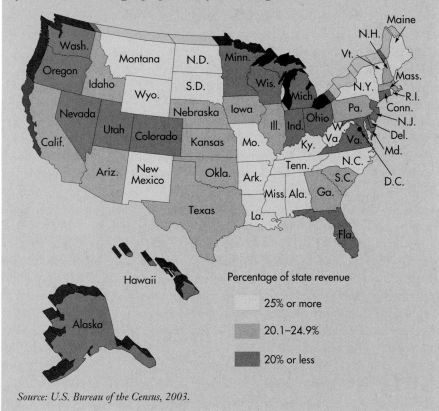

Percentage of state revenue

- 25% or more
- 20.1–24.9%
- 20% or less

Source: U.S. Bureau of the Census, 2003.

Cash grants to states and localities have extended Washington's influence over policy.[32] State and local governments can reject a grant-in-aid, but if they accept it, they must spend it in the way specified by Congress. And since most grants require states to contribute matching funds, the federal programs in effect also determine how states will allocate some of their own tax dollars. Federal grants have also pressured state and local officials to accept broad national goals, such as the elimination of racial and other forms of discrimination. A building constructed with the help of federal funds, for example, must be accessible to persons with disabilities.

Nevertheless, federal grants-in-aid also serve the policy interests of state and local officials. They have often complained that federal grants contain too many restrictions and infringe too much on their authority, but they have been eager to obtain the money, since it permits them to offer services they could not otherwise provide. An example is a 1994 federal grant program that enabled local governments to put seventy-five thousand additional police officers on the streets.

Categorical and Block Grants State and local governments receive two major types of assistance, categorical grants and block grants, which differ in the extent to which Washington defines the conditions of their use.

Categorical grants are the more restrictive; they can be used only for a designated activity. An example is funds directed for use in school lunch programs. These funds can be used only in support of school lunches; they cannot be diverted for other school purposes, such as the purchase of textbooks or the hiring of teachers. **Block grants** are less restrictive. The federal government specifies the general area in which the funds must be used, but state and local officials select the specific projects. A block grant targeted for the health area, for example, might give state and local officials leeway in deciding whether to use the money on hospital construction, medical equipment, or some other health care activity.

State and local officials have naturally preferred federal money that comes with fewer strings attached, so they have favored block grants. On the other hand, members of Congress have at times preferred categorical grants, since this form of assistance gives them more control over how state and local officials will spend federal funds.[33] Recently, however, officials at all levels have looked to block grants as the key to a more workable form of federalism. This tendency is part of a larger trend—that of devolution.

A New Federalism: Devolution

Devolution is the idea that American federalism will be improved by a shift in authority from the federal government to the state and local governments.

Devolution is reshaping American federalism and is attributable to both practical and political developments.

Budgetary Pressures and Public Opinion As a practical matter, the growth in federal assistance had slowed by the early 1980s. The federal government was facing huge budget deficits, and large new grants-in-aid to states and localities were not feasible.

As budgetary pressures intensified, relations among national, state, and local officials became increasingly strained. A slowdown in the annual increase in federal assistance had forced states and localities to pay an increasingly larger share of the costs of joint programs. As state and local governments raised taxes or cut other services to meet the costs, taxpayer anger intensified. Some of the grant programs, such as AFDC, food stamps, and housing subsidies, had not been very popular before the budget crunch and now came under even heavier criticism.

By the early 1990s, American federalism was positioned for a change. Two decades earlier, three-fourths of Americans had expressed confidence in Washington's ability to govern effectively. Less than half the public now held this view. A 1993 CBS News/New York Times survey indicated that 69 percent of Americans believed that "the federal government creates more problems than it solves."

The Republican Revolution When the Republican party scored a decisive victory in the 1994 congressional elections, Newt Gingrich declared that "1960s-style federalism is dead." Republican lawmakers proposed to cut some programs, but even more, they sought to increase state and local control. They proposed to lump dozens of categorical grants into a few block grants, thus giving states and localities more control of how money would be spent.

That Republicans would lead the move to a more decentralized form of federalism was no surprise. Although members of both parties had supported expansions of federal authority, Republicans had more often questioned the overall result. Republican presidents Richard Nixon and Ronald Reagan, for example, proposed versions of a "new federalism" in which some areas of public policy for which the federal government had assumed responsibility would be returned to state and localities.[34]

Upon taking control of Congress in 1995, Republican lawmakers acted to reduce *unfunded mandates*, the federal programs that require action by states or localities but provide no or insufficient funds to pay for it. For example, states and localities are required by federal law to make their buildings accessible to the physically handicapped, but Washington pays only part of the cost of these accommodations. In the Unfunded Mandates

When the 1994 elections were over, Newt Gingrich declared that "1960s-style federalism is dead." As Speaker of the House of Representatives, Gingrich then helped enact major changes in federal-state relations.

Reform Act of 1995, Congress eliminated some of these mandates, although under threat of a presidential veto it exempted those that deal with civil rights and liberties. The GOP-controlled Congress also took action to lump additional categorical grants into block grants, thus giving states more control over how federal money would be spent.

The most significant legislative change came a year later, when the Republican Congress enacted the sweeping 1996 Welfare Reform Act. Its key element is the Temporary Assistance for Needy Families block grant (TANF), which ended the decades-old program that granted cash assistance to every poor family with children. TANF restricts a family's eligibility for federal assistance to five years, and after two years, a family head normally has to go to work or the benefits cease. Moreover, TANF gives states wide latitude in setting benefit levels, eligibility criteria, and other regulations affecting aid for poor families. Ironically, TANF actually increased the level of federal grant spending because Washington picked up a larger share of welfare costs. But states gained more control over how the funds would be spent. (TANF and other aspects of the 1996 welfare reform legislation are discussed further in later chapters.)

After passage of the 1996 Welfare Reform Act, congressional efforts to reduce federal authority declined sharply. Devolution had hardly rolled back a half century of Washington-centered federalism, nor had it blunted new federal assistance programs. Among the federal initiatives enacted recently are grants for classroom modernization and the hiring of additional teachers. The war on terrorism has also expanded Washington's power. The federal Department of Homeland Security was created in 2002 to coordinate governmental efforts to deal with the terrorist threat. State and local agencies will be on the front lines of any response to a terrorist attack on U.S. soil, just as they were in New York City on September 11, 2001, but the coordination of their efforts as well as most of the investigative and intelligence work will be centered in Washington.

Thus, devolution has resulted in a modification of fiscal and cooperative federalism rather than their demise. States and localities have recaptured some of their authority, but there are limits on how far the process can go. Because of the complexity of modern policy issues and the interdependency of American society, the states will never again have the level of autonomy that they exercised early in the twentieth century.

Devolution, Judicial Style In the five decades after the 1930s, the Supreme Court granted Congress broad discretion in the enactment of policies affecting state and local governments. In *Garcia v. San Antonio Authority* (1985), for example, the Court held that federal minimum wage standards apply even to employees of state and local governments.[35] States and localities are prohibited from paying their employees less than the federally mandated minimum wage.

In recent years, however, the Supreme Court has restricted congressional authority somewhat. Chief Justice William Rehnquist and some of the other Republican appointees on the Supreme Court believe that Congress in some instances has encroached on powers properly belonging to state governments. In *United States v. Lopez* (1995), for example, the Court cited the Tenth Amendment in striking down a federal law that prohibited the possession of guns within a thousand feet of a school. Congress had justified the law as an exercise of its commerce power, but the Court stated that the ban had "nothing to do with commerce, or any sort of economic activity."[36] Two years later, in *Printz v. United States* (1997), the Court struck down that part of the federal Handgun Violence Prevention Act (the so-called Brady bill) that required local law-enforcement officers to conduct background checks on prospective handgun buyers. The Court concluded that the provision violated the Tenth Amendment in that it compels state officials "to administer or enforce a federal regulatory program."[37] In *Kimel v. Florida Board of Regents* (2000), the Supreme Court held that Congress did not have the authority under the Fourteenth Amendment to require state governments to comply with the federal law that bars discrimination against older workers. Age discrimination is not among the forms of discrimination expressly prohibited by the U.S. Constitution, and the Court declared that states have the power to decide for themselves the age-related policies that will apply to their employees.[38] In a 2002 case, *Board of Trustees of the University of Alabama v. Garrett*, the Court extended this ban to include people with disabilities, saying they cannot sue a state for violations of the Americans With Disabilities Act. In rejecting a law suit for monetary damages against the state of Alabama by a cancer patient who had been demoted after returning to her job with the state, the Supreme Court held that Alabama was immune from the suit because of the Eleventh Amendment, which protects a non-consenting state from being sued by private individuals in a federal court. An exception occurs when a state is in violation of the Fourteenth Amendment. The Supreme Court held that disability discrimination is not among the forms of discrimination expressly protected by the Fourteenth Amendment and, accordingly, that states cannot be sued without their consent in such cases.[39]

Through these and other recent decisions, the Court has sought to expand states' immunity from federal authority. However, the Court has not repudiated the principle established in the 1930s that Congress's commerce and spending powers are broad and substantial. In *Reno v. Condon* (2000), for example, the Court ruled that the states have to comply with a federal law barring them from selling to private firms or groups their databases of personal information obtained from automobile license applicants. The majority opinion, which was written by Chief Justice Rehnquist, declared that the information in these databases is "an article of commerce" and thus is subject to regulation through Congress's commerce power. The Court noted that the law also applied to "private resellers" and was aimed at regulating "the owners of databases," which in this case includes the states.[40]

THE PUBLIC'S INFLUENCE: SETTING THE BOUNDARIES OF FEDERAL-STATE POWER

The ebb and flow in Washington's power in the twentieth century coincided closely with public opinion. The American people have had a decisive voice in determining the relationship between the federal and state governments.

During the Great Depression, when it was clear that the states would be unable to help, Americans turned to Washington for relief. For people without jobs, the fine points of the Constitution were of little consequence. President Roosevelt's programs were a radical departure from the past but quickly gained public support.[41] The second great wave of federal social programs—President Johnson's Great Society—was also driven by public demands. Income and education levels had risen dramatically after the Second World War, and Americans wanted more and better services from government. When the states were slow to respond, Americans pressured federal officials to act.[42] Public opinion was also behind the recent rollback in federal authority. The Republican takeover in 1995 was in large part a result of Americans' increased dissatisfaction with the performance of the federal government.[43]

The public's role in defining the boundaries between federal and state power would come as no surprise to the Framers of the Constitution. For them, federalism was a pragmatic issue, one to be decided by the nation's needs rather than by inflexible rules. And indeed, each succeeding generation of Americans has seen fit to devise a balance of federal and state power that would serve its interests. The historian Daniel Boorstin said the true genius of the American people is their pragmatism; their willingness to try new ways when the old ones stop working.[44] In few areas of governing has this ingenuity been more apparent than in Americans' approach to federalism.

Summary

A foremost characteristic of the American political system is its division of authority between a national government and the states. The first U.S. government, established by the Articles of Confederation, was essentially a union of the states.

In establishing the basis for a stronger national government, the U.S. Constitution also made provision for safeguarding state interests. The  result was the creation of a federal system in which sovereignty was vested in both national and state governments. The Constitution enumerates the general powers of the national government and grants it implied powers through the "necessary and proper" clause. Other powers are reserved to the states by the Tenth Amendment.

From 1789 to 1865, the nation's survival was at issue. The states found it convenient at times to argue that their sovereignty took precedence over national authority. In the end, it took the Civil War to cement the idea that the United States was a union of people, not of states. From 1865 to 1937, federalism reflected the doctrine that certain policy areas were the exclusive responsibility of the national government, whereas other policy areas belonged exclusively to the states. This constitutional position permitted the laissez-faire doctrine that big business was largely beyond governmental control. It also allowed the states in their public policies to discriminate against African Americans. Federalism in a form recognizable today began to emerge in the late 1930s.

In the areas of commerce, taxation, spending, civil rights, and civil liberties, among others, the federal government now has an important role, one that is the inevitable consequence of the increasing complexity of American society and the interdependence of its people. National, state, and local officials now work closely together to solve the country's problems, a situation that is described as cooperative federalism. Grants-in-aid from Washington to the states and localities have been the chief instrument of national influence. States and localities have received billions in federal assistance; in accepting that money, they have also accepted both federal restrictions on its use and the national policy priorities that underlie the granting of the money.

In recent years, the relationship between the nation and the states has again become a priority issue. Power is shifting downward to the states, and a new balance in the ever-evolving system of U.S. federalism is taking place. This change, like changes throughout U.S. history, has sprung from the demands of the American people.

Key Terms

block grants	fiscal federalism
categorical grants	grants-in-aid
commerce clause	implied powers
confederacy	"necessary and proper" clause
cooperative federalism	(elastic clause)
devolution	reserved powers
dual federalism	sovercignty
enumerated powers (expressed	supremacy clause
powers)	unitary system
federalism	

Suggested Readings

Beer, Samuel H. *To Make a Nation: The Rediscovery of American Federalism.* Cambridge, Mass.: The Belknap Press of Harvard University Press, 1993. An innovative interpretive framework for understanding the impact of federalism and nationalism on the nation's development.

Conlan, Timothy. *From New Federalism to Devolution*. Washington, D.C.: Brookings Institution Press, 1998. A careful analysis of the changing nature of modern federalism.

Cornell, Saul. *The Other Founders: Anti-Federalism and the Dissenting Tradition in America*. Chapel Hill: University of North Carolina Press, 1999. An analysis of Anti-Federalist thought, its origins, and its legacy.

Elkins, Stanley, and Eric McKitrick. *The Age of Federalism: The Early American Republic, 1788–1800*. New York: Oxford University Press, 1993. An award-winning book on the earliest period of American federalism.

Ross, William G. *A Muted Fury: Populists, Progressives, and Labor Unions Confront the Courts, 1890–1937*. Princeton, N.J.: Princeton University Press, 1993. A valuable study of the political conflict surrounding the judiciary's laissez-faire doctrine in the period from 1890 to 1937.

Thompson, Tommy. *Power to the People: An American State at Work*. New York: HarperCollins, 1996. An argument for state-centered federalism by one of its leading practitioners, the former governor of Wisconsin.

Walker, David B. *The Rebirth of Federalism*, 2d ed. Chatham, N.J.: Chatham House Publishers, 2000. An optimistic assessment of the state of today's federalism.

LIST OF WEBSITES

http://lcweb2.loc.gov/ammem/amlaw/lawhome.html A site containing congressional documents and debates from 1774 to 1873.

http://www.statesnews.org The site of the Council of State Governments; includes current news from each of the states and basic information about their governments.

http://www.temple.edu/federalism The site of the Center for the Study of Federalism, located at Temple University; it offers information and publications on the federal system of government.

http://www.yale.edu/lawweb/avalon/federal/fed.htm A documentary record of the Federalist Papers, the Annapolis Convention, the Articles of Confederation, the Madison Debates, and the U.S. Constitution.

POLITICS IN THEORY AND PRACTICE

Thinking: How have interdependency and the federal government's superior taxing power contributed to a larger policy role for the national government? Do you think these factors will increase or decrease in importance in the future? What will this trend mean for the future of American federalism? (You might find it helpful to think about these questions in the context of a specific policy area, such as the terrorist threat facing the country.)

Acting: Federalism can be a contentious system in that a policy outcome may depend on whether the issue is settled at the national or state level. Oregon's physician-assisted suicide law (see the chapter's opening example) is a case in point. Consider writing a letter expressing your view of what ought to be done in that case to John Ashcroft, the attorney general of the United States (U.S. Department of Justice, 950 Pennsylvania Avenue NW, Washington DC 20530-0001 or Ask DOJ@usdoj.gov). In preparing your letter, you will need to address two questions: What is your opinion on the issue of physician-assisted suicide? What is your opinion on the question of whether an issue of this type should be properly decided at the state or federal level? Note that your opinion on the issue may be at odds with your opinion on whether state or federal authority should prevail—for example, you may conclude that the issue should be decided by Oregon even though you personally oppose physician-assisted suicide.

𝔈𝔥𝔢 𝔑𝔢𝔴 𝔜𝔬𝔯𝔨 𝔗𝔦𝔪𝔢𝔰   reading 3

The Nation: 5-to-4, Now and Forever; At the Court, Dissent over States' Rights Is Now War

by Linda Greenhouse

In recent years, the Supreme Court in a series of decisions has placed limits on the power of Congress to enact policy binding on the states. Nearly all of these decisions have been decided by a 5-4 vote with the same justices each time aligned on opposite sides of the issue. In this June 9, 2002, New York Times article, correspondent Linda Greenhouse tells just how deeply the justices are divided over the issue of federalism.

WASHINGTON—There are dissenting opinions at the Supreme Court, and then there are declarations of war. These days, federalism means war.

The court's majority has been expanding the states' immunity from the reach of federal law for some time, and their latest such move provoked four justices into signing an unusual dissenting opinion in which they made clear that they were not simply disagreeing with the decision at hand. Rather, they were taking a public vow to remain in dissent from the majority's open-ended view of the sovereign powers of the individual states. "Today's decision

reaffirms the need for continued dissent," Justice Stephen G. Breyer wrote at the end of a 17-page opinion that was also signed by Justices John Paul Stevens, David H. Souter and Ruth Bader Ginsburg. The opinion explained how, in the view of the four, the outcome in *Federal Maritime Commission v. South Carolina* was not just a mistake but the result of a fundamentally flawed understanding of the role of the states within the federal system.

The majority opinion, written by Justice Clarence Thomas, interpreted the 11th Amendment, which speaks of state immunity from "the judicial power of the United States," to shield states from proceedings in which federal agencies would rule on private complaints. In doing so, the majority embraced an open-ended concept of state immunity that sees it as an aspect of the states' "dignity" as "sovereign entities," rather than anchored in the actual constitutional text.

It was the latest of several 5-to-4 decisions that have unsettled the modern "basic understanding" of federal supremacy, as Justice Breyer put it, opening a new chapter in a 200-year-old debate over the country's most basic structural arrangements and stirring the deep judicial passions that the dissenters' stance reflected.

Justice Breyer offered one qualification: continued dissent might be unnecessary, he said, if "the consequences of the court's approach prove anodyne, as I hope, rather than randomly destructive, as I fear." But this was a throwaway line, coming as it did after a long description of the dangers the dissenters saw resulting from the decision. At its core, their opinion was a declaration that could fairly be translated as: "We will never surrender."

By themselves, dissenting opinions are hardly unusual. There were dissents in 47 of the 79 cases the court decided in its last term. In a lecture last week to the Supreme Court Historical Society, Justice Sandra Day O'Connor—whose position at the court's center of gravity makes her an infrequent dissenter, with only nine dissenting votes last term—discussed the role of dissent. "The citizens of this nation are educated and aware enough to understand that the questions that come before the court rarely have easy answers," Justice O'Connor said. "The existence of dissent demonstrates, indeed embodies, the struggles we undergo in reaching our decisions."

Most often, the message of the dissent is that the majority has misinterpreted the law or has invoked a legal principle for a set of facts that it does not really fit. Precedents may well be found not to apply, perhaps disingenuously; justices are very good at sending cases off on oblique paths when a direct route, like adherence to what appears to be a directly relevant precedent, is unappealing.

Rarely, however, do they confront an entire body of precedent, openly denounce it, and publicly vow to keep on dissenting.

It is easy to understand why. Most people want to think of judges as open-minded, engaged in intellectual struggle, willing to be persuaded by the best argument.

Many political scientists believe this to be a naive view. Harold J. Spaeth and Jeffrey A. Segal have written a series of books and articles, including most recently a revised version of their 1993 "The Supreme Court and the Attitudinal Model," arguing that personal ideology rather than fidelity to legal principles best explains the justices' behavior. Their work is based on a vast database of voting patterns that the two authors have maintained for years.

Despite the academic cynicism, the public holds a more romantic view of judicial behavior. Any judicial nominee foolish enough to confess fealty to an idee fixe, no matter how well defended, would probably not be confirmed. Justice William J. Brennan Jr. encountered criticism for his refusal to acquiesce to the court's death-penalty precedents, adhering instead to the view that capital punishment was unconstitutional under all circumstances.

In a 1985 speech titled "In Defense of Dissents," Justice Brennan explained what he referred to "a special kind of dissent: the repeated dissent in which a justice refuses to yield to the views of the majority although persistently rebuffed by them."

He acknowledged that some found his position "simply contrary, tiresome, or quixotic," but added: "Yet, in my judgment, when a justice perceives an interpretation of the text to have departed so far from its essential meaning, that justice is bound, by a larger constitutional duty to the community, to expose the departure and point toward a different path. This type of dissent constitutes a statement by the judge as an individual: 'Here I draw the line.'"

THE two original dissenters in the *Roe v. Wade* abortion ruling, William H. Rehnquist and Byron R. White, never accepted that case as valid precedent. Justice White, who retired in 1993 and died this year, also dissented from the Miranda decision in 1966. But he eventually accepted Miranda, even writing the court's decision in a 1981 case, *Edwards v. Arizona,* which clarified and built on Miranda's protections for criminal suspects.

One unusual characteristic of the four federalism dissenters is that there are four of them. They have held together in a series of cases since 1995, when the majority's states'-rights agenda came into full focus.

"It sends a certain kind of signal not only to litigants but to the political system," said Howard Gillman, a political scientist and Supreme Court specialist at the University of Southern California. The cohesion of the four, he commented in an interview, puts squarely on the table the question of a future fifth vote and insures high visibility for the federalism issue, "the biggest and deepest disagreement about the nature of our constitutional system," in future confirmation debates.

"At some level, the country will eventually decide which of these two visions will triumph," Professor Gillman said. "The country will be the referee."

What's Your Opinion?

Which side in this dispute has the stronger constitutional argument? Why?

CHAPTER 4

CIVIL LIBERTIES: PROTECTING INDIVIDUAL RIGHTS

"A bill of rights is what the people are entitled to against every government on earth, general or particular, and what no just government should refuse, or rest on inference.**"**

THOMAS JEFFERSON[1]

Robert and Sarisse Creighton and their three children were asleep when FBI agents and local police broke into their home in the middle of the night. Brandishing guns, the officers searched the house for a relative of the Creightons who was suspected of bank robbery. When asked to show a search warrant, the officers said, "You watch too much TV." The suspect was not there, and the officers left as abruptly as they had entered. The Creightons sued the FBI agent in charge, Russell Anderson, for violating their Fourth Amendment right against unlawful search.

The Creightons won a temporary victory when the U.S. Circuit Court of Appeals for the Eighth Circuit—noting that individuals are constitutionally protected against warrantless searches unless officers have good reason ("probable cause") for a search and unless they have good reason ("exigent circumstances") for conducting that search without a warrant—concluded that Anderson had been derelict in his duty. In the judgment of the appellate court, Anderson should have sought a warrant from a judge, who would have decided whether a search of the Creightons' home was justified.

The Supreme Court of the United States overturned the lower court's ruling. The Court's majority opinion said: "We have recognized that it is inevitable that law enforcement officials will in some cases reasonably but mistakenly conclude that probable cause is present, and we have indicated that in such cases those officials . . . should not be held personally liable." Justice John Paul Stevens and two other justices sharply dissented. Stevens accused the Court's majority of showing "remarkably little fidelity" to the Fourth Amendment.[2] Civil liberties groups claimed that the Court's decision gave police an open invitation to invade people's homes on the slightest pretext. On the other hand, law enforcement officials praised the decision, saying that a ruling in the Creightons' favor would have made them hesitant to pursue suspects for fear of a lawsuit whenever the search failed to produce the culprit.

As this case illustrates, issues of individual rights are complex and political. No right is absolute. For example, the Fourth Amendment protects Americans not from *all* searches but from *unreasonable* searches. The public would be unsafe if law officials could never pursue a suspect into a home. Yet the public would also be unsafe if police could invade homes anytime they wanted. The challenge to a civil society is to establish a level of police authority that balances the demands of public safety with those of personal freedom. The balance point, however, is always subject to dispute. Did FBI agent Anderson have sufficient cause for a warrantless search of the Creightons' home? Or was his evidence so weak that his forcible entry constituted an unreasonable search? Law enforcement officials and civil liberties groups had widely different opinions on these questions. Nor did the justices of the Supreme Court have a uniform view. Six of the justices sided with Anderson and three backed the Creightons' position.

This chapter examines issues of **civil liberties:** specific individual rights, such as freedom of speech and protection against self-incrimination, that are constitutionally protected against infringement by government. As seen in Chapter 2, the Constitution's failure to enumerate individual freedoms led to demands for the **Bill of Rights.** Enacted in 1791, these first ten amendments to the Constitution specify certain rights of life, liberty, and property that the national government is obliged to respect. A later amendment, the Fourteenth, became the basis for protecting these rights from actions by state and local governments.

Rights have full meaning only as protected in law. A constitutional guarantee of free speech, for example, is worth no more than the paper on which it is written if authorities are able to stop people from speaking freely. Judicial action is important in defining what people's rights mean in practice and in setting and enforcing limits on official action that may infringe on these rights. In some areas, the judiciary devises a specific test to determine whether government action is lawful. A test applied in the area of free speech, for example, is whether general rules (such as restrictions on the time and place of a public gathering) are applied fairly to all groups. Government officials do not meet this test if they apply one set of rules for groups that they like and a harsher set of rules for those they dislike.

Issues of individual rights have become increasingly complex and important. The writers of the Constitution could not possibly have foreseen the United States of the early twenty-first century, with its huge national government, enormous corporations, pervasive mass media, urban crowding, and vulnerability to terrorist acts. These developments are potential threats to individual liberty, and the judiciary in recent decades has seen fit to expand the rights to which individuals are entitled. However, these rights are constantly being balanced against competing individual rights and society's collective interests. The Bill of Rights operates in an untidy world where people's highest aspirations collide with their worst passions, and it is at this juncture that issues of civil liberties arise. Should an admitted murderer be entitled to recant a confession? Should the press be allowed to print military secrets whose publication might jeopardize national security? Should prayer be allowed in the public schools? Should extremist groups be allowed to publicize their messages of prejudice and hate? Such questions are among the subjects of this chapter, which focuses on the following major points:

* *Freedom of expression is the most basic of democratic rights, but like all rights, it is not unlimited.* Free expression recently has been strongly supported by the Supreme Court.
* *"Due process of law" refers to legal protections (primarily procedural safeguards) that are designed to ensure that individual rights are respected by government.*
* *During the last half century particularly, the civil liberties of individual Americans have been substantially broadened in law and given greater judicial protection from action by all levels of government.* Of special significance has been the Supreme Court's use of the Fourteenth Amendment to protect these individual rights from action by state and local governments.
* *Individual rights are constantly being weighed against the demands of majorities and the collective needs of society.* All political institutions are involved in this process, as is public opinion, but the judiciary plays the central role in it and is the institution that is most partial to the protection of civil liberties.

Protesters in San Francisco demonstrate against the possibility of war with Iraq. Freedom of expression is widely regarded as the most basic of rights since other aspects of a free society, such as open and fair elections, are dependent on it.

FREEDOM OF EXPRESSION

Freedom of political expression is the most basic of democratic rights. Unless citizens can openly express their political opinions, they cannot properly influence their government or act to protect their other rights. As the Supreme Court concluded in 1984, "The freedom to speak one's mind is not only an aspect of individual liberty—and thus a good unto itself—but also is essential to the common quest for truth and the vitality of society as a whole."[3]

It is for such reasons that the First Amendment provides the foundation for **freedom of expression**—the right of individual Americans to hold and communicate views of their choosing. For many reasons, such as a desire to conform to social pressure or a fear of harassment, Americans do not always choose to express themselves freely. Moreover, freedom of expression, like other rights, is not absolute. It does not entitle individuals to say or do whatever they want, to whomever they want, whenever they want. Free expression can be denied, for example, if it endangers national security, wrongly damages the reputations of others, or deprives others of their basic freedoms. Nevertheless, the First Amendment provides for freedom of expression by prohibiting laws that would abridge the freedoms of conscience, speech, press, assembly, and petition.

In recent decades, free expression has been vigorously protected by the courts. Today, under most circumstances, Americans can freely express their political views without fear of governmental interference. In earlier times, however, Americans were less free to express their opinions.

The Early Period: The Uncertain Status of the Right of Free Expression

The first legislative attempt by the U.S. government to restrict free expression was the Sedition Act of 1798, which made it a crime to print false or malicious newspaper stories about the president or other national officials. Thomas Jefferson called the Sedition Act an "alarming infraction" of the Constitution and, upon replacing John Adams as president in 1801, pardoned those who had been convicted under it. Because the Supreme Court did not review the sedition cases, however, the judiciary's position on free expression remained an open question. The Court also did not rule on free speech during the Civil War era, when the government severely restricted individual rights.

In 1919 the Court finally ruled on a case that challenged the national government's authority to restrict free expression. The defendant had been convicted under the 1917 Espionage Act, which prohibited forms of dissent, including the distribution of antiwar leaflets, that could harm the nation's effort in World War I. In *Schenck v. United States* (1919), the Court unanimously ruled that the Espionage Act was constitutional. In the opinion written by Justice Oliver Wendell Holmes, the Court said that Congress could restrict speech that was "of such a nature as to create a clear and present danger" to the nation's security. In a famous passage, Holmes argued that not even the First Amendment would permit a person to falsely yell "fire" in a crowded theater and create a panic that could kill or injure innocent people.[4]

Although the Schenck decision upheld a law that limited free expression, it also established a standard—the **clear-and-present-danger test**—for determining when government had exceeded its constitutional authority to restrict speech. Political speech that was not a clear and present danger could not be banned by government. (The clear-and-present-danger test was later replaced by an even more stringent standard—the imminent-lawless-action test—that is discussed later in the chapter.)

The Modern Period: Protecting Free Expression

Until the twentieth century, the tension between national security interests and free expression was not a pressing dilemma for the United States. The country's great size and ocean barriers provided protection from potential enemies, minimizing concerns of internal subversion. World War I, however, intruded on America's isolation, and World War II brought it to an abrupt end. Since then, Americans' rights of free expression have been defined largely in the context of national security concerns.

This tendency is clearly evident in recent government actions in the war on terrorism, including the USA Patriot Act of 2001 (see Chapter 1). The government's powers of surveillance and detention have been expanded, which has narrowed the legal protections provided to those people who are even remotely suspected of having ties to terrorist activity. Although these new powers have not yet been substantially reviewed by the judiciary, their legality is sure to be tested in future cases.

Free Speech and Assembly During the cold war that developed after World War II, many Americans perceived the Soviet Union as bent on destroying the United States, and the Supreme Court allowed government to put substantial limits on free expression. In 1951, for example, the Court upheld the convictions of eleven members of the U.S. Communist party who had been prosecuted under a law that made it illegal to express support for the forceful overthrow of the U.S. government.[5]

By the late 1950s, however, fear of internal communist subversion was subsiding, and the Supreme Court expanded the scope of permissible speech.[6] The Court implicitly embraced a legal doctrine first outlined by Justice Harlan Fiske Stone in 1938. Stone argued that First Amendment rights of free expression are the basis of Americans' liberty and ought to have a "preferred position" in the law. If government can control what people know and say, it can manipulate their opinions and thereby deprive them of the right to decide for themselves how they will be governed. Therefore, government should be broadly prohibited from restricting free expression.[7]

This philosophy has led the Supreme Court to rule that government officials must show that national security is directly and substantially imperiled before they can lawfully prohibit citizens from speaking out or assembling. For example, during the Vietnam era, despite the largest sustained protest movement in America's history, not a single individual was convicted solely for speaking out against the government's war policy. (Some dissenters were found guilty on other grounds, such as inciting riots and assaulting the police.)

After the terrorist attacks on the World Trade Center and the Pentagon, the American flag suddenly appeared on offices, homes, and vehicles throughout the country. Kevin Sabia of Kent, Connecticut, chose to paint his house like a flag. Americans can also choose to burn the flag. In 1989, the Supreme Court declared flag burning to be a constitutionally protected right of free expression.

The Supreme Court's protection of **symbolic speech** has been less substantial than its protection of verbal speech. For example, the Court in 1968 upheld the conviction of a Vietnam protester who had burned his draft registration card. The Court said that government can prohibit action that threatens a legitimate public interest as long as the main purpose of the policy is not to restrict free expression. The Court concluded that the federal law prohibiting the destruction of draft cards was designed primarily to protect the military's need for soldiers, not to prevent people from criticizing government policy.[8]

The Supreme Court, however, has not granted the government broad power to restrict symbolic speech. In 1989, for example, the Court ruled that the burning of the American flag is a protected form of free expression. The ruling came in the case of Gregory Lee Johnson, a member of the Communist Youth Brigade, who had set fire to a U.S. flag outside the hall in Dallas where the 1984 Republican National Convention was being held. The Supreme Court rejected the state of Texas's argument that flag burning is, in every instance, an imminent danger to public safety. "If there is a bedrock principle underlying the First Amendment," the Court ruled in the *Johnson* case, "it is that the Government may not prohibit the expression of an idea simply because society finds the idea itself offensive or disagree-able."[9] (A year later the Court struck down a new federal statute that made it a federal crime to burn or deface the flag.)[10]

Press Freedom and Prior Restraint Freedom of the press has also re-ceived strong judicial support in recent decades. In *New York Times Co. v. United States* (1971), the Court ruled that the *Times*'s publication of the "Pentagon papers" (secret government documents revealing official decep-tion about the success of the Vietnam war policy) could not be blocked by the Department of Justice, which claimed that publication would hurt the war effort. The documents had been illegally obtained by antiwar activists, who had turned them over to the *Times* for publication. The Court ruled that "any system of prior restraints" on the press is unconstitutional unless the government can clearly justify the restriction.[11]

The unacceptability of **prior restraint**—government prohibition of speech or publication before the fact—is basic to the current doctrine of free expression. The Supreme Court has said that any attempt by govern-ment to prevent expression carries "a 'heavy presumption' against its con-stitutionality."[12] News organizations and individuals are legally responsible after the fact for what they report or say (for example, they can be sued by an individual whose reputation is wrongly damaged by their words), but generally government cannot stop them in advance from expressing their views. One exception is the reporting on U.S. military operations during wartime. The courts have allowed the government to censor reports filed by journalists who are granted access to the battlefront. The courts have also upheld the government's authority to ban uncensored publications by certain past and present government employees, such as CIA agents, who have taken part in classified national security activities.

Free Expression and State Governments

In 1790 Congress rejected a proposed amendment to the Constitution that would have applied the Bill of Rights to the states. Thus the freedoms guar-anteed in the Bill of Rights were initially protected only from action by the national government, a constitutional arrangement that the Supreme Court upheld in *Barron v. Baltimore* (1833).[13] The effect was that the Bill of Rights had little practical meaning in the lives of ordinary Americans because state and local governments carry out most of the activities, such as law enforce-ment, in which people's rights are at issue.

Not until the twentieth century did the Supreme Court begin to protect individual rights from infringement by state and local governments. The vehicle for this change was the **due process clause of the Fourteenth Amendment** to the Constitution.

The Fourteenth Amendment and Selective Incorporation Ratified in 1868, the Fourteenth Amendment includes a clause that forbids a state from depriving any person of life, liberty, or property without due process of law (due process refers to the legal procedures that have been established as a means of protecting individuals' rights). Six decades later, the Supreme Court in *Gitlow v. New York* (1925) decided that the Fourteenth Amendment applied to state action in the area of freedom of expression. The Court upheld Benjamin Gitlow's conviction for violating a New York law that prohibited advocacy of the violent overthrow of the U.S. government, but warned that the states were not completely free to limit expression:

> For present purposes we may and do assume that freedom of speech and of the press—which are protected by the First Amendment from abridgement by Congress—are among the fundamental personal rights and "liberties" protected by the due process clause of the Fourteenth Amendment from impairment by the states.[14]

There is no indication that Congress, when it passed the Fourteenth Amendment after the Civil War, meant it to protect First Amendment rights from state action. The Supreme Court justified its new interpretation in the *Gitlow* case by reference to **selective incorporation**—the incorporation into the Fourteenth Amendment of certain provisions of the Bill of Rights, particularly freedom of speech and press, so that these rights can be protected from infringement by the states. The Court reasoned that the Fourteenth Amendment's due process clause would be largely meaningless if states had the power to stop their residents from speaking openly.

This interpretation of the Fourteenth Amendment provided the Court with a legal basis for striking down state laws that infringed unreasonably on free expression. But the Supreme Court acts only in the context of specific cases; it does not have the authority to issue blanket rulings. Accordingly, further action by the Court could not occur until appropriate cases arose and reached the Court on appeal from lower courts. Within a dozen years (see Table 4–1), the Court had received four cases that enabled it to invalidate state laws that restricted expression in the areas of speech (*Fiske v. Kansas*), press (*Near v. Minnesota*), religion (*Hamilton v. Regents, University of California*), and assembly and petition (*DeJonge v. Oregon*).[15] The *Near* decision is most famous of these rulings. Jay Near was the publisher of a Minneapolis weekly newspaper that regularly made scurrilous attacks on blacks, Jews, Catholics, and labor union leaders. His paper was closed down on authority of a state law that banned "malicious, scandalous, or defamatory" publications. Near appealed the shutdown, and the Supreme Court ruled in his favor, saying that the Minnesota law was "the essence of censorship."[16]

TABLE 4-1 SELECTIVE INCORPORATION OF RIGHTS OF FREE EXPRESSION

In the 1920s and 1930s, the Supreme Court selectively incorporated the free-expression provisions of the First Amendment into the Fourteenth Amendment so that these rights would be protected from infringement by the states.

Supreme Court Case	Year	First Amendment Right at Issue
Gitlow v. New York	1925	First Amendment's applicability to free speech
Fiske v. Kansas	1927	Free speech
Near v. Minnesota	1931	Free press
Hamilton v. Regents, U. of California	1934	Religious freedom
DeJonge v. Oregon	1937	Freedom of assembly and of petition

Limiting the Authority of States to Restrict Expression Since the 1930s, the Supreme Court has broadly protected freedom of expression from action by the states and by local governments, which derive their authority from the states. The Court has held that the states cannot restrict free expression except when such expression is almost certain to result in imminent lawlessness. A leading free speech case was *Brandenburg v. Ohio* (1969). The appellant was a Ku Klux Klan member who, in a speech delivered at a Klan rally, said that "revenge" might have to be taken if the national government "continues to suppress the white Caucasian race." He was convicted of advocating force under an Ohio law prohibiting criminal syndicalism, but the Supreme Court reversed the conviction, saying the First Amendment prohibits a state from suppressing speech that advocates the unlawful use of force "except where such advocacy is directed to inciting or producing imminent lawless action, and is likely to produce such action."[17] This test—the likelihood of **imminent lawless action**—is a strong limit on the government's power to restrict expression. It is rare when words alone incite others to resort to immediate unlawful action.

The Court has broadly held that hate speech cannot be silenced. This ruling came in a unanimous 1992 opinion that struck down a St. Paul, Minnesota, ordinance making it a crime to engage in speech likely to arouse "anger or alarm" on the basis of "race, color, creed, religion or gender." The Court said the First Amendment prohibits government from "silencing speech on the basis of its content."[18] This protection of violent *speech* does not, however, extend to violent *crimes*, such as assault, motivated by racial or other forms of prejudice. A Wisconsin law that provided for increased sentences for such crimes was challenged as a violation of the First Amendment. In a unanimous 1993 opinion, the Court said that the law was aimed at "conduct unprotected by the First Amendment" rather than the defendant's speech.[19]

In a key case involving freedom of assembly, the U.S. Supreme Court in 1977 upheld a lower-court ruling against local ordinances of Skokie, Illinois, which had been invoked to prevent a parade there by the American Nazi party.[20] Skokie had a large Jewish population, including many survivors of Nazi Germany's concentration camps. The Supreme Court held that the right of free expression takes precedence over the mere *possibility* that exercising the right may have undesirable consequences. Before government can lawfully prevent a speech or rally, it must offer persuasive evidence that an evil will almost certainly result from the event and must also demonstrate the lack of alternative ways (such as assigning police officers to control the crowd) to prevent the evil from happening.

The Supreme Court has recognized that freedom of speech and assembly may conflict with the routines of daily life. Accordingly, individuals do not have the right to hold a public rally in the middle of a busy intersection during rush hour, nor do they have the right to command immediate access to a public auditorium. The Court has held that public officials can regulate the time, place, and conditions of public assembly, provided that these regulations are reasonable and are applied evenhandedly to all groups, including those that hold unpopular views.[21]

In general, the Supreme Court's position is that the First Amendment makes any government effort to regulate the *content* of a message highly suspect. In the flag-burning case, Texas was regulating the content of the message—contempt for the flag and the principles it represents. Texas could not have been regulating the act itself, for the Texas government's own method of disposing of worn-out flags is also to burn them. But a content-neutral regulation (no public rally can be held in the middle of a busy intersection at rush hour) is acceptable as long as it is reasonable and does not discriminate against certain groups or ideas.

Libel and Slander

The constitutional right of free expression is not a legal license to avoid responsibility for the consequences of what is said or written. If false information that greatly harms a person's reputation is published (**libel**) or spoken (**slander**), the injured party can sue for damages. The ease of winning such suits has obvious implications for free expression. Individuals and organizations are less likely to express themselves openly if they stand a good chance of subsequently losing a libel or slander suit.

Libel is the more compelling issue for the political process because it affects the news media's ability to criticize public officials. A leading decision in this area is *New York Times Co. v. Sullivan* (1964), in which the Court overruled an Alabama state court that had found the *Times* guilty of libel for printing an advertisement criticizing Alabama officials for physically assaulting black civil rights demonstrators. The Court ruled that libel of a public official requires proof of actual malice, which was defined as a knowing or reckless disregard for the truth.[22] It is very difficult to prove that a publication acted with reckless or deliberate disregard for the truth. In fact, no federal official has won a libel judgment against a news organization in the three decades since the *Sullivan* ruling. (The press has less protection against a libel judgment when its target is a private person rather than a public official. The courts regard the communication of information about private individuals as less basic to the democratic process than information about public officials, and therefore the press must take greater care in ascertaining the validity of claims about an ordinary citizen.)

The *Sullivan* decision notwithstanding, the greatest protection against a libel judgment is truthfulness. The Court has held that expressions of opinion deserve "full constitutional protection" against the charge of libel as long as they do not contain "a provably false factual connotation."[23]

Obscenity

Obscenity is a form of expression that is not protected by the First Amendment. However, the Supreme Court has found it difficult to define which publicly disseminated sexual materials are obscene and which are not. The Court has struggled to develop a standard that gives predictability to the law without endangering First Amendment rights.

The Court's first test was established in *Roth v. United States* (1957), when the Court defined obscenity as material that "taken as a whole" appealed to "prurient interest" and had no "redeeming social significance." The perspective was to be that of "the average person, applying contemporary community standards."[24] The test proved unworkable. Even the justices, when personally examining allegedly obscene material, would argue over whether it appealed to prurient interest and was without redeeming social value. In the end, they usually concluded that it had at least some social significance.

In *Miller v. California* (1973), the Court narrowed the "contemporary community standards" to the local level. The court said that what might offend residents of "Mississippi might be found tolerable in Las Vegas."[25] But even this test proved too restrictive. The Court subsequently ruled that material cannot be judged obscene simply because the "average" local resident might object to it. "Community standards" were to be judged in the context of a "reasonable person"—someone whose outlook is broad enough to evaluate the material on its overall merit rather than its most objectionable feature. The Court later also modified its content standard, saying that the material must be of a "particularly offensive type."[26] These efforts illustrate the difficulty of defining obscenity and, even more, of developing a legal standard that can be applied evenhandedly by courts when an obscenity case arises.

The Supreme Court has distinguished between obscene materials in public places and in the home. A unanimous ruling in 1969 held that what adults read and watch in the privacy of their homes cannot be made a crime.[27] The Court created an exception to this rule in 1990 by upholding an Ohio law making it a crime to possess pornographic photographs of children.[28] The Court reasoned that the purchase of such material encouraged producers to use children in the making of pornographic materials, which is a crime. Consistent with this reasoning, the Court in *Ashcroft v. Free Speech Coalition* (2002) held that pictures of adults, digitally altered to look like children, cannot be banned because children are not used in the production of this type of material.[29]

The shielding of children from the effects of the demand for sexually explicit material has also affected cable television policy. In 1996, the Supreme Court held that although cable operators are not required to scramble the signal of channels that provide adult programming, they must do so for individual subscribers who request that the signal be scrambled.[30]

The Internet can also be a source of indecent material. To prevent such material from reaching children, Congress in 1996 passed the Communications Decency Act, which made it a federal crime to use the Internet to transmit obscene material to someone under eighteen years of age or to post material in a way that made it available to minors. In a 1997 ruling, *Reno v. ACLU*, the Supreme Court declared the Decency Act to be unconstitutional on the grounds that its restrictions were so broad that they had the effect of suppressing material intended for adults.[31] Congress responded with the Child Online Protection Act (COPA) of 1998, which defines indecency according to "contemporary community standards." In *Ashcroft v. ACLU* (2002), the Supreme Court in a narrow ruling upheld the community standards test for web content. This test could become a stringent one. Because the Internet reaches into homes everywhere, content could be limited to what is found acceptable in more traditional communities rather than in communities where, in the Court's words, "avant garde culture is the norm."[32]

The Supreme Court in 1997 invalidated the Communications Decency Act, which had broadly outlawed indecent material on the Internet. The Court held that the law was so broad and so punitive that it would censor "a large amount of speech."

FREEDOM OF RELIGION

Free religious expression is the precursor of free political expression, at least within the English tradition of limited government. England's Glorious, or Bloodless, Revolution of 1689 centered on the issue of religion and resulted in the Act of Toleration, which gave members of all Protestant sects the right to worship freely and publicly. The English philosopher John Locke (1632–1704) extended this principle, arguing that legitimate government could not inhibit free expression, religious or otherwise. The First Amendment reflects this tradition, providing for freedom of religion along with freedom of speech, press, assembly, and petition.

In regard to religion, the First Amendment reads: "Congress shall make no law respecting an establishment of religion, or prohibiting the free exercise thereof." The prohibition on laws aimed at "establishment of religion" (the establishment clause) and its "free exercise" (the free-exercise clause) applies to states and localities through the Fourteenth Amendment.

The Establishment Clause

The **establishment clause** has been interpreted by the courts to mean that government may not favor one religion over another or support religion over no religion. (This position contrasts with that of a country such as England, where Anglicanism is the official, or "established," state religion, though no religion is prohibited.) The Supreme Court's interpretation of the establishment clause has been described as maintaining a "wall of separation" between

The First Amendment's protection of free expression includes religious freedom, which has led the courts to hold that government should not in most instances promote or interfere with religious practices.

church and state, which includes a prohibition on nondenominational support for religion.[33] The Court has taken a pragmatic approach, however, by permitting some establishment activities but disallowing others. The Court has permitted states to provide secular textbooks for use by church-affiliated schools,[34] for instance, but has forbidden states to pay part of the salaries of teachers in church-affiliated schools.[35] Such distinctions follow no strict logic but are based on judgments of whether government action involves "*excessive* entanglement with religion."[36] In allowing public funds to be used by religious schools for secular textbooks but not for teachers' salaries, the courts have indicated that, whereas it is relatively easy to ascertain whether the content of a particular textbook promotes religion, it would be much harder to determine whether a particular teacher was promoting religion in the classroom.[37]

In a key 2002 decision, however, the Supreme Court upheld an Ohio law that allows students in Cleveland's failing public schools to receive a tax-supported voucher to attend private or parochial school. The Court's majority argued in *Zelman v. Simmons-Harris* that the program did not violate the establishment clause because students had a choice between secular and religious education. Four members of the Court dissented sharply with the majority's reasoning. Justice Stevens said the ruling had removed a "brick from the wall that was once designed to separate religion from government."[38]

Yet the Court has held firm in its position, first announced in *Engel v. Vitale* (1962), that the establishment clause prohibits the reciting of prayers in public schools.[39] A year later the Court struck down Bible readings in public schools.[40] Religion is a powerful force in American life, and the Supreme Court's school-prayer position has evoked strong opposition. An Alabama law attempted to circumvent the prayer ruling by permitting public schools to set aside one minute each day for silent prayer or meditation. In 1985, the Court declared the law unconstitutional, ruling that "government must pursue a course of complete neutrality toward religion."[41] The Court in 2000 reaffirmed the ban by extending it to include organized student-led prayer at public school football games.[42]

The Free-Exercise Clause

The First and Fourteenth Amendments also prohibit governmental interference with the free exercise of religion. The idea underlying the **free-exercise clause** is clear: Americans are free to hold any religious belief they choose.

Although people are free to believe what they want, they are not always free to act on their beliefs. The courts have allowed government interference in the exercise of religious beliefs when such interference is the secondary result of an overriding social goal. An example is the legal protection of children with life-threatening illnesses whose parents refuse to permit medical treatment on religious grounds. A court may order that such children be given medical assistance because the social good of saving their lives overrides their parents' free-exercise rights.

In some circumstances, exceptions to certain laws have been permitted on free-exercise grounds. The Supreme Court ruled in 1972 that Wisconsin could not compel Amish parents to send their children to school beyond the eighth grade because this policy violates a centuries-old Amish religious practice of having children leave school and begin work at an early age.[43] In upholding free exercise in such cases, the Court may be said to have violated the establishment clause by granting preferred treatment to people who hold a particular religious belief. The Court has recognized the potential conflict between the free-exercise and establishment clauses and, as in other such situations, has tried to strike a reasonable balance between the competing claims.

When the free-exercise and establishment clauses cannot be balanced, the Supreme Court has been forced to make a choice. In 1987, the Court overturned a Louisiana law requiring that creationism (the Bible's account of how the world was created) be taught along with the theory of evolution in public school science courses. Creationism, the Court concluded, is a religious doctrine, not a scientific theory; thus its inclusion in public school curricula violates the establishment clause by promoting a religious belief.[44] Creationists viewed the Court's decision as a violation of their right to the free exercise of religion; they argued that their children were being forced to study a theory of evolution that contradicts the biblical account of human origins.

THE RIGHT OF PRIVACY

Until the 1960s, Americans' constitutional rights were confined largely to those enumerated in the Bill of Rights. This situation prevailed despite the Ninth Amendment, which reads: "The enumeration in the Constitution, of certain rights, shall not be construed to deny or disparage others retained by the people."

In 1965, however, the Supreme Court added to the list of individual rights, declaring that Americans have "a right of privacy." This judgment arose from the case of *Griswold v. Connecticut*, which challenged a state law prohibiting the use of birth control devices, even by married couples. The Supreme Court invalidated the statute, concluding that a state had no business interfering with a married couple's decision regarding contraception. The Court did not base its decision on the Ninth Amendment, but reasoned instead that the freedoms in the Bill of Rights imply an underlying right of privacy. Individuals have, said the Court, a "zone of [personal] privacy" that government cannot lawfully infringe upon.[45]

The right of privacy was the basis for the Supreme Court's ruling in *Roe v. Wade* (1973), which gave women full freedom to choose abortion during the first three months of pregnancy.[46] In overturning a Texas law prohibiting abortion except to save the life of the mother, the Supreme Court said that the right to privacy is "broad enough to encompass a woman's decision whether or not to terminate her pregnancy."

After *Roe*, antiabortion activists sought to reverse or weaken the Court's ruling. Attempts to pass a constitutional amendment that would ban abortions were unsuccessful, but abortion foes succeeded in a campaign to prohibit the use of government funds to pay for abortions for poor women. Then, in *Webster v. Reproductive Health Services* (1989), the Supreme Court upheld a Missouri law that prohibits abortions in its public hospitals and by its public employees.[47]

The *Webster* decision was followed in 1992 by a judgment in the Pennsylvania abortion case *Planned Parenthood v. Casey*. Pennsylvania's law placed a twenty-four-hour waiting period on women who sought an abortion, required doctors to counsel women on abortion and alternatives to abortion, required a minor to have a parent's consent or a judge's approval before having an abortion, and required a married woman to notify her husband before obtaining an abortion. Antiabortion advocates saw the Pennsylvania law as an opportunity for the Supreme Court to overturn the *Roe* precedent.

However, in a decision that surprised many observers, the Court by a 5-4 margin reaffirmed the "essential holding" of *Roe v. Wade:* that a woman, because of the constitutional guarantee of privacy, has a right to abortion during the early months of pregnancy. The Court also ruled, however, that states can regulate abortion as long as they do not impose an "undue burden" on women seeking abortion. The Court concluded that the twenty-four-hour waiting period, physician counseling, and the informed-consent requirement for minors were not undue burdens and were therefore permissible. The spousal notification requirement, however, was judged to place a "substantial obstacle" in the path of women seeking abortion and was thereby declared unconstitutional.[48]

In a controversial 2000 ruling, *Stenberg v. Carhart,* the Supreme Court ruled that states may not ban partial-birth abortion (where the fetus's life is terminated during delivery), because it is sometimes the most appropriate medical procedure for protecting the life or health of the mother.[49] The ruling was applauded by pro-choice groups and condemned by pro-life groups.

Although a right of privacy has been established in some areas of personal conduct, the Supreme Court has declined to extend it to other areas. In *Bowers v. Hardwick* (1986), for example, the Court upheld a Georgia law prohibiting sodomy, concluding that the right of privacy did not include homosexual acts among consenting adults.[50] States can choose to permit these acts, but the Constitution of the United States does not require states to permit them. (In 1998, the Georgia Supreme Court invalidated the state's sodomy law, concluding that it violated "the Georgia Constitution's protection of the right of privacy.")

The U.S. Supreme Court has also held that the right of privacy does not extend to the terminally ill who might want medical help in taking their own lives. This ruling came in response to New York and Washington state laws that ban physician-assisted suicide. The Court held that a state has a legitimate interest in protecting vulnerable people. Although the Court did not say so, it hinted in its ruling that a state might choose to permit physician-assisted suicide if there were proper safeguards in its use. But the Court made it clear that "liberty" in the Fourteenth Amendment does not give residents of a state the constitutional right to doctor-assisted suicide.[51]

Privacy questions are among the most contentious in American politics because of the moral and ethical issues they raise. The abortion issue, for example, has provoked intense debate for three decades, and there is no end in sight to the controversy. The American public is divided on the issue, and there are many deeply committed activists on both sides. As with other rights, the abortion issue is not only, or even primarily, fought out in the courts. Abortion opponents have waged demonstrations outside clinics in an effort to stop the practice. Some of these protests have erupted in violent acts toward women and staff who tried to enter the clinics. In 1994, Congress made it unlawful to block the entrance to abortion clinics or otherwise prevent people from entering. (The Supreme Court upheld the law, concluding that it regulated abortion protesters' actions as opposed to their words and thus did not violate their right to free speech.)[52]

RIGHTS OF PERSONS ACCUSED OF CRIMES

Due process refers to legal protections that have been established to preserve the rights of individuals. The most significant form of these protections is **procedural due process;** the term refers primarily to procedures that authorities must follow before a person can legitimately be punished for an offense.

The U.S. Constitution provides for several procedures designed to protect a person from wrongful arrest, conviction, and punishment. According to Article I, Section 9, any person taken into police custody is entitled to seek a writ of habeas corpus, which requires law enforcement officials to bring the suspect into court and to specify the legal reason for the detention. The Fifth and Fourteenth Amendments provide generally that no person can be deprived of life, liberty, or property without due process of law. And specific procedural protections for the accused are spelled out in the Fourth, Fifth, Sixth, and Eighth Amendments:

- *The Fourth Amendment* forbids the police to conduct searches and seizures unless they have probable cause to believe that a crime has been committed.
- *The Fifth Amendment* protects against double jeopardy (being prosecuted twice for the same offense); self-incrimination (being compelled to testify against oneself); indictment for a crime except through grand jury proceedings; and loss of life, liberty, and property without due process of law.
- *The Sixth Amendment* provides the right to have legal counsel, to confront witnesses, to receive a speedy trial, and to have a trial by jury in criminal proceedings.
- *The Eighth Amendment* protects against excessive bail or fines and prohibits the infliction of cruel and unusual punishment on those convicted of crimes.

These procedural protections have always been subject to interpretation. The Sixth Amendment, for example, provides the right to have legal counsel. But what if a person cannot afford a lawyer? For most of the nation's

LIBERTY, EQUALITY & SELF-GOVERNMENT
What's Your Opinion?

Procedural Due Process

"The history of liberty has largely been the history of the observance of procedural guarantees," said Justice Felix Frankfurter in *McNabb v. United States* (1943). No system of justice is foolproof. Even in the most honest systems, innocent people have been wrongly accused, convicted, and punished with imprisonment or death. But the scrupulous application of procedural safeguards, such as a defendant's right to legal counsel, greatly increases the likelihood that justice will prevail.

However, as recent police scandals in Dallas, Los Angeles, New York, and several other cities would indicate, constitutional guarantees are no assurance that people will be treated justly. Wrongful arrests and cooked-up evidence are not by any means the norm in U.S. law enforcement. But they occur with enough frequency to be a cause of concern to anyone committed to the principle of legal justice.

What do you think can be done to safeguard individuals' due process rights? Do you share the view of social theorists who say that when procedural due process is violated, the fault lies more with a public that is willing to tolerate abuses than with the few errant law enforcement officials who commit these abuses?

---

history, poor people had almost no choice but to act as their own attorneys. They had a right to counsel but could avail themselves of it only if they had the money to hire a lawyer. Today, if a person is accused of a serious crime and cannot afford a lawyer, the government must provide one. This change came about not through a constitutional amendment but through Supreme Court rulings that gave new meaning in practice to the Sixth Amendment.

Selective Incorporation of Procedural Rights

For most of the nation's history, the procedural protections in the Bill of Rights applied only to the actions of the national government. States in their criminal proceedings were not bound by them. There were limited exceptions, such as a 1932 Supreme Court ruling that a defendant charged in a state court with a crime carrying the death penalty had to be provided with an attorney.[53] Nevertheless, even as the Court was moving to protect free-expression rights from state action in the 1930s, it held back on doing the same for the rights of the accused. The Court claimed that free-expression

| TABLE 4-2 | SELECTIVE INCORPORATION OF RIGHTS OF THE ACCUSED |

In the 1960s, the Supreme Court selectively incorporated the fair-trial provisions of the Fourth through Eighth Amendments into the Fourteenth Amendment so that these rights would be protected from infringement by the states.

Supreme Court Case	Year	Constitutional Right (Amendment) at Issue
Mapp v. Ohio	1961	Unreasonable search and seizure (Fourth)
Robinson v. California	1962	Cruel and unusual punishment (Eighth)
Gideon v. Wainwright	1963	Right to counsel (Sixth)
Malloy v. Hogan	1964	Self-incrimination (Fifth)
Pointer v. Texas	1965	Right to confront witnesses (Sixth)
Miranda v. Arizona	1966	Self-incrimination (Fifth)
Klopfer v. North Carolina	1967	Speedy trial (Sixth)
Duncan v. Louisiana	1968	Jury trial in criminal cases (Sixth)
Benton v. Maryland	1968	Double jeopardy (Fifth)

rights were more deserving of federal protection because they are more "fundamental" to the preservation of liberty. Such rights, the Court said in a 1937 ruling, are "the indispensable condition of nearly every other form of freedom."[54]

This view changed abruptly in the 1960s when the Supreme Court broadly required states to safeguard procedural rights. Changes in public education and communication made Americans more aware of their rights, and the civil rights movement dramatized the fact that rights were administered very unequally: the poor and minority group members had many fewer rights in practice than other Americans did. In response, the Supreme Court in the 1960s "incorporated" Bill of Rights protections for the accused by ruling that these rights are protected against state action by the Fourteenth Amendment's guarantee of due process of law (see Table 4–2).

This selective incorporation process began with *Mapp v. Ohio* (1961). Dollree Mapp's home had been entered by Cleveland police, who, though they failed to find what they were looking for, happened to discover some pornographic material. Mapp's conviction for its possession was overturned by the Supreme Court on the grounds that she had been subjected to unreasonable search and seizure.[55] The Court ruled that illegally obtained evidence could not be used in state courts.

Two years later, the Court's decision in *Gideon v. Wainwright* (1963) required the states to furnish attorneys for poor defendants in all felony cases. Clarence Gideon, an indigent drifter, had been convicted and sentenced to prison in Florida for breaking into a poolroom. He successfully appealed on the grounds that he had been denied due process because he could not afford to pay an attorney.[56]

During the 1960s the Court also ruled that defendants in state criminal proceedings cannot be compelled to testify against themselves,[57] have the rights to remain silent and to have legal counsel when arrested,[58] have the right to confront witnesses who testify against them,[59] must be granted a speedy trial,[60] have the right to a jury trial,[61] and cannot be subjected to double jeopardy.[62] The most famous of these cases is *Miranda v. Arizona* (1966), as a result of which police are required to inform suspects of their rights at the time of arrest. Ernesto Miranda had confessed during police interrogation to kidnapping and raping a young woman. His confession led to his conviction, which he successfully appealed to the Supreme Court on the grounds that he had not been informed of his rights to remain silent and to have legal counsel present during interrogation. Using other evidence of Miranda's crime, the state of Arizona then retried and convicted him again. He was paroled from prison in 1972 and four years later was stabbed to death in a bar fight. Ironically, Miranda's assailant was read his "Miranda rights" when police arrested him. By now the wording has become familiar: "You have the right to remain silent. . . . Anything you say can and will be used against you in a court of law. . . . You have the right to an attorney."

In a 2000 case, *Dickerson v. United States,* the Supreme Court reaffirmed the *Miranda* decision, saying that because it had established "a constitutional rule," it was not subject to change by legislative action.[63]

Limits on Defendants' Rights

In the courtroom, the rights to counsel, to confront witnesses, and to remain silent are of paramount importance. Before that phase in a criminal proceeding, the key protection is the Fourth Amendment's restriction on illegal search and seizure. This restriction holds that police must have suspicion of wrongdoing before they can search your person, your car, or your residence, although involvement in an offense can lead to a permissible search that uncovers wrongdoing of another kind. Without search and seizure protection, individuals could be subject to unrestricted police harassment and intimidation, which are characteristic of a totalitarian state, not a free society.

The Fourth Amendment, however, does not provide blanket protection against searches. In 1990, for example, the Supreme Court held that roadside checkpoints at which police stop drivers to check them for signs of

The Bill of Rights:
A Selected List of Constitutional Protections

First Amendment

Speech: You are free to say almost anything except that which is obscene, slanders another person, or has a high probability of inciting others to take imminent lawless action.

Assembly: You are free to assemble, although the time and place may be regulated in the interests of public safety and convenience.

Religion: You are protected from having the religious beliefs of others imposed on you, and you are free to believe what you like.

Fourth Amendment

Search and seizure: You are protected from unreasonable searches and seizures, although you forfeit that right if you knowingly waive it.

Arrest: You are protected from arrest unless authorities have probable cause to believe you have committed a crime.

Fifth Amendment

Self-incrimination: You are protected against self-incrimination, which means that you have the right to remain silent and to be protected against coercion by law enforcement officials.

Double jeopardy: You cannot be tried twice for the same crime if the first trial results in a verdict of innocence.

Due process: You cannot be deprived of life, liberty, or property without proper legal proceedings.

Sixth Amendment

Counsel: You have a right to be represented by an attorney and can demand to speak first with an attorney before responding to questions from law enforcement officials.

Prompt and reasonable proceedings: You have a right to be arraigned promptly, to be informed of the charges, to confront witnesses, and to have a speedy and open trial by an impartial jury.

Eighth Amendment

Bail: You are protected against excessive bail or fines.

Cruel and unusual punishment: You are protected against cruel and unusual punishment, although this provision does not protect you from the death penalty or from a long prison term for a minor offense.

intoxication are legal as long as the action is systematic and not arbitrary (for example, stopping young drivers only would be unconstitutional). The Court justified its decision by saying roadblocks serve a public safety purpose.[64] However, the Court does not allow the same types of roadblocks to check for drugs in the car. In *Indianapolis v. Edmund* (2001), the Court held that narcotics roadblocks, because they serve a general law enforcement purpose rather than one specific to highway safety, violate the Fourth Amendment's requirement that police have suspicion of wrongdoing before they can search an individual's auto.[65]

The Court also ruled in 2001 (*Kyllo v. United States*) that police may not use a thermal-imaging device in order to detect whether unusual heat sources are found in a home. The Court held that police cannot enter a home without a warrant based on suspicion of wrongdoing and that searches based on modern technology must meet the same standard.[66]

The Fourth Amendment protects individuals in their persons as well as in their homes and vehicles. The police cannot arbitrarily stop and search someone on the street or in other settings. In *Ferguson vs. Charleston* (2001), for example, the Court held that patients in public hospitals cannot be forced to take a test for illegal drugs if the purpose is to turn over to the police those patients who test positive. Such action, said the Court, constitutes an illegal search of the person.[67] Yet the Court in *Board of Education of Independent School District No. 92 of Pottawatomie County v. Earls* (2002) held that random drug testing of high school students involved in extracurricular activities does not violate the ban on unreasonable searches.[68]

The Exclusionary Rule In general, the Supreme Court in recent decades has reduced but not eliminated the protections afforded to the accused by *Mapp* and other 1960s rulings. This reduction can be seen in the application of the **exclusionary rule,** which bars the use in trials of evidence obtained in violation of a person's constitutional rights. The rule was formulated in a 1914 Supreme Court decision,[69] and its application was further expanded in federal cases. The *Mapp* decision extended the exclusionary rule to state trial proceedings as well. Subsequent decisions of the Supreme Court broadened its application to the point where almost any type of illegally obtained evidence was considered inadmissible in a criminal trial. In the 1980s, the Supreme Court reversed the trend by placing restrictions on the rule's application, concluding that illegally obtained evidence can sometimes be admitted in trials if the procedural errors are inadvertent or if the prosecution can show that it would have discovered the evidence anyway.[70]

Recent decisions have also lowered the standard that must be met for a lawful search and seizure to occur. In the 1960s, the Court developed the

In recent decades the Supreme Court has restricted the scope of the "exclusionary rule." This rule excludes from use in court proceedings any evidence that is illegally obtained by law enforcement officials.

principle that police had to have a solid basis ("probable cause") for believing that an individual was involved in a specific crime before they could stop a person and engage in search-and-seizure activity. This principle has been modified, as illustrated by *Whren v. United States* (1996), which upheld the conviction of an individual who had been found with drugs in the front seat of his car. The police had no evidence (no "probable cause") to believe that drugs were in the car but they suspected that the driver was involved in drug dealing and they used a minor traffic infraction as a pretext to stop and check him. The Supreme Court accepted defense arguments that the police had no clear evidence for their suspicion, that the traffic infraction was not the real reason the individual was stopped, and that police usually do not stop a person for the infraction in question (turning a corner without signaling). But the Court concluded that the officers' motive was irrelevant, as long as an officer in some situations might reasonably stop a car for the infraction that occurred. Thus, the stop-and-search action was deemed to meet the Fourth Amendment's reasonableness standard.[71]

The Court's objective has been to weaken the exclusionary rule without giving police unlimited discretion. In *U.S. v. Drayton et al.* (2002), for example, the Court upheld the conviction of two bus passengers who had been found with cocaine after voluntarily agreeing to a police search. They were not told of their right to refuse the search, and their attorneys argued that the evidence was therefore inadmissible. The Supreme Court said police are not required by the Fourth Amendment "to advise bus passengers of their right . . . to refuse consent to searches." However, the Court also said police cannot tell passengers they must submit to a search and cannot threaten them into permitting one.[72]

Habeas Corpus Appeals Legal protection for the accused has also been reduced by a restriction on the habeas corpus appeals to federal courts by individuals who have been convicted of crimes in state courts. (Habeas corpus gives defendants access to federal courts in order to argue that their rights under the Constitution of the United States were violated when they were convicted in a state court.) A 1960s Supreme Court precedent had assured prisoners of the right to have their petitions heard in federal court unless they had "deliberately bypassed" the opportunity to first make the appeal in state courts.[73]

This precedent was overturned in 1992 when the Court held that inmates can lose the right to a federal hearing even if a lawyer's mistake is the reason they failed to first present their appeal properly in state courts.[74] Another significant habeas corpus defeat for inmates occurred in 1993 when the Supreme Court held that federal courts cannot overturn a state conviction on the basis of constitutional error unless the prisoner can demonstrate that the error contributed to the conviction.[75] Previously, the burden of proof was on the state: it had to prove that the error did not affect the case's outcome. Then, in *Felker v. Turpin* (1996), the Court upheld a recent federal law that prohibits in most cases federal habeas corpus appeals by state prison inmates who have already filed one.[76]

Through these decisions, the Supreme Court has sought to prevent frivolous and multiple federal court appeals. State prisoners had used habeas corpus appeals to contest even small issues, and some—particularly those on death row—had filed appeal after appeal. An effect was to clog the federal courts and delay other cases. A majority of Supreme Court justices concluded that a more restrictive policy toward these appeals is required. They have held that it is fair to ask inmates to first pursue their options in state courts and then, except in unusual cases,[77] to confine themselves to a single federal appeal. Civil liberties groups have objected to the change, arguing that no procedure that would protect the innocent from wrongful punishment—particularly when the death penalty is at issue—is too big a burden to place on the courts.

Nevertheless, no one claims that recent decisions mark a return to the lower procedural standards that prevailed before the 1960s. Many of the vital precedents set in that decade remain in effect, including the most important one of all: the principle that procedural protections guaranteed to the accused by the Bill of Rights must be observed by the states as well as by the federal government.

★ ‖ STATES IN THE NATION

The Death Penalty

Most crimes and punishments in the United States are defined by state law. Nowhere is this arrangement more obvious than in the application of the death penalty. Some states prohibit it, and others apply it liberally. Texas, Florida, and Virginia are far and away the leaders in its application. Roughly a third of all executions in the past quarter-century have taken place in Texas alone.

Q: What do many of the states that prohibit capital punishment have in common?

A: States without the death penalty are concentrated in the North. Most of these states are relatively affluent, rank high on indicators of educational attainment, and have a small minority-group population.

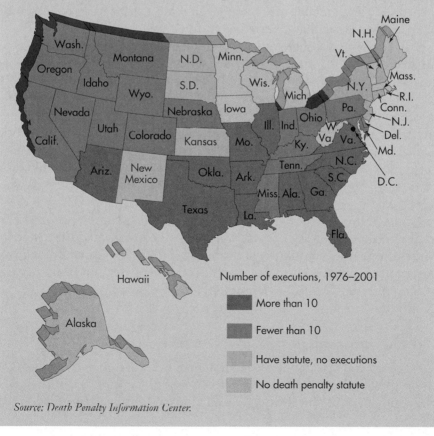

Number of executions, 1976–2001

More than 10

Fewer than 10

Have statute, no executions

No death penalty statute

Source: Death Penalty Information Center.

Rights and the War on Terrorism

The rules that apply to the government's intelligence-gathering activities are less stringent than those that apply to criminal proceedings. After the terrorist attacks of September 11, 2001, the Bush administration received legislative authority for greater flexibility in treating persons suspected of terrorist activity. The Bush administration argued that terrorist activity is a special case because it must be detected and disrupted before it occurs. Although many of the legal issues raised by the new rules have not yet been tested in the courts, the judiciary so far has said that some degree of departure from normal practices is acceptable.

The new rules include a lowering of wiretap standards. Authorities have more discretion and a lower burden of proof when seeking to place a wiretap on a group or individual suspected of terrorist activity than when ordinary criminal activity is at issue. Moreover, under the USA Patriot Act of 2001 (see Chapter 1), information gathered by intelligence investigators can now be shared with criminal investigators. Previously, information gathered through intelligence activity could not be shared if obtained by a standard lower than that for criminal proceedings.

The new rules also give authorities broad discretion to name and confine suspected terrorists. If the president designates individuals as enemy combatants, they can be held indefinitely without charge and without access to a lawyer or family members even if they are U.S. citizens. Moreover, noncitizens can be deported without being told of the charges against them and without an opportunity to defend themselves. As of early 2003, two U.S. citizens and an unspecified number of noncitizens were being held under these conditions. When the U.S. began its war on Iraq in March of 2003, FBI agents detained a large number of Iraqis living in America who were thought to be possible security risks.

Critics argue that these policies are an unwise departure from America's legal tradition. They say that the United States hands terrorists a victory when it lowers its constitutional protections. "No one is questioning the government's authority to prosecute spies and terrorists," says Ann Beeson of the American Civil Liberties Union. "But we do not need to waive the Constitution to do so."[78]

Crime, Punishment, and Police Practices

The theory and practice of procedural guarantees are often two quite different things, as Adrienne Cureton discovered on January 2, 1995. She is a plainclothes police officer who, with a uniformed partner, was called to the scene of a domestic dispute. A struggle ensued, and her partner radioed for help. When the officers arrived, Cureton and her partner had already hand-cuffed the homeowner. The officers barged in and mistook Cureton, an African American, for the other person involved in the dispute. They grabbed her by the collar, dragged her by the hair onto the porch, and clubbed her repeatedly with flashlights, despite her screams that she was a police officer.[79]

There is no reliable estimate of how often Americans' rights are violated in practice, but infringements of one sort or another are commonplace. Minorities and the poor are the more likely victims. *Racial profiling* (the assumption that certain groups are more likely to commit particular crimes) is a common police practice and results in the unequal treatment of minorities. A 1999 American Civil Liberties Union study found that although minority and white motorists were about equally likely to commit traffic infractions, 80 percent of the motorists stopped and searched by Maryland State Police on Interstate 95 were minorities and only 20 percent were white, despite the fact that white motorists constituted 75 percent of all drivers. A 1999 report by the New Jersey Attorney General's Office revealed a similar pattern in that state.

/pattersonwtp5

Profiling of a different kind came to the forefront after the terrorist attacks of September 11, 2001, when males of Middle Eastern descent were stopped and searched for reasons of appearance alone in airports and other places where further attacks were feared. Sixty-eight percent of Americans in one poll said they favored allowing police to stop and search people who might fit a terrorist profile.[80]

Another issue of justice in America is whether adherence to proper legal procedures produces reasonable outcomes. The Eighth Amendment prohibits "cruel and unusual punishment" for those convicted of crime, but judgments in this area are subjective. Although the Supreme Court has ordered officials to relieve inmate overcrowding and to improve prison facilities in a few instances, it has concluded that inmates cannot sue over prison conditions unless prison officials show "deliberate indifference" to conditions.[81] The severity of a sentence can also be an Eighth Amendment issue.[82] A divided Supreme Court in 2003 upheld California's "three-strikes" law that resulted in life imprisonment for a thrice-convicted felon who, the third time, was convicted of stealing video tapes worth $100. In general, the Court has shied away from Eighth Amendment decisions, preferring to leave those decisions to legislative bodies. In *Atkins v. Virginia* (2002), however, the Supreme Court outlawed the death penalty for the mentally retarded, saying it constitutes "cruel and unusual

In the aftermath of the September 11, 2001, terrorist attacks, Arab Americans were subject to ethnic profiling at airports and other locations. Shown here is an Arab American protesting the practice of profiling.

punishment." The Court noted that thirty states and nearly all countries in the world prohibit such executions.[83] (In another 2002 death penalty case, *Ring v. Arizona*, the Court held that the Sixth Amendment right to a jury trial prohibits judges—as opposed to juries—from deciding whether the death penalty will be imposed.)[84]

In recent years, legislators in the United States have taken a tougher stance on crime. Congress and most states have mandated stiffer sentences, and the number of federal and state prisoners has more than doubled in the past decade. The United States has a larger proportion of its people behind bars than any country in the world (see "How the United States Compares").

As the prison population has increased and the sentencing has become more severe, debate over America's criminal justice system has intensified. The severest criticisms have been directed at the death penalty and the incarceration of non-violent drug users. In these areas, U.S. policies are at odds with those of other industrialized countries, nearly all of which have outlawed the death penalty and nearly all of which rely more heavily on treatment programs than prisons in dealing with drug users. Critics have also cited the studies that indicate minorities and the poor are punished more severely than are middle-class white Americans who commit the same crimes. In 2003, outgoing Illinois governor George Ryan acted on his belief that the justice system is flawed. Claiming that the death penalty process is "arbitrary and capricious, and therefore immoral," Ryan pardoned four Illinois death-row inmates who had been convicted on false evidence and commuted to life in prison the sentences of the other 167 death-row inmates. Ryan's unprecedented action was applauded by some observers but was swiftly condemned by others, including prosecutors and some of the victims' relatives.

THE COURTS AND A FREE SOCIETY

A free and democratic nation has a vital stake in maintaining individual freedoms. The United States was founded on the belief that individuals have an innate right to personal liberty—to speak their minds, to worship as they choose, to be free of police intimidation. Yet, a majority of Americans have sometimes preferred policies that would diminish the freedom of those who hold minority views, have unconventional lifestyles, or simply "look different" than they do.

Americans are very supportive of rights and freedoms in the abstract but are much less supportive—and in some cases antagonistic—when confronted with these same rights in concrete situations. For example, after the terrorist attacks of September 11, 2001, polls indicated that a third of Americans would favor putting Arab Americans under special surveillance, half said they would favor requiring Arab Americans to carry special identification cards, and a fourth said they would approve of special detention facilities for members of suspect groups.[85] Two-fifths even said they would not allow as a college speaker someone who says that terrorism is the result of U.S. foreign policy (see Figure 4–1).

Support for individual rights is stronger among the political elite. They are also better positioned than the ordinary citizen to express their beliefs. However, they are not always willing to act on what they believe. Often, the exercise of rights involves society's least savory characters—its murderers,

HOW THE UNITED STATES COMPARES

Law and Order

Individual rights are a cornerstone of the American governing system and receive strong protection from the courts. The government's ability to restrict free expression is severely limited, and the individual's right to a fair trial is protected through elaborate due process guarantees.

According to Amnesty International, a watchdog group that monitors human rights achievements and violations around the world, the United States has a good record in terms of its constitutional protection of civil liberties. Nevertheless, Amnesty International does not rank the United States as high as the countries of northern Europe in terms of respect for human rights. Among other problems, Amnesty International faults police in the United States for "excessive force" in their treatment of prisoners and faults U.S. immigration officials for the forcible return of asylum seekers to their countries of origin without granting them hearings.

Although human rights groups admire America's elaborate procedural protections for those accused of crime, they are critical of its sentencing and incarceration policies. The United States is the world leader in the number of people it places behind bars and in the length of sentences for various categories of crime. More than half of the people in prison were convicted of nonviolent offenses, such as drug use or a crime against property. Whatever the reasons, the United States is rivaled only by Russia in the proportion of its people who are in prisons.

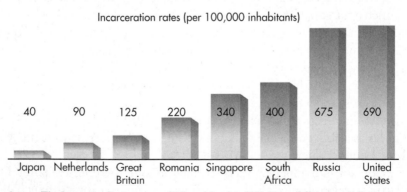

Incarceration rates (per 100,000 inhabitants)

Japan	Netherlands	Great Britain	Romania	Singapore	South Africa	Russia	United States
40	90	125	220	340	400	675	690

Source: The Sentencing Project, 2001 (U.S. and Russia); U.K. Home Office, 2001 (all others).

"Should someone who says that terrorism is the fault of how our country behaves in the world be allowed to make a speech at a college?"

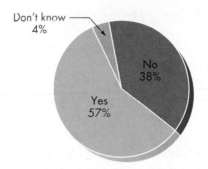

Don't know
4%

No
38%

Yes
57%

FIGURE 4-1 OPINIONS ON SPEECH ABOUT TERRORISM CAUSES ON COLLEGE CAMPUSES

Two-fifths of Americans would deny a college speaking opportunity to someone who claims terrorism is the result of U.S. policies abroad.
Source: National Public Radio/Kaiser Family Foundation/Kennedy School of Government Poll, Oct. 31– Nov. 12, 2001.

rapists, drug dealers, and hate peddlers. They are not the type of people who engender public support at any level.

The courts are not isolated from the public mood. They inevitably balance society's demand for safety and order against the rights of the individual. Nevertheless, the judicial branch can normally be expected to grant more consideration to the rights of the individual, however unpopular his or her views or actions, than will the general public or elected officials. How far the courts will go in protecting a person's rights depends on the facts of the case, the existing status of the law, prevailing social needs, and the personal views of the judges. Nevertheless, the courts regard the protection of individual rights as one of their most significant responsibilities, a perspective that is owed in no small measure to the Bill of Rights. It transformed the inalienable rights of life, liberty, and property into legal rights, thus putting them under judicial protection.[86]

The judiciary alone, however, cannot provide adequate protection for individual rights. A civil society rests also on open-minded representatives and a tolerant citizenry. If, for example, politicians and the public encourage police to infringe the rights of vaguely threatening minorities or nonconformists, the judiciary's protection of persons accused of crimes will not ensure justice. It may be said that the test of a truly civil society is not its treatment of popular ideas and of its best citizens but its willingness to tolerate ideas that the majority detests and to respect equally the rights of its least popular citizens.

SUMMARY

In their search for personal liberty, Americans added the Bill of Rights to the Constitution shortly after its ratification. These amendments guarantee certain political, procedural, and property rights against infringement by the national government. Freedom of expression is the most basic of democratic rights. People are not free unless they can freely express their views.

Nevertheless, free expression may conflict with the nation's security needs during times of war and insurrection. The courts at times have allowed government to limit expression substantially for purposes of national security. In recent decades, however, the courts have protected a very wide range of free expression in the areas of speech, press, and religion.

The guarantees embodied in the Bill of Rights originally applied only to the national government. Under the principle of selective incorporation of these guarantees into the Fourteenth Amendment, the courts extended them to state governments, though the process was slow and uneven. In the 1920s and 1930s, First Amendment guarantees of freedom of expression were given protection from infringement by the states. The states continued to have wide discretion in criminal proceedings until the early 1960s, when most of the fair-trial rights in the Bill of Rights were given federal protection.

Due process of law refers to legal protections that have been established to preserve individual rights. The most significant form of these protections consists of procedures or methods (for example, the right of an accused person to have an attorney present during police interrogation) designed to ensure that an individual's rights are upheld. A major controversy in this area is the breadth of the exclusionary rule, which bars the use in trials of illegally obtained evidence. The right of privacy, particularly as it applies to the abortion issue, is also a source of controversy. So too is the issue of constitutional rights in the pursuit of the war on terrorism.

Civil liberties are not absolute but must be balanced against other considerations (such as national security or public safety) and against one another when different rights come into conflict. The judicial branch of government, particularly the Supreme Court, has taken on much of the responsibility for protecting and interpreting individual rights. The Court's positions have changed with time and conditions, but the Court has generally been more protective of and sensitive to civil liberties than have elected officials or popular majorities.

Key Terms

Bill of Rights

civil liberties

clear-and-present-danger test

due process clause (of the
  Fourteenth Amendment)

establishment clause

exclusionary rule

free-exercise clause

freedom of expression

imminent-lawless-action test

libel

prior restraint

procedural due process

selective incorporation

slander

symbolic speech

Suggested Readings

Abraham, Henry J. *Freedom and the Court.* New York: Oxford University Press, 1998. A comprehensive analysis of the Supreme Court's work on civil rights and civil liberties.

Epstein, Lee, and Thomas G. Walker. *Constitutional Law for a Changing America*, 2d ed. Washington, D.C.: Congressional Quarterly Press, 2000. An accessible introduction to U.S. constitutional law.

Hull, N. E. H., and Peter Charles Hoffer. *Roe v. Wade: The Abortion Rights Controversy in American History.* Lawrence: University Press of Kansas, 2001. A thorough assessment of both sides of the abortion conflict, beginning with the *Roe v. Wade* decision.

Lewis, Anthony. *Gideon's Trumpet.* New York: Random House, 1964. The riveting story of Clarence Gideon and the effects of his case on the right to legal counsel.

Nagel, Robert F. *Judicial Power and American Character.* New York: Oxford University Press, 1996. Concludes that the real protection for legal rights resides in political action rather than judicial decisions.

Perry, Michael J. *Religion in Politics: Constitutional and Moral Perspectives.* New York: Oxford University Press, 1997. A legal and philosophical analysis of the role of religion in politics.

Wirenius, John F. *First Amendment, First Principles.* New York: Holmes and Meier, 2000. Analysis of verbal acts and freedom of speech.

LIST OF WEBSITES

http://oyez.nwu.edu/ Includes information on Supreme Court rulings; particularly useful when studying nineteenth-century cases.

http://www.aclu.org/ The American Civil Liberties Union sites; it provides information on current civil liberties and civil rights issues, including information on recent and pending Supreme Court cases.

http://www.findlaw.com/casecode/supreme.html An excellent source of information on Supreme Court and lower-court rulings.

http://www.mitretek.org/business_areas/justice/cjlinks/ A site dedicated to criminal justice questions with links to many additional sites that focus on particular issues.

POLITICS IN THEORY AND PRACTICE

Thinking: What is the process of selective incorporation, and why is it important to the rights you possess today?

Acting: Although their right of free expression is protected by law, Americans often choose not to exercise this right for fear of social pressure or official reprisal. Yet constitutional rights tend to wither when people fail to exercise them. Think of an issue that you favor but that is unpopular on your campus or in your community. Consider writing a letter expressing your opinion to the editor of your college or local newspaper. (Practical advice: Keep the letter short and to the point; write a lead sentence that will get readers' attention; provide a convincing argument for your position; and be sure to sign the letter and provide a return address so the editor can contact you if there are questions.)

𝕿𝖍𝖊 𝕹𝖊𝖜 𝖄𝖔𝖗𝖐 𝕿𝖎𝖒𝖊𝖘   reading 4

Judges Ban Pledge of Allegiance from Schools, Citing "Under God"

by Evelyn Nieves

In 2002, controversy erupted when a three-judge federal appeals court ruled that recitation of the Pledge of Allegiance in public schools is a violation of the First Amendment's establishment clause because the pledge contains the words "under God." In this June 27, 2002, article, New York Times reporter Evelyn Nieves describes the ruling and reactions to it. Most observers expect the ruling to be overturned either by appeals court en banc or by the Supreme Court. Nevertheless, the ruling illustrates the controversy that surrounds the issue of the separation of church and state.

SAN FRANCISCO—A federal appeals court here declared today that the Pledge of Allegiance is unconstitutional because the phrase "one nation under God" violates the separation of church and state.

In a decision that drew protest across the political spectrum, a three-member panel of the United States Court of Appeals for the Ninth Circuit ruled that the pledge, as it exists in federal law, could not be recited in schools because it violates the First Amendment's prohibition against a state endorsement of religion. In addition, the ruling, which will certainly

be appealed, turned on the phrase "under God" which Congress added in 1954 to one of the most hallowed patriotic traditions in the nation.

From a constitutional standpoint, those two words, Judge Alfred T. Goodwin wrote in the 2-to-1 decision, were just as objectionable as a statement that "we are a nation 'under Jesus,' a nation 'under Vishnu,' a nation 'under Zeus,' or a nation 'under no god,' because none of these professions can be neutral with respect to religion."

If it stands, the decision by the nation's most liberal appellate court would take effect in several months, banning the pledge from being recited in schools in the nine Western states under the court's jurisdiction: Alaska, Arizona, California, Hawaii, Idaho, Montana, Nevada, Oregon and Washington.

The panel's decision prompted an immediate reaction in Washington, where senators unanimously passed a resolution condemning the ruling and where dozens of House members gathered on the Capitol steps to recite the pledge and sing "God Bless America."

The White House spokesman, Ari Fleischer, said President Bush called the decision "ridiculous," and many legal experts said they expected it to be reversed on appeal.

The ruling came in a lawsuit filed in Federal District Court in Sacramento by an atheist, Michael A. Newdow, whose daughter attended elementary school in the Elk Grove Unified School District near the state capital.

Although under a 1943 ruling by the United States Supreme Court, children cannot be forced to recite the pledge, Dr. Newdow, an emergency room doctor with a law degree acting as his own lawyer, argued that his daughter's First Amendment rights were harmed because she was forced to "watch and listen as her state-employed teacher in her state-run school leads her classmates in a ritual proclaiming that there is a God, and that ours is 'one nation under God.'"

The National Conference of State Legislatures says half the states require the pledge as part of the school day and half a dozen more recommend it. In the burst of patriotism that followed the Sept. 11 terrorism attacks, bills to make the oath mandatory have been introduced in Colorado, Connecticut, Illinois, Indiana, Minnesota, Mississippi and Missouri.

The Ninth Circuit panel's majority consisted of Judge Goodwin, a 79-year-old jurist appointed in 1971 by President Richard M. Nixon, and Stephen Reinhardt, a 71-year-old member of the court since 1980, when President Jimmy Carter appointed him. Writing for the majority, Judge Goodwin said the school district is "conveying a message of state endorsement of a religious belief when it requires public school teachers to recite, and lead the recitation of the current form of the pledge."

"Given the age and impressionability of schoolchildren," he added, "particularly within the confined environment of the classroom, the policy is highly likely to convey an impermissible message of endorsement to some and disapproval to others of their beliefs regarding the existence of a monotheistic God."

The "under God" clause of the pledge, the panel argued, was added by Congress solely to advance religion in order to differentiate the United States from nations under atheistic Communist rule.

"Such a purpose," Judge Goodwin wrote, runs counter to the Establishment Clause of the First Amendment, "which prohibits the government's endorsement or advancement not only of one particular religion at the expense of other religions, but also of religion at the expense of atheism."

The two judges issuing the decision acknowledged that the Supreme Court had occasionally commented in nonbinding decisions that the presence of "one nation under God" in the Pledge of Allegiance is constitutional. But, the judges said, "the court has never been presented with the question directly."

The panel also noted that the Supreme Court had ruled that students could not hold religious invocations at graduations.

In 1984, several liberal members of the Supreme Court, including Thurgood Marshall, Harry A. Blackmun, John Paul Stevens and William J. Brennan Jr., said references like "In God We Trust," which appears on United States currency and coins, were protected from the Establishment Clause because their religious significance had been lost through rote repetition.

The dissenting judge in today's ruling, Ferdinand F. Fernandez, expressed concern that the ruling could be applied to other expressions of patriotism.

"We will soon find ourselves prohibited from using our album of patriotic songs in many public settings," wrote Judge Fernandez, 63, who was appointed in 1989 by President Bush's father. "'God Bless America' and 'America the Beautiful' will be gone for sure, and while the first and second stanzas of 'The Star-Spangled Banner' will still be permissible, we will be precluded from straying into the third."

Praise for the panel's decision was muted. Joe Conn, a spokesman for Americans United for Separation of Church and State, said that while he supported the decision, it should not be seen as a finding against the entire pledge.

"They didn't strike down the Pledge of Allegiance," Mr. Conn said. "All they said is Congress made a mistake when they added God to the pledge."

Arthur Hayes, a law professor at Quinnipiac University, called the decision a "well-reasoned opinion that is certain to enrage the Christian right."

But criticism of the decision was swift and, mostly, harsh. The Senate halted debate on a military bill to work on a resolution criticizing the ruling. Politicians of all political stripes reeled off faxes to reporters condemning the decision. Gov. George E. Pataki of New York called the decision "junk justice." Senator Tom Daschle of South Dakota, the Democratic leader, called it "nuts."

Steve Duprey, the retired chairman of the New Hampshire Republican Party, who is still active in national Republican politics, said that the decision was "so out of tune with what Americans believe, I don't think it will be a hot political issue in this campaign, because I don't think Republicans or Democrats will agree with it."

The most vehement reactions came from conservative religious groups.

"I think the opinion is absurd," said Jay Sekulow, chief counsel of the American Center for Law and Justice, which is aligned with the Christian Coalition. "This is the first court to hold the pledge with the phrase 'with one nation under God' is unconstitutional. They've created a constitutional crisis for no reason."

The Rev. Jerry Falwell said the ruling was "appalling."

"This is probably the worst ruling of any federal appellate court in history," Mr. Falwell said, adding that he had started a petition drive this afternoon to gather a million signatures by Friday to urge the Supreme Court to reverse the panel's ruling immediately.

Legal experts said today's decision would most likely be reversed by the full appeals court, if not the Supreme Court.

Christopher Landau, an appellate lawyer with Kirkland & Ellis in Washington, and a former clerk for Justices Antonin Scalia and Clarence Thomas, said he was certain that the Supreme Court would reverse the decision.

"In their heart of hearts, I don't think the justices would ever think that this kind of a practice is unconstitutional," Mr. Landau said. "And I think that they'll probably say that this is a tradition and that it is primarily ceremonial."

Mr. Newdow told The Associated Press today that the decision validated his point that it was wrong to force his daughter to listen to the pledge.

He also said that he and his family had been threatened because of the lawsuit and that the threats were "personal and scary."

"I could be dead tomorrow," Mr. Newdow said.

What's Your Opinion?

Should the Pledge of Allegiance be banned from public schools as a violation of the First Amendment's establishment clause?

CHAPTER 5

EQUAL RIGHTS: STRUGGLING TOWARD FAIRNESS

❝ I have a dream that one day this nation will rise up and live out the true meaning of its creed: "We hold these truths to be self-evident: that all men are created equal. **❞**

MARTIN LUTHER KING JR.[1]

The producers of ABC television's *PrimeTime Live* put hidden cameras on two young men, equally well dressed and groomed, and then sent them on different routes to do the same things—search for an apartment, shop for a car, look at albums in a record store. The cameras recorded the reactions the two men received. One was greeted with smiles and was provided with quick service. The other man was often greeted with suspicious looks and was sometimes made to wait. Why the difference? The explanation was simple: the young man who was routinely well received was white; the young man who was treated poorly was an African American.

The Urban Institute conducted a similar experiment. The experiment used pairs of specially trained white and black male college students who were the same in all respects—education, work experience, speech patterns, physical builds—except for their race. The students responded individually to nearly five hundred classified job advertisements in Chicago and Washington, D.C. The black applicants got fewer interviews, had shorter interviews, and were given fewer job offers than were the white applicants. An Urban Institute spokesperson said, "The level of reverse discrimination [favoring blacks over whites] that we found was limited, was certainly far lower than many might have been led to fear, and was swamped by the extent of discrimination against black job applicants."[2]

These two experiments suggest why some Americans are still struggling for equal rights. In theory, Americans are equal in their rights, but in reality, they are not now equal, nor have they ever been. African Americans, women, Hispanic Americans, the disabled, Jews, Native Americans, Catholics, Asian Americans, homosexuals, and members of nearly every other minority group have been victims of discrimination in fact and in law. The nation's creed—"all men are created equal"—has encouraged minorities to believe that they deserve equal justice and has given weight to their claims for fair treatment. But inequality is built into almost every aspect of U.S. society. Here is but one example: African Americans with a correctable heart problem are only half as likely to receive the necessary surgery as are whites with the same problem.[3]

This chapter focuses on **equal rights**, or **civil rights**—terms that refer to the right of every person to equal protection under the laws and equal access to society's opportunities and public facilities. Chapter 4 explained that civil liberties refer to specific *individual* rights, such as freedom of speech, that are protected from infringement by government. Equal rights, or civil rights, have to do with whether individual members of differing *groups*—racial, sexual, and the like—are treated equally by government and, in some areas, by private parties. To oversimplify, civil liberties deal with issues of personal freedom, and civil rights deal with issues of equality.

Although the law refers to the rights of individuals first and to those of groups in a secondary and derivative way, this chapter concentrates on groups because the history of civil rights has been largely one of group claims to equality. The chapter emphasizes the following main points:

★ *Disadvantaged groups have had to struggle for equal rights.* African Americans, women, Native Americans, Hispanic Americans, Asian Americans, and others have all had to fight for their rights in order to come closer to equality with white males.

★ *Americans have attained substantial equality under the law.* They have, in legal terms, equal protection of the laws, equal access to accommodations and housing, and an equal right to vote. Discrimination by law against persons because of race, sex, religion, and ethnicity is now almost nonexistent.

★ *Legal equality for all Americans has not resulted in de facto equality.* African Americans, women, Hispanic Americans, and other traditionally disadvantaged groups have a disproportionately small share of America's opportunities and benefits. Existing inequalities, discriminatory practices, and political pressures are still major barriers to their full equality. Affirmative action and busing are policies designed to help the disadvantaged achieve full equality.

THE STRUGGLE FOR EQUALITY

Equality has always been the least fully developed of America's founding concepts. Not even Thomas Jefferson, who had a deep admiration for the "common man," believed that precise meaning could be given to the claim of the Declaration of Independence that "all men are created equal."[4]

The history of America shows that disadvantaged groups have rarely achieved a greater measure of justice without a struggle.[5] Their gains have nearly always occurred through intense and sustained political action, such as the civil rights movement of the 1960s, that has forced entrenched interests to relinquish or share their privileged status (see Chapter 7).

Disadvantaged groups have a shared history of political exclusion, struggles for empowerment, and policy triumphs, but they also have distinctive histories, as is evident by a brief look at the equal rights efforts of African Americans, women, Native Americans, Hispanic Americans, Asian Americans, and other groups.

African Americans

No Americans have faced greater hardship than have its black people. Their ancestors came to this country as slaves, after having been captured in Africa, shipped in chains across the Atlantic, and sold in open markets in Charleston, Boston, and other seaports.

The Civil War brought slavery, but not racism, to an end. When federal troops withdrew from the South in 1877, the region's whites regained power and enacted laws that prohibited black citizens from using the same public facilities as whites.[6] In *Plessy v. Ferguson* (1896), the Supreme Court endorsed these laws, ruling that "separate" facilities for the two races did not violate the Constitution as long as the facilities were "equal." "If one race be inferior to the other socially," the Court argued, "the Constitution of the United States cannot put them on the same plane."[7] The *Plessy* decision became a justification for the separate and *unequal* treatment of African Americans. Black children, for example, were forced into separate schools that rarely had libraries and had few teachers; they were given worn-out books that had been used previously in white schools.

Two police dogs attack a black civil rights activist (*center left of picture*) during the 1963 Birmingham demonstrations. Such images of hatred and violence shook many white Americans out of their complacency regarding race relations.

Black Americans challenged these discriminatory policies through legal action, but not until the late 1930s did the Supreme Court begin to acknowledge their plight. The Court began modestly by ruling that where no separate public facilities existed for African Americans, they must be allowed to use those reserved for whites.[8] When Oklahoma, which had no law school for blacks, was ordered to admit Ada Sipuel in 1949, it created a separate law school for her—she sat alone in a roped-off corridor of the state capitol building. The white students, meanwhile, continued to meet at the University of Oklahoma's law school in Norman, twenty miles away.

The Brown Decision Substantial judicial relief for African Americans was finally achieved in 1954 with *Brown v. Board of Education of Topeka*, arguably the most significant ruling in Supreme Court history. The case began when Linda Carol Brown, a black child in Topeka, Kansas, was denied admission to an all-white elementary school that she passed every day on her way to her all-black school, which was twelve blocks farther away. In its decision, the Court fully reversed its *Plessy* doctrine by declaring that racial segregation of public schools "generates [among black children] a feeling of inferiority as to their status in the community that may affect their hearts

and minds in a way unlikely ever to be undone. . . . Separate educational facilities are inherently unequal."[9]

A 1954 Gallup poll indicated that a substantial majority of southern
whites opposed the *Brown* decision. The same poll found that a slim majority of whites outside the South agreed with the decision.

The Black Civil Rights Movement After *Brown*, the struggle of African
Americans for their rights became a political movement. Perhaps no single
event turned national public opinion so dramatically against segregation as
a 1963 march led by Dr. Martin Luther King Jr. in Birmingham, Alabama.[10]
As the nation watched in disbelief on television, police officers led by Birmingham's sheriff, Eugene "Bull" Connor, attacked King and his followers
with dogs, cattle prods, and fire hoses.

The modern civil rights movement peaked with the triumphant March
on Washington for Jobs and Freedom of August 2, 1963. Organized by Dr.
King and other civil rights leaders, it attracted 250,000 marchers, one of the
largest gatherings in the history of the nation's capital. "I have a dream," the
Reverend King told the gathering, "that my four little children will one day
live in a nation where they will not be judged by the color of their skin but
by the content of their character."

A year later, after a months-long fight in Congress that was marked by
every parliamentary obstacle that racial conservatives could muster, the
Civil Rights Act of 1964 was enacted. The legislation provided African
Americans and other minorities with equal access to public facilities and
prohibited job discrimination. President Lyndon Johnson, who had been a

Martin Luther King Jr.
(1929–1968)

Martin Luther King Jr. is the only American of
the twentieth century to be honored with a national holiday. The civil rights leader was the
pivotal figure in the movement to gain legal
and political rights for black Americans. The
son of a Baptist minister, King used rhetorical
skills and nonviolent protest to sweep aside a
century of governmental discrimination and to inspire other groups,
including women and Hispanics, to assert their rights. Recipient of the
Nobel Peace Prize in 1964 (the youngest person ever to receive that
honor), King was assassinated in Memphis in 1968.

decisive force in the battle to pass the Civil Rights Act, called for new legislation that would also end racial barriers to voting.[11] Congress's answer was the 1965 Voting Rights Act.

The Aftermath of the Civil Rights Movement Although the most significant progress in history toward the legal equality of all Americans occurred during the 1960s, Dr. King's dream of a color-blind society has remained elusive.[12] Even the legal rights of African Americans do not, in practice, match the promise of the civil rights movement.[13] Studies have found, for example, that African Americans accused of crime are more likely to be convicted and to receive stiffer sentences than are white Americans on trial for comparable offenses. Federal statistics indicate, for example, that black Americans account for more than 75 percent of crack cocaine convictions but only about 35 percent of crack cocaine users.[14]

One area in which African Americans have made substantial progress since the 1960s is elective office (see "States in the Nation"). Although the percentage of black elected officials is still far below the proportion of African Americans in the population, it has risen sharply over recent decades.[15] As of 2000, there were more than twenty black members of Congress and four hundred black mayors—including the mayors of some of this country's largest cities.

Women

The United States carried over from English common law a political disregard for women, forbidding them to vote, hold public office, and serve on juries.[16] Upon marriage, a woman essentially lost her identity as an individual and could not own and dispose of property without her husband's consent. Even the wife's body was not fully hers. A wife's adultery was declared by the Supreme Court to be a violation of the husband's property rights![17]

The first women's rights convention in America was held in 1848 in Seneca Falls, New York, after Lucretia Mott and Elizabeth Cady Stanton had been barred from the main floor of an antislavery convention.[18] Thereafter, however, the struggle for women's rights became closely aligned with the abolitionist movement, but the passage of the post–Civil War constitutional amendments proved to be a setback for the women's movement. The Fifteenth Amendment, for example, said that the right to vote could not be abridged on account of race or color, but said nothing about sex.[19] It was not until passage of the Nineteenth Amendment in 1920 that women gained the right to vote.

Women's Legal and Political Gains Ratification of the Nineteenth Amendment encouraged leaders of the women's movement to propose in

★ STATES IN THE NATION

Black and Latino Representation in State Legislatures

For a long period in U.S. history, there were almost no minorities among the ranks of state legislators. Minorities are still underrepresented relative to their numbers in the population. Although one in every three Americans is a minority-group member, only one in eight state legislators comes from such a group.

Q: What accounts for differences between the states in the percentage of minority-group members in their legislatures?

A: States with large populations of minorities tend to have a larger percentage of legislators from minority groups. Alabama and Mississippi have large black populations and have the highest proportion of African American legislators. New Mexico with its large Hispanic population has the highest proportion of Latino lawmakers.

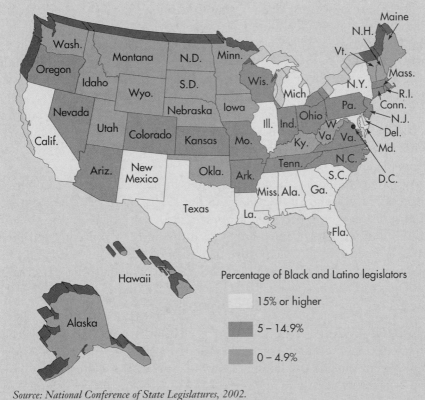

Percentage of Black and Latino legislators

- 15% or higher
- 5 – 14.9%
- 0 – 4.9%

Source: National Conference of State Legislatures, 2002.

1923 a constitutional amendment that would guarantee equal rights for women. Congress rejected that proposal and several subsequent ones. In 1973, however, Congress approved the Equal Rights Amendment (ERA) and submitted it to the states for ratification or rejection. The ERA failed by three states to get the three-fourths majority required for ratification.[20]

Although the ERA did not become part of the Constitution, it helped bring women's rights to the forefront at a time when developments in Congress and the courts were contributing significantly to legal equality for women.[21] Among the congressional initiatives were the Equal Pay Act of 1963, which prohibits sex discrimination in salary and wages by some categories of employers; the Civil Rights Act of 1964, which prohibits sex discrimination in federally funded programs; Title IX of the Education Amendment of 1972, which prohibits sex discrimination in education; and the Equal Credit Act of 1974, as amended in 1976, which prohibits sex discrimination in the granting of financial credit.

Women have made substantial gains in the area of appointive and elective offices.[22] In 1981, President Reagan appointed the first woman to serve on the Supreme Court, Sandra Day O'Connor. When the Democratic party in 1984 chose Geraldine Ferraro as its vice presidential nominee, it was the first time a woman ran on the national ticket of a major political party. The elections of California's Dianne Feinstein and Barbara Boxer in 1992 marked the first time that women occupied both U.S. Senate seats from a state.

Despite such signs of progress, women are still a long way from political equality with men.[23] Women occupy fewer than 15 percent of congressional seats and only 20 percent of statewide and city council offices (see "How the United States Compares").

Although women are underrepresented in political office, their vote is becoming increasingly powerful. Until the 1970s, there was almost no difference in the voting patterns of women and men. Today, there is a substantial **gender gap:** women and men differ in their opinions and their votes. Women are more supportive than men of government programs for the poor, minorities, children, and the elderly. They also have a greater tendency to cast their votes for Democratic candidates (see Figure 5–1). The gender gap is discussed further in Chapter 6.

Job–Related Issues: Family Leave, Comparable Worth, and Sexual Harassment In recent decades, increasing numbers of women have sought employment outside the home. Government statistics indicate that more than two-thirds of employment-age women work outside the home compared with only one in eight a half century ago. Women have made gains in

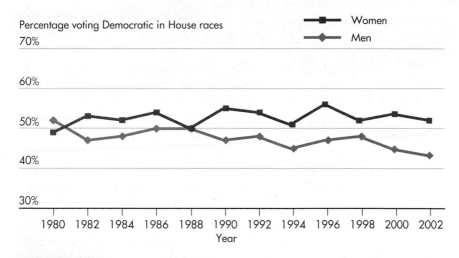

FIGURE 5-1 THE GENDER GAP IN CONGRESSIONAL VOTING

Women and men differ, on average, in their political behavior. For example, women are more likely than men to vote Democratic, as shown by the difference between the women's vote and the men's vote for Democratic candidates in U.S. House races.
Source: National Election Studies (1988–1998); estimated from multiple polls (2000, 2002).

many traditionally male-dominated fields. For example, women now make up a third of the new lawyers who enter the job market each year. The change in women's work status is also reflected in education statistics. A few decades ago, more white, black, and Hispanic men than women enrolled in college. Throughout the past decade, the reverse has been true: more women than men of each group were enrolled.

The increased presence of women in the workplace has created demands for the expansion of programs such as day care centers and parental leave. In 1993, Congress passed the Family and Medical Leave Act, which provides up to twelve weeks of unpaid leave for employees, male or female, to care for a new baby or a seriously ill family member. Upon return from leave, employees must ordinarily be restored to their original or equivalent positions with equivalent pay, benefits, and other employment terms.

Nevertheless, women are less than equal to men when it comes to job opportunities. Although women increasingly hold managerial positions, they are less likely than men to be appointed to the top positions. The term *glass ceiling* refers to the invisible but nonetheless real barrier to advancement that talented women encounter after having reached the middle-management level.

How the United States Compares

Women's Inequality

The one form of inequality common to all nations is that of gender: nowhere are women equal to men in law or in fact. But there are large differences between countries. A study by the Population Crisis Committee ranked the United States third overall in women's equality, behind only Sweden and Finland. Based on five measures—jobs, education, social relations, marriage and family, and health—the study rated the status of U.S. women at 82.5 percent that of men.

The inequality of women is underscored by their underrepresentation in public office. There is no country in which women comprise as many as half the members of the national legislature. The Scandinavian countries rank highest in terms of the percentage of female lawmakers. Other northern European countries have lower levels, but the levels are higher than that of the United States. The accompanying figure indicates the approximate percentage of seats held by women in the largest chamber of each country's national legislature:

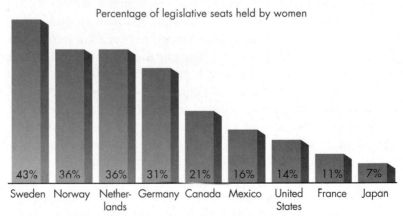

Percentage of legislative seats held by women

Sweden	Norway	Nether-lands	Germany	Canada	Mexico	United States	France	Japan
43%	36%	36%	31%	21%	16%	14%	11%	7%

Source: For non–U.S. countries, Inter-Parliamentary Union, 2001; for U.S., U.S. House of Representatives, 2003.

Women are also more likely than men to work in low-wage job positions. Although the disparity is decreasing, the average pay for full-time women employees is only about three-fourths that of full-time men employees. This situation has led to demands by women for equal pay for

The majority of women with preschool children work outside the home, a situation that has created demands for government support of day care centers, parental leave, and other programs and services.

work that is of similar difficulty and responsibility and that requires similar levels of education and training—a concept called **comparable worth.** Advocates gained an early victory when the Supreme Court held in 1981 that female guards at a prison had to be paid the same wages as male guards even if their work assignments differed.[24] In general, however, proponents of comparable worth have had only limited success in persuading public and private employers to institute the policy.[25]

Workplace discrimination against women includes sexual harassment. Lewd comments and unwelcome advances are a part of everyday life for many working women, and the courts have increasingly held firms liable if they tolerate this type of behavior.[26]

Native Americans

When white settlers began arriving in America in large numbers during the seventeenth century, nearly ten million Native Americans were living in the territory that would become the United States. By 1900, the Native American population had plummeted to less than a tenth that number. Diseases

brought by white settlers had taken a toll on the various Indian tribes, but
so had wars and massacres. "The only good Indian is a dead Indian" is not
simply a hackneyed expression from cowboy movies. It was part of a strategy of westward expansion, as settlers and U.S. troops alike mercilessly
drove the eastern Indians from their ancestral lands to the Great Plains and
then took those lands as well.

Today Native Americans number more than one million, about half of
whom live on or close to reservations set aside for them by the federal government. Reservations are governed by treaties signed when they were established. State governments have no direct authority over federal reservations,
and the federal government's authority is limited by the terms of a particular
treaty. Although U.S. policy toward the reservations has changed over time,
the current policy is to promote self-government and economic self-
sufficiency.[27]

Native Americans are less than half as likely to attend college as other
Americans, their life expectancy is more than ten years lower than the national average, and their infant mortality rate is more than three times
higher than that of white Americans. In recent years, some Native American tribes have erected gaming casinos on reservation land. The casinos
have brought jobs and income to the reservations but have also brought
controversy—traditionalists argue that the casinos are destroying their
tribal cultures.

The civil rights movement of the 1960s at first did not include Native
Americans. Then, in the early 1970s, militant Native Americans occupied the
Bureau of Indian Affairs in Washington, D.C., and later seized control of the
village of Wounded Knee on a Sioux reservation in southwestern South
Dakota, exchanging gunfire with U.S. marshals. These episodes brought attention to the grievances of Native Americans and may have contributed to
the passage in 1974 of legislation that granted Native Americans on reservations a greater measure of control over federal programs that affected them.
Native Americans had already benefited from the legislative climate created
by the civil rights movement of the 1960s. In 1968, Congress had enacted the
Indian Bill of Rights, which gives Native Americans on reservations constitutional guarantees that are similar to those held by other Americans.

In recent years Native Americans have filed suit to reclaim lost ancestral
lands and have won a few settlements. But they stand no realistic chance of
getting back even those lands that had been granted them by federal treaty
but were later sold off or simply taken forcibly by federal authorities. Native
Americans were not even official citizens of the United States until an act of
Congress in 1924. This status came too late to be of much help; their traditional way of life had already been destroyed.

Hispanic Americans

The fastest-growing minority in the United States is that of Hispanic Americans, that is, people of Spanish-speaking background. Hispanics are also one of the country's oldest ethnic groups. Some Hispanics are descendants of people who helped colonize the areas of California, Texas, Florida, New Mexico, and Arizona before those areas were annexed by the United States. But most Hispanics are recent immigrants or their descendants.

Hispanics recently surpassed African Americans as the nation's largest racial or ethnic minority group. There are roughly 35 million Hispanics living in the United States, an increase of 40 percent over the 1990 census. They have emigrated to the United States primarily from Mexico and the Caribbean islands, mainly Cuba and Puerto Rico. About half of all Hispanics in the United States were born in Mexico or claim a Mexican ancestry. Hispanics are concentrated in their states of entry; thus Florida, New York, and New Jersey have large numbers of Caribbean Hispanics, while California, Texas, Arizona, and New Mexico have many immigrants from Mexico. More than half the population of Los Angeles is of Hispanic—mostly Mexican—descent.

The term *Hispanic* can be misleading if it is construed to mean a group of people who all think alike (see Table 5–1). Hispanics cover a wide political spectrum, from the conservative Republican-leaning Cuban Americans of

TABLE 5–1   HISPANICS' PARTY IDENTIFICATION, BY NATIONAL ORIGIN

Hispanics share a common language and ancestry but differ substantially in their political leanings.

Party Identification	Puerto Rican Americans	Mexican Americans	Cuban Americans
Democratic	64%	60%	19%
Independent	22	24	17
Republican	14	16	64
	100%	100%	100%

Source: Reported in Rudolpho O. de la Garza, Angelo Falcon, F. Chris Garcia, and John A. Garcia, "Hispanic Americans in the Mainstream of U.S. Politics," The Public Perspective, *July/August 1992, p. 19. © The Roper Center for Public Opinion Research, University of Connecticut. Reprinted with permission.*

southern Florida to the liberal Democratic-leaning Puerto Ricans of the Northeast. Hispanic Americans share a common ancestral language, Spanish, but they are not monolithic in their politics.[28]

Legal and Political Action Hispanic Americans have benefited from laws and court rulings aimed primarily at protecting other groups. Thus, although the Civil Rights Act of 1964 was largely a response to the condition of black people, its provisions against discrimination apply broadly to other groups as well.

Nevertheless, Hispanics had their own civil rights movement. Its most publicized actions were the farm workers' strikes of the late 1960s and the 1970s that aimed at achieving basic labor rights for migrant workers. Migrants were working long hours for low pay, were living in shacks without electricity or plumbing, and were unwelcome in many local schools and in some local hospitals as well. Farm owners at first refused to bargain with the workers, but a well-organized national boycott of California grapes and lettuce forced that state to pass a law giving migrant workers the right to bargain collectively. The strikes were led in California by Cesar Chavez, who himself grew up in a Mexican American migrant family. Chavez's tactics were copied in other states, particularly Texas, but the results were less successful.

Cesar Estrada Chavez
(1927–1993)

Cesar Chavez led the first successful farm workers' strike in U.S. history. Founder of the United Farm Workers of America, Chavez was called "one of the heroic figures of our time" by Robert F. Kennedy and is widely regarded as the most influential Latino leader in modern U.S. history. A migrant worker as a child, Chavez knew firsthand the deprivations suffered by farm laborers. Like Martin Luther King Jr., Chavez was an advocate of nonviolent protest, and he organized food boycotts that eventually caused agricultural firms to improve wages and working conditions for farm workers. In 1994, Chavez was posthumously awarded the Presidential Medal of Freedom, the highest civilian honor that an American can receive.

Hispanics face some distinctive problems. The fact that many do not speak English led to a 1968 amendment to the 1964 Civil Rights Act that funds public school programs offering English instruction in the language of children for whom English is a second language. In addition, many Hispanics are illegal aliens and do not have the full rights of citizens. In *De Canas v. Bica* (1976), for example, the Supreme Court upheld a state law barring illegal aliens from employment.[29]

The issue of illegal aliens was also addressed through California's controversial Proposition 187. Placed on the state's ballot in 1994 through a citizen petition, Proposition 187 received the votes of a majority of Californians even though most of the state's Mexican Americans voted against it. The initiative aimed to cut off public services to illegal immigrants, the great majority of whom are Mexicans. They would no longer receive state-funded food stamps, welfare, and medical care except in life-threatening circumstances, and they would no longer be eligible for public schooling at any level. To many of California's Mexican Americans, the initiative was a thinly disguised attempt to discourage additional people from Mexico from entering the state. The implementation of Proposition 187 was delayed pending a court ruling on its constitutionality, and most of its key provisions were subsequently judged to be unconstitutional.

Growing Political Power Hispanic Americans are an important political force in several states and communities, and their influence is likely to increase substantially in the future. Hispanics are projected to become the largest single population group in California in the current century. Their political involvement, like that of other immigrant groups, can be expected to increase as they become more firmly rooted in society. At present, about half of all Hispanic citizens are not registered to vote, and only about a third actually vote, which limits the group's political power. Nevertheless, the sheer size of the Hispanic population in states such as Texas and California makes the group a potent political force, as was evident in the 2002 midterm elections when both parties mounted a massive effort to woo Hispanic voters.

More than four thousand Hispanic Americans nationwide hold public office. Hispanics have been elected to statewide office in several states, including New Mexico and Arizona. About twenty Hispanic Americans currently serve in the House of Representatives.

Asian Americans

Chinese and Japanese laborers were brought into western states during the late 1800s to work in mines and to build railroads. When the need for this labor declined, Congress in 1892 ordered a temporary halt to this immigration.

Over the next three decades, informal agreements kept all but a few Asians from entering the country. In 1930, Congress completely blocked the entry of Japanese. Japan had protested a California law that prohibited persons of Japanese descent from buying property in the state. Rather than finesse what was called "the California problem," Congress bluntly told Japan that its people were not wanted in the United States.[30]

Discrimination against Asians did not ease substantially until 1965, when Congress enacted legislation that adjusted the immigration quotas to favor those who had previously been assigned very small numbers. This change in the law was a product of the 1960s civil rights movement, which increased public awareness of all forms of discrimination. About half a million people now emigrate to the United States each year, and a majority come from Asian and Latin American countries. Asian Americans numbered about twelve million in the 2000 census, or roughly 4 percent of the total U.S. population. Most Asian Americans live on the West Coast, particularly in California. China, Japan, Korea, India, Vietnam, and the Philippines are the ancestral homes of most Asian Americans.

The rights of Asian Americans have been expanded primarily by court rulings and legislation, such as the Civil Rights Act of 1964, that were responses to the problems of other minorities. In a few instances, however, the rights of minorities have been defined by actions of Asian Americans. For example, in *Lau v. Nichols* (1974), a case involving Chinese Americans, the Supreme Court ruled that public schools with a large proportion of children for whom English is a second language must offer English instruction in the children's first language.[31]

In 1998, the second-language issue arose in the form of Proposition 227, a California ballot measure that called for a ban on bilingual education in the state's public schools. The measure received the support of a majority of voters despite opposition from teachers' groups and many within California's Hispanic and Asian communities. Children for whom English is a second language would have to take their courses in English after their first year in school. The constitutionality of Proposition 227 was challenged unsuccessfully in the courts, but some teachers do not abide by its provisions.

Asian Americans are an upwardly mobile group. The values of most Asian cultures include a commitment to hard work, which, in the American context, has included an emphasis on academic achievement. For example, Asians make up a disproportionate share of the students at California's leading public universities, which base admission primarily on high school grades and standardized test scores. However, Asian Americans are still underrepresented in certain areas of the workplace. According to U.S. government figures, Asian Americans account for about 5 percent of professionals

Asian Americans studying in a high school classroom. Many Asian American families emphasize academic achievement as a basis of personal advancement.

and technicians, slightly more than their percentage of the total population. Yet they hold less than 2 percent of managerial jobs; past and present discrimination has kept them from obtaining their fair share of top business positions. They are also underrepresented politically. It was not until 1996, for example, that the first Asian American was elected governor of a state other than Hawaii.

Other Groups and Their Rights

Although civil rights efforts have been directed mainly at women and at racial and ethnic minorities, other groups are also involved.

One such group is the roughly 40 million Americans who have a physical or mental disability that prevents them from performing a critical function, such as seeing, hearing, or walking. A goal of the disabled is equal access to society's opportunities, which was facilitated by the 1990 Americans with Disabilities Act. It grants the disabled the same employment and other protections enjoyed by other disadvantaged groups. In addition, the Education for All Handicapped Children Act of 1975 mandates that all children, however severe their disability, receive a free, appropriate education. Before the legislation, 4 million children with disabilities were getting either no education or an inappropriate one (as in the case of a blind child who is not taught Braille).

Older Americans are also protected from discrimination. The Age Discrimination Act of 1975 and the Age Discrimination in Employment Act of 1967 prohibit discrimination against older workers in hiring for jobs in which age is not clearly a crucial factor in job performance. More recently, mandatory retirement ages for most jobs have been eliminated by law.

Forced retirement for reasons of age is permissible only if justified by the nature of a particular job or the performance of a particular employee.

A group that until very recently had not received substantial legal protection is homosexuals. In *Bowers v. Hardwick* (1986), the Supreme Court upheld a state law banning sexual acts between consenting homosexual adults, ruling that the constitutional right of privacy does not extend to such acts.[32] Gay rights also were dealt a setback when the Supreme Court in 2000 ruled that the Boy Scouts, as a private organization that has a right to freedom of association, can ban gays because homosexuality is prohibited by the Scouts' creed.[33] Gays and lesbians are also prohibited from serving in the military but can be dismissed only if they engage in overt verbal or behavioral displays of homosexuality (the so-called don't ask, don't tell policy).

However, gays and lesbians gained a significant legal victory when the Supreme Court in *Romer v. Evans* (1996) struck down a Colorado constitutional amendment that nullified all existing and any new legal protections for homosexuals. In a 6-3 ruling, the Court said the Colorado law violated the Constitution's guarantee of equal protection because it subjects individuals to employment and other forms of discrimination simply because of their sexual preference. The Court concluded that the law had no reasonable purpose but was instead motivated by hostility toward homosexuals.[34]

Gay rights activists have petitioned state governments to recognize civil unions that would grant to same-sex couples the legal status and rights that married couples enjoy. So far, Vermont is the only state to do so. In contrast, numerous states have recently passed "defense of marriage acts" that explicitly deny civil union to gay and lesbian couples, which means that individuals in these relationships have no legal claim on their partner's health care benefits, property, and the like. The number of same-sex couples has increased dramatically, which means that the issue of civil union for gays and lesbians will remain a focus of political action in coming years.

EQUALITY UNDER THE LAW

The catchphrase of nearly every group's claim to a more equal standing in American society has been "equality under the law." Once secure in their legal rights, people are in a stronger position to insist that their rights be respected and find it easier to pursue equality in other arenas, such as the economic sector. Americans' claims to legal equality are contained in a great many laws, a few of which are particularly noteworthy.

Equal Protection: The Fourteenth Amendment

The Fourteenth Amendment, which was ratified in 1868, declares in part that no state shall "deny to any person within its jurisdiction the equal protection of the laws." Through this **equal-protection clause,** the courts have protected such groups as African Americans and women from discrimination by state and local governments.

The Fourteenth Amendment's equal-protection clause does not require government to treat all groups or classes of people the same way in all circumstances. By law, for example, twenty-one-year-olds can drink alcohol but twenty-year-olds cannot. The judiciary allows such inequalities because they are held to be "reasonably" related to a legitimate government interest. In applying this **reasonable-basis test,** the courts require government only to show that a particular law has a sound basis. For example, the courts have held that the goal of reducing fatalities from alcohol-related accidents involving young drivers is a valid reason for imposing a twenty-one-year minimum age requirement for the purchase of alcohol.

The reasonable-basis test does not apply, however, to racial or ethnic classifications, particularly when these categories serve to discriminate against minority group members (see Table 5–2). Any law that treats people differently because of race or ethnicity is subject to the **strict-scrutiny test,** under

TABLE 5–2 LEVELS OF COURT REVIEW FOR LAWS THAT TREAT AMERICANS DIFFERENTLY

Test	Applies to	Standard Used
Strict-scrutiny	Race, ethnicity	Suspect category—assumed unconstitutional in the absence of an overwhelming justification
Intermediate-scrutiny	Gender	Almost suspect category—assumed unconstitutional unless the law serves a clearly compelling and justified purpose
Reasonable-basis	Other categories (such as age and income)	Not suspect category—assumed constitutional unless no sound rationale for the law can be provided

Although women are excluded by law from having to register for the draft, they serve with distinction in the U.S. military.

which such a law is unconstitutional in the absence of an overwhelmingly convincing argument that it is necessary. The strict-scrutiny test has virtually eliminated race and ethnicity as permissible classifications when the effect is to place a hardship on members of a minority group. The Supreme Court's position is that race and national origin are **suspect classifications**—in other words, that legal classifications based on race and ethnicity are presumed to have discrimination as their purpose and are therefore unconstitutional.

The strict-scrutiny test emerged after the 1954 *Brown* ruling and became a basis for invalidating laws that discriminated against black people. As other groups, especially women, began to organize and assert their rights in the late 1960s and early 1970s, the Supreme Court gave early signs that it might expand the scope of suspect classifications to include gender. In the end, however, the Court announced in *Craig v. Boren* (1976) that sex classifications were permissible if they served "important governmental objectives" and were "substantially" related to the achievement of those objectives.[35] The Court thus placed sex distinctions in an intermediate (or almost suspect) category, to be scrutinized more closely than some other classifications (for example, income or age levels) but, unlike racial classifications, justifiable in some instances. In *Rostker v. Goldberg* (1980), for example, the policy of male-only registration for the military draft was upheld on grounds that the exclusion of women from involuntary combat duty serves a legitimate and important purpose.[36]

The inexactness of the **intermediate-scrutiny test** has led some scholars to question its usefulness as a legal principle. Nevertheless, when evaluating claims of sex discrimination, the judiciary applies a stricter level of scrutiny than is required by the reasonable-basis test. Rather than giving government broad leeway to treat men and women differently, the Supreme Court has recently invalidated most of the laws it has reviewed that contain sex classifications. A leading case is *United States v. Virginia* (1996), in which the Supreme Court determined that the male-only admissions policy of Virginia Military Institute (VMI), a 157-year-old state-supported college, was unconstitutional. The state had developed an alternative program for women at another college, but the Court concluded it was no substitute for the unique education and other opportunities that attendance at VMI could provide. (The VMI decision also had the effect of ending the all-male admissions policy of the Citadel, a state-supported military college in South Carolina.)[37]

Equal Access: The Civil Rights Acts of 1964 and 1968

The Fourteenth Amendment applies only to action by government. It does not prohibit discrimination by private parties. As a result, for a long period in the nation's history, owners could legally bar black people from restaurants, hotels, and other accommodations, and employers could freely discriminate in their job practices. Since the 1960s private firms have had much less freedom to discriminate for reasons of race, sex, ethnicity, or religion.

Accommodations and Jobs The Civil Rights Act of 1964 entitles all persons to equal access to restaurants, bars, theaters, hotels, gasoline stations, and similar establishments serving the general public. The legislation also bars discrimination in the hiring, promotion, and wages of employees of medium-sized and large firms. A few forms of job discrimination are still lawful under the Civil Rights Act. For example, an owner-operator of a small business can discriminate in hiring his or her coworkers, and a religious school can take the religion of a prospective teacher into account.

The Civil Rights Act of 1964 has nearly eliminated the most overt forms of discrimination in the area of public accommodations. Some restaurants and hotels may provide better service to white customers, but outright refusal to serve African Americans or other minority group members is rare. Such a refusal is a violation of the law and could easily be proved in many instances. It is harder to prove discrimination in job decisions; accordingly, the act has been less effective in rooting out employment discrimination— a subject that will be discussed in detail later in this chapter.

Housing In 1968, Congress passed civil rights legislation designed to prohibit discrimination in housing. A building owner cannot refuse to sell or rent housing because of a person's race, religion, ethnicity, or sex. An exception is allowed for owners of small multifamily dwellings who reside on the premises.

LIBERTY, EQUALITY, & SELF-GOVERNMENT

What's Your Opinion?

Private Discrimination

The courts have ruled that private organizations are often within their rights in discriminating against individuals because of color, gender, creed, national origin, or other characteristics. The Fifth and Fourteenth Amendments only prohibit discrimination by government bodies.

Jews, Catholics, and blacks are among the groups that historically have been denied membership in private clubs and organizations. The most celebrated recent incident was the decision of the Boy Scouts of America (BSA) to revoke the membership of Scoutmaster James Dale. Dale is gay, and the BSA excludes homosexuals from membership. Dale's suit against the BSA went to the Supreme Court, which ruled in 2000 that the BSA, as a private organization, had the right to deny membership to homosexuals.

Issues of liberty and equality are at the forefront of such cases. Liberty is enhanced when private organizations are free to pick their members. But equality is diminished when people are denied opportunities because of their physical characteristics or lifestyles.

What's your opinion on the Dale-BSA dispute? What general limits, if any, would you impose on the discriminatory acts of private organizations?

Despite legal prohibitions on discrimination, housing in America remains highly segregated. Less than a third of all African Americans live in a neighborhood that is mostly white. One reason is that the annual income of most black families is substantially below that of most white families. Another reason is banking practices. At one time, banks contributed to housing segregation by redlining—refusing to grant mortgage loans in certain neighborhoods. This practice drove down the selling prices of homes in these neighborhoods, which led to an influx of African Americans and an exodus of whites. Redlining is prohibited by the 1968 Civil Rights Act, but many of the segregated neighborhoods that it helped to create still exist.

Recent studies indicate that minority status is still a factor in the lending practices of some banks.[38] A report of the U.S. Conference of Mayors indicated that, among applicants with average or slightly higher incomes relative to their community, Hispanics and African Americans were twice as likely as whites to be denied a mortgage.[39]

Equal Ballots: The Voting Rights Act of 1965, as Amended

Free elections are perhaps the foremost symbol of American democracy, yet the right to vote has only recently become a reality for many Americans, particularly for African Americans.

The Nineteenth Amendment, which in 1920 gave women the right to vote, effectively ended resistance to women's suffrage; paradoxically, resistance to black suffrage was intensified by the Fifteenth Amendment, which in 1870 gave black persons the right to vote. Southern whites invented a series of devices, including whites-only primaries, poll taxes, and rigged literacy tests to keep African Americans from registering and voting.[40] For example, almost no votes were cast by African Americans between the years 1920 and 1946 in North Carolina.[41]

Barriers to black participation in elections began to crumble in the mid-1940s, when the Supreme Court declared that whites-only primary elections were unconstitutional.[42] Two decades later, through the Twenty-fourth Amendment, poll taxes were outlawed.

The major step toward equal voting rights for African Americans was passage of the Voting Rights Act of 1965, which forbids discrimination in voting and registration.[43] The legislation empowers federal agents to register voters and to oversee participation in elections. The Voting Rights Act, as interpreted by the courts, also eliminates literacy tests: local officials can no longer deny registration and voting for reasons of illiteracy. Although civil rights legislation has seldom had a large and immediate impact on people's behavior, the Voting Rights Act was an exception. In the 1960 presidential election, voter turnout among African Americans was barely 30 percent nationwide. In 1968, three years after passage of the legislation, their turnout rate exceeded 40 percent

Congress renewed the Voting Rights Act in 1970, 1975, and 1982. The 1982 extension is noteworthy because it renewed the act for twenty years and requires states and localities to clear with federal officials any electoral change that has the effect, intended or not, of reducing the voting power of a minority group. When congressional district boundaries were redrawn after the 1990 census (see Chapter 11), the 1982 extension became the basis for the creation of districts that included a majority of Hispanic or African American voters. The result was the election of an unprecedented number of minority group members to Congress in 1992; the number of Hispanic and African American representatives jumped from 27 to 63.

However, in three separate cases that were each decided by 5–4 margins, the Supreme Court ruled that the redistricting of several congressional districts in Texas, North Carolina, and Georgia was unconstitutional because race had been the "dominant" factor in their creation. The Court held that the redistricting violated the rights of white voters under the Fourteenth Amendment's equal-protection clause, and the states were ordered to redraw the districts. Three of the justices in the majority indicated, however, that there *might* be instances in which race, along with other factors, could be taken into account in redistricting decisions. But the Court's majority was insistent in the claim that race cannot be the *deciding* factor in redistricting arrangements.[44]

In a 2001 decision, *Easley v. Cromartie*, the Court granted states considerably more flexibility in drawing district lines. The Court held that as long as a district's boundaries were based on partisan considerations, the fact that a large number of minority group members were concentrated in a district did not violate the equal-protection clause. State legislatures routinely draw district boundaries in ways designed to increase the likelihood that the congressional seat will be won by a particular party. The Court has long held that this action is permissible. In *Easley v. Cromartie*, the Court said that even though the North Carolina district in question contained a large proportion of black Americans, it was drawn with the goal of creating a safe Democratic seat and, as such, did not violate the Fourteenth Amendment.[45]

EQUALITY OF RESULT

America's disadvantaged groups have made significant progress toward equal rights, particularly during the past few decades. Through acts of Congress and rulings of the Supreme Court, most forms of government-sponsored discrimination—from racially segregated public schools to gender-based pension plans—have been banned.

However, civil rights problems involve deeply rooted conditions, habits, and prejudices and affect whole categories of people. For these reasons, a new civil rights policy rarely produces a sudden and dramatic change in society. Despite their greater equality in law, America's traditionally disadvantaged groups are still substantially unequal in their daily lives. Consider the issue of income disparity (see Figure 5–2). The average Hispanic or African American's income is only about 60 percent of the average white person's income.

Such figures reflect **de facto discrimination,** which is discrimination that is a consequence of social, economic, and cultural biases and conditions. This type of discrimination is different from **de jure discrimination,** which is discrimination based on law, as in the case of segregation in southern public schools during the pre-*Brown* period. De facto discrimination is difficult to root out because it is embedded not in the law but in the very structure of society. **Equality of result** is the aim of policies intended to

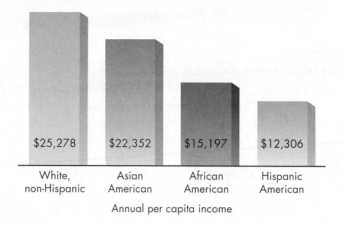

| $25,278 | $22,352 | $15,197 | $12,306 |

White,   Asian   African   Hispanic
non-Hispanic   American   American   American

Annual per capita income

FIGURE 5–2   U.S. PER CAPITA INCOME, BY RACE AND
ETHNICITY

The average income of white Americans is substantially higher than that of most other Americans.
Source: U.S. Bureau of the Census, 2002.

reduce or eliminate de facto discriminatory effects. Such policies are inherently more controversial because many Americans believe that government's responsibility extends no further than the removal of legal barriers to equality. This attitude reflects the culture's emphasis on *individualism* and helps explain the lack of any large-scale government effort to reduce the economic and social gaps between Americans of varying racial and ethnic backgrounds. Nevertheless, a few policies—notably affirmative action and busing—have been implemented to achieve equality of result.

Affirmative Action: Workplace Integration

The difficulty of converting newly acquired legal rights into everyday realities is illustrated by the 1964 Civil Rights Act. Although the legislation prohibited discrimination in employment, women and minorities did not suddenly obtain jobs for which they were qualified. Many employers maintained a deliberate though unwritten preference for white male employees. Other employers adhered to established employment procedures that continued to keep women and minorities at a disadvantage; membership in many union locals, for example, was handed down from father to son. Moreover, the Civil Rights Act did not require employers to prove that their hiring practices were not discriminatory. Instead, the burden of proof was on the woman or minority group member who had been denied a particular job. It was costly and often difficult to prove in court that one's sex or race was the reason that one had not been hired. In addition, a victory in court helped only the individual in question; these case-by-case settlements did not affect the millions of other women and minorities facing job discrimination.

A broader remedy was obviously required, and the result was the emergence during the late 1960s of affirmative action programs. **Affirmative action** is a deliberate effort to provide full and equal opportunities in employment, education, and other areas for members of traditionally disadvantaged groups. Affirmative action requires corporations, universities, and other organizations to establish programs designed to ensure that all applicants are treated fairly. Affirmative action also places the burden of proof on the providers of opportunities; to some extent, they must be able to demonstrate that any disproportionate granting of opportunities to white males is not the result of discriminatory practices.

Few issues in recent years have provoked more controversy than has affirmative action.[46] Although most Americans say they believe that minorities and women deserve a truly equal chance at jobs and other opportunities, they also say they worry that aggressive affirmative action programs will discriminate against more qualified males, an outcome that is called *reverse discrimination.*

Affirmative Action in the Law

Most issues that pit individuals against each other in a struggle over society's benefits eventually end up in the courts, and affirmative action is no exception (see Table 5–3). The policy was first tested before the Supreme Court in *University of California Regents v. Bakke* (1978). Alan Bakke, a white man, had twice been denied admission to a University of California medical school, even though his admission test scores were higher than those of several minority group students who had been accepted. Bakke sued, claiming the school had a quota system for minorities that discriminated against white males. The Court ruled in Bakke's favor but did not invalidate affirmative action per se. The Court said only that rigid racial quotas could not be used in determining medical school admissions.[47]

Bakke was followed by two rulings in favor of affirmative action programs, one of which—*Fullilove v. Klutnick* (1980)—upheld a quota system that required 10 percent of federal public works funds to be set aside for minority-owned firms.[48]

In the 1980s, the appointment of more conservative justices to the Supreme Court narrowed the scope of affirmative action policy. The Court held, for example, that preferential treatment of minorities could normally be justified only in cases where discrimination had been severe and that affirmative action could be applied only in a way that did not infringe on the rights of white employees to keep their jobs (thus restricting the use of race

TABLE	5–3	Key Decisions in the History of Affirmative Action Policy

Year	Action
1969	Nixon administration's Department of Labor initiates affirmative action policy.
1978	Supreme Court in *Bakke* invalidates rigid quotas for medical school admissions but does not invalidate affirmative action
1980	Supreme Court in *Fullilove* upholds a quota system for minority-owned firms in granting of federal contracts
1980s	Supreme Court in a series of decisions narrows situations in which preferential treatment of minorities will be permitted
1995	Supreme Court in *Adarand* eliminates fixed quotas in the granting of government contracts
1996	California voters enact Proposition 209, which bans public employment, education, and contracting programs based on race, ethnicity, or sex

as a basis for determining which employees would be terminated in the case of job layoffs).[49]

Proponents of affirmative action succeeded, however, in shifting some of the burden of proof about discrimination from employees to employers. After the Supreme Court in the 1980s allowed business firms more latitude in defending their hiring practices,[50] Congress responded with the Civil Rights Act of 1991, which requires larger firms in some instances to prove why their overwhelmingly male or white work force is the result of business necessity (such as the nature of the work or the locally available labor pool) and not the result of systematic discrimination against women or minorities.

In a key 1995 decision, *Adarand v. Pena*, the Supreme Court sharply curtailed the federal government's affirmative action authority. The case arose when Adarand Constructors filed suit over a federal contract that was awarded to a Hispanic-owned company even though Adarand had submitted a lower bid. The Court in a 5-4 ruling said that the government had to prove that a preference program for minorities was a response to specific past acts of discrimination, not just historical discrimination in a general sense. This decision reversed earlier precedents that allowed the federal government to give a preference to minority applicants. The Supreme Court held that set-aside contracts for minority applicants are lawful only in situations where it can be conclusively shown that such applicants have been discriminated against. Even in such situations, the remedy must be "narrowly tailored" to

Students at a California state university demonstrate against Proposition 209. The initiative proposed to end all racial, ethnic, and gender preferences in the awarding of university admissions, jobs, and government contracts in the state. The initiative passed by a 54 percent to 46 percent vote margin in 1996.

the situation—that is, it must be designed specifically to fix the problem at issue.[51] In other words, the government cannot issue general requirements (such as an automatic 10 percent set-aside of contracts for minority firms) as a means of remedying past discrimination.

Even supporters of affirmative action concluded that the *Adarand* decision likely marked the end of the era of extensive racial and gender preferences. By holding that affirmative action must be narrowly tailored and based on specific past acts of discrimination, the Court substantially restricted the authority of federal authorities to mandate broad affirmative action remedies. Earlier, the Court had restricted the authority of state and local governments to institute such requirements.

Another blow to affirmative action proponents was the California Civil Rights Initiative, which bans in California any public employment, education, or contracting program that is based on race, ethnicity, or sex. Known as Proposition 209, the initiative was placed on the 1996 ballot by citizen petition and approved 54 percent to 46 percent by California voters. The vote divided along racial, ethnic, and gender lines, with white males most strongly in favor and blacks and Hispanics most strongly opposed. The constitutionality of Proposition 209 was challenged by opponents, but the Supreme Court upheld it in 1997. Black and Hispanic enrollment in the entering classes at University of California campuses fell by more than 30 percent in 1998.

Further restrictions on affirmative action are possible. For example, the University of Michigan's points system for admission, which granted twenty points (out of a total of one hundred and fifty possible points) to minority applicants, was challenged in 2003 on the grounds that it was a de facto quota system. In any event, it is unlikely that affirmative action will be eliminated entirely, given the statistical evidence that indicates women and minorities, overall, are still at a substantial disadvantage to white males in the terms of job hiring, pay, and promotion. Affirmative action policy in the future could take the form of aggressive recruiting of women and minority applicants, coupled with consideration of factors specific to an individual's background. For example, minority applicants from poor families could have a better chance of admission at a selective college than equally qualified white or minority applicants from upper-middle-class families.

In 1998, the state of Texas devised an innovative response to the problem of equal opportunity. Recognizing the disparity in the quality of its public schools and other factors that result in lower average scores on standardized tests for minorities, the state es-tablished a policy that guarantees admission at the public university campus of his or her choice to any Texas high school student who graduates in the top 10 percent of the class. The 10 percent rule has met with little opposition from even the most outspoken critics of affirmative action, and those who favor affirmative action support this program "because it eliminates suspicion that students may have been admitted solely on the basis of race."[52]

School Integration: Busing

The 1954 *Brown* ruling mandated an end to *forced segregation* of public schools. Government would no longer be permitted to prevent minorities from enrolling in white schools. *Brown* did not, however, mandate school *integration*. Government was not required by *Brown* to take action to require white and minority children to attend school together, and *Brown* did little to change the face of America's schools. Ten years after *Brown*, less than 3 percent of black children were attending schools that were predominantly white. The proportion jumped to roughly 20 percent after passage of the 1964 Civil Rights Act, but the fact that black and white children lived in mostly separate neighborhoods meant that they would continue to attend separate schools. This situation set the stage for one of the few public policies that forced whites into close regular contact with blacks: the busing of children to achieve racial balance in schools.

The Swann Decision and Its Aftermath In 1971, the Supreme Court took the controversial step of requiring the busing of children in some circumstances. Affirming a lower-court decision, the Supreme Court held in *Swann v. Charlotte-Mecklenburg County Board of Education* that the busing of children from one neighborhood to another was a permissible way for courts to compel the integration of public schools in which past years of official segregation had created residential patterns that had the effect of keeping the races in separate schools.[53]

Few policies of recent times provoked so much controversy as the introduction of forced busing.[54] Surveys indicated that more than 80 percent of white Americans and a majority in Congress disapproved of forced busing. Angry demonstrations lasting weeks took place in Charlotte. When busing was ordered in Detroit and Boston, the protests turned violent. Unlike *Brown*, which affected mainly the South, *Swann* also applied to northern communities in which African Americans and whites lived apart as a result of economic and cultural differences as well as discriminatory real estate practices and local housing ordinances.

Despite the widespread protests, busing became a part of national policy. Busing's application was narrowed, however, by court-imposed restrictions on its use. The Supreme Court in 1974—perhaps in response to the protests over busing—held that it could be applied *across* school districts only in situations where it could be shown that district boundaries were purposely drawn so as to segregate the races.[55] Because school districts in most states coincide with community boundaries, the ruling meant that most suburbs would not be affected by busing.

Does Busing Work? Studies indicate that busing has contributed to more positive racial attitudes among children. Studies also show that the performance of black children on standardized tests improves when they attend white-majority schools and that the test performance of the white children is not adversely affected.[56]

However, busing has contributed to whites' departure from public schools, which, along with population and residential shifts, has made it increasingly difficult to achieve diversity in city schools. In Boston, for example, less than 20 percent of public school children today are white, compared with more than 50 percent when busing began there in 1974.

Busing also fragmented neighborhoods and forced children into long bus rides to and from school. Many black and white families alike were affected by what came to be called "busing fatigue." Parents asked, in effect, whether busing was worth the costs. That debate led the Prince George's County (Maryland) school board, which had a black majority, to abandon busing in 1998 and replace it with improved funding for neighborhood schools. Alvin Thornton, chair of the Prince George's County school board and a Howard University professor, argued that the change would increase "the sense of community" among the county's African Americans.[57]

Diversity and America's Schools Prince George's County is among dozens of communities—including Seattle, Jacksonville, Minneapolis, Mobile, and Boston—that have dismantled their school busing programs in recent years. In 1999, the school district where busing policy began—Charlotte-Mecklenberg—joined the list. The trend is consistent with Supreme Court rulings in the 1990s that held that busing was intended as a temporary, not permanent, solution to the problem of segregated schools[58] and that communities can devise alternative programs to replace their busing programs.[59]

The cutback in busing has contributed to a decrease in racial mixing in the schools. Nationwide, integration peaked in the late 1980s and has declined steadily since then (see Figure 5–3). Only about one in three black children

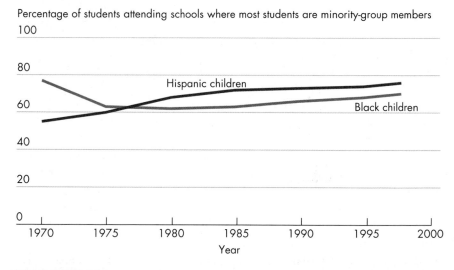

Percentage of students attending schools where most students are minority-group members

FIGURE 5–3 **Segregation in Public Schools Has Been Increasing**

In the past two decades, racial and ethnic segregation in America's public schools has increased. More than two-thirds of black and Hispanic children today attend a school in which most of the students are members of a minority group. An increase in the number of Non-Hispanic white students attending private schools and a decrease in racial busing are factors in the trend.

Source: U.S. Department of Education, 2002.

today attend a predominantly white school, which is about the same proportion as in 1970, before busing began. The proportion is even higher for Hispanic children—only about one in four of them attend a predominantly white school.

The trend is unlikely to be reversed anytime soon through public policy because *diversity*, unlike *equality*, has no explicit constitutional status. Government is compelled by the Constitution to treat people equally; it is not required to promote diversity. "Some say that diversity should be a compelling governmental purpose," says George Mason University professor David J. Armor, "but the Supreme Court says no."[60]

As busing recedes, the focus has shifted to parity in school financing. In comparison with predominantly white schools, those schools with mostly minority children have significantly larger classroom sizes, fewer certified teachers, and fewer resources, including library materials, computers, and science laboratories.[61] In Prince George's County and other communities that have dismantled busing programs, local and state governments have promised to increase the funding for predominantly minority schools.

PERSISTENT DISCRIMINATION: SUPERFICIAL DIFFERENCES, DEEP DIVISIONS

In 1944, the Swedish sociologist Gunnar Myrdal gained fame for his book *An American Dilemma*, whose title referred to deep-rooted racism in a country that idealized equality.[62] Since then, legal obstacles to the mixing of the races have been nearly eliminated, and public opinion has softened significantly. In the early 1940s, a majority of white Americans believed that black children should not be allowed to go to school with white children; today less than 5 percent of white Americans express this belief. There are also visible signs of black progress. In the past two decades, increasing numbers of African Americans have attended college, received undergraduate degrees, obtained jobs as professional and managers, and moved into suburban neighborhoods.

Nevertheless, true equality for all Americans has remained elusive. The realities of everyday American life are still very different for its white and black citizens. For example, a black child born in the United States has more than twice the chance of dying before reaching his or her first birthday than a white child does. The difference in the infant mortality rates of whites and African Americans reflects differences in their nutrition, medical care, and education—in other words, differences in their access to the most basic resources of a modern society.

The history of equality in America is one of progress and of setbacks and, always, of new challenges. The latest is the treatment of Arab Americans and

Muslims in the aftermath of the terrorist attacks of September 11, 2001. Shortly afterward, a radio talk-show host suggested that all recent immigrants from the Middle East should be deported, a message eerily reminiscent of what some people once said about black Americans and Irish Americans and, more recently, about Latin Americans. Although the great majority of Americans have a lot more sense than was displayed by this particular talk show host, they do not necessarily fully embrace the notion that the United States is "one people and one nation." They accept that idea in the abstract but often find it difficult to apply in everyday life. Equality is a difficult idea in practice because it requires people to shed preconceived and often deeply embedded notions about how other people think, behave, and feel. It is difficult for nearly everyone to see beyond superficial differences—whether those differences relate to skin color, national origin, religious preference, sex, or lifestyle—to the shared humanity that unites people of all backgrounds. Myrdal called discrimination "America's curse." He could have broadened the generalization. Discrimination is civilization's curse, as evident in the scores of ethnic, national, and religious conflicts that have marred human history. But America is a special case because, as Lincoln said in his Gettysburg address, it was a nation founded "on the proposition that all men are created equal." No greater challenge faces America, today as throughout its history, than the challenge of living out the full meaning of its most imposing ideal.

SUMMARY

During the past few decades, the United States has undergone a revolution in the legal status of its traditionally disadvantaged groups, including African Americans, women, Native Americans, Hispanic Americans, and Asian Americans. Such groups are now provided equal protection under the law in areas such as education, employment, and voting. Discrimination by race, sex, and ethnicity has not been eliminated from American life but is no longer substantially backed by the force of law.

/pattersonwtp5

Traditionally disadvantaged Americans have achieved fuller equality primarily as a result of their struggle for greater rights. The Supreme Court has been an important instrument of change for minority groups. Its ruling in *Brown v. Board of Education* (1954), which declared racial segregation in public schools to be an unconstitutional violation of the Fourteenth Amendment's equal-protection clause, was a major breakthrough in equal rights. Through its busing, affirmative action, and other rulings, the Court has also mandated the active promotion of integration and equal opportunities.

However, because civil rights policy involves large issues of social values and the distribution of society's resources, questions of civil rights are politically explosive. For this reason, legislatures and executives as well as the courts have been deeply involved in such issues, siding at times with established groups and sometimes backing the claims of underprivileged groups.

In recent years, affirmative action programs—designed to achieve equality of result for African Americans, women, Hispanic Americans, and other disadvantaged groups—have become a civil rights battleground. Affirmative action has had the strong support of civil rights groups and has won the qualified endorsement of the Supreme Court but has been opposed by those who claim that it unfairly discriminates against white males. Busing is another issue that has provoked deep divisions within American society.

KEY TERMS

affirmative action
civil rights
comparable worth
de facto discrimination
de jure discrimination
equal-protection clause
equal rights

equality of result
gender gap
intermediate-scrutiny test
reasonable-basis test
strict-scrutiny test
suspect classifications

SUGGESTED READINGS

Armor, David. *Forced Justice: School Desegregation and the Law.* New York: Oxford University Press, 1995. An evaluation that concludes that the federal courts have overstretched their legal mandate by requiring school integration rather than simply school desegregation.

Bergmann, Barbara A. *In Defense of Affirmative Action.* New York: Basic Books, 1997. An economist's analysis of affirmative action that concludes that the policy is necessary for women and broadly beneficial to society.

Howard, John R. *The Shifting Wind.* Albany: State University of New York Press, 1999. A review of the Supreme Court and civil rights from Reconstruction to the *Brown* decision.

McClain, Charles J. *In Search of Equality: The Chinese Struggle Against Discrimination in Nineteenth-Century America.* Berkeley: University of California Press, 1994. A careful study of how Chinese in nineteenth-century California used the legal system to fight racism and injustice.

Nagel, Joane. *American Indian Ethnic Renewal: Red Power and the Resurgence of Identity and Culture.* New York: Oxford University Press, 1996. Explores the meaning of activism for Native Americans' ethnic identification.

Pinello, Daniel R. *Gay Rights and American Law.* New York: Cambridge University Press, 2003. A careful study of recent appellate-court decisions dealing with gay rights issues.

Reeves, Keith. *Voting Hopes or Fears? White Voters, Black Candidates, and Racial Politics in America.* New York: Oxford University Press, 1997. A critical assessment of race and politics in American society.

Skrentny, John David. *The Ironies of Affirmative Action: Politics, Culture, and Justice in America.* Chicago: University of Chicago Press, 1996. An empirical analysis of affirmative action and its impact.

Stavans, Ilan. *The Hispanic Condition: Reflections on Culture and Identity in America.* New York: HarperPerennial, 1996. An analysis of the behavioral and cultural differences and similarities among the major Hispanic groups.

LIST OF WEBSITES

http://www.airpi.org/ The website for the American Indian Policy Center, which was established by Native Americans in 1992; includes a political and legal history of Native Americans and examines current issues affecting them.

http://www.naacp.org The website of the National Association for the Advancement of Colored People (NAACP); includes historical and current information on the struggle of African Americans for equal rights.

http://www.nclr.org The website for the National Council of La Raza (NCLR), an organization dedicated to improving the lives of Hispanics; contains information on public policy, immigration, citizenship, and other subjects.

http://www.rci.rutgers.edu/~cawp The website of the Center for the American Woman and Politics (CAWP) at Rutgers University's Eagleton Institute of Politics.

Politics in Theory and Practice

Thinking: What role have political movements played in securing the legal rights of disadvantaged groups? How has the resulting legislation contributed to a furtherance of their rights?

Acting: Think of a disadvantaged group that you would like to assist. It could be one of the federal government's designated groups (such as Hispanics), one of the other groups mentioned in the chapter (such as the disabled), or some other group (such as the homeless). Contact a college, community, national, or international organization that seeks to help this group and volunteer your assistance. (The Internet provides the names of thousands of organizations, such as Habitat for Humanity, that are involved in helping the disadvantaged.)

The New York Times   reading 5

The World: What's in a Name?; Redefining Minority

by Susan Sachs

The 2000 census found that Hispanics were overtaking African Americans as America's largest minority group. Yet some observers question even the use of the term minority in the case of Hispanics. In this March 11, 2001, article, New York Times *reporter Susan Sachs explores this issue.*

IT'S OFFICIAL, at least according to raw numbers from the 2000 census. Latinos are on the verge of becoming the nation's biggest minority group, just about to edge out blacks.

The news comes as no surprise to politicians from California to New York, who have been courting Latinos, or to analysts who have tracked the Latin inroads into popular culture and mass marketing. Still, the rise of a specific Latino identity challenges many traditional American conventions about what a minority group will demand of society as a whole and how it defines itself.

The term Latino is itself a recent construct, born on American soil, to define its members as something other than mainstream Americans. But relying on a classic view of minority to understand this robust, diverse and politically fickle group is risky. Indeed, the sheer concentration of Spanish-speaking immigrants in some states, like California and Texas, and in some cities like New York and Miami, turns the image of minority status inside out.

"In California, we are not using the word minority much anymore," said Jewelle Taylor Gibbs, a retired University of California at Berkeley professor and the author of "Preserving Privilege: California Politics, Propositions and People of Color," a book on varied minority groups due out this month.

The book examines the vibrant growth of the population, its influence on state culture and how statewide ballot propositions to ban bilingual education and eliminate social services for illegal immigrants helped create Latino political solidarity in the 1990's.

"Latinos are now the largest ethnic group in California other than whites," Dr. Taylor Gibbs said. "One out of three people speaks Spanish or is of Spanish descent. By 2021, they will be the largest ethnic group in California. So they don't feel much like a minority. There's a very, very strong sense of empowerment."

Political scientists and immigration experts have long debated just how to think about this population that the census-takers, for only the last 30 years, have categorized ethnically as Hispanics. Is it a minority group in the meaning typically applied to blacks, that is, an oppressed group with common historic grievances against white society? Or is it simply another immigrant group, with its own characteristics, that will eventually lose its cohesion in pursuit of a place in American society?

Even Latino scholars do not answer with one voice.

"There are forks in the road for the Hispanic community," said Harry P. Pachon, director of the Tomas Rivera Policy Institute. "It all depends on how absorptive American society is to Hispanics. If there is upward mobility, that group identity loses its hold."

Certainly, Latinos are united by an intimate affinity for the Spanish language. But they include people on vastly different trajectories, some already successful and some mired in the economic underclass. They are also divided by national origin, historical memory, shades of skin color and religion—just about every element that has bound other immigrant and racial groups in their formation of a shared identity.

Numerically, of course, Latinos are by definition a minority in a nation still dominated by non-Hispanic whites. But here, too, they defy the classic political and social meaning of the term. Public policies toward minorities, including affirmative action and school desegregation, were undertaken to redress historic wrongs done to African-Americans whose ancestors arrived as slaves rather than voluntarily.

Still, nurturing the idea of Latinos as a politically and socially aggrieved minority has helped the diverse components of the population—people from every country in the Spanish-speaking Caribbean, Central and South America and Mexico—find a unified voice on the national stage.

To do so, many national pan-Latino advocacy groups that became active in the past decade adopted the blueprint of the black civil rights movement. They maintain that Mexicans (the largest component nationally of the overall Latino population) experienced wide-ranging exploitation like African-Americans, that dark-skinned Latinos suffer racial discrimination, that Latinos are negatively in the media stereotyped in ways similar to blacks and that anti-immigrant laws target them as an entire ethnic group.

"The national Latino organizations take the view that the legacy of the civil rights movement is to redress issues of discrimination and if you are a person of color, you need to be protected from that as well, even if you just got here yesterday," said Angelo Falcon, a senior policy executive at the Puerto Rican Legal Defense and Education Fund in New York City.

"You have people who come here and say, 'I don't know what this Latino and minority stuff is all about. I'm Colombian,'" he said, "Then one day you wind up in the wrong neighborhood." At the first insult denigrating Latinos, "all of the sudden you're a minority."

Besides African-Americans, anyone with an Irish or Jewish or Italian grandparent who came to the United States in the early 20th century heard of similar ethnic and racial slurs directed against their ancestors. American history has no lack of examples of discriminatory laws against specific immigrant groups. Indeed, the principal determinant of who was allowed into the country for decades, until the laws changed in 1965, was white European ancestry.

Immigration experts say Latinos—and others—respond differently to such experiences today because they are different from those earlier waves in significant ways. True, some have fled civil war and repression, but many more feel free to move back and forth between their native land and new homeland. The United States, with its historic links to the Spanish-speaking world, also feels less foreign to Latino immigrants.

And American society and its demands on immigrants have changed. Though multiculturalism is often criticized for diluting American identity, it is also more acceptable now to retain a distinct ethnic identity.

Ethnic solidarity, the traditional wedge that immigrants used to clear a space for themselves to become Americans, is now celebrated for its own sake.

Whether it will persist as an identity as opposed to a political grouping is not so clear.

Studies of immigrant children in general show that the impulse to assimilate is still strong, as it has been for more than 100 years. But they also show that today's

Latinos are more sensitive to perceived discrimination than earlier immigrants and the desire to become an unhyphenated American can be crippled when youngsters believe that mainstream society judges them by ethnicity, race or national origin.

"Ethnicity is a subjective feeling as well as an imposed category," said Dr. Pachon of the Tomas Rivera institute. "If it's imposed, because people make assumptions about you if you are dark-skinned and speak with an accent, then you have no option but to consider yourself Hispanic."

"In the Latino community now, there is a selective assimilation going on," he added. "But acculturation is also very strong."

What's Your Opinion?

Are Hispanics a minority group in the traditional sense or are they simply another immigrant group with its own characteristics and culture?

CHAPTER 6

PUBLIC OPINION AND POLITICAL SOCIALIZATION: SHAPING THE PEOPLE'S VOICE

" To speak with precision of public opinion is a task not unlike coming to grips with the Holy Ghost. **"**

V. O. KEY JR.[1]

As facts emerged about who might have been responsible for the terrorist attacks of September 11, 2001, most Americans were at a loss to supply information of their own in forming a judgment about what the next step should be. Few could recall even hearing about Osama bin Laden or an Islamic terrorist network. Most Americans were unable even to say where Afghanistan was located. Opinion surveys indicated, however, that nine of ten Americans wanted and expected retaliatory action.

Americans' response to the terrorist attacks is a revealing example of the nature of public opinion. Citizens' thoughts about most policy issues are not deeply informed by facts. Moreover, public opinion is normally not a guide to an exact course of action. President Bush was not forced by public opinion to launch a massive military attack on the Taliban regime in Afghanistan. However, public opinion did require that he take decisive action of some form and of some duration. The nature of that action was for Bush and his advisors to decide. When he announced that he had decided on a long-term "war on terrorism" through military, economic, intelligence-gathering, and

In late 2001, the United States launched a massive air attack on the Taliban regime and its Al Qaeda ally in Afghanistan. In taking action, the Bush administration was responding to public opinion even though the air assault itself was a policy decided on in closed deliberations among President Bush and his advisors.

diplomatic means, the public embraced that action as an appropriate response.

Public opinion has a central place in democratic government because of the idea that any such government should reflect the will of the people. However, public opinion is not the well-formed phenomenon that commentators sometimes suggest. Public opinion is seldom exact when it comes to questions of how to resolve society's problems. Political leaders typically have leeway in deciding a course of action. Rather than choosing to topple the regime in Afghanistan, for example, Bush could have chosen targeted attacks on terrorist groups around the globe. He perhaps even had the option of a law enforcement response, relying on police efforts throughout the world to flush out and eliminate terrorist cells.

This chapter discusses public opinion and its influence on the U.S. political system. A major theme is that public opinion is a powerful and yet inexact force in American politics. The policies of the U.S. government cannot be understood apart from public opinion; at the same time, public opinion is not a precise determinant of public policy. This apparent paradox is explained by the fact that *self-government* in a large and complex country involves a division of labor between the public and its representatives. The public ordinarily affects only the general direction of its government whereas the lawmakers decide the specific actions. The main points made in this chapter are the following:

★ *Public opinion consists of those views held by ordinary citizens that are openly expressed.* Public officials have many means of gauging public opinion but increasingly have relied on public opinion polls to make this determination.

★ *The process by which individuals acquire their political opinions is called political socialization.* This process begins during childhood, when, through family and school, Americans acquire many of their basic political values and beliefs. Socialization continues into adulthood, during which peers, political institutions and leaders, and the news media are major influences.

★ *Americans' political opinions are shaped by several frames of reference. Four of the most important are ideology, group attachments, partisanship, and political culture.* These frames of reference form the basis for political consensus and conflict among the general public.

★ *Public opinion has an important influence on government but ordinarily does not directly determine what officials will do.* Public opinion works primarily to place limits on the choices made by officials.

THE NATURE OF PUBLIC OPINION

Public opinion is a relatively new concept in the history of political ideas. Not until democracy surfaced in the eighteenth century did the need arise for a term that refers to the political beliefs of the mass public.

Public opinion is now a widely used term. It is typically applied in ways that suggest that the public has a common set of concerns. However, it is ordinarily not very meaningful to lump all citizens together as if they constitute a coherent whole.[2] There is, to be sure, an occasional issue of such power and breadth that it captures the attention of nearly all citizens. The large majority of issues, however, attract the attention of some citizens but not most citizens. Agricultural conservation programs, for example, are of intense interest to some farmers, hunters, and environmentalists, but of little interest to other people. The tendency is so pervasive that opinion analysts have described America as a nation of *many* publics.[3]

There are numerous issues about which there is literally no majority opinion. On issues such as agricultural conservation programs, a form of *pluralist* democracy usually prevails. Government responds to the views of an intense minority. In other cases, *elitist* opinion prevails. On the question of U.S. relations with Finland, for example, there is little likelihood that ordinary citizens would know or care what the U.S. government does. In such instances, the policy opinions of an elite group of business and policy leaders ordinarily prevail. *Majority* opinion also can be decisive, but its influence is normally confined to a few broad issues that elicit widespread attention and concern, such as social security and employment. This situation may suggest a limited role for popular majorities, but such issues, although few in number, typically have the greatest impact on society as a whole.

Hence, any definition of the term *public opinion* cannot be based on the assumption that all citizens, or even a majority, are actively interested and have a preference about all aspects of political life. *Public opinion* can be defined as those opinions held by ordinary citizens that they are willing to express openly.[4] This expression need not be verbal. It could also take the form, for example, of a protest demonstration or a vote for one candidate rather than another. The crucial point is that a person's private thoughts on an issue become public opinion when expressed openly.

How Informed Is Public Opinion?

There are practical obstacles to government by public opinion in all instances. One obstacle is that people have differing opinions; in responding to one side of an issue, government is compelled to reject other preferences. Public opinion is also contradictory in many cases. Polls indicate, for example, that Americans would like better schools, health care, and other public services while they also favor a reduction in taxes (see Figure 6–1). A significant increase in the quantity and quality of social services cannot be accomplished without additional taxes. Which opinion of the people should govern—their desire for more services or their desire for lower taxes?

Another limitation on the role of public opinion is the public's relatively low level of political information. Some citizens pay close attention to politics, but most do not. When asked in a Times Mirror survey five simple questions on people and events that were currently at the top of the news about international affairs, only 6 percent of the respondents answered all five questions correctly. A total of 21 percent correctly answered only one question, and 37 percent could answer none of the questions. In other words, more than half knew little or nothing when asked relatively simple questions about world developments. (Citizens in several other countries were asked the same five questions; the results are summarized in "How the United States Compares.")

Although people with lower education levels are more likely to be uninformed, many college-educated people also lack basic information. A survey of Ivy League students found that a third could not identify the British

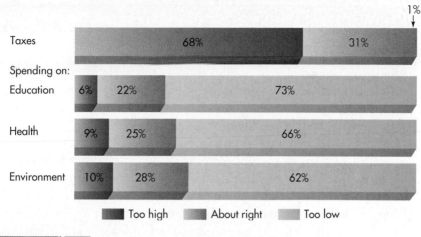

FIGURE 6-1 OPINIONS ON TAXING AND SPENDING

People's opinions are sometimes contradictory. Americans say, for example, that taxes are too high and yet also say government is spending too little in areas such as health, education, and the environment.

Source: Used by permission of National Opinion Research Center, University of Chicago.

prime minister, half could not name both U.S. senators from their state, and three-fourths could not identify Abraham Lincoln as the author of the phrase "a government of the people, by the people, and for the people."[5]

The public's lack of information is not as significant a factor as it might seem. Citizens do not necessarily have to be well informed about a situation to have a reasonable opinion about it. Opinions stem more from people's general beliefs, values, and policy orientations than from precise information about policy alternatives. Many people's opinions on the abortion issue, for example, derive from deep-seated religious beliefs. The fact that most individuals have only a foggy notion of Supreme Court rulings on the abortion issue does not make their opinions any less relevant. Similarly, people can have a considered view of how the United States should respond to foreign aggression without a detailed knowledge of global affairs.

Nevertheless, the public's lack of information restricts the role it can play in policy formation. The choice of one policy over another requires knowledge of the likely consequences of the various alternatives. Citizens typically lack this knowledge.

The Measurement of Public Opinion

Woodrow Wilson once said he had spent nearly all his adult life in government and yet had never seen a "government." What Wilson was

How the United States Compares

Citizens' Awareness of Public Affairs

Americans' knowledge of public affairs is relatively low. Even the simplest facts sometimes elude the average citizen's grasp. A 1994 Gallup poll found, for example, that a third of Americans were unable to name the vice president of the United States.

Low levels of public information are characteristic of most countries, but Americans rank lower than citizens of other Western democracies by some indicators. In a seven-country survey conducted in 1994 by the Times-Mirror Center for the People and the Press, Americans ranked next to last in terms of their ability to respond correctly to five questions about world leaders and events. Americans did their best on a question that asked them to name the president of Russia: 50 percent said Boris Yeltsin, but this was far lower than the 94 percent of Germans who named Yeltsin. In light of America's leading role in the world, its citizens might be expected to be uniquely well informed about international affairs. However, they are less knowledgeable in this area than Europeans, who live in closer proximity to other countries and who thus may be more attentive to world politics.

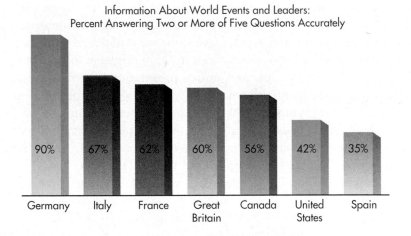

Information About World Events and Leaders:
Percent Answering Two or More of Five Questions Accurately

Germany	Italy	France	Great Britain	Canada	United States	Spain
90%	67%	62%	60%	56%	42%	35%

saying, in effect, was that government is a system of relationships. A government is not a building or a person; it is not tangible in the way that a car or a bottle of soda is. So it is with public opinion. No one has ever seen a "public opinion," and thus it cannot be measured directly. It must be assessed indirectly.

A time-honored method of interpreting public opinion is election re-turns. The vote is routinely interpreted by the press and politicians as an in-dicator of the public's mood—whether liberal or conservative, angry or satisfied, quiet or intense. Letters to the editor in newspapers, e-mail mes-sages to elected officials, and the size of crowds at mass demonstrations are other means of judging public opinion. Yet another device is the activity of lobbyists, who bring the concerns of their constituents to government's attention.

All these indicators are important and deserve the attention of those in power. Each of these indicators, however, has shortcomings as a guide to what is on people's minds. Elections offer citizens only a yes-or-no choice between candidates, and different voters will make the same choice for quite different reasons. The winning candidate may claim that the public has based its choice on a particular issue or inclination, but election returns always mask a more complex reality. As for letter writers and demonstra-tors, they are not at all representative of the general population. Less than 1 percent of Americans participate each year in a mass demonstration, and fewer than 10 percent write to the president or a member of Congress. Studies have found that the views of letter writers and demonstrators are more extreme than those of other citizens.[6]

Public Opinion Polls

In an earlier day, such indicators as elections and letters to the editor were the only means by which public officials could gauge what the public was thinking. Today, they can also rely on polls or surveys, which provide a more systematic method of estimating public sentiment.

In a *public opinion poll*, a relatively few individuals—the *sample*—are inter-viewed in order to estimate the opinions of a whole *population*, such as the students of a college, the residents of a city, or the citizens of a country. If a sufficient number of individuals are chosen at random, their views will tend to be representative—that is, roughly the same as the views held by the population as a whole.

How is it possible to measure the thinking of a large population on the basis of a relatively small sample? How can interviews with, say, one thou-sand Americans provide a reliable estimate of what 250 million are think-ing? The answer is found in the theory of probability. Opinion sampling is based on the mathematical laws of probability, which can be illustrated by the hypothetical example of a huge jar filled with a million marbles, half of them red and half of them blue. If a blindfolded person reaches into the jar, the likelihood of selecting a marble of a given color is fifty-fifty. And if one thousand marbles are chosen in this random way, it is likely that about half of them will be red and half will be blue. Opinion sampling works in the same way. If respondents are chosen at random from a population, their opinions will be approximately the same as those of the population as a whole.

Many people assume that a poll of the United States, with its 250 million people, must utilize a much larger sample to achieve the same level of accuracy as, say, a poll of Massachusetts or Arizona. In fact, the mathematics of polling are such that sample size is the critical factor. Thus, a sample of one thousand people will have nearly the same level of accuracy whether the population is that of the nation, a state, or a large city.

The accuracy of a poll is usually expressed in terms of *sampling error*, which indicates the likelihood that the responses of the sample accurately represent the view of the population. As would be expected, the larger the size of the sample, the greater the likelihood that the sample's opinions will accurately reflect those of the population. Thus, the larger the sample is, the smaller the sampling error is.

A properly drawn sample of one thousand individuals has a sampling error of about plus or minus 3 percent, which is to say that the proportions of the various opinions expressed by the people in the sample are likely to be within 3 percent of those of the whole population. For example, if 55 percent of a sample of one thousand respondents say that they intend to vote for the Republican candidate for president, then the chances are high that 52 to 58 percent (55 percent plus or minus 3 percent) of the whole population plan to vote for the Republican.

The impressive record of the Gallup poll in predicting the outcomes of presidential elections indicates that the theoretical accuracy of polls can be matched in practice. For example, the Gallup poll predicted that the 2000 election would divide 47 percent for Bush, 45 percent for Gore, and 4 percent for Nader. The actual result was 48 percent, 48 percent, and 3 percent respectively. The Gallup organization has erred badly only once: it stopped polling several weeks before the 1948 election and missed a late trend that carried Harry Truman to victory.

Problems with Polls

Mathematical estimations of poll accuracy require a *probability sample*—a sample in which each individual in the population has a known probability of being selected at random for inclusion. In practice, pollsters can only approximate this ideal. Because pollsters rarely have a list of all individuals in a population from which to draw a random sample, they usually base their sample on telephones. Pollsters use computers to randomly pick telephone numbers, which are then dialed by interviewers to reach respondents. Because the computer is as likely to pick one telephone number as any other and because 95 percent of U.S. homes have a telephone, a sample selected in this way is usually assumed to be reasonably representative of the population.

Some polls are not based on probability sampling. For example, news reporters sometimes conduct "people-in-the-street" interviews to obtain individual responses to political questions. Although a reporter may say that the opinions of those interviewed reflect the views of the general public, this claim is faulty. The sample will be biased by where and when the reporter chooses to conduct the interviews. For example, interviews conducted on a downtown street at the noon hour will include a disproportionate number of business employees who are taking their lunch breaks. Housewives, teachers, and factory workers, not to mention farmers, are among the many groups that would be underrepresented in such a sample.

Polls can also be misleading if they include poorly worded questions or ask people about remote topics. For example, a Roper poll received national attention when it found that a third of Americans expressed doubt about whether the Holocaust had actually happened. However, the poll question was a double negative ("Does it seem possible or does it seem impossible to you that the Nazi extermination of the Jews never happened?"), and some analysts suggested that the survey respondents may have been confused by the wording of the question. In fact, they were. A follow-up poll that asked a straightforward question found that less than one in ten Americans said they doubted the Holocaust had occurred.

Despite these and other sources of error, the poll or survey is the most relied-upon method of measuring public opinion. More than one hundred organizations are in the business of conducting public opinion polls. Some, like the Gallup Organization, conduct polls that are then released to the news media by syndication. Most large news organizations also have their own in-house polls; one of the foremost of these is the CBS News/New York Times poll. Finally, there are polling firms that specialize in conducting surveys for candidates and officeholders.

mhhe
.com
/pattersonwtp5

POLITICAL SOCIALIZATION: HOW AMERICANS LEARN THEIR POLITICS

Analysts have long been interested in the process by which public opinion is formed. The learning process by which people acquire their political opinions, beliefs, and values is called *political socialization*. Just as a language, a religion, or an athletic skill is acquired through a learning process, so too are people's political orientations. Political beliefs are not ingrained; they are acquired. Americans believe that free elections are the proper method

Students in a North Carolina school reciting the Pledge of Allegiance. Such childhood socialization experiences can have a profound impact on an individual's basic political beliefs.

of choosing leaders. People in some parts of the world find that other methods are perfectly natural.

For most Americans, the socialization process starts in the family with exposure to the political loyalties and opinions of the parents. The schools later contribute to the process, as do the mass media, friends, work associates, and other agents. Political socialization is thus a lifelong process.

The Process of Political Socialization

The process of political socialization in the United States has several major characteristics. First, although socialization continues throughout life, most people's political outlook is substantially influenced by their childhood learning. The *primacy tendency* refers to the fact that what is learned first is often lodged most firmly in one's mind.[7] Basic ideas about race, gender, and political party, for example, are often formed uncritically in childhood, much in the way that belief in a particular religion, typically the religion of one's parents, is acquired.

A second characteristic of political socialization is that it is cumulative. The *structuring tendency* refers to the tendency of earlier learning to structure later learning.[8] The beliefs that people hold will affect their response to new ideas and developments. Of course, people's beliefs are not completely fixed. Change in a person's views is possible, especially when previous and current experiences are at odds with one another. However, individuals have psychological defense mechanisms that protect their ingrained beliefs. When faced with situations that might challenge their original views, they often come up with reasons for holding onto them.

Widespread political change is rare, and when it has occurred, it has nearly always been preceded by a catastrophic event. Younger adults are usually more responsive to such events because their beliefs are less firmly rooted than those of older adults. The *age-cohort tendency* holds that a significant change in the pattern of political socialization is almost always concentrated among younger citizens. For example, President Franklin Roosevelt's New Deal, which sought to alleviate the economic hardship of the Great Depression, prompted many younger Republicans, but not many older ones, to shift their loyalty to the Democratic party.

The Agents of Political Socialization

The socialization process takes place through a variety of agents, including family, schools, peers, mass media, and political leaders and events. It is helpful to consider briefly some of these *agents of socialization* and how they affect political learning.

Families The family is a powerful agent of socialization because it has a near-monopoly on the attention of the young child, who also places great trust in what a parent says. By the time the child is a teenager and is not likely to listen to any advice a parent might offer, many of the beliefs and values that will stay with the child throughout life are already in place. Many adults are Republicans or Democrats today largely because their parents backed that party. They now can give all sorts of reasons for preferring their party to the other. But the reasons come later in life; the loyalty comes first, during childhood. The family also contributes to basic orientations that, while not directly political, have political significance. For example, the American family tends to be more egalitarian than families in other nations, and American children often have a voice in family decisions. Such basic American values as equality, individualism, and personal freedom have their roots in patterns of family interaction.[9]

Schools The school, like the family, has its major impact on children's basic political beliefs rather than on their opinions about specific issues. Teachers at the elementary level extol the exploits of national heroes such as George Washington, Abraham Lincoln, and Martin Luther King Jr. and praise the country's economic and political systems.[10] Although students in the middle and high school grades receive a more nuanced version of American history, it tends to emphasize the nation's great moments—for example, its decisive role in the two world wars. U.S. schools are probably more instrumental in building support for the nation than are the schools in other democracies. The Pledge of Allegiance, which is recited daily in many U.S. schools, has no equivalent in European countries. Schools also contribute to Americans' sense of social equality. Most American children, regardless of family income, attend public schools and study a fairly standard curriculum. In many countries, even some in Europe, school children are separated at an early age; some of them are placed in courses that train them to became manual laborers while others take courses that will prepare them for college.

Mass Media The mass media are another powerful socializing agent. The themes and images that prevail in the media affect people's perceptions of their world. For example, exposure to crime and lawlessness on television can lead people to believe that society itself is more violent than it actually is (see Chapter 10) and may even provoke violence in some people. Similarly, people's perceptions of political leaders are affected to some extent by how these leaders are portrayed in the media. When leaders are repeatedly said to be manipulative and self-interested, for example, people tend to see them as manipulative and self-interested.[11]

Peers Peer groups—friends, neighbors, and coworkers—tend to reinforce what a person already believes. One reason is that most people trust the opinions of their friends and associates. Many individuals are also unwilling to deviate too far from what their peers think. In *Spiral of Silence*, Elisabeth Noelle-Neumann contends that most individuals are conformists and are reluctant to speak out against prevailing opinions. An effect, she argues, is to make such opinions appear to be more widely held than they are, which can lead public officials to give them more attention than they may deserve.[12]

Political Institutions and Leaders Citizens look to political leaders and institutions, particularly the president and political parties, as guides to opinion. In the period immediately after the terrorist attacks on the World Trade Center and the Pentagon on September 11, 2001, most Americans were confused about who the enemy was and how the attack should be dealt with. That opinion changed dramatically ten days later after a televised speech by President Bush in which he identified the Al Qaeda and Taliban forces in Afghanistan as the immediate target of what would become a war on terrorism. In polls taken after the speech, about 90 percent of Americans said they agreed with Bush's plan of action.

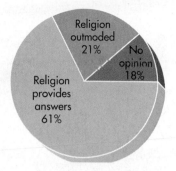

FIGURE 6-2 **OPINIONS ON RELIGION AS AN ANSWER TO TODAY'S PROBLEMS**

Most Americans say that religion can answer all or most of today's problems; only a minority believe religion is old-fashioned and out of date.
Source: Gallup poll, December, 2001. Used with permission.

Churches Since the seventeenth-century Puritans, churches have played a substantial role in shaping Americans' social and political opinions. Most Americans say they believe in God, most attend church at least once in a while, and most belong to a religion that includes teachings on the proper nature of society. Moreover, most Americans say that religion has answers to many of the problems facing today's society (see Figure 6–2). In these various respects, churches and religion are a more powerful force in the United States than in most other Western countries.

Scholars have not studied the impact of churches on political socialization as closely as they have studied other influences, such as the schools and the media. Nevertheless, churches are a source of political attitudes, including ones related to society's obligations to children, the poor, and the unborn. (The impact of religion is discussed further in a later section of this chapter.)

FRAMES OF REFERENCE: HOW AMERICANS THINK POLITICALLY

What are the frames of reference that guide the political thinking of Americans? The question is important in at least two respects. First, the ways in which citizens think politically provide clues about the way in which public opinion is likely to affect government. The government in a democratic system is expected to act more often in accordance with public opinion than against it.

Religion is a powerful socializing force in American life. Churches, synagogues, mosques, and temples are places where Americans acquire values and beliefs that can affect their opinions about politics.

A second reason it is important to understand how the people think politically is that a shared frame of reference can bring citizens together in the pursuit of a common goal. The opinions of millions of Americans would mean almost nothing if each of these opinions were different from all the others. If enough people think the same way, however, they may be able to exert political power.

The subject of how Americans think politically fills entire books. Outlined here are four of the major frames of reference through which Americans evaluate political alternatives. The first tends to unite Americans; the other three give rise to differences of opinion among them.

Cultural Thinking: Common Ideas

As was indicated in Chapter 1, Americans embrace a common set of ideals. Such principles as liberty, equality, and individualism have always meant somewhat different things to Americans but nonetheless are a source of agreement. For example, government programs aimed at redistributing wealth from the rich to the poor are popular among Europeans but are less appealing to Americans, who have a deeper commitment to individualism.

There are limits, of course, to the degree to which Americans' basic beliefs shape their policy opinions. For nearly two centuries African Americans were inferior by law to white Americans, despite the American creed that "all men are created equal." Such inconsistencies speak to the all-too-human capacity to voice one idea and live another.

Nevertheless, Americans' political ideals have a powerful influence on their opinions. These ideals affect the way in which disputes are argued and affect what Americans regard as reasonable and desirable. These ideals place boundaries on political action.

Ideological Thinking: The Outlook for Some

Commentators on public opinion in the United States often use such ideological words as *liberal* and *conservative* in describing how ordinary citizens think about political issues. In the early 1980s, for example, analysts spoke of a "conservative tide" that was supposedly sweeping the country and displacing the liberal trend that had dominated American politics for most of the preceding fifty years.

Liberal and *conservative* are ideological terms. So too are such terms as *populist*, *progressive*, *libertarian*, *communist*, and *fascist*. An *ideology* is a consistent pattern of opinion on particular issues that stems from a core or basic belief. Communism, for example, is rooted in a belief in material equality, and a communist therefore would be expected to support wage and welfare policies designed to spread wealth more evenly across society.

LIBERTY, EQUALITY & SELF-GOVERNMENT
What's Your Opinion?

Americans' Ideologies

In the United States, the key dimensions of political conflict occur around the extent of government intervention in the economic marketplace and in the maintenance of traditional values. Government intervention in either sphere has implications for liberty—how much freedom you should have in deciding your lifestyle and in your economic choices. Government intervention in the economic sphere can also affect equality: government has been the principal means of providing economic security for those vulnerable to market forces.

You can test your own ideology—and thus in a way your own conception of liberty and equality—by asking yourself the measurement questions used in Gallup surveys. Should government do more or do less in terms of leveling out the effects of the marketplace? Should government do more or do less in terms of promoting traditional social values? You are a libertarian if you favor less government action in both spheres. You are a populist if you favor more government action in both spheres. You are a conservative if you favor less intervention but more in the realm of social values. And you are a liberal if you favor more intervention in the marketplace and less in the realm of social values.

Although ideological terms are often used to describe mass publics, they do not accurately describe how most people think about politics.[13] Nearly everyone has basic beliefs that affect their opinions, but most people do not apply them consistently across a wide range of issues. They may say, for example, that they favor free trade among nations but then oppose it in particular cases where it works to the disadvantage of U.S. firms or workers. Research indicates that no more than a third of Americans, and perhaps as few as a tenth, have a pattern of opinions on issues that is consistent enough to be described as a manifestation of a true ideology.[14]

Nevertheless, analysts sometimes find it useful to measure the public's ideological tendencies. A standard method is to ask survey respondents whether they think of themselves as liberal, moderate, or conservative. Although people readily label themselves by these terms, many individuals are unable to say what the terms mean, or they provide inexact or inappropriate definitions. For this reason, pollsters have recently developed a less-direct method. They ask respondents two questions: "Do you support or oppose an activist role for government in determining the distribution of economic benefits in society?" and "Do you support or oppose activist government as a means of promoting a particular set of social values?" This method does not require that respondents know the meaning of ideological terms and yet provides a measure of people's general beliefs about government action in the broad areas of economic and social policy.

Responses to the two questions have been the basis for identifying four ideological types: conservatives, liberals, populists, and libertarians (see Figure 6–3). Conservatives are defined as individuals who oppose an activist role for government in providing economic benefits but look to government to uphold traditional social values. In contrast, liberals favor activist government as an instrument of economic redistribution but reject the notion that government should favor a particular set of social values. True liberals and conservatives could be expected to differ, for instance, on the issues of homosexual rights (a social values question) and government-guaranteed health care (an economic distribution question). Liberals would view homosexuality as a private issue and believe that government should ensure that everyone has access to adequate medical care. Conservatives would oppose government-mandated access to health care and favor government policies that actively discourage homosexual lifestyles. Populists are defined as individuals who share with conservatives a concern for traditional values but, like liberals, favor an active role for government in providing economic security. Libertarians are opposed to government intervention in both the economic and social spheres.

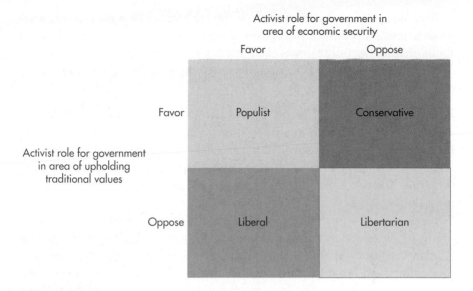

FIGURE **6-3** TYPES OF IDEOLOGIES

Americans can be classified as liberals, conservatives, populists, or libertarians, depending on their attitudes toward the government's role in the areas of economic security and social values.

In sum, libertarians are the most committed to individual freedom, and populists are the most committed to government activism. Conservatives and liberals are committed to individual freedom in one area (the economic sphere for conservatives, the social sphere for liberals) but to government activism in the other (the social sphere for conservatives, the economic sphere for liberals). Of these ideological types, conservatives are the largest group. A Gallup poll, for example, estimated that 31 percent of Americans are conservatives, 24 percent are libertarian, 17 percent are populist, and 13 percent are liberal.[15]

Group Thinking: The Outlook of Many

For most citizens, groups are a more important reference than is ideology.[16] Many Americans see politics through the lens of a group to which they belong or with which they identify. Farmers, for example, are more likely to follow agricultural issues than they are labor-management issues. A group outlook is a source of both consensus and conflict. Farmers generally approve of government price supports for commodities; this opinion unites farmers but pits them against other groups, including consumers.

Because of the country's great size, its settlement by various immigrant groups, and its economic pluralism, Americans are a very diverse people. Later chapters examine group tendencies more fully, but it is useful here to mention a few of the major group orientations: religion, class, region, race and ethnicity, gender, and age.

Religion Religious differences have always been a source of solidarity within a group and a source of conflict with outsiders. As Catholics and Jews came to America in large numbers in the nineteenth and early twentieth centuries, they encountered intense hostility from Protestant reactionaries. Today, Catholics, Protestants, and Jews have similar opinions on most policy issues.

Nevertheless, some important religious differences remain, although the opposing sides are not always the same. Fundamentalist Protestants and Roman Catholics oppose legalized abortion more strongly than do other Protestants and Jews. In contrast, on welfare issues such as food programs for the poor, Catholics and Jews are more supportive than are Protestants. Such differences have at least a partial basis in religious beliefs. A belief in self-reliance, for example, is part of the so-called Protestant ethic. Attitudes on abortion are tied to religious beliefs about whether human life begins at conception or at a later stage in the development of the fetus.

The most powerful religious force in contemporary American politics is the so-called religious right, which consists primarily of individuals who see themselves as born-again Christians and view the Bible as the infallible truth. Their views on such issues as homosexual rights, abortion, and school prayer differ significantly from those of the population as a whole. A Time/CNN survey found, for example, that born-again Christians are 37 percent more likely than other Americans to agree that "the Supreme Court and the Congress have gone too far in keeping religious and moral values like prayer out of our laws, schools, and many areas of our lives."

Class Economic class has less influence on political opinion in the United States than in Europe, but it is nevertheless related to opinions on certain economic issues. For example, lower-income Americans are more supportive of social welfare programs, business regulation, and progressive taxation than are those in higher-income categories. An obstacle to class-based politics in the United States is that people with similar incomes but differing occupations do not share the same opinions. Support for collective bargaining, for example, is substantially higher among factory workers than among small farmers, service workers, and those in the skilled crafts. The interplay of class and opinion will be examined more closely in Chapter 9, which discusses interest groups.

Economic class is related to Americans' opinions on a range of social and economic issues. Shown here is a work crew constructing formed wooden beams.

Region Region has declined as a basis of political opinions. The increased mobility of the U.S. population has resulted in the relocation of millions of Americans from the Northeast and Midwest to the South and West. Their beliefs on issues such as social welfare tend to be more liberal than those of people who are native to these regions. Nevertheless, regional differences are still evident in the areas of social welfare, civil rights, and national defense. Conservative opinions on these issues are more prevalent in the southern and mountain states than elsewhere (see "States in the Nation").

Race and Ethnicity Race and ethnicity, as Chapter 5 pointed out, have a significant influence on opinions. Whites and African Americans, for example, differ on issues of integration: black people are more in favor of affirmative action, busing, and other measures designed to promote racial equality and integration. Racial and ethnic groups also differ on economic issues, largely as a result of the differences in their economic situations. The crime issue is another area in which opinion differences are pronounced and predictable: minorities are less trusting of police and the judicial system. An American Bar Association poll found, for example, that only one in four nonwhites believe that "law enforcement officials and police try to treat whites and minorities alike."

Gender Although male-female differences of opinion are small on most issues, gender does affect opinion in some policy areas. Women are slightly

★‖ STATES IN THE NATION

Conservatives and Liberals

In the United States, self-identified conservatives substantially out-number those who call themselves liberals. Only in twelve states and the District of Columbia are liberals greater or nearly equal in number to conservatives.

Q. Why is the concentration of conservatives especially high in the southern, plains, and mountain states?

A. The southern, plains, and mountain states are less urbanized. Accordingly, their residents traditionally have been less dependent on and less trusting of government.

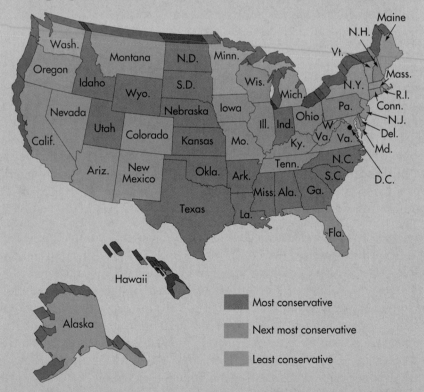

Most conservative

Next most conservative

Least conservative

Source: CNN exit polls, 2000. Classification based on the difference in the proportions of self-identified conservatives and liberals in each state.

more supportive than men, for example, of abortion rights and affirmative action. A 2000 Gallup poll found a 63 percent to 53 percent difference in support for affirmative action. The difference is even larger on some social welfare issues, such as poverty and education assistance.[17] A 2000 Washington Post/ABC News poll, for example, found that 72 percent of women compared with 57 percent of men favored increased spending for education. Some analysts suggest that such differences are accounted for in part by a tendency for women to think more in terms of the community as a whole and for men to think more in terms of self-reliance.

Women and men differ also in their opinions on the use of military force. In nearly every case, women are less supportive of military action than men are. The terrorist attacks on the World Trade Center and the Pentagon on September 11, 2001, produced an exception to the normal pattern. Men and women were almost equally likely (90 percent and 88 percent, respectively) to favor a military response. But they differed in expected ways when questioned about how the terrorist threat should be countered. Women were more likely than men to favor a narrowly targeted war on terrorism (see Figure 6–4).

Differences such as these are a factor in the gender gap that was discussed in Chapter 5. Women and men do not differ greatly in their political views, but there are persistent and predictable differences that lead them to respond somewhat differently to issues, events, and candidates. The politics of gender will be discussed further in Chapter 8.

Age Age has always affected opinions, but the gap between young and old is growing. In her book *Young v. Old*, the political scientist Susan MacManus notes that the elderly tend to oppose increases in public school funding while supporting increases in social security and Medicare (government-assisted medical care for retirees). MacManus predicts that issues of age will increasingly dominate American politics and that the elderly have the political clout to prevail. They vote at a much higher rate than do young people, are better organized politically (through groups such as the powerful AARP), and are increasing in number as a result of lengthened life spans (the so-called graying of America).[18] (The politics of age is also discussed in Chapters 8 and 9.)

Crosscutting Cleavages Although group loyalty can have a powerful impact on people's opinions, this influence is diminished when identification with one group is offset by identification with other groups. In a pluralistic society such as the United States, groups tend to be "crosscutting"—that is,

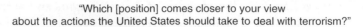

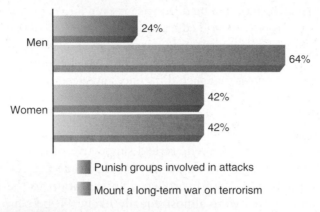

| FIGURE | 6-4 | GENDER AND THE TERRORIST THREAT |

Compared with men, women are somewhat less inclined to see military force as the answer to conflict. This difference was evident shortly after the terrorist attacks of September 11, 2001, when women were more inclined than men to prefer a carefully targeted attack on terrorists as opposed to a long-term war on terrorism.
Source: Gallup poll, September 21-22, 2001.

each group includes individuals who also belong to many other groups. Crosscutting cleavages tend to produce moderate opinions. Faced with conflicting feelings arising out of identification with several groups, most people seek a balanced opinion. However, in societies such as Northern Ireland where group loyalties are reinforcing rather than crosscutting (Catholics tend to have much lower incomes, Protestants much higher ones), opinions are intensified by group identifications, and deep hatreds among the opposing camps can result. In America, Catholics and Protestants are not at each other's throats, largely because each group includes people of varying income, education, region, and so on.

Partisan Thinking: The Line That Divides

In the everyday play of politics, no source of opinion more clearly divides Americans than that of their partisanship. Figure 6–5 provides examples, but they show only a few of the differences. On nearly every major political issue, Republicans and Democrats have views that are at least somewhat different. In many cases, such as spending programs for the poor, the differences are substantial.

Party identification refers to a person's ingrained sense of loyalty to a political party. Party identification is not formal membership in a party but

Percentage expressing agreement

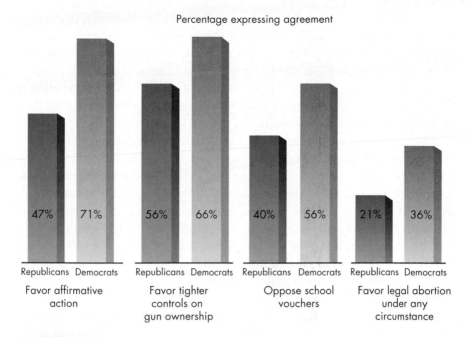

| Republicans Democrats | Republicans Democrats | Republicans Democrats | Republicans Democrats |
| Favor affirmative action | Favor tighter controls on gun ownership | Oppose school vouchers | Favor legal abortion under any circumstance |

FIGURE 6-5 PARTISANSHIP AND ISSUE OPINIONS

Republicans and Democrats differ significantly in their opinions on many policy issues.

Source: In order of questions: Washington Post/ABC News, 2000; ABC News, 2002; Gallup, 2000; Gallup, 2000.

instead an emotional attachment to a party—the feeling that "I am a Democrat" or "I am a Republican." Scholars and pollsters have typically measured party identification with a question of the following type: "Generally speaking, do you think of yourself as a Republican, a Democrat, an Independent, or what?" About two-thirds of adults call themselves Democrats or Republicans. Of the third who prefer the label "Independent," most say they lean toward one party or the other.

Early studies concluded that party loyalties were highly stable and seldom changed over the course of adult life.[19] Subsequent studies have shown that party loyalties are more fluid than originally believed; they can be influenced by the issues and candidates of the moment.[20] Nevertheless, most adults do not switch their party loyalties easily, and a substantial proportion never waver from an initial commitment to a party, which can often be traced to childhood influences.

Once acquired, partisanship affects how people perceive and interpret events. For example, when the U.S. Supreme Court ruled against a manual recount of Florida votes, which decided the 2000 presidential election in George W. Bush's favor, 53 percent of Democrats and 25 percent of Independents but only 12 percent of Republicans said in a national poll that they had "less respect" for the Court because of its action.

For most people, partisanship is not simply a blind faith in the party of their choice. Some Republicans and Democrats know very little about their party's policies, and they unthinkingly embrace its candidates. However, party loyalties are not randomly distributed across the population but follow a pattern that would be predicted from the parties' traditions. The Democratic party, for example, has been the driving force behind social welfare and workers' rights policies, while the Republican party has been the spearhead for pro-business and tax reform policies. The fact that most union workers are Democrats and most businesspeople are Republicans is not a coincidence. Their partisanship is rooted in their different economic circumstances and the different policy traditions of the two parties.

Partisanship is a strong force in American politics, but its influence is declining. In recent decades, the proportion of voters who identify with the Democratic or Republican party has declined and the proportion of Independents has increased. As a result, elections are more volatile than in the past. People are less likely to vote on the basis of a long-standing party loyalty and more likely to base their choice on the issues and candidates of the moment. This and other issues of partisanship are examined in depth at various points later in this book, particularly in Chapters 7, 8, 11, and 12.

THE INFLUENCE OF PUBLIC OPINION ON POLICY

Yet unanswered in the discussion is the central question about public opinion: what impact does it have on government?

The fundamental principle of democracy is that the people's view ought to prevail on public issues. This principle is difficult to put into practice. In any society of appreciable size, it is simply not possible for the people to directly formulate public policies and programs. However, democracy can be said to exist once officials take the public's views into account when making policy decisions and once the people have recourse to free and fair elections when they believe their opinions are being ignored.[21]

Some analysts argue that the public's views do not count for enough; the elites, it is claimed, are so entrenched and remote that they pay little attention to the preferences of ordinary citizens.[22] The most comprehensive study ever conducted of the relationship between public opinion and policy, however, concluded otherwise. In a study spanning fifty years of trends, Benjamin Page

Bags containing the bodies of American soldiers killed in the Vietnam War await shipment back to the United States. The large numbers of American casualties during the war helped to turn public opinion against U.S. involvement in Vietnam. As public opinion turned, U.S. policymakers had little choice but to plan a phased withdrawal from Vietnam.

and Robert Shapiro found a substantial relationship between changes in public opinion and subsequent changes in public policy, particularly on highly visible issues. More often than not, policy changed when opinion changed. Furthermore, the more important the issue, the more likely it was that policy changed in the direction of public opinion. Page and Shapiro concluded that U.S. officials are reasonably responsive to public opinion.[23]

Not all scholars have interpreted the evidence on public opinion and policy so favorably,[24] but there is little question that the public's views do have an impact. Public opinion is rarely powerful enough to force officials into a specific course of action, but public opinion does serve as a guiding force in public policy. There are many actions, for example, that officials dare *not* take for fear of public retribution. No politician who wants to stay in office is likely to say, for example, that social security for the elderly should be abolished. And there are many actions that politicians willingly take in order to appeal to the public.[25] In late 1999, for example, the GOP-controlled Congress passed a budget that included funding to hire thousands of new public school teachers. Congressional Republicans had opposed the measure, but education ranked near the top in polls of Americans' policy priorities and the 2000 election was just around the corner. Republicans, reluctant to hand the Democrats a potent campaign issue, enacted the funding measure.

Such examples, however, do not provide an answer to the question of whether government is *sufficiently* responsive to public opinion. This question is a normative one, the answer to which rests on assumptions about the proper relationship between people's everyday opinions and what government does. The question is also complicated by the fact that politics includes a battle over the control of public opinion. People's views are neither fixed nor simply a product of personal circumstances. Public opinion is dynamic and can be changed, activated, and crystallized through political action.

In fact, one of the best indicators of the power of public opinion is the effort of political leaders to harness it in support of their goals. In American politics, popular demand for a policy is a powerful argument for that policy. For this reason and others, great effort is made to organize and represent public opinion through elections (Chapter 7), political parties (Chapter 8), interest groups (Chapter 9), the news media (Chapter 10), and political institutions (Chapters 11 to 14).

SUMMARY

Public opinion can be defined as those opinions held by ordinary citizens that they openly express. Public officials have many ways of assessing public opinion, such as the outcomes of elections, but have increasingly come to rely on public opinion polls. There are many possible sources of error in polls, and surveys sometimes present a misleading portrayal of the public's views. However, a properly conducted poll can provide an accurate indication of what the public is thinking and can dissuade political leaders from thinking that the views of the most vocal citizens (such as demonstrators and letter writers) are also the views of the broader public.

The process by which individuals acquire their political opinions is called political socialization. During childhood the family and schools are important

 sources of basic political attitudes, such as beliefs about the parties and the nature of the U.S. political and economic systems. Many of the basic orientations that Americans acquire during childhood remain with them in adulthood, but socialization is a continuing process. Major shifts in opinion during adulthood are usually the consequence of changing political conditions; for example, the Great Depression of the 1930s was the catalyst for wholesale changes in Americans' opinions on the government's economic role. There are also short-term fluctuations in opinion that result from new political issues, problems, and events. Individuals' opinions in these cases are affected by prior beliefs, peers, political leaders, and the news media. Events themselves are also a significant short-term influence on opinions.

The frames of reference that guide Americans' opinions include cultural beliefs, such as individualism, that result in a range of acceptable and unacceptable policy alternatives. Opinions can also stem from ideology, although most citizens do not have a strong and consistent ideological attachment. In addition, individuals develop opinions as a result of group orientations, notably religion, income, occupation, region, race, ethnicity, gender, or age. Partisanship is perhaps the major source of political opinions; Republicans and Democrats differ in their voting behavior and views on many policy issues. However, party loyalty has declined in importance in recent decades as a frame of reference for people's opinions.

Public opinion has a significant influence on government but seldom determines exactly what government will do in a particular instance. Public opinion serves to constrain the policy choices of officials. Some policy actions are beyond the range of possibility because the public will not accept change in existing policy or will not seriously consider policy that seems clearly at odds with basic American values. Evidence indicates that officials are reasonably attentive to public opinion on highly visible and controversial issues of public policy.

KEY TERMS

- age-cohort tendency
- agents of socialization
- conservatives
- ideology
- liberals
- libertarians
- party identification
- political socialization
- population

- populists
- primacy tendency
- probability sample
- public opinion
- public opinion poll
- sample
- sampling error
- structuring tendency

SUGGESTED READINGS

Delli Carpini, Michael X., and Scott Keeter. *What Americans Know About Politics and Why It Matters*. New Haven, Conn.: Yale University Press, 1996. A synthesis of the American public's knowledge about politics.

Dunn, Charles W., and J. David Woodard. *The Conservative Tradition in America*. Lanham, Md.: Rowman & Littlefield, 1996. A study of the philosophical and political roots of conservatism from its origins to the present.

Jacobs, Lawrence, and Robert Shapiro. *Politicians Don't Pander*. Chicago: University of Chicago Press, 2000. An analysis that concludes politicians are not driven by polls.

MacManus, Susan A. *Young v. Old: Generational Combat in the Twenty-First Century*. Boulder, Colo.: Westview Press, 1996. A study of the emerging conflict in the political self-interest of younger and older Americans.

Noelle-Neumann, Elisabeth. *The Spiral of Silence*, 2d ed. Chicago: University of Chicago Press, 1993. An intriguing theory of how public opinion is formed and muted.

Sobel, Richard. *The Impact of Public Opinion on U.S. Foreign Policy Since Vietnam*. New York: Oxford University Press, 2001. A study of the relationship between public opinion and foreign policy.

Traugott, Michael W., and Paul J. Lavrakas. *The Voter's Guide to Election Polls*, 2d ed. Chatham, N.J.: Chatham House, 2000. A clear guide to survey methods and analysis with an emphasis on election polling.

Zaller, John R. *The Nature and Origins of Mass Opinion*. New York: Cambridge University Press, 1992. A superb analysis of the nature of public opinion.

LIST OF WEBSITES

http://www.gallup.com/ The website of the renowned Gallup Organization; includes the results of recent Gallup polls.

http://www.policy.com/ A nonpartisan site that provides a wealth of information about current public issues.

http://www.princeton.edu/~abelson/ The Princeton Survey Research Center's site; offers results from surveys conducted by a variety of polling organizations.

http://www.publicagenda.org/ The nonpartisan Public Agenda's site; it provides opinions, analyses, and educational materials on current policy issues.

Politics in Theory and Practice

Thinking: What factors limit the influence of public opinion on the policy choices of public officials?

Acting: At the website of a polling organization such as the Pew Research Center on the People and the Press (www.people-press.org), examine the poll results on a current policy issue. Study the extent to which opinions differ, if at all, among men and women and among Republicans and Democrats. Would an informal poll of the people you know result in a similar distribution of opinion? Why or why not?

The New York Times

Wrong Number: The Unbearable Lightness of Public Opinion Polls

by Adam Clymer

Until scientific polling was developed, policymakers relied on less precise indicators to judge people's opinions on public policy issues. Yet polls themselves are subject to various types of error. In this July 22, 2001, article, The New York Times's *Adam Clymer examines two sources of polling error—the wording of poll questions and the polling of people who have given little thought to an issue.*

WASHINGTON—After a week during which one politician or interest group after another brandished a poll to prove conclusively that the public backs federal funding of human embryonic stem cell research, it may come as a surprise to learn that American public opinion on the subject doesn't exist—at least not yet. The subject is just too new and too complicated.

Polls seem to say otherwise. There is a NBC News/ Wall Street Journal poll with 69 percent in favor and 23 percent opposed, a Gallup Poll for CNN and USA Today that found 54 percent in favor and a poll done by ABC News and Beliefnet, a religious Web site, that found 58 percent support. A survey done for the Conference of Catholic

Bishops, on the other hand, found only 24 percent approval, while the Juvenile Diabetes Foundation, as part of the Coalition for the Advancement of Medical Research, came up with a 70 percent figure. The advocates of stem cell research certainly believe the numbers should persuade President Bush—who promised in the 2000 campaign to oppose funding— that the politically smart course is to change course.

Representative Connie Morella, a moderate Republican from Maryland, said last week, "Three to one, the Americans, when polled, are in favor of stem cell research under particular strong guidelines." About the same time, the Juvenile Diabetes Foundation ran an advertisement in The Washington Times claiming, "A recent national survey shows conclusively that 70 percent support human embryonic stem cell research, including Catholics (72 percent) . . . ."

But the large variations in the polls cited, which can generally be traced to how the poll questions were worded, suggest that the opinions of respondents are not fully formed, or firmly held. And that is very much the case in the matter of stem cell research, as a crucial finding in the Gallup poll, ignored by the combatants, shows.

Before having the issue explained to them, 57 percent of the public said they did not know enough to say whether they favored or opposed stem cell research (the pollsters then offered some information and pressed for opinions). The Gallup survey was the only one that specifically offered respondents that choice.

And a no-opinion number that high, said Herbert L. Asher, a professor of political science at Ohio State University, indicated that all these polls "are measuring nonattitudes."

Some professional pollsters disagree sharply. A firm defense of polling on questions about which the public may not yet have strong feelings comes from Peter Hart, a Democratic pollster who does the NBC/ Journal poll with Robert Teeter, a Republican. He argues that "wording is all-important," and that even if the poll question itself is the first thing someone has heard on a subject, it at least shows the potency various arguments will have once the subject becomes part of a public dialogue.

In the case of stem cell research, Mr. Hart and his colleagues at other polling organizations tried to write questions that fairly stated both sides of the argument.

Writing a balanced question, especially one that is not so long that the respondent hangs up in the middle, is a difficult art, not a science. Honest pollsters try to avoid phrasing that leads respondents toward one answer or another, though they don't always succeed. But can the argument against human embryo research be adequately conveyed by saying it involves "potentially viable human embryos," as the Journal/NBC poll asked?

The key question in the bishop's poll, on the other hand, included a line that read, "the live embryos would be destroyed in their first week of development."

This question, which also used phrases like "your federal tax dollars" and speaks only of "experiments," not the lofty goals of the research, was not written by a pollster but by the bishops' chief lobbyist on the issue, Richard A. Doerflinger. And it was ridiculed by other pollsters. As Professor Asher said, "It's loaded."

Whatever their language, all the polls on stem cell research asked long, involved questions. And that is a tipoff that the issue is remote from most people, said Bernard Roshco, a former editor of Public Opinion Quarterly.

"Americans are acquiescent so they'll give you an answer," he said. But "the mere fact that you've got to offer a lengthy summary implies that it's too early to sort it out."

Pollsters regularly prove that point by eliciting opinions from people on nonexistent laws and even nonexistent people. This strongly suggests that the opinions people offer on subjects that are real but remote may be equally unreliable.

One safeguard is to ask a lot of questions, using different phrasings, and asking things like, "Would you still support X if you knew . . ." But that costs money. So it is not easy for pollsters and their clients to take the advice of academics like Professor Asher or Stanley Presser of the University of Maryland, and explore difficult issues with a series of questions.

Without such persistence, said Professor Presser, a past director of the university's survey research center, pollsters and the politicians who seek their wisdom can be trapped by eager-to-please respondents, who answer questions not based on fully formed attitudes and strong feelings, but who, in effect, are "constructing them as the interview progresses."

Which means that, sometimes, the pollsters are measuring phantoms, and the politicians are calling on them for support.

What's Your Opinion?

Are poll responses to questions about new and complicated issues largely meaningless? Or can something be learned from such responses?

CHAPTER 7

POLITICAL PARTICIPATION AND VOTING: EXPRESSING THE POPULAR WILL

❝ We are concerned in public affairs, but immersed in our private ones. **❞**

WALTER LIPPMANN[1]

At stake in the 2002 elections was control of the Congress. Which party would have the leading voice on legislation affecting education, health, welfare, and the environment? Which party would have the greater say in how America responded to the legislative challenges posed by the domestic and global economies? Which party would be entrusted with national security legislation? With so much at stake, it might be thought that Americans would have been eager to cast their ballots for the party of their choice. But in fact more than 60 percent of American adults did not vote in the 2002 elections. Despite a concerted get-out-the-vote campaign by the news media and public service groups, the number of people who did not vote was far greater than the number of votes the winning party received in the congressional races.

Voting is a form of **political participation**—a sharing in activities designed to influence public policy and leadership. Political participation involves other activities in addition to voting, such as joining political parties and interest groups, writing to elected officials, demonstrating for political causes, and giving money to political candidates.

202

Democratic societies are distinguished by their emphasis on citizen participation. The concept of self-government is based on the idea that ordinary people have a right to participate in the affairs of state. Related issues include whether they exercise that right and whether participation is evenly spread across society. As it happens, the United States is an unusual case relative to other democracies, as this chapter will show. The major points made in this chapter are the following:

★ *Voter turnout in U.S. elections is low in comparison with that of other democratic nations.* The reasons for this difference include the nature of U.S. election laws, particularly those pertaining to registration requirements and the scheduling of elections.

★ *Most citizens do not participate actively in politics in ways other than voting.* Only a small proportion of Americans can be classified as political activists.

★ *Most Americans make a sharp distinction between their personal lives and national life.* This attitude reduces their incentive to participate and contributes to a pattern of participation dominated by citizens with higher levels of income and education.

VOTER PARTICIPATION

At the nation's founding, **suffrage**—the right to vote—was restricted to property-owning males. Tom Paine ridiculed this policy in *Common Sense*. Observing that a man whose only item of property was a jackass would lose his right to vote if the jackass died, Paine asked, "Now tell me, which was the voter, the man or the jackass?" It was not until 1840 that all states extended suffrage to propertyless white males, a change made possible by their continued demand for the vote and by the realization on the part of the wealthy that the nation's abundance and openness were natural protections against an assault on property rights by the voting poor.

Women did not secure the vote until 1920, with the ratification of the Nineteenth Amendment. In the 1870s, Susan B. Anthony tried to vote in her hometown of Rochester, New York, asserting that she had a right to do so as a U.S. citizen. The men who placed her under arrest charged her with "illegal voting" and insisted that her proper place was in the home. By 1920, men had run out of excuses for keeping the vote from women. As Senator Wendell Phillips observed: "One of two things is true: either woman is like man—and if she is, then a ballot based on brains belongs to her as well as to him. Or she is different, and then man does not know how to vote for her as she herself does."[2]

After a hard-fought, decades-long campaign, American women finally won the right to vote in 1920.

African Americans had to wait nearly fifty years longer than women to be granted full suffrage. Blacks seemed to have won the right to vote with passage of the Fifteenth Amendment after the Civil War, but as was explained in Chapter 5, they were effectively disenfranchised in the South by a number of electoral tricks, including poll taxes, literacy tests, and whites-only primary elections. The poll tax was a fee of several dollars that had to be paid before one could register to vote. Since most blacks in the South were too poor to pay it, the poll tax barred them from voting. Not until the ratification of the Twenty-fourth Amendment in 1964 was the poll tax outlawed in federal elections. Supreme Court decisions and the Voting Rights Act of 1965 swept away other legal barriers to fuller participation by African Americans.

In 1971, the Twenty-sixth Amendment extended voting rights to include citizens eighteen years of age or older. Previously, nearly all states had restricted voting to those twenty-one years of age or older.

Today virtually any American—rich or poor, man or woman, black or white—who is determined to vote can legally and actually do so. Americans attach great importance to the power of their votes. They claim that voting is their greatest source of influence over political leadership and their strongest protection against an uncaring or corrupt government.[3] They also claim that voting is a basic act of citizenship (see Table 7–1). In view of this

TABLE 7-1   OPINIONS ON OBLIGATIONS OF CITIZENS

Americans rank voting as one of the essential obligations of citizenship.

	Essential Obligation	Very Important Obligation	Somewhat Important	Personal Preference
Treating all people equally regardless of race or ethnic background	57%	33%	6%	4%
Voting in elections	53	29	9	9
Working to reduce inequality and injustice	41	42	12	6
Being civil to others with whom we may disagree	35	45	14	6
Keeping fully informed about the news and other public issues	30	42	19	10
Donating blood or organs to help with medical needs	20	37	18	26
Volunteering time to community service	16	42	26	16

Source: Used by permission of the 1996 Survey of American Political Culture, James Davison Hunter and Carol Bowman, directors, University of Virginia.

attitude and the historical struggle of various groups to gain voting rights, the surprising fact is that millions of Americans choose not to vote regularly, a tendency that sets them apart from citizens of most other Western democracies.

Factors in Voter Turnout: The United States in Comparative Perspective

Voter turnout is the proportion of persons of voting age who actually vote in a given election. Since the 1960s the turnout level in presidential elections has not reached 60 percent (see Figure 7–1). In the 1996 and 2000 elections, only about half of adults cast a vote for president.

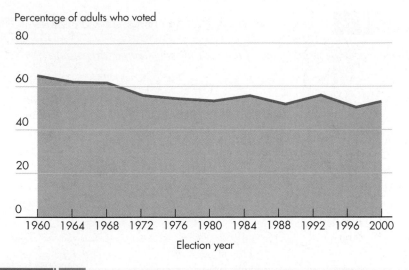

VOTER TURNOUT IN PRESIDENTIAL ELECTIONS, 1960–2000

Voter turnout has declined substantially since the 1960s.
Source: U.S. Bureau of the Census.

Turnout is even lower in the midterm congressional elections that take place between presidential elections. Midterm election turnout has not reached 50 percent since 1920, nor made it past the 40 percent mark since 1970. After one midterm election, the cartoonist Rigby showed an election clerk eagerly asking a stray cat that had wandered into a polling place, "Are you registered?"[4]

Nonvoting is far more prevalent in the United States than in nearly all other democracies (see "How the United States Compares"). In recent decades, turnout in major national elections has averaged less than 60 percent in the United States, compared with more than 90 percent in Belgium, and more than 80 percent in France, Germany, and Denmark.[5] The disparity in turnout between the United States and other nations is not as great as these official voting rates indicate. Some nations calculate turnout solely on the basis of eligible adults, whereas the United States bases its figures on all adults, including noncitizens and other ineligible groups. Nevertheless, even when such statistical disparities are corrected, turnout in U.S. elections is relatively low.

Contributing to the relatively low turnout in U.S. elections are registration requirements, ballot counting procedures, the frequency of elections, and the lack of clear-cut differences between the political parties.

How the United States Compares

Voter Turnout

The United States ranks near the bottom among the world's democracies in the percentage of eligible citizens who participate in national elections. One reason for the low voter turnout is that individual Americans are responsible for registering to vote, whereas in most other democracies, voters are automatically registered by government officials. In addition, unlike some other democracies, the United States does not encourage voting by holding elections on the weekend or imposing penalties, such as fines, on those who do not participate.

Another factor affecting the turnout rate in the United States is the absence of a major labor or socialist party, which would serve to bring lower-income citizens to the polls. In democracies where such parties exist, the turnout difference between upper- and lower-income groups is relatively small. In the United States, however, lower-income persons are much less likely to vote than higher-income persons are.

Country	Approximate Voter Turnout	Automatic Registration?	Social Democrat, Socialist, or Labor Party?	Election Day a Holiday or Weekend Day?
Belgium	90%	Yes	Yes	Yes
Germany	85%	Yes	Yes	Yes
Denmark	85%	Yes	Yes	No
Italy	80%	Yes	Yes	Yes
Austria	80%	Yes	Yes	Yes
France	80%	No	Yes	Yes
Great Britain	60%	Yes	Yes	No
Canada	60%	Yes	No	No
Japan	60%	Yes	Yes	Yes
United States	50%	No	No	No

Source: Developed from multiple sources.

Registration Requirements Before Americans are allowed to vote, they must be registered—that is, their names must appear on an official list of eligible voters. **Registration** began around 1900 as a way of preventing voters from casting more than one ballot during an election. Fraudulent voting had become a favorite tactic of political party machines in communities where the population was too large for residents to be personally known to poll watchers. However, the extra effort involved in registering placed an added burden on honest citizens. Because citizens could now vote only if they had registered beforehand, those people who forgot or otherwise failed to do so found themselves unable to participate on election day. Turnout in U.S. elections declined steadily after registration was instituted.[6]

Although other democracies also require registration, they place this responsibility on government. In most European nations, public officials have the duty to enroll citizens on registration lists. The United States—in keeping with its *individualistic* culture—is one of the few democracies in which registration is the individual's responsibility.[7] In addition, registration laws have traditionally been established by the state governments, and some states make it relatively difficult for citizens to qualify. Registration periods and locations are usually not highly publicized, and many citizens simply do not know when or where to register.[8] Eligibility can also be a problem. In most states, a citizen must establish legal residency by living in the same place for a minimum period, usually thirty days, before becoming eligible to register.

States with a tradition of lenient registration laws generally have a higher turnout than other states do. Idaho, Maine, Minnesota, New Hampshire, Wisconsin, and Wyoming, which are states that allow people to register at their polling place on election day, have high turnout rates. Those states that have erected the most barriers are in the South, where restrictive registration was originally intended to prevent black people from voting. These historical differences continue to be reflected in state voter turnout levels (see "States in the Nation").

In 1993, in an effort to increase registration levels nationwide, Congress enacted a voting registration law known as "motor voter." It requires states to permit people to register to vote when applying for a driver's license and when applying for benefits at certain state welfare offices. Registration does not occur automatically in these situations; the citizen must fill out an application form. Congressional Republicans made their support of the legislation contingent on this nonmandatory provision. They had blocked the legislation for several years, believing that the bill as written would increase the proportion of lower-income Americans on the registration rolls and thereby help the Democratic party.

★ STATES IN THE NATION

Voter Turnout in Presidential Elections

The United States has a low voter turnout relative to most other western democracies. However, the state-to-state variation is considerable. In the 2000 presidential election, for example, Minnesota ranked highest, with a 68.8 percent voting rate among its adult population, while Hawaii ranked lowest, with a 40.5 percent rate.

Q. Why does the South have lower turnout than do other regions? And why do states in the southwest have relatively low turnout rates?

A. Southern states have more poverty and a tradition of more restrictive registration laws (dating to the Jim Crow era of racial segregation). Both factors are associated with lower voting rates. States with large populations of recent immigrants, including those states in the southwest, also tend to have lower voting rates.

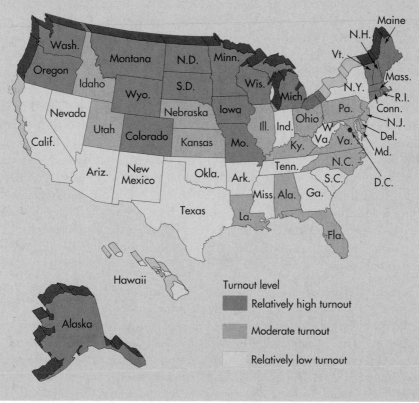

Turnout level

Relatively high turnout

Moderate turnout

Relatively low turnout

According to Federal Election Commission estimates, the motor-voter law has increased the registration rolls by roughly ten million people. (A larger number of people have been registered through the law, but many of them would have registered anyway under the old system.) Nevertheless, the overall turnout rate has not increased since the law was passed. Other factors have combined to offset the gain in voters attributable to the legislation. Clearly, the registration requirement is only one of the factors underlying America's low turnout rate.

Ballots Cast but Not Counted In the 2000 election, more than one hundred million votes were officially recorded as having been cast for president. However, more than two million other votes were cast but not counted. Some could not be read by a voting machine because the voter had not marked the ballot clearly or had placed a mark outside the designated space. Some were punch-card ballots that could not be read because the hole in the card was not punched through completely.

It has been estimated that 2 percent of all ballots cast in U.S. elections are spoiled for one reason or another. These votes rarely get attention because they do not affect an election's outcome. In the 2000 presidential election, however, they may have been decisive. George W. Bush won the presidency on the basis of a 537-vote victory in Florida, where tens of thousands of ballots went uncounted. His opponent, Al Gore, mounted a legal challenge to get the ballots counted, but it failed when the U.S. Supreme Court intervened to stop a hand recount on the grounds that the standards for determining a legal ballot were vague (see Chapter 14). The Florida vote highlighted a glaring weakness in the conduct of U.S. elections. Many communities are unable or unwilling to invest public funds in balloting systems that have a low error rate. Most of the inadequate machinery is found in minority areas. In Chicago, for example, the error rate is three times lower in white neighborhoods than in African American neighborhoods, where older and less reliable balloting methods are used. By comparison, many Western European countries have uniform national standards for balloting and, apparently, a smaller percentage of uncounted ballots than does the United States.

Frequency of Elections The United States holds more elections than any other nation. No other democracy has elections for the lower chamber of its national legislature (the equivalent of the U.S. House of Representatives) as often as every two years, and none schedules elections for chief executive as often as every four years.[9] In addition, elections of state and local officials in the United States are often scheduled separately from national races. Four-fifths of the states elect their governors in nonpresidential election years,[10]

Volunteers at a community event attempt to interest citizens in registering so that they can vote in the next election. Nearly all democracies have automatic voter registration. The United States does not, which makes voter registration efforts an important factor in election turnout.

and 60 percent of U.S. cities hold elections of municipal officials in odd-numbered years.[11]

The frequency of U.S. elections reduces turnout by increasing the effort required to participate in all of them.[12] Most European nations have less frequent elections, and the responsibility of voting is thus less burdensome. Many European nations also schedule their elections on Sundays or declare election day to be a national holiday, thus making it more convenient for working people to vote. In the United States, elections are traditionally held on Tuesdays, and most people must vote before or after work.

Party Differences A final explanation for low voter turnout in the United States has to do with voters' perception that there is not much difference between the major political parties (see Figure 7–2). More than half of Americans claim that it does not make a big difference whether the Republicans or the Democrats gain control of government.[13] This belief is not entirely unfounded. The two major American political parties do not normally differ sharply in their policies. Each party depends on citizens of all economic interests and social backgrounds for support; consequently, neither party can afford to take an extreme position that would alienate any sizable segment of the electorate. For example, both parties share a

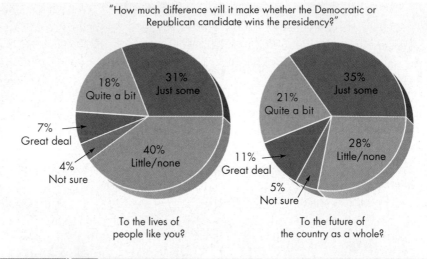

"How much difference will it make whether the Democratic or Republican candidate wins the presidency?"

To the lives of
people like you?

To the future of
the country as a whole?

FIGURE 7-2   THE PERCEIVED CONSEQUENCES OF ELECTING
REPUBLICAN OR DEMOCRATIC PRESIDENT
(2000)

Most Americans believe that their lives and the country as a whole will not be greatly affected by whether the Republican or Democratic candidate wins the presidency.
Source: Used by permission of the Shorenstein Center Poll for the Vanishing Voter Project.

commitment to the private enterprise system and to social security for the elderly (see Chapter 8).

European voters have more clearly defined choices. Nearly all European democracies have three or more significant political parties. Moreover, European parties (although less sharply today than a few decades ago) tend to divide along class lines, with one or more parties representing the working class and one or more parties representing middle- and upper-class interests. In some European countries, the parties also divide along religious and social lines. European voters thus have a greater opportunity through elections to pursue their policy interests than Americans do.[14] European parties, particularly those on the left, also tend to work more closely with other organizations, such as labor unions, in efforts to mobilize the electorate.[15]

Why Some Americans Vote and Others Do Not

Even though turnout is lower in the United States than in other democracies, some Americans do vote regularly while other Americans seldom or never vote. Among the factors that explain this difference are age, education, income, and civic attitudes.

Civic Attitudes Regular voters are characterized by a strong sense of **civic duty.** They believe that citizens are obliged to vote, regardless of the expected outcome of an election. In 1996, for example, it was clear from the polls that Bill Clinton would handily defeat Bob Dole, yet regular voters were undeterred. Although they knew their votes would not sway the election, they voted anyway in order to fulfill their duty as citizens. Civic duty is an attitude that is usually acquired as part of childhood socialization. When parents vote regularly and take an interest in politics, their children are likely to acquire the belief that voting is an obligation of citizenship.

Many citizens do not have a strong sense of civic duty, and some of them display almost no interest in politics. **Apathy** is the term that describes a general lack of interest in or concern with politics. Just as some people would not attend the Super Bowl even if it were free and being played across the street, some people would not bother to vote even if a ballot were delivered to their door. As with civic duty, a sense of apathy is often the consequence of childhood socialization. When parents disparage voting and other forms of political participation, their children are likely to hold a similar view when they reach voting age.

Alienation is the term that describes a sense of personal powerlessness that includes the notion that government does not care about the opinions of people like oneself.[16] Alienation diminishes people's interest in political participation.[17] It might be thought foolish for alienated citizens to withdraw from politics as opposed to getting more deeply involved in an effort to shake up the system. However, citizens recognize that a single vote is unlikely to make a difference, and they may choose not to cast their vote if they believe government is unresponsive to their interests.

Citizens who trust government are more likely to vote than those who do not.[18] For this reason, some analysts predicted that turnout would increase as a result of the September 11, 2001, terrorist attacks. Trust in government rose after the attacks. Nevertheless, turnout in the 2002 congressional elections was largely unchanged from the previous level. This development may owe to Americans' growing disenchantment with campaign politics. Most Americans believe, for example, that money plays too large a role in determining who gets elected and that candidates will say almost anything to get themselves elected (see Table 7–2). As long as Americans feel so negatively about campaigns, increased trust in government might not be enough to draw them to the polls in larger numbers.

Age When viewers tuned in MTV at various times in the 2000 presidential campaign, they might have thought at first that they had selected the wrong channel. Rather than a video of their favorite rock star, they saw the presidential candidates urging young people to vote.

TABLE | 7-2 OPINIONS ON ELECTION POLITICS

Americans are generally dissatisfied with election politics.

	Agree	Disagree	Don't Know
Political candidates are more concerned with fighting each other than with solving the nation's problems.	70%	26%	4%
Most political candidates will say almost anything in order to get themselves elected.	78	18	4
Political campaigns today seem more like theater or entertainment than like something to be taken seriously.	65	30	5
Interest groups and donors who give large sums of money to political campaigns have way too much influence on what candidates do once they are elected.	80	16	4

Source: National poll by The Vanishing Voter Project, Joan Shorenstein Center on the Press, Politics, and Public Policy, John F. Kennedy School of Government, Harvard University, October 20-24, 2000. Used by permission of the Director, Vanishing Voter Project.

The candidates had targeted the right audience for their get-out-the-vote message. Young adults are much less likely to vote than middle-aged citizens are. Even senior citizens, despite the infirmities of old age, have a far higher turnout rate than do voters under the age of thirty. Young people are less likely to have the political concern that can accompany such lifestyle characteristics as homeownership, a permanent career, and a family.[19] In fact, citizens under the age of thirty have the lowest turnout rate of any major demographic group.

Young voters account for much of the decline in voter turnout in recent decades. Of the eligible eighteen- to twenty-four-year-olds, about half voted in 1972 compared with less than a third in 2000. During this same period, turnout among those forty-five years of age and older declined only a few percentage points.

Education What does your college education mean? One thing it means is that you have a higher likelihood of becoming an active citizen. Persons with a college education are about 40 percent more likely to vote than are persons with a grade school education. Education generates an interest in politics,

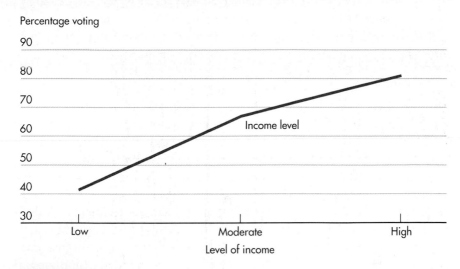

Percentage voting

FIGURE 7-3   VOTER TURNOUT AND INCOME

Lower income Americans are much less likely to vote than higher-income Americans, which is different than the situation in European democracies, where income level has only a marginal impact on turnout level.
Source: U.S. Bureau of the Census.

confidence that one can make a difference politically, and peer pressure to participate—all of which are related to the tendency to vote.[20]

Education is the single best predictor of voter turnout. This fact led analysts in the 1950s to conclude that increasing the overall level of education was the way to increase levels of turnout. Paradoxically, the overall education level of the American people has increased greatly since then, but turnout has dropped. The positive effect of increased education levels has been more than offset by people's declining political interest and party loyalties.

Economic Class Turnout is also closely related to economic status (see Figure 7–3). Americans at the bottom of the income ladder are only half as likely to vote in presidential elections as are those at the top.[21]

In European democracies, economic status does not affect turnout to such a high degree. Europeans of lower income levels are encouraged to participate by class-based organizations and traditions—strong socialist parties, politically oriented trade unions, and class-based political ideologies.[22] The United States does not have, and never has had, a major socialist or labor party.[23] Although the Democratic party by and large represents the working class and the poor, it is more attentive to the middle class, which, because of its size and voting regularity, is the key to victory in U.S.

elections. In 2000, Americans in the bottom third by income were 30 percent more likely than those in the top third to say that the election's outcome would have no appreciable effect on their lives.[24]

The Impact of the Vote

Through their votes, the people choose the representatives who will govern
in their name. But what effect does the vote have on these representatives?
Fuller answers to this question will be provided later (see Chapters 8, 11,
and 12), but it is useful to consider at least a partial response at this point.

Elections do *not* ordinarily produce a policy mandate for the winning
candidate. A mandate requires voters to consciously choose between candidates on the basis of the promises they make during the campaign. A difficulty with this interpretation of election results is that voters are not usually
well informed about candidates' policy positions. In most campaigns, fewer
than half the voters can identify the candidates' positions on major issues.[25]

Several influences combine to limit the voters' issue awareness. The candidates do not always make their positions clear, either because they fear
that taking a firm stand will lose them votes or because they do not have
specific policies in mind. Many candidates have dodged the abortion issue
in recent years by expressing personal opposition to it while at the same
time promising to uphold a woman's right to choose as long as the courts
permit it. Additionally, the news media concentrate on election strategy and
tactics rather than on the candidates' policy positions. Finally, voters can
hardly be aware of issues if they are not paying attention. Most citizens do
not follow campaigns closely and do not necessarily gain knowledge of even
highly publicized issues.[26] In 2000, only about half of adults could identify
Bush's and Gore's positions even on the candidates' top issues—tax cuts and
prescription drugs for the elderly, respectively.[27]

There are, to be sure, some voters who are highly informed on the issues
and cast their ballots on this basis. **Prospective voting** is a term used to describe this forward-looking type of voting. Prospective voting occurs when
voters know the issue stands of the candidates and choose the candidate
whose positions best match their own.

A more prevalent form of voting is **retrospective voting,** which is the
situation in which voters support the incumbent candidate or party when
they are pleased with its performance and oppose it when they are dis-
pleased. Bill Clinton's victories in 1992 and 1996 illustrate the importance
that voters attach to past governmental performance. The U.S. economy
in 1992 was in its longest recession since World War II, and the situation
soured voters on the incumbent president George Bush. Three-fourths of
the American public expressed dissatisfaction with his handling of the
economy, and their dissatisfaction translated into Bush's defeat. He lost by

a substantial margin to Clinton, who, despite people's reservations about his personal character, represented the prospect of change. According to the National Election Studies survey, about 80 percent of the voters who supported Bush in 1988 but who deserted him in 1992 believed that the economy was the nation's most important problem.

By 1996, the nation's economy had recovered. Economic growth was strong, jobs were plentiful, and consumer confidence was high. Clinton's opponent, Bob Dole, tried to persuade voters that Clinton's personal character was reason enough to deny him a second term. But voters were satisfied with Clinton's handling of the economy and returned him to office.

As in these cases, economic conditions are usually the key factor in the electorate's retrospective judgments. When voters' confidence in the in-party's handling of the economy has been high, its nominee has usually won the presidential election. Conversely, its nominee has usually lost when the voters are dissatisfied with the economy.[28]

Retrospective voting is a weaker form of public control than prospective voting, because it occurs after the fact: government has already acted, and nothing can change what has taken place. Nevertheless, retrospective voting can be an effective form of popular control over policy. The fear that they might be voted out of office because of their policies leads officials to take public opinion into account in their decisions.[29]

CONVENTIONAL FORMS OF PARTICIPATION OTHER THAN VOTING

In one sense, voting is an unrivaled form of citizen participation. Free and open elections are the defining characteristic of democratic government, so voting is regarded as the most basic duty of citizens.[30] Voting is also the only form of citizen participation engaged in by a majority of adults in every democratic country.[31]

In another sense, however, voting is a restricted form of participation. Citizens have the opportunity to vote only at a particular time and place, and only on those items listed on the ballot. Other activities, such as campaign work or community participation, offer citizens a greater opportunity to express themselves.

Campaign Activities

A citizen may engage in such campaign-related activities as working for a candidate or a party, attending election rallies, contributing money, and wearing a campaign button. The more demanding of these activities, such as doing volunteer work for a candidate or a party, require a lot more time

Voters have turned out in relatively low numbers in recent U.S. elections. Some analysts think the terrorist attacks on New York and Washington, D.C., in 2001 might reverse the trend.

than voting does. These activities are also less imbued with notions of civic duty than is voting.[32] Not surprisingly, the proportion of citizens who engage in these activities is relatively small. For example, less than one in twenty adult Americans say they worked for a party or a candidate within the past year.

Nevertheless, campaign participation is higher in the United States than in Europe. A five-country comparative study found that Americans were more likely to contribute money and time to election campaigns than citizens of Germany, Austria, the Netherlands, and Great Britain.[33] One reason Americans are more active in campaigns, even though they vote at a lower rate, is that they have more opportunities to become active.[34] The United States is a federal system with campaigns for national, state, and local offices. A citizen who wishes to participate is almost certain to find an opportunity at one level of office or another. Most of the governments of Europe are unitary in form (see Chapter 2), which means that there are fewer elective offices and thus fewer campaigns in which to participate.

Community Activities

Many Americans participate in public affairs not through campaigns and political parties but through local organizations such as parent-teacher associations, neighborhood groups, business clubs, church-affiliated groups, and hospital auxiliaries. The actual number of citizens who participate actively in a community group is difficult to estimate, but the number is

Youthful volunteers work to fix up a children's playground. Americans are more likely than citizens of other democracies to take part in voluntary community activities.

surely in the tens of millions. The United States has a tradition of local participation that goes back to colonial days. Moreover, compared with cities and towns in Europe, those in the United States have more authority over policy issues, which is an added incentive to participation. Because of increased mobility and other factors, Americans may be less tied to their local communities than in the past and therefore less involved in community action. Nevertheless, half of Americans claim that they volunteer time to groups and community causes, compared with 20 percent or less in most European countries. When it comes to donating money to a group, Americans also have an edge on Europeans.

In a widely publicized book entitled *Bowling Alone*, Harvard's Robert Putnam claims that America is undergoing a decline in its **social capital** (the sum of the face-to-face civic interactions among citizens in a society).[35] Putnam attributes the decline to television and other factors that are drawing people inward and away from participation in civic and political groups. Not all scholars accept Putnam's interpretation of trends in civic involvement (some indicators point toward a rise in certain types of participation),[36] but no one challenges his assumption about the importance of civic participation. It brings people together, gives them an understanding of other points of view, and builds skills that make them more effective as citizens.

Lobbying Group Activities

Increasingly, Americans are also involved in public affairs through membership in lobbying groups. This form of participation seldom consists of more than the contribution of annual dues that enable a national organization to pressure government officials or otherwise attempt to influence public policy. Examples of these groups are the National Organization for Women, Common Cause, the Christian Moral Government Fund, the American Civil Liberties Union, and the National Conservative Political Action Committee. Chapter 9 discusses lobbying groups more fully.

Following Politics in the Media

Campaign work and community participation are active forms of political involvement. There is also a passive form: following politics in the news. It can safely be said that no act of political participation takes up more of people's time than does news consumption. The news is important to citizen participation: if people are to participate effectively and intelligently in politics, they must be aware of what is taking place in their communities, in their nation, and in the world.

News about politics is within easy reach of nearly all Americans. More than 95 percent of U.S. homes have a television set, and about 50 percent of Americans receive a daily newspaper. However, the regular audience for news is much smaller than these figures suggest. The mere fact of having a television or getting a daily paper does not mean that a person pays close attention to the news. About a third of Americans regularly read a newspaper's political sections or watch a television newscast. Another third follows the news intermittently, catching an occasional newscast or scanning a paper's news sections somewhat often. The final third pays no appreciable attention to the news either on television or in a newspaper.

Television is the medium of choice for most Americans (see Figure 7–4). Citizens who say television is their main source of news substantially outnumber those who rely mainly on a newspaper. Radio and magazines account for even smaller proportions. The figures are somewhat misleading in that people are asked where they get "most" of their news, not how much news they actually get. Some of the people who say they get "most" of their news from television do not watch the news a lot. They do not read a newspaper at all, so that even a little exposure to television news makes it their leading news source.

The news audience has been shrinking. Newspapers have lost audience to television newscasts, which in turn have lost audience to entertainment broadcasts. Before cable television was widely available, many television viewers had no alternative to a newscast during the dinner hour. With cable, viewers always have a variety of choices, and many viewers, as many as 40 percent by some estimates, choose to ignore the news unless a sensational event occurs.

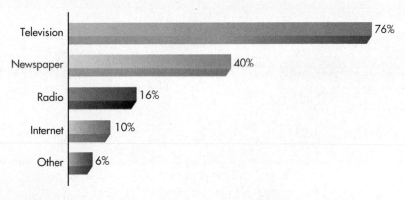

FIGURE 7-4 AMERICANS' MAJOR NEWS SOURCES

When most Americans are asked where they get most of their news, they mention television most often.
Source: Pew Research Center for the People and the Press, February 2001. Totals to more than 100% due to multiple responses.

The audience for major televised political events has also fallen off. Although they are still a major attraction, even the October presidential debates get less attention than before. The four Kennedy-Nixon debates in 1960 each attracted roughly 60 percent of all households with television sets. When debates resumed with Carter and Ford in 1976, viewers again flocked to their TVs, as they also did for the single Reagan-Carter face-off in 1980. Since then, however, debate audiences have declined. The 2000 debates drew on average about 30 percent of households with television sets, which was half the level of the 1960 debates.[37]

Young Americans in particular are ignoring politics. Today's young adults are less politically interested and informed than any cohort of young people on record. They watch a lot of television but do not pay much attention to television news. Many of them apparently cannot be bothered with news in any form.[38]

Virtual Participation

The prospect of an entire generation of politically inattentive citizens is a disturbing one to many observers. Yet there is a glimmer of hope—the Internet. It is used more heavily by younger people and is packed with political information and participation possibilities.

Nevertheless, it is unclear whether the Internet will actually serve as an entry into the world of politics for large numbers of citizens. Most people use it primarily for entertainment, school assignments, shopping,

A student works on the computer in her room. The Internet has vast but as yet unrealized potential as an instrument of mass political participation.

and personal and business communication. On the other hand, there are thousands of chat rooms in which politics and public affairs are discussed. In addition, nearly every interest group and political campaign has its own website.

According to a recent survey, 10 percent of Americans get most of their news of public affairs from the Internet. The full impact of this new medium on citizen participation, however, is not likely to be known until its technological capacity is fully developed and today's computer-literate generation reaches adulthood.

Unconventional Activism: Social Movements and Protest Politics

Before mass elections became prevalent, the public often resorted to protest as a way of expressing dissatisfaction with government. Tax and food riots were commonplace. The advent of elections allowed the masses to communicate their views in an institutionalized and less disruptive way. Elections are double-edged, however. Although they are commonly viewed as a means by which the people control the government, *elections are also a means by which the government controls the people.*[39] Because representatives are freely chosen by the people, they can claim that their policies reflect the popular will. It is difficult for people to argue they are justified in rioting against government policy that has been enacted by representatives they themselves placed in office.

Voting in elections is also limited to the options listed on the ballot. America's voters effectively have only two choices: the Democratic or Republican party. No other party has much chance of victory, and citizens who are dissatisfied with both parties have no realistic way to exercise power through the ballot.

Social movements are an alternative form of influence. **Social movements,** or **political movements** as they are sometimes called, refer to broad efforts to achieve change by citizens who feel that government is acting improperly.[40] These efforts are sometimes channeled through traditional forms of participation, such as political lobbying, but citizens can also take to the streets in protest against government. A dramatic example occurred in late 1999 when a host of activists—trade unionists, environmentalists, and others—engaged police in what became known as the "Battle in Seattle." The World Trade Organization (WTO) was meeting in Seattle to discuss global economic issues, and the activists were protesting the weak environmental and labor provisions that had marked earlier trade agreements. In 2003, as the Bush administration was preparing for war with Iraq, major protest demonstrations were held in several U.S. cities, including Washington and San Francisco.[41]

Social movements do not always succeed, but they sometimes enable otherwise politically weak persons to force government to respond to their desires. For example, the timing and scope of the landmark 1964 Civil Rights Act and 1965 Voting Rights Act can be explained only as a response by Congress to the pressure created by the civil rights movement. Another effective social movement in the 1960s was the farm workers' movement, whose protests led to improved working and living conditions for migrant workers.

Protest politics in America goes back to the Boston Tea Party and earlier, but it has taken on new forms in recent years. Protest was traditionally a desperate act that began, often spontaneously, when a group had lost hope that it could succeed through more conventional methods. Today, however, protest is usually a calculated act—a means of bringing added attention and impetus to a cause.[42] These tactical protests often involve a great deal of planning, including, in some instances, the busing of thousands of people to Washington for a rally staged for television. Civil rights, environmental, agricultural, and pro- and antiabortion groups are among those that have staged tactical protests in Washington within the past few years.

Police and protesters clashed in 1999 at the World Trade Organization (WTO) meeting in Seattle. Although protest movements are an American tradition, they rarely receive strong public support. Moreover, unlike other forms of participation, younger adults are more likely than older ones to get involved in protest activities.

Citizens who participate in social movements tend to be younger than nonparticipants, which is a reversal of the situation with voting. [43] Participants in social movements also tend to emphasize nonmaterial values more than do nonparticipants. Social movements often develop in response to real or perceived injustices and thus attract idealists. [44]

Protest movements seldom gain broad public support. In May 1970, unarmed students at Kent State University and Jackson State University were shot to death by national guardsmen while protesting the Vietnam War. Opinion polls indicated a majority of Americans blamed the students and not the guardsmen for the tragedy. Most citizens apparently believe the proper way to express disagreement over public policy is through voting and not through protesting.

PARTICIPATION AND THE POTENTIAL FOR INFLUENCE

Although Americans claim that political participation is important, most of them do not practice what they preach. Most citizens take little interest in participation except to vote, and a significant minority cannot even be persuaded that voting is worth their while. However, Americans are not completely apathetic: many millions of them give their time, effort, and money to political causes, and roughly a hundred million go to the polls in presidential elections.

Yet sustained political activism does not engage a large proportion of the public. Moreover, many of those who do participate are drawn to politics by a habitual sense of civic duty rather than by an intense concern with current issues. The emphasis that American culture places on *individualism* tends to discourage a sense of urgency about political participation. "In the United States, the country of individualism *par excellence*," William Watts and Lloyd Free write, "there is a sharp distinction in people's minds between their own personal lives and national life."[45] Although wars and severe recessions can lead the American public to turn to government, most people under most conditions expect to solve their own problems. This is not to say that Americans have a disdain for collective action. In their communities particularly, citizens frequently take part in collective efforts to support a local hospital, improve the neighborhood, and the like. But most Americans tend not to see their material well-being as greatly dependent on involvement in politics of the traditional kind.[46]

This tendency contributes to a class bias in American politics. For one thing, it helps maintain a relatively sharp distinction between that which is properly public (political) and that which is properly private (economic). The private component, which includes most economic relationships, is largely beyond the realm of political debate and action. Americans, said political scientist Robert Lane, prefer to see benefits distributed primarily through the economic marketplace rather than through the policies of government.[47] For example, access to medical care in the United States, unlike in Europe where government-provided health care is available to all, is to some degree based on a person's ability to pay for it. There are nearly forty million Americans who do not have access to adequate health care because they cannot afford health insurance.

Lower-income Americans are a relatively weak force in the nation's politics. Citizens of higher economic status are more likely to have the financial resources and communication skills that encourage participation and make it personally rewarding. Among citizens who are most active in politics, three times as many have incomes in the top third as in the bottom third.[48] This difference is much greater than in other Western democracies, where poorer citizens are assisted through automatic voter registration and by the presence of class-based political organizations. By comparison, the poor in the United States must arrange their own registration and must choose between two political parties that are attuned primarily to middle-class interests.

The low participation rate of lower-income Americans reduces their influence on public policy. Studies indicate that representatives are more

LIBERTY, EQUALITY, & SELF-GOVERNMENT
What's Your Opinion?

Voting: A Right?

On election day, officials unfailingly urge Americans "to get out and vote." Some of these officials are not to be taken seriously. On the whole, U.S. elections are conducted fairly and openly with the support of tens of thousands of public-minded officials and volunteer poll watchers. Lurking in the shadows, however, are official actions that serve to depress the vote. Registration closing dates, early poll closings, and flawed voting machines are obstacles to fuller participation, just as in the past such actions as whites-only primaries and poll taxes were obstacles.

More so than in other Western democracies, voting in the United States has been subject to political manipulation. America's electoral history is replete with examples of public policies designed to deny or suppress the vote. Voting has been treated as a privilege rather than an inalienable right, something to be earned (or, in some cases, arbitrarily withheld) rather than something so intrinsic to citizenship that government makes every reasonable effort to promote its exercise.

What, in your opinion, explains the historical tendency? Do you think Americans' claim to self-government has been diminished by the tendency?

responsive to the demands of participants than to those of nonparticipants,[49] although it must be kept in mind that participants do not always promote only their own interests. It would be a mistake, however, to conclude that large numbers of people regularly support policies that would mainly benefit others. For example, a turning point in the defeat of President Bill Clinton's health care reform proposal came when middle-class Americans decided that it might increase the cost and reduce the quality of their own medical care. According to Time/CNN polls, support for the Clinton plan dropped from 57 percent to 37 percent between September 1993 and July 1994. Although this decline reflected a loss of support among all groups, the drop was particularly severe among middle-income and higher-income groups. A majority of lower-income individuals still favored the plan. They would have been the principal beneficiaries of the Clinton plan, which called for universal health care insurance. On the other hand, most middle-income people and virtually all higher-income people already had health insurance, either through an individual policy or an employment-related group policy.

In sum, the pattern of individual political participation in the United States parallels the distribution of influence that prevails in the private sector. Those who have the most power through participation in the marketplace also have the most power through participation in the political arena. However, the issue of individual participation is only one piece of the larger puzzle of who rules America and for what purposes. Subsequent chapters will provide additional pieces.

SUMMARY

Political participation is involvement in activities designed to influence public policy and leadership. A main issue of democratic government is the question of who participates in politics and how fully they participate.

Voting is the most widespread form of active political participation among Americans. Yet voter turnout is significantly lower in the United States than in other democratic nations. The requirement that Americans must personally register in order to establish their eligibility to vote is one reason for lower turnout among Americans; other democracies place the burden of registration on government officials rather than on the individual citizen. The fact that the United States holds frequent elections also discourages some citizens from voting regularly. Finally, the major American political parties, unlike many of those in Europe, do not clearly represent the interests of opposing economic classes; thus the policy stakes in American elections are less high. Some Americans do not vote because they think that policy will not change greatly regardless of which party gains power.

Prospective voting is one way the people can exert influence on policy through their participation. It is the most demanding approach to voting: voters must develop their own policy preferences and then educate themselves about the candidates' positions. Most voters are not well-enough informed about the issues to respond in this way. Retrospective voting demands less from voters: they need only decide whether the government has been performing well in terms of the goals and values they hold. The evidence suggests that the electorate is, in fact, reasonably sensitive to past governmental performance, particularly in relation to economic prosperity.

Only a minority of citizens engage in the more demanding forms of political activity, such as work on community affairs or on behalf of a candidate during a political campaign. The proportion of Americans who engage in these more demanding forms of activity exceeds the proportion of Europeans who do so. Nevertheless, only about one in every four Americans will take an active part in a political organization at some point in their lives.

Most political activists are individuals of higher income and education; they have the skills and material resources to participate effectively and tend to take greater interest in politics. More than in any other Western democracy, political participation in the United States is related to economic status.

Social movements are broad efforts to achieve change by citizens who feel that government is not properly responsive to their interests. These efforts sometimes take place outside established channels; demonstrations, picket lines, and marches are common means of protest. Protesters are younger and more idealistic on average than are other citizens, but they are a very small proportion of the population. In addition, protest activities do not have much public support, despite the country's tradition of free expression.

Overall, Americans are only moderately involved in politics. They are concerned with political affairs but mostly immersed in their private pursuits, a reflection in part of this culture's emphasis on individualism. The lower level of participation among low-income citizens has particular significance in that it works to reduce their influence on public policy and leadership.

KEY TERMS

alienation

apathy

civic duty

political participation

prospective voting

registration

retrospective voting

social capital

social (political) movements

suffrage

voter turnout

SUGGESTED READINGS

Burns, Nancy, Kay Lehman Schlozman, and Sidney Verba. *The Private Roots of Public Action: Gender, Equality, and Public Action*. Cambridge, Mass.: Harvard University Press, 2001. An analysis of gender differences in political participation and their roots in patterns of everyday life.

Leighley, Jan. *Strength in Numbers: The Political Mobilization of Racial and Ethnic Minorities*. Princeton, N.J.: Princeton University Press, 2001. A study of the factors that motivate blacks and Hispanics to participate in politics.

Neuman, W. Russell, Marion R. Just, and Ann N. Crigler. *Common Knowledge: News and the Construction of Meaning*. Chicago: University of Chicago Press, 1992. An assessment of how citizens interpret and use the news they receive.

Patterson, Thomas E. *The Vanishing Voter*. New York: Knopf, 2002. A study of the decline in electoral participation and what might be done to reverse the trend.

Putnam, Robert. *Bowling Alone*. New York: Simon and Schuster, 2000. A provocative analysis of the trend in civic participation.

Rimmerman, Craig A. *The New Citizenship: Unconventional Politics, Activism, and Service*. Boulder, Colo.: Westview Press, 1997. An assessment of citizenship in the modern age.

Schudson, Michael. *The Good Citizen: A History of American Civic Life*. New York: Free Press, 1998. A thoughtful history of civic participation in America.

Verba, Sidney, Kay Schlozman, and Henry Brady. *Voice and Equality*. Cambridge, Mass.: Harvard University Press, 1995. A careful study of political attitudes and participation.

LIST OF WEBSITES

http://www.rockthevote.org/ Rock the Vote is an organization dedicated to helping young people realize and utilize their power to affect the civic and political life of their communities.

http://www.umich.edu/~nes/ The University of Michigan's National Election Studies (NES) site provides survey data on voting, public opinion, and political participation.

http://www.vanishingvoter.org/ Harvard University's election study site provides data and analysis of public involvement in the 2000 presidential campaign.

http://www.vote-smart.org/ Project Vote Smart includes information on Republican and Democratic candidates and officials; it also has the latest in election news.

POLITICS IN THEORY AND PRACTICE

Thinking: Why does economic class—differences in people's incomes—make such a large difference in political participation levels? What are the policy consequences of this difference?

Acting: If you are not currently registered to vote, consider doing so. You can obtain a registration form from the election board or clerk in your community of residence. (Check the web or the telephone book to get the number to call.) If you are already registered, consider participating in a registration or voting drive on your campus. Although students typically register and vote at relatively low rates, they will often participate if encouraged to do so.

The New York Times   reading 7

Election Day Curtain Call

by Maura J. Casey

*By European standards, the voting rate
in U.S. elections is low. And if the
question is whether turnout could go
even lower, the answer is yes. Since the
1960s, voting rates have fallen
dramatically in elections of all types and
at all levels. In a November 3, 2002,
article,* New York Times *reporter
Maura Casey describes the situation in
one state—Connecticut. She singles out
young voters as a factor in the decline.*
ON ELECTION DAY 2000, galvanized by
Senator Joseph Lieberman's bid for vice
president, more than three-quarters of
registered voters in [Connecticut] cast
ballots, the third-highest voter participation
rate in the country.

But don't count on that happening
Tuesday. Not only do elections for governor
traditionally lure far fewer voters than
presidential election years, but the highest
turnout of registered voters two years ago
masked a longer and more disturbing trend.
The percentage of registered voters who
vote has been declining in the state for
more than 40 years. Voter participation two
years ago may have set a record nationally,
but it was still lower than the percentage of
state voters who turned out in any
presidential election during the 1950's and
1960's, and far lower than the staggering
93.5 percent of the electorate who cast
ballots in the presidential race of 1960. The
percentage of registered voters casting
ballots for governor peaked decades ago.

And the last election for governor was
greeted by a yawn from voters from one
end of the state to another: just over
56 percent of registered voters showed up,
the lowest voter participation rate recorded
in a governor's race since 1950.

So will even fewer voters turn out on
Tuesday?

A bad sign, some registrars of voters
said, was the record-breaking low turnout
that occurred in the Republican primary
held in the First Congressional District on
Sept. 10, when only 3 percent of the voters
showed up to choose between the
candidates Phil Steele and Miriam J.
Masullo. In Manchester, only 216 people
out of the 6,474 registered Republicans cast
ballots, making the primary, which cost
$12,000 to hold, expensive indeed;
taxpayers paid $56 for each vote cast, said
Barbara King, the Republican registrar.

Yet observers said the election wasn't
well-publicized and, since the district hasn't
elected a Republican since 1956, the low
turnout there isn't necessarily a predictor of
how many will go to the polls statewide on
Tuesday.

Secretary of the State Susan Bysiewicz
is optimistic.

"I think there is going to be a strong
turnout," she said.

It helps, she said, that there's a race in
the Second Congressional District between
former State Rep. Joe Courtney and United
States Rep. Robert Simmons that has

attracted widespread interest. In addition, the newly redistricted Fifth Congressional District has become an old-fashioned slugfest between two incumbent members of Congress, Nancy L. Johnson and James H. Maloney.

Another promising sign is that more races for General Assembly this year are contested. Two years ago about one-third of statehouse races had just one candidate with no opposition; this year fewer races, about one-quarter, have candidates running unopposed. This is important to voter turnout, Ms. Bysiewicz said.

"The General Assembly candidates are the foot soldiers who influence the number of people voting," she said. "They are making the phone calls and going door to door."

Fewer races were unopposed years ago when political parties were stronger in Connecticut, said Clyde McKee, a political science professor at Trinity College.

Party strength was aided by the fact that each voting booth included a party lever that allowed voters to cast ballots, with the flick of one switch, for all the candidates of one of the two major parties, guaranteeing a strong vote. The party lever was outlawed in the mid-1980's, and the power of parties declined soon after, Mr. McKee said.

Public opinion has also hastened party decline, he said.

"You have the media, beating up on the candidates, the public dumping on politicians, and politicians shooting themselves in the foot," Mr. McKee said. "It's weakened parties' abilities to recruit candidates."

The chairman of the Republican party, Chris DePino, said that when the party lever was outlawed, voters more frequently cast ballots for individuals, not for the parties they represented.

"It's a blessing and a curse," he said. "It's a blessing because that's the way it should be in a democracy. It's a curse because only if you are an incumbent or a formidable challenger do you stand a good chance of winning. And formidable challengers are few and far between."

A general lack of people who feel civic minded may contribute to a lack of voter turnout, many said, along with pressures on time.

Yet there's at least one very simple reason a lower percentage of people have been voting than did residents in the past, said Joe Loy, an elections officer in the secretary of the state's office. The 26th Amendment, ratified and added to the Constitution in 1971, expanded the number of potential voters by lowering the voting age from 21 to 18. Yet 18-to-21-year-olds are precisely the age group less likely to cast ballots, Mr. Loy said.

"It's a good thing to register them, but they don't all vote," he said. "You increase the number of voters registered, you may decrease the percentage turnout."

Ms. Bysiewicz agreed. "Nationally, 20 percent of 20-year-olds vote, and 80 percent of 80-year-olds vote," she said.

A Quinnipiac University poll conducted three years ago showed that younger voters are less likely to cast ballots. In the 1999 survey of 1,465 Connecticut residents, 34 percent of people 18 to 34 said they always vote, but 83 percent of those 54 and older said they always vote.

In addition, just 31 percent of 18-to-34-year-olds agreed with the statement, "Politics has an impact on their lives," but 54 percent of the older generation agreed.

Yet the fact that the young don't vote as much as their elders may help create a Catch-22. The more older citizens vote, the more politics appears geared toward the concerns of the elderly to the exclusion of the needs of the younger generation. That's the way it seemed to several students discussing the issue in a class last week at Three Rivers Community College in Norwich.

"I really don't know much about politics and I really don't care," said James Conner,

18. "Politicians don't seem to care about teenagers and college kids."

Audrey Blackburn, 25, said she hadn't voted in several years.

"Those under 30 don't seem to matter to politicians," she said. "All they talk about are issues like Social Security, which isn't relevant to me because I don't think it will be around when I'm 65. And it seems every time you turn around, a politician is doing something wrong. We're almost desensitized to it."

But others were more optimistic. "I vote because otherwise I have no right to complain," said Katherine Reissner, 21, who said she registered to vote while still in high school. "You can't just walk by and not get involved."

The reasons why younger voters feel less connected are debatable, but to Mr. McKee, it gets back to the problem of too few candidates. "Twenty-five percent of our elections are noncompetitive. If you are a bright college student, faced with a no-contest election, why vote?" he said.

Representative Diana Urban, a Republican of Stonington, a college professor and legislator completing her first term, said the young mistrust the political system.

"They think the whole system is bogus," she said. "The need for campaign finance reform has a lot to do with it."

She said college students waited all day to speak at legislative hearings on a proposed system to publicly finance campaigns that came up in the General Assembly and it ultimately failed.

"The reason I voted for the campaign finance reform bill was for the kids, to let them know that we are not bought and paid for," Representative Urban said. "That's how you galvanize them," she said. "You tell them the process is for real."

What's Your Opinion?

What might be done to encourage young adults to vote at a higher rate?

CHAPTER

8

POLITICAL PARTIES, CANDIDATES, AND CAMPAIGNS: DEFINING THE VOTER'S CHOICE

❝Political parties created democracy and . . . modern democracy is unthinkable save in terms of the parties.❞

E. E. SCHATTSCHNEIDER[1]

On opposite coasts and two weeks apart, the two parties faced off, each offering its own plan for a better America.

The Republicans met first, in Philadelphia. Their 2000 platform included a steep cut in personal income taxes, a limit on abortions, parental choice of schools, business deregulation, a partial privatization of the social security system, and a delegation of authority to state and local governments. The Republicans chose Texas governor George W. Bush, the son of former President George Bush, as their presidential nominee. Wyoming's Dick Cheney was selected as his running mate.

The Democrats met in Los Angeles, the same city where thirty-two years earlier Robert F. Kennedy had been assassinated at the end of a bitter Democratic nominating campaign that had nearly torn the party apart over the issue of the Vietnam War. This time, however, the Democrats were a united party. The Democrats chose Vice President Al Gore, a native of

231

Tennessee, as their presidential nominee. His running mate was Senator Joseph Lieberman of Connecticut, the first Jewish American to be named to the national ticket of a major U.S. party. The Democrats' lengthy platform included tax benefits for low- and middle-income families, restrictions on handguns, protection of social security, reproductive freedom for women, and pledges to strengthen the nation's environmental, educational, and health systems.

The political parties, as their nominees and platforms illustrate, are in the business of offering the voting public a choice. The party is the one institution that develops broad policy and leadership choices and then presents them to the voting public to accept or reject. This competitive process is what allows citizens, through elections, to influence how they will be governed. "It is the competition of political organizations that provides the people with an opportunity to make a choice," the political scientist E. E. Schattschneider once wrote. "Without this opportunity popular sovereignty amounts to nothing."[2]

A **political party** is an ongoing coalition of interests joined together in an effort to get its candidates for public office elected under a common label.[3] As such, a party is actually three election parties in one. There is, first, the *party in the electorate*, which consists of the voters who identify with it and support its candidates. This component of the party was discussed in Chapter 6 and is also addressed briefly in this chapter. The main subjects of this chapter, however, are the other two components: the *party as organization*, staffed and led by party activists, and the *party as candidates*, which consists of those individuals who run for public office under its label.[4]

A theme of this chapter is that party organizations are alive and well in America but are also secondary to candidates as the driving force in contemporary campaigns. **Party-centered politics** is an important dimension of U.S. elections, but much of what goes on in the campaign is better described by the term **candidate-centered politics**. For the most part, candidates for the presidency and Congress raise their own funds, form their own campaign organizations, and choose for themselves the issues on which they will run.

This chapter explains this development and also explores the history of U.S. parties, the patterns of party politics, and the conduct of candidate-centered campaigns. The following points are emphasized in this chapter:

★ *Political competition in the United States has centered on two parties, a pattern that is explained by the nature of America's electoral system, political institutions, and political culture.* Minor parties exist in the United States but have been unable to compete successfully for governing power.

★ *To win an electoral majority, candidates of the two major parties must appeal to a diverse set of interests; this necessity normally leads them to advocate moderate and somewhat overlapping policies.* Only during periods of stress are America's parties likely to present the electorate with starkly different choices.

★ *U.S. party organizations are decentralized and fragmented.* The national organization is a loose collection of state organizations, which in turn are loose associations of autonomous local organizations. This feature of U.S. parties can be traced to federalism and the nation's diversity, which have made it difficult for the parties to act as instruments of national power.

★ *The ability of America's party organizations to control nominations and election to office is weak, which in turn enhances the candidates' role.*

★ *Candidate-centered campaigns are based on the media and utilize the skills of professional consultants.* Money, strategy, and televised advertising are key components of today's presidential and congressional campaigns.

PARTY COMPETITION AND MAJORITY RULE: THE HISTORY OF U.S. PARTIES

Through their numbers, citizens have the potential for great influence, but that potential cannot be realized unless they have the capacity to act together. Parties give them that capacity. When Americans go to the polls, they have a choice between the Republican and Democratic parties. This **party competition** narrows their options to two and in the process enables people with different opinions to render a common judgment. In electing a party, the voters choose its candidates, its philosophy, and its policies over those of the opposing party.

The history of democratic government is virtually synonymous with the history of parties. When the countries of eastern Europe gained their freedom more than a decade ago, one of their first steps toward democracy was the legalization of parties. When the United States was founded two centuries ago, the formation of parties was also a first step toward the building of its democracy. The reason is simple: it is the competition among parties that gives popular majorities a chance to determine how they will be governed.[5]

The First Parties

America's early leaders mistrusted parties. George Washington in his farewell address warned the nation of the "baneful effects" of parties, and

James Madison likened parties to special interests. However, Madison's initial misgivings about parties gradually gave way to a grudging admiration; he recognized that they provided a way for like-minded people to work together to achieve their mutual goals.

America's parties originated in the rivalry within George Washington's administration between Thomas Jefferson, a supporter of states' rights and small landholders, and Alexander Hamilton, who promoted a strong national government and commercial interests (see Figure 8–1). When Hamilton's ideas prevailed in Congress, Jefferson and his followers formed a political party, the Republicans. By adopting this label, which was associated with popular government, the Jeffersonians sought to portray themselves as the rightful heirs to the American Revolution's legacy of self-government and political equality.

Hamilton responded by organizing his supporters into a formal party—the Federalists—and in the process created America's first competitive party system. The Federalists took their name from the faction that had supported ratification of the Constitution, thereby implying that they were the Constitution's true defenders. However, the Federalists' preoccupation with commercial and wealthy interests fueled Jefferson's claim that the Federalists were bent on establishing a government for the rich and wellborn. After

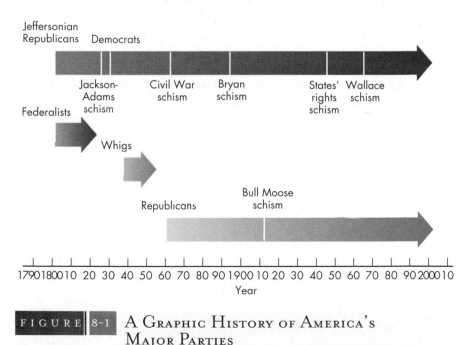

FIGURE 8-1   A GRAPHIC HISTORY OF AMERICA'S MAJOR PARTIES

The U.S. party system has been remarkable for its continuity. Competition between two major parties has been a persistent feature of the system.

Adams's defeat by Jefferson in the election of 1800, the Federalists and their philosophy never again held sway.

During the so-called Era of Good Feeling, when James Monroe ran un-opposed in 1820 for a second presidential term, it appeared as if the politi-cal system might operate without parties. Yet by the end of Monroe's second term, policy differences had split the Republicans. The dominant faction, led by Andrew Jackson, retained Jefferson's commitment to the in-terests of ordinary people. This faction called itself Democratic Republi-cans, later shortened to Democrats. Thus, the Republican party of Jefferson is the forerunner of today's Democratic party rather than today's Republi-can party.

Andrew Jackson and Grassroots Parties

For all its shortcomings, competition between parties is the only system that can regularly mobilize collective influence on behalf of the many who are individually powerless against those few who have extraordinary wealth and prestige.[6]

This realization led Jackson during the 1820s to develop a **grassroots party.** Whereas Jefferson's party had been well organized only at the lead-ership level, Jackson sought a party that was built from the bottom up. Jack-son's Democratic party consisted of committees and clubs at the local, state, and national levels, with membership open to all eligible voters. These or-ganizational activities, along with more liberal suffrage laws, contributed to a nearly fourfold rise in voter turnout during the 1830s.[7] At the peak of Jacksonian democracy, Alexis de Tocqueville wrote, "The People reign in the American political world as the Deity does in the universe."[8] Although

Andrew Jackson
(1767-1845)

Andrew Jackson rose to national fame when, as a major general, he defeated the British at the Battle of New Orleans during the War of 1812. A Tennessee native, he won the presi-dency in 1828 after having lost in 1824 despite having received the most popular votes. He in-stituted political changes including grassroots parties that were designed to strengthen popular rule. The term *Jack-sonian Democracy* became synonymous with his belief that ordinary people were capable of governing themselves.

Tocqueville exaggerated the people's true power, he caught the spirit of popular government that was behind the development of grassroots parties under Andrew Jackson.

In this period, a new opposition party, the Whigs, emerged to challenge the Democrats. The Whigs were a catch-all party. Its followers were united not by a coherent philosophy of their own but by their opposition for one reason or another to the policies of the Jacksonian Democrats.

Competition between the Whigs and the Democrats was relatively short-lived. During the 1850s the slavery issue began to tear both parties apart. The Whig party began to disappear, and a northern-based new party, the Republicans, arose as the main challenger to the Democrats. In 1860, the Democratic party's northern faction nominated for president Stephen A. Douglas, who held that the question of whether a new territory permitted slavery was for a majority of its voters to decide, while the southern faction nominated John C. Breckinridge, who called for the legalization of slavery in all territories. The Democratic vote in the fall election was split sharply along regional lines between these two candidates—with the result that the Republican nominee, Abraham Lincoln, was able to win the presidency with only 40 per cent of the popular vote. However, the U.S. party system collapsed in 1860, for the only time in the nation's history.[9] The issue of slavery was too explosive to be settled peaceably through competition between political parties.

Republicans Versus Democrats: Realignments and the Enduring Party System

After the Civil War, the nation settled into the pattern of competition between the Republican and Democratic parties that has prevailed ever since. The durability of these two parties is due not to their ideological consistency but to their remarkable ability to adapt during periods of crisis. By abandoning at these crucial times their old ways of doing things, the Republican and Democratic parties have repeatedly remade themselves—with new bases of support, new policies, and new public philosophies.

These periods of great political change are known as *realignments*. A **party realignment** involves four basic elements:

1. The disruption of the existing political order because of the emergence of one or more unusually powerful and divisive issues
2. An election contest in which the voters shift their support strongly in favor of one party
3. A major change in policy through the action of the stronger party
4. An enduring change in the party coalitions, which works to the lasting advantage of the dominant party

Realignments are rare. They do not occur simply because one party wrests control of government from the other. They involve deep and lasting changes in the party system that affect not just the most recent election but later ones as well. By this standard, there have been three clear-cut realignments since the 1850s.

The Civil War realignment, for example, brought about a thorough change in the party system. The Republicans replaced the Democrats as the nation's majority party. The Republicans were the dominant party in the larger and more populous North; the Democratic party was left with a stronghold in what became known as "the Solid South." During the next three decades, the Republicans held the presidency except for Grover Cleveland's two terms of office and had a majority in Congress for all but four of those years.

The 1896 election resulted in a further realignment of the Republican-Democratic party system. Three years earlier, an economic panic following a bank collapse had resulted in a severe depression. The Democrat Cleveland was president when the crash happened, and people blamed him and his party. When the Democrats then nominated William Jennings Bryan in 1896 on a cheap-credit platform (unlimited coinage of silver) that frightened many voters into believing that inflation would destroy their savings and the economy, the Republicans made additional gains in the Northeast and Midwest, solidifying their position as the nation's dominant party. During the four decades between the 1890s realignment and the next one in the 1930s, the Republicans held the presidency except for Woodrow Wilson's two terms and had a majority in Congress for all but six years.

The Great Depression of the 1930s triggered a thoroughgoing realignment of the American party system. The Republican Herbert Hoover was president when the stock market crashed in 1929, and many Americans blamed Hoover, his party, and its business allies for the economic catastrophe that followed. The Democrats became the country's majority party, and their political and policy agenda called for an expanded social and economic role for the national government. Franklin D. Roosevelt's presidency was characterized by unprecedented policy initiatives in the areas of business regulation and social welfare (see Chapter 3). His election in 1932 began a thirty-six-year period of Democratic presidencies that was interrupted only by Dwight D. Eisenhower's two terms in the 1950s. In this period, the Democrats also dominated Congress, losing control only in 1947–1948 and 1953–1954.

The reason realignments have such a substantial effect on future elections is that they affect voters' *party identification* (see Chapter 6). Young voters in particular are likely to identify with the newly ascendant party, and

The new order begins: Franklin D. Roosevelt rides to his inauguration with outgoing president Herbert Hoover after the realigning election of 1932.

they tend to maintain that identity, giving the party a solid base of support for years to come. In the 1930s, for example, the Democratic party's image as the party of the common people, jobs, and social security was vastly more appealing to young voters than the Republican party's image as the party of business and wealthy interests. First-time voters in the 1930s came to identify by a two-to-one margin with the Democratic party, which established it as the nation's majority party and enabled it to dominate national politics for the next three decades.[10]

A New Realignment or a Dealignment?

A party realignment inevitably loses strength over time, because the issues that gave rise to it cannot remain dominant indefinitely. By the late 1960s, when the Democratic party was divided over the Vietnam War and civil rights, it was apparent that the era of New Deal politics was over.[11]

A realignment affecting part of the nation was soon evident. The South, which had been solidly Democratic at all levels, was becoming staunchly Republican in presidential elections and more competitive at the state and local levels. As the Democratic party became increasingly identified as the party of civil rights and social change, it had less and less appeal to conservative white southerners.[12]

Yet Republican inroads were otherwise less dramatic or temporary. After 1968, the Republicans held the presidency for more years than the Democrats, and in 1994, they won a landslide midterm election victory that gave

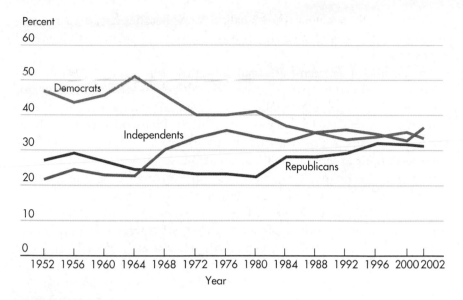

FIGURE 8-2 PARTISAN IDENTIFICATION

Party loyalties weakened in the late 1960s, and the proportion of Independents increased.

Source: Compiled from multiple sources.

the GOP control of both houses of Congress for the first time in four elections. But at no time has the GOP been able to dominate presidential and congressional elections time after time the way that Democrats did during the height of the New Deal era. Nor has the GOP succeeded in gaining a decisive edge in terms of party identification. The proportion of Americans who call themselves Democrats has usually equaled or exceeded that of those who say they are Republicans. A lasting realignment favorable to the Republican party could be taking place, but if so, it is unlike past ones—slower, more fitful, and less encompassing. And if such a realignment is taking place, it will be evident only after Republicans enjoy a period of sustained dominance.

An alternative explanation for what has been happening in American elections is put forth by advocates of the dealignment thesis. They argue that the U.S. electoral system, rather than undergoing a realignment favorable to one party, has been in the process of **dealignment,** a partial but enduring weakening of voters' partisan loyalties.[13] In recent decades, the number of voters who describe themselves as Independents has increased substantially (Figure 8–2). Advocates of the dealignment thesis also point to an increase in **split-ticket voting,** in which the voter selects candidates of both parties for different offices when casting a ballot. A few decades ago, the large majority of voters engaged in **straight-ticket voting,** supporting candidates of one party only.

The decline of partisanship began during the 1960s and 1970s when divisive issues arose and disrupted existing loyalties. The civil rights issue, for example, was unsettling not only to many southern Democrats but also to some white northern Democrats, particularly blue-collar workers from newer immigrant groups who felt that African Americans were making progress at their expense.[14] Vietnam, abortion, social welfare, and a host of other issues also divided followers of each party. Americans' trust in their elected representatives declined, as did their faith in parties.

Party loyalties have been weaker ever since, and advocates of the dealignment thesis see no likelihood of a dramatic reversal. For one thing, voters today are better educated and more likely to believe they can judge the candidates for themselves on the basis of what they hear through the media rather than on the basis of party labels. Moreover, people today are protected by programs like social security and Medicare from the economic hardships that in the past fueled party realignments. Finally, Americans today want higher incomes and lower taxes, but they also want a cleaner environment, services for the elderly, and better schools. As a result, they are less likely to be drawn fully to either the Republican argument for a less active government or the Democratic argument for a more active one.[15]

If advocates of the dealignment thesis are correct, neither party will enjoy the prolonged success of the type the Democratic party had from the 1930s on. The predicted scenario is one of shifting support, with the Republicans prevailing at some times and the Democrats doing so at other times.

ELECTORAL AND PARTY SYSTEMS

The United States traditionally has had a **two-party system:** Federalists versus Jeffersonian Republicans, Whigs versus Democrats, and Republicans versus Democrats. These have not been the only American parties, but they have been the only ones with a realistic chance of acquiring political control. A two-party system, however, is the exception rather than the rule (see "How the United States Compares"). Most democracies have a **multiparty system,** in which three or more parties have the capacity to gain control of government, separately or in coalition. Why the difference? Why three or more major parties in most democracies but only two in the United States?

The Single-Member-District System of Election

A chief reason for the persistence of America's two-party system is the fact that the nation chooses its officials through plurality voting in **single-member districts**.[16] Each constituency elects a single candidate to a particular office, such as U.S. senator or representative; only the party that gets the most votes (a plurality) in a district wins the office. This system discourages minor parties. Assume, for example, that a minor party received exactly 20 percent of the vote in each of the nation's 435 congressional races. Even though one in five voters nationwide backed the minor party, it would not win any seats in Congress because none of its candidates had placed first in any of the 435 single-member-district races. The winning candidate in each case would be the major-party candidate who received the larger proportion of the remaining 80 percent of the vote.

By comparison, most European democracies use some form of **proportional representation,** in which seats in the legislature are allocated according to a party's share of the popular vote. This type of electoral system provides smaller parties an incentive to organize and compete for power. In the 2002 German elections, the Green party gained nearly 9 percent of the national vote and thereby won 55 seats in the 603-seat Bundestag, the German parliament. If the Greens had been competing under American electoral rules, they would not have won any seats and would have had no chance of exercising a share of legislative power. In Germany, the Greens even gained a share of executive power. The Social Democratic party won the most legislative seats in the 2002 German election but failed to gain an outright majority. The Social Democrats formed a coalition with the Green party, which received cabinet posts in return for its backing of a Social Democrat–led government.

Policies and Coalitions in the Two-Party System

The overriding goal of a major American party is to gain power by getting its candidates elected to office. Because there are only two major parties, however, the Republicans or Democrats can win consistently only by attracting majority support. In Europe's multiparty systems, a party can hope for a share of power if it has the firm backing of a minority faction. Not so in the United States. If either party confines its support to a narrow segment of society, it forfeits its chance of gaining control of government.

Seeking the Center, Usually American parties, Clinton Rossiter said, are "creatures of compromise."[17] The two parties typically try to develop stands that have broad appeal, or at least will not alienate significant blocs of voters. Any time a party makes a pronounced shift toward either

How the United States Compares

Party Systems

Electoral competition in the United States centers on the Republican and Democratic parties. By comparison, most democracies have a multi-party system, in which three or more parties receive substantial support from voters. The difference is significant. In a two-party system, the parties tend to have overlapping coalitions and programs, because each party must appeal to the middle-of-the-road voters who provide the margin of victory. In multiparty systems, particularly those with four or more strong parties, the parties tend to separate themselves, as each tries to secure the enduring loyalty of voters who have a particular viewpoint.

Whether a country has a two-party or a multiparty system depends on several factors, but particularly the nature of its electoral system. The United States has a single-member plurality district system that is biased against smaller parties; even if they have some support in a great many races, they win nothing unless one of their candidates places first in an electoral district. By comparison, in proportional representation systems, each party gets legislative seats in proportion to its share of the total vote. All the countries in the chart that have four or more parties also have a proportional representation system of election.

Number of Competitive Parties		
Two	*Three*	*Four or More*
United States	Canada (at times)	Belgium
	Great Britain	Denmark
		France
		Germany
		Italy
		Netherlands
		Sweden

extreme, the political center is left open for the opposing party. Barry Goldwater, the Republican presidential nominee in 1964, proposed the elimination of mandatory social security and said he might consider the tactical use of small nuclear weapons in such wars as the Vietnam conflict—extreme positions that cost him many votes. Eight years later, the Democrat nominee, George McGovern, took positions on Vietnam and income security that alarmed many voters and, like Goldwater, got buried in one of the greatest landslides in presidential history.

It is impossible to understand the dynamics of the U.S. party system without a recognition that the true balance of power in American elections rests with the moderate voters in the center rather than those who hold more extreme positions. When congressional Republicans mistook their 1994 election victory as a mandate to trim assistance programs for the elderly, the poor, and children, they alienated many of the moderate voters who had contributed to their 1994 victory. These voters wanted "less" government but not a government that neglected society's most vulnerable citizens. After weak showings in the 1996 and 1998 elections, congressional Republicans shifted course. They unseated Speaker Newt Gingrich, replacing him with a more pragmatic conservative, Dennis Hastert. "We still need to prove that we can be conservative without being mean," was how one Republican member of Congress described the change in strategy.[18] The change in Republican outlook was also apparent in GOP presidential candidate George W. Bush's 2000 campaign slogan: "compassionate conservatism." These adjustments reflect a basic truth about U.S. politics: party ideology is acceptable as long as it is tinged with moderation.

Nonetheless, the Republican and Democratic parties do offer somewhat different alternatives and, at times, a clear choice. When Roosevelt was elected president in 1932, Johnson in 1964, and Reagan in 1980, the parties were relatively far apart in their priorities and programs. Roosevelt's New Deal, for example, was an extreme alternative within the American political tradition and caused a decisive split along party lines. A lesson of these periods is that the center of the American political spectrum can be moved. Candidates risk a crushing defeat by straying too far from established ideas during normal times, but they may do so with some chance of victory during turbulent times.

Another lesson of such periods is that public opinion is the critical element in partisan change. Critics who say that the Democratic and Republican parties fail to offer the voters a real choice ignore the parties' tendency to tailor their appeals to majority opinion.[19] When the public's mood shifts, the parties usually also shift. The Republicans' Contract with America in

1994, for example, was a response to public discontent with the federal government's taxing and spending policies. When the Republicans won in 1994, many Democratic officeholders also embraced cutbacks in federal power, thus shifting the entire party system toward the right. Perhaps GOP leaders misjudged just how far right the public was willing to go, but they nonetheless redirected the nation's politics. President Clinton, a Democrat, summed up the change in his 1996 State of the Union address when he said: "The era of big government is over."

Party Coalitions The groups and interests that support a party are collectively referred to as the **party coalition.** In multiparty systems, each party is supported by a relatively narrow range of interests. European parties tend to divide along class lines, with the center and right parties drawing most of their votes from the middle and upper classes and the left parties drawing theirs from the working class. By comparison, America's two-party system requires each party to accommodate a wide range of interests in order to gain the voting plurality necessary to win elections.[20] The Republican and Democratic coalitions are therefore very broad. Each includes a substantial proportion of voters of nearly every ethnic, religious, regional, and economic grouping. There are only a few sizable groups that are tightly aligned with a party. African Americans are the clearest example; they vote about 85 percent Democratic in national elections.

Although the Republican and Democratic coalitions overlap, they are hardly identical (see Figure 8–3). Each party likes to appear to be all things to all Americans, but in fact each builds its coalition through a process of both unification and division. If a party did not stand for something—if it never took sides—it would lose all support.

Since the 1930s, the major policy differences between the Republicans and the Democrats have involved the national government's role in solving social and economic problems. Each party has supported government action to promote economic security and social equality, but the Democrats have consistently favored a greater degree of governmental involvement. Virtually every major assistance program for the poor, elderly, and low-wage workers has been initiated by the Democrats. To some extent, the Democratic coalition draws support disproportionately from society's underdogs—blacks, union members, the poor, city dwellers, Hispanics, Jews, and other "minorities."[21] For a long period, the Democratic party was also the clear choice of the nation's elderly as a result of its support for old-age assistance programs and because the basic political loyalties of the elderly were acquired during the New Deal era, a period favorable to the Democrats. Recently, however, elderly voters have split their vote nearly evenly between the parties.

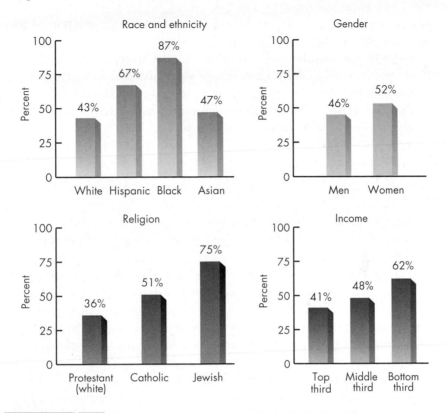

FIGURE 8-3   THE VOTE OF SELECTED DEMOGRAPHIC
GROUPS IN RECENT PRESIDENTIAL ELECTIONS

Although the Democratic and Republican coalitions overlap substantially, there are
important differences, as illustrated by the Democratic party's percentage of the two-
party vote among some major demographic groups in recent elections.
Source: Compiled by author from various sources.

The Democratic party's biggest gains recently have been with women,
who traditionally had a voting pattern very similar to that of men. In recent
elections, however, there has been a gender gap (see Chapter 6). Women
have voted disproportionately for the Democratic party, apparently as a result of its positions on issues such as abortion rights, education spending,
employment policies, and gun control.

The Republican coalition consists mainly of white middle-class Protestants. The GOP has historically been the party of tax cuts and business incentives. The GOP has also been more supportive of traditional values, as
reflected, for example, in its support of school prayer and its opposition to
abortion. Not surprisingly, the GOP has generally been the stronger party in
the suburbs and other areas, such as the West and Midwest, where traditional

values and a desire for lower taxes and less government regulation of economic activity are more pronounced.

The GOP has made big gains in recent decades among white fundamentalist Christians. They have been drawn to the GOP by its positions on abortion, school prayer, affirmative action, and other social issues. In recent presidential elections, the Republican nominee has garnered the votes of roughly 70 percent of fundamentalist Christians.

Minor Parties

Although the U.S. electoral system discourages the formation of third parties, the nation has always had minor parties—more than a thousand during the nation's history.[22] Most of them have been short-lived, and only a few have had a lasting impact. Only one minor party, the Republican party, has ever achieved majority status.

Minor parties in the United States have formed largely to promote policies that their followers believe are not being adequately represented by either of the two major parties. A major party is always somewhat captive to its past, which is the source of many of its ideas and most of its followers. When conditions change, major parties are often slow to respond, and a minor party can capitalize on the neglected issues.

When a minor party gains a large following, as has happened a few times in history, the major parties are forced to pay attention to the problems that are driving people to look outside the two-party system for leadership. In such a situation, one or both major parties typically awaken to the new issues, at which time the minor party usually begins to lose support. Nevertheless, the minor party will have served the purpose of making the major parties more responsive to the public's concerns.

Single-Issue Parties Some minor parties form around a single issue of overriding interest to their supporters, such as the present-day Right-to-Life party, which was formed to oppose the legalization of abortion. Some single-issue parties have seen their policy goals enacted into law. The Prohibition party contributed to the ratification in 1919 of the Eighteenth Amendment, which prohibited the manufacture, sale, and transportation of alcoholic beverages (but which was repealed in 1933). Single-issue parties usually disband when their issue is favorably resolved or fades in importance.[23]

Factional Parties Although the Republican and Democratic parties are normally adept at managing internal divisions, there have been times when internal conflict has led a faction to break away and form its own party.

The most successful of these factional parties at the polls was Theodore Roosevelt's Bull Moose party. In 1908 Roosevelt, after having served eight years as president, declined to seek a third term and handpicked William Howard Taft for the Republican nomination. When Taft as president showed neither Roosevelt's enthusiasm for a strong presidency nor his commitment to the goals of the Progressive movement, Roosevelt unsuccessfully challenged Taft for the 1912 Republican nomination. Roosevelt led a Progressive walkout to form the Bull Moose party (a reference to Roosevelt's claim that he was "as strong as a bull moose"). Roosevelt won 27 percent of the presidential vote to Taft's 25 percent, but the split within Republican ranks enabled the Democratic nominee, Woodrow Wilson, to win the presidency.

The States' Rights party in 1948 and George Wallace's American Independent party in 1968 are other examples of strong factional parties. These parties were formed by southern Democrats angered by northern Democrats' support of racial desegregation.

Deep divisions within a party give rise to factionalism and can lead eventually to a change in its coalition. The conflict over civil rights that began within the Democratic party during the Truman years continued for the next quarter-century, leading many southern whites to shift their party loyalty to the GOP.

Ideological Parties Other minor parties are characterized by their ideological commitment to a broad and radical philosophical position, such as redistribution of economic resources. Modern-day ideological parties include the Citizens party, the Socialist Workers party, and the Libertarian party, each of which operates on the fringe of American politics.

One of the strongest ideological parties in the nation's history was the Populist party. Its candidate in the 1892 presidential election, James B. Weaver, gained 8.5 percent of the national vote and won twenty-two electoral votes in six western states. The party began as an agrarian protest movement in response to an economic depression and the anger of small farmers over low commodity prices, tight credit, and the high rates charged by railroad monopolies to transport farm goods. The Populists' ideological platform called for government ownership of the railroads, a graduated income tax, low tariffs on imports, and elimination of the gold standard.[24]

The strongest minor party today is the Green party, an ideological party that holds liberal positions on the environment, labor, taxation, social welfare, and other issues. Its 2000 presidential nominee, consumer-rights advocate Ralph Nader, received 3 percent of the national vote. According to polls, Nader's support came primarily from voters who otherwise would have supported Democrat Al Gore, which tipped the election to the more

Republican presidential nominee George W. Bush reaches out to shake a voter's hand during the 2000 campaign. Bush sought to reverse Republican losses in recent elections by positioning the GOP closer to the political center.

conservative Republican nominee, George W. Bush. This outcome stirred a debate within Green party ranks. Some argued that the party should concentrate on local and state races, concluding that its participation in the 2000 presidential campaign served to elect a candidate whose policy goals were opposite its own. Others said that the Green party should continue to contest the presidential election so as to force the Democratic party to move toward more liberal policy positions.

Before the 2000 presidential election, the Reform party was America's strongest minor party. It originated in the 1992 independent candidacy of Ross Perot, who gained 19 percent of the presidential vote (second only to Roosevelt's 1912 percentage among candidates who were not major-party nominees). Perot's campaign was based on middle-class discontent with the major parties, was conducted almost entirely on television, and was funded by more than $60 million of his own money. Perot ran again in 1996 but as the nominee of the Reform party, which he had founded. This time, Perot accepted public funds for his campaign, which limited his spending to roughly $30 million (see Chapter 12). He ran a media-based campaign that attracted 8 percent of the vote, which qualified the Reform party for public funding again in 2000. When Perot chose not to run in 2000, however, the Reform party nomination became a contest between its party regulars and supporters of conservative Pat Buchanan. Buchanan's nomination splintered the party, and he received less than 1 percent of the presidential vote.

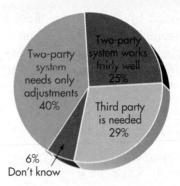

FIGURE 8-4   AMERICANS' OPINIONS ABOUT THE NEED FOR A STRONG THIRD PARTY

Most Americans say the two-party system works well or needs only some adjustments, but some believe that a strong third party is needed if the party system is to work effectively.

Source: Vanishing Voter Project National Survey, Joan Shorenstein Center on the Press, Politics, and Public Policy, Harvard University, 2000.

It appears doubtful that the Reform party will recover from its 2000 debacle, which included the defection of its most prominent officeholder, Jesse Ventura, a former professional wrestler who was elected governor of Minnesota in 1998.

Are Conditions Ripe for a Strong Third Party? The Perot and Nader candidacies are the first substantial third-party presidential candidacies in a quarter-century. Do they indicate that a strong third party will soon emerge in American politics?

The long history of the American party system would discourage almost anyone who is hoping that a strong third party will surface and remain strong for more than an election or two. As we have seen, the U.S. electoral system frustrates smaller parties by denying them anything but a symbolic victory in national politics. In addition, most Americans identify with either the Republican or the Democratic party, and the large majority of them regularly support their party's nominee. Finally, there is no powerful issue on the horizon that could serve as a rallying point for a strong third-party movement. Without such an issue, third parties, even if they do well in a single election (as Perot did in 1992), lack enduring appeal.

Nevertheless, Americans are increasingly dissatisfied with the way the two major parties are operating. According to a 2000 Harvard survey, about 30 percent of Americans believe that a third party is needed, even if they would not necessarily vote for its presidential candidate (see Figure 8–4).

Americans are disgruntled by the partisan bickering that they think increasingly defines the relationship between Republican and Democratic officeholders. They also believe that money has come to play too large a role in Republican and Democratic politics and that candidates' campaign promises are too often broken once they take office.

PARTY ORGANIZATIONS

The Democratic and Republican parties have organizational units at the national, state, and local levels. The main purpose of these **party organizations** is the contesting of elections.

A century ago, party organizations enjoyed almost complete control of nominations and elections. The party organizations still perform all the activities they formerly engaged in. They recruit candidates, raise money, develop policy positions, and canvass for votes. But they do not control these activities as completely as they once did.[25] For the most part, these activities are now directed by the candidates themselves.[26]

The Weakening of Party Organizations

Nomination refers to the selection of the individual who will run as the party's candidate in the general election. Until the early twentieth century, nominations were entirely the responsibility of party organizations. To be nominated, an individual had to be loyal to the party organization, a requirement that included a willingness to share with it the spoils of office: government jobs and contracts. The situation allowed party organizations to acquire campaign workers and funds, but also enabled unscrupulous party leaders to extort money from those seeking political favors. Reform-minded Progressives argued that the power to nominate should rest with ordinary voters rather than with the party leaders (see Chapter 2).

The result was the introduction of the **primary election** (or **direct primary**) as a method of choosing nominees. In place of party-designated nominees, the primary system placed nomination in the hands of voters (see Chapters 2 and 12).

Primary elections take several forms. Most states conduct closed primaries, in which participation is limited to voters registered or declared at the polls as members of the party whose primary is being held. Other states use open primaries, a form that allows independents and voters of either party to vote in a party's primary, although voters are prohibited by law from participating in both parties' primaries simultaneously. A few states have a third form of primary, known as the blanket primary. These states provide a single primary ballot listing both the Republican and

Democratic candidates by office. Each voter can cast only one vote per office, but can select a candidate of either party. Louisiana has a variation on this form in which all candidates are listed on the ballot but are not identified by party.

In most states, the winner of a primary election is the candidate who receives the largest number of votes, even if not a majority. In some border and southern states, however, there is a provision for a runoff primary if no candidate receives a majority of the vote (or, in North Carolina, 40 percent of the vote) in the regular primary. Slightly more than half the states have a sore-loser law that prevents a candidate who loses a primary from running as an independent or third-party candidate in the general election.

Primaries are the severest impediment imaginable to the strength of the party organizations. If primaries did not exist, candidates would have to work through party organizations in order to gain nomination, and they could be denied renomination if disloyal to the party's goals. Because of primaries, however, candidates have the option of seeking office on their own, and once elected (with or without the party's help), they can build an independent electoral base that effectively places them beyond the party's direct control.

Party organizations also lost influence over elections because of a decline in patronage. When a party won control of government a century ago, it also gained control of public jobs, which were doled out to loyal party workers. However, as government jobs in the early twentieth century shifted from patronage to the merit system (see Chapter 13), the party organizations lost control of many of these positions. Today, because of the expanded size of government, thousands of patronage jobs still exist. These government employees help staff the party organizations (along with volunteers), but most of them are more indebted to an individual politician than to a party organization. The people who work for members of Congress, for example, are all patronage employees, but they owe their jobs and their loyalty to their senator or representative, not their party.

In the process of taking control of nominations, candidates have also acquired control of most campaign money. At the turn of the last century, when party machines were at their peak, most campaign funds passed through the hands of party leaders. Today, most of the money spent on congressional and presidential campaigns goes to the candidates without first passing through the parties.

In Europe, where there are no primary elections, the situation is very different. Parties control their nominations, and because of this, they also control campaign money and workers. A party's candidates are expected to campaign on the national platform and, if elected as a governing majority, to support its planks, which are formulated in conjunction with organizational leaders. A candidate who repudiates the party's platform is likely to be denied renomination in the next election.

The Structure and Role of Party Organizations

Although the influence of party organizations has declined, parties are not about to die out. Political leaders and activists need an ongoing organization through which they can work together, and the party serves that purpose. Moreover, certain activities, such as voter registration drives and get-out-the-vote efforts on election day, affect all of a party's candidates and are therefore more efficiently conducted through the party organization. Indeed, parties have staged a comeback of sorts.[27] National and state party organizations in particular have developed the capacity to assist candidates with fund-raising, polling, research, and media production, which are essential ingredients of a successful modern campaign.

Structurally, U.S. parties are loose associations of national, state, and local organizations (see Figure 8–5). The national party organizations cannot

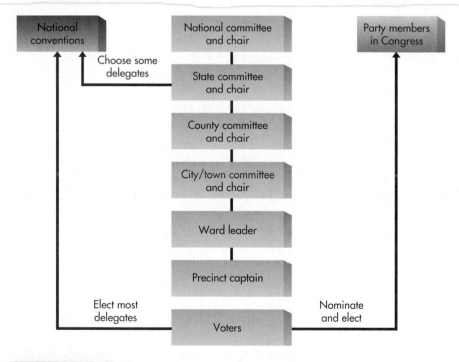

FIGURE 8-5 ORGANIZATION OF THE POLITICAL PARTY

U.S. parties today are loosely structured alliances of national, state, and local organizations.

dictate the decisions of the state organizations, which in turn do not control the activities of local organizations. However, there is communication between the levels because they all have a common interest in strengthening the party's position.[28]

Local Party Organizations In a sense, U.S. parties are organized from the bottom up, not the top down. There are about five hundred thousand elective offices in the United States, of which fewer than five hundred are contested statewide and only two—the presidency and vice presidency—are contested nationally. All the rest are local offices; not surprisingly, at least 95 percent of party activists work within local organizations.

It is difficult to generalize about local parties because they vary greatly in their structure and activities. Today only a few local parties, including the Democratic organizations in Albany, Philadelphia, and Chicago, bear even a faint resemblance to the fabled old-time party machines that, in return for jobs and even welfare services, were able to control the vote on election day. Nevertheless, local parties tend to be strongest in urban areas and in the Northeast and Midwest, where parties traditionally have been more highly organized. In any case, local parties tend to specialize in elections that coincide with local electoral boundaries. Campaigns for mayor, city council, state legislature, county offices, and the like motivate most local parties to a greater degree than do congressional, statewide, and national contests.

In most urban areas, the party organizations do not have enough workers to staff even a majority of local precincts (voting districts) on an ongoing basis. However, they do become more active during campaigns, when they open campaign headquarters, conduct registration drives, send mailings or deliver leaflets to voters, and help get out the vote. These activities are not trivial. Most local campaigns are not well funded, and the party's backing of a candidate can make the difference.

In most suburbs and towns, the party's role is less substantial. The parties exist organizationally but typically have little money and few workers; hence they cannot operate effectively as electoral organizations. The individual candidates must carry nearly the entire burden.

State Party Organizations At the state level, each party is headed by a central committee made up of members of local party organizations and local and state officeholders. These state central committees do not meet regularly, and they provide only general policy guidance for the state organizations. Day-to-day operations and policy are directed by a chairperson, who is a full-time, paid employee of the state party. The central committee appoints the chairperson, but it often accepts the individual

recommended by the party's leading politician, usually the governor or a
U.S. senator.

In recent decades the state parties have expanded their budgets and staffs
considerably and, therefore, have been able to play a more active electoral
role.[29] In contrast, forty years ago about half of the state party organizations
had no permanent staff at all. The increase in state party staff is largely due
to improvements in communication technology, such as computer-assisted
direct mail, which have made it easier for political organizations of all
kinds, parties included, to raise funds. Having acquired the ability to pay for
permanent staffs, state parties have used them to expand their activities,
which range from polling to issues research to campaign management.

State party organizations concentrate on statewide races, including those
for governor and U.S. senator,[30] and also focus on races for the state legislature. They play a smaller role in campaigns for national or local offices,
and in most states, they do not endorse candidates in statewide primary
contests.

National Party Organizations The national party organizations are
structured much like those at the state level: they have a national committee, a national party chairperson, and a support staff. The national
headquarters for the Republican and Democratic parties are located in
Washington, D.C. Although in theory the national parties are run by
their committees, neither the Democratic National Committee (DNC)
nor the Republican National Committee (RNC) has great power. The

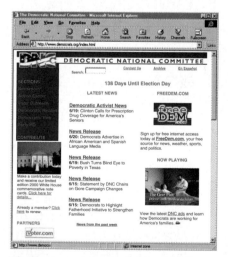

The home pages of the websites of the Democratic National Committee (DNC) and the
Republican National Committee (RNC).

RNC (with more than 150 members) and the DNC (with more than 300 members) are too cumbersome to act as deliberative bodies. They meet only periodically, and their power is largely confined to setting organizational policy, such as determining the site of the party's presidential nominating convention and the rules governing the selection of convention delegates. They have no power to decide nominations or to determine candidates' policy positions.

The national party's day-to-day operations are directed by a national chairperson chosen by the national committee, although the committee defers to the president's choice when the party controls the White House. The national chairperson is supported by a permanent staff that concentrates on providing assistance in presidential and congressional campaigns.

This focus began in the 1970s when Republican leaders decided that a revamped national party organization could play a larger contributing role in campaigns. The RNC developed campaign-management "colleges" and "seminars" for candidates and their staffs, compiled massive amounts of computer-based electoral data, and sent field representatives to assist state and local party leaders in modernizing their operations. The range of services the RNC provides is impressive. For example, the RNC tapes C-SPAN's televised coverage of congressional debate and can instantly retrieve the statement of any speaker on any issue. Republican challengers use this material to create attack ads directed at Democratic incumbents, while Republican incumbents use it to show themselves speaking out on issues of concern to their constituents. The Republican model has also filtered down to the state Republican party committees, which, in varying degrees, provide the types of media, data research, and educational services that the national committee offers. In every recent election, Republicans have raised and spent substantially more money than the Democrats have (see Figure 8–6), reflecting the greater affluence of the GOP's constituents.

The DNC in the early 1980s followed the Republicans' example, but its later start and less affluent followers have kept the Democrats behind. Modern campaigns, as David Adamany notes, are based on "cash," and Democrats are relatively cash-poor.[31]

The Parties and Money The parties' major role in campaigns is the raising and spending of money. The RNC and the DNC are major sources of campaign funds, as are the party campaign committees in the House and the Senate: the Democratic Congressional Campaign Committee (DCCC), the National Republican Congressional Committee (NRCC), the Democratic Senatorial Campaign Committee (DSCC), and the National Republican Senatorial Committee (NRSC).

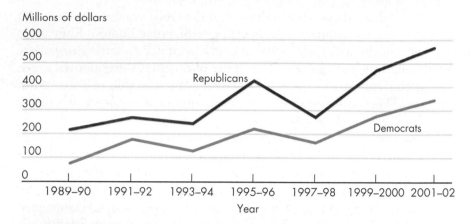

FIGURE 8-6 NATIONAL PARTY FUND-RAISING, 1989-2002

FIGURE 8-6 **NATIONAL PARTY FUND-RAISING, 1989-2002**
Over the years, the Republican party has raised significantly more money than the
Democratic party has. The figures include fund-raising by the DNC, RNC, DCCC,
NRCC, DSCC, and NRSC. Soft-money (nonfederal) fund-raising is not included.
Source: Federal Elections Commission, 2003.

These committees have more of a **service relationship** than a power relationship with their party's candidates. The party offers help to virtually
any of its candidates who have a chance of victory. Without the ability to
control the nominating process, the party has little choice but to embrace a
strong candidate who runs under its banner. If the candidate wins, the party
at least has denied the office to the opposing party. Of course, the party will
acquire some additional loyalty from officeholders as a result of the contributions it makes to their campaigns. But since the party is more or less willing to support any candidate whatever his or her policy positions, its money
does not give it substantial control over how party members conduct themselves after they take office.

A party can legally give $10,000 directly to a House candidate and
$37,500 to a Senate candidate. This funding, along with the money a can-
didate receives from individual contributors ($2,000 is the maximum per
contributor) and interest groups ($5,000 is the maximum per group), is
termed **hard money,** since it goes directly to the candidate and can be spent
as he or she chooses.

Limits on party contributions were established when the campaign finance
laws were reformed in the 1970s in response to the Watergate scandal. However, a loophole in the laws was exposed when a court ruling gave the parties
a nearly unlimited opportunity to raise and spend campaign funds provided
the funds were not channeled directly to a party's candidates. Although the

law limited how much an individual could give directly to a candidate for federal office, it did not restrict individual contributions to a political party. Thus, whereas a wealthy contributor could legally give a candidate only a limited amount, that same contributor could give an unlimited amount to the candidate's party. These contributions were **soft money** in the sense that a party could not hand it over directly to a candidate. But the party could use these contributions to support party activities such as voter registration efforts, get-out-the-vote drives, and party-centered televised ads that could indirectly benefit its candidates. The party could also funnel soft money to state and local party organizations and, by concentrating it on organizations in areas with close races, could influence the outcome of those races. In some cases, the line between the use of hard and soft money was hard to distinguish. In 1996, for example, the Democratic Party ran a $100 million ad campaign that did not directly urge voters to support Clinton but did include pictures of him and references to his accomplishments as president.

In his surprisingly strong bid for the 2000 Republican presidential nomination, John McCain proposed a ban on soft money, which contributed to heightened interest within Congress in closing the loophole. Revelations that the bankrupt Enron Corporation had given soft money contributions as part of its strategy to influence national energy policy strengthened the drive to end the practice. In the previous decade, Enron had contributed $4.4 million to Republican candidates and committees and $1.5 million to Democratic candidates and committees. Prodded by these revelations, Congress in 2002 placed restrictions on soft money contributions, but few believe that the legislation will solve the problem of money in politics once and for all. Every effort at campaign finance reform has encountered pitfalls, usually in the form of a loophole of one kind or another. In the case of the soft money ban, which applies only to the national parties, some analysts predict that the money will now flow into the coffers of the state parties. Just as water always runs downhill, money always seems to find its way into election politics.

THE CANDIDATE-CENTERED CAMPAIGN

Although competition between the Republican and Democratic parties provides the backdrop to today's campaigns, the campaigns themselves are largely controlled by the candidates, particularly in congressional, statewide, and presidential races. Each candidate has a personal organization, created especially for the campaign and disbanded once it is over.

Today's candidates tend to be self-starters. Some candidates still rise through the ranks of the party or are drafted because no other qualified persons are willing to run. But most candidates seek high office because they aspire to careers in politics. They are entrepreneurs who play what the political consultant Joe Napolitan called "the election game."[32] The game begins with money, lots of it.

Seeking Funds: The Money Chase

Campaigns for high office are expensive, and the costs keep rising. In 1980, about $250 million was spent on all Senate and House campaigns combined. The figure had jumped to $425 million by 1990 and topped $1 billion ($1,000 million) in 2000.

Because of the high cost of campaigns, candidates are forced to spend much of their time raising funds, which come primarily from individual contributors, interest groups (through PACs, discussed in Chapter 9), and political parties. The **money chase** is relentless.[33] It has been estimated that a U.S. senator must raise $10,000 a week on average throughout the entire six-year term in order to raise the $3 million or so that it takes to run a competitive Senate campaign in most states. A Senate campaign in a large state can cost several times that amount. In 2000, Representative Rick Lazio and First Lady Hillary Clinton raised nearly $70 million for the New York Senate race. House campaigns are less costly, but expenditures of $1 million or more are commonplace.[34] As for presidential elections, even the nominating race is expensive. It was thought that a candidate needs at least $20 million to have a realistic chance of gaining nomination, but even that figure is now too low. In 2000, Texas governor George W. Bush raised more than $75 million for his nominating campaign. (In presidential races, but not congressional ones, candidates are eligible to receive federal funds, a topic discussed in Chapter 12).

As might be expected, incumbents have a distinct advantage in fund-raising. They have contributor lists from past campaigns and have acquired the public visibility and political clout that donors like. In recent House and Senate races, incumbents have outspent their challengers by more than two to one.[35]

Creating Organization: Hired Guns

The "old politics" emphasized party rallies and door-to-door canvassing, which required organizations built around campaign volunteers. The "new politics" is based on the mass media and requires a much different kind of organizational structure. The key operatives are campaign consultants, pollsters, media producers, and fund-raising specialists. They are **hired guns** who charge hefty fees for their services. The "new king-makers" is the way the writer David Chagall characterized these pros.[36]

★ | STATES IN THE NATION

Public Funding of State Elections

About half the states have public funding of election campaigns. Some of them give the money to political parties, which allocate it to candidates or spend it on party activities, such as get-out-the-vote efforts. Other states give funds directly to candidates, although this funding is typically limited to candidates for designated offices, such as governor.

Q. What might explain the fact that there is no clear-cut regional pattern to the public funding of state elections?

A: Public funding of elections is relatively new, so additional states may adopt it in the next decade or two, at which time a regional tendency could emerge. (If your state does not have public funding, do you think it is likely to adopt it anytime soon? Why?)

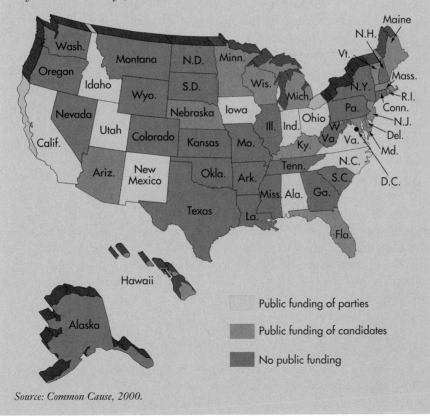

Public funding of parties

Public funding of candidates

No public funding

Source: Common Cause, 2000.

Some of the hired guns are specialists in campaign management. Inexperienced candidates often think that campaigns are simple to run and entrust the job to an amateur, who is often a relative or friend. They soon discover that their campaign is headed nowhere. At this point, if they have the money, they hire a seasoned professional. Over the years, some of these operatives, like James Carville, Joe Napolitan, Ed Rollins, Dick Morris, and Roger Ailes, have developed almost legendary reputations.

Fund-raising specialists are also part of the new politics. Direct-mail operators have developed contributor lists for every state and nearly every type of candidacy, and they flood the mail with computer-generated letters. There are also numerous specialty mailing lists, such as EMILY's List (early money is like yeast, "it makes the dough rise"). EMILY's List was started in the 1980s to provide seed money for liberal women candidates. Effective fund-raisers also know how to tap into the networks of large contributors and interest groups who give to election campaigns (see Chapter 9).

Polling is another ingredient of the modern campaign. Although candidates make use of the public polls conducted by Gallup, the news media, and other organizations, they also hire their own pollsters.[37] They also rely on focus groups, which are small groups of voters assembled to talk at length about the issues and candidates and, in some instances, to evaluate proposed themes and materials, such as televised political ads. Polls and focus groups enable candidates to identify messages that are likely to resonate with the voters. At one point in the 2000 presidential race, for example, George W. Bush shifted from the issue of taxes to issues of education and health care after polls indicated these issues were having a larger impact on undecided voters.

Media consultants are another staple of the modern campaign. These experts are adept at producing televised political advertising and creating the "photo-ops" and other staged events that attract news coverage. They also teach the candidates how to use the media properly. Inexperienced candidates soon discover that they cannot "just be themselves" when talking with journalists or participating in televised debates. They have to conform to the demands of the media, such as the preference of television journalists for sound bites: short, pithy statements that add zest and zing to a news story.[38]

Devising Strategy: Packaging the Candidate

In the old days, candidates were nearly prepackaged. They were labeled as Democrats or Republicans, which was about all the guidance most voters wanted or needed. Party labels are still meaningful, but today's campaigns are also based on media images.

No presidential first lady had run for elective office until Hillary Clinton did so in 2000. She moved to New York and won the state's U.S. Senate race. Clinton is shown here campaigning in Jamestown, New York.

Often depicted as hollow deceptions, images are more typically rooted in factual arguments.[39] They are constructed by placing aspects of the candidate's partisanship, policy positions, record, and personality in the context of the voters' "ideal" candidate, a process known as the **packaging** of a candidate.[40] The voters want a representative who is honest, able, straightforward, resolute, and responsive to their interests, but there are limits on the claims a candidate can reasonably make. It would be difficult, for example, for Democratic incumbents who have been long-time advocates of domestic spending programs to convincingly portray themselves as fiscal conservatives. Instead, they would base their images as responsive legislators on other issues, such as education and social security. In any case, officeseekers try to create a favorable portrayal of their candidacy that is also plausible. In a way, this type of packaging is as old as politics itself. Andrew Jackson's self-portrayal as "the champion of the people" is an image that any modern candidate could appreciate. What is new is the need to fit the image to the requirements of a media campaign. It must conform to a world of sound bites, thirty-second ads, and televised debates.

/pattersonwtp5

The battleground of the modern campaign is the mass media. Televised advertising in particular enables candidates to communicate directly, and on their own terms, with the voters.[41] Candidates spend heavily on the production and airing of televised ads, which account for more than half the

TABLE 8-1   TELEVISION CAMPAIGN PRACTICES IN
SELECTED DEMOCRACIES

In many democracies, free television time is provided to political parties, and candidates are not allowed to buy advertising time. The United States provides no free time to parties and allows candidates to purchase air time. Television debates are also a feature of many U.S. campaigns.

Country	Paid TV Ads Allowed?	Unrestricted Free TV Time Provided?	Are TV Debates Held?
Canada	Yes	Yes	Yes
France	No	Yes	Yes
Germany	Yes	Yes	Yes
Great Britain	No	Yes	No
Italy	No	Yes	Yes
Netherlands	No	No	Yes
United States	Yes	No	Yes

Source: Compiled from various sources.

expenditures in every presidential campaign and most congressional races. Indeed, televised ads are usually cited as the main reason for the high cost of U.S. campaigns. In most democracies, televised campaigning takes place through parties, which receive *free* air time to make their pitch. Many democracies even prohibit the purchase of televised advertising time by candidates (see Table 8–1).

Air wars is the term that the political scientist Darrell West applies to candidates' use of televised ads. Candidates increasingly play off each other's ads, seeking to gain the strategic advantage.[42] Modern production techniques enable well-funded candidates to get new ads on the air within a few hours' time, which allows them to rebut attacks and exploit fast-breaking developments. *Rapid-response* was the term used by the Clinton campaign in 1992 and 1996 for its capacity to counter Republican charges. For example, when Bush ads in the 1992 campaign accused Clinton of having raised taxes when governor of Arkansas, Clinton aired an immediate rebuttal based on his interpretation of his tax record.[43] Rapid-response has become a standard tactic in high-profile contests; both the Bush and the Gore campaigns employed the tactic in 2000.

The media campaign also takes place through news outlets, but coverage varies depending on the race and location. Many House candidates are nearly ignored by their local news media. The New York City media market, for example, includes more than a score of House districts in New York, New Jersey, Pennsylvania, and Connecticut, and candidates in these districts get little or no coverage from the New York media. The presidential campaign, in contrast, gets daily coverage from both national and local media. Between these extremes are Senate races and House races in less populated areas; they always get some news coverage and, if hotly contested, may get heavy coverage.

The media campaign also includes debates and talk-show appearances. Debates are particularly important because they often attract a large and attentive audience. But they are also risky encounters, since they give viewers a chance to directly compare the candidates. A weak or bumbled performance can seriously damage a candidate's chances in a close race. To reduce the risks, candidates often spend the day or two before a debate rehearsing their presentation.

Internet Politics: In the Web

New communication technology usually makes its way into campaign politics, and the Internet is no exception. Every presidential candidate in 2000 had a website. Each site was packed with information, but its main purposes were to generate public support, to raise money, and to attract and organize volunteers. Republican candidate John McCain raised more than $5 million for his campaign through Internet contributions.

Although television is still the principal mechanism of election politics, some observers believe that the Internet may eventually replace it, particularly in congressional races. E-mail is much cheaper than television advertising (or, for that matter, traditional mail) and can be more easily directed at supporters and swing voters. Because it is a targeted medium, the Internet may become a channel through which candidates deliver narrowly targeted messages to particular groups and interests.

PARTIES, CANDIDATES, AND THE PUBLIC'S INFLUENCE

Candidate-centered campaigns have some distinct advantages. First, they lend flexibility to and infuse new blood into electoral politics. When political conditions and issues change, self-directed candidates quickly adjust, bringing new ideas into the political arena. Strong party organizations are rigid by comparison. Until recently, for example, the British Labour party

LIBERTY, EQUALITY, & SELF-GOVERNMENT
What's Your Opinion?

Parties and Equality

Historically, parties have given weight to the voice of disadvantaged people. Their strength is in their numbers rather than in their wealth or status, and elections give them a chance to exercise that strength if they act together. It is no accident that the Jacksonians created the first American grassroots party in order to mobilize lower-class voters. The role of the political party in giving voice to the lower classes is even more evident in Europe, where labor and socialist parties emerged out of workers' movements.

As U.S. parties have weakened in recent decades, so has the political influence of Americans of lower income levels. The voting rate of citizens at the bottom of the income ladder is now about half that of those at the top. Party conflict, in the first half of the twentieth century centered on the working class. It now inhabits the periphery of policy debates. The candidate-centered politics of today is mainly a politics of media and money and is primarily responsive to middle-class interests.

What do you make of this development? Is there a good alternative to the political party as an instrument for the aspirations of lower-income Americans? What might be done to increase the parties' responsiveness to their interests?

---

was controlled by old-line activists who refused to concede that changes in the British economy called for changes in the party's trade unionist and economic policies. The result was a series of humiliating defeats to the Conservative party that ended only after Tony Blair and other proponents of "New Labour" successfully rebuilt the party's image.

Second, candidate-centered campaigns encourage national officeholders to be responsive to local interests. In building personal followings among their state and district constituents, members of Congress respond to local needs. Nearly every significant domestic program enacted by Congress is adjusted to accommodate the interests of states and localities that would otherwise be hurt by the policy. Members of Congress are not obliged to support the legislative position of their party's majority, and they often extract favors for their constituents as the price of their support. Where strong national parties exist, national interests take precedence over local concerns. In both

France and Britain, for example, the pleas of representatives of underdeveloped regions have often gone unheeded by their party's majority.

In other respects, however, candidate-centered campaigns have some real disadvantages. Often they degenerate into mere personality contests and are fertile ground for powerful special interest groups, which contribute much of the money that underwrites candidates' campaigns. Many groups give large sums of money to incumbents of both parties, which enables them to insulate themselves from an election's outcome. Whether the Republicans win or the Democrats win, these contributors are assured of having friends in high places.

Candidate-centered campaigns also blur the connection between electing and governing by making it easier for officeholders to deny responsibility for government's actions. If national policy goes awry, an incumbent can always say that he or she is only one vote out of many and that the real problem resides with the president or with "others" in Congress.[44] The problem of accountability in the U.S. system is illustrated by surveys that have asked Americans about their confidence in Congress. Although most citizens do not have a high opinion of Congress as a whole, most citizens also say they have confidence in their own representative in Congress. This paradoxical attitude prevails in so many districts that the net result in most elections is a Congress whose membership is not greatly changed from the previous one (see Chapter 11). In the 2000 elections, despite a widespread view that Congress was bogged down in narrow-minded partisanship, less than 3 percent of incumbents seeking reelection were defeated.

In sum, candidate-centered campaigns strengthen the relationship between the voters and their individual representative while at the same time weakening the relationship between the full electorate and their representative institutions. Whether this arrangement serves the public's interest is debatable. Most citizens are not even sure. A 2000 Harvard poll found that 68 percent of Americans agreed with the statement that today's politics "seem more like theater or entertainment than like something to be taken seriously." Nevertheless, it is clear that Americans do not want truly strong parties. Parties survived the shift to candidate-centered campaigns and will persist, but their heyday has passed. (Congressional and presidential campaigns are discussed further in Chapters 11 and 12, respectively.)

SUMMARY

Political parties serve to link the public with its elected leaders. In the United States, this linkage is provided by the two-party system; only the

/pattersonwtp5

Republican and Democratic parties have any chance of winning control of government. The fact that the United States has only two major parties is explained by several factors: an electoral system—characterized by single-member districts—that makes it difficult for third parties to compete for power; each party's willingness to accept differing political views; and a political culture that stresses compromise and negotiation rather than ideological rigidity.

Because the United States has only two major parties, each of which seeks to gain majority support, their candidates normally tend to avoid controversial or extreme political positions. Candidates typically pursue moderate and somewhat overlapping policies. Nonetheless, Democratic and Republican candidates sometimes do offer sharply contrasting policy alternatives, particularly in times of political unrest.

America's parties are decentralized, fragmented organizations. The national party organization does not control the policies and activities of the state organizations, and they in turn do not control the local organizations. Traditionally the local organizations have controlled most of the party's work force because most elections are contested at the local level. Local parties, however, vary markedly in their vitality. Whatever their level, America's party organizations are relatively weak. They lack control over nominations and elections. Candidates can bypass the party organization and win nomination through primary elections. Individual candidates also control most of the organizational structure and money necessary to win elections. Recently the state and national party organizations have expanded their capacity to provide candidates with modern campaign services. Nevertheless, party organizations at all levels have few ways of controlling the candidates who run under their banners. They assist candidates with campaign technology, workers, and funds, but cannot compel candidates' loyalty to organizational goals.

American political campaigns, particularly those for higher-level office, are candidate centered. Most candidates are self-starters who become adept at "the election game." They spend much of their time raising campaign funds, and they build their personal organizations around hired guns: pollsters, media producers, and election consultants. Strategy and image making are key components of the modern campaign, as is televised political advertising, which accounts for roughly half of all spending in presidential and congressional races.

Because America's parties cannot control their candidates or coordinate their policies at all levels, they are unable to consistently present the voters with coherent, detailed platforms for governing. The national electorate as a whole is thus denied a clear choice among policy alternatives and has difficulty exerting a decisive and predictable influence through elections.

KEY TERMS

air wars	party competition
candidate-centered politics	party organizations
dealignment	party realignment
grassroots party	political party
hard money	primary election (direct primary)
hired guns	proportional representation
money chase	service relationship
multiparty system	single-member districts
nomination	soft money
packaging (of a candidate)	split-ticket voting
party-centered politics	straight-ticket voting
party coalition	two-party system

SUGGESTED READINGS

Aldrich, John H. *Why Parties? The Origin and Transformation of Political Parties in America*. Chicago: University of Chicago Press, 1995. An insightful analysis of what parties are and how they emerge and develop.

Flanigan, William H., and Nancy H. Zingale. *Political Behavior of the American Electorate*, 10th ed. Washington, D.C.: Congressional Quarterly Press, 2002. A study of Americans' electoral behavior.

King, Anthony. *Running Scared: The Victory of Campaigning over Governing in America*. New York: Free Press, 1997. An analysis of why America's leaders have succumbed to the pressure of the permanent campaign.

Lijphardt, Arend. *Electoral Systems and Party Systems: A Study of Twenty-Seven Democracies, 1945–1990*. New York: Oxford University Press, 1994. A comprehensive study of the relationship between electoral systems and party systems.

Patterson, Kelly D. Political *Parties and the Maintenance of Liberal Democracy*. New York: Columbia University Press, 1996. A systematic look at the effects of political parties on American government and politics.

Pomper, Gerald M. *The Election of 2000: Reports and Interpretations*. New York: Seven Bridges Press, 2001. An edited volume of assessments of the 2000 election by a team of thoughtful scholars and observers.

Rosenstone, Steven J., Roy L. Behr, and Edward H. Lazarus. *Third Parties in America*, 2d ed. Princeton, N.J.: Princeton University Press, 1996. An analysis of America's third parties and their impact on the two-party system.

Stonecash, Jeffrey. *Class and Party in American Politics*. Boulder, Colo.: Westview Press, 2001. An insightful analysis that argues class is still very much a part of America's party politics.

West, Darrell M. *Air Wars: Television Advertising in Election Campaigns, 1952–1992*, 3rd ed. Washington, D.C.: Congressional Quarterly Press, 2001. A thorough study of the role of televised advertising in election campaigns.

LIST OF WEBSITES

http://www.democrats.org/ The Democratic National Committee's site; it provides information on the party's platform, candidates, officials, and organization.

http://www.greenparties.org The Green party's website; it contains information on the party's philosophy and policy goals.

http://www.rnc.org/ Home page of the Republican National Committee; it offers information on Republican leaders, policy positions, and organizations.

http://www.jamescarvillesoffice.com The website of James Carville, one of the nation's top campaign consultants and a frequent guest on talk-show programs.

POLITICS IN THEORY AND PRACTICE

Thinking: Why are elections conducted so differently in the United States than in European democracies? Why are the campaigns so much longer, more expensive, and more candidate centered?

Acting: Consider becoming a campaign volunteer. The opportunities are numerous. Candidates at every level from the presidency on down seek volunteers to assist in organizing, canvassing, fund-raising, and other campaign activities. As a college student, you have communication and knowledge skills that would be valuable to a campaign. You might be pleasantly surprised by the tasks you are assigned.

The New York Times

reading 8

The 2002 Campaign: The Commercials; A Softer Spin on the Mean Season

By Lizette Alvarez

Although competition between the Republican and Democratic parties is a defining feature of today's campaigns, the campaigns themselves center largely on the candidates. Money is the name of the game, and televised political advertising is the major battleground in national and statewide campaigns. During the past few decades, this advertising has become more negative in tone. Even though most Americans say they dislike negative political ads, the candidates' consultants believe such ads are usually more effective than positive ones. In this October 24, 2002, article, New York Times *reporter Lizette Alvarez examines the use of negative ads in the 2002 midterm elections.*

WASHINGTON—For a brief moment this year, as the nation prepared to commemorate the Sept. 11 attacks, television screens were mostly free of mud-slinging political commercials; some consultants wondered whether good cheer and optimism in advertising were here to stay.

Now, as Election Day draws closer, they have stopped wondering. "Look around the country at the tough races," Alex Castellanos, a Republican media consultant,

said. "I'd be hard pressed to find a lot of subtlety. The old rule applies: The more things change, the more they stay the same." If anything, media consultants say they have gotten shrewder about how to make the negative commercials seem less overt, while ensuring that they are as tough as always.

Increasingly, the commercials use women narrators whose softer voices sound less hostile even when delivering scorching messages. More advertisements now feature newspaper headlines in an effort to project an image of legitimacy onto the accusations.

That does not mean that the candidates, their campaigns, their parties and outside interest groups are abandoning shock value.

In the race for Oklahoma governor, where Steve Largent is the front-runner, one candidate has broadcast a commercial with the image of the World Trade Center collapsing and a country singer singing, "Where were you when the world stopped turning on that September day?" A narrator supplies an answer: "Largent was hunting in Idaho, out of touch, while Congress was in session." Viewers in Georgia watched Osama bin Laden's face pop up on the screen as a narrator questioned the commitment of Senator Max Cleland, a Democrat, to domestic security.

Others have employed a touch of cleverness.

In Georgia, one Democratic commercial asked, "Don't we have enough confused people in Congress already?"

A report released today by the Wisconsin Advertising Project at the University of Wisconsin, which tracks political commercials in the major media markets, found that commercials were decidedly more positive prior to Sept. 11. But since then, campaigns have pushed the negative advertising to nearly the same levels as in 2000.

"Political advertising, generally, has been more positive in 2002 than 2000," said Ken Goldstein, professor of political science at the University of Wisconsin and the project's director. "But after a crescendo around the 9/11 anniversary, it's back to negative as usual."

The weeks leading up to an election are usually crammed with negative political advertisements as candidates go all-out to win votes. This year, there are more advertisements than ever, in part because the number of third-party groups has grown.

As is often true, the tighter the race, the more negative the tone of the commercials. The New Jersey Senate race has featured the most negative advertisements, Mr. Goldstein said. Senator Robert G. Torricelli, the Democrat plagued by muddy ethics charges, dropped out of that race earlier this month. Only 18 percent of the advertisements in New Jersey were labeled positive, Mr. Goldstein said.

Coming in second is the Senate race in Colorado, which is perhaps the closest match-up this year, followed by the Iowa race, where Senator Tom Harkin, a Democrat, is in a tight contest against Representative Greg Ganske, a Republican.

Media consultants, recognizing that voters are tuning out or turning against partisan attacks, have grown a little wiser about how to frame negative attacks to make them more palatable. The bottom line is that it is much harder to get a message across to viewers than it was a few years ago when, consultants estimated, it took three commercials to get noticed. Now, it can take 15 repetitions, consultants say.

"There is one big difference," Steve Murphy, a media consultant for Murphy Putnam Media who represents Democrats, said. "Harsh negatives are not working. Harsh, vitriolic, dripping with sarcasm, that's not working. And if you want to draw a contrast on an issue, or present negative information, you better do it factually and with a tone that is not offensive to the viewer.

The more typical negative advertisement this year contrasts a candidate's stance on an issue with past votes or the candidate's own words, a technique that is most evident in the battle over who can be trusted with Social Security. Consultants have learned to use headlines to back up their claims, which are more closely vetted nowadays by the media.

Media consultants are relying more on feminine voices and they are using expressions of sorrow or disappointment, rather than anger or rage. They are letting candidates speak for themselves, a method Elizabeth Dole, who is running for Senate in North Carolina, and many others have used this year to blunt an opponent's attack advertisements.

Candidates and their parties are also more likely to respond to a negative advertisement with a negative commercial that talks about their opponents as shamelessly using negative advertisements. The Wisconsin Advertising Project found that 9 percent of the advertisements it studied complained about negative advertising by a candidate's opponent.

Perhaps the most infamous negative commercial this year has been the one used by the state Democratic Party in Montana. The advertisement showed the Republican candidate Mike Taylor dressed in a 1980's leisure suit with wide lapels, massaging another man's face as he explained cosmetic tips. The footage was of Mr. Taylor when he was the host of a TV show in Colorado.

Already badly trailing in the race, Mr. Taylor, who is married with children, dropped out soon after the commercial was broadcast, citing the advertisement as the primary reason. He re-entered the race today, saying he wants to "save democracy from smear campaigns."

"When you have footage like that, you can't go wrong," said Rick Reed, a Republican media consultant for Stevens Reed Curcio & Co. "If I could do an ad like that and drive the guy out of the race. Wow. That's effective."

What's Your Opinion?

The writer and columnist Joe Klein claims that political consultants and their negative ads are ruining American elections. Do you agree?

CHAPTER 9

INTEREST GROUPS: ORGANIZING FOR INFLUENCE

❝ The flaw in the pluralist heaven is that the heavenly chorus sings with a strong upper-class bias. **❞**

E. E. SCHATTSCHNEIDER[1]

They launched their attack within hours of the announcement that congressional Republicans had included Medicare in their balanced-budget proposal. The GOP lawmakers planned a $1.1 trillion reduction in federal spending over seven years, including a $270 billion cut in health care for the elderly. Senior-citizen groups assailed the plan and quickly organized a mass demonstration outside the Capitol. The next step was an orchestrated campaign of thousands of angry calls, letters, telegrams, and faxes from retirees to their congressional representatives.

President Clinton sided with the seniors' lobby, promising to veto the Republican bill, which led to a showdown between Congress and the White House that forced a temporary shutdown of the federal government. In January 1996, after a six-week battle and with their poll ratings dropping almost daily, Republican lawmakers shelved their balanced-budget proposal.

The campaign against the Republicans' Medicare initiative suggests why interest groups are both admired and feared. On the one hand, groups have a legitimate right to express their views on public policy issues. It is entirely appropriate for senior citizens or any other group—whether farmers,

269

consumers, business firms, or college students—to actively promote their interests through collective action. In fact, the *pluralist* theory of American politics (see Chapter 1) holds that society's interests are most effectively represented through the efforts of groups.

Yet groups can wield too much power. If a group gets its way at an unreasonable cost to the rest of society, the public interest is harmed. When the Republican budget package was prepared in Congress, polls indicated that most Americans wanted a balanced federal budget and were willing to bear a fair share of the costs. Did the senior-citizen lobby, in pursuit of its own interest, derail a sound budgetary proposal? Or did the Republican package, which also included tax cuts for upper-income Americans, place on the elderly too much of the burden of a balanced budget?

Opinions on these questions differ widely, but there is no doubt that the special interest in some cases wrongly prevails over the general interest. Indeed, most observers are of the opinion that groups have achieved too much influence over public policy in recent decades. Some analysts describe the situation as the triumph of **single-issue politics:** separate groups organized around nearly every conceivable policy issue, with each group pressing its demands and influence to the utmost, at whatever cost to the broader society. The structure of the American political system provides fertile ground for group influence. The system's elaborate checks and balances make it relatively easy for a group, if it has strong support even within a single corner of government, to pursue its goals effectively. (This "Madisonian dilemma" will be explored more fully in the chapter's concluding section.)

Also called a "faction" or "pressure group" or "special interest," an **interest group** has two characteristics: an organized membership and the pursuit of policy goals that stem from its members' shared interest. Thus, a bridge club or an amateur softball team is not an interest group because it does not seek to influence the political process. Organizations such as the Association of Wheat Growers, Common Cause, the National Organization for Women, the World Wildlife Fund, the National Rifle Association, and the Anti-Defamation League of B'nai B'rith are interest groups because, despite their differences, each is an organized entity and each seeks to further its members' interests through political action.

Interest groups are similar to political parties in certain respects, but the two types of organizations differ in important ways. Major political parties address a broad range of issues so as to appeal to diverse blocs of voters. Parties exist to contest elections. They change their policy positions as the voters' preferences change; for the party, winning is almost everything. In comparison, interest groups focus on specific issues of immediate concern to their members; farm groups, for example, concentrate on agricultural

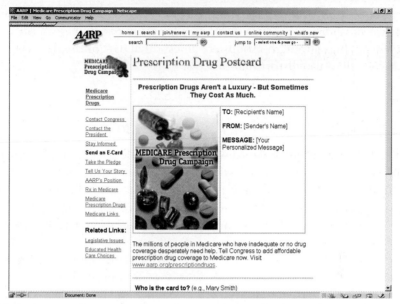

AARP (the American Association of Retired Persons) has roughly thirty million members and is the largest citizens' group. It regularly encourages its members to contact Congress on issues facing retirees, as in this electronic message on prescription drugs.

policy. A group may involve itself in elections, but its purpose is to influence public policy.

This chapter examines the degree to which various interests in American society are represented by organized groups, the process by which interest groups exert influence, and the costs and benefits of group politics in regard to the public good. The main points made in the chapter are the following:

★ *Although nearly all interests in American society are organized to some degree, those associated with economic activity, particularly business enterprises, are by far the most thoroughly organized.* Their advantage rests on their superior financial resources and on the fact that they offer potential members private goods (such as wages and jobs).

★ *Groups that do not have economic activity as their primary function often have organizational problems.* They pursue public or collective goods (such as a safer environment) that are available even to individuals who are not group members, and so individuals may choose not to pay the costs of membership.

★ *Lobbying and electioneering are the traditional means by which groups communicate with and influence political leaders.* Recent developments, including grassroots lobbying and PACs, have given added visibility to groups' activities.

★ *The interest-group system overrepresents business interests and higher-income groups and fosters policies that serve a group's interest more than the public interest.* Thus, although groups are an essential part of the democratic process, they also distort that process.

THE INTEREST-GROUP SYSTEM

In the 1830s, the Frenchman Alexis de Tocqueville wrote that the "principle of association" was nowhere more evident than in America.[2] The country's tradition of free association has always made it easy for Americans to join together for political purposes, and their diverse interests have given them reason to seek influence through specialized groups (see "How the United States Compares").

However, the nation's various interests are not equally well organized. Organizations develop when people with shared interests have the opportunity and the incentive to join together. Some individuals have the skills, money, contacts, or time to participate effectively in group politics, but others do not. Moreover, some groups are inherently more attractive to potential members than others are and thus find it easier to build large or devoted followings. Organizations also differ in their access to financial resources and thus differ also in their capacity for political action.

Therefore, a first consideration in regard to group politics in America is the issue of how thoroughly various interests are organized. Interests that are highly organized stand a good chance of having their views heard by policymakers. Poorly organized interests run the risk of being ignored.

Economic Groups

No interests are more fully or effectively organized than those that have economic activity as their primary purpose. An indication of their advantage is the fact that Washington lobbyists who represent economic groups outnumber those of all other groups by more than two to one.

Economic groups include corporations, labor unions, farm groups, and professional associations. They exist primarily for economic purposes: to make profits, provide jobs, improve pay, or protect an occupation. For the sake of discussion, such organizations will be called **economic groups**, although it is important to recognize that their political goals can include policies that transcend the narrow economic interests of their members. Although the AFL-CIO, for example, concentrates on labor policies, it also takes positions on other foreign and domestic issues.

How the United States Compares

Groups: "A Nation of Joiners"

"A nation of joiners" is how the Frenchman Alexis de Tocqueville described the United States during his visit to this country in the 1830s.

Even today, Americans are more actively involved in groups and community causes than are Europeans. The American tradition of group activity is only one reason. Another is the structure of the U.S. political system. Because of federalism and the separation of powers, the American system offers numerous points at which groups can try to influence public policy. If unsuccessful with legislators, groups can turn to executives or the courts. If thwarted at the national level, groups can turn to state and local governments. By comparison, the governments of most other democratic nations are not organized in ways that facilitate group access and influence. France's unitary government, for example, concentrates power at the national level.

Such differences are reflected in citizens' participation rates. Americans are more likely to belong to groups than Europeans are, as the accompanying figures from the World Values Survey indicate.

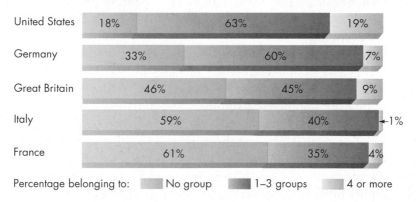

	No group	1–3 groups	4 or more
United States	18%	63%	19%
Germany	33%	60%	7%
Great Britain	46%	45%	9%
Italy	59%	40%	←1%
France	61%	35%	4%

Percentage belonging to: ■ No group   ■ 1–3 groups   ■ 4 or more

An Organizational Edge One reason for the abundance of economic groups is their access to financial resources. Political activity does not come cheap. If a group is to make its views known, it normally must have a headquarters, an expert staff, and communication facilities. Economic groups can obtain the requisite money and expertise from their economic activities.

Corporations have the greatest built-in advantage. They do not have to charge membership dues or conduct fund-raisers to support their lobbying. Their political money comes from their business activity.

Some economic groups do depend on dues for their support, but they can offer prospective members a powerful incentive to join: **private (individual) goods,** which are the benefits that a group can grant directly to the individual member. For example, workers in the state of Michigan cannot hold automobile assembly jobs unless they belong to the United Auto Workers (UAW). The UAW has a **material incentive**—the economic lure of a high-paying job—to attract potential members. Economic groups are highly organized in part because they serve the economic needs of potential members. The predominance of economic interests was predicted in *Federalist* No. 10, in which James Madison declared that property is "the most common and durable source of factions." Stated differently, nothing seems to matter quite so much to people as their pocketbooks and livelihoods.

Types of Economic Groups Most economic groups are of four general types: business groups, labor groups, agricultural groups, and professional groups.

Business Groups More than half of all groups formally registered to lobby Congress are business organizations. Nearly all large corporations and many smaller ones are politically active. They concentrate their activities on policies that touch directly on business interests, such as tax, tariff, and regulatory decisions.

Business firms are also represented through associations, such as the U.S. Chamber of Commerce, which includes nearly three million businesses of all sizes. Other business associations, such as the American Petroleum Institute, are confined to a single trade or industry. Because each trade association represents a single industry, it can promote the interests of member corporations even when these interests conflict with those of business generally. Thus, while the Chamber of Commerce promotes a global free trade policy, some trade associations seek protective tariffs because their member firms want barriers against foreign competition.

Business interests have the advantage of what the economist Mancur Olson calls "the size factor."[3] Although large groups can claim that government should pay more attention to them because they represent more people, small groups are usually more cohesive. Everyone is a consumer, but most consumers do not see any benefit in belonging to a consumer advocacy group. On the other hand, because business firms in a particular industry are few in number, they are likely to recognize the significance of working together. When the "Big Three" U.S. automakers—General Motors, Ford,

and Chrysler—fought federally mandated safety and mileage-efficiency standards, the defection of any one of them would likely have meant defeat. But
they stayed together and won concessions from the government. In the
process, each automaker saved hundreds of millions of dollars in design and
production costs on new autos. In one instance, the automakers gained a mul-
tiyear delay in the installation of air bags in all new cars. Their gain came at
an unknown cost to consumers, whose newly purchased automobiles were
less safe than they could have been.

Labor Groups Since the 1930s, organized labor has been politically active on
a large scale. Its goal has been to promote policies that benefit workers in
general and union members in particular. Although there are some major
independent unions, such as the United Mine Workers, the dominant labor
group is the AFL-CIO, which has its national headquarters in Washington,
D.C. The AFL-CIO has more than thirteen million members in its ninety-
seven affiliated unions, which include the International Brotherhood of
Electrical Workers, the Sheet Metal Workers, the Communication Workers of America, and the International Brotherhood of Teamsters.

At one time, about a third of the U.S. work force was unionized, but today only about a seventh of all workers belong to unions. Skilled and unskilled laborers have been the core of organized labor, but their numbers are
decreasing while professionals, technicians, and service workers are increasing in number. Professionals have shown little interest in union organization, perhaps because they identify with management or see themselves as
economically secure. Service workers and technicians are also difficult for
unions to organize because they work closely with managers and, often, in
small offices.

Nevertheless, unions have made inroads in recent decades in their efforts
to organize service and public employees. Teachers, postal workers, police,
firefighters, and social workers are among the public employee groups that
have become increasingly unionized. Today, the nation's largest unions are
those that represent service and public employees rather than skilled and
unskilled laborers.

Agricultural Groups Farm organizations represent another large economic
lobby. The American Farm Bureau Federation is the largest of the farm
groups, with more than four million members. The National Farmers
Union, the National Grange, and the National Farmers Organization are
smaller farm lobbies. Agricultural groups do not always agree on policy issues. For instance, the Farm Bureau sides with agribusiness and owners of
large farms, while the Farmers Union promotes the interests of smaller
"family" farms.

There are also numerous specialty farm associations, including the Association of Wheat Growers, the American Soybean Association, and Associated Milk Producers. Each association acts as a separate lobby to try to obtain policies beneficial to its members' specific interest.

Professional Groups Most professions have lobbying associations. Among the most powerful of these groups is the American Medical Association (AMA), which, with nearly three hundred thousand members, represents about half the nation's physicians. The AMA has consistently opposed any government policy that would limit physicians' autonomy. Other professional groups are the American Bar Association and the American Association of University Professors, each of which maintains a lobbying office in Washington.

Citizens' Groups

Although economic interests are the best organized groups, they do not have a monopoly on group activity. There are a great number and variety of other organized interests, which are referred to collectively as **citizens' groups** (or **noneconomic groups**). The members of groups in this category are drawn together not by the promise of direct economic gain but by **purposive incentives**—opportunities to promote a cause in which they believe.[4] Whether a group's goal is to protect the environment, reduce the threat of nuclear war, return prayer to the public schools, feed the poor at home or abroad, or whatever, there are citizens who are willing to participate simply because they believe the cause is a worthy one.[5]

In comparison with economic groups, citizens' groups have a harder time acquiring the resources necessary for organization. These groups do not generate profits or fees as a result of economic activity. Moreover, the incentives they offer prospective members are not exclusive. Unlike the private or individual goods provided by many economic groups, most noneconomic groups offer **collective goods** (or **public goods**) as an incentive for membership. Collective goods are, by definition, benefits that must be shared; they cannot be granted or withheld on an individual basis. The air people breathe and the national forests people visit are examples of collective goods. They are available to one and all, those who pay dues to a clean-air group or a wilderness group and those who do not.

The Free-Rider Problem This characteristic of collective goods creates what is called the **free-rider problem:** individuals can receive the good even when they do not contribute to the group's effort. Take the case of National Public Radio (NPR). Although NPR's programs are funded primarily through listeners' donations, those who do not contribute can also hear the programs. The noncontributors are free riders: they receive the benefit

One of the most successful citizen lobbying campaigns in history was conducted largely through the Internet. It was a global campaign aimed at the elimination of land mines, and its chief organizer, Jody Williams, (shown here accepting the peace flame) won the Nobel Peace Prize in 1997. By linking together activists and groups throughout the world, Williams succeeded in getting one hundred countries to agree to an international treaty that bans the use of land mines.

without paying any of the costs of providing it. About 90 percent of people who regularly listen to NPR do not contribute to their local station.

As the economist Mancur Olson noted, it is not rational, in a purely economic sense, for individuals to contribute to a group when they can obtain its benefit without paying for it.[6] Moreover, the dues paid by any single member are too small to affect the group's success one way or another. Why pay dues to an environmental group when any improvements in the air, water, or wildlife from its lobbying efforts are available to everyone and when one's contribution is too small to make a real difference? Although many people do join such groups anyway, there is no doubt that the free-rider problem is a reason why citizens' groups are less highly organized than economic ones.

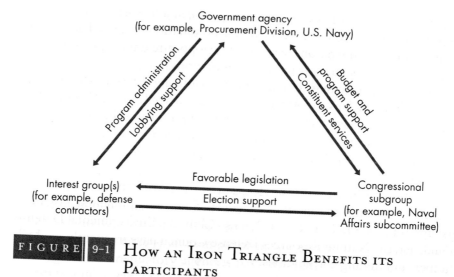

FIGURE 9-1   How an Iron Triangle Benefits its
Participants

An iron triangle works to the advantage of each of its participants: an interest group, a congressional subgroup, and a government agency.

and Senate agriculture committees. Figure 9–1 summarizes the benefits that flow to each member of an iron triangle.

Issue Networks Iron triangles represent the pattern of influence only in certain policy areas and are less common now than in the past. A more frequent pattern of influence today is the **issue network,** which is an informal grouping of officials, lobbyists, and policy specialists (the "network") who are brought together temporarily by their shared interest in a particular policy problem (the "issue").

Issue networks are a result of the increasing complexity of policy problems. Participants must have specialized knowledge of the issue at hand in order to participate effectively. Thus, unlike iron triangles, where one's position is everything, an issue network is built around specialized interests and information. On any given issue, the participants might come from a variety of executive agencies, congressional committees, interest groups, and institutions such as universities or think tanks. And, unlike iron triangles, issue networks are less stable. As the issue develops, new participants may join the debate and old ones drop out. Once the issue is resolved, the network disbands.[21]

An example of an issue network is the set of participants who would come together over the issue of whether a large tract of old forest should be opened to logging. A few decades ago, that issue would have been settled in an iron triangle consisting of the timber companies, the U.S. Forest Service, and relevant members of the House and Senate agriculture committees. But as forestlands have diminished and environmental concerns have grown, such issues can no longer be contained within the cozy confines of an iron triangle. Today, an issue network would form that included logging interests, the U.S. Forest Service, House and Senate agriculture committee members, research scientists, and representatives of environmental groups, the housing industry, and animal-rights groups. Unlike the old iron triangle, which was confined to like-minded interests, this issue network would include opposing interests (for example, the loggers and the environmentalists). And unlike an iron triangle, the issue network would dissolve once the issue was resolved; after it was settled, the various parties would go their separate ways.

Issue networks, then, differ substantially from iron triangles. In an iron triangle, it is a common interest that brings the participants together in a stable, long-lasting, and mutually beneficial relationship. In an issue network, it is an immediate issue that brings the participants together in a temporary network that is based on their ability to address the issue in a sophisticated way and where they play out their separate interests before disbanding once the issue is settled.

Iron triangles and issue networks, however, do have one thing in common. They are arenas in which organized interests operate. The interests of the general public may be taken into account in these webs of influence, but the interests of the participating groups are paramount.

OUTSIDE LOBBYING: SEEKING INFLUENCE THROUGH PUBLIC PRESSURE

Although an interest group may rely solely on inside lobbying, this approach is not likely to be successful unless the group can demonstrate convincingly that its concerns reflect those of a vital constituency. Accordingly, groups make use of constituency connections when it is advantageous to do so. They engage in **outside lobbying,** which involves bringing public ("outside") pressure to bear on policymakers (see Table 9–2).[22]

Constituency Advocacy: Grassroots Lobbying

One form of outside pressure is **grassroots lobbying**—that is, pressure designed to convince government officials that a group's policy position has popular support.

No group illustrates grassroots lobbying better than the AARP (American Association of Retired Persons). With more than thirty million members

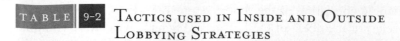

TABLE 9-2 TACTICS USED IN INSIDE AND OUTSIDE LOBBYING STRATEGIES	
Inside lobbying and outside lobbying are based on different tactics.	
Inside Lobbying	**Outside Lobbying**
Developing contacts with legislators and executives	Encouraging group members to write or phone their representatives in Congress
Providing information and policy proposals to key officials	Seeking favorable coverage by news media
Forming coalitions with other groups	Encouraging members to support particular candidates in elections
	Targeting group resources on key election races
	Making PAC contributions to candidates

and a staff of sixteen hundred employees, AARP is a powerful lobby on retirement issues such as social security and Medicare. When major legislation affecting retirees is pending, AARP swings into action. Congress gets more mail from members of the AARP than it does from members of any other group.[23]

As with other forms of lobbying, the precise impact of grassroots campaigns is usually difficult to assess. Some members of Congress downplay its influence, but all congressional offices monitor letters and phone calls as a way of tracking constituents' opinions.

Electoral Action: Votes and PAC Money

An "outside" strategy can also include election campaigns. "Reward your friends and punish your enemies" is a political adage that loosely describes how interest groups view elections. Organized groups work to elect their supporters and defeat their opponents. The possibility of electoral opposition from a powerful group can keep an officeholder from openly obstructing its goals. For example, opposition from the three-million-member National Rifle Association is a major reason the United States has lagged behind other Western societies in its handgun control laws, despite polls that show most Americans favor such laws.

The principal way in which interest groups try to gain influence through elections is by contributing money to candidates' campaigns. As one lobbyist

The Houston headquarters of the now-bankrupt Enron Corporation. Until its collapse from illegal business practices, Enron was one of the nation's largest corporations and one of the most active lobbying groups in Washington.

said, "Talking to politicians is fine, but with a little money they hear you better."[24] Members of Congress sometimes get into hot water by listening too closely to the groups that fund their campaigns. When the Enron Corporation collapsed into bankruptcy in 2002, depleting the retirement accounts of its employees in the process, its deep connections in Washington quickly became known. In the previous decade, Enron and its top officials had contributed $6 million in campaign funds. Some members of Congress found themselves in the embarrassing position of holding investigative hearings on a company that they had consulted on policy issues and from which they had taken money.

A group's election contributions are given through its **political action committee (PAC).** A group cannot give organizational funds (such as corporate profits or union dues) to candidates; but through its PAC, a group can raise money for election campaigns by soliciting voluntary contributions from members or employees. A PAC is legally limited in the amount it can contribute to the campaign of a candidate for federal office. The ceiling is $10,000 per candidate—$5,000 in the primary campaign and $5,000 in the general election campaign; there is no legal limit on the number of candidates a PAC can support. These financial limits do not apply to candidates for state and local office. Their campaigns are regulated by state laws, and many states allow PACs to make unlimited campaign contributions.

PACs increased eightfold after favorable changes were made in campaign finance laws in 1974. There are now more than four thousand PACs, and PAC contributions account for roughly a third of total contributions to congressional campaigns. Their role is less significant in presidential campaigns, which are larger in scale and publicly funded in part and therefore less dependent on PAC contributions.

PACs contribute more than five times as much money to incumbents as to their challengers. PACs are well aware of the fact that incumbents are likely to win and thus to remain in a position to make policy. One PAC director, expressing a common view, said, "We always stick with the incumbent when we agree with them both."[25]

The tendency of PACs to back incumbents has to some extent blurred long-standing partisan divisions in campaign funding. Business interests are especially pragmatic. Although they tend to favor Republican candidates, they are reluctant to anger Democratic incumbents. The result is that Democratic incumbents, particularly in House races, have received substantial support over the years from business-related PACs.[26] Other PACs, of course, are less pragmatic. The Christian Moral Government Fund, for example, backs only candidates who take conservative stands on issues such as school prayer and abortion.

More than 40 percent of all PACs are associated with corporations (see Figure 9–2). Examples include the Ford Motor Company Civic Action Fund, the Sun Oil Company Political Action Committee (Sunpac), and the Coca-Cola PAC. The next largest group of PACs consists of those linked to citizens' groups (that is, public-interest, single-issue, and ideological groups), such as the liberal People for the American Way and the conservative NCPAC (National Conservative Political Action Committee). Ranking third are PACs tied to trade and professional associations, such as AMPAC (American Medical Association) and R-PAC (National Association of Realtors). Labor unions were once the major source of group contributions, but they now rank fourth.

Advocates of PACs claim that groups have a right to be heard, which includes the right to express themselves with money. Advocates also say that a campaign finance system based on pooled contributions by individuals is superior to one in which candidates rely on a few wealthy donors.[27]

Critics argue, however, that PACs give interest groups altogether too much influence with public officials.[28] Opposition to PACs has increased in recent years as citizens have come to believe that interest groups have

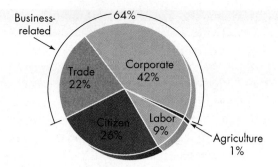

FIGURE 9-2 **PERCENTAGE OF PACS BY CATEGORY**

Most PACs represent business; corporate and trade association PACs make up 64 percent of the total.
Source: Federal Election Commission figures, 2003.

gained too much power over public policy. Although members of Congress deny that they are unduly influenced, there has been a growing sentiment even within Congress to place some restrictions on PACs. Agreement on the changes, however, has been difficult to achieve because of differences in the ways that Democrats and Republicans would reform the process and also because some incumbents are unwilling to support any change that would reduce the advantage they derive from the present system.

THE GROUP SYSTEM: INDISPENSABLE BUT BIASED

As was noted in the chapter's introduction, pluralist theory holds that organized groups are a source of sound governance. On one level, this claim is beyond dispute. Without groups to carry their message, most of society's interests would find it difficult to get government's attention and support. Yet the issue of representation is also a question of whether all interests in society are fairly represented through the group system, and here the pluralist argument is less compelling.

The Contribution of Groups to Self-Government: Pluralism

Group activity is an essential part of self-government. A major obstacle to popular sovereignty is the difficulty that public officials encounter in trying to discover what the people want from government. To discern their wishes, lawmakers consult public opinion polls, meet with constituents, and assess

★ ‖ STATES IN THE NATION

Limits on PAC Contributions

Elections of state officials (such as governors and state legislators) are regulated by state law rather than by federal law. In some states, there is no law limiting how much PACs can contribute to a candidate. Of the states that limit PAC contributions, only New York and Nevada allow contributions in excess of $10,000.

Q. Why might states located to the west of the Mississippi River (which runs down the eastern borders of Minnesota, Iowa, Missouri, Arkansas, and Louisiana) place fewer limits on PAC contributions than other states?

A. A possible explanation is that the political cultures of the westernmost states, as a result of their frontier heritage, are less accepting of government restraints on economic and political activity.

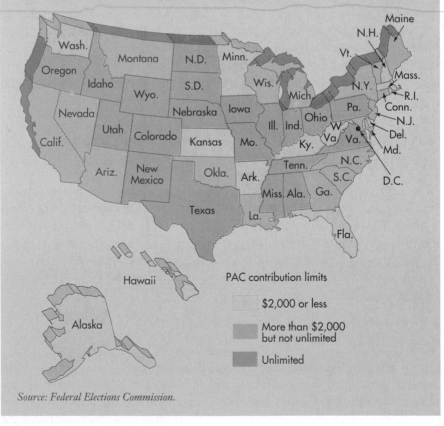

PAC contribution limits

$2,000 or less

More than $2,000 but not unlimited

Unlimited

Source: Federal Elections Commission.

election results. The activities of organized groups are also a clue to what people are seeking.[29] On any given issue, the policy positions that are likely to be expressed most clearly and intensely are those held by organized interests.

Moreover, government does not exist simply to serve majority interests. The fact that most people are not retirees or labor union members or farmers or college students or Hispanics does not mean that the concerns of such "minorities" are unworthy of attention. And what better instrument exists for promoting their interests than organizations formed by them?

Some pluralists even question the usefulness of such terms as *the common good* and *the collective interest*. If people disagree on society's goals and priorities, as they always do, how can it be said that people have a "common" or "collective" interest? As an alternative, pluralists contend that, because society has so many interests, the common good is ultimately best served by a process that enables a great many interests to gain favorable policies. Thus, if manufacturing interests prevail on one issue, environmentalists on another, farmers on a third, minorities on a fourth, and so on until many interests are served, the collective interest of society will have been promoted.[30]

Finally, interest groups often take up issues that are neglected by the party system. Party leaders typically shy from issues, such as affirmative action and abortion, on which the party's voters disagree. Such issues would get less notice if not for the groups that promote them. And when groups succeed in drawing attention to these issues, the parties are nearly compelled also to address them. In this sense, as the political scientist Jack Walker noted, the party and group systems "are complementary and together constitute a more responsive and adaptive system than either would be if they somehow operated on their own."[31]

Flaws in Pluralism: Interest-Group Liberalism and Economic Bias

Although pluralist theory includes some compelling arguments, it also has questionable aspects. In a direct attack on pluralism, Theodore Lowi argues that there is no concept of society's collective interest in a system that allows special interests to determine for themselves which policy benefits they receive, regardless of how many interests are served.[32] When each group makes its own choice, the basis of decision in each case is not majority (collective) rule but minority (special-interest) rule.

It is seldom safe to assume that what most people would favor is what a special-interest group wants. Consider the case of the federal law that required auto dealers to list the known defects of used cars on window stickers. The law was repealed after an extensive lobbying campaign financed by

Sometimes the interests of a group clearly diverge from majority opinion, as when the National Association of Auto Dealers lobbied successfully against legislation that would have required automobile dealers to inform customers about any defects in used cars.

contributions of more than $1 million by the National Association of Automobile Dealers to the reelection campaigns of members of Congress.

Lowi uses the term **interest-group liberalism** to describe the tendency of officials to support the policy demands of the interest group or groups that have a special stake in a policy. In practical terms, it is the group as much as the government that decides policy. The adverse effects include an inefficient use of society's resources: groups get what they want, whether or not their priorities match those of society as a whole.

Another flaw in the pluralist argument resides in its claim that the group system is representative. Pluralists recognize that better-organized interests have more influence but argue that the group process is relatively open and that few interests are at a serious disadvantage. These claims contain an element of truth but are far from the complete truth.

As this chapter has pointed out, organization is a political resource that is distributed unequally across society. Economic interests, particularly corporations, are the most highly organized, and some analysts argue that group politics works chiefly to the advantage of business.[33] Of course, economic groups do not dominate everything, nor do they act unchecked. Many of the public interest groups formed in the past three decades were deliberately

LIBERTY, EQUALITY & SELF GOVERNMENT
What's Your Opinion?

Interest Groups

Rarely is the tension between liberty and equality more evident than in the activities of interest groups. "Liberty is to faction what air is to fire," wrote James Madison in *Federalist* No. 10. Madison was lamenting the self-interested behavior of factions or, as they are called today, interest groups. Yet Madison recognized that the only way to suppress this behavior was to destroy the liberty that allows people to organize.

Interest groups tend to strengthen the already powerful and thus contribute to political inequality. As the political scientist E. E. Schattschneider said, the group system "sings with a strong upper-class bias."

Numerous efforts have been made to harness the power of groups without infringing on Americans' rights of free expression, assembly, and petition. Laws have been enacted that require lobbyists to register, report their lobbying expenditures, and identify the issues on which they are working. Other laws restrict group contributions to candidates for public office. Yet nothing in the end seems to be all that effective in harnessing the self-interested actions of groups. Is there an answer to "Madison's dilemna"? Or are the excesses of group politics simply one of the costs of living in a free society?

created to check and balance the influence of corporate lobbies.[34] Activist government has also brought the group system into closer balance; the government's poverty programs have spawn groups that act to protect these programs. Nevertheless, nearly two-thirds of all lobbying groups in Washington are business-related. The interest-group system is biased toward America's economically oriented groups, particularly its corporations.

The group system is also slanted toward the interests of upper-middle-class Americans. Studies indicate that individuals of higher socioeconomic status are disproportionately represented among group members and even more so among group leaders. Educated and affluent Americans have the money, communication skills, and savvy to participate effectively in special-interest politics. The poor, minorities, women, and the young are greatly underrepresented in the group politics system. A lack of organization does not ensure an interest's failure, just as the existence of organization does not guarantee success. However, organized interests are obviously in a better position to promote their views.

The business and class bias of the group system is especially significant because the most highly organized interests are, in a sense, those least in need of political clout. Corporations and affluent citizens already control the largest share of society's wealth.

A Madisonian Dilemma

James Madison recognized the dilemma inherent in group activity. Although he worried that government would fall under the control of a dominant interest, whether of the majority or of the minority, he realized that a free society is obliged to permit the advocacy of self-interest. Unless people can promote the separate opinions that stem from differences in their talents, needs, values, and possessions, they do not have liberty.

Ironically, Madison's constitutional solution to the problem of factions has become part of the problem. The American system of checks and balances, with a separation of powers at its core, was designed primarily to prevent a majority faction from trampling on the interests of others. Indeed, throughout the nation's history, majorities have been frustrated in their efforts to gain full power by America's elaborate system of divided government.

This same system, however, makes it relatively easy for minority factions—or, as they are called today, special-interest groups—to gain government support. If they can get the backing of even a small number of well-placed policymakers, as in the case of iron triangles, they are likely to get many of the benefits they seek. Because of the system's division of power, they have numerous points at which to exert influence. Often, they need only to find an ally in one place, whether that be a congressional committee or an executive agency or a federal court, to get at least some of what they want. And once they obtain a government benefit, it is likely to persist. Benefits are hard to eliminate because concerted action by the executive and both houses of Congress is usually required. If a group has strong support in even a single institution, it can usually fend off attempts to eliminate its benefits. This support is ordinarily easy to acquire, because the group has resources—information, money, and votes—that officeholders want. (Chapters 11 and 13 discuss further the issue of interest-group power).

SUMMARY

A political interest group is composed of a set of individuals organized to promote a shared political concern. Most interest groups owe their existence to factors other than politics. They form for economic reasons, such as the pursuit of profit, and maintain themselves by making profits (in the case of corporations) or by providing their members with private goods, such as

/pattersonwtp5

jobs and wages. Such interest groups include corporations, trade associations, labor unions, farm organizations, and professional associations. Collectively, economic groups are by far the largest set of organized interests. The group system tends to favor interests that are already economically and socially advantaged.

Citizens' groups do not have the same organizational advantages as economic groups. They depend on voluntary contributions from potential members who may lack interest and resources or who recognize that they will get the collective good from a group's activity even if they do not participate (the free-rider problem). These citizens' groups include public-interest, single-issue, and ideological groups. Their numbers have increased dramatically since the 1960s despite their organizational problems.

Organized interests seek influence largely by lobbying public officials and contributing to election campaigns. Using an inside strategy, lobbyists develop direct contacts with legislators, government bureaucrats, and members of the judiciary in order to persuade them to accept their group's perspective on policy. Groups also use an outside strategy, seeking to mobilize public support for their goals. This strategy relies in part on grassroots lobbying—encouraging group members and the public to communicate their policy views to officials. Outside lobbying also includes efforts to elect officeholders who will support group aims. Through political action committees (PACs), organized groups now provide nearly a third of all contributions received by congressional candidates.

The policies that emerge from the group system bring benefits to many of society's interests, and in some instances these benefits also serve the general interest. But when groups can essentially dictate policies, the common good is not served. The majority's interest is subordinated to group (minority) interests. In most instances, the minority consists of individuals who already have a substantial share of society's benefits.

Key Terms

citizens' (noneconomic) groups
collective (public) goods
economic groups
free-rider problem
grassroots lobbying
inside lobbying
interest group
interest-group liberalism
iron triangle

issue network
lobbying
material incentive
outside lobbying
political action committee (PAC)
private (individual) goods
purposive incentive
single-issue politics

SUGGESTED READINGS

Berry, Jeffrey M. *The New Liberalism: The Rising Power of Citizen Groups*. Washington, D.C.: Brookings Institution Press, 1999. An exploration of the influence that citizen groups exercise.

Browne, William P. *Cultivating Congress: Constituents, Issues, and Interests in Agriculture Policymaking*. Lawrence: University Press of Kansas, 1995. An analysis of the limits of "iron triangles" as a description of congressional policymaking.

Cigler, Allan J., and Burdett A. Loomis. *Interest Group Politics*, 5th ed. Washington, D.C.: Congressional Quarterly Press, 1998. A comprehensive analysis of interest-group politics.

Gatz, Thomas L. *Improper Influence: Campaign Finance Law, Political Interest Groups, and the Problem of Equality*. Ann Arbor: University of Michigan Press, 1996. An analysis of how PACs have changed the process of representation through groups.

Grossman, Gene M. and Elhanan Helpman. *Interest Groups and Trade Policy*. Princeton, N.J.: Princeton University Press, 2002. An examination of the impact of groups' campaign and lobbying activities on trade policy.

Herrnson, Paul S., Ronald G. Shaiko, and Clyde Wilcox, eds. *The Interest Group Connection: Electioneering, Lobbying, and Policymaking in Washington*. Chatham, N.J.: Chatham House Publishers, 1998. Essays and commentaries on groups and officials and the linkages between them.

Lowi, Theodore J. *The End of Liberalism*, 2d ed. New York: Norton, 1979. A thorough critique of interest groups' influence on American politics.

Olson, Mancur, Jr. *The Logic of Collective Action*, rev. ed. Cambridge, Mass.: Harvard University Press, 1971. A pioneering analysis of why some interests are more fully and easily organized than others.

LIST OF WEBSITES

http://www.fec/gov/ The Federal Election Commission site; it offers information on elections, voting, campaign finance, parties, and PACs. It also includes a citizens' guide to campaign contributions.

http://www/pirg.org/ The Public Interest Research Group (PIRG) site; PIRG has chapters on many college campuses and the site provides state-by-state policy and other information.

http://www.sierraclub.org/ The Sierra Club site; this organization, one of the oldest environmental protection interest groups, promotes conservation. Its website provides information on its activities.

http://www.townhall.com/ The website of the American Conservative Union (ACU); it includes policy and political information and has a lively chat room.

POLITICS IN THEORY AND PRACTICE

Thinking: Why are there so many more organized interests in the United States than elsewhere? Why are so many of these groups organized around economic interests—particularly business interests?

Acting: Consider contributing to a citizens' interest group. Such groups depend on members' donations for operating funds. Citizens' groups cover the political spectrum from right to left and touch on nearly every conceivable public issue. You will not have difficulty locating a group through the Internet that has policy goals consistent with your beliefs and values.

The New York Times   reading 9

Lobbyists Waitin' on the Levy for Their Ship to Come In

by Jill Abramson

The nation's capital is teeming with lobbyists, and no interest is more fully represented through the group system than is American business. Corporations and trade associations account for well over half of all Washington lobbyists and for an even larger proportion of the money spent on lobbying activities. Business firms are particularly active when the Republicans control the White House or Congress. In this March 4, 2001, article, New York Times correspondent Jill Abramson describes how the business lobby responded when George W. Bush assumed the presidency.

WASHINGTON—A new president whose road to the White House was paved with hundreds of millions of dollars in corporate donations, the prospect of huge tax cuts and the presence of many comrades in top Bush administration jobs has spread jubilation on K Street, Washington's legendary boulevard of lobbying.

The celebratory mood, built on the prospect of signing new clients, charging heftier fees, and securing special breaks, was already evident during the inauguration, as lobbying firms and corporations vied to flaunt their ties to the new Bush White House. There was General Motors' gaudy Kennedy Center reception for Andrew H. Card Jr., the White House chief of staff and former G.M. lobbyist. There was Patton Boggs's soiree for Benjamin L. Ginsberg, who argued Bush v. Gore in Florida, the case that gave Mr. Bush the White House. No sooner had President Bush sent his $1.6 million tax-cutting plan to Congress last week than lobbyists and trade associations representing everything from software makers to manufacturers of energy-efficient appliances began salivating over their own share of the tax-cut bonanza.

"Lobbying groups and corporations invested a lot in the Bush presidency," said John B. Judis, author of "The Paradox of American Democracy," a book analyzing the growth and power of special interests. "They all now see a payoff with a Bush presidency, with control of the House and Senate and the tax-writing committees."

But when President Bush invited K-Streeters, including the veteran tax lobbyist Charls E. Walker, to the White House for sandwiches and a tete-a-tete in the Cabinet room, his message was hardly music to their ears. "We should focus on people first, not corporations," he said. Then, at his first

CHAPTER

10

THE NEWS MEDIA: COMMUNICATING POLITICAL IMAGES

❝The press in America . . . determines what people will think and talk about—an authority that in other nations is reserved for tyrants, priests, parties, and mandarins.**❞**

THEODORE H. WHITE[1]

Early on the morning of April 22, 2000, the television networks interrupted their coverage to report a breaking story from Miami. Federal agents had just forced their way into the home where six-year-old Elian Gonzalez was staying and had rushed him to a waiting plane that would fly him to Washington to be reunited with his father. During the next few days, Elian's seizure and the reactions to it filled the airwaves and front pages. The seizure was the latest episode in a running news story that had begun months earlier when Elian was rescued at sea after his mother had drowned while trying to escape Cuba by boat. The young boy became the object of a political tug-of-war between Florida's Cuban American community and Cuba's Fidel Castro. Every move and countermove provoked a torrent of news coverage.

Not all developments receive such intensive news coverage. More new immigrants have arrived in the United States in the past two decades than during any comparable period in the nation's history. Their sheer number has strained the capacity of schools and other public organizations. In some

Federal agents seize Elian Gonzalez from the home of his Miami relatives. The Gonzalez story was one of the most heavily covered news events of recent years.

communities, mobile homes have been converted into makeshift school-rooms simply to get a roof over all students' heads. This great wave of immigration will affect U.S. communities and public policies for years to come. Yet this development has only occasionally been mentioned in the news, let alone emblazoned in the headlines month after month.

Although the news has been compared to a mirror held up to society, it is actually a highly selective portrayal of reality. The **news** is mainly an account of obtruding events, particularly those that are *timely* (new or unfolding developments rather than old or static ones), *dramatic* (striking developments rather than commonplace ones), and *compelling* (developments that arouse people's emotions).[2] These tendencies have a number of origins, not the least of which is that the news organizations seek to make a profit, which leads them to prefer news stories that will attract and hold an audience. Thus, Elian Gonzalez became headline news the instant he was plucked from the sea, and he remained newsworthy while the political and legal process surrounding his status unfolded. The larger issue of the influx of immigrants into the United States during the past two decades is not considered particularly newsworthy because it is a slow and steady process, dramatic only in its long-term implications. The columnist George Will notes that a development requires a defining event before it can become big news.[3] Without such an event, reporters have no peg on which to hang their stories.

News organizations and journalists, of either the print media (newspapers and magazines) or the broadcast media (radio and television), are referred to collectively as the **press** or the **news media.** The press is an increasingly important political actor. Its heightened influence is attributable in part to changes within the media. New technology, from television to cable to satellites, has dramatically increased the reach and speed of communication. In addition, the press has filled some of the void created by the decline in political parties and other political institutions.

In some ways, the press is better positioned than parties or groups to serve the public. On a daily basis, Americans connect to politics more through the news than through the activities of parties or groups. This chapter argues, however, that the news media are a very different kind of intermediary than either parties or interest groups and that problems arise when the press is expected to perform the same functions as these organizations. The chapter begins with a review of the media's historical development and the current trends in news reporting. It concludes with an analysis of the roles the press can and cannot perform adequately in the American political system. The main ideas represented in this chapter are the following:

★ *The American press was initially tied to the nation's political party system (the partisan press) but gradually developed an independent position (the objective press).* In the process, the news shifted from a political orientation, which emphasizes political values and ideas, to a journalistic orientation, which stresses newsworthy information and evaluations.

★ *Although the United States has thousands of separate news organizations, they present a common version of the news that reflects journalists' shared view of what the news is.* Freedom of the press in the United States does not result in a robust marketplace of ideas.

★ *In fulfilling its responsibility to provide public information, the news media effectively perform three significant roles—those of signaler (the press brings relevant events and problems into public view), common carrier (the press serves as a channel through which political leaders can address the public), and watchdog (the press scrutinizes official behavior for evidence of deceitful, careless, or corrupt acts).* These roles are within the news media's capacity because they fit with the values, incentives, and accountability of the press.

★ *The press cannot do the job of political institutions, even though it increasingly tries to do so.* The nature of journalism as it has evolved is incompatible with the characteristics required for the role of public representative.

THE DEVELOPMENT OF THE NEWS MEDIA: FROM PARTISANSHIP TO OBJECTIVE JOURNALISM

Democracy requires a free flow of information. Communication enables a free people to keep in touch with one another, with their leaders, and with important events.

America's early leaders were quick to recognize the importance of the press. At Alexander Hamilton's urging, the *Gazette of the United States* was founded by John Fenno to promote the policies of George Washington's administration. Hamilton was secretary of the treasury and supported Fenno's paper by granting it the Treasury Department's printing contracts. Thomas Jefferson, who was secretary of state and Hamilton's political adversary, complained that the newspaper's content was "pure Toryism." Jefferson persuaded Philip Freneau to start the *National Gazette* as the opposition Republican party's publication and supported it by granting Freneau authority to print State Department documents.

Early newspapers were printed on flat presses, a process that limited production and kept the cost of each copy beyond the reach of ordinary citizens—most of whom were illiterate anyway. Leading papers such as the *Gazette of the United States* had fewer than fifteen hundred subscribers and could not have survived without party support. Not surprisingly, the "news" they printed was a form of party propaganda.[4] In this era of the **partisan press,** publishers openly took sides on partisan issues. Their employees were expected to follow the party line. President James K. Polk once persuaded a leading publisher to fire an editor who was critical of Polk's policies.[5]

From a Partisan Press to an "Objective" One

Technological changes helped bring about the gradual decline of America's partisan press. After the introduction of the telegraph in 1837, editors could receive timely information on developments in Washington and the state capital, and they had less reason to fill their pages with partisan arguments.[6] The invention in 1815 of the rotary press enabled publishers to print their newspapers more rapidly and cheaply.[7] The *New York Sun* was the first paper to pass on the benefit of higher-speed printing to subscribers by reducing the price of a daily copy from six cents to a penny. The *Sun's* circulation rose to five thousand in four months and to ten thousand in less than a year.[8] Increased circulation meant increased advertising revenue, which freed newspapers from their dependence on government printing contracts.

By the late nineteenth century, helped along by the invention of newsprint and power-driven presses, many American newspapers were printing fifty thousand or more copies a day, and their large circulations enabled them to charge high prices for advertising. The period marked the height of newspapers' power and the low point in their sense of public responsibility.[9] A new style of reporting—"yellow journalism"—had emerged as a way of boosting circulation.[10] It was "a shrieking, gaudy, sensation-loving, devil-may-care kind of journalism which lured the reader by any possible means."[11] A circulation battle between William Randolph Hearst's *New York Journal* and Joseph Pulitzer's *New York World* is believed to have contributed to the outbreak of the Spanish-American War through sensational (and largely inaccurate) reports on the cruelty of Spanish rule in Cuba. A young Frederic Remington (who later became a noted painter and sculptor), working as a news artist for Hearst, planned to return home because Cuba appeared calm and safe, but Hearst cabled back, "Please remain. You furnish the pictures and I'll furnish the war."[12]

The excesses of yellow journalism led some publishers to consider ways of reporting the news more responsibly. One step was to separate the newspaper's advertising department from its news department, thus reducing the influence of advertisers on news content. A second development was a new model of reporting called **objective journalism**, which was based on the reporting of "facts" rather than opinions and was "fair" in that it presented both sides of partisan debate.[13]

A chief advocate of this new form of journalism was Adolph Ochs of *The New York Times*. Ochs bought the *Times* in 1896, when its circulation was 9,000; four years later, its readership had grown to 82,000. Ochs told his reporters that he "wanted as little partisanship as possible . . . as few judgments as possible."[14] The *Times*'s approach to reporting appealed particularly to educated readers, and by the early twentieth century it had acquired a reputation as the country's best newspaper. Objective reporting was also promoted through newly formed journalism schools. Among the first of these professional schools were those at Columbia University and the University of Missouri.

Objective journalism is still a component of news coverage. Although most newspapers have a partisan bias on their editorial pages, they tend to treat the Republican and Democratic parties equally on their news pages. Nevertheless, the influence of objective journalism is waning. Newspapers increasingly rely on an **interpretive style of reporting,** in which the journalist's job is to analyze, evaluate, and explain developments rather than merely report them. The older form of objective journalism (called

descriptive reporting, because of its straightforward description of events) required that reporters stick to the "facts." The newer interpretive style allows them to speculate on what the facts mean. As explained later in the chapter, interpretive reporting has greatly increased journalists' ability to shape the news to fit their own biases, including their skeptical opinion of politicians' motives and accomplishments.

The Development of the Broadcast Media

Radio and Television: The Truly National Media Until the early twentieth century, the print media were the only form of mass communication. Within a few decades, however, there were hundreds of radio stations throughout the nation. Broadcasting was the first truly *national* mass medium. Newspapers had local readerships, whereas radio could reach millions of Americans across the country simultaneously.

Television followed radio, and by the late 1950s more than 90 percent of American homes had a television set. However, television newscasts of the 1950s were brief, lasting no more than fifteen minutes, and relied on news gathered by other organizations, particularly the Associated Press and other wire services. In the early 1960s, the three commercial networks—CBS, NBC, and ABC—expanded their evening newscasts to thirty minutes, and their audience ratings increased.[15] Simultaneously, they increased the size and funding of their news divisions, and television soon became the principal news medium of national politics.

Today, television provides a twenty-four-hour forum of political news and information. The creation of the Cable News Network (CNN) and C-SPAN in the late 1970s brought Americans round-the-clock public-affairs coverage. Television talk shows, such as *Larry King Live*, have broadened the range of choices available to politically interested viewers. A parallel development is the emergence of radio talk shows. Nearly a sixth of the American public claims to listen regularly to a politically oriented radio talk show, most of which have a conservative slant.

Even more so than their newspaper counterparts, television journalists rely on an interpretive style of reporting. The reason is that television journalists use a narrative or storytelling mode in order to appeal to an audience accustomed to entertainment programming. "Facts" alone do not tell a story; they have to be interpreted in a way that makes them into a story. Reuven Frank, a network executive and pioneer in television journalism, once told his correspondents: "Every news story should, without any sacrifice of probity or responsibility, display the attributes of fiction, of drama. It should have structure and conflict, problem and denouement, rising action and falling action, a beginning, a middle and an end."[16]

★ STATES IN THE NATION

In the News, or Out?

Most of the news that reaches Americans wherever they might live originates with a handful of news outlets, such as NBC News. This coverage, however, concentrates on events in a few places. The map shows the relative frequency with which each of the fifty states was mentioned on NBC News during a recent one-year period.

A. Why do some states get more coverage than other states do?

B. The heavily covered states are the more populous ones, which increases the likelihood a newsworthy event will occur. In NBC's case, coverage is also heavier in states where one of its news bureaus is located. NBC has bureaus in New York, Washington, Los Angeles, Dallas, Atlanta, Chicago, and Boston.

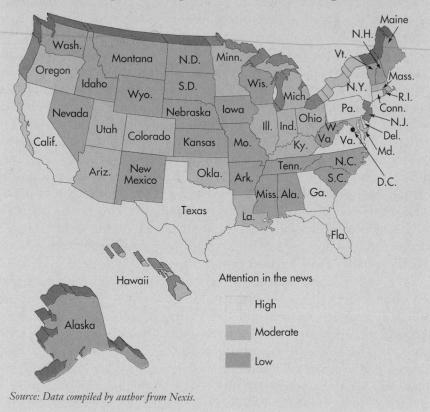

Source: Data compiled by author from Nexis.

Government Licensing and Regulation of Broadcasters At first the government did not carefully regulate broadcasting. Chaos was the result. Nearby stations often used the same or adjacent radio frequencies, interfering with each other's transmissions. Finally, in 1934, Congress passed the Communications Act, which requires that broadcasters be licensed and meet certain performance standards. Congress established the Federal Communications Commission (FCC) to administer the act through regulations pertaining to such matters as signal strength, advertising rates, and political coverage.

The principle of scarcity justifies the licensing and regulation of broadcast media. Because the number of available broadcasting frequencies is limited, those few individuals who are granted a broadcasting license are expected to serve the public interest in addition to their own. In principle, licensing is a means of controlling broadcasting. If a station fails to comply with federal broadcast regulations, the FCC can withdraw its license. However, the FCC seldom even threatens to revoke a license, for fear of being accused of restricting freedom of the press. A broadcast station can apply for renewal of its license by postcard and is virtually guaranteed FCC approval, which covers seven years for radio and five for television.

Because broadcast frequencies are a scarce resource, licensees are required by law to be somewhat evenhanded during election campaigns. Section 315 of the Communications Act imposes on broadcasters an "equal-time" restriction, which means that they cannot sell or give air time to a political candidate without granting equal opportunities to the other candidates running for the same office. (Election debates are an exception; broadcasters can televise them even if participation is limited to the Republican and Democratic nominees only.)

The Emergence of the Internet Although the First Amendment protects each individual's right to press freedom, the right in practice has been reserved for a tiny few. The journalist A. J. Liebling wrote that freedom of the press belongs to those with the money to own a broadcast station or newspaper.[17] Even a smaller broadcast station or daily newspaper costs millions to buy; the larger are worth hundreds of millions.

Access to the Internet is no substitute for ownership of a major news outlet, but it provides ordinary citizens an opportunity to exercise their free-press rights. By creating a website, the ordinary citizen can post information about public affairs, harangue officials, argue for public policies, and attempt to mobilize the support of others. There is no assurance of a wide audience, and in fact, most citizens have neither a personal website nor, if they do, a

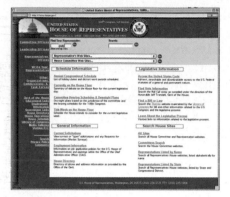 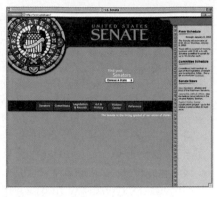

The Internet has weakened the traditional news media's control of the political information that Americans receive. Through the Internet, citizens and political leaders alike can communicate widely without having their messages filtered through the news media. Pictured here are the home pages of the U.S. House and Senate.

large following. But the Internet has reduced the barriers to citizen communication to a level not seen since the colonial days, when citizen-produced pamphlets were the major form of political expression. The Internet has also provided political leaders and organizations a direct channel to the public. At all political levels, officeholders, parties, and interest groups now have websites that are used to inform and mobilize their followers.

Freedom and Conformity in the U.S. News Media

Some democracies impose significant legal restraints on the press. The news media in Britain are barred from reporting on anything that the government has labeled an "official secret," and the nation's tough libel laws inhibit the press from publishing unsubstantiated personal attacks.

In the United States, as pointed out in Chapter 4, the First Amendment gives the press substantial protection. The courts have consistently upheld the right of U.S. newspapers to report on politics as they choose. Broadcasters, as the equal-time restriction indicates, have less freedom under the law, but they are subject to much less government control than are broadcasters in Europe. In the case of both U.S. newspapers and broadcasters, the government cannot block publication of a news story unless it can convincingly demonstrate in court that the information would jeopardize national security. Although most Americans would permit censorship in time of armed conflict (see Figure 10–1), the courts have limited the government's ability to restrict press freedom even when the nation is at war. U.S.

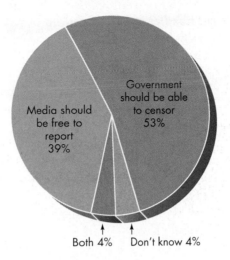

FIGURE   10-1   OPINIONS ON PRESS CENSORSHIP IN TIME OF WAR

When U.S. forces were attacking Afghanistan, more Americans said they would support government censorship than said they would give the press free rein in its reporting.

Source: Pew Research Center Survey, November 13-19, 2001.

libel laws also strongly favor the press. A public figure who is attacked in a news story cannot collect libel damages unless he or she can demonstrate convincingly that the news organization was false in its accusations and knowingly or recklessly careless in its search for the truth.

Moreover, the U.S. government gives the news media a lot of economic support. Newspapers and magazines have a special postal rate that helps them keep their circulation costs low, and broadcasters pay only a few dollars annually in license fees for broadcasting rights that are worth hundreds of billions of dollars. Such policies have contributed to the development of a truly enormous news industry in the United States: 1,600 daily newspapers; 8,500 weeklies; 9,500 radio stations; 6 national television news networks; 850 local television stations; and 10,500 cable television systems.[18]

The audience reach of leading news organizations is substantial. Each weekday evening, more than twenty million Americans tune into a network newscast. *The New York Times, The Wall Street Journal, USA Today,* and the *Los Angeles Times* have daily circulations exceeding one million readers. Three dozen other newspapers have circulations in excess of 250,000 readers. The average daily circulation of America's newspapers is roughly forty million; on Sunday, newspaper circulation jumps to sixty million.[19]

In view of the great number and the freedom of news organizations in the United States, it might be expected that Americans would have a lot of choice in the news they receive. However, the opposite is true. Each day, newspapers and broadcast stations from coast to coast tend to highlight the same national news stories and to interpret them in similar ways. Any number of terms—*pack journalism, groupthink, media concentration*—have been used to describe this tendency.

The basic reason the news is pretty much the same everywhere is that America's reporters, unlike their counterparts in some European democracies, do not take sides in partisan disputes. They do sometimes differ on which facts, events, and issues are the most important, but these polite disagreements are a far cry from the lively disputes that characterized the nineteenth-century partisan press.

LIBERTY, EQUALITY, AND SELF-GOVERNMENT
What's Your Opinion?

Press Freedom

In the United States, government has little power to block the press from reporting information that could damage national security. The principle of "no prior restraint" holds that government cannot stop a publication or broadcast program unless it can convince a court that grave harm to the nation would result from release of the information. The U.S. press is also protected, as was explained in Chapter 4, by an imposing legal standard for libel. It is nearly impossible for a U.S. official to win a libel suit against a newspaper, magazine, or broadcast organization even in situations where his or her reputation has been destroyed by false allegations.

By comparison, Britain's government has the power to prevent news organizations from reporting on national security issues. For example, there was a long period during which British journalists were prohibited from reporting stories on the Irish separatist issue that presented the conflict from the terrorists' viewpoint. British law also differs from American law when it comes to libel. Although libel judgements in Britain typically result in relatively small monetary awards, libel is much easier to prove in British courts than in American courts.

Which model of press freedom—the American or the British—do you prefer? What arguments would you make for and against each model?

Of course, today's news organizations differ in the way they tell a given story. Broadcast news tends to be, in effect, headline news with pictures. A thirty-minute network news broadcast typically presents a dozen or so stories in the roughly twenty minutes allotted to news content (the other ten minutes being devoted to commercials). Newspapers have the space to present news developments in greater depth; some, like *The New York Times* (which labels itself "the newspaper of record"), provide substantial detail. The reporting styles of news organizations also vary. Although most of them present the news in an understated way, others tend toward sensationalism. For example, when Jeffrey Dahmer, a convicted murderer who had cannibalized his victims, was himself murdered in a Wisconsin prison in 1994, the *New York Post* gave its whole front page to the headline: "Death of a Monster." *The New York Times*, in contrast, gave the story a standard-size front-page headline, "Jeffrey Dahmer, Multiple Killer, Is Bludgeoned to Death in Prison." Such differences in approach, however, do not disguise the fact that most news organizations tell their audiences the same stories each day.

Domination of News Production

Another reason for the lack of diversity in national news reporting is that a few news organizations generate most of it. The Associated Press (AP) is the major producer of news stories. It has three hundred full-time reporters stationed throughout the country and the world to gather news stories, which are relayed by satellite to subscribing newspapers and broadcast stations. More than 95 percent of the nation's dailies are serviced by AP, and some also subscribe to other wire services, such as Reuters and The New York Times.[20] Smaller dailies lack the resources to gather news outside their own localities and thus depend on wire service reports for their national and international coverage.[21]

Television news production is similarly dominated by just a few organizations. The six major networks—ABC, CBS, NBC, PBS, Fox, and CNN—generate most of the news coverage of national and international politics. For news of the nation and the world, local stations depend on video transmissions fed to them by the networks.

News Values and Imperatives

Competitive pressures also lead the producers of news to report the same stories. No major news organization wants to miss an important story that others are reporting.[22]

The networks, wire services, and a few elite dailies, including *The New York Times, Washington Post, The Wall Street Journal, Los Angeles Times,* and *Chicago*

Tribune, establish a national standard of story selection. Whenever one of them highlights a story, the others jump on the bandwagon. The top trendsetter is *The New York Times*, which has been described as "the bulletin board" for other major newspapers, newsmagazines, and television networks.[23]

The imperatives of the fast pace of daily journalism also tend to make the news homogeneous.[24] Journalists have the task each day of filling a newspaper or broadcast with stories. Thus editors assign reporters to such beats as the White House and Congress, which can be relied on for a steady supply of news. On these beats the reporters of various news organizations see and hear the same things, exchange views on what is important, and not surprisingly, produce similar news stories.

Finally, shared professional values guide journalists in their search for news.[25] Reporters are on the lookout for aspects of situations that lend themselves to interesting news stories—novel, colorful, and compelling developments.[26] Long practice at reporting leads journalists to develop a common understanding of what the news is.[27] After the White House press corps has listened to a presidential speech, for example, nearly all the journalists in attendance are in agreement on what was most newsworthy about the speech, often only a single statement within it.

"Megamedia": Mergers, Profits, and the News

Over the past two decades and at an accelerating pace, media ownership has become increasingly concentrated. The ABC network and its news division, for example, are part of the Disney corporation, while CNN is part of AOL Time Warner. The trend reflects the high profitability of the media business and the economies of scale—the larger the media organization, the more it can leverage advertisers and achieve efficiencies in the production of news and entertainment. The net result is that U.S. news is largely in the hands of what the political scientist Dean Alger calls the "megamedia."[28]

Should so few entities control so much of what Americans see and hear through the mass media? Some observers say that the change is not all that significant because there is still competition between news organizations and because there is a degree of independence for news organizations within their corporate structures. Alger is not convinced:

> It is . . . vital for democracy to have a truly diverse set of media
> sources present in the public arena. . . . The continued advance of
> megamedia and their increasing domination of the prime mass media
> spell a profound constriction of that diversity and a severe diminution
> of the marketplace of ideas, and thus a danger to democracy.[29]

Another issue is the impact of media conglomerates on the quality of news content. As news organizations have been absorbed by larger corporations, they have been pressured to increase their profit margins. A result has been a cutback in news-gathering capacity. ABC, CBS, and NBC News, for example, have closed many of their overseas news bureaus. This cost-saving measure placed the networks in a weak position to report accurately on global terrorism in the immediate aftermath of the September 11, 2001, attacks on the World Trade Center and the Pentagon. The networks did not have seasoned reporters on station in Pakistan or Afghanistan when the attacks occurred.

News divisions have also been directed to compete more aggressively for audiences, because audience size determines advertising revenues. As a consequence, the news has become increasingly entertainment oriented. Critics say it is "infotainment" rather than real news. A study of network evening newscasts found that, over the past decade, the amount of news time devoted to government, politics, and public affairs has declined significantly while the amount given to lifestyle issues, celebrities, and human-interest subjects has risen sharply.[30]

THE NEWS MEDIA AS LINK: ROLES THE PRESS CAN AND CANNOT PERFORM

When the objective model of reporting came to dominate American news coverage, the relationship between the press and the public was fundamentally altered. The nineteenth-century partisan press gave its readers overt cues as to how to evaluate political issues and leaders. In the presidential election campaign of 1896, the *San Francisco Call* devoted 1,075 column-inches of photographs to the Republican ticket of McKinley-Hobart and only 11 inches to the Democrats, Bryan and Sewell.[31] Many European newspapers still function in this way, guiding their readers by applying partisan or ideological values to current events. The *Daily Telegraph*, for example, is an unofficial but fiercely loyal mouthpiece of Britain's Conservative party (see "How the United States Compares").

In contrast, U.S. news organizations do not routinely and consistently take sides in partisan conflict. Their main task is to report and analyze events. The media are thus very different from political parties and interest groups, the other major links between the public and its leaders. Parties and groups exist to promote political positions. The media are driven by the search for interesting and important stories.

This distinction provides a basis for determining what roles the media can and cannot be expected to fulfill. The press is capable of fulfilling only those public responsibilities that are compatible with journalistic values: the signaler role, the common-carrier role, and the watchdog role. The media

How the United States Compares

Partisan Neutrality as a News Value

In the nineteenth century, the United States had a partisan press. Journalists were partisan actors, and news was a blend of reporting and advocacy. This type of reporting gradually gave way to a model of journalism that emphasizes the "facts" and covers the two parties more or less equally. For example, a political scandal, whether it involves a Democrat or Republican, is a big story for any major U.S. news organization.

European news organizations are less committed to partisan neutrality. Many European newspapers are aligned with specific parties, and although they focus on events, their coverage has a partisan component. In Great Britain, for example, the *Daily Telegraph* often serves as a voice of the Conservative party, while the *Guardian* favors the liberal side. A political scandal involving a Conservative party leader would be reported differently in the two newspapers.

The difference between the U.S. and European media is evident in a five-country survey that asked journalists whether they thought journalists should remain neutral in reporting on political parties. Compared with their counterparts in Great Britain, Germany, Sweden, and Italy, U.S. journalists were more likely to believe in partisan neutrality.

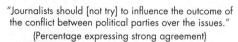

"Journalists should [not try] to influence the outcome of
the conflict between political parties over the issues."
(Percentage expressing strong agreement)

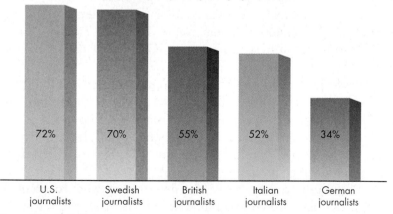

| U.S. journalists | Swedish journalists | British journalists | Italian journalists | German journalists |
| 72% | 70% | 55% | 52% | 34% |

Source: Thomas E. Patterson, Media and Democracy Project, in progress.

are less successful in their attempts to perform a fourth and more politically oriented role: that of public representative.

The Signaler Role

As journalists see it, their responsibilities include the **signaler role.** They seek to alert the public to important developments as soon as possible after they happen: a state visit to Washington by a foreign leader, a bill that has just been passed by Congress, a change in the nation's unemployment level, a terrorist bombing in a foreign capital.

The U.S. media are well equipped to play the signaler role. They are poised to converge on any fast-breaking major news event anywhere in the nation and nearly anywhere in the world. For instance, as the United States prepared to launch air strikes on Afghanistan in late 2001, hundreds of U.S. journalists descended on that part of the world. Their news stories kept Americans abreast of the progress of the war effort and the subsequent effort to create a post-Taliban government in Afghanistan.

The media are particularly well suited to signal developments from Washington. More than half of all national news coverage emanates from the nation's capital, most of it from the White House and Congress. Altogether, more than ten thousand people in Washington work in the news business. The key players are the leading correspondents of the television networks and major newspapers, the heads of the Washington news bureaus, and a few top editors.[32]

The press, in its capacity as signaler, has the power to focus the public's attention. The term **agenda setting** has been used to describe the media's ability to influence what is on people's minds.[33] By covering the same events, problems, issues, and leaders—simply by giving them space or time in the news—the media place them on the public agenda.[34] The press, as Bernard Cohen notes, "may not be successful much of the time in telling people what to think, but it is stunningly successful in telling them what to think about."[35] This influence is most obvious in such situations as the U.S. conflict with Iraq, a development that held Americans' attention for months on end in 2003.

The Common-Carrier Role

The press also plays a **common-carrier role** in that it provides political leaders a channel through which to communicate with the public. The importance of this role to officials and citizens alike is obvious. Citizens cannot very well support or oppose a leader's plans and actions if they do not know about them. And leaders need news coverage if they are to get the public's attention. Indeed, national news is mainly about the actions of political leaders and institutions, as is reflected in the hundreds of reporters who station themselves regularly at the Capitol and White House.

Officials try to get the most favorable news coverage they can. For example, the White House Press Office and the White House Office of Communications try to shape information in a way favorable to the president. Sometimes they succeed in placing their spin (that is, the president's interpretation) on the media's coverage of events.

Even though the president and Congress can expect coverage, the press increasingly places its own spin on these stories. Journalists, because of their increased celebrity status, their heightened skepticism of politicians since Vietnam and Watergate, and the greater latitude afforded them by the interpretive style of reporting, have become accustomed not only to covering what newsmakers say but also to having their own say. In 2002, as the Bush administration was trying to focus domestic coverage on its attempts to stimulate the economy, the press was concentrating on the Enron Corporation scandal and its links to the White House.

In fact, the news today is as much journalist centered as it is newsmaker centered. For every minute that the presidential candidates spoke on the network newscasts during coverage of the 2000 campaign, for example, the journalists who were covering them talked for six minutes. At one time, a candidate's sound bite (the length of time within a television story that the

U.S. journalists covering the war against the Taliban and Al Qaeda in Afghanistan. Most of the war correspondents were from the major networks, the wire services, and leading newspapers such as *The New York Times*. These news organizations supply most of the national and international news that Americans receive.

candidate speaks without interruption) was more than forty seconds in length on average.[36] In recent campaigns, the average sound bite has been less than ten seconds, which is barely enough time for the candidate to utter a full sentence.

The Watchdog Role

Traditionally, the American press has accepted responsibility for protecting the public from deceitful, careless, incompetent, and corrupt officials.[37] In this **watchdog role,** the press stands ready to expose any official who violates accepted legal, ethical, and performance standards.

The most notable exercise of the watchdog role in recent decades took place during the Watergate scandal. Bob Woodward and Carl Bernstein of the *Washington Post* spent months uncovering evidence that high-ranking officials in the Nixon White House were lying about their role in the burglary of the Democratic National Committee's headquarters and in the subsequent cover-up. Virtually all the nation's media picked up on the *Post*'s revelations. Nixon was forced to resign, as was his attorney general, John Mitchell. The Watergate episode is a dramatic reminder that a vigilant press is one of society's best safeguards against abuses of political power.

There is an inherent tension between the watchdog role and the common-carrier role. The watchdog role demands that the journalist maintain a skeptical view of political leaders and keep them at a distance. The common-carrier role requires the journalist to maintain close ties with political leaders. In the period before Watergate, the common-carrier role was clearly the dominant orientation. It perhaps still is, but journalists have become increasingly critical of political leaders and institutions.

Some of this criticism revolves around scandals such as the Iran-Contra episode (President Reagan) and the Monica Lewinsky affair (President Clinton). Most of the criticism, however, is leveled at the day-to-day conduct of politics. Journalists are intent on publicizing the missteps of political leaders. Given the enormous size of the U.S. government, there is plenty to criticize if journalists want to focus on it. The media's preference for "bad news" can be seen, for example, in the fact that the negative coverage of presidential candidates has risen steadily in recent decades and now exceeds the positive coverage (see Figure 10–2).

"Bad news" characterizes the coverage of Democrats and Republicans alike. Although surveys indicate that most journalists lean toward the Democratic party in their personal beliefs, studies have found partisan bias to be a relatively small factor in political coverage.[38] Other influences, including the norm of objectivity, counterbalance the effect of partisanship on journalists' news decisions. On the other hand, there is no

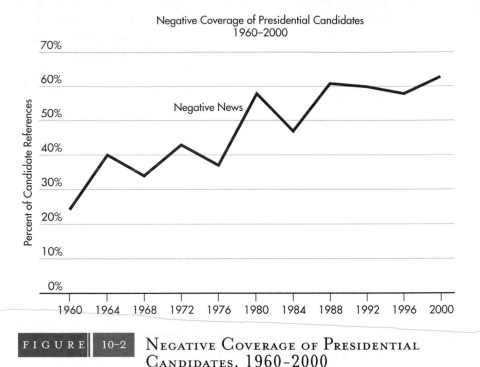

Source: Thomas E. Patterson, Out of Order, (New York: Vintage, 1994), 20, for 1960-1992; Center for Media and Public Affairs, for 1996, 2000.

FIGURE 10-2 NEGATIVE COVERAGE OF PRESIDENTIAL CANDIDATES, 1960–2000

In the 1960s, candidates received largely favorable news coverage. Today, their coverage is mostly negative.

rule of journalism that limits negativity.[39] Coverage of the Democrat-controlled Congress of 1993–1994 by the national media was nearly 70 percent negative; when the Congress shifted to Republican hands in 1995–1996, its coverage too was nearly 70 percent negative in tone.[40] The fact is, the real bias of the press is not liberal as opposed to conservative, but a pronounced tendency to report what is wrong with politics and politicians rather than what is right.

Critics argue that the press has gone too far in its search for bad news, claiming that it now faults nearly everything that politicians say and do, thereby undermining the public trust on which effective leadership is built. Critics also complain that the press no longer has any respect for public officials' private lives—that everything from their bedroom behavior to decades-old "skeletons in the closet" are grist for news stories. Journalists claim that they are merely doing their job—that the public is better served by a highly skeptical and intrusive press than a compliant one.

CNN correspondent Bob Franken said, "We historically are not supposed to be popular, and it's almost our role to be bearer of bad news."[41]

The Public-Representative Role

Traditionally, the **public-representative role**—that of spokesperson for and advocate of the public—has belonged to political leaders, political institutions, and political organizations. Today, however, many reporters believe they also have a mandate to represent the public. "[Our] chief duty," newscaster Roger Mudd claims, "is to put before the nation its unfinished business."[42]

Although the press has to some degree always acted as a stand-in for the people, the desire of journalists to play the role of public advocate has increased significantly since the 1960s.[43] As journalists' status rose, they became more assertive, a tendency sharpened by the trend toward interpretive reporting. Vietnam and Watergate also contributed to the change; these events convinced many journalists that their judgments were superior to those of political leaders. James Reston of *The New York Times* said of Vietnam, "Maybe the historians will agree that the reporters and cameras were decisive in the end. They brought the issue of the war to the people, before the Congress and the courts, and forced the withdrawal of American power from Vietnam."[44]

Nevertheless, there are at least two basic reasons for concluding that journalists are not nearly as well suited as political leaders to the role of public representative. First, the news media are not subject to the level of public accountability required of a public representative. Political institutions are made responsible to the public by a formal mechanism of accountability—elections. The vote gives officeholders a reason to act in the majority's interest, and it offers citizens an opportunity to boot from office anyone they feel has failed them. Thousands of elected officials have lost their jobs this way. The public has no comparable hold over the press. Journalists are neither chosen nor removable by the people.

A second obstacle to journalists' attempts to play the role of public representative is that representation requires a point of view. Politics is essentially the mobilization of bias—that is, it involves the representation of particular values and interests. Political parties and interest groups, as explained in Chapters 8 and 9, exist to represent particular interests in society. But what political interests do the media represent? CBS News executive Richard Salant once said that his reporters covered stories "from nobody's point of view."[45] What he was saying, in effect, was that journalists do not consistently represent the political concerns of any segment of society. They respond to news opportunities, not to political interests. Above all, they prize good stories.

The Gary Condit–Chandra Levy story is a prime example. Levy's disappearance in 2001 amid allegations of an affair with Representative Condit was for several months the nation's top story. It received more news coverage than health care, unemployment, drug abuse, education, and every other national problem.

Underlying the press's obsession with the dramatic story is its quest for profits. The bottom line, rather than the public interest, increasingly drives news coverage. Audience competition has intensified with the spread of cable television, and the news has become increasingly sensational. "All Monica All the Time" was how some critics described the press's coverage of the Lewinsky scandal. One network, MSNBC, chose to make the scandal nearly the sole focus of its programming, hoping that higher audience ratings and correspondingly higher advertising revenues would be the result.

Even the media's terrorism coverage after September 11, 2001, gradually came to rest on commercial considerations. In the first months following the terrorist attacks on the World Trade Center and the Pentagon, the news media devoted vast amounts of news space and time to the terrorism issue. Americans heard things they had never been told before about Afghanistan, Pakistan, terrorism networks, and Islamic militants. Many

The audience reach of the U.S. news media is truly substantial. More than twenty million Americans each evening watch a network newscast, and about half the adult population reads a daily paper. However, the news audience is shrinking, which has caused alarm among those in the news industry and those who believe that attention to news is critical to an informed citizenry.

daily newspapers added an extra section to accommodate the heavy coverage. However, once the U.S. military attack on Al Qaeda and Taliban forces in Afghanistan quieted down, the press reverted to the pattern of its earlier coverage. A Center for Responsible Journalism study revealed that six months after the terrorist attacks, network newscasts were once again filled with lifestyle, celebrity, and similar stories.

A burst of international coverage occurred again in 2003 when the Bush administration built toward and then declared war on Iraq. However, the news was dominated by war stories. More complicated subjects such as differences within the Arab world regarding terrorist activity were largely ignored. The imbalance affected public opinion. According to a CNN/USA Today poll, two-thirds of Americans believed, contrary to available evidence, that Iraq's Saddam Hussein had been heavily supporting the Al-Qaeda terrorist group.

The relentless search for attention-getting stories weakens the press's ability to provide citizens a clear understanding of what is broadly at issue in politics. The journalist Walter Lippmann put it plainly when he said:

> The press is no substitute for [political] institutions. It is like the beam of a searchlight that moves restlessly about, bringing one episode and then another out of darkness into vision. Men cannot do the work of the world by this light alone. They cannot govern society by episodes, incidents, and interruptions.[46]

ORGANIZING THE PUBLIC IN THE MEDIA AGE

Lippmann's point was not that news organizations are somehow inferior to political organizations but that each has a different role and responsibility in society. Democracy cannot operate effectively without a free press that fulfills its signaler, common-carrier, and watchdog roles. Citizens must have access to timely and uncensored news about public affairs. However, the media cannot also be expected to do the job of political institutions.

As previous chapters have emphasized, the problem of citizen influence is the problem of organizing the public so that people can act together effectively. The news media merely appear to solve this problem. The fact that millions of people each day receive the same news about their government does not mold them into an organized community. The news creates a pseudo-community: citizens feel they are part of a functioning whole until they try to act on their news awareness. The futility of media-centered democracy was dramatized in the movie *Network* when its central character, a television anchorman, became enraged at the nation's political leadership and urged his viewers to go to their windows and yell, "I'm mad as hell and I'm not going to take it anymore!" Citizens heeded his instructions, but the main effect was to raise the network's ratings. It was not clear what officials in Washington were expected to do about several milli n people leaning o t their windows and shouting a vague slogan. The film vividly illustrated the fact that the news can raise public consciousness as a prelude to action, but the news itself cannot organize the public in any meaningful way. When public opinion on an issue is already formed, the media can serve as a channel for the expression of that opinion. But when society's choices are in their formative stage, the media are not ordinarily an adequate guide to the action that should be taken.[47]

SUMMARY

In the nation's first century, the press was allied closely with the political parties and helped the parties mobilize public opinion. Gradually the press freed itself from this relationship and developed a form of reporting, known as objective journalism, that emphasizes the fair and accurate reporting of newsworthy developments. The foundation of modern American news rests on the presentation and evaluation of significant events, not on the advocacy of partisan ideas. The nation's news organizations do not differ greatly in their reporting; broadcast stations and newspapers throughout the country emphasize many of the same events, issues, and personalities, following the lead of the major broadcast networks, a few elite newspapers, and the wire services.

/pattersonwtp5

   The press performs four basic roles in a free society. In their signaler role, journalists communicate information to the public about events and problems that they consider important, relevant, and therefore newsworthy. The press also serves as a common carrier in that it provides political leaders with a channel for addressing the public. Third, the press acts as a public protector, or watchdog, by exposing deceitful, careless, or corrupt officials. The American media can and, to a significant degree, do perform these roles adequately.

   The press is less well suited, however, to the other role it plays, that of public representative. This role requires a consistent political viewpoint and public accountability, neither of which the press possesses. The media are not a substitute for effective political institutions. The press's strength lies ultimately in its capacity to inform the public, not in its attempts to serve as the public's representative.

KEY TERMS

agenda setting
common-carrier role
descriptive reporting
interpretive reporting
news
objective journalism

partisan press
press (news media)
public-representative role
signaler role
watchdog role

SUGGESTED READINGS

Bagdikian, Ben H. *The Media Monopoly*, 6th ed. Boston: Beacon Press, 2000. An examination of the growing power of the press, including tendencies toward monopolies of ownership and news production.

Cook, Timothy E. *Governing with the News: The News Media as a Political Institution*. Chicago: University of Chicago Press, 1997. An analysis of the press in its role as a political institution.

Downie, Leonard, Jr., and Robert G. Kaiser. *The News About the News: American Journalism in Peril*. New York: Knopf, 2002. A critical assessment of today's news media by two *Washington Post* journalists.

Kurtz, Howard. *Spin Cycle: Inside the Clinton Propaganda Machine*. New York: Free Press, 1998. A look at the Clinton White House's attempts to manage its news coverage.

Maltese, John Anthony. *Spin Control: The White House Office of Communications and the Management of Presidential News*. Chapel Hill: University of North Carolina Press, 1994. An assessment of how presidents attempt to manage news coverage.

Patterson, Thomas E. *Out of Order*. New York: Vintage Books, 1994. An analysis of how election news coverage has changed in recent decades.

Sabato, Larry J., Mark Stencel, and S. Robert Lichter. *Peep Show: Media and Politics in the Age of Scandal*. Lanham, Md.: Rowman and Littlefield, 2000. A penetrating critique of today's news.

Sparrow, Bartholomew H. *Uncertain Guardians*. Baltimore, Md.: Johns Hopkins University Press, 1999. A systematic assessment of the news media's political role and tendencies.

LIST OF WEBSITES

http://www.cmpa.com The website for the Center for Media and Public Affairs (CMPA), a nonpartisan organization that analyzes news coverage on a continuing basis; its website provides analyses of news content that are useful to anyone interested in the media's political coverage.

http://www.drudgereport.com The website through which Matt Drudge (The Drudge Report) has challenged the traditional media's control of the news.

http://www.fcc.gov The Federal Communications Commission (FCC) website, which provides information on broadcasting regulation and current issues.

http://www.newslink.org/ Provides access to more than a thousand news organizations, including most U.S. daily newspapers.

POLITICS IN THEORY AND PRACTICE

Thinking: Why does almost every U.S. news outlet, despite having the freedom to say nearly anything it wants, cover virtually the same national stories in virtually same way as other news organizations?

Acting: If you are like most citizens, news consumption is the politically related activity that takes up most of your time. And if you are like most citizens, you will spend this time without thinking critically about what you are seeing and hearing. The next time you watch a television newscast or read a newspaper, pay attention to how a story is constructed. Is it framed in terms of conflict? Does it sensationalize the material? Is it framed critically—that is, does it present a negative view of a development, institution, or leader? How else might the same factual information have been presented? Do significant items of information or points of view seem to be missing from the story?

The New York Times   reading 10

Mideast Turmoil: The News Outlets; Some U.S. Backers of Israel Boycott Dailies Over Mideast Coverage That They Deplore

by Felicity Barringer

The news media are the one institution that specializes in revealing the flaws and failings of other institutions. Yet the media themselves are often criticized for the decisions they make. The mainstream press, for example, has long been accused of a liberal bias. Some criticisms of the press are more pointed. In this New York Times *article of May 23, 2002, Felicity Barringer describes how some Americans responded to Mideast coverage that they believed was biased against Israel.*

INTENSE PUBLIC REACTION to coverage of the violence of the Middle East conflict has prompted unusually harsh attacks on several news media outlets and has led to boycotts of *The New York Times, The Los Angeles Times* and *The Washington Post*.

Broadcast news operations, including CNN and National Public Radio, have also been criticized. The general manager of one public radio station, WBUR-FM in Boston, said it had lost more than $1 million in underwriting and pledges this year—nearly 4 percent of its annual budget—because some supporters of Israel encouraged people not to give. The criticism has come largely from supporters of Israel, and it reached a climax in recent weeks in the aftermath of the suicide bombing at a Passover seder in Netanya, which killed 28 Israelis, and the subsequent incursion by Israeli troops into West Bank cities like Ramallah, Bethlehem and Jenin, where the destruction of homes and loss of life among Palestinians was highly visible.

The swift communications of the Internet era apparently help fan the intensity of the criticism.

For instance, an account of supposedly anti-Israel remarks made by a CNN correspondent in Jerusalem was widely

CONGRESS: BALANCING NATIONAL GOALS AND LOCAL INTERESTS

❝ There are really two Congresses, not just one. Often these two Congresses are widely separated; the tightly knit, complex world of Capitol Hill is a long way from the world of [the member's district or state]—not only in miles, but in perspective and outlook as well. **❞**

ROGER DAVIDSON AND WALTER OLESZEK[1]

In 1998, for the first time in a generation, the federal government had the luxury of a budget surplus. How would Congress use it? To cut taxes? To underwrite the future of the social security system? To provide a cushion against some future day when the economy turned sour and federal expenditures exceeded revenues?

As it happened, a first use of the surplus was to help fund the most expensive transportation bill in the nation's history. It was hard to argue that it was a bad use of the money. The nation's transportation infrastructure had been neglected for years, and there were plenty of bridges, roads, and mass transit systems in need of repair and expansion. Yet the $200 billion transportation bill was attractive to Congress in part because it provided public works projects and jobs for virtually every state and every congressional district in the nation. It was good policy, but it was also very good politics. When they ran for reelection, members of Congress could point

325

to all the jobs and transportation improvements they had given their constituents.

The story of the 1998 transportation bill illustrates the dual nature of Congress: it is both a lawmaking institution for the country and a representative assembly for states and districts.[2] Members of Congress have both an individual duty to serve the interests of their separate constituencies and a collective duty to protect the interests of the nation as a whole. Attention to constituency interests is the common denominator of a national institution in which each member must please the voters back home in order to win reelection.[3]

This chapter examines Congress, beginning with congressional election and organization and concluding with congressional policymaking. The following points are emphasized in this chapter:

★ Congressional elections tend to have a strong local orientation and to favor incumbents. Congressional office provides incumbents with substantial resources (free publicity, staff, and legislative influence) that give them (particularly House members) a major advantage in election campaigns. However, incumbency also has some liabilities that contribute to turnover in congressional membership.

★ Although party leaders in Congress provide collective leadership, the work of Congress is done mainly through its committees and subcommittees, each of which has its separate leadership and policy jurisdiction. The committee system of Congress allows a broad sharing of power and leadership, which serves the power and reelection needs of Congress's members but fragments the institution.

★ Congress lacks the direction and organization required for the development of comprehensive national policies, but it is well organized to handle policies of relatively narrow scope. At times, Congress takes the lead on broad national issues, but ordinarily it does not do so.

★ Congress's policymaking role is based on three major functions: lawmaking, representation, and oversight.

Congress as a Career: Election to Congress

In the nation's first century, service in the Congress was not a career for most of its members. Before 1900 at least a third and sometimes as many as half the seats in Congress changed hands at each election. Most members left voluntarily. Because travel was slow and arduous, serving in the nation's capital required members to spend months away from their families. And

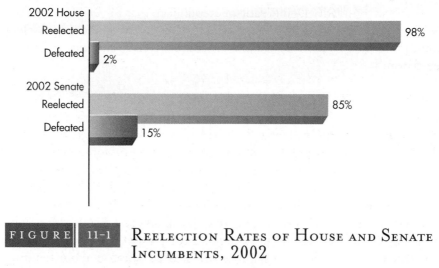

FIGURE   11-1   REELECTION RATES OF HOUSE AND SENATE INCUMBENTS, 2002

Congressional incumbents have a very good chance of being relected, particularly if they serve in the House. The reelection rate of House members in 2002 was about average for the past few elections. The Senate reelection in 2002 was below the recent average.

because the national government was not the center of power and politics that it is today, many politicians preferred to serve in state capitals.

The modern Congress is very different. Most of its members are professional politicians, and a seat in the U.S. Senate or House is as high as most of them can expect to rise in politics. The pay (about $150,000 a year) is reasonably good, and the prestige of their office is substantial, particularly if they serve in the Senate. A lengthy career in Congress is the goal of most of its members.[4]

Incumbents have a good chance of being reelected (see Figure 11–1). In the past few elections, more than 95 percent of House incumbents and 85 percent of Senate incumbents seeking another term have been reelected.[5] These figures overestimate slightly an incumbent's chances of reelection. A few incumbents retire from Congress when faced with a campaign they fear they will lose. Moreover, incumbents must win reelection again and again in order to have a congressional career. A single loss will halt or interrupt it.

On balance, however, incumbents have a clear edge over their opponents, as their margin of victory indicates. In recent elections, two-thirds of House incumbents and nearly half of Senate incumbents seeking reelection have received 60 percent or more of the vote. Even when voters are convinced that Congress as an institution is performing badly, they reelect a large majority of its members. One reason is that many congressional districts and a few states are so lopsidedly Democratic or Republican that the candidate of the weaker party has no realistic chance of victory. In recent congressional elections, more than 10 percent of House incumbents have run unopposed for reelection.

Using Incumbency to Stay in Congress

An incumbent promotes his or her reelection prospects by catering to the **constituency:** the body of citizens eligible to vote in their state or district. Members of Congress pay attention to constituency opinions when choosing positions on legislation,[6] and they work hard to get their share of **pork barrel projects** (a term referring to legislation that funds a special project for a particular locale, such as a new highway or hospital).

They also respond to their constituents' individual needs, a practice known as the **service strategy.** Whether a constituent is seeking information about a government program, expressing an opinion about pending legislation, or looking for help in obtaining a federal benefit, the representative's staff is ready to assist.[7] Congressional staffers spend most of their time not on legislative matters but on constituency service and public relations—efforts that pay off on election day.[8] Each House member receives an office allowance of $750,000 a year, which supports a personal staff of about twenty full-time staff members.[9] Senators receive allowances that vary according to the population size of the state they represent. Senators' personal staffs average about forty employees.[10] Each member of Congress is also permitted several free mailings annually to constituent households, a privilege known as the frank.

Finally, incumbents have a decided advantage when it comes to raising campaign funds. Congressional elections have become increasingly expensive in recent decades because of the high cost of polling, televised advertising, and other modern techniques (see Figure 11–2). Today a successful House campaign will often cost a million dollars or more. The price of victory in competitive Senate races is much higher, ranging from several million dollars in small states to $15 million or more in larger states. A study by the *Congressional Quarterly* found that only 10 percent of incumbents said they had trouble raising enough money to conduct an effective campaign, compared with 70 percent of challengers.[11] Many challengers are able to raise only enough money for a token campaign.[12]

Incumbents obtain a fund-raising advantage from their past campaigns and constituent service, which enable them to develop mailing lists of potential contributors. Individual contributions, most of which are $100 or less, account for about 50 percent of all funds raised by candidates and are obtained mainly through fund-raising events and direct-mail solicitation.

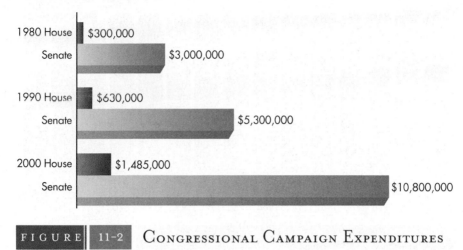

1980 House	$300,000
Senate	$3,000,000
1990 House	$630,000
Senate	$5,300,000
2000 House	$1,485,000
Senate	$10,800,000

FIGURE   11-2   CONGRESSIONAL CAMPAIGN EXPENDITURES

The cost of running for congressional office has risen sharply as campaign techniques—television advertising, opinion polling, and so on—have become more elaborate and sophisticated. The increase in spending can be seen from a comparison of the approximate median spending level by both candidates per House or Senate seat at ten-year intervals, beginning in 1980.
Source: Federal Elections Commission.

Incumbents also have an edge with political action committees, or PACs, which are the fund-raising arm of interest groups (see Chapter 9). Most PACs are reluctant to oppose an incumbent unless it is clear that the candidate is vulnerable. More than 85 percent of PAC contributions in recent elections have been given to incumbents; their challengers got less than 15 percent (see Figure 11–3).[13] "Anytime you go against an incumbent, you take a minute and think long and hard about what your rationale is," said Desiree Anderson, director of the Realtors PAC.[14] (A race without an incumbent—called an **open-seat election**—usually brings out a strong candidate from each party and involves heavy spending, especially when the parties are evenly matched in the state or district.)

The Pitfalls of Incumbency

Incumbency is not without its liabilities. The potential pitfalls include troublesome issues, personal misconduct, variation in turnout, strong challengers, and for some House members, redistricting.[15]

Troublesome Issues Disruptive issues are a potential threat to incumbents. Although most elections are not waged against the backdrop of strong issues, those that are tend to produce the largest turnover in Congress. In the period from 1992 to 1994, when the public was angry over

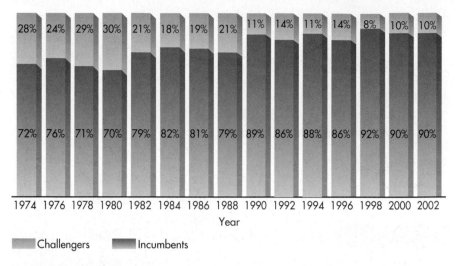

28%	24%	29%	30%	21%	18%	19%	21%	11%	14%	11%	14%	8%	10%	10%
72%	76%	71%	70%	79%	82%	81%	79%	89%	86%	88%	86%	92%	90%	90%

1974 1976 1978 1980 1982 1984 1986 1988 1990 1992 1994 1996 1998 2000 2002
Year

▮ Challengers   ▮ Incumbents

FIGURE 11-3   ALLOCATION OF PAC CONTRIBUTIONS
BETWEEN INCUMBENTS AND CHALLENGERS
IN CONGRESSIONAL RACES THAT INCLUDED
AN INCUMBENT, 1974–2002

In allocating campaign contributions, PACs favor incumbent members of Congress
over their challengers by a wide margin.
Source: Federal Elections Commission.

economic and social conditions and believed Congress was performing
poorly, the number of incumbents who were defeated exceeded 10 percent.
After that, the economy improved and the number dropped to roughly 5
percent.

Personal Misconduct Members of Congress can also fall prey to scandal.
Life in Washington can be fast paced, glamorous, and expensive, and some
members of Congress get caught up in influence peddling, sex scandals, and
other forms of misconduct. Roughly a fourth of House incumbents who
lost their bid for reelection in the past decade were shadowed by ethical
questions. "The first thing to being reelected is to stay away from scandal,
even minor scandal," says the political scientist John Hibbing.[16] Representative Gary Condit found that out in 2002 when he was defeated in the
Democratic primary. A married man, Condit had been romantically linked
to Chandra Levy, an intern in his office who was missing and later found
dead from foul play. Even top congressional leaders are not immune from
the effects of scandal, as illustrated by the experience of former House
Ways and Means Committee Chairman Dan Rostenkowski. Accused of

U.S. Representative William (Bill) Clay represents a heavily Democratic district in St. Louis. The biggest reelection obstacles for House members from one-sided districts are redistricting, personal impropriety, scandal, and a well-funded primary election opponent. In the absence of any such factor, as in Clay's case, reelection is nearly a sure thing.

gross misuse of congressional funds, he lost his House seat in 1994, despite having won by 20 percentage points two years earlier and outspending his 1994 opponent by more than ten to one.

Turnout Variation: The Midterm Election Problem Historically, the party holding the presidency loses seats in the midterm congressional elections, particularly in the House of Representatives. The 2002 midterm elections, when the Republicans had George W. Bush in the White House and picked up a handful of House seats, was only the fourth time in more than a century that the president's party gained seats.

The pattern is largely attributable to a dropoff in turnout for midterm elections.[17] The voters who go the polls only during presidential election years tend to have weaker party loyalties and are therefore more responsive to the issues of the moment. In any given election, these issues tend to favor one party, which contributes to the success of its congressional candidates as well as its presidential nominee. Most of the party's congressional candidates who win narrowly owe their margin of victory to these voters. However, these voters stay home during midterm elections. Thus, unless these incumbents can make inroads among midterm voters who backed their opponent two years earlier, they stand a good chance of losing. Since many of these voters are strong partisans, they are not easily swayed, and the typical result is the midterm defeat of some of these incumbents.

Strong Challengers: A Problem for Senators Incumbents are also vulnerable to strong challengers. Senators are particularly likely to face formidable opponents: after the presidency, the Senate is the top rung of the political ladder. Governors and House members are frequent challengers for Senate seats, and they have the electoral base, reputation, and experience to compete effectively. Moreover, the U.S. Senate lures wealthy challengers. Maria Cantwell spent $10 million of her own money to defeat Senator Slade Gorton for the state of Washington's Senate seat in 2000. Cantwell made her fortune as an executive with RealNetworks, a high-tech company.

House incumbents have less reason to fear strong challengers. A House seat is often not attractive enough to induce prominent local politicians, such as mayors or state legislators, to risk their political careers in a challenge to an incumbent.[18] This situation leaves the field open to weak opponents with little or no governmental or political experience.[19]

Redistricting: A Problem for House Members Every ten years, after each population census, the 435 seats in the House are reallocated among the states in proportion to their population. This process is called **reapportionment.** States that have gained population since the last census may acquire additional House seats, while those that have lost population may lose seats. New York and Illinois were among the states that lost one or more House seats as a result of the 2000 census; Arizona and Washington were among the states that gained one or more seats. (The Senate is not affected by population change, since each state has two senators regardless of its size.)

The responsibility for redrawing House election districts after a reapportionment—a process called **redistricting**—rests with the state gov-

Constitutional Qualifications for Serving in Congress

Representatives: "No person shall be a Representative who shall not have attained to the age of twenty-five years, and been seven years a citizen of the United States, and who shall not, when elected be an inhabitant of that State in which he shall be chosen" (Article I, section 2).

Senators: "No person shall be a Senator who shall not have attained to the age of thirty years, and been nine years a citizen of the United States, and who shall not, when elected, be an inhabitant of the State for which he shall be chosen" (Article I, section 3).

ernments. States are required by law to make their districts as nearly equal in population as possible. There are many ways, however, to divide a state into districts of nearly equal size, and the party in power in the state legislature will do so in a way that favors candidates of its party. One method is to stack a few districts with overwhelming numbers of voters from the opposing party. This tactic ensures that the opposing party will win easily in these districts, but it also reduces the number of voters from that party in other districts, thus placing it at a disadvantage in most races. The process by which one party draws district boundaries to its advantage is called **gerrymandering.**

Reapportionment, redistricting, and gerrymandering are a potential threat to House incumbents. Turnover in House elections is typically higher after a new census than in previous elections. The newly redrawn districts include voters who are unfamiliar with the incumbent, thereby diminishing an advantage that incumbents typically have over their challengers. Moreover, when a state loses congressional seats, there are fewer districts than there are incumbents, who may end up running against each other. Finally, incumbents of the party that does not control the state legislature may find themselves having to compete in redrawn districts that are stacked with the opposition party's voters.

Safe Incumbency and Representation

Although incumbents can and do lose their reelection bids, they normally win easily. An effect is to reduce Congress's responsiveness to political change. Research indicates that incumbents tend to hold relatively stable policy positions during their time in office.[20] Thus, because few congressional seats normally change hands during an election, Congress does not normally change its direction all that much from election to election. Even when people are dissatisfied with national conditions, congressional elections sometimes produce only a small turnover in congressional membership.

Safe incumbency weakens the public's influence on Congress. Democracy depends on periodic shifts in power between the parties to bring public policy into closer alignment with public opinion. In European democracies, incumbents tend to win or lose depending on the popularity of their political party, which can change markedly from one election to the next. In the United States, incumbents are often able to overcome adverse political change through constituency service and other efforts on behalf of the residents of their particular state or district. It is worth noting that national legislators in other democracies do not have the large personal staffs and the substantial travel and publicity budgets that members of Congress have.

Who Are the Winners in Congressional Elections?

Although members of the House and Senate are elected to represent their constituents, the average representative is very different from the average American in virtually every respect.[21] Although only 1 in every 350 Americans is a lawyer, about 1 in 3 members of Congress has studied law. Attorneys are attracted to politics in part by Congress's role in lawmaking and by the public visibility that a campaign for office helps build, which can make a private law practice more successful. Along with lawyers, such professionals as business executives, educators, bankers, and journalists account for more than 90 percent of congressional membership.[22] Blue-collar workers, clerical employees, and homemakers are seldom elected to Congress. Farmers and ranchers are not as rare; a fair number of House members from rural districts have agricultural backgrounds.

Finally, members of Congress are disproportionately white and male. Minority group members and women each account for only about 10 percent of the Congress (see Chapter 5). This proportion, however, is twice that of a decade ago. Safe incumbency is a major obstacle to the election to Congress of more women and minorities. They have been no more successful than other challengers in dislodging congressional incumbents. In elections to state and local office, where incumbency is less important, women and minority candidates have made greater inroads (see "States in the Nation").[23]

CONGRESSIONAL LEADERSHIP

The way in which Congress works is related to the way in which its members win election. Because of their independent power base in their state or district, members of Congress have substantial independence within the institution they serve. The Speaker of the House and the other top leaders in Congress are crucial to its operation, but unlike their counterparts in European legislatures, they cannot demand the loyalty of the members they lead. There is an inherent tension in Congress between the institution's need for strong leadership at the top and the individual member's need to exercise power on behalf of constituents. The result is an institution where the power of the top leaders rests on the willingness of other members to support them.

Party Leadership in Congress

The House and Senate are organized along party lines. When members of Congress are sworn in at the start of a new two-year session, they automatically are members of either the Republican or Democratic **party caucus** in

★ | STATES IN THE NATION

Women in the State Legislatures

Nearly one in four state legislators is a woman, a five-fold increase since 1970. The state of Washington has the highest proportion of women legislators—nearly 40 percent—while Alabama with fewer than 10 percent has the lowest.

Q. Why do the northeastern and western regions have the most women legislators?

A. The northeastern and western regions have a higher proportion of college-educated women in the work force than do other regions. College-educated women are more likely to run for public office and to actively support those who do run.

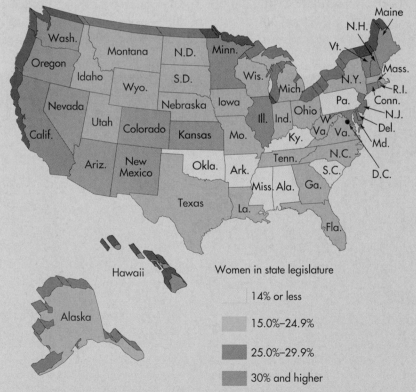

Women in state legislature

- 14% or less
- 15.0%–24.9%
- 25.0%–29.9%
- 30% and higher

Source: Created from data gathered by Center for the American Woman and Politics (CAWP). National Information Bank on Women in Public Office. Eagleton Institute of Politics, Rutgers University, 2002.

their chamber. Through the caucuses, the Democrats and Republicans in each chamber meet periodically to plan strategy and discuss their differences in the process of settling on the party's legislative program. The caucuses also select the **party leaders** who represent the party's interests in the chamber and give direction to the party's goals.

The House Leadership The main party leaders in the House are the Speaker, majority leader, majority whip, minority leader, and minority whip. The Constitution provides only for the post of Speaker, who is elected by a vote of the entire House. In practice, this provision means that the Speaker is chosen by the majority party's members, because only they have enough votes to elect one of their own. (Table 11–1 shows the party composition in Congress during recent years.)

The Speaker is often said to be the second most powerful official in Washington, after the president. The Speaker is active in developing the party's positions on issues and in persuading party members in the House to support these positions.[24] Although the Speaker cannot force party members to support this program, they look to the Speaker for leadership. The Speaker also has certain formal powers, including the right to speak first on

The U.S. Capitol in Washington, D.C., with the House wing in the foreground. The Senate meets in the wing to the right of the central rotunda (under the dome). The offices of the House and Senate party leaders—Speaker, vice president, majority and minority leaders and whips—are located in the Capitol building. Other members of Congress have their offices in nearby buildings.

| TABLE | 11-1 | **Number of Democrats and Republicans in House of Representatives and Senate, 1993–2004** |

	93-94	95-96	97-98	99-00	01-02	03-04
House						
Democrats	259	205*	207*	212*	213	206
Republicans	176	230	228	223	222	229
Senate						
Democrats	56	46*	45*	45*	51*	49
Republicans	44	54	55	55	49	51

*Chamber not controlled by the president's party. Independents are included in the total for the party with which they caucused.

legislation during House debate and the power to recognize members—that is, give them permission to speak from the floor. Because the House places a time limit on floor debate, not everyone has a chance to speak on a bill, and the Speaker can sometimes influence legislation simply by exercising the power to decide who will speak and when.[25] The Speaker also chooses the chairperson and majority-party members of the powerful House Rules Committee, which controls the scheduling of bills for debate. Legislation that the Speaker wants passed is likely to reach the floor under conditions favorable to its enactment; for example, the Speaker may ask the Rules Committee to delay sending a bill to the floor until there is enough support for its passage. The Speaker has other ways of directing the work of the House. The Speaker assigns bills to committees, places time limits on the reporting of bills out of committees, and assigns members to conference committees. (The importance of these powers over committee action will become apparent later in this chapter.)

The Speaker is assisted by the House majority leader and the House majority whip, who are elected by the majority party's members. The majority leader acts as the party's floor leader, organizing the debate on bills and working to line up legislative support. The whip has the important job of soliciting votes from party members and of informing them when critical votes are scheduled. As voting is getting under way on the House floor, the whip will sometimes stand at a location that is easily seen by party members and let them know where the leadership stands on the bill by giving them a thumbs-up or thumbs-down signal.

The minority party has its own leaders in the House. The House minority leader heads the party's caucus and its policy committee and plays the leading role in developing the party's legislative positions. The minority leader is assisted by a minority whip.

The Senate Leadership In the Senate, the most important party leadership position is that of the majority leader, who heads the majority-party caucus. The majority leader's role is much like that of the Speaker of the House in that the majority leader formulates the majority party's legislative agenda and encourages party members to support it. Like the Speaker, the Senate majority leader chairs the party's policy committee and acts as the party's voice in the chamber.[26] The majority leader is assisted by the majority whip, who sees to it that members know when important votes are scheduled and ensures that the party's strongest advocates on a legislative measure are present for the debate. The Senate also has a minority leader and minority whip, whose roles are comparable to those performed by their counterparts in the House.

Unlike the Speaker of the House, the Senate majority leader is not the chamber's presiding officer. The Constitution assigns this responsibility to the vice president of the United States. However, because the vice president is allowed to vote in the Senate only to break a tie, the vice president seldom presides over Senate debates. The Senate has a president *pro tempore*, who, in the absence of the vice president, has the right to preside over the Senate. President *pro tempore* is largely an honorary position that by tradition is usually held by the majority party's senior member. The presiding official has limited power, since each senator has the right to speak at any length on bills under consideration.

The Senate's tradition of unlimited debate stems mainly from its relatively small size (only 100 members, compared with the House's 435 members). Moreover, senators like to view themselves as the equals of all others in their chamber and are thus reluctant to take orders from their leadership. For such reasons, the Senate majority leader's position is weaker than that of the Speaker of the House.

The Power of Party Leaders The power of all party leaders, in the Senate and House alike, rests largely on the trust placed in them by the members of their party. They do not have the strong formal powers of parliamentary leaders (see "How the United States Compares"), but they are expected to lead. If they are adept at promoting ideas and building coalitions, they can exercise considerable power within their chamber. By the same token, their power is diminished if they make a mistake that hurts their party. In 2002,

Republican Senate leader Trent Lott of Mississippi resigned his post after he placed his party at the center of an unwanted controversy by publicly praising the South's segregated past.

Party leaders are in a stronger position today than a few decades ago as a result of changes in the composition of the congressional parties. The GOP once had a substantial progressive faction within it, but this faction has been eclipsed by its conservative wing. At the same time, the Democratic party's conservative wing, represented by its southern lawmakers, has withered away almost entirely. As congressional Republicans have become more alike in their thinking and different from congressional Democrats, each group has found it easier to band together and to stand against the opposing party. Accordingly, the party leaders through the party caucus have found it easier to bring their party's lawmakers together on legislative issues.

/pattersonwtp5

In a different way, however, House and Senate members are less deferential to their leaders than in the past. Until a few decades ago, congressional folkways dictated that newer members, particularly on the House side, would mostly listen and learn, awaiting the day when through seniority they were positioned to assume a larger role in the institution. There were always a few mavericks, but most new members willingly took a back seat. Of course, a back seat in the Senate was not the same as one in the House. Because the Senate is a small body and operates on rules that are more egalitarian, a junior senator could rise to prominence more quickly than a junior House member could. Nevertheless, the Senate too had a tight inner circle dominated by its more senior members.[27]

Today, junior House and Senate members are less deferential. They are elected in a system that rewards self-starters. They want the attention that comes with a more visible role in Washington policy debates.[28] They also are likely to have close ties to the special interests that support their campaigns, and they are expected by these groups to vigorously pursue legislative goals. Finally, television has provided a path to prominence for junior members who are articulate and engaging. The visibility they obtain outside Congress through the media magnifies their voice within the institution. The old axiom that junior members "should be seen and not heard" is no longer an accurate description of life in Congress.

Committee Chairs: The Seniority Principle

Party leaders are not the only important leaders in Congress. Most of the work of Congress takes place in the meetings of its thirty-five standing (permanent) committees and their numerous subcommittees, each of which

How the United States Compares

Unity and Fragmentation in National Legislatures

The U.S. House and the U.S. Senate are separate and coequal chambers, each with its own legislative structure and rules. This type of legislative structure is not found in most democracies. Although many of them have a bicameral legislature like the U.S. Congress, nearly all power is vested in just one of the two chambers. In such a situation, legislative power is more concentrated and easier to exercise.

National legislatures also differ in their degree of party unity. All democratic legislatures are organized by party, but they differ greatly in the degree of control exercised by parties. At one extreme (for example, in Great Britain and Germany), a single legislative chamber dominates, one party has a majority in that chamber, and the members of the majority party are united behind the party leadership. Party control of the U.S. Congress is less pronounced. For one thing, Republicans may control one chamber while the Democrats control the other. For another, Congress is not characterized by unbending party unity. Members sometimes vote against their party's position on important legislation. This lack of an ironclad party majority weakens the ability of Congress and its party leaders to set the nation's policy agenda.

Country	Form of Legislature
Canada	One house dominant
France	One house dominant
Germany	One house dominant (except on regional issues)
Great Britain	One house dominant
Israel	One house only
Italy	Two equal houses
Japan	One house dominant
Mexico	Two equal houses
United States	Two equal houses

is headed by a chairperson. A committee chair schedules committee meetings, determines the order in which committee bills are considered, presides over committee discussions, directs the committee's majority staff, and can choose to lead the debate when a committee bill reaches the floor of the chamber for a vote by the full membership.

Committee chairs are always members of the majority party, and they usually have the most **seniority** (the most consecutive years of service on a particular committee). Seniority is based strictly on time served on a committee, not on time spent in Congress. If a member switches committees, the years spent on the first committee do not count toward seniority on the second one.

The seniority principle for selecting committee chairs is not absolute. In 2001, for example, Representative Bill Thomas of California was appointed chair of the House Ways and Means Committee even though he had less seniority than another Republican on the committee. In most cases, however, seniority determines who will chair House and Senate committees.[29]

The seniority system has several important advantages: it reduces the number of bitter power struggles that would occur if the chairs were decided each time by open competition, it provides experienced and knowledgeable committee leadership, and it enables members to look forward to the reward of a position as chair after years of service on the same committee. A drawback of the seniority system is that it places the committee chairs outside the direct control of the House and Senate's elected leaders.[30]

Congressional organization and leadership extend into subcommittees, which are smaller units within each committee formed to conduct specific aspects of the committee's business. Altogether there are about two hundred subcommittees in the House and Senate, each with a chairperson who decides its order of business, presides over its meetings, and coordinates its staff. In both chambers, a subcommittee chair is often the most senior member on the panel, but seniority is not as important in these appointments as it is in the designation of committee chairs.

Oligarchy or Democracy: Which Principle Should Govern?

In 1995, House Republicans gave committee chairs the power to select the chairs of their subcommittees and to appoint all majority-party staff members, including those who work for the subcommittees. The changes were designed to give committee chairs more control over legislation.[31] The changes reversed House reforms of the 1970s that gave subcommittees and their chairs greater authority in order to make the House "more democratic" in its organization.[32]

The opposing forces embedded in the 1970s and 1995 reforms have played themselves out many times in the history of Congress. The institution is at once a place for conducting the nation's business and for promoting constituency interests. At times, the position of top leaders has been strengthened. At other times, the position of rank-and-file members has been enhanced. At all times, there has been an attempt to create a workable balance of the two. The result is an institution very different from European parliaments, where power is thoroughly concentrated at the top (an arrangement reflected even in the name for rank-and-file members: "backbenchers"). The distinguishing feature of congressional power is its division among the membership, with provision for added power at the top.

THE COMMITTEE SYSTEM

As indicated earlier, most of the work in Congress is conducted through **standing committees,** which are permanent committees with responsibility for a particular area of public policy. At present there are twenty standing committees in the House and sixteen in the Senate (see Table 11–2). Both the House and the Senate, for example, have a standing committee that specializes in handling foreign policy issues. Other important standing committees are those that deal with agriculture, commerce, the national budget, the interior (natural resources and public lands), defense, government spending, labor, the judiciary, and taxation. House committees, which average about thirty-five to forty members each, are about twice the size of the Senate committees. Each standing committee has legislative authority in that it can draft and rewrite proposed legislation and can recommend to the full chamber the passage or defeat of the legislation it considers.

Each standing committee in Congress has its own staff. Unlike the members' personal staffs, which concentrate on constituency relations, the committee staffs perform an almost entirely legislative function. They help draft legislation, organize hearings, and participate in altering bills within committee. In fact, experienced staffers sometimes play as large a role in the writing of legislation as do the members themselves.

In addition to its standing committees, Congress also has a number of **select committees,** which are created to perform specific tasks and are disbanded after they have done so; **joint committees,** composed of members

| TABLE | 11-2 | THE STANDING COMMITTEES OF CONGRESS |

House of Representatives	Senate
Agriculture	Agriculture, Nutrition, and Forestry
Appropriations	Appropriations
Armed Services	Armed Services
Banking and Financial Services	Banking, Housing, and Urban Affairs
Budget	Budget
Education and the Workforce	Commerce, Science, and Transportation
Energy and Commerce	Energy and Natural Resources
Government Reform	Environment and Public Works
House Administration	Finance
International Relations	Foreign Relations
Judiciary	Governmental Affairs
Resources	Health, Education, Labor, and Pensions
Rules	Judiciary
Science	Rules and Administration
Small Business	Small Business
Standards of Official Conduct	Veterans' Affairs
Transportation and Infrastructure	
Veterans' Affairs	
Ways and Means	

of both houses, which perform advisory or coordinating functions for the House and the Senate; and **conference committees,** which are joint committees formed temporarily to work out differences in House and Senate versions of a particular bill. The role of conference committees is discussed more fully later in the chapter.

Congress could not possibly handle its workload without the help of its committee system. About ten thousand bills are introduced during each two-year session of Congress. The sheer volume of this legislation would paralyze the institution if it did not have a division of labor. Yet the very existence of committees and subcommittees helps fragment Congress: each of these units is relatively secure in its power, jurisdiction, and membership.[33]

Committee Membership

Each committee includes Republicans and Democrats, but the majority party holds the majority of seats on each committee and subcommittee. The ratio of Democrats to Republicans on each committee is approximately the same as the ratio in the full House or Senate, but there is no fixed rule on this matter, and the majority party decides what the ratio will be (mindful that at the next election it could become the chamber's minority). Members of the House typically serve on only two committees. Senators often serve on four, although they can sit on only two major committees, such as Foreign Relations and Finance. There are also limits on subcommittee assignments; no House member, for example, can serve on more than five subcommittees.

Each standing committee has a fixed number of members, and a committee must have a vacancy before a new member can be appointed. These vacancies usually occur at the start of a new congressional session, when the committee positions of members who have retired or been defeated for reelection are reallocated. On nearly all committees, members retain their seats unless they decide to relinquish them or are forced to do so by changes in party ratios or committee size. The biggest change in committee memberships comes when a party loses control of the House or Senate; several Democrats had to relinquish committee assignments when the Republicans took control of the Senate in the 2002 midterm elections.

Each party has a special committee in each chamber with responsibility for deciding who will fill vacancies on standing committees. Several factors influence these decisions, including the preferences of the legislators themselves. Most newly elected members of Congress receive a committee assignment that they have requested.[34] New members usually ask for assignment to a committee on which they can serve their constituents' interests and at the same time increase their reelection prospects.[35] For example, when Hillary Clinton was elected to the Senate in 2000 from New York, a state that depends heavily on human services programs, she asked for and received an appointment on the Senate Health, Education, Labor, and Pensions Committee.

Members of Congress also prefer membership on one of the most important committees, such as Foreign Relations or Finance in the Senate and Appropriations or Ways and Means in the House. Such factors as members' intelligence, experience, party loyalty, ideology, region, length of congressional service, and work habits weigh heavily in the determination of appointments to these prestigious committees.[36]

Subcommittee assignments are handled differently. The members of each party on a committee decide who among them will serve on each of its subcommittees. The members' preferences, seniority, and personal backgrounds and the interests of their constituencies are key influences on subcommittee assignments.

Committee Jurisdiction

The 1946 Legislative Reorganization Act requires that each bill introduced in Congress be referred to the proper committee. An agricultural bill introduced in the Senate must be assigned to the Senate Agriculture Committee, a bill dealing with foreign affairs must be sent to the Senate Foreign Relations Committee, and so on. This requirement is a major source of each committee's power. Even if its members are known to oppose certain types of legislation, bills clearly within its **jurisdiction**—the policy area in which it is authorized to act—must be sent to it for deliberation.

However, policy problems are increasingly complex, and jurisdiction has accordingly become an increasingly contentious issue, particularly on major bills. Which House committee, for example, should handle a major bill addressing the role of financial institutions in global trade? Is it the Banking Committee? Or the Commerce Committee? Or the International Relations Committee? Since all committees seek legislative influence and since each is jealous of its jurisdiction, bills that overlap committee boundaries provoke conflict. The political scientist David King describes these conflicts as "turf wars." They also involve the party leaders, who are in charge of assigning bills to committee. The party leaders can take advantage of these situations by shuttling a bill to the committee that is most likely to handle it in the way they would like. But party leaders depend on the committee chairs for support, so they cannot regularly ignore a committee that has a strong claim to a bill. At times, party leaders have responded by dividing up a bill, handing over some of its provisions to one committee and other provisions to a second committee.

House and Senate subcommittees also have relatively secure jurisdictions. Thus responsibility in Congress is thoroughly divided, with each subcommittee having authority over a small area of public policy. The House International Relations Committee, for instance, has five subcommittees: International Economic Policy and Trade, International Operations and Human Rights, Asia and the Pacific, Western Hemisphere, and Africa. Each subcommittee has about a dozen members, and these few individuals do most of the work and have the major voice in the disposition of most bills in their policy domain.

How A Bill Becomes Law

Parties, party leaders, and committees are critical actors in the legislative process. Their role and influence, however, vary with the nature of the legislation under consideration.

Committee Hearings and Decisions

The formal process by which bills become law is shown in Figure 11–4. A **bill** is a proposed legislative act. Many bills are prepared by executive agencies, interest groups, or other outside parties, but members of Congress also draft bills, and only they can formally submit a bill for consideration by their chamber. Once a bill is introduced by a member of the House or Senate, it is given a number and a title and is then sent to the appropriate committee, which assigns it to one of its subcommittees. Most bills that reach a subcommittee are tabled on the grounds that they are not worthwhile. Only about 10 percent of the bills that committees consider reach the floor for a vote; the others are "killed" when committees decide that they do not warrant further consideration and table them. The full House or Senate can overrule these committee decisions, but this seldom occurs.

The fact that committees kill 90 percent of the bills submitted in Congress does not mean that committees exercise 90 percent of the power in Congress. A committee rarely decides fully the fate of legislation that is important to the majority party or its leadership. Most bills die in committee because they are of little interest to anyone other than a few members of Congress or are so poorly conceived that they lack merit. Some bills are not even supported by the members who introduce them. A member may submit a bill to appease a powerful constituent group and then quietly inform the committee to ignore it.

If a bill seems to have merit, the subcommittee will schedule hearings on it. The subcommittee invites testimony on the proposed legislation by lobbyists, administrators, and experts, who inform members about the suggested policy, provide an indication of the support the bill has, and disclose possible weaknesses in the proposal. After the hearings, if the subcommittee still feels that the legislation is warranted, members recommend the bill to the full committee, which can hold additional hearings. In the House, both the full committee and a subcommittee can "mark up," or revise, a bill; in the Senate, markup is usually reserved for the full committee.

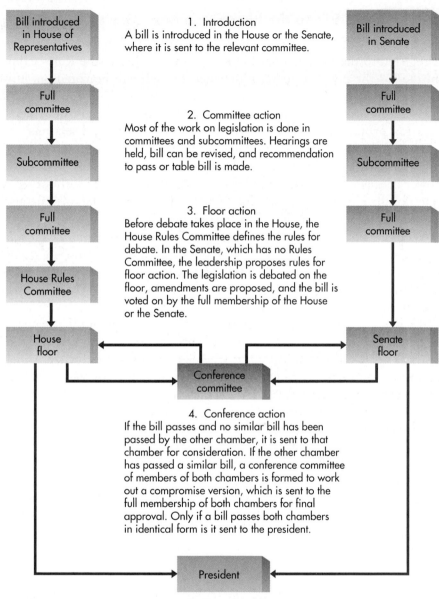

1. Introduction
A bill is introduced in the House or the Senate, where it is sent to the relevant committee.

Bill introduced in House of Representatives

Bill introduced in Senate

Full committee

Full committee

2. Committee action
Most of the work on legislation is done in committees and subcommittees. Hearings are held, bill can be revised, and recommendation to pass or table bill is made.

Subcommittee

Subcommittee

3. Floor action
Before debate takes place in the House, the House Rules Committee defines the rules for debate. In the Senate, which has no Rules Committee, the leadership proposes rules for floor action. The legislation is debated on the floor, amendments are proposed, and the bill is voted on by the full membership of the House or the Senate.

Full committee

Full committee

House Rules Committee

House floor

Senate floor

Conference committee

4. Conference action
If the bill passes and no similar bill has been passed by the other chamber, it is sent to that chamber for consideration. If the other chamber has passed a similar bill, a conference committee of members of both chambers is formed to work out a compromise version, which is sent to the full membership of both chambers for final approval. Only if a bill passes both chambers in identical form is it sent to the president.

President

5. Executive action
If the president signs the bill, it becomes law. A presidential veto can be overridden by a two-thirds majority in each chamber.

FIGURE   11-4   HOW A BILL BECOMES A LAW

Although the legislative process can be short-circuited in many ways, this diagram describes the steps that may be required for a bill to become a law.

From Committee to the Floor

If a majority of the committee votes to recommend passage of the bill, it is referred to the full chamber for action. In the House, the Rules Committee has the power to determine when the bill will be voted on, how long the debate on the bill will last, and whether the bill will receive a "closed rule" (no amendments will be permitted), an "open rule" (members can propose amendments relevant to any of the bill's sections), or something in between (for example, only certain sections of the bill will be subject to amendment). The Rules Committee has this scheduling power because the House is too large to operate effectively without strict rules for the handling of legislation by the full chamber. The rules are also a means by which the majority party controls legislation. House Democrats employed closed rules to prevent Republicans from proposing amendments to major bills, a tactic House Republicans said they would forgo when they took control in 1995. Once in control, however, the Republicans applied closed rules to a number of major bills. The tactic was too effective to ignore.

The Senate has no Rules Committee, relying instead on the majority leader to schedule bills. All Senate bills are subject to unlimited debate unless a three-fifths majority of the full Senate votes for **cloture,** which limits debate to thirty hours. Cloture is a way of thwarting a Senate **filibuster,** a procedural tactic whereby a minority of senators prevent a bill from coming to a vote by holding the floor and talking until other senators give in and the bill is withdrawn from consideration. The Senate also differs from the House in that its members can propose any amendment to any bill. Unlike House amendments, those in the Senate do not have to be germane to a bill's content. For example, a senator may propose an antiabortion amendment to a bill dealing with defense expenditures. Such an amendment is called a **rider,** and they are frequently introduced.

Leadership and Floor Action

Committee action is usually decisive on bills that address small issues. If a majority of committee members favor such a bill, it normally is passed by the full chamber, often without amendment. In a sense, the full chamber merely votes to confirm or modify decisions made previously by committees and subcommittees. Of course, these units do not operate in a vacuum. In making its decisions, a committee takes into account the fact that its action can be reversed by the full chamber, just as a subcommittee recognizes that the full committee can overrule its decision.[37] Partisanship also serves as a check on committee action. When a committee's vote is sharply divided along party or regional lines, other members may conclude that they need to look more closely at the bill before deciding whether to support it.

On major bills, the party leaders are the critical actors. They will have worked closely with the committee during its deliberations and may assume leadership of the bill when it clears the committee. (In the case of "minor" bills, leadership during floor debate is normally provided by committee members.)

In her book *Unorthodox Lawmaking: New Legislative Processes in the U.S. Congress,* Barbara Sinclair notes that the majority party's leaders (particularly in the House) have increasingly set the legislative agenda and defined the debate on major bills.[38] They shape the bills' broad outlines and set the boundaries of the floor debate. In these efforts, they depend on the support of their party's members. To obtain it, they consult their members informally and through the party caucus. **Party discipline**—the willingness of a party's House or Senate members to act together as a cohesive group—is increasingly important in congressional action and is the key to party leaders' ability to shape major legislation. (The role of parties in Congress is discussed further in the section on Congress's representation function.)

Conference Committees and the President

For a bill to pass, it must receive the support of a simple majority (50 percent plus one) of the House or Senate members voting on it. To become a law, however, a bill must be passed in identical form by both the House and the Senate. About 10 percent of all proposals that are approved by both chambers—the proportion is larger for major bills—differ in important respects in their House and Senate versions and are referred to conference committees to resolve their differences. Each **conference committee** is formed temporarily to handle a particular bill; its members are usually appointed from the House and Senate standing committees that worked on the bill originally. The conference committee's job is to bargain over the differences in the House and Senate versions and to develop a compromise version. It then goes to the House and Senate floors, where it can be passed, defeated, or returned to conference, but not amended.

Legislation that is passed by the House and the Senate is not assured of becoming a law. The president also has a role. If the president signs the bill it becomes a **law.** If the president exercises the **veto,** a refusal to sign a bill, it is sent back to its originating chamber with the president's reasons for the

mhhe
com
/pattersonwtp5

veto. Congress can override a veto by a two-thirds vote of each chamber; the bill then becomes law. If the president fails to sign a bill within ten days (Sundays excepted) and Congress has remained in session, the bill automatically becomes law anyway. If the president fails to sign a bill within ten days and Congress has adjourned for the term, the bill does not become law. This last situation is called a pocket veto and forces Congress in its next session to start from the beginning: The bill must again pass both chambers and is again subject to presidential veto.

CONGRESS'S POLICYMAKING ROLE

The Framers of the Constitution expected Congress to be the leading branch of the national government. It was to the legislature—the embodiment of representative government—that the people were expected to look for policy leadership. During most of the nineteenth century, Congress, not the president, was clearly the dominant national institution. Aside from a few strong leaders such as Jackson and Lincoln, presidents did not play a major legislative role (see Chapter 12). However, as national and international forces combined to place greater leadership and policy demands on the federal government, the president became a vital part of the national legislative process. Today Congress and the president substantially share the legislative effort, although their roles differ greatly.[39]

Congress's policymaking role revolves around its three legislative functions: lawmaking, representation, and oversight. In practice, the three functions overlap, but they are conceptually distinct.

The Lawmaking Function of Congress

Under the Constitution, Congress is granted the **lawmaking function:** the authority to make the laws necessary to carry out the powers granted to the national government. However, whether Congress takes the lead in the making of laws depends heavily on the type of policy at issue.

Broad Issues: The Limits of Fragmentation on Congress's Role

Congress is structured in a way that makes agreement on large issues difficult to obtain. Congress is not one house, but two, each with its own authority and constituency base. Neither the House nor the Senate can enact legislation without the other's approval, and they are hardly two versions of the same thing. California and North Dakota have exactly the same representation in the Senate, but in the House, which is apportioned by population, California has fifty-three seats compared to North Dakota's one.

Congress also includes a lot of people: 100 members of the Senate and 435 members of the House. They come from different constituencies and represent different and sometimes opposing interests. Since each member has a separate power base, and depends on it for reelection, the members can be expected to take different positions on legislative issues, even when they agree on the general goal. Nearly every member of Congress, for example, supports the principle of global free trade. When it comes to specific trade provisions, however, they often disagree. Foreign competition means different things to manufacturers that produce automobiles, computer chips, or underwear; it means different things to farmers who produce corn, sugar, or grapes; and it means different things to firms that deal in international finance, home insurance, or student loans. And because it means different things to different people in different parts of the country, members of Congress who represent these areas have conflicting views on what the nation's trade policy should be.

For such reasons, Congress often has difficulty taking the lead on broad issues of national policy. A legislative institution can easily lead on such issues only if it assigns this authority to its top leadership. Although the rise in party discipline in Congress has strengthened leaders' role, the fact remains that House and Senate members are relatively free to go their separate ways if they so choose. For this reason, Congress often struggles when faced with the task of developing comprehensive policies that address broad national problems.

The fragmented nature of Congress enables the president to assume leadership of many of these issues. The presidency is better suited to the task. First, whereas Congress's authority is divided, the presidency's authority is not.[40] Executive power is vested constitutionally in the hands of a single individual—the president. As a result, the presidency is capable of a degree of policy planning and coordination that is far beyond the normal capacity of Congress. Second, whereas members of Congress see issues mainly from the perspective of their state or district, the president has a national outlook. The president cannot ignore specific state and local interests, but must concentrate on broad national ones in order to retain power.

Presidential leadership means that Congress will normally pay attention to White House proposals, not that it will adopt them. Congress typically accepts a presidential initiative only as a starting point in its deliberations. It may reject the proposal outright—particularly when the president is from the opposite party—but any such proposal provides Congress a tangible bill on which to focus. If the proposal is at all close to what a congressional majority would regard as acceptable, Congress will modify it in large or small ways to fit the demands of its membership.

The president gains leverage because of the veto power. When the president threatens a veto, and is clearly willing to carry out the threat, Congress

Supported by staff assistants, Senate members of the Health, Education, Labor, and Pensions Committee work during a break in hearings.

is nearly forced into taking the president's position into account in shaping the legislation, since it is exceedingly difficult to muster the two-thirds majority in each chamber that is required to override a presidential veto. Of course, Congress can dare the president to veto the bill, hoping that public anger will be directed at the White House. But any such showdown is risky, and Congress and the White House normally bargain their way to a bill that accommodates their separate interests. (The legislative roles of Congress and the president are discussed further in Chapter 12.)

In its lawmaking activities, Congress has the support of three congressional agencies. One is the Congressional Budget Office (CBO), which was created as part of the Budget Impoundment and Control Act of 1974. Before this time, the president, through the Office of Management and Budget (OMB), had a significant advantage in budgetary matters. Congress had no independent way to systematically assess the president's budgetary proposals or their projected impact. The CBO gives Congress this capacity. Its two hundred employees provide Congress with general economic projections, overall estimates of government expenditures and revenues, and specific estimates of the costs of proposed programs. Since the CBO's inception, its calculations have often been at odds with those of the OMB. For example, the OMB's estimates of the cost of presidential initiatives are usually optimistic, and the CBO's figures have been a basis by which Congress has trimmed or rejected these proposals. (The budgetary process is described more fully in later chapters.)

A second congressional agency is the General Accounting Office (GAO). With thirty-five hundred employees, the GAO is the largest congressional agency. Formed in 1921, it has primary responsibility for overseeing executive agencies' spending of money that has been appropriated by Congress.[41] The programs that the executive agencies administer are authorized and funded by Congress. The GAO's responsibility is to ensure that executive agencies operate in the manner prescribed by Congress.

The third congressional agency is the Congressional Research Service (CRS). It is the oldest congressional agency, has a staff of one thousand employees, and operates as a nonpartisan reference agency. It conducts research and provides information upon request from congressional committees and members.

Congress in the Lead: Fragmentation as a Policymaking Strength

Congress occasionally does take the lead on large issues. Except during Roosevelt's New Deal, Congress has been a chief source of major labor legislation. Environmental legislation, federal aid to education, and urban development are other areas in which Congress has played an initiating role.[42] The Republicans' Contract with America that was introduced during the 1994 election is yet another example of congressional policy leadership. The contract included broad fiscal, regulatory, and social initiatives. In 1996, for example, the Republican-controlled Congress led the way on legislation that fundamentally changed the nation's welfare system. Nevertheless, Congress does not routinely develop broad policy programs and carry them through to passage. "Congress remains organized," James Sundquist notes, "to deal with narrow problems but not with broad ones."[43]

As it happens, the great majority of the hundreds of bills that Congress considers each session deal with narrow issues. The leading role in the disposition of these bills falls not on the president but on Congress and, in most cases, on a relatively small number of its members. The same fragmentation that makes it difficult for Congress to take the lead on a broad issue makes it easy for Congress to tackle scores of narrow issues simultaneously. Most of the legislation passed by Congress is "distributive"—that is, it distributes benefits to a particular group while spreading the costs among the general public. Veterans' benefits and business tax incentives are examples.[44]

Such legislation, because it directly benefits a constituent group, is the type of policy that members of Congress are most inclined to support. It is also the type of policy that Congress, through its committee system, is organizationally best suited to handle. Most committees parallel a major constituent interest, such as agriculture, commerce, or labor.

The Representation Function of Congress

In the process of making laws, the members of Congress represent various interests within American society, giving them voice and attention in the national legislature. The proper approach to the **representation function** has been debated since the nation's founding. A recurrent issue has been whether the primary concern of a representative should be the interests of the nation as a whole or those of his or her own constituency. These interests overlap to some degree but rarely coincide exactly. Policies that are of benefit to the full society are not always equally advantageous to particular localities and can even cause harm to some constituencies.

Representation of States and Districts The choice between national and local interests is not a simple one, even for a legislator who is inclined toward either orientation. To be fully effective, a member of Congress must be reelected time and again, a necessity that compels him or her to pay attention to local demands. Yet, as part of the nation's legislative body, no member can easily put aside his or her judgment as to the nation's needs. In making the choice, most members of Congress, it appears, tend toward a local orientation. They are particularly reluctant to oppose local sentiment on issues of intense concern. Support for gun control legislation, for example, has always been much lower among members of Congress from rural areas where sporting guns are part of the fabric of everyday life.

Local representation also occurs through the committee system.[45] Although studies indicate that the views of committee members are not radically different from the views of the full House or Senate membership,[46] senators and representatives typically sit on committees and subcommittees with policy jurisdictions that coincide with state or district interests. For example, farm-state legislators dominate the membership of the House and Senate Agriculture committees, and westerners dominate the Interior committees (which deal with federal lands and natural resources, most of which are concentrated in the West). Committees are also where most of the congressional **logrolling** takes place (logrolling is the practice of trading one's vote with another member so that each gets what he or she most wants). It is not uncommon, for example, for agriculture committee members from livestock-producing states of the North to trade votes with committee members from the South where crops such as cotton, tobacco, and peanuts are grown.

LIBERTY, EQUALITY & SELF-GOVERNMENT

What's Your Opinion?

Minority Redistricting

Congressional representatives tend naturally to favor the opinions of the voters who supported them. This tendency can result in the underrepresentation of minority group members because only rarely will they constitute an electoral majority in a congressional district. In 1982, Congress decided that race could be taken into account in congressional redistricting, and after the 1990 census, the boundaries of some House districts were drawn so that black Americans were a voting majority. In a 1996 decision, the Supreme Court held that race cannot be the determining factor in redistricting decisions (because this action violates the Fourteenth Amendment's equal protection clause), although there might be circumstances in which it could be considered along with other factors. Then, in a 2001 decision, the Court held that racial redistricting is permissible if it is the consequence of a reapportionment plan motivated by partisan rather than racial considerations (for example, if the primary purpose was to create a district favorable to the Democratic candidate).

What's your view on racial redistricting? What's your view on partisan redistricting?

Nevertheless, representation of constituency interests has its limits. A representative's constituents have little interest in most issues that come before Congress and even less information about them. Whether the government should appropriate a few million dollars in foreign aid for Bolivia or should alter patent requirements for copying machines is not the sort of issue that local people are likely to know or care about. Moreover, members of Congress often have no choice but to go against the wishes of a significant portion of their constituency. The interests of small and large farmers in an agricultural state, for example, can differ considerably.

Representation of the Nation Through Parties When a clear-cut and vital national interest is at stake, members of Congress can be expected to respond to that interest. The difficulty of using the common good as a routine basis for thinking about representation, however, is that Americans often disagree on what constitutes the common good and what government should do to further it.

Most Americans believe, for example, that the nation's education system requires strengthening. The test scores of American schoolchildren on standardized reading, math, and science examinations are significantly below those of children in many other industrial democracies. This situation creates pressure for political action. But what action is necessary and desirable? Does more money have to be funneled into public schools, and which level of government—the federal, state, or local—would provide it? Or does the problem rest with teachers? Should they be subject to higher certification and performance standards? Or is the problem a lack of competition for excellence? Should schools be required to compete for students and the tax dollars they represent? Should private schools be part of any such competition, or would their participation wreck the public school system? There is no general agreement on such issues. The quality of America's schools is of vital national interest, and quality schools would serve the common good. But the means to that end are subjects of endless dispute.

In Congress, debates over national goals occur primarily along party lines.[47] Republicans and Democrats have different perspectives on national issues because their parties differ philosophically and politically. In the end-of-the-year budget negotiations in 1998 and 1999, for example, Republicans and Democrats were deadlocked on the issue of new funding to hire thousands of public school teachers. The initiative had come from President Clinton and was supported by congressional Democrats but opposed by congressional Republicans, who objected to spending federal (as opposed to state and local) funds for that purpose and who also objected to the proposed placement of the new teachers (most would be placed in overcrowded schools, most of which are in Democratic constituencies). Democrats and Republicans alike agreed that more teachers were needed, but they disagreed on how that goal should be reached. In the end, through concessions in other areas, Clinton and the congressional Democrats obtained federal funding for new teachers, but it was obtained through an intensely partisan process.

Partisanship is the main source of division within Congress.[48] There are real and substantial differences between members of the two parties, such that they often vote on the opposite sides of legislative issues. Party-line voting has been relatively high in the past two decades, reflecting the rise of party discipline in Congress and the widening gap between the Democrats and Republicans who serve there. There are now in Congress fewer liberal Republicans and fewer conservative Democrats, as well as fewer moderates of both parties.

Partisanship also affects the president's relationship with Congress. Presidents serve as legislative leaders not so much for the whole Congress as for members of their own party. More than half the time, opposition and support for presidential initiatives divide along party lines. Accordingly, the president's legislative success can depend on which party controls the Congress. After Republicans in the 2002 midterm elections took full control of Congress, President Bush was in a stronger position to get his major programs enacted into law.

In short, any accounting of representation in Congress that minimizes the influence of party is faulty. If constituency interests drive the thinking of many members of Congress, so do partisan values. In fact, constituent and partisan influences are often difficult to separate in practice. In the case of conflicting interests within their constituencies, members of Congress naturally side with those that align with their party. When local business and labor groups take opposing sides on issues before Congress, for example, Republican members tend to back business's position, while Democratic members tend to line up with labor.

The Oversight Function of Congress

Although Congress enacts the nation's laws and appropriates the money to implement them, the administration of these laws is entrusted to the executive branch. Congress has the responsibility to see that the executive carries out the laws faithfully and spends the money properly, a supervisory activity that is referred to as the **oversight function** of Congress.[49]

Oversight is carried out largely through the committee system of Congress and is facilitated by the parallel structure of the committees and the executive bureaucracy: the House International Relations and Senate Foreign Relations committees oversee the work of the State Department, the House and Senate Agriculture committees look after the Department of Agriculture, and so on. The Legislative Reorganization Act of 1970 spells out each committee's responsibility for overseeing its parallel agency:

> Each standing committee shall review and study, on a continuing basis, the application, administration, and execution of those laws, or parts of laws, the subject matter of which is within the jurisdiction of that committee.

However, oversight is easier to mandate than to carry out. If congressional committees were to try to monitor all the federal bureaucracy's activities, they would have no time or energy to do anything else. Most members of Congress are more interested in working out new laws and looking after constituents than in laboriously keeping track of the bureaucracy. Although Congress is required by law to maintain "continuous watchfulness" over programs, committees have little incentive to take a hard look at programs that they have enacted or on which their constituent groups depend. Oversight normally is not pursued aggressively unless members of Congress are annoyed with an agency, have discovered that a legislative authorization is being grossly abused, or are reviewing a program for possible major changes.[50]

When an agency is suspected of serious abuses, a committee is likely to hold hearings. Except in cases involving *executive privilege* (the right to withhold confidential information affecting national security), executive-branch officials are compelled to testify at these hearings. If they refuse, they can be cited for contempt of Congress, which is a criminal offense. Congress's investigative power is not listed in the Constitution, but the judiciary has not challenged the power, and Congress has used it extensively.

Most federal programs must have their funding renewed every year, a requirement that gives Congress crucial leverage in its ongoing oversight function. If an agency has acted improperly, Congress may reduce the agency's appropriation or tighten the restrictions on the way its funds can be spent. A major difficulty is that the House and Senate Appropriations committees must review nearly the entire federal budget, a task that limits the amount of attention they can give any particular program.

Oversight conducted after the bureaucracy has acted has an obvious drawback: If a program has been administered improperly, some damage has already been done. For this reason, Congress in recent years has developed

Senate Majority Leader Trent Lott of Mississippi (left) addresses the Senate impeachment trial on the day that the Senate voted to acquit President Clinton on two articles of impeachment. Four years later, Lott was himself a center of controversy for praising America's segregated past.

ways of limiting the bureaucracy's discretion in advance. One method is to include detailed instructions in appropriations bills. Such instructions serve to limit bureaucrats' flexibility when they spend funds on programs and provide a firmer basis for holding them accountable if they disregard the intent of Congress. Another oversight device is the **sunset law,** which fixes a date on which a program will end (or "fade into the sunset") unless it is renewed by Congress. Sunset provisions help to prevent a program from outliving its usefulness, because once its expiration date is reached, Congress can reestablish it only by passing a new law. The "legislative veto" is a more intrusive and controversial oversight tool. It requires that an executive agency have the approval of Congress before it can take a specified action. Legislative vetoes are under challenge as an unconstitutional infringement on executive authority, and their future is unclear.

The biggest obstacle to effective oversight is the sheer magnitude of the task. With its hundreds of agencies and thousands of programs, the bureaucracy is beyond comprehensive scrutiny. Even some of Congress's most publicized oversight activities are relatively trivial when viewed against the sheer scope of the bureaucracy. For example, congressional investigations into the Defense Department's purchase of small hardware items, such as wrenches and hammers, at many times their market value do not begin to address the issue of whether the country is overspending on the military. Overpriced hand tools represent pocket change in a defense budget of billions of dollars. The real oversight question is whether the defense budget as a whole provides cost-effective national security. It is a question that Congress has neither the capacity nor the determination to investigate fully.

Congress's zeal for oversight changes dramatically when allegations of scandal or wrongdoing attract national media attention. Then, members of Congress use the oversight process to hold high-profile hearings. The collapse of the Enron Corporation as a result of financial manipulation is an example. Several congressional committees held hearings in 2002 to grill Enron officials on the practices that led stockholders to lose billions of dollars and Enron employees to lose their retirement pensions. The hearings in the Democratic-controlled Senate were the more heated. Enron had close ties to President Bush and Vice President Cheney, and the Enron hearings gave Senate Democrats a chance to embarrass and to pressure the White House. Four years earlier, the parties' roles were reversed. Then, Republicans were in control of the House and Senate, and they held hearings on President Clinton's relationship with Monica Lewinsky, which led to Clinton's impeachment by the House and trial (in which he was acquitted) by the Senate. (Chapter 12 describes the impeachment process and the Lewinsky scandal in greater detail.)

CONGRESS: TOO MUCH PLURALISM?

Congress is an institution divided between service to the nation and service to the separate constituencies within it. Its members have responsibility for the nation's laws. Yet for reelection they depend on the voters of their states and districts and are highly responsive to constituency interests. This focus is facilitated by the committee system, which is organized around particular interests. Agriculture, labor, education, banking, and commerce are among the interests represented through this system. It is hard to conceive of a national legislature structured to respond to special interests more closely than the Congress of the United States. It is even harder to conceive of a national legislature that gives as much real power to these interests through committees as Congress does.

Pluralists admire this feature of Congress. They argue that the United States has a majoritarian institution in the presidency and that Congress is a place where a *diversity* of interests are represented. Critics of this view say that Congress is sometimes so responsive to particular interests that the overall national interest is neglected. This criticism is blunted from time to time by a strong majoritarian impulse in Congress. The current period is one of these moments. The high level of party discipline in recent years, coupled with a widening ideological gap between the parties, has placed Congress at the center of many national policy debates, including the issue of the balance of power between Washington and the states.

The fact is, Congress cannot be an institution that is highly responsive both to diverse interests and to the national interest. These interests often conflict, as the rise and fall of former Speaker Newt Gingrich illustrates. He sought to make the Republican congressional majority into the driving force in American national politics, but was ousted from his position when the conflicts generated by the uncompromising pursuit of conservative policy goals began to weaken the GOP's support in the states and districts, thereby threatening the reelection chances of Republican incumbents. This inherent tension between Congress's national role and local base has replayed itself many times in U.S. history. In a real sense, the strengths of Congress are also its weaknesses. The features of congressional election and organization that make Congress responsive to separate constituencies are often the very same ones that make it difficult for Congress to act as a strong instrument of a national majority. The perennial challenge for members of Congress is to find a workable balance between what Roger Davidson and Walter Oleszek call the "two Congresses": the one embodied by the Capitol in Washington and other embodied by the members' separate districts and states.[51]

SUMMARY

Members of Congress, once elected, are likely to be reelected. Members of Congress can use their office to publicize themselves, pursue a service strat-

/pattersonwtp5
egy of responding to the needs of individual constituents, and secure pork barrel projects for their states or districts. House members gain a greater advantage from these activities than do senators, whose larger constituencies make it harder for them to build close personal relations with voters and whose office is more likely to attract strong challengers. Incumbency does have some disadvantages. Members of Congress must take positions on controversial issues, may blunder into political scandal or indiscretion, must deal with changes in the electorate, or may face strong challengers; any of these conditions can reduce their reelection chances. By and large, however, the advantages of incumbency far outweigh the disadvantages. Incumbents' advantages extend into their reelection campaigns. Their influential positions in Congress make it easier for them to raise campaign funds from PACs and individual contributors.

Congress is a fragmented institution. It has no single leader; the House and Senate have separate leaders, neither of whom can presume to speak for the other chamber. The principal party leaders of Congress are the Speaker of the House and the Senate majority leader. They share leadership power with committee and subcommittee chairpersons, who have influence on the policy decisions of their committee or subcommittee.

It is in the committees that most of the day-to-day work of Congress is conducted. Each standing committee of the House or the Senate has jurisdiction over congressional policy in a particular area (such as agriculture or foreign relations), as does each of its subcommittees. In most cases, the full House and Senate accept committee recommendations about passage of bills, although amendments to bills are quite common and committees are careful to take other members of Congress into account when making legislative decisions. Congress is a legislative system in which influence is widely dispersed, an arrangement that suits the power and reelection needs of its individual members. However, partisanship is a strong and binding force in Congress. It is the basis for party leaders' ability to build support for major legislative initiatives. On this type of legislation, party leaders and caucuses rather than committees are the central actors.

The major function of Congress is to enact legislation. Yet the role it plays in developing legislation depends on the type of policy involved. Because of its divided chambers and committee structure, as well as the concern of its members with state and district interests, Congress, through its party leaders and caucuses, only occasionally takes the lead on broad national issues. Congress typically looks to the president for this leadership; nevertheless, presidential initiatives are passed by Congress only if they meet its members' expectations and usually only after a lengthy process of compromise and negotiation. Congress is more adept at handling legislation that deals with problems of narrow interest. Legislation of this sort is decided mainly in congressional committees, where interested legislators, bureaucrats, and groups concentrate their efforts on issues of mutual concern.

A second function of Congress is the representation of various interests. Members of Congress are highly sensitive to the state or district on which they depend for reelection. Members of Congress do respond to overriding national interests, but for most of them, local concerns generally come first. National and local representation often work through party representation, particularly on issues that divide the Democratic and Republican parties and their constituent groups.

Congress's third function is oversight, the supervision and investigation of the way the bureaucracy is implementing legislatively mandated programs. Although oversight is a difficult process, it is an important means of control over the actions of the executive branch.

KEY TERMS

bill	party discipline
cloture	party leaders
conference committee	pork barrel projects
constituency	reapportionment
filibuster	redistricting
gerrymandering	representation function
jurisdiction	rider
law	seniority
lawmaking function	service strategy
logrolling	standing committee
open-seat election	sunset law
oversight function	veto
party caucus	

SUGGESTED READINGS

Galderisi, Peter, Marni Ezra, and Michael Lyons, eds. *Congressional Primaries and the Politics of Representation.* Latham, Md.: Rowman and Littlefield, 2001. A set of readings on the dynamics of congressional primary elections.

Hibbing, John R., and Elizabeth Theiss-Morse. *Congress as Public Enemy: Public Attitudes Toward American Political Institutions.* New York: Cambridge University Press, 1995. An analysis through survey and focus group data of Americans' attitudes toward Congress.

Jacobson, Gary C. *The Politics of Congressional Elections,* 5th ed. New York: Longman, 2001. An overview of the congressional election process and its impact on policy and representation.

King, David C. *Turf Wars: How Congressional Committees Claim Jurisdiction.* Chicago: University of Chicago Press, 1997. An innovative study on how congressional committees claim jurisdiction.

Krasno, Jonathan S. *Challenges, Competition, and Reelection: Comparing Senate and House Elections.* New Haven, Conn.: Yale University Press, 1995. A comparison of the competitiveness of House and Senate races that uses National Election Study (NES) data as evidence.

Sinclair, Barbara. *Unorthodox Lawmaking: New Legislative Processes in the U.S. Congress.* Washington, D.C.: Congressional Quarterly Press, 1997. A detailed analysis of the American legislative process.

Witt, Linda, Karen M. Paget, and Glenna Matthews. *Running as a Woman: Gender and Power in American Politics.* New York: Free Press, 1993. A comprehensive study of the problems faced by women candidates.

LIST OF WEBSITES

http://www.rollcall.com The online version of *Roll Call*, the newspaper of Capitol Hill; the site provides an insider's view of current developments within Congress.

http://thomas.loc.gov Library of Congress site, named after Thomas Jefferson, that provides information about the congressional process, including the status of pending legislation.

http://www.house.gov The U.S. House of Representatives' web page; it has information on party leaders, pending legislation, and committee hearings as well as links to each House member's office and website.

http://www.senate.gov The U.S. Senate's website, which is similar to that of the House and provides links to each senator's website.

POLITICS IN THEORY AND PRACTICE

Thinking: How does the structure of Congress (for example, its two houses and its committee system) affect its policymaking role?

Acting: Each year, thousands of college students serve as interns in Congress or state legislatures. Many internships are unpaid, but students often can get college credit for the work experience. If a legislative internship is of interest to you, information can be obtained from the American Political Science Association (www.apsa.org). In addition, there are organizations in Washington that arrange Congressional internships. Many of these organizations charge a fee, so you might want to contact a legislative office directly. Students normally get a better response when they contact their own legislator (representative or senator) rather than one from another district or state. You could also check with the student services office at your college or university. Some of these offices have information on internship programs; some even offer application assistance.

The New York Times

Unlikely Allies Press to Add Conservation to Farm Bill

by Elizabeth Becker

Congress is a place in which local interests play a large part in the thinking of the legislators. Members of Congress prefer legislation that allows them to pursue national goals while also taking care of constituent groups. When large amounts of money are at issue, the informal rule within Congress is to spread the money around so that as many members as possible can claim to have taken care of their constituents. Such was the case recently with a major farm bill, which is discussed in this June 18, 2001, news story by New York Times *reporter Elizabeth Becker.*

WASHINGTON—A coalition of more than 100 environmental and hunting organizations, from the Sierra Club to the National Rifle Association, is trying to turn the measure that will set farm policy for the coming years into the major conservation act of this Congress.

With the recently enacted $1.3 trillion tax cut squeezing out most new spending programs, the conservationists are focusing on what is typically known as the farm bill as their best bet for recovering millions of acres of wetlands, prairies, grassland and forests and protecting the wildlife that live on the land. Few other bills offer both the money—$79 billion in new financing over the next five years—and the assurance that the legislation will become law. The bill pays for the subsidies that have for decades underwritten farmers who grow major crops like corn, wheat, rice and soybeans.

But in the last 15 years, since conservation programs were added to the farm program, farmers have lined up for cash payments in return for taking their land out of production and letting it return to the wild.

Already, farmers have voluntarily set aside more than 35 million acres as nature reserves and another million acres of wetlands as part of the two major conservation programs supported by the farm program. There is a backlog of farmers and ranchers who have applied for $3.7 billion in payments for setting aside an additional 68 million acres, but the programs have run out of money.

Conservation and hunting groups support payments to farmers for returning some of their acreage to a natural state because it not only helps sustain wildlife but also helps farmers hold on to their property. In addition, it slows the encroachment of suburbs into the countryside.

"The conservation programs in the farm bill have really helped the farmer hold the line against developers," said Susan Lamson of the National Rifle Association, making points more often associated with the Friends of the Earth.

The environmental and hunting groups are asking that a new farm bill include money for the protection of another million acres of wetlands and 10 million more acres of land through the conservation reserve program. They are going up against the powerful farm and agribusiness lobbies that have helped persuade Congress to increase crop subsidies, which last year reached a record $22 billion in commodity payments to farmers.

Environmental groups argue that these subsidies encourage overproduction of the major crops, which not only keeps prices flat but also pollutes rivers and soil with chemicals.

"When farms go into overproduction you have dirty water and dirty air," said Brett Hulsey of the Sierra Club. "With conservation programs, you have clean water, reduced flooding and more open space."

In Congress, these environmentalists, as well as the hunting and fishing groups, the so-called hooks-and-bullets crowd, have found natural allies among senators and representatives from states where farmers receive little of the $20 billion annual subsidies for the major crops. More than 120 House members wrote to the Agriculture Committee chairman this week asking for support for the conservation programs.

"We could turn this farm bill into the great conservation bill of the 21st century," said Representative Ron Kind, Democrat of Wisconsin, who is leading the movement in the House to rewrite the farm bill with conservation as its centerpiece.

Congress has begun considering how to rewrite the farm bill, which was last passed in 1996 as the Freedom to Farm Act.

Representative Larry Combest, Republican of Texas and chairman of the Agriculture Committee, has concluded that the major commodity subsidy programs should be more predictable, with farmers receiving less money when their crops fetch higher prices. He has yet to recommend how much money should go to conservation.

"This is a work in progress," said an aide to Mr. Combest. "When the environmentalists discovered the farm bill, they made it trendy. Now the conservation programs are more oriented to Eastern farmers. Mr. Combest prefers the more traditional point of view of protecting soil banks that would give more money to the Western areas."

That geographic split is evident throughout Congress. In the Senate, a group of 43 Republicans and Democratic senators from New England and mid-Atlantic states have formed an informal caucus to support farm conservation programs. Most of the farmers from Maine to Maryland either grow vegetables and fruits or are dairy farmers and therefore ineligible for the major commodity subsidy programs. But they can and have taken advantage of the conservation programs.

In the current farm bill, conservation payments have become so popular they rank third, behind payments for growing corn and wheat. Over five years, government payments to corn farmers were $24.3 billion, to wheat farmers $13.2 billion and to conservation programs $8.24 billion.

"In many parts of farm country, conservation is now the single most important source of government assistance to agriculture, especially for small and medium-size farms," said Ken Cook, president of Environmental Working Group.

During the Republican revolution in which Newt Gingrich was House speaker, the conservation programs were nearly lost. When the House wrote the initial Freedom to Farm Act of 1996, the bill excluded financing for conservation. But Representative Sherwood Boehlert, Republican of New York, offered an amendment to reinstate the programs, and the measure won by a vote of 372 to 37, establishing the now classic divide between Eastern and Western farm states over financing.

"Conservation used to be considered the purview of the Midwest and its eroded soil," Mr. Boehlert said in an interview. "With the expanded programs it has worked wonders for our Eastern farmers who were on the edge."

With so much money at stake in the new revision of the farm bill, Mr. Combest has vowed to present a new farm bill to the House by the end of July, nearly a year in advance of the Senate. For their part, the environmentalists in the House say they will offer legislation this month to expand the conservation programs.

"Our competition is the commodity payments, and there is only so much money in the bill," said Scott Sutherland of Ducks Unlimited, a conservation group supported by hunters. "We want funding put back for the wetlands and we know there are members of Congress who are hunters and anglers who will want to preserve those wetlands."

What's Your Opinion?

The proposed legislation will make local farmers, conservationists, and hunters happy and, in the process, will promote the reelection prospects of members of Congress. Is the national purpose also served by this legislation?

CHAPTER 12

THE PRESIDENCY: LEADING THE NATION

❝ [The president's] is the only voice in national affairs. Let him once win the admiration and confidence of the people, and no other single voice will easily overpower him. **❞**

WOODROW WILSON[1]

George W. Bush was sinking in the polls. His approval rating, which had been above 60 percent, was less than 55 percent. The economy was weakening and the president was being criticized for not doing enough to reverse the downtrend. Bush was also getting heat for the defection of Senator James Jeffords of Vermont, which cost Republicans control of the Senate. The press was also starting to attack the president. Journalists had given him the honeymoon period traditionally accorded a new president, but they were now turning on him.

Everything changed on September 11, 2001. The terrorist attacks on the World Trade Center and the Pentagon led Americans to rally around their president. Bush vowed that America would not rest until the terrorists were brought to justice and the international network of which they were a part was destroyed. His presidential approval rating reached 96 percent, the highest level ever recorded. Not even Franklin Roosevelt and Harry Truman had received approval ratings that high during the Second World War. The *Washington Post's* David Broder compared Bush's response to the terrorist attacks to Abraham Lincoln's leadership at the outset of the Civil War.

The Bush story is but one in the saga of the ups and downs of the modern presidency. Lyndon Johnson's and Richard Nixon's dogged pursuit of the Vietnam War led to talk of "the imperial presidency," an office so powerful that constitutional checks and balances were no longer an effective constraint on it. Within a few years, because of the undermining effects of Watergate and of changing international conditions during the Ford and Carter presidencies, the watchword was "the imperiled presidency," an office too weak to meet the nation's demands for executive leadership. Reagan's policy successes before 1986 renewed talk heard in the Roosevelt and Kennedy years of "a heroic presidency," an office that is an inspirational center of American politics. After the Iran-Contra scandal in 1986, Reagan was more often called a lame duck. The first George Bush's handling of the Gulf crisis—leading the nation in 1991 into a major war and emerging from it with a stratospheric public approval rating bolstered the heroic conception of the office. A year later, Bush was on his way to being removed from office by the voters. Bill Clinton overcame a fitful start to his presidency to become the first Democrat since Franklin D. Roosevelt in the 1930s to win reelection. As Clinton was launching an aggressive second-term policy agenda, however, he got entangled in an affair with a White House intern, Monica Lewinsky, that led to his impeachment by the House of Representatives and weakened his claim to national leadership.

No other political institution has been subject to such varying characterizations as the modern presidency. One reason is that the formal powers of the office are somewhat limited, and thus presidential power changes with national conditions, political circumstances, and the personal capacity of the office's occupant.[2] The American presidency is always a central office in that its occupant is a focus of national attention. Yet the presidency is not an inherently powerful office in the sense that presidents routinely get what they want. Presidential power is conditional. It depends on the president's own abilities, but even more on the circumstances—on whether the situation demands strong leadership and whether the political support for that leadership exists. When conditions are favorable, the president will look powerful. When conditions are adverse, the president will appear vulnerable.

This chapter examines the roots of the presidential power, the presidential selection process, the staffing of the presidency, and the factors associated with the success and failure of presidential leadership. The main ideas of this chapter are these:

★ *Public expectations, national crises, and changing national and world conditions have required the presidency to become a strong office.* Underlying

President George W. Bush addresses troops of the 101st Airborne Division. Standing next to Bush is General Tommy Franks. The president's constitutional authority as commander in chief of the nation's armed forces was the basis for the U.S. attack on Iraq in 2003.

this development is the public support that the president acquires from being the only nationally elected official.

★ *The modern presidential election campaign is a marathon affair in which self-selected candidates must plan for a strong start in the nominating contests and center their general election strategies on media, issues, and a baseline of support.* The lengthy campaign process heightens the public's sense that the presidency is at the center of the U.S. political system.

★ *The modern presidency could not operate without a large staff of assistants, experts, and high-level managers, but the sheer size of this staff makes it impossible for the president to exercise complete control over it.*

★ *The president's election by national vote and position as sole chief executive ensure that others will listen to the president's ideas; but to lead effectively, the president must have the help of other officials and, to get their help, must respond to their interests as they respond to the president's.*

★ *Presidential influence on national policy is highly variable.* Whether
presidents succeed or fail in getting their policies enacted depends
heavily on the force of circumstance, the stage of their presidency,
partisan support in Congress, and the foreign or domestic nature of the
policy issue.

FOUNDATIONS OF THE MODERN PRESIDENCY

The writers of the Constitution knew what they wanted from a president—national leadership, statesmanship in foreign affairs, command in
time of war or insurgency, enforcement of the laws—but could devise only
general phrases to describe the president's constitutional authority. Compared with Article I, which enumerates Congress's specific powers, Article
II of the Constitution contains relatively vague statements on the president's powers.[3]

Over the course of American history, each of the president's constitutional powers has been extended in practice beyond the Framers' intention.
For example, the Constitution grants the president command of the nation's military, but only Congress can declare war. In *Federalist* No. 69,
Alexander Hamilton wrote that a surprise attack on the United States was
the only justification for war by presidential action. Nevertheless, the nation's presidents have sent troops into military action abroad more than two
hundred times. Of the more than a dozen wars included in that figure, only
five were declared by Congress.[4] All of America's most recent wars—the
Korean, Vietnam, Persian Gulf, Balkans, Afghanistan, and Iraq conflicts—
have been undeclared.

The Constitution also empowers the president to act as diplomatic
leader with the authority to appoint ambassadors and to negotiate treaties
with other countries, subject to approval by the Senate. The Framers anticipated that Congress would define the nation's foreign policy objectives,
while the president would oversee their implementation. However, the
president has become the principal architect of U.S. foreign policy and has
even acquired the power to make treaty-like arrangements with other nations, in the form of executive agreements. In 1937, the Supreme Court
ruled that such agreements, signed and approved only by the president,
have the same legal status as treaties, which require approval by a two-
thirds vote of the Senate.[5] Since World War II, presidents have negotiated
more than ten thousand executive agreements, compared to fewer than one
thousand treaties ratified by the Senate.[6]

The Constitution also vests "executive power" in the president. This power includes the responsibility to execute the laws faithfully and to appoint major administrators, such as heads of the various departments of the executive branch. In *Federalist* No. 76, Hamilton indicated that the president's real authority as chief executive was to be found in this appointive capacity. Presidents have indeed exercised substantial power through their appointments, but they have found their administrative authority—the power to execute the laws—to be of even greater value, because it enables them to determine how laws will be interpreted and applied. President Ronald Reagan used his executive power to *prohibit* the use of federal funds by family-planning clinics that offered abortion counseling. President Bill Clinton exerted the same power to *permit* the use of federal funds for this purpose. The *same* act of Congress was the basis for each of these actions. The act authorizes the use of federal funds for family-planning services, but it neither requires nor prohibits their use for abortion counseling, which enables the president to decide this issue.

Finally, the Constitution provides the president with legislative authority, including use of the veto and the opportunity to recommend proposals to Congress. The Framers expected this authority to be used in a limited and largely negative way. George Washington acted as the Framers anticipated: he proposed only three legislative measures and vetoed only two acts of Congress. Modern presidents have a different, more activist view of their legislative role. They routinely submit legislative proposals to Congress and often veto legislation they find disagreeable.

The presidency is a more powerful office than the Framers envisioned for many reasons, but two features of the office in particular—*national election* and *singular authority*—have enabled presidents to make use of changing demands on government to claim the position of leader of the American people. It is a claim that no other elected official can routinely make, and it is a key to understanding the role and power of the president.

Asserting a Claim to National Leadership

The first president to forcefully assert a claim to popular leadership was Andrew Jackson, who had been swept into office in 1828 on a tide of public support that broke the hold of the upper classes on the presidency. Jackson used his popular backing to challenge Congress's claim to national policy leadership, contending that he was "the people's tribune."

However, Jackson's view was not shared by most of his successors during the nineteenth century, because national conditions did not routinely call for strong presidential leadership. The prevailing conception was the **Whig theory,** which held that the presidency was a limited or constrained

LIBERTY, EQUALITY, & SELF-GOVERNMENT

What's Your Opinion?

The Presidency

When the Constitution was drafted, fear of executive power was widespread. The Framers worried that a too-powerful executive would threaten Americans' hard-won liberty, equality, and self-government.

Ironically, presidents have been in the vanguard of efforts to enlarge the practice of these principles. Thomas Jefferson, Abraham Lincoln, Franklin Roosevelt, and Lyndon Johnson are among the presidents whose names are nearly synonymous with such efforts. Johnson's leadership, for example, was critical to passage of the 1964 Civil Rights Act and the 1965 Voting Rights Act.

Can this development be explained by the nature of executive power? Unlike legislative power, which is widely shared, executive power is vested in a single individual. Have presidents taken the lead on issues of liberty, equality, and self-government simply because of their greater capacity for assertive action?

office whose occupant was confined to the exercise of expressly granted constitutional authority. The president had no implicit powers for dealing with national problems but was primarily an administrator, charged with carrying out the will of Congress. "My duty," said President James Buchanan, a Whig adherent, "is to execute the laws . . . and not my individual opinions."[7]

Theodore Roosevelt rejected the Whig tradition upon taking office in 1901; he attacked the business trusts, pursued an aggressive foreign policy, and pressured Congress to adopt progressive domestic policies. Roosevelt embraced the **stewardship theory,** which calls for an assertive presidency that is confined only at points specifically prohibited by law, not by undefined inherent restrictions. As "steward of the people," Roosevelt said, he was permitted "to do anything that the needs of the Nation demanded unless such action was forbidden by the Constitution or by the laws."[8]

Roosevelt's image of a strong presidency was shared by Woodrow Wilson, but his other immediate successors reverted to the Whig notion of the limited presidency.[9] Herbert Hoover's restrained conception of the presidency prevented him from taking decisive action even during the devastation of the Great Depression. Hoover said that he lacked the constitutional authority to establish public relief programs for jobless Americans. However, Hoover's successor, Franklin D. Roosevelt, shared the stewardship theory of his distant cousin Theodore Roosevelt, and FDR's New Deal signaled the end of the limited presidency. As FDR's successor, Harry Truman, wrote in his memoirs: "The power of the President should be used in the interest of the people and in order to do that the President must use whatever power the Constitution does not expressly deny him."[10]

Today the presidency is an inherently strong office.[11] The modern presidency becomes a more substantial office in the hands of a persuasive leader such as Ronald Reagan, but even a less forceful person such as Jimmy Carter is now expected to act assertively. This expectation not only is the legacy of former strong presidents but also stems from changes that have occurred in the federal government's national and international policy responsibilities.

The Need for Presidential Leadership of an Activist Government

During most of the nineteenth century (the Civil War being the notable exception), the United States did not need a strong president. The federal government's policymaking role was small, as was its bureaucracy. Moreover, the nation's major issues were of a sectional nature (especially the North-South split over slavery) and thus suited to action by Congress, which represented state and local interests. The U.S. government's role in world affairs was also small. As these conditions changed, however, the presidency also changed.

Foreign Policy Leadership The president has always been the nation's foreign policy leader, but the role was initially a rather undemanding one. The United States avoided entanglement in the turbulent affairs of Europe, and though it was involved in foreign trade, it was preoccupied by internal development. By the end of the nineteenth century, however, the nation was seeking to expand the world market for its goods. President Theodore Roosevelt advocated an American economic empire and looked south toward Latin America and west toward Hawaii, the Philippines, and China (the "Open Door" policy) for new markets. However, the United States's tradition of isolationism remained a powerful influence on national policy. The United States fought in World War I but immediately thereafter demobilized its armed forces. Over President Woodrow Wilson's objections, Congress then voted against the entry of the United States into the League of Nations.

World War II fundamentally changed the nation's international role and the president's role in foreign policy. In 1945 the United States emerged as a global superpower, a giant in world trade, and the recognized leader of the noncommunist world. The United States today has a military presence in nearly every part of the globe and an unprecedented interest in trade balances, energy supplies, and other international issues affecting the nation.[12]

The effects of these developments on America's political institutions has been one-sided.[13] Because of the president's constitutional authority as chief diplomat and military commander and the special demands of foreign policy leadership, the president, not Congress, has taken the lead in addressing the nation's increased responsibilities in the world. Foreign policy requires singleness of purpose and, at times, fast action. Congress—a large, divided, and unwieldy institution—is poorly suited to such a response. In contrast, the president, as sole head of the executive branch, can act quickly and speak authoritatively for the nation as a whole in its relations with other nations.

This capacity was rarely more evident than after the terrorist attacks of September 11, 2001. The initiative in the war on terrorism rested squarely with the White House. President Bush decided the U.S. response to the attacks and took the lead in obtaining international support for U.S. military, intelligence, and diplomatic initiatives. Congress backed these actions enthusiastically but, in reality, had little choice but to endorse whatever

The White House contains, on the first floor, the president's Oval Office, other offices, and ceremonial rooms. The First Family's living quarters are on the second floor.

policies he chose. In other situations, of course, Congress is less compliant. In recent decades, it has contested presidential positions on issues such as global trade and international human rights. Nevertheless, the president remains the dominant force in U.S. foreign policy and the leader to whom many countries turn when global problems surface. (The changing shape of the world and its implications for presidential power and leadership are discussed more fully later in the chapter.)

Domestic Policy Leadership The change in the president's domestic leadership has also been substantial. Throughout most of the nineteenth century Congress jealously guarded its constitutional powers, making it clear that domestic policy was its business. James Bryce wrote in the 1880s that Congress paid no more attention to the president's views on legislation than it did to the editorial positions of prominent newspaper publishers.[14]

By the early twentieth century, however, the national government was taking on regulatory and policy responsibilities imposed by the nation's transition from an agrarian to an industrial society, and the executive branch was growing ever larger. In 1921, Congress conceded that it lacked the centralized authority to coordinate the growing national budget and enacted the Budget and Accounting Act, which provided for an executive budget.[15] Federal departments and agencies would no longer submit their annual budget requests directly to Congress. The president would oversee the initiation of the budget by working the various agencies' requests into a comprehensive budgetary proposal, which would then be submitted to Congress as a starting point for its deliberations.

During the Great Depression of the 1930s, Franklin D. Roosevelt's New Deal responded to the public's demand for economic relief with a broad program that involved a level of policy planning and coordination that was beyond the capacity of Congress. In addition to initiating public works projects and social welfare programs aimed at providing immediate relief, the New Deal made the government a partner in nearly every aspect of the nation's economy. If economic regulation was to work, unified and continuous policy leadership was needed, and only the president could routinely provide it.

Presidential authority has continued to grow since Roosevelt's time. In response to pressures from the public, the national government's role in such areas as education, health, welfare, safety, and protection of the environment has expanded greatly, which in turn has created additional demands for presidential leadership.[16] Big government, with its emphasis on comprehensive planning and program coordination, has favored executive authority at the expense of legislative authority. All democracies have seen a shift in power from their legislature to their executive. In Britain, for example, the prime minister has taken on responsibilities that once belonged to the cabinet or the parliament.

CHOOSING THE PRESIDENT

As the president's policy and leadership responsibilities changed during the nation's history, so did the process of electing presidents. The changes do not parallel each other exactly, but they are related politically and philosophically. As the presidency drew ever closer to the people, their role in selecting the president grew ever more important.[17] The United States in its history has had four systems of presidential selection, each more "democratic" than its predecessor (See Table 12-1). The justification for each new electoral system was **legitimacy,** the idea that the

TABLE **12-1** THE FOUR SYSTEMS OF PRESIDENTIAL SELECTION

Selection System	Period	Features
1. Original	1788–1828	Party nominees are chosen in congressional caucuses.
		Electoral College members act somewhat independently in their presidential voting.
2. Party convention	1832–1900	Party nominees are chosen in national party conventions by delegates selected by state and local party organizations.
		Electoral College members cast their ballots for the popular-vote winner in their respective states.
3. Party convention, primary	1904–1968	As in system 2, except that a *minority* of national convention delegates are chosen through primary elections (the majority still being chosen by party organizations).
4. Party primary, open caucus	1972–present	As in system 2, except that a *majority* of national convention delegates are chosen through primary elections.

choice of a president should be based on the will of the people as expressed through their votes.

Toward a More "Democratic" System of Presidential Election

The delegates to the constitutional convention of 1787 feared that popular election would make the presidency too centralized and too powerful, which would undermine the principles of federalism and separation of powers. The Framers devised a novel system, which came to be called the Electoral College. Under the Constitution, the president is chosen by a vote of electors who are appointed by the states; the candidate who receives the majority of electoral votes is elected president. Each state is entitled to an elector for each member it has in Congress (House and Senate combined).

In choosing the nation's first presidents, electors acted somewhat independently, exercising their own judgment in casting their votes. This pattern changed after the election in 1828 of Andrew Jackson, who believed the people's will had been denied four years earlier when he placed first in the popular voting but failed to gain an electoral majority. Jackson could not persuade Congress to support a constitutional amendment that would have eliminated the Electoral College but did obtain the next-best alternative: he persuaded the states to tie their electoral votes to the popular vote. Under Jackson's reform, which is still in effect today, each party in a state has a separate slate of electors who gain the right to cast a state's electoral votes if their party's candidate places first in the state's popular voting. Thus the popular vote for the candidates directly affects their electoral vote and one candidate is likely to win both forms of the presidential vote. Since Jackson's time, only Rutherford B. Hayes (in 1876), Benjamin Harrison (in 1888), and George W. Bush (in 2000) have won the presidency after having lost the popular vote.

Jackson also championed the national convention as a means of nominating the party's presidential candidate (before this time, nominations were made by party caucuses in Congress and in state legislatures). The parties had their strength at the grass roots, among the people, and Jackson saw the convention process as a means of bringing the citizenry and the presidency closer together. Since Jackson's time, presidential nominees have been formally chosen at national party conventions. Each state party sends delegates to the national convention, and these delegates select the nominee.

Jackson's system of presidential nomination remained fully intact until the early twentieth century, when the Progressives devised the primary election as a means of curbing the power of the party bosses (see Chapter 2). State party leaders had taken control of the nominating process by

Should the Electoral College Be Abolished?

As the votes in the 2000 election were counted, the country was thrown into turmoil by the existence of the electoral vote system. The president is chosen by an indirect system of election. Voters cast ballots for candidates but their votes choose only each state's electors, whose subsequent ballots then result in the actual selection of the president. Electoral votes are apportioned by states based on their representation in Congress, which creates the possibility that the candidate who gets the most popular votes will not get the most electoral votes and thus not be elected president. The 2000 election renewed calls for the abolition of the electoral system.

Yes: Only the President and Vice President of the United States are currently elected indirectly by the Electoral College—and not by the voting citizens of this country. All other elected officials, from the local officeholder up to United States senator, are elected directly by the people. Our bill will replace the complicated electoral college system with the simple method of using the popular vote to decide the winner of a presidential election. By switching to a direct voting system, we can avoid the result of electing a President who failed to win the popular vote.

—U.S. Representative Ray LaHood (R-Illinois)

No: Abolishing the Electoral College would be fine—as long as the American people are also willing to abolish the Senate. They serve a similar purpose in our democracy. When the Founding Fathers laid the foundation for our form of government, they created the Senate as a balance of power in Congress and as a means of equality between the states. When it came time to create a rule of law governing the election of a president, the Founding Fathers continued down this constitutional path of every state's right to a more equal voice, and established the Electoral College.

—U.S. Representative Richard Burr (R-N.C.)

handpicking their states' delegates. The Progressives sought to shift control to the voters by allowing them to select the convention delegates. Such a process is called an *indirect primary*, since the voters are not choosing the nominees directly (as they do in House and Senate races) but rather are choosing delegates who in turn select the nominees.

The Progressives were able to persuade only a minority of states to switch to the primary system. As a result, party leaders continued to control a majority of the delegates and therefore continued to have the larger voice in the nominating process.

In 1968, the Democratic nomination went to Vice President Hubert Humphrey, who had not entered a single primary and was closely identified with the Johnson administration's Vietnam policy. After Humphrey narrowly lost the 1968 general election to Richard Nixon, reform-minded Democrats forced changes in the nominating process. The new rules gave rank-and-file party voters more control by requiring that states choose their delegates through either primary elections or **open party caucuses** (meetings open to any registered party voter who wants to attend). Although the Democrats initiated the change, the Republicans were also affected by it. Most states that adopted a presidential primary in order to comply with the Democrats' new rules also required Republicans to select their convention delegates through a primary.

Today it is the voters in state primaries and open caucuses who play the decisive role in the selection of the Democratic and Republican presidential nominees.[18] A state's delegates are awarded to candidates in accordance with how well they do in the state's primary or caucus. Thus, to win the majority of national convention delegates necessary for nomination, a candidate must place first in a lot of states and do at least reasonably well in most of the rest. (About forty states choose their delegates through a primary election; the others use a caucus system.)

In sum, the presidential election system has changed from an elite-dominated process to one that is based on voter support. This arrangement has strengthened the presidency by providing the office with the reserve of power that popular election confers on democratic leadership.

The Campaign for Nomination

The fact that voters pick the nominees has opened the nominating races to any politician with the energy and resources to run a major national campaign. Nominating campaigns, except those in which an incumbent president is seeking reelection, typically attract a half-dozen contenders. They begin their planning and organizing far in advance of the election year. Once the 2002 midterm elections were concluded, several Democratic hopefuls—including John Kerry, John Edwards, Richard Gephardt, Carol Mosley-Brown, Bob Graham, Wesley Clark, Joseph Lieberman, Al Sharpton, and Howard Dean—talked with party leaders and donors across the country to determine whether they should toss their hat into the ring for 2004.

A key to success in the nominating campaign is **momentum**—a solid showing in the early contests that leads to a buildup of public support in subsequent ones. If candidates start off strongly, the press will cover them more heavily, contributors will provide them more funding, and voters will give more thought to supporting them. For these reasons, presidential contenders now give extraordinary attention to the early contests, particularly the first caucuses in Iowa and the first primary in New Hampshire.[19]

Money, always a critical factor in elections, has become increasingly important in the last two decades because states have moved their primaries and caucuses to the early weeks of the nominating period in order to increase their influence on the outcome. To compete effectively in so many contests in such a short period, candidates need money—lots of it. A candidate can only be in one place at a time, which requires that the campaign be carried to other voters through televised political advertising. Ads are expensive to produce and broadcast, and analysts claim that it takes at least $20 million to $30 million to run a competitive nominating campaign. George W. Bush raised more than $75 million in 2000 for his successful nominating campaign, far more than any of his Republican rivals. In *every* nominating race from 1984 to 2000, the winner was the candidate who had raised the most money before the start of the primaries.

Candidates in primary elections receive federal funding if they meet the eligibility criteria. The Federal Election Campaign Act of 1974 (as amended in 1979) provides for federal matching funds to be given to any candidate who raises at least $5,000 in individual contributions of up to $250 in each of twenty states. Candidates who accept matching funds must agree to limit their expenditures for the nominating phase to a set amount ($45.6 million in 2000), which is adjusted each election year to account for inflation. (Because Bush exceeded the spending limit in 2000, he was ineligible for matching funds.)

After the state primaries and caucuses have been held, the national party conventions occur. The leading candidate has usually acquired enough delegates in the primaries and caucuses to lock up the nomination before the convention begins. Nevertheless, the party convention is a major event. It brings together the delegates elected in state caucuses and primaries, who then vote to approve a party platform and to nominate the party's presidential and vice presidential candidates.

By tradition, the choice of the vice presidential nominee rests with the presidential nominee. Critics have argued that the vice presidential nomination should be decided in open competition, since the vice president stands a good chance of becoming president someday (see Table 12-2). The chief argument for the existing method is that the president needs a trusted and like-minded vice president.

TABLE 12-2 THE PATH TO THE WHITE HOUSE

President	Years in Office	Highest Previous Office	Second-Highest Office
Theodore Roosevelt	1901–1908	Vice president*	Governor
William Howard Taft	1909–1912	Secretary of war	Federal judge
Woodrow Wilson	1913–1920	Governor	None
Warren G. Harding	1921–1924	U.S. senator	Lieutenant governor
Calvin Coolidge	1925–1928	Vice president*	Governor
Herbert Hoover	1929–1932	Secretary of commerce	War relief administrator
Franklin D. Roosevelt	1933–1945	Governor	Assistant secretary of Navy
Harry S. Truman	1945–1952	Vice president*	U.S. senator
Dwight D. Eisenhower	1953–1960	None (Army general)	None
John F. Kennedy	1961–1963	U.S. senator	U.S. representative
Lyndon Johnson	1963–1968	Vice president*	U.S. senator
Richard Nixon	1969–1974	Vice president	U.S. senator
Gerald Ford	1974–1976	Vice president*	U.S. representative
Jimmy Carter	1977–1980	Governor	State senator
Ronald Reagan	1981–1988	Governor	None
George Bush	1989–1992	Vice president	Director, CIA
Bill Clinton	1993–2000	Governor	State attorney general
George W. Bush	2000–	Governor	None

*Became president on death or resignation of incumbent.

The Campaign for Election

The winner in the November general election is almost certain to be either the Republican or the Democratic nominee. A minor-party or independent candidate, such as George Wallace in 1968, Ross Perot in 1992 and 1996, or Ralph Nader in 2000, stands almost no chance of victory. Although party loyalty has declined in recent decades (see Chapters 6 and 8), two-thirds of the nation's voters still identify themselves as Democrats or Republicans, and a substantial majority of them support the party's presidential candidate. Even Democrat George McGovern, who had the lowest level of party support among recent nominees, was backed in 1972 by 60 percent of his party's voters. To overcome this inherent disadvantage, a minor-party candidate would have to win the support of nearly every independent voter, many of whom have a latent Democratic or Republican preference. It is an impossible task for a candidate even as strong as Ross Perot was in 1992. He gained just 30 percent of the independent vote—an extraordinary showing for a third-party candidate, but far short of what was required for victory.

On the other hand, a third-party candidate can draw enough votes away from a major-party nominee to tip the balance in a close election. The Green party's presidential nominee Ralph Nader got only 3 percent of the national vote in the 2000 election, but it came primarily at the expense of the Democratic nominee Al Gore (see Figure 12-1). If Nader had not been on the ballot, Gore would have received enough votes in the decisive state of Florida to beat his Republican rival George W. Bush in the presidential race.

Election Strategy The candidates' strategies in the general election are shaped by many considerations, including the constitutional provision that each state shall have electoral votes equal in number to its representation in Congress. Each state thus gets two electoral votes for its Senate representation and a varying number of electoral votes depending on its House representation. Altogether, there are 538 electoral votes (including 3 for the District of Columbia, even though it has no voting representatives in Congress). To win the presidency, a candidate must receive at least 270 votes, an electoral majority. (If no candidate receives a majority, the election is decided in the House of Representatives. No president since 1824 has been elected in this way. The procedure is defined by the Constitution's Twelfth Amendment, which is reprinted in this book's appendix.)

The importance of the electoral votes is magnified by the existence of the **unit rule;** all the states except Maine and Nebraska grant all their electoral votes as a unit to the candidate who wins the state's popular vote. For this reason, candidates are particularly concerned with winning the most populous states, such as California (with 55 electoral votes), Texas (34),

Nader voters

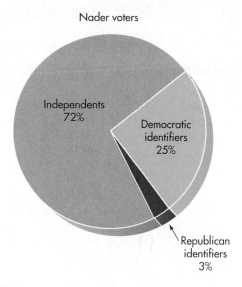

Nader voters

Independents
72%

Democratic
identifiers
25%

Republican
identifiers
3%

FIGURE **12-1**   Support for Ralph Nader's 2000
Presidential Candidacy

Although Ralph Nader drew most of his 3 percent of the presidential vote from
independents, he fared better with Democrats than Republicans, which contributed to
the Democratic presidential candidate Al Gore's defeat in 2000.
Source: *The Vanishing Voter Project, Joan Shorenstein Center on the Press, Politics, and Public Policy, John F. Kennedy
School of Government, Harvard University, 2000. Published by permission of The Vanishing Voter Project.*

New York (31), Florida (27), Pennsylvania (21), Illinois (21), and Ohio (20).
Victory in the eleven largest states alone would provide an electoral majority, and presidential candidates therefore spend most of their time campaigning in those states.[20]

In 2000, Bush was elected with 271 electoral votes, one more than required, even though he received 540,000 fewer popular votes than Gore.
Bush is the first president since Harrison in 1888 to win the presidency despite losing the popular vote. The 2000 election was decided when Bush received Florida's electoral votes by a virtue of 537-vote margin that excluded
ballots that could not be read by voting machines. The U.S. Supreme
Court blocked a count of these ballots (see Chapter 14).

Media and Money The modern presidential campaign is a media campaign. At one time, candidates relied heavily on party organization and rallies to carry their messages to the voters, but now they rely on the media,
particularly television.[21] Candidates strive to produce the pithy ten-second
sound bites that the television networks prefer to highlight on the evening

newscasts. They also rely on the power of the "new media," making frequent appearances on such programs as *Larry King Live* and creating their own Internet websites.

Television is the forum for the major confrontation of the fall campaign: the presidential debates. The first televised debate took place in 1960 between Kennedy and Nixon, and an estimated one hundred million people saw at least one of their four debates.[22] Televised debates resumed in 1976 and have become an apparently permanent fixture of presidential campaigns. Elections are sometimes decided by a small margin, and the debates can make a difference. In 2000, Gore had an edge in the polls before the first debate. He was also the more experienced debater and had a firmer grasp of policy issues. But Gore drew a negative response from viewers when he huffed and grimaced while Bush was talking. Meanwhile, Bush gave a stronger performance than pundits had expected, which led them to conclude he had helped his candidacy. Gore was unable in the second and third debates to overcome fully the image created by his performance in the first debate, which some analysts believe was a turning point in the 2000 campaign.

The television campaign includes political advertising. Televised commercials are by far the most expensive part of presidential campaigns, accounting for about half the candidates' general election expenditures.

The Republican and Democratic nominees are each eligible for federal funding of their general election campaigns even if, as in Bush's case in 2000, they did not accept it during the primaries. The amount for the general election was set at $20 million in 1975 and has been adjusted for inflation in succeeding elections. The major-party nominees in the 2004 presidential election will each receive more than $70 million. The only string attached to this money is that candidates who accept it can spend no additional funds on their campaigns (although the party can spend additional money on their behalf; see Chapter 8).

Candidates can choose not to accept public funds, in which case the amount they spend is limited only by their ability to raise money privately. However, all major-party nominees since 1976 have accepted public funding. Other candidates for the presidency qualify for federal funding if they receive at least 5 percent of the vote and do not spend more than $50,000 of their own money on the campaign. Such candidates receive an amount of funds equal to the proportion of their vote to the average of that of the two major-party nominees. In 1992, Perot spent over $60 million of his own money and thus was ineligible for federal funding. He accepted federal funding in 1996, receiving about half as much as the major-party nominees, since in 1992 his vote total was roughly half that averaged by the two major-party candidates. In 2000, Perot's party, the Reform party, received more than $10 million in federal funding by virtue of Perot's 8 percent of the vote in 1996.

Presidents rely heavily on their top-ranking cabinet officers and personal assistants in making major policy decisions. During the Cuban missile crisis in 1962, this group of advisers to President John F. Kennedy met regularly to help decide on a naval blockade as a means of forcing the Soviet Union to withdraw its missiles from Cuba.

The Winners The Constitution specifies only that the president must be at least thirty-five years old, a natural-born U.S. citizen, and a U.S. resident for at least fourteen years. Yet the holding of high public office is nearly a prerequisite for gaining the presidency. Except for four army generals, all presidents had previously served as vice presidents, members of Congress, state governors, or top federal executives.

All presidents have been white and male, but it is likely only a matter of time before the nation has its first minority-group president or its first woman president. Until the early 1950s, a majority of Americans in polls said they would not vote for a woman for president. By the 1990s, however, fewer than 10 percent held this view. A similar change of opinion preceded John Kennedy's election to the presidency in 1960. Kennedy was the nation's first Catholic president and only the second Catholic to have received a major party's nomination.

STAFFING THE PRESIDENCY

When Americans go to the polls on election day, they have in mind the choice between two individuals, the Democratic and the Republican presidential nominees. In effect, however, they are choosing a lot more than a single executive leader. They are also picking a secretary of state, the director of the FBI, the chair of the Federal Reserve Board, and a host of other executives. Each of them is a presidential appointee.

Presidential Appointees

Newly elected presidents gain important advantages from their appointment powers. First, their appointees are a source of policy information. Modern policymaking requires a detailed understanding of policy issues, and this knowledge is a source of considerable power in Washington. Second, these appointees extend the president's reach into the huge federal bureaucracy, exerting influence on the day-to-day workings of the agencies they head. Not surprisingly, presidents have tended to appoint individuals who are members of their political party.

The Executive Office of the President The key staff organization is the Executive Office of the President (EOP), which Congress created in 1939 to provide the president with the staff necessary to coordinate the activities of the executive branch.[23] The EOP has since become the command center of the presidency.[24] It currently consists of the Office of the Vice President and ten other organizations (see Figure 12-2). They include the White House Office (WHO), which consists of the president's closest personal advisers; the Office of Management and Budget (OMB), which consists of experts who formulate and then administer the federal budget; the National Security Council (NSC), which advises the president on foreign and military affairs; and the Council of Economic Advisers (CEA), which advises the president on the national economy.[25]

The Vice President Although the vice president works in the White House, no constitutional executive authority comes along with this office. Accordingly, the president decides the role the vice president will play. Earlier presidents often refused to assign any significant duties to their vice presidents, which diminished the office's appeal. Nomination to the vice presidency was refused by many leading politicians, including Daniel Webster and Henry Clay. Said Webster, "I do not propose to be buried until I am really dead."[26] Recent presidents, however, have assigned important duties to their vice presidents. George W. Bush, for example, chose Dick Cheney as his running mate in part because of Cheney's experience as White House chief of staff and secretary of defense during previous Republican administrations.

The White House Office Of the EOP's ten other organizations, the White House Office serves the president most directly and personally. The WHO consists of the president's personal assistants, including close personal advisers, press agents, legislative and group liaison aides, and special assistants for domestic and international policy. They work in the White

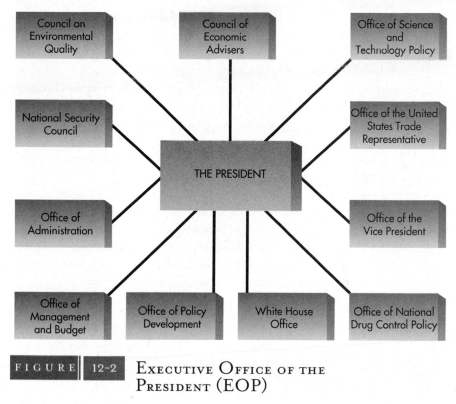

Council on
Environmental
Quality

Council of
Economic
Advisers

Office of Science
and
Technology Policy

National Security
Council

Office of the United
States Trade
Representative

THE PRESIDENT

Office of
Administration

Office of the
Vice President

Office of
Management
and Budget

Office of Policy
Development

White House
Office

Office of National
Drug Control Policy

FIGURE   12-2   EXECUTIVE OFFICE OF THE
PRESIDENT (EOP)

The EOP Helps the president to manage the rest of the executive branch and
promotes the president's policy and political goals.
Source: Executive Office of President, 2003.

House, and the president can hire and fire them at will. The personal assistants do much of the legwork for the president and serve as a main
source of advice. Most of them are skilled at developing political strategy,
recognizing political opportunities, and communicating with the public,
Congress, key groups, and the news media. Because of their closeness and
loyalty to the president, they are among the most powerful individuals in
Washington.

Policy Experts The president is also served by the policy experts in the EOP's
other organizations, who include economists, legal analysts, national security specialists, and others. The president is advised on economic issues, for
example, by the National Economic Council (NEC). The NEC gathers information to develop indicators of the economy's strength and applies economic theories to various policy alternatives. Modern policymaking cannot
be conducted in the absence of such expert advice and knowledge.

The President's Cabinet The heads of the fifteen executive departments, such as the Department of Defense and the Department of Agriculture, constitute the president's **cabinet.** They are appointed by the president, subject to confirmation by the Senate. Although the cabinet once served as the president's main advisory group, it has not played this role since Herbert Hoover's administration. As national issues have become increasingly complex, the cabinet has become outmoded as a policymaking forum: department heads are likely to understand issues only in their respective policy areas.[27] Cabinet meetings have been largely reduced to gatherings at which only the most general matters are discussed.

Nevertheless, cabinet members, as individuals who head major departments, are important figures in any administration. The president chooses them for their prominence in politics, business, government, or the professions. Many of them, like Colin Powell and Donald Rumsfeld, President Bush's secretary of state and secretary of defense respectively, also bring to their office a high level of experience in public affairs.[28]

Other Presidential Appointees In addition to cabinet secretaries, the president appoints the heads and the top deputies of federal agencies and commissions. Altogether, the president appoints more than five thousand executive officials. However, most of these appointees are selected at the agency level or are part-time workers. This still leaves nearly seven hundred appointees who serve the president more or less directly, a much larger number than is appointed by the chief executive of any other democracy.[29]

The Problem of Control

Although the president's appointees are a valuable asset, they also pose a problem: because they are so numerous, the president has difficulty controlling them. President Truman had a wall chart in the Oval Office listing more than one hundred officials who reported directly to him and often told visitors, "I cannot even see all of these men, let alone actually study what they are doing."[30] Since Truman's time, the number of bureaucratic agencies has more than doubled, compounding the problem of presidential control over subordinates.[31]

The nature of the control problem varies with the type of appointee. The advantages of having the advice of policy experts, for example, are offset somewhat by the fact that these experts often have little political experience and tend to exaggerate the importance of their particular policy interests. As a result, their proposals are sometimes impractical or politically unacceptable. On the other hand, top political appointees, while adept at politics, have a tendency to act too independently. WHO assistants tend naturally to skew information in a direction that supports the course of action they favor.[32]

The problem of presidential control is even more severe in the case of appointees who work outside the White House, in the departments and agencies. The loyalty of agency heads and cabinet secretaries is often split between a desire to promote the president's goals and an interest in boosting themselves or the agencies they lead.[33] In late 2002, Harvey Pitt, appointed by President Bush to chair the Securities and Exchange Commission (SEC), resigned amid charges that he had not aggressively pursued corporate accounting irregularities. The Enron, WorldCom, and other corporate scandals had put regulatory action in the spotlight, and Pitt's apparent favoritism toward accounting firms, which he had represented as a lawyer before his appointment to the SEC, was an embarrassment to the Bush administration.

Lower-level appointees within the departments and agencies pose a different type of problem. The president rarely, if ever, sees them, and they are typically political novices (most have fewer than two years of government experience) and not very knowledgeable about policy. These appointees are often "captured" by the agency in which they work because they depend for advice on the agency's career bureaucrats. (Chapter 13 examines further the relationship between presidential appointees and career bureaucrats.)

In sum, the modern presidency is a double-edged sword. Presidents today have greater responsibilities than their predecessors, and the increase in responsibilities expands their opportunities to exert power. At the same time, the range of these responsibilities is so broad that presidents must rely on staffers who may or may not act in the president's best interests. The modern president's recurring problem is to find some way of making sure that aides serve the interests of the presidency above all others. (The subject of presidential control of the executive branch will be discussed further in Chapter 13.)

FACTORS IN PRESIDENTIAL LEADERSHIP

The president operates within a system of separate institutions that share power (see "How the United States Compares"). Significant presidential action normally depends on the approval of Congress, the cooperation of the bureaucracy, and sometimes the acceptance of the judiciary. Since other officials have their own priorities, presidents do not always get their way. Congress in particular—more than the courts or the bureaucracy—holds the key to presidential success. Without congressional authorization and funding, most presidential proposals are nothing but ideas, empty of action.

▌HOW THE UNITED STATES COMPARES

Systems of Executive Policy Leadership

The United States instituted a presidential system in 1789 as part of its constitutional checks and balances. This form of executive leadership was copied in Latin America but not in Europe. European democracies adopted parliamentary systems, in which executive leadership is provided by a prime minister, who is a member of the legislature. In recent years some European prime ministers have campaigned and governed as if they were a singular authority rather than the head of a collective institution. In the 1960s, France created a separate chief executive office but retained its parliamentary form of legislature.

The policy leadership of a president can differ substantially from that of a prime minister. As a singular head of an independent branch of government, a president does not have to share executive authority, but nevertheless depends on the legislative branch for support. By comparison, a prime minister shares executive leadership with a cabinet, but once agreement within the cabinet is reached, he or she is almost assured of the legislative support necessary to carry out policy initiatives.

Presidential System	Presidential/ Parliamentary System	Parliamentary System
Mexico	Finland	Australia
United States	France	Belgium
Venezuela		Canada
		Germany
		Great Britain
		Italy
		Japan
		Netherlands
		Sweden

Whether a president's initiatives succeed or fail depends substantially on several factors, including the force of circumstance, the stage of the president's term, the nature of the issue, the president's support in Congress, and the level of public support for the president's leadership. The remainder of this chapter examines each of these factors.

The Force of Circumstance

During his first months in office and in the midst of the Great Depression, Franklin D. Roosevelt accomplished the most sweeping changes in domestic policy in the nation's history. Congress moved quickly to pass nearly every New Deal initiative he proposed. In 1964 and 1965, Lyndon Johnson pushed landmark civil rights and social welfare legislation through Congress on the strength of the civil rights movement, the legacy of the assassinated President Kennedy, and large Democratic majorities in the House and Senate. When Ronald Reagan assumed the presidency in 1981, high unemployment and inflation had greatly weakened the national economy and created a mood for significant change, which enabled Reagan to persuade Congress to support some of the most notable taxing and spending changes in history.

From such presidencies has come the popular impression that presidents single-handedly decide national policy. However, each of these periods of presidential dominance was marked by a special set of circumstances: a decisive election victory that gave added force to the president's leadership, a compelling national problem that convinced Congress and the public that bold presidential action was needed, and a president who was mindful of what was expected and who vigorously advocated policies consistent with those expectations.

When conditions are favorable, the power of the presidency appears awesome. The problem for most presidents is that conditions are not normally conducive to strong leadership. The political scientist Erwin Hargrove suggests that presidential influence depends largely on circumstance.[34] Some presidents serve in periods when resources are scarce or when important problems are surfacing in American society but have not yet become critical. Such a situation, Hargrove contends, works against the president's efforts to accomplish significant policy change. In 1994, reflecting on the constraints of budget deficits and other factors beyond his control, Bill Clinton said he had no choice but "to play the hand that history had dealt" him.

The Stage of the President's Term

If conditions conducive to great accomplishments occur infrequently, it is nonetheless the case that nearly every president has favorable moments. Such moments tend to come during the first months in office. Most newly elected presidents enjoy a **honeymoon period** during which Congress, the press, and the public anticipate initiatives from the Oval Office and are more predisposed than usual to support these initiatives.

Not surprisingly, presidents have put forth more new programs in their first year in office than in any subsequent year. James Pfiffner uses the term

strategic presidency to refer to a president's need to move quickly on priority items to take advantage of the policy momentum that is gained from the election.[35] Later in their terms, presidents tend to do less well in presenting initiatives and getting them enacted. They may run out of good ideas, get caught up in scandal, or exhaust their political resources: the momentum of their election is gone and sources of opposition have emerged. Even highly successful presidents like Johnson and Reagan tended to have weak records in their final years. Franklin Roosevelt began his presidency with a remarkable period of achievement—the celebrated "Hundred Days"—but during his last six years in office, few of his major domestic proposals were enacted.

An irony of the presidency, then, is that presidents are usually most powerful when they are least knowledgeable—during their first months in office. These months can, as a result, be times of risk as well as times of opportunity. An example is the Bay of Pigs fiasco during the first year of John Kennedy's presidency, in which a U.S.-backed invasion force of anti-communist Cubans was easily defeated by Fidel Castro's army.

The Nature of the Issue: Foreign or Domestic

In the 1960s, the political scientist Aaron Wildavsky wrote that although the nation has only one president, it has two presidencies: one domestic and one foreign.[36] Wildavsky was referring to Congress's greater tendency to defer to presidential leadership on foreign policy issues than on domestic policy issues. He had in mind the broad leeway Congress had granted Truman, Eisenhower, Kennedy, and Johnson in their foreign policies. Wildavsky's thesis is now regarded as a somewhat time-bound conception of presidential influence. He wrote before the Vietnam War had weakened congressional support for presidential leadership in foreign affairs. Today, many of the same factors that affect a president's success on domestic policy, such as the partisan composition of Congress, also affect success on foreign policy.[37]

Nevertheless, presidents are still somewhat more likely to get what they want when the issue is foreign policy, because they have more authority to act on their own and are more likely to get support from the opposite party in Congress.[38] The clash between powerful interest groups that occurs on many domestic issues is less prevalent in the foreign policy area. Additionally, the president is recognized by other nations as America's voice in world affairs, and members of Congress will sometimes back the president in order to maintain America's credibility abroad. In some cases, Congress effectively has no choice but to accept presidential leadership. When President Bush in 2002 pursued a congressional resolution to use force against Iraq if it did not disarm, even some members of Congress who questioned such a broad grant of war-making authority to the president supported it, realizing that defeat of the resolution might lead Iraq's Saddam Hussein to conclude that America lacked the unity and determination to stop his weapons development programs. Five months later, Bush ordered U.S. forces to attack Iraq.

Presidents also gain some leverage in foreign and defense policy because of their commanding position with the defense, diplomatic, and intelligence agencies. These are sometimes labeled "presidential agencies." As chief executive, the president is in charge of all federal agencies, but in practice the president's influence is strongest in those agencies that connect with his constitutional authority as chief diplomat and commander in chief, such as the departments of State and Defense and the CIA. These agencies have a tradition of deference to presidential authority that is not found in agencies that deal primarily with domestic policy. The Department of Agriculture, for example, responds to presidential direction but is also responsive (perhaps even more responsive) to farm-state senators and representatives.

Relations with Congress

Although the presidency is not nearly as powerful as most Americans assume, the capacity of presidents to influence the agenda of national debate is unrivaled, reflecting their unique claim to represent the whole country. Whenever the president directs attention to a particular issue or program, members of Congress take notice. But will they take action? The answer is sometimes yes and sometimes no, depending in part on whether the president takes their concerns into account.

Seeking Cooperation from Congress As the center of national attention, presidents can easily start to believe that their ideas should prevail over those of Congress. This line of reasoning invariably gets any president into trouble. Jimmy Carter had not held national office before he was elected in 1976, so he had no clear understanding of how Washington operates.[39] Soon after taking office, Carter deleted from his budget nineteen public works projects that he believed were a waste of taxpayers' money, ignoring the importance that members of Congress attach to obtaining federally funded projects for their constituents. Carter's action set the tone for a conflict-ridden relationship with Congress.

In order to get the help of members of Congress, the president must respond to their interests as they respond to the president's. The political scientist Fred Greenstein concludes that "whatever else his qualities, the president needs to be a working politician who can work with or otherwise win over the Washington community."[40]

The use of the presidential veto illustrates the point. Presidents can sometimes force Congress to accommodate their views through the use or threatened use of the veto. When a major civil rights bill was being debated in Congress in 1991, George Bush said flatly that he would veto any bill that imposed hiring "quotas" on employers; his ultimatum forced Congress to alter provisions of the bill. Yet the veto is more effective as a presidential restraint on Congress than as a device by which Congress can be forced to take positive action on the president's proposals.

The most basic fact about presidential leadership is that it takes place in the context of a system of divided powers. Although the president gets most of the attention, Congress has most of the constitutional authority in the American system. The powers of the presidential office are insufficient by themselves to keep the president in a strong position. Even the president's most direct legislative tool, the veto, has clear limits.[41] Congress can seldom muster the two-thirds majority in each chamber required to override a presidential veto, and so the threat of a veto can make Congress bend to the president's demands. Yet, as the presidential scholar Richard Neustadt argues, the veto is as much a sign of presidential weakness as it is of strength, because it comes into play when Congress refuses to go along with the president's ideas.[42]

Congress is a constituency that all presidents must serve if they expect to get its support.[43] Neustadt concludes that presidential power, at base, is "the power to persuade."[44] Like any singular notion of presidential power, Neustadt's has limitations. Presidents at times have the power to command and to threaten. But Congress can never be taken for granted. Theodore Roosevelt expressed the wish that he could "be the president and Congress, too," if only for a day, so that he would have the power to enact as well as propose laws.

Benefiting from Partisan Support in Congress For most presidents, the next-best-thing to being "Congress, too" is to have a Congress filled with members of their own party. The sources of division within Congress are many. Legislators from urban and rural areas, wealthier and poorer constituencies, and different regions of the country often have very different views of the national interest. To obtain majority support in Congress, the president must find ways to overcome these differences.

No source of unity is more important to presidential success than partisanship. Presidents are more likely to succeed when their own party controls Congress (see Figure 12-3). Between 1954 and 1992, each Republican president—Eisenhower, Nixon, Ford, Reagan, and Bush—had to contend with a Democratic majority in one or both houses of Congress. Congress

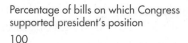

Percentage of bills on which Congress
supported president's position

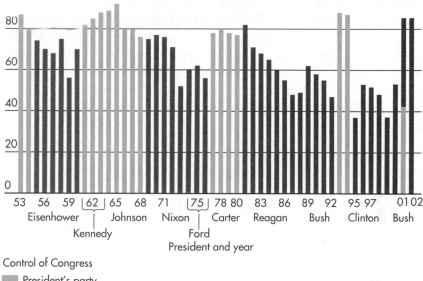

Control of Congress

 President's party
Other party (one or both houses)

FIGURE   12-3   **PERCENTAGE OF BILLS PASSED BY CONGRESS
ON WHICH THE PRESIDENT ANNOUNCED A
POSITION, 1953–2002**

In most years, presidents have been supported by Congress on a majority of policy
issued on which they have taken a stand. Presidents fare better when their party
controls Congress.
Source: Congressional Quarterly Weekly Report, various dates. Used by permission.

passed a smaller percentage of the initiatives supported by each of these
presidents than by any Democratic president of the period: Kennedy, Johnson, or Carter.[45] In his first two years in office, backed by Democratic majorities in the House and Senate, Clinton had a high proportion of his
initiatives enacted into law. After Republicans took control of Congress in
1995, Clinton's legislative success rate sank to the lowest of any recent
Democratic president, a dramatic illustration of the way presidential power
is affected by whether the president's party controls Congress.

In 2001, George W. Bush had an 87 percent success rate, the highest
since Lyndon Johnson's 93 percent in 1965. Bush's extraordinary success in
winning congressional support was achieved in a way never before seen.

When he took office, his Republican party controlled both the House and the Senate, which virtually ensured a responsive Congress. In mid-summer, however, Senator James Jeffords of Vermont bolted the GOP, leaving the Democrats in control of the Senate. This shift occurred shortly before Congress's summer recess, which meant few bills were considered in the first weeks after Jeffords's defection. Then, shortly after Congress resumed its work, terrorist attacks on the World Trade Center and the Pentagon led congressional members of both parties to rally behind the president. After September 11, Bush won eleven of twelve House votes and thirty of thirty-one Senate votes, contributing to the highest presidential success rate in more than three decades.

Colliding with Congress On rare occasions, presidents have pursued their goals so zealously that Congress has been compelled to take steps to curb their use of power.

The ultimate sanction of Congress is its constitutional power to impeach and remove the president from office. The House of Representatives decides whether the president should be impeached (placed on trial), and the Senate conducts the trial and then votes on the president's guilt, with a two-thirds vote required for removal from office. In 1868, Andrew Johnson was impeached and came within one Senate vote of being removed from office for his opposition to Congress's harsh Reconstruction policies after the Civil War. In 1974, Richard Nixon's resignation halted congressional proceedings on the Watergate affair that would almost certainly have ended in his impeachment and removal from office.

The specter of impeachment arose again in 1998 when the House of Representatives by a vote of 258 to 176 authorized an investigation of President Clinton's conduct. He was accused of lying under oath about his relationship with Monica Lewinsky and of obstructing justice by trying to conceal the affair. The gravity of the allegations was leavened by the circumstances. The charges had grown out of an extramarital affair rather than a gross abuse of executive power and were tied to a controversial five-year $40-million investigation by independent counsel Kenneth Starr. For

/pattersonwtp5

their part, the American people were ambivalent about the whole issue. Most people approved of Clinton's handling of the presidency and did not believe his actions warranted removal from office, but they were also critical of his relationship with Lewinsky. Not surprisingly, congressional Republicans and Democrats differed sharply on the impeachment issue. At all formal stages of the process—the House vote to authorize an inquiry, the House vote on

Impeaching, Convicting, and Removing the President

In October 1998, for only the third time in American history, the Congress authorized an official impeachment investigation of the president. Bill Clinton joined Andrew Johnson and Richard Nixon as presidents whose legacy will be forever linked with the word *impeachment*.

Although *impeachment* technically applies only to the indictment stage of congressional action, it is commonly used to refer also to the conviction stage. But these are constitutionally separate stages. The House is granted under Article I, section 2 of the Constitution the power to impeach (indict) the president. The Senate under Article I, section 3 has the power to try, convict, and remove the president.

Article II, section 4 of the Constitution states that impeachable acts are "Treason, Bribery, or Other High Crimes and Misdemeanors" but does not spell out what these other high crimes and misdemeanors shall include. Nevertheless, it is clear from the historical record that the Framers deliberately created a process that would make it difficult to remove the president from office in order to discourage Congress from seeking to get rid of a president for purely political reasons.

The steps that Congress would take would take in removing the president from office are the following:

1. The House of Representatives by simple majority vote would authorize an investigation of the president.
2. The House Judiciary Committee would conduct the inquiry and submit its findings to the full House.
3. The House through simple majority vote would indict the president on one or more charges (thus "impeaching" the president).
4. The Senate would hold a trial on the charges; the chief justice of the Supreme Court would preside over the trial.
5. The Senate through a two-thirds majority would convict, causing the president's removal from office.

The Clinton impeachment process ended with step 4; the Senate did not vote to convict. The course of Andrew Jackson's impeachment was the same, although the Senate, in his case, came within one vote of conviction. Nixon resigned shortly before the House vote on impeachment (step 3).

the articles of impeachment, and the Senate vote on whether to convict the president—the vote divided largely along party lines. In the end, Clinton was acquitted by the Senate, but his legacy will forever be tarnished by his impeachment by the House.

The gravity of impeachment action makes it an unsuitable basis for curbing presidential power except in rare instances. More often, Congress has responded legislatively to executive abuses. An example is the Budget Impoundment and Control Act of 1974, which prohibits a president from refusing to release funds that have been appropriated by Congress. The legislation was enacted in response to the Nixon administration's practice of withholding funds from programs it disliked.

Congress's most significant effort in history to curb presidential power, however, is the War Powers Act. During the Vietnam War, presidents Johnson and Nixon repeatedly misled Congress, supplying it with intelligence estimates that painted a falsely optimistic picture of the military situation. This information contributed to the willingness of Congress to appropriate the funds necessary for continuation of the war. However, congressional support changed abruptly in 1971 with *The New York Times's* publication of classified documents (the so-called Pentagon Papers) that revealed the Vietnam situation to be much worse than portrayed by Johnson and Nixon.

Richard M. Nixon
(1913–1994)

Richard Nixon is one of the most controversial presidents in the nation's history. His presidency saw major triumphs, including the reestablishment of relations with China and the reduction of tensions with the Soviet Union. However, his presidency also included major reversals. He was forced to resign his office because of the Watergate scandal, and his high-handed actions led Congress to enact the War Powers Act and the Budget Impoundment Act, which restricted presidential authority. Before gaining the presidency, Nixon served as a U.S. representative, U.S. senator, and vice president. He narrowly lost to John F. Kennedy in the 1960 presidential election. He gained the presidency by narrowly defeating Hubert Humphrey in 1968.

To prevent future presidential wars, Congress in 1973 passed the War Powers Act. Nixon vetoed the measure, but Congress overrode his veto. The act requires the president to notify Congress of the reason for committing combat troops within forty-eight hours of their deployment; requires that hostilities must end within sixty days unless Congress extends the period; gives the president an additional thirty days to withdraw the troops from hostile territory, although Congress can shorten the period; and requires the president to consult with Congress whenever feasible before dispatching troops into a hostile situation.

Every president since Nixon has claimed that the act infringes on his constitutional power as commander in chief, and each has refused to accept it fully. Nevertheless, the War Powers Act is a potentially significant constraint on the president's war-making power.

Thus the effect of executive efforts to circumvent congressional authority is heightened congressional opposition. Even if presidents gain in the short run by acting on their own, they undermine their capacity to lead in the long run by failing to keep in mind that Congress is a coequal branch of the American governing system.

Public Support

Public support affects a president's ability to achieve policy goals.[46] Presidential power rests in part on a claim to national leadership, and the legitimacy of that claim is roughly proportional to the president's public support. With public backing, the president's leadership cannot easily be dismissed by other Washington officials. If the president's public support sinks, officials are less inclined to accept presidential leadership.[47]

Every recent president has had the public's confidence at the very start of the term of office. When asked in polls whether they "approve or disapprove of how the president is doing his job," most Americans have expressed approval during the first months of the term. Sooner or later, however, all **presidential approval ratings** have slipped below this high point, and several recent presidents have left office with a rating below 50 percent.

Events and Issues The public's support for the president is affected by national and international conditions. Threats from abroad tend to produce a patriotic "rally 'round the flag" reaction that initially creates widespread support for the president. Every foreign policy crisis in the past four decades has followed this pattern. Americans were deeply divided in 2003 over the wisdom of war with Iraq, but, once the war began, a substantial majority expressed support for President Bush's action.

★ | STATES IN THE NATION

Divided Power in the Executive

The president operates in a system of divided power in which joint action by Congress is often required for the president's programs to be adopted. The chief executives in the American states are the governors, and nearly all of them must contend with a further division: a separation of power within the executive itself. Maine and New Jersey are the only states in which executive power is vested solely in a governor. Five other states have separately elected and (unlike the vice president) constitutionally empowered lieutenant governors. In most of the other states, other major executive officials, such as the attorney general and secretary of state, are also elected. Finally, there are twelve states in which even minor executive officials, such as commissioner of education, are chosen by the voters. In the case of the federal government, these other major and minor officials are appointed by the president.

Elected officials:

Governor or governor and lt. governor only

Also other major officials (e.g., attorney general)

Also other minor officials (e.g., commissioner of education)

Ongoing crises, however, can eventually erode a president's support if they are not resolved or pursued successfully. Jimmy Carter's approval rating jumped by twenty points when Iranian extremists stormed the U.S. embassy in Teheran in November 1979 and took fifty-nine Americans hostage.[48] However, when months passed without a resolution of the hostage situation, Carter's popularity began to sink, which contributed to his defeat in the 1980 election.

Economic downswings tend to reduce the public's confidence in the president.[49] Ford, Carter, and the first President Bush lost their reelection bids when their popularity plummeted after the economy swooned. In contrast, Clinton's popularity rose in 1995 and 1996 as the economy strengthened, contributing to his reelection in 1996. The irony is that presidents do not actually have all that much control over the economy. If they did, it would always be strong.

The Televised Presidency A major advantage that presidents enjoy in their efforts to nurture public support is their access to the media, particularly television.[50] Only the president can expect the television networks to provide free air time on occasion, and in terms of the amount of news coverage, the president and top advisors receive half again as much coverage as all members of Congress combined.

The political scientist Samuel Kernell calls it "going public" when the president bypasses inside bargaining with Congress and promotes "himself and his policies by appealing to the American public for support."[51] Such appeals are at least as old as Theodore Roosevelt's use of the presidency as a "bully pulpit" but have increased substantially in recent years.[52] As the president has moved from the role of administrative leader to that of policy advocate and agenda setter, public support has become increasingly important to presidential success.[53] Television has made it easier for presidents to go public with their programs. Ronald Reagan was called the "Great Communicator" in part because of his ability to use television to generate public support for his initiatives.

However, the press is also adept at putting its own spin on events and tends to play up adverse developments. For example, although presidents get some credit in the press when the economy is doing well, they get mounds of negative coverage when the economy is doing poorly. Scandal is the biggest threat to a president's ability to influence news coverage. When scandal strikes, a media "feeding frenzy" ensues, and power shifts from the White House to the press and the president's political opponents. The Clinton-Lewinsky scandal is a prime example. Throughout 1998, it was at the top of the news. Clinton's efforts to direct the nation's attention to other

Bush press secretary Ari Fleischer briefs reporters in the cramped space of the White House briefing room. Effective communication is an essential part of the modern presidency.

issues, such as the financial crisis spreading across Asia, were unsuccessful. In less dramatic fashion, the flurry of accounting scandals that came to light in 2002 enabled the press to disrupt the Bush administration's efforts to control the policy agenda. The press played up the contributions that Enron and WorldCom had made to Bush's 2000 campaign and also dug up embarrassing facts about business dealings by Bush and by Vice President Cheney. For example, when Bush announced his support of legislation that would prohibit business firms from giving low-interest personal loans to their officers, the press was quick to point out that Bush himself had been the beneficiary of two such loans when he was on the board of Harken Energy Corporation in the 1980s.

The Illusion of Presidential Government Presidents have no choice but to try to counter this type of press coverage with their own version of their accomplishments. A public relations effort can carry a president only so far, however. National conditions ultimately determine the level of public confidence in the president. Indeed, presidents run a risk by trying to build up their images through public relations. Through their frequent television appearances and claims of success, presidents contribute to the public's belief that the president is in charge of the national government, a perception that the political scientist Hugh Heclo calls "the illusion of presidential government."[54]

Because the public expects so much from its presidents, they get too much credit when things go well and too much blame when things go badly. Therein lies an irony of the presidential office. More than from any constitutional grant, more than from any statute, and more than from any crisis, presidential power derives from the president's position as the sole official who can claim to represent the whole American public. Yet because presidential power rests on a popular base, it erodes when public support declines. The irony is that the presidential office typically grows weaker as problems mount: just when the country could most use effective leadership, that leadership is often hardest to achieve.[55]

/pattersonwtp5

SUMMARY

The presidency has become a much stronger office than the Framers envisioned. The Constitution grants the president substantial military, diplomatic, legislative, and executive powers, and in each case the president's authority has increased measurably. Underlying this change is the president's position as the one leader chosen by the whole nation and as the sole head of the executive branch. These features of the office have enabled presidents to claim broad authority in response to the increased demands placed on the federal government by changing world and national conditions.

During the course of American history, the presidential selection process has been altered in ways that were intended to make it more responsive to the preferences of ordinary people. Today, they have a vote not only in the general election, but also in the selection of nominees. To gain nomination, a presidential hopeful must gain the support of the electorate in state primaries and open caucuses. Once nominated, the candidates receive federal funds for their general election campaigns, which are based on televised appeals.

Although the campaign tends to personalize the presidency, the responsibilities of the modern presidency far exceed any president's personal capacities. To meet their obligations, presidents have surrounded themselves with large staffs of advisers, policy experts, and managers. These staff members enable the president to extend control over the executive branch while providing the information necessary for policymaking. All recent presidents have discovered, however, that their control of staff resources is incomplete and that some things that others do on their behalf actually work against what they are trying to accomplish.

As sole chief executive and the nation's top elected leader, presidents can always expect that their policy and leadership efforts will receive attention. However, other institutions, particularly Congress, have the authority to make this leadership effective. No president has come close to winning approval of all the programs he has placed before Congress, but the presidents' records of success have varied considerably. The factors in a president's success include the presence or absence of national conditions that require strong leadership from the White House and whether the president's party has a majority in Congress.

To retain an effective leadership position, the president depends on the backing of the American people. Recent presidents have made extensive use of the media to build support for their programs. Yet they have had difficulty maintaining that support throughout their terms of office. A major reason is that the public expects far more from its presidents than they can deliver.

KEY TERMS

cabinet
honeymoon period
legitimacy (of election)
momentum
open party caucuses

presidential approval rating
stewardship theory
unit rule
Whig theory
Strategic presidency

SUGGESTED READINGS

Cohen, Jeffrey E. *Presidential Responsiveness and Public Policymaking: The Publics and the Policies That Presidents Choose.* Ann Arbor: University of Michigan Press, 1997. An accounting of presidential responsiveness and public policymaking.

Jackson, John S., and William J. Crotty. *The Politics of Presidential Selection.* New York: Longman, 2001. A careful look at the presidential election process by two of its finest analysts.

Jones, Charles. *Separate But Equal Branches.* New York: Chatham House, 1999. An insightful analysis of presidential power in a system of divided powers.

Kernell, Samuel. *Going Public: New Strategies of Presidential Leadership,* 3d ed. Washington, D.C.: Congressional Quarterly Press, 1997. An examination of presidential use of going public to gain support.

Kessel, John H. *Presidents, the Presidency, and the Political Environment.* Washington, D.C.: Congressional Quarterly Press, 2001. An insightful assessment of the politics of the presidency.

Neustadt, Richard E. *Presidential Power and the Modern Presidents: The Politics of Leadership from Roosevelt to Reagan.* New York: Free Press, 1990. The classic analysis of the limitations on presidential power.

Pfiffner, James P. *The Strategic Presidency: Hitting the Ground Running,* 2d ed. Chicago: Dorsey Press, 1996. A study of the way a newly elected president can convert electoral support into power in office.

Relyea, Harold C., and Charles V. Arja. *Vice Presidency of the United States: Evolution of the Modern Office.* Huntington, N.Y.: Nova Science Publishers, 2002. An assessment of how the vice presidency has changed into the office that it is today.

Walcott, Charles E., and Karen M. Hult. *Governing the White House: From Hoover through LBJ.* Lawrence: University Press of Kansas, 1995. An innovative study of how the organization of the White House affects presidential performance.

List of Websites

http://sunsite.unc.edu:80/lia/president A site with general information on specific presidents and links to the presidential libraries.

http://www.ipl.org/ref/POTUS Profiles of the nation's presidents, their cabinet officers, and key events during their time in office.

http://www.vote-smart.org/executive Information on the presidency and the Executive Office of the President as well as links to key executive agencies and organizations.

http://www.whitehouse.gov The White House's home page; it has an e-mail guest book and includes information on the president, the vice president, and current White House activities.

Politics in Theory and Practice

Thinking: Why is presidential power "conditional"—that is, why is it affected so substantially by circumstance, the makeup of Congress, and popular support? (The separation of powers should be part of your answer.)

Acting: Consider writing a letter or sending an e-mail to the president or a top presidential appointee that expresses your opinion on an issue that is currently the object of executive action. You can inform yourself about the administration's policy or stance on the issue through the website of the White House (www.whitehouse.gov) or of the agency in question (for example, the State Department's site is www.state.gov).

The New York Times   reading 12

After the Attacks: Assessment; President Seems to Gain Legitimacy

by R. W. Apple Jr.

Although the presidency is always a center of national attention, the power of the office varies significantly, depending on circumstances. Nothing does more to strengthen the office than a national crisis. During such periods, the president becomes the rallying point for Americans' hopes and fears. In this article, written on September 16, 2001, five days after the terrorist attacks on the World Trade Center and the Pentagon, New York Times correspondent R. W. Apple Jr. describes the transforming effect of the attacks on the presidency of George W. Bush.

WASHINGTON—With the eyes of a nervous nation fixed upon him, George W. Bush began coming of age as president this weekend.

In the capital and in New York City, in settings both formal and informal, Mr. Bush sought to lift the spirits of the American people in the wake of Tuesday's horrific terrorist attacks. He sought to console the bereaved, comfort the wounded, encourage the heroic, calm the fearful and, by no means incidentally, rally the country for the struggle and sacrifice ahead. In the process, he made significant progress toward easing the doubts about his capacity for the job

and the legitimacy of his election that have clung stubbornly to him during his eight difficult months in the Oval Office. You could almost see him growing into the clothes of the presidency.

"I'm impressed," said Representative Richard A. Gephardt, the Democratic leader in the House. "He's been very strong these last few days."

A Democratic elder said, "We all desperately want him to succeed, and there is nothing more valuable to a president than that emotion."

A man who had seldom traveled abroad before seeking the presidency, who came to office determined to focus on domestic issues like education and taxes, Mr. Bush now finds thrust upon him the role of wartime president, or something like it. He will be measured by how well he fulfills his own vision of "our responsibility to history," which he said was "to answer these attacks and rid the world of evil."

It is no small goal, reminiscent in a way of Woodrow Wilson's promise that World War I would make the world safe for democracy.

Palpable early progress in the effort to identify those who carried out Tuesday's suicide missions provided Mr. Bush with

Protection Agency (EPA), which monitors and prevents industrial pollution. Table 13-1 lists some of the regulatory agencies and other noncabinet units of the federal bureaucracy.

Beyond their executive functions, regulatory agencies have legislative and judicial functions. They issue regulations and judge whether individuals or

TABLE 13-1   SELECTED U.S. REGULATORY AGENCIES, INDEPENDENT AGENCIES, GOVERNMENT CORPORATIONS, AND PRESIDENTIAL COMMISSIONS

Central Intelligence Agency	National Labor Relations Board
Commission on Civil Rights	National Railroad Passenger Corporation (Amtrak)
Consumer Product Safety Commission	National Science Foundation
Environmental Protection Agency	National Transportation Safety Board
Equal Employment Opportunity Commission	Nuclear Regulatory Commission
Export-Import Bank of the United States	Occupational Safety and Health Review Commission
Farm Credit Administration	Office of Personnel Management
Federal Communications Commission	Peace Corps
Federal Deposit Insurance Corporation	Securities and Exchange Commission
Federal Election Commission	Selective Service System
Federal Energy Regulatory Commission	Small Business Administration
Federal Maritime Commission	Tennessee Valley Authority
Federal Reserve System, Board of Governors of the	U.S. Arms Control and Disarmament Agency
Federal Trade Commission	U.S. Information Agency
General Services Administration	U.S. International Development Cooperation Agency
National Aeronautics and Space Administration	U.S. International Trade Commission
National Archives and Record Administration	U.S. Postal Service
National Foundation on the Arts and the Humanities	Women's History Commission

Source: The U.S. Government Manual.

organizations have complied. The SEC, for example, can impose fines and other penalties on business firms that violate regulations pertaining to the trading of stocks and bonds.

Some regulatory agencies, particularly the older ones (such as the SEC), are "independent" by virtue of their relative freedom from ongoing political control. They are headed by a commission of several members who are appointed by the president and confirmed by Congress but who are not subject to removal by the president. Commissioners serve a fixed term, a legal stipulation intended to free their agencies from political interference. The newer regulatory agencies (such as the EPA) lack such autonomy. They are headed by a presidential appointee who can be removed at the president's discretion.

Government Corporations **Government corporations** are similar to private corporations in that they charge clients for their services and are governed by a board of directors. However, government corporations receive federal funding to help defray operating expenses, and their directors are appointed by the president with Senate approval. The largest government corporation is the U.S. Postal Service, with roughly eight hundred thousand employees. Other government corporations include the Federal Deposit Insurance Corporation (FDIC), which insures savings accounts against bank failures, and the National Railroad Passenger Corporation (Amtrak), which provides passenger rail service.

Presidential Commissions Some **presidential commissions** are permanent bodies that provide ongoing recommendations to the president in particular areas of responsibility. Two such commissions are the Commission on Civil Rights and the Commission on Fine Arts. Other presidential commissions are temporary and disband after making recommendations on specific issues. An example is the commission on racial reconciliation that was appointed by President Clinton in 1997; it concluded its work in 1998.

Federal Employment

The roughly 2.5 million civilian employees of the federal government include professionals who bring their expertise to the problems of governing a large and complex society, service workers who perform such tasks as the typing of correspondence and the delivery of mail, and middle and top managers who supervise the work of the various federal agencies.

More than 90 percent of federal employees are hired by merit criteria, which include educational attainment, employment experience, and performance on competitive tests (such as the civil service and foreign service examinations). The merit system is intended to protect the public from the inept or discriminatory administrative practices that can result if partisanship is the employment criterion.

Federal employees are underpaid in comparison with their counterparts in the private sector. The large majority of federal employees have a GS (Graded Service) job ranking. The rankings range from GS-1 (the lowest rank) to GS-18 (the highest). College graduates who enter the federal service usually start at the GS-5 level, which provides a salary of about $22,000 for a beginning employee. With a master's degree, the level is GS-9 at a $33,000 salary. Federal employees' salaries increase with rank and length of service. Public employees receive substantial fringe benefits, including full health insurance, secure retirement plans, and generous vacation time and sick leave.

Public service has its drawbacks. Federal employees can form labor unions, but their unions by law have limited authority: the government maintains full control of job assignments, compensation, and promotion. Moreover, the Taft-Hartley Act of 1947 prohibits strikes by federal employees and permits the firing of workers who do go on strike. When federal air traffic controllers went on strike anyway in 1981, they were fired by President Reagan. There are also some limits on the partisan activities of civil servants. The Hatch Act of 1939 prohibited them from holding key positions in election campaigns. In 1993, Congress relaxed this prohibition but retained it for certain high-ranking career bureaucrats.

The Federal Bureaucracy's Policy Responsibilities

The Constitution mentions executive departments but does not grant them any powers. Their authority derives from grants of power to the three constitutional branches: Congress, the president, and the courts. Nevertheless, the bureaucracy is far more than an administrative extension of the three branches. It never merely follows orders. The primary function of administrative agencies is **policy implementation,** which is to say that they carry out decisions made by Congress, the president, and the courts.

Although implementation is sometimes described as "mere administration," it is a highly significant and creative function. In the course of their work, administrators come up with policy ideas that are then brought to the attention of the president or members of Congress. Administrative agencies also develop public policy in the process of implementing it.[7] Most legislative acts identify general goals, which bureaucrats translate into specific programs. The Telecommunications Act of 1996, for example, had the stated goal "to promote competition and reduce regulation in order to secure lower prices and higher quality services for American telecommunication consumers and encourage the rapid deployment of new telecommunications

The U.S. Postal Service, the largest government corporation, moves more mail and does so more cheaply and reliably than do the postal bureaucracies of most other industrialized nations. Yet the U.S. Postal Service, like most other federal agencies, has a poor public image.

technologies." Although the act included specific provisions, its implementation was left in large part for the Federal Communications Commission (FCC) to decide. The FCC decided, for example, that regional telephone companies (the Bell companies) had to open their networks to AT&T and other competitors at wholesale rates that were far below what they were charging their retail customers. The purpose was to enable AT&T and other carriers to compete with the Bell companies for local phone customers; in other words, the FCC was responding to its legislative mandate to promote "competition." But it was the FCC, not Congress, that determined the wholesale rates and many of the interconnection rules. This development of policy—through rule making that determines how laws will work in practice—is perhaps the chief way that administrative agencies exercise real power.

Agencies are also charged with the delivery of services—carrying the mail, processing welfare applications, approving government loans, and the like. Such activities are governed by rules, and in most instances the rules decide what gets done. But some services allow agency employees enough discretion that laws end up being applied arbitrarily, a situation that Michael Lipsky describes as "street-level bureaucracy."[8] For example, FBI agents are more diligent in their pursuit of organized crime than of white-collar crime, even though the laws do not say that white-collar criminals should somehow get more lenient treatment.

In sum, administrators necessarily exercise discretion in carrying out their policy responsibilities. They initiate policy, develop it, evaluate it, apply it, and determine whether others are complying with it. The bureaucracy does not simply administer policy, it also *makes policy*.

DEVELOPMENT OF THE FEDERAL BUREAUCRACY: POLITICS AND ADMINISTRATION

Agencies are responsible for carrying out programs that serve the society, and yet each agency was created and is maintained in response to partisan interests. Each agency thus confronts two simultaneous but incompatible demands: that it administer programs fairly and competently and that it respond to partisan claims.

Historically, this conflict has worked itself out in ways that have made the organization of the modern bureaucracy a blend of the political and the administrative. This dual line of development is clearly reflected in the mix of management systems that characterizes the bureaucracy today—the *patronage, merit,* and *executive leadership* systems.

Small Government and the Patronage System

The federal bureaucracy was originally small (three thousand employees in 1800, for instance). The federal government's role was confined mainly to defense and foreign affairs, currency and interstate commerce, and the delivery of the mail. The nation's first six presidents, from George Washington through John Quincy Adams, believed that only distinguished men should be entrusted with the management of the national government. Nearly all top presidential appointees were men of education and political experience, and many of them were members of socially prominent families. They often remained in their jobs year after year.

The nation's seventh president, Andrew Jackson, did not share his predecessors' admiration for the wellborn. In Jackson's view, government would be more responsive to the people if it were administered by common men of good sense.[9] Jackson also believed that top administrators should remain in office for short periods, so that there would be a steady influx of fresh ideas.

Jackson's version of the **patronage system** was popular with the public, but critics labeled it a **spoils system**—a device for placing political cronies in government office as a reward for partisan service. Although Jackson was motivated as much by a concern for democratic government as by his desire to reward partisan supporters, later presidents were often more interested in distributing the spoils of victory. Jackson's successors extended patronage to all levels of administration.[10]

Growth in Government and the Merit System

Because the government of the early nineteenth century was relatively small and limited in scope, it could be managed by employees who had little or no administrative training or experience. As the century advanced, however, the nature of the country changed rapidly and the bureaucracy changed along with it. The Industrial Revolution brought with it massive economic shifts, which prompted groups to look to government for assistance. Farmers were among these groups, and in 1889, Congress created the Department of Agriculture. Business and labor interests also pressed their claims, and in 1903 Congress established the Department of Commerce and Labor to "promote the mutual interest" of the nation's firms and workers. (The separate interests of business and labor proved stronger than their shared concerns, and so in 1913 Labor became a separate department.)[11]

By 1930, federal employment had reached six hundred thousand, a sixfold increase over the level of the 1880s (see Figure 13-2).[12] During the 1930s, as a result of President Franklin Roosevelt's New Deal, the federal work force again expanded, climbing to 1.2 million. Public demand for relief from the economic hardship and uncertainty of the Great Depression led to the formation of economic and social welfare agencies such as the Securities and Exchange Commission and the Social Security Board. An effect was to give the federal government an ongoing role in promoting Americans' economic well-being.

A large and active government requires skilled and experienced personnel. In 1883, Congress passed the Pendleton Act, which established a **merit system** (or **civil service system**) whereby certain federal employees were hired through competitive examinations or by virtue of having special qualifications, such as an advanced degree in a particular field. The transition to a career civil service was gradual. Only 10 percent of federal positions in 1885 were filled on the basis of merit. But the pace accelerated when the

Number of civilian federal employees

FIGURE

FIGURE **13-2** NUMBER OF PERSONS EMPLOYED BY THE
FEDERAL GOVERNMENT, 1791–2003

The federal bureaucracy grew slowly until the 1930s, when an explosive growth began
in programs that required ongoing administration by the federal government.
Source: U.S. Office of Personnel Management, 2003.

Progressives (see Chapter 2) promoted the merit system as a way of eliminating partisan graft and corruption in the administration of government.
By 1920, as the Progressive era was concluding, more than 70 percent of
federal employees were merit appointees. Since 1950, the proportion of
merit employees has not dipped below 80 percent.[13]

The Pendleton Act created the Civil Service Commission to establish
job classifications, administer competitive examinations, and oversee merit
employees. The commission was replaced by two independent agencies in
1978. The Merit Service Protection Board handles appeals of personnel actions, and the Office of Personnel Management (OPM) supervises the hiring and classification of federal employees.

The administrative objective of the merit system is **neutral competence.**[14] A merit-based bureaucracy is "competent" in the sense that employees are hired and retained on the basis of their skills, and it is "neutral"
in the sense that employees are not partisan appointees and thus are expected to do their work on behalf of everyone, not just those who support
the incumbent administration.

Although the merit system contributes to the impartial and proficient
administration of government programs, it has its own sources of bias and
inefficiency. Career bureaucrats tend to place their agency's interests ahead
of those of other agencies and typically oppose substantial efforts to trim

their agency's activities. They are not partisans in the sense of Democratic or Republican politics, but they are partisans when it comes to protecting their own positions and agencies, as will be explained more fully later in the chapter.

Big Government and the Executive Leadership System

As problems with the merit system surfaced after the early years of the twentieth century, reformers looked to a strengthened presidency—an **executive leadership system**—as a means of coordinating the bureaucracy's activities to increase its efficiency and responsiveness.[15] The president was to provide the general leadership that would overcome agency fragmentation and provide a common direction. As Chapter 12 described, Congress in 1939 provided the president with some of the tools needed for improved coordination of the bureaucracy. The Office of Management and Budget (OMB) was created to give the president the authority to coordinate the annual budgetary process. Agencies would be required to prepare their budget proposals under the direction of the president, who would then submit the overall budget to Congress for its approval and modification. The president was also authorized to develop the Executive Office of the President, which oversees the agencies' activities on the president's behalf, assisting in the development and implementation of policy programs.

Like the merit and patronage systems, the executive leadership system has brought problems as well as improvements to the administration of government. The executive leadership concept, if carried too far, can threaten the balance between executive power and legislative power on which the U.S. constitutional system is based, and it can make the president's priorities, not fairness, the criterion by which provision of services is determined. Richard Nixon abused the system, for example, by ordering the OMB to impound (that is, fail to spend) more than $40 billion in appropriated funds of programs he disliked. (The courts ruled that Nixon's action was an unlawful infringement on Congress's constitutional authority over spending. To prevent a recurrence of the problem, Congress in 1974 passed legislation that gives the president the authority to withhold funds for only forty-five days unless Congress passes legislation to rescind the appropriation.)

The executive leadership system is not a panacea but, along with the patronage and merit systems, is a necessary component of any effective strategy for managing the modern federal bureaucracy.[16] The federal bureaucracy today embodies aspects of all three systems, a situation that reflects the tensions inherent in governmental administration. The bureaucracy is expected

TABLE 13-2	STRENGTHS AND WEAKNESSES OF MAJOR SYSTEMS FOR MANAGING THE BUREAUCRACY	
System	**Strengths**	**Weaknesses**
Patronage	Makes the bureaucracy more responsive to election outcomes by allowing the president to appoint some executive officials.	Gives executive authority to individuals chosen for their partisan loyalty rather than administrative or policy expertise; can favor interests that supported the president's election.
Merit	Provides for *competent* administration in that employees are hired on the basis of ability and allowed to remain on the job and thereby become proficient, and provides for *neutral* administration in that civil servants are not partisan appointees and are expected to work in an evenhanded way.	Can result in fragmented, unresponsive administration since career bureaucrats are secure in their jobs and tend to place the interests of their particular agency ahead of those of other agencies or the nation's interests as a whole.
Executive leadership	Provides for presidential leadership of the bureaucracy in order to make it more responsive and to coordinate and direct it (left alone, the bureaucracy tends toward fragmentation).	Can upset the balance between executive and legislative power and can make the president's priorities, not fairness or effective management, the basis for administrative action.

to carry out programs fairly, but it is also expected to respond to political forces and to principles of effective management. The first of these requirements is addressed primarily through the merit system, the second through the patronage system, and the third through the executive leadership system (see Table 13-2).

THE BUREAUCRACY'S POWER IMPERATIVE

A common misperception is that the president, as the chief executive, has the sole claim on the bureaucracy's loyalty. In fact, each of the elected institutions has reason to claim proprietorship: the president as chief executive and Congress as the source of the authorization and funding of the bureaucracy's programs. One presidential appointee asked a congressional committee whether it had any problem with his plans to reduce one of his agency's programs. The committee chairman replied, "No, you have the problem, because if you touch that bureau I'll cut your job out of the budget."[17]

The U.S. system of separate institutions sharing power results in a natural tendency for each institution to guard its turf. In addition, the president and members of Congress differ in their constituencies and thus in the interests to which they are most responsive. For example, although the agricultural sector is just one of many concerns of the president, it is of vital interest to senators and representatives from farm states. Finally, because the president and Congress are elected separately, the White House and one or both houses of Congress may be in the hands of opposing parties. Since 1968, this source of executive-legislative conflict has been more often the rule than the exception.

If agencies are to operate successfully in this system, they must seek support where they can find it—if not from the president, then from Congress. In other words, agencies must play politics.[18] Any agency that is content to sit idly by while new priorities for money and policy are determined is virtually certain to lose out to other agencies that are willing to fight for power.

The Agency Point of View

Administrators have little choice but to look out for their agency's interests, a perspective that is called the **agency point of view**.[19] This perspective comes naturally to most high-ranking civil servants. More than 80 percent of all top careerists reach their high-level positions by rising through the ranks of the same agency.[20] As one top administrator said when testifying before the House Appropriations Committee, "Mr. Chairman, you would not think it proper for me to be in charge of this work and not be enthusiastic about it . . . would you? I have been in it for thirty years, and I believe in it."[21]

Professionalism also cements agency loyalties. High-level administrative positions have increasingly been filled by scientists, engineers, lawyers, educators, physicians, and other professionals. Most of them take jobs in an agency whose mission they support, as in the case of the aeronautical engineers who work for NASA.

Studies confirm that bureaucrats believe in the importance of their agency's work. One study found that social welfare administrators are three times as likely as other civil servants to believe that social welfare programs should be a high policy priority.[22]

Sources of Bureaucratic Power

In promoting their agency's interests, bureaucrats rely on their specialized knowledge, the support of interests that benefit from the programs they run, and the backing of the president and Congress.

The Power of Expertise Most of the policy problems that the federal government confronts do not lend themselves to simple solutions. Whether the issue is space travel or hunger in America, expert knowledge is essential to the development of effective public policy. Much of this expertise is held by bureaucrats. They spend their careers working in a particular policy area, and many of them have had scientific, technical, or other specialized training.[23]

By comparison, elected officials are generalists. To some degree, members of Congress do specialize through their committee work, but they rarely have the time or inclination to acquire a commanding knowledge of a particular issue. The president's understanding of policy issues is even more general. Not surprisingly, the president and members of Congress regularly depend on the bureaucracy for policy advice and guidance.

All agencies acquire some power through their careerists' expertise. No matter how simple a policy issue may appear at first, it invariably involves a lot more than meets the eye. A recognition that the United States has a trade deficit with Japan, for example, can be the premise for policy change, but this recognition does not begin to address such basic issues as the form that the new policy might take, its probable cost and effectiveness, and its links to other issues, such as America's relations with Japan's neighbors. Among the officials most likely to understand these issues are the career bureaucrats in the Commerce Department and the Federal Trade Commission.

The Power of Clientele Groups Most agencies have **clientele groups,** which are special interests that benefit directly from an agency's programs. Clientele groups assist agencies by placing pressure on Congress and the president to support the programs from which they benefit.[24] For example, when House Speaker Newt Gingrich threatened in 1995 to "zero out" funding for the Corporation for Public Broadcasting, audience members and groups such as the Childrens Television Workshop wrote, called, faxed, and cajoled members of Congress, saying that programs like *Sesame Street* and *All Things Considered* were irreplaceable. Within a few weeks, Gingrich had retreated from his position, saying a complete cessation of funding was not what he had in mind.

In general, agencies assist and are assisted by the clientele groups that depend on the programs they administer.[25] Many agencies were created for the purpose of promoting particular interests in society. For example, the Department of Agriculture's career bureaucrats are dependable allies of

HOW THE UNITED STATES COMPARES

Educational Backgrounds of Bureaucrats

To staff its bureaucracy, the U.S. government tends to hire persons with specialized educations to hold specialized jobs. This approach heightens the tendency of bureaucrats to take the agency point of view. By comparison, Great Britain tends to recruit its bureaucrats from the arts and humanities, on the assumption that general aptitude is the best qualification for detached professionalism. The continental European democracies also emphasize detached professionalism, but in the context of the supposedly impartial application of rules. As a consequence, high-ranking civil servants in Europe tend to have legal educations. The college majors of senior civil servants in the United States and other democracies reflect these tendencies.

College Major of Senior Civil Servants	Norway	Germany	Great Britain	Italy	Belgium	United States
Natural science/ engineering	8%	8%	26%	10%	20%	32%
Social science/ humanities/ business	38	18	52	37	40	50
Law	38	63	3	53	35	18
Other	16	11	19	—	5	—
	100%	100%	100%	100%	100%	100%

Adapted from THE POLITICS OF BUREAUCRACY, 5th ed. By B. Guy Peters. Copyright 2001 by Routledge. Printed by permission.

farm interests year after year. The same cannot be said of the president, Congress as a whole, or either political party; they must balance farmers' demands against those of other interests.

The Power of Friends in High Places Although members of Congress and the president sometimes appear to be at war with the bureaucracy, they need it as much as it needs them. An agency's resources—its programs, expertise, and group support—can assist elected officials in their efforts to

The popular children's program *Sesame Street* is produced through the Corporation for Public Broadcasting, a government agency that gains leverage in budgetary deliberations from its public support. The singer Garth Brooks is shown here with two muppets during his appearance on *Sesame Street*

achieve their goals. When President George W. Bush announced plans in 2001 for a war on terrorism, he needed the help of careerists in the Central Intelligence Agency, the Department of Defense, and the Justice Department to make his efforts successful. At a time when other agencies were feeling the pinch of a tight federal budget, these agencies received substantial new funding.

Bureaucrats also seek favorable relations with members of Congress. Congressional support is vital because agencies' funding and programs are established through legislation. Agencies that offer benefits to major constituency interests are particularly likely to have close ties to Congress. In some policy areas, more or less permanent alliances—iron triangles—form among agencies, clientele groups, and congressional subcommittees. In other policy areas, temporary issue networks form among bureaucrats, lobbyists, and members of Congress. As seen in Chapters 9 and 11, these alliances are a means by which an agency can gain support from legislators and groups that are positioned to support its goals.

BUREAUCRATIC ACCOUNTABILITY

Even though most Americans say that they have a favorable impression of their most recent personal experience with the bureaucracy (as, say, when a senior citizen applies for social security), they have an unfavorable impression

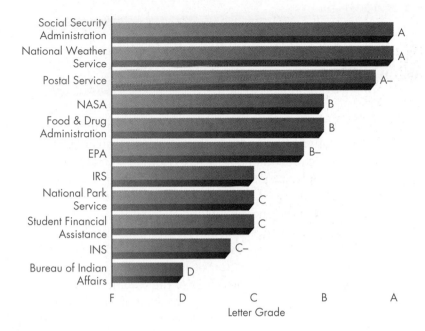

Source: Created from data in Anne Laurent, "Managing for Results," Government Executive, April 2001, pp. 8–12.

FIGURE 13-3   RATING FEDERAL AGENCIES, SELECTED EXAMPLES

The Federal Performance Project evaluates federal agencies and gives them a "report card" based on the quality of their management of finances, human resources, programs, information, and physical assets. The Social Security Administration is one of the top-rated agencies. The Bureau of Indian Affairs is one of the lowest rated agencies.

of the bureaucracy as a whole. This view is somewhat unfair—the effectiveness of the U.S. federal bureaucracy has been found in studies to compare favorably with that of other governmental bureaucracies at home and abroad.[26] (Figure 13-3 shows the relative effectiveness of selected federal agencies.)

Nevertheless, it is easy to understand why Americans believe otherwise. For one thing, the news media more or less ignore the bureaucracy unless it makes a large mistake, fostering the impression that the bureaucracy does more harm than good. In addition, the bureaucracy is the symbol of "big government" and thus a convenient target for political candidates who claim that taxpayers' money is being wasted on unnecessary programs. (The irony is that the bureaucracy has no power to create programs or authorize spending; these decisions are made by elected officials.) When combined with Americans' traditional mistrust of concentrated political power, it is no

LIBERTY, EQUALITY, & SELF-GOVERNMENT

What's Your Opinion?

Bureaucracy and Self-Government

The power of the bureaucracy is both undeniable and difficult to reconcile with the concept of self-government. Bureaucracy entails hierarchy, command, permanence of office, appointment to office, and fixed rules, whereas self-government involves equality, consent, rotation of office, election to office, and open decisions. At base, the conflict between bureaucracy and self-government centers on the degree of power held by unelected officials.

Eliminating the bureaucracy is not an answer to the problem. American society would collapse without the defense establishment, the education and welfare programs, the regulation of business, the transportation systems, and the hundreds of other activities of the federal bureaucracy.

Oversight by Congress, the president, and the judiciary has been America's answer to the problem. Can you think of ways this oversight might be made more effective? Can you also think of ways of reorganizing the bureaucracy that would enhance accountability? For example, do you think the bureaucracy would be more accountable if civil servants rotated from one agency to another every few years, much as military personnel rotate in their assignments? What would be the disadvantages of a personnel system of this kind?

surprise that Americans have qualms about the federal bureaucracy and want it more closely controlled.

Adapting the requirements of the bureaucracy to those of democracy has been a persistent challenge for public administration (see "Liberty, Equality, and Self-Government").[22] The issue is **accountability:** the capacity of the public to hold officials responsible for their actions. In the case of the bureaucracy, accountability works primarily through other institutions: the presidency, Congress, and the courts.

Accountability Through the Presidency

The president can only broadly influence, not directly control, the bureaucracy. "We can outlast any president" is a maxim of bureaucratic politics. Each agency has its clientele and its congressional supporters as well as statutory authority for its existence and activities. No president can unilaterally eliminate an agency or its funding and programs. Nor can the president be indifferent to the opinions of career civil servants—not without losing their support and expertise in developing and implementing presidential policy objectives.

To encourage the bureaucracy to act responsibly, the president can apply management tools that have developed out of the "executive leadership" concept discussed earlier in this chapter. These tools include reorganization, presidential appointees, and the executive budget.

Reorganization The bureaucracy's extreme fragmentation—its hundreds of separate agencies—makes presidential coordination of its activities difficult. Agencies pursue independent, even contradictory paths, resulting in an undetermined amount of waste and duplication of effort. For example, more than one hundred units are responsible for different pieces of education policy.

All recent presidents have tried to streamline the bureaucracy and make it more accountable.[28] Such changes seldom greatly improve things, but they can produce marginal gains.[29] For George W. Bush, the challenge came after the terrorist attacks on the World Trade Center and the Pentagon. Breakdowns in the FBI and CIA had undermined whatever chance there might have been to prevent the attacks. These agencies had not shared or vigorously pursued the intelligence information they had gathered. Bush concluded, and Congress agreed, that a reorganization of the FBI and CIA, as well as the creation of the Department of Homeland Security, was necessary. Nevertheless, neither the White House nor Congress was under the illusion that this reorganization would fully correct the coordination problems plaguing the agencies charged with stopping terrorist attacks on American soil.

Presidential Appointments Although there is almost no direct confrontation with a bureaucrat that a president cannot win, the president does not have time to deal personally with every troublesome careerist or make sure that the bureaucracy has complied with every presidential order. The president relies on political appointees in the agencies to ensure that directives are followed.

The power of presidential appointees is greater in those agencies where wide latitude exists in the making of decisions. Although the Social Security Administration has a huge budget and gives monthly payments to more than forty million Americans, the eligibility of recipients is determined by relatively fixed rules. In contrast, most regulatory agencies have broad discretion over regulatory policy, and a change in leadership can have a substantial impact. For example, President Reagan's appointee to head the Federal Trade Commission, James Miller III, was a strong-willed economist who shared

Reagan's belief that consumer protection policy had gone too far and was adversely affecting business interests. In Miller's first year as head of the FTC, the commission dropped one-fourth of its pending cases against business firms.[30] Overall, enforcement actions declined by about 50 percent during Miller's tenure compared with the previous period.

However, as was noted in Chapter 12, there are limits to what a president can accomplish through appointments. High-level presidential appointees number in the hundreds, and their turnover rate is high: the average appointee remains in the administration for less than two years before moving on to other employment.[31] No president can keep track of all appointees, much less instruct them in detail on all intended policies.

The Executive Budget Faced with the difficulty of controlling the bureaucracy, presidents have come to rely heavily on their personal bureaucracy, the Executive Office of the President (EOP).

In terms of presidential management, the key unit within the EOP is the Office of Management and Budget (OMB). Funding, programs, and regulations are the mainstays of every agency, and the OMB has substantial influence on each of these areas. No agency can issue a major regulation without the OMB's verification that the regulation's benefits outweigh its costs, and no agency can propose legislation to Congress without the OMB's approval. However, the OMB's greatest influence over agencies

The Old Executive Office Building is adjacent to the west wing of the White House. Its occupants are part of the Executive Office of the President (EOP) and serve as contacts between the president and agency bureaucrats.

derives from its budgetary role. At the start of the annual budget cycle, the OMB assigns each agency a budget limit in accord with the president's directives. The agency's tentative allocation requests are sent back to the OMB, which then conducts a final review of all requests before sending the full budget to Congress in the president's name.

In most cases, an agency's overall budget does not change much from year to year. This fact indicates that a significant portion of the bureaucracy's activities persist regardless of who sits in the White House or Congress.[32] It must be noted, however, that the bulk of federal spending is for programs such as social security that, although enacted in the past, have the continuing support of the president, Congress, and the public.

Accountability Through Congress

Congress has powerful means of influencing the bureaucracy. All agencies depend on Congress for their existence, authority, programs, and funding.

The most substantial control that Congress exerts on the bureaucracy is through its power to authorize and fund programs. Without authorization or funding, a program simply does not exist, regardless of the priority an agency claims it deserves. Congress can also void an administrative decision through legislation that prohibits it or mandates an alternative course of action. However, Congress lacks the institutional capacity to work out complex policies down to the last detail.[33] Congress has no option in most cases but to give the bureaucracy leeway in its decisions. The government would grind to a halt if the bureaucracy had to clear all its major policy decisions with Congress.

Congress also exerts some control through its oversight function, which involves monitoring the bureaucracy's work to ensure compliance with legislative intent.[34] As was noted in Chapter 11, however, oversight is a difficult and relatively unrewarding task, and members of Congress ordinarily place less emphasis on oversight than on their other major duties. Only when an agency has clearly stepped out of line is Congress likely to take decisive corrective action by holding hearings to ask tough questions and to warn of legislative punishment.[35]

Because oversight is so difficult and unrewarding, Congress has shifted much of its oversight responsibility to the General Accounting Office (GAO). The GAO's primary function once was to keep track of the funds spent within the bureaucracy; now it also monitors the implementation of policies. The Congressional Budget Office (CBO) also does oversight studies. When the GAO or CBO uncovers a major problem with an agency's handling of a program, it notifies Congress, which can then take remedial action.

Of course, bureaucrats are kept in line by an awareness that misbehavior can trigger a response from Congress. Nevertheless, oversight cannot correct mistakes or abuses that have already occurred. Recognizing this limit on oversight, Congress has devised ways to constrain the bureaucracy *before* it acts. The simplest method is to draft laws that contain very specific provisions that limit bureaucrats' options when they implement policy. Another restrictive device is the sunset law, which establishes a specific date when a law will expire unless it is reenacted by Congress. Advocates of sunset laws see them as a means to counter the bureaucracy's reluctance to give up programs that have outlived their usefulness. Because members of Congress usually want their policies to last far into the future, however, most legislation does not include a sunset provision.

Accountability Through the Courts

The judiciary's influence on agencies is less direct than that of the elected branches, but the courts too can and do act to ensure the bureaucracy's compliance with Congress's requirements. Legally, the bureaucracy derives its authority from acts of Congress, and an injured party can bring suit against an agency on the grounds that it has failed to carry out the law properly. Judges can then order an agency to change its application of the law.[36]

However, the courts have tended to support administrators if their actions seem at all consistent with the laws they are administering. The Supreme Court has held that agencies can choose rule-making procedures that meet the minimal threshold set down by Congress, that agencies can apply any reasonable interpretation of statutes unless Congress has specifically stated something to the contrary, and that agencies in many instances have wide discretion in deciding whether to enforce statutes.[37] These positions reflect the need for flexibility in administration. The bureaucracy and the courts would both grind to a halt if judges routinely chose to substitute their interpretations of the law for those of administrators. The judiciary cannot conduct a decision-by-decision oversight of the bureaucracy. Judges recognize that constraints on the bureaucracy must work mainly through the Congress and the president. The judiciary has promoted bureaucratic accountability primarily by encouraging administrators to act responsibly in their dealings with the public and by protecting individuals and groups from the bureaucracy's worst abuses.

Accountability Within the Bureaucracy Itself

A recognition of the difficulty of ensuring adequate accountability of the bureaucracy through the presidency, Congress, and the courts has led to the development of mechanisms of accountability within the bureaucracy itself. Two measures, whistle-blowing and demographic representativeness, are particularly noteworthy.

The U.S. Coast Guard is the federal agency with the mission of safeguarding the nation's ports, waterways, and coastlines. Lifesaving is one of the Coast Guard's missions. About 4,000 mariners a year are estimated to owe their lives to Coast Guard assistance.

Whistle-Blowing Although the bureaucratic corruption that is rampant in some countries is relatively uncommon in the United States, a certain amount of waste, fraud, and abuse is inevitable in a bureaucracy as big as that of the federal government. **Whistle-blowing,** the act of reporting instances of corruption or mismanagement by one's fellow bureaucrats, is a potentially effective internal check.[38] A case in point is Colleen Rowley, a Minneapolis-based FBI agent, who accused top FBI officials of blocking an investigation that might have prevented the September 11, 2001, terrorist attacks. Agents in Minneapolis had wanted to investigate Zacarias Moussaoui, who was being held in Minnesota on immigration charges. Moussaoui had been enrolled in flight school, and the agents suspected he might be part of a terrorist plot. Rowley's revelation that FBI headquarters had blocked the investigation led to Senate hearings in which Rowley was the star witness.[39]

However, whistle-blowing has not been a highly successful policy. Many federal employees will not report instances of mismanagement because they fear reprisals from their superiors. When FBI agent Rowley traveled to Washington for her Senate testimony, the FBI failed to provide her with an escort or a vehicle, despite the hoard of news reporters with which she had to contend. To encourage whistle-blowers to come forward with their information, Congress enacted the Whistle Blower Protection Act to protect them from retaliation. Federal law also provides whistle-blowers with financial rewards in some cases.

Demographic Representativeness Although the bureaucracy is an unrepresentative institution in the sense that its officials are not elected by the people, it can be representative in the demographic sense. If bureaucrats were a demographic microcosm of the general public, they presumably would treat the various groups and interests in society more fairly.[40]

At present, the bureaucracy is not demographically representative at its top levels (see Table 13-3). Roughly 60 percent of managerial and professional positions are held by white males. However, the employment status of women and, to a lesser extent, minorities has improved somewhat in recent years, and top officials in the bureaucracy include a greater proportion of women and minorities than is found in Congress or the judiciary. Moreover, if all levels of the federal bureaucracy are considered, it comes reasonably close to being representative of the nation's population.[41]

Demographic representativeness is only a partial answer to the problem of bureaucratic accountability. A fully representative civil service would still be required to play agency politics. The careerists in, say, defense agencies and welfare agencies are not very different in their demographic backgrounds, but they differ markedly in their opinions about policy. Each group believes that the goals of its agency should take priority. The inevitability of agency politics is the most significant of all political facts about the U.S. federal bureaucracy.[42]

REINVENTING GOVERNMENT

There have been numerous attempts during the twentieth century to enhance the bureaucracy's efficiency, responsiveness, and accountability.

| TABLE | 13-3 | FEDERAL JOB RANKINGS (GS) OF VARIOUS DEMOGRAPHIC GROUPS |

Women and minority group members are underrepresented in the top jobs of the federal bureaucracy but their representation has been increasing.

Grade Level*	Women's Share 1976	Women's Share 2000	Blacks' Share 1982	Blacks' Share 2000	Hispanics' Share 1982	Hispanics' Share 2000
GS 1–4 (lowest ranks)	78%	68%	23%	27%	5%	9%
GS 5–8	60	68	19	25	4	8
GS 9–12	20	45	10	15	4	7
GS 13–15 (highest ranks)	5	31	5	10	2	4

*In general, the higher-numbered grades are managerial and professional positions, and the lower-numbered grades are clerical and manual labor positions.

Source: Office of Workforce Information, 2002.

Another wave of this reform effort began in the 1990s, and it seeks to improve the administration of government by the reduction of its size, cost, and lines of authority.

In *Reinventing Government*, David Osborne and Ted Gaebler argue that the bureaucracy of today was created in response to earlier problems, particularly those spawned by the Industrial Revolution and a rampant spoils system. They claim that the information age requires a different kind of administrative structure, one that is more flexible and less hierarchical. Instead of the provision of goods and services, the bureaucracy ought to be in the business of creating incentives that will encourage individuals to make their own way and ought to foster competition among and between agencies and private firms. This approach requires a more decentralized form of administration that is oriented toward consumers and results. Osborne and Gaebler would empower lower-level employees to make decisions that previously were made at the top of the bureaucracy.[43]

This concept informed the Clinton administration's National Performance Review and is now embedded in some laws and administrative practices. An example is a law that requires agencies to monitor their performance by standards such as efficiency, responsiveness, and outcomes. These standards have long been considered gauges of administrative effectiveness but have often been overlooked as bureaucrats went about their customary ways of doing business. The law seeks to overcome this inertia by *requiring* agencies to actively monitor their performance.

Some analysts question the logic and presumed consequences of the new philosophy of administration. They have asked, for example, whether the principles of decentralized management and market-oriented programs are as sound as their advocates claim. The delegation of control to lower-level administrators weakens the hierarchical connection between elected and administrative officials. A reason for hierarchy is to ensure that decisions made at the bottom of the bureaucracy are faithful to the laws made by Congress. Free to act on their own, lower-level administrators, as they did under the spoils system, might favor certain people and interests over others.[44] There is also the issue of the identity of the "customers" in a market-oriented administration.[45] Who are the Security and Exchange Commission's customers—firms, brokerage houses, or shareholders? Will not some agencies inevitably favor their more powerful customers at the expense of the less powerful ones?

Furthermore, there are practical limits on how much the federal bureaucracy can be trimmed. Some activities can be delegated to states and localities, and others can be privatized, but most of Washington's programs cannot be reassigned. National defense, social security, and Medicare are but three examples, and they alone account for more than half of all federal spending. National problems require national solutions, which is why national crises inevitably bring about an expansion of federal activity and authority. The war on terrorism that began in 2001, for example, has resulted in large increases in federal spending on military defense, intelligence gathering, law enforcement, and homeland security. Nor does the delegation of programs necessarily result in better performance. When the space shuttle Columbia exploded upon reentry in 2003, some analysts suggested that the tragedy was rooted in NASA's decision to assign many of the shuttle program's safety checks to private contractors in order to cut costs.

Thus, although the current wave of administrative reform is unique in its specific elements, it involves long-standing issues about the bureaucracy and about America's national needs.

How can the federal government be made more efficient and yet accomplish all that Americans expect of it? How can it be made more responsive and yet act fairly? How can it be made more creative and yet be held accountable? There are, as history makes clear, no easy or final answers to these questions.

SUMMARY

Bureaucracy is a method of organizing people and work. It is based on the principles of hierarchical authority, job specialization, and formalized rules. As a form of organization, bureaucracy is the most efficient means of getting people to work together on tasks of great magnitude and complexity. It is also a form of organization that is prone to waste and rigidity, which is why efforts are being made to "reinvent" it.

The United States could not be governed without a large federal bureaucracy. The day-to-day work of the federal government, from mail delivery to provision of social security to international diplomacy, is done by the bureaucracy. Federal employees work in roughly four hundred major agencies, including cabinet departments, independent agencies, regulatory agencies, government corporations, and presidential commissions. Yet the bureaucracy is more than simply an administrative giant. Administrators exercise considerable discretion in their policy decisions. In the process of implementing policy, they make important policy and political choices.

Each agency of the federal government was created in response to political demands on national officials. Because of its origins in political demands, the administration of government is necessarily political. An inherent conflict results from two simultaneous but incompatible demands on the bureaucracy: that it respond to the preferences of partisan officials but also that it administer programs fairly and competently. These tensions are evident in the three concurrent personnel management systems under which the bureaucracy operates: patronage, merit, and executive leadership.

Administrators are actively engaged in politics and policymaking. The fragmentation of power and the pluralism of the American political system result in a policy process that is continually subject to conflict and contention. There is no clear policy or leadership mandate in the American system, and hence government agencies must compete for the power required to administer their programs effectively. Accordingly, civil servants tend to have an agency point of view: they seek to advance their agency's programs and to repel attempts by others to weaken their position. In promoting their agency, civil servants rely on their policy expertise, the backing of their clientele groups, and support from the president and Congress.

Administrators are not elected by the people they serve, yet they wield substantial independent power. Because of this, the bureaucracy's accountability is a central issue. The major checks on the bureaucracy are provided by the president, Congress, and the courts. The president has some power to reorganize the bureaucracy and the authority to appoint the political head of each agency. The president also has management tools (such as the executive budget) that can be used to limit administrators' discretion. Congress has influence on bureaucratic agencies through its authorization and funding powers and through various devices (including sunset laws and oversight hearings) that hold administrators accountable for their actions. The judiciary's role in ensuring the bureaucracy's accountability is smaller than that of the elected branches, but the courts do have the authority to force agencies to act in accordance with legislative intent, established procedures, and constitutionally guaranteed rights. Nevertheless, administrators are not fully accountable. They exercise substantial independent power, a situation that is not easily reconciled with democratic values.

The National Performance Review is among recent efforts to scale down the federal bureaucracy. The reduction has included cuts in budgets, staff, and organizational units and also has involved changes in the way the bureaucracy does its work. This process is a response to political forces and also to new management theories.

KEY TERMS

accountability	demographic representativeness
agency point of view	executive leadership system
bureaucracy	formalized rules
cabinet (executive) departments	government corporations
clientele groups	hierarchical authority

independent agencies   policy implementation
job specialization   presidential commissions
merit (civil service) system   regulatory agencies
neutral competence   spoils system
patronage system   whistle-blowing

SUGGESTED READINGS

Aberbach, Joel D., and Bert A. Rockman. *In the Web of Politics: Two Decades of the U.S. Federal Executive.* Washington, D.C.: Brookings Institution, 2000. An evaluation of the federal bureaucracy and its evolving nature.

Brehm, John, and Scott Gates. *Working, Shirking, and Sabotage: Bureaucratic Response to a Democratic Public.* Ann Arbor: University of Michigan Press, 1996. A generally favorable assessment of the bureaucracy's responsiveness to the public it serves.

Cook, Brian J. *Bureaucracy and Self-Government: Reconsidering the Role of Public Administration in American Politics.* Baltimore, Md.: Johns Hopkins University Press, 1996. A thorough history of public administration in American politics.

Kettl, Donald F., Patricia W. Ingraham, Ronald P. Sanders, and Constance Horner. *Civil Service Reform: Building a Government That Works.* Washington, D.C.: Brookings Institution Press, 1996. A careful analysis of government management.

Osborne, David, and Ted Gaebler. *Reinventing Government: How the Entrepreneurial Spirit Is Transforming the Public Sector.* New York: Addison-Wesley, 1992. The book that Washington policymakers in the 1990s regarded as the guide to transforming the bureaucracy.

Sagini, Meshack M. *Organizational Behavior: The Challenges of the New Millennium.* Lanham, Md.: University Press of America, 2001. A comprehensive assessment of bureaucratic structures and behaviors.

Wood, B. Dan, and Richard W. Waterman. *Bureaucratic Dynamics: The Role of Bureaucracy in a Democracy.* Boulder, Colo.: Westview Press, 1994. A penetrating analysis of bureaucratic agencies and their power relationships with the president, Congress, and constituent groups.

LIST OF WEBSITES

http://iccweb.com/federal A site for those interested in finding employment with the federal government. The site provides job applications and other information for the various federal agencies.

http://www.census.gov Website of the Census Bureau; the bureau is the best source of statistical information on Americans and the government agencies that administer programs affecting them.

http://www.whistleblower.org The Government Accountability Project's website; this project is designed to protect and encourage whistle-blowers by providing information and support to federal employees.

http://www.whitehouse.gov/WH/Cabinet Lists the cabinet secretaries and provides links to each cabinet-level department.

POLITICS IN THEORY AND PRACTICE

Thinking: What are the major sources of bureaucrats' power? What mechanisms for controlling that power are available to the president and Congress?

Acting: If you are considering a student internship, you might want to look into working for a federal, state, or local agency. Compared with legislative interns, executive interns are more likely to get paid and to be given significant duties. (Many legislative interns spend the bulk of their time answering phones or responding to mail.) Internship information can often be obtained through an agency's website. You should apply as early as possible; some agencies have application deadlines.

The New York Times   **reading 13**

Signing Homeland Security Bill, Bush Appoints Ridge as Secretary

by Richard W. Stevenson

Each agency of the federal government has been created in response to political demands on national officials. And the creation of each new agency has been accompanied by questions of its likely effectiveness. In this November 26, 2002, article, New York Times *reporter Richard Stevenson describes the creation of the newest cabinet-level agency–the Department of Homeland Security–and the challenges awaiting it.*

WASHINGTON—President Bush signed legislation today creating a Department of Homeland Security and named Tom Ridge, the former Pennsylvania governor who has been the White House's domestic security coordinator, to run it.

Mr. Bush's signature on the bill, which won final Congressional approval last week after a bitter political fight, set in motion a vast bureaucratic reorganization that the president said would "focus the full resources of the American government on the safety of the American people." By nightfall, 60 days before he was required by law to do so, Mr. Bush had sent to Congress his detailed plan for bringing the department into being. The plan called for getting the department largely up and running by March 1, with the process to be completed, at least in organizational terms, by Sept. 30.

In announcing that he would nominate Mr. Ridge as the first secretary of homeland security, Mr. Bush was entrusting him not just to oversee what is sure to be a difficult merger of disparate government agencies but also to elevate defense of Americans at home to a new level in the face of what officials say are ever-evolving terrorist threats.

"He has a monumental task in front of him," said Senator Joseph I. Lieberman, the Connecticut Democrat who was one of the original proponents of creating the cabinet-level department. "It's like asking Noah to build the ark after the rain has started to fall."

Mr. Bush also began filling other top posts in the department. He nominated Gordon R. England, a former military contracting executive who is the Navy secretary, to be Mr. Ridge's deputy, and Asa Hutchinson, a former Republican congressman from Arkansas who is the administrator of the Drug Enforcement Administration, as undersecretary for border and transportation security.

The birth of the department flowed from a bipartisan consensus after last year's terrorist attacks that the nation needed to do more to protect its citizens at home. It will require the largest reshuffling of governmental responsibilities since the founding of the Defense Department after World War II, a process sure to encompass turf battles and culture clashes even as the country parries a steady stream of terrorist threats and girds for possible war with Iraq.

It will bring together nearly 170,000 workers from 22 agencies with widely varying histories and missions, like the Coast Guard, the Secret Service, the federal security guards in airports and the Customs Service. The goal is to improve security along and within the nation's borders, strengthen the ability of federal, state and local authorities to respond to an attack, better focus research into nuclear, chemical and biological threats and more rigorously assess intelligence about terrorists.

"The continuing threat of terrorism, the threat of mass murder on our own soil, will be met with a unified, effective response," said Mr. Bush, who had at first resisted calls for creation of the new cabinet-level department and embraced them only after political pressure mounted last spring.

"Dozens of agencies charged with homeland security will now be located within one cabinet department with the mandate and legal authority to protect our people," he said as he prepared to sign the bill in the East Room before an audience of cabinet members, Republicans and Democrats from Capitol Hill and law enforcement officials from around the country. "America will be better able to respond to any future attacks, to reduce our vulnerability and, most important, prevent the terrorists from taking innocent American lives."

But Mr. Bush also injected a note of caution, saying, "No department of government can completely guarantee our safety against ruthless killers, who move and plot in shadows."

Led by Clay Johnson, the White House personnel director, a transition team has been working since summer to allow the administration to move quickly to deal with details like establishing systems for better evaluating intelligence reports.

To help oversee the integration into the new department of one of its most troubled components, the Immigration and Naturalization Service, Mr. Bush today named Michael Garcia, an assistant commerce secretary and former federal prosecutor, as acting immigration commissioner. The service has come under widespread criticism for failing to keep track of immigrants, most recently in a report last week by the General Accounting Office that said immigration authorities had been unable to find nearly half of more than 4,000 registered immigrants the government wanted to interview after the Sept. 11 terrorist attacks.

With many agencies struggling to deal with deeply entrenched problems, experts said improvements to domestic security would not take place with the stroke of Mr. Bush's pen today or even the submission of the reorganization plan. They said it could be years before the department could be expected to operate at full effectiveness.

"The first challenge is to lower expectations," said Paul C. Light, who studies government organization at the Brookings Institution, a liberal-leaning research organization. "People should think they will be safer, but remember we have a long way to go."

Some Democrats also suggested that there were risks that the reorganization could be a distraction to some of the agencies most directly involved in domestic security, especially since government employee unions are already concerned that Mr. Bush wants to scale back Civil Service protections for workers in the new department.

Moreover, some Democrats said, the administration is not providing the department with the money it will need to do its job effectively.

"We didn't reorganize the Pentagon in the middle of World War II," said Representative David R. Obey of Wisconsin, the senior Democrat on the House Appropriations Committee. He said the administration was "shortchanging" the department in areas like safeguarding nuclear materials and assisting state and local governments with the financial burden of the roles they must take on.

The bill came to Mr. Bush's desk only after generating deep partisan differences through much of the year. The idea of a cabinet-level department was first pushed more than a year ago by Mr. Lieberman and other Democrats on the Senate Governmental Affairs Committee. Mr. Bush said at the time that the job could be better done, at least initially, by an office within the White House rather than by creating a new bureaucracy.

Mr. Bush endorsed the idea in June, after pressure grew in both parties to address weaknesses in the government's performance in battling terrorism. But the two parties in Congress then became enmeshed in an argument over whether to grant the president broad powers to hire and fire federal workers and move them among jobs.

Republicans said Democrats were obstructing the bill at the bidding of union leaders representing government employees, an assertion that Republicans used to attack two incumbent Democratic senators in the election this fall, Max Cleland of Georgia and Jean Carnahan of Missouri. Both lost, and Democrats largely gave in to Mr. Bush's demands after the election, leaving them with some bitterness about what they viewed as politicization of the issue by Mr. Bush and his party.

What's Your Opinion?

What are the possible advantages of entrusting homeland security to a cabinet-level agency rather than to an office within the White House? What are the possible disadvantages?

THE FEDERAL JUDICIAL SYSTEM: APPLYING THE LAW

❝It is emphatically the province and duty of the judicial department to say what the law is. Those who apply the rule to particular cases, must of necessity expound and interpret that rule. If two laws conflict with each other, the courts must decide on the operation of each.❞

JOHN MARSHALL[1]

Through its ruling in *Bush v. Gore*, the U.S. Supreme Court effectively ended the 2000 presidential election.[2] At issue was whether the "under-votes" in Florida—ballots on which counting machines had detected no vote for president—would be tabulated by hand. Florida's top court had ordered a statewide manual recount, but the U.S. Supreme Court by a narrow 5-4 margin had issued a rare emergency order halting the action. Three days later, the Supreme Court's majority delivered its ruling, saying that the manual recount violated the constitution's equal protection clause. Florida's high court had said that officials should base the hand count on the "intent of the voter." The Supreme Court held that this standard gave county officials in Florida too much leeway and violated the right of citizens to have their votes counted fairly and equally.

The ruling brought charges that the Supreme Court had acted politically rather than on any strict interpretation of the law. In issuing a halt to the recount, the Court had divided sharply along ideological lines. The majority consisted of its most conservative members, all of whom were Republican appointees: Chief Justice William Rehnquist and associate justices Sandra Day O'Connor, Anthony Kennedy, Antonin Scalia, and Clarence Thomas. In a dissenting opinion, Justice John Paul Stevens said: "Preventing the re-count from being completed will inevitably cast a doubt upon the legitimacy of the election." Stevens argued that the Florida high court's de-cision had properly reflected "the basic principle, inherent in our Constitu-tion and our democracy, that every legal vote should be counted."

Bush v. Gore illustrates three key points about court decisions. First, the judiciary is an extremely important policymaking body. Some of its rulings are as consequential as a law passed by Congress or an executive action taken by the president. Second, the judiciary has considerable discretion in its rulings. The *Bush v. Gore* ruling was not based on any literal reading of the law: the justices invoked *their* individual interpretations. Third, the ju-diciary is a political as well as legal institution. The *Bush v. Gore* case was a product of contending political forces, was developed through a political process, had political content, and was decided by political appointees.

This chapt r describes the federal judiciary and the work of its judges and justices. J ike the executive and legislative branches, the judiciary is an independent ɹranch of the U.S. government, but unlike the two other branches, its top officials are not elected by the people. The judiciary is not

Demonstrators rally outside the U.S. Supreme Court building during hearings on the *Bush v. Gore* case that effectively brought the 2000 presidential election to an end. At times, the policy rulings of the judiciary are as significant as the decisions of the president or Congress.

a democratic institution, and its role is different from and, in some areas, more controversial than those of the executive and legislative branches. This chapter explores this issue in the process of discussing several main points:

★ *The federal judiciary includes the Supreme Court of the United States, which functions mainly as an appellate court; courts of appeals, which hear appeals; and district courts, which hold trials.* Each state has a court system of its own, which for the most part is independent of supervision by the federal courts.

★ *Judicial decisions are constrained by applicable constitutional law, statutory and administrative law, and precedent.* Nevertheless, political factors have a major influence on judicial appointments and decisions; judges are political officials as well as legal ones.

★ *The judiciary has become an increasingly powerful policymaking body in recent decades, which has raised the question of the judiciary's proper role in a democracy.* The philosophies of judicial restraint and judicial activism provide different answers to this question.

The Federal Judicial System

The writers of the Constitution were determined that the judiciary would be a separate and independent branch of the federal government but, for practical reasons, did not fully define the structure of the federal court system. The Framers established the Supreme Court of the United States but granted to Congress the power to decide the structure of the lower federal courts.

Federal judges are nominated by the president, and if confirmed by the U.S. Senate, they are appointed by the president to the office. The Constitution states that judges "shall hold their offices during good behavior." However, the Constitution does not contain a precise definition of "good behavior," and no Supreme Court justice and only a very small number of lower-court judges have been removed from office through impeachment and conviction by Congress. In practice, federal judges and justices serve until they retire or die.

Unlike the offices of president, senator, and representative, the Constitution places no age, residency, or citizenship qualifications on federal judicial office. Nor does the Constitution require a judge to have legal training. Tradition alone dictates that federal judges have an educational or professional background in the law.

The Supreme Court of the United States

The Supreme Court of the United States is the nation's highest court. The chief justice of the United States presides over the Supreme Court and, like the eight associate justices, is selected by the president and is subject to Senate confirmation. The chief justice has the same voting power as the other justices but has usually exercised additional influence because of the position's leadership role.

The Constitution grants the Supreme Court both original and appellate jurisdiction. A court's **jurisdiction** is its authority to hear cases of a particular type. **Original jurisdiction** is the authority to be the first court to hear a case. The Supreme Court's original jurisdiction embraces legal disputes involving foreign diplomats and those in which the opposing parties are state governments. The Court in its entire history has convened as a court of original jurisdiction only a few hundred times and has rarely done so in recent years.

The Supreme Court does its most significant work as an appellate court. **Appellate jurisdiction** is the authority to review cases that have already been heard in lower courts and are appealed to the higher court by the losing party; such courts are called appeals courts or appellate courts. The Supreme Court's appellate jurisdiction extends to cases arising under the Constitution, federal law and regulations, and treaties. The Court also hears appeals involving admiralty or maritime issues and legal controversies that cross state or national boundaries. Appellate courts, including the Supreme Court, do not retry cases; rather, they determine whether a trial court acted in accord with applicable law.

Selecting and Deciding Cases
The primary function of the judiciary is to interpret the law in such a way that rules made in the past (for example, the Constitution or legislation) can be applied reasonably in the present. This function gives the courts—all courts—a role in policymaking. Antitrust legislation, for example, is designed to prevent uncompetitive business practices, but like all such legislation, it is not self-enforcing. It is up to the courts to decide whether and how these laws apply to the case at hand.

As the nation's highest court, the Supreme Court is particularly important in establishing legal precedents that guide lower courts. A *precedent* is a judicial decision that serves as a rule for settling subsequent cases of a similar nature. Lower courts are expected to follow precedent—that is, to resolve cases of a like nature in ways consistent with upper-court rulings. However, for reasons that will be explained later in this chapter, they do not always do so.

The Supreme Court's ability to set legal precedent is strengthened by its nearly complete discretion in choosing the cases it will hear. The large majority of cases that reach the Supreme Court do so through a **writ of certiorari** in which the losing party in a lower-court case explains in writing why its case should be ruled on by the Court. Four of the nine justices must agree to accept a particular case before it is granted a writ. Each year roughly seven thousand parties apply for certiorari, but the Court accepts only about a hundred cases for a full hearing and signed ruling. The Court issues another one hundred to two hundred per curiam (unsigned) decisions, which are made summarily without a hearing and simply state the facts of the case and the Court's decision. The Court is most likely to grant certiorari when the U.S. government through the solicitor general (the high-ranking Justice Department official who serves as the government's lawyer in Supreme Court cases) requests it.[3]

The Court seldom accepts a routine case, even if the justices believe that a lower court has erred. The Supreme Court's job is not to correct every mistake of other courts, but to resolve broad legal questions. As a result, the justices usually choose cases that involve substantial legal issues. This criterion is vague but essentially means that a case must center on an issue of significance not merely to the parties involved but to the nation. As a result, most of the cases heard by the Court raise major constitutional issues, or affect the lives of many Americans, or address issues that are being decided inconsistently by the lower courts, or are in conflict with a previous Supreme Court ruling.[4] When the Court does accept a case, chances are that most of the justices disagree with the lower court's ruling. In recent years about three-fourths of the Supreme Court's decisions have reversed the judgments of lower courts.[5]

Once the Supreme Court accepts a case, it sets a date on which the attorneys for the two sides will present their oral arguments. Strict time limits, usually thirty minutes per side, are placed on these arguments, because each side has already submitted written arguments to the justices.

The open hearing is far less important than the **judicial conference** that follows, which is attended only by the nine justices. The conference's proceedings are kept strictly confidential. This secrecy allows the justices to speak freely about a case and to change their minds as the discussion unfolds.[6] After the discussion, the justices vote on the case; the least senior justice usually votes first and the chief justice votes last.

Issuing Decisions and Opinions After a case has been decided on in conference, the Court prepares and issues its ruling, which consists of a decision and one or more opinions. The **decision** indicates which party the Court supports and by how large a margin. The **opinion** explains the reasons behind the decision. The opinion is the most important part of a Supreme

Court ruling because it informs others of the justices' interpretations of laws. For example, in the landmark *Brown v. Board of Education of Topeka* (1954) opinion, the Court held that government-sponsored school segregation was unconstitutional because it violated the Fourteenth Amendment provision that guarantees equal protection under the laws to all citizens. This opinion became the legal basis by which communities throughout the southern states were ordered by lower courts to end their policy of segregating students in their public schools by race.[7]

/pattersonwtp5

When a majority of the justices agree on the legal basis of a decision, the result is a **majority opinion.** In some cases there is no majority opinion because a majority of the justices agree on the decision but cannot agree on the legal basis for it. The result is a **plurality opinion,** which presents the view held by most of the justices who side with the winning party. Another type of opinion is a **concurring opinion,** which is a separate view written by a justice who votes with the majority but disagrees with its reasoning.

Justices on the losing side can write a **dissenting opinion** to explain their reasons for disagreeing with the majority position. Sometimes these dissenting views become a later Court's majority position. In a 1942 dissenting opinion, Justice Hugo Black wrote that defendants in state felony trials should

Types of Supreme Court Opinions

Per curiam: Unsigned decision of the Court that states the facts of the case and the Court's ruling.

Majority opinion: A written opinion of the majority of the Court's justices stating the reasoning underlying their decision on a case.

Plurality opinion: A written opinion that in the absence of a majority opinion presents the reasoning of most of the justices who side with the winning party.

Concurring opinion: A written opinion of one or more justices who support the majority position but disagree with the majority's reasoning on a case. This opinion expresses the reasoning of the concurring justices.

Dissenting opinion: A written opinion of one or more justices who disagree with the majority's decision and opinion. This opinion provides the reasoning underlying the dissent.

have legal counsel, even if they could not afford to pay for it. Two decades later, in *Gideon v. Wainwright* (1963), the Court adopted this position.[8]

When part of the majority, the chief justice decides which of the justices will write the majority opinion. Otherwise, the senior justice in the majority determines the author. Chief justices have often given themselves the influential task of writing the majority opinion in important cases. John Marshall did so often: *Marbury v. Madison* (1802) and *McCulloch v. Maryland* (1819) were among the opinions he wrote. The justice who writes the Court's majority opinion has the responsibility to express accurately the majority's reasoning. The vote on a case is not considered final until the decision is made public, so plenty of give-and-take can occur during the writing stage.

Other Federal Courts

There are more than one hundred federal courts but there is only one Supreme Court, and its position at the top of the country's judicial system gives the Supreme Court unparalleled importance. It is a mistake, however, to conclude that the Supreme Court is the only court of consequence. Judge Jerome Frank once wrote of the "upper-court myth," which is the view that appellate courts and in particular the Supreme Court make up the only truly significant judicial arena and that lower courts just dutifully follow the rulings handed down by the appellate level.[9] The reality is very different, as the following discussion will explain.

U.S. District Courts The lowest federal courts are the district courts (see Figure 14-1). There are more than ninety federal district courts altogether—at least one in every state and as many as four in some states. District court judges, who number about eight hundred in all, are appointed by the president with the consent of the Senate. Federal cases usually originate in district courts, which are trial courts where the parties argue their sides. District courts are the only courts in the federal system in which juries hear testimony. Most cases at this level are presented before a single judge.

Lower federal courts unquestionably rely on and follow Supreme Court decisions in their own rulings. The Supreme Court reiterated this requirement in a 1982 case, *Hutto v. Davis:* "Unless we wish anarchy to prevail within the federal judicial system, a precedent of this Court must be followed by the lower federal courts no matter how misguided the judges of those courts may think it to be."[10]

However, the idea that lower courts are guided strictly by Supreme Court rulings is part of the upper-court myth. District court judges may misunderstand the Supreme Court's position and deviate from it for that

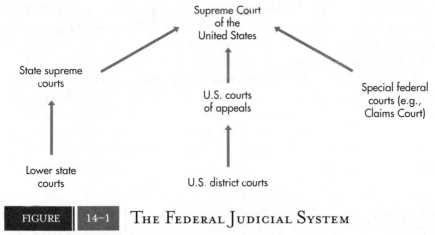

FIGURE | 14-1 THE FEDERAL JUDICIAL SYSTEM

This simplified diagram shows the relationships among the various levels of federal courts and between state and federal courts. The losing party in a case can appeal a lower-court decision to the court at the next-highest level, as the arrows indicate. Decisions can be removed from state courts to federal courts only if they raise a constitutional question.

reason. In addition, the facts of a case before a district court are seldom identical to those of a case settled by the Supreme Court. The lower-court judge must decide whether a different legal principle should be invoked. Finally, it is not unusual for the Supreme Court to issue a general ruling that is ambiguous enough to give lower courts some flexibility in deciding similar cases that come before them. Trial court judges then have a creative role in judicial decision making that rivals that of appellate court judges.

Most federal cases end with the district court's decision; the losing party does not appeal the decision to a higher court. This fact is another indication of the highly significant role of district court judges.

U.S. Courts of Appeals When cases are appealed from district courts, they go to a federal court of appeals. These appellate courts make up the second level of the federal court system. Courts of appeals do not use juries. No new evidence is submitted in an appealed case; appellate courts base their decisions on a review of lower-court records. Appellate judges act as supervisors in the legal system, reviewing trial court decisions and correcting what they consider to be legal errors. Facts (i.e., the circumstances of a case) found by district courts are presumed to be correct.

The United States has twelve general appeals courts, each of which serves a "circuit" that is comprised of between three and nine states, except the one that serves the District of Columbia only. There is also the U.S. Court of Appeals for the Federal Circuit, which specializes in appeals of cases involving patents and international trade. Between four and twenty-six judges sit on each court of appeals, but each case is usually heard by a panel of three judges. On rare occasions, all the judges of a court of appeals sit as a body (*en banc*) in order to resolve difficult controversies, typically ones that have resulted in conflicting decisions within the same circuit.

Courts of appeals offer the only real hope of reversal for many appellants, since the Supreme Court hears so few cases. The Supreme Court reviews less than 1 percent of the cases heard by federal appeals courts.

Special U.S. Courts In addition to the Supreme Court, the courts of appeals, and the district courts, the federal judiciary includes a few specialty courts. Among them are the U.S. Claims Court, which hears cases in which the U.S. government is being sued for damages; the U.S. Court of International Trade, which handles cases involving appeals of U.S. Customs Office rulings; and the U.S. Court of Military Appeals, which hears appeals of military courts-martial. Some federal agencies and commissions also have adjudicative powers, and their decisions can be appealed to a federal court of appeals.

The State Courts

The American states are separate governments within the United State's federal system. The Tenth Amendment protects each state in its sovereignty, and each state has its own court system. Like the federal courts, state court systems have trial courts at the bottom level and appellate courts at the top.

Each state decides for itself the structure of its courts and the method of judicial appointment. In some states, judges are appointed by the governor, but judgeships are *elective offices* in most states. The common form involves competitive elections of either a partisan or nonpartisan nature, although some states use a system called the *merit plan* (also called the "Missouri Plan" because Missouri was the first state to use it) under which the governor selects a judge from a short list of acceptable candidates provided by a judicial selection commission. To stay on the bench, the judge selected must periodically receive the voters' support in a "yes" or "no" election (see "States in the Nation").

Besides the upper-court myth, there exists a "federal court myth," which holds that the federal judiciary is the most significant part of the judicial system and that state courts play a subordinate role. This view is inaccurate as

★ STATES IN THE NATION

Principal Methods of Selecting State Judges

The states use a variety of methods for selecting the judges on their highest court, including the merit plan, election, and political appointment. The states that appoint judges grant this power to the governor, except in Virginia, Connecticut, and South Carolina, where the legislature makes the choice.

Q. What might explain why a bloc of states in the middle of the nation use the merit plan for selecting judges?

A. The merit plan originated in the state of Missouri. Innovations in one state sometimes spread to adjacent states that have similar political cultures.

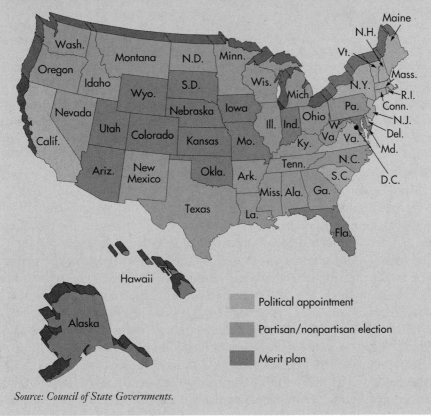

Political appointment

Partisan/nonpartisan election

Merit plan

Source: Council of State Governments.

The Florida Supreme Court hears the arguments that led it to order a statewide canvas of uncounted ballots in the Bush-Gore presidential contest. Less than a day after it was rendered, the court's order was blocked by the U.S. Supreme Court. It was a rare intervention. Upwards of 95 percent of the nation's legal cases are decided entirely within the state court system, an indication of the "federal-court myth."

well. More than 95 percent of the nation's legal cases are decided in state courts. Most crimes (from shoplifting to murder) and most civil controversies (such as divorces and corporate disputes) are defined by state or local law. Moreover, nearly all cases that originate in state courts also end there. The federal courts never come into the picture because the case does not involve a federal issue.

In state criminal cases, after a person has been convicted and after all avenues of appeal in the state court system have been exhausted, the defendant can seek a writ of habeas corpus from a federal district court (see Chapter 4). The federal court often confines itself to the federal aspects of the matter, such as whether the defendant in a criminal case received the protections guaranteed by the U.S. Constitution. In addition, the federal court must accept the facts determined by the state court unless such findings are clearly in error. In short, legal and factual determinations of state courts can bind the federal courts—a clear contradiction of the federal court myth.

However, cases traditionally within the jurisdiction of the states can become federal cases through rulings of federal courts. In *Roe v. Wade* (1973), for example, the Supreme Court concluded that women had the right under the Constitution to choose an abortion, thus making abortion rights, which had been a state issue, also a federal one.[11]

FEDERAL COURT APPOINTEES

The quiet dignity of the courtroom and the lack of fanfare with which a court delivers its decisions give the impression that the judiciary is as far removed from the world of politics as a governmental institution can possibly be. The reality is different. Federal judges and justices are political officials who exercise the authority of a separate and powerful branch of government. All federal jurists bring their political views with them to the courtroom and have regular opportunities to promote their political beliefs through the cases they decide. Accordingly, the process by which federal judges are appointed is a partisan one.

The Selection of Supreme Court Justices and Federal Judges

The formal mechanism for appointments to the Supreme Court and the lower federal courts is the same: the president nominates and the Senate confirms or rejects. Beyond that basic similarity, however, there are significant differences.

Supreme Court Nominees A Supreme Court appointment is a critical choice for a president.[12] The cases that come before the Court tend to be controversial and have far-reaching implications. And since the Court is a small body, each justice's vote can be crucial to the decisions it makes. Because most justices retain their positions for many years, presidents can influence judicial policy through their appointments long after they have left office. The careers of some Supreme Court justices provide dramatic testimony to the enduring effects of judicial appointments. Franklin D. Roosevelt appointed William O. Douglas to the Supreme Court in 1939, and for thirty years after Roosevelt's death in 1945, Douglas remained a strong liberal influence on the Court.

Presidents invariably seek nominees who share their political philosophy, but they also must take into account a nominee's acceptability to others. Every nominee is closely scrutinized by the legal community, interested groups, and the media; must undergo an extensive background check by the FBI; and then must gain the approval of a Senate majority. Within the Senate, the key body is the Judiciary Committee, whose members have responsibility for conducting hearings on judicial nominees and recommending their confirmation or rejection by the full Senate.

Nearly 20 percent of presidential nominees have been rejected by the Senate on grounds of judicial qualification, political views, personal ethics,

The Justices of the U.S. Supreme Court pose for a photo. From left, they are Clarence Thomas, Antonin Scalia, Sandra Day O'Connor, Anthony Kennedy, David Souter, Stephen Breyer, John Paul Stevens, Chief Justice William Rehnquist, and Ruth Bader Ginsburg.

or partisanship. Most of these rejections in the country's history occurred before 1900, and partisan politics was the main reason. Today a nominee with strong professional and ethical credentials is less likely to be blocked for partisan reasons alone. An exception was Robert Bork, whose 1987 nomination by President Reagan was rejected primarily because of strong opposition from Senate Democrats who disagreed with his judicial philosophy. The Senate almost always approves middle-of-the-road, noncontroversial nominees. One such nominee, Ruth Bader Ginsburg, was confirmed by a 96-to-3 Senate vote in 1993.

Lower-Court Nominees The president normally gives the deputy attorney general the task of screening potential nominees for lower-court judgeships.[13] **Senatorial courtesy** is also a consideration in these appointments: this tradition, which dates back to the 1840s, holds that a senator from the state in which a vacancy has arisen should be given a say in the nomination if the senator is of the same party as the president.[14] If not consulted, the senator involved can request that confirmation be denied, and other senators will normally grant the request as a "courtesy" to a fellow senator.[15] Not surprisingly, presidents have preferred to give senators a voice in judicial appointments.

Although the president does not become as personally involved in selecting lower-court nominees as in naming potential Supreme Court justices, lower-court appointments are collectively a significant factor in the impact of a president's administration. Recent presidents have appointed about two hundred judges each term.

Justices and Judges as Political Officials

Presidents generally manage to appoint jurists who have a similar political philosophy. Although Supreme Court justices are free to make their own decisions, their legal positions can usually be inferred from their prior activities. A study by the judicial scholar Robert Scigliano found that about three of every four appointees have behaved on the Supreme Court approximately as presidents could have expected.[16] Of course, a president has no guarantee that a nominee will fulfill his hopes. Justices Earl Warren and William Brennan proved more liberal than President Dwight D. Eisenhower would have liked. When he was asked whether he had made any mistakes as president, Eisenhower replied, "Yes, two, and they are both sitting on the Supreme Court."[17]

The Role of Partisanship In nearly every instance, presidents chose members of their own party as Supreme Court nominees. Partisanship is also decisive in nominations to lower-court judgeships. More than 90 percent of recent district and appeals court nominees have been members of the president's own party.[18]

The fact that judges and justices are chosen through a partisan political process should not be interpreted to mean that they engage in blatant partisanship while on the bench. Judges and justices are officers of a separate branch and prize their judicial independence. All Republican appointees do not vote the same way on cases, nor do all Democrats. Nevertheless, the partisan backgrounds of judges are a significant influence on their decisions. A study of the voting records of appellate court judges, for example, found that Republican appointees tend to be more conservative than Democratic appointees in their civil rights and civil liberties decisions.[19]

Other Characteristics of Judicial Appointees In recent years, increasing numbers of federal justices and judges have had prior judicial experience; the assumption is that such individuals are best qualified for appointment to the federal bench. Most recent appellate court appointees have been district or state judges or have worked in the office of the attorney general.[20] Elective office (particularly a seat in the U.S. Senate) was once a common route

| TABLE | 14-1 | JUSTICES OF THE SUPREME COURT, 2003 |

Most recent appointees held an appellate court position before being nominated to the Supreme Court.

Justice	Year of Appointment	Nominating President	Position Before Appointment
William Rehnquist*	1971	Nixon	Assistant attorney general, Department of Justice
John Paul Stevens	1975	Ford	Judge, U.S. Courts of Appeals
Sandra Day O'Connor	1981	Reagan	Judge, Arizona Courts of Appeals
Antonin Scalia	1986	Reagan	Judge, U.S. Courts of Appeals
Anthony Kennedy	1988	Reagan	Judge, U.S. Courts of Appeals
David Souter	1990	Bush	Judge, U.S. Courts of Appeals
Ruth Bader Ginsburg	1993	Clinton	Judge, U.S. Courts of Appeals
Stephen Breyer	1994	Clinton	Judge, U.S. Courts of Appeals

*Appointed chief justice in 1986.

to the Supreme Court,[21] but now justices have typically held an appellate court judgeship before their appointment (see Table 14-1).

White males are greatly overrepresented on the federal bench, just as they dominate in Congress and at the top levels of the executive branch.[22] However, the number of women and minority-group judges increased substantially as a result of the appointments of President Clinton. About a third of Clinton's appointees were women compared with a seventh of the appointees of the two previous presidents (Reagan and Bush).

The Supreme Court itself is demographically unrepresentative. Until 1916, when Louis D. Brandeis was appointed to the Court, no Jewish justice had ever served. At least one Catholic, but at most times only one, has been on the Court almost continuously for nearly a century. Thurgood Marshall in 1967 became the first black justice, and Sandra Day O'Connor in 1981 became the first woman. Antonin Scalia in 1986 became the Court's first justice of Italian descent. No person of Hispanic or Asian descent has ever been a member of the Court.

The Nature of Judicial Decision Making

Federal judges and justices are political officials: they constitute one of three coequal branches of the national government. Yet, unlike members of Congress or the president, judges serve in a legal institution and make their decisions in a legal context. As a consequence, their discretionary power is less than that of elected officials. Article III of the Constitution bars a federal court from issuing a decision except in response to an actual case presented to it. As federal judge David Bazelon noted, a judge "can't wake up one morning and simply decide to give a helpful little push to a school system, a mental hospital, or the local housing agency."[23]

Another major restriction on the courts is the law itself. Although a president or Congress can make almost any decision that is politically acceptable, the judiciary must justify its decision in terms of existing provisions of the law.[24] When asked by a friend to "do justice," Oliver Wendell Holmes Jr. replied, "That is not my job. My job is to play the game according to the rules."[25] In playing according to the rules, judges engage in a creative legal process that requires them to identify the facts of the case, determine and sometimes formulate the relevant legal principles or rules, and then apply them to the case at hand.

The Constraints of the Facts

A basic distinction in any legal case is between "the facts" and "the laws." The **facts** of a case, as determined by trial courts, are the relevant circumstances of a legal dispute or offense. In the case of a person accused of murder, for example, key facts would include evidence about the murder and whether the rights of the accused were respected by police in the course of their investigation. The facts of a case are crucial because they determine which law or laws are applicable to the case. The courts must respond to the facts of a dispute. This restriction is a very substantial one. A murder case cannot be used as an occasion to pronounce judgment on freedom of religion.

The Constraints of the Law

In deciding cases, the judiciary is also constrained by existing **laws.** To use an obvious comparison, the laws that apply to a case of alleged murder differ from those that apply to a case of alleged shoplifting. A judge must treat a murder case as a murder case, applying to it the laws that define murder and the penalties that can be imposed when someone is found guilty of that crime.

The Constitution and Its Interpretation The Constitution of the United States is the nation's highest law, and the judges and justices are sworn to uphold it. When a case raises a constitutional issue, a court has the duty to apply the Constitution to the case. For example, the Constitution prohibits the states from printing their own currency. If a state decided that it would do so anyway, a federal judge would be obligated to rule against the practice.

Nevertheless, constitutional provisions are open to interpretation in some cases. For example, the Fourth Amendment of the Constitution protects individuals against "unreasonable searches and seizures," but the meaning of "unreasonable" is not specified. Judges must decide upon its meaning in particular situations. Take, for example, the question of whether wiretapping, which was not invented until 150 years after ratification of the Fourth Amendment, is included in the prohibition on unreasonable searches and seizures. Reasoning that the Fourth Amendment was intended to protect individuals from government intrusion in their private lives, judges have ruled that indiscriminate wiretapping is unconstitutional. It is legal only when law enforcement officials can persuade a judge that they have sufficient evidence to justify a tap on a person's phone.

Sources of Law That Constrain the Federal Judiciary's Decisions

U.S. Constitution: The federal courts are bound by the provisions of the U.S. Constitution. The sparseness of its wording, however, requires the Constitution to be applied in the light of particular circumstances. Thus judges are accorded a substantial degree of discretion in their constitutional judgments.

Statutory and administrative law: The Supreme Court is constrained by statutes and by administrative regulations derived from the provisions of statutes. Most laws, however, are somewhat vague in their provisions and often have unanticipated applications. As a result, judges have some freedom in deciding cases based on statutes.

Precedent: Federal courts tend to follow precedent (or stare decisis), which is a legal principle developed in earlier court decisions. Because times change and not all cases have a clear precedent, judges have some discretion in their evaluation of the way earlier cases apply to a current case.

Statutes, Administrative Laws, and Their Interpretation The vast majority of cases that arise in courts involve issues of statutory and administrative law rather than constitutional law. Most criminal acts (such as murder and assault) and civil actions (such as divorce and contract disputes) are covered by laws (statutes) created by legislative action or by administrative regulations that have been developed by government agencies on the basis of statutory law.

All federal courts are bound by federal statutes (laws passed by Congress) and by federal administrative regulations as well as by treaties. When hearing a case involving statutory law or administrative regulation, judges must work within the limits of the applicable law or regulation. A company that is charged with violating federal environmental law will be judged within the context of that law—what it permits and what it prohibits, and the penalties that would apply if the company is found to have broken the law.

When hearing such a case, judges will often try to determine whether the meaning of the statute or regulation can be determined by common sense (the "plain meaning rule"). The question for the judge is what the law or regulation was intended to safeguard (such as a particular issue of environmental protection). In most instances the law or regulation is clear enough that when the facts of the case are judged against it, a reasonable decision can be reached. Not all cases, however, are clear-cut in their facts or in the applicable law or laws. In these instances, courts have no choice but to exercise their judgment.

Legal Precedents (Previous Rulings) and Their Interpretation The U.S. legal system developed from the English common-law tradition, which includes the principle that a court's decision on a case should be consistent with previous judicial rulings. This principle is known as **precedent** and reflects the philosophy of stare decisis (Latin for "to stand by things that have been settled"): the doctrine that principles of law, once established, should be accepted as authoritative in all subsequent similar cases. Judges and justices often cite past rulings as a justification for their decisions in the cases before them.

Precedent is important because it gives predictability to the application of law. If courts routinely ignored how similar cases had been decided in the past, they would create confusion and uncertainty among those who must make choices on the basis of their understanding of how the law has been applied in previous situations.[26] A business firm that is seeking to comply with environmental protection laws, for example, can develop company policies that will keep the company safely within the law if court decisions in this area are predictable. But if courts routinely ignore precedent, a firm

might unintentionally engage in activity that a court could arbitrarily conclude was unlawful.

Government has an obligation to citizens and firms alike to make clear
what its laws are and how they are being applied. Precedent is one of the
means by which greater consistency in the application of the law can be
achieved.

POLITICAL INFLUENCES ON
JUDICIAL DECISIONS

Although judicial rulings are constrained by existing laws, judges nearly always have some degree of discretion in their decisions.[27] The Constitution
is a sparsely worded document and must be adapted to new and changing
situations. The judiciary also has no choice at times but to apply its own
judgment to statutory law. Congress often cannot anticipate or reach agreement on all the specific applications of a legislative act and therefore uses
general language to state the act's purpose. The judiciary must decide what
this language means in the context of a specific case arising under the act.
Precedent is even less precise as a guide to decision. Precedent is more a
rule of thumb than a strict command; its significance must be weighed
against the changes that have occurred since it was established. In the words
of Justice Oliver Wendell Holmes Jr., precedent must be judged against the
"felt necessities of the time."

The Supreme Court's ruling in a 1998 case (*Faragher v. Boca Raton*) involving sexual harassment in the workplace illustrates the ambiguity that
can exist in the written law. The Court developed its ruling in the context
of the antidiscrimination provisions of the Civil Rights Act of 1964. The act
itself contains no description of, or even reference to, job-related sexual harassment. Nevertheless, the act does prohibit workplace discrimination, and
the Court was unwilling to dismiss sexual harassment as an irrelevant form
of job-related discrimination. In judging the case, however, the Court had
no choice except to determine for itself which actions in the workplace are
instances of harassment and which are not. In this sense, the Court was
"making" law; it was deciding how legislation enacted by Congress applied
to actions that Congress had not addressed when it wrote the legislation.[28]

In sum, judges have leeway in their decisions. As a consequence, their
rulings reflect not only legal influences but political ones, which come from
both outside and inside the judicial system.

Outside Influences on Court Decisions

The courts can and do make unpopular choices, but in the long run, judicial decisions must be seen as fair if they are to be obeyed. In other words,

The Supreme Court building is located across from the Capitol in Washington, D.C. The courtroom, the justices' offices, and the conference room are on the first floor. Administrative staff offices and the Court's records and reference materials occupy the other floors.

the judiciary cannot ignore the expectations of the general public, interest groups, and elected representatives.

Judges are responsive to public opinion, although much less so than are elected officials. In some cases, for example, the Supreme Court has tailored its rulings in an effort to gain public support or dampen public resistance. In the *Brown* case, the justices, recognizing that school desegregation would be an explosive issue in the South, required only that desegregation take place "with all deliberate speed" rather than immediately or on a fixed timetable. The Supreme Court has typically stayed close enough to public opinion to avoid seriously eroding public support for its decisions.[29]

Organized groups make their opinions known to the judiciary through the lawsuits they file. The range of interests that use lawsuits as a policy tactic includes traditional advocacy groups such as the American Civil Liberties Union (ACLU) and newer ones such as the Christian Legal Society's Center for Law and Religious Freedom. Groups also participate in cases brought by others through amicus curiae ("friend of the court") briefs, which they file in support of one of the parties to a case.[30]

Groups and the general public also make an impact on the judiciary indirectly, through their elected representatives. Both Congress and the president

have powerful means of influencing the federal judiciary. Congress is constitutionally empowered to establish the Supreme Court's size and appellate jurisdiction, and Congress can rewrite legislation that it feels the judiciary has
misinterpreted. Although Congress seldom undermines the judiciary directly,
its members often express displeasure with judicial action. In a 1998 Senate
speech, the chair of the Judiciary Committee, Orrin Hatch (R-Utah), lashed
out at judges who he claimed were "making laws instead of interpreting the
law."[31] Other Republicans on the Judiciary Committee shared Hatch's view,
and they delayed confirmation of a number of President Clinton's judicial
nominees on the grounds that they were unlikely to be "strict construction-
ists." (*Strict constructionism* holds that a judicial officer should apply a narrow
interpretation of the laws, whereas *loose constructionism* holds that a judicial officer can apply an expansive interpretation.) Senate Democrats got their
chance to influence the nominating process when they became the Senate
majority in 2001. They slowed down confirmation on several dozen of President Bush's judicial nominees. When the Republicans retook control of the
Senate after the 2002 midterm elections, one of their first steps was to expe-
dite the delayed nominations.

    The president also has ways to influence the judiciary. The president is
responsible for enforcing court decisions and has some control over the
types of cases that come before the courts. Under President Ronald Reagan, for instance, the Justice Department pushed lawsuits that challenged
the constitutionality of affirmative action programs. Judicial appointments
also provide the president with opportunities to influence the judiciary's direction.[32] When Democrat Bill Clinton took office in 1993, more than a
hundred federal judgeships were vacant. President Bush had expected to
win reelection and had not moved quickly to fill vacancies as they arose. By
the time it was apparent that Bush might lose the election, the Democrat-
controlled Congress was able to delay action on the appointments. This enabled Clinton to fill the positions with loyal Democrats who could be
expected to partially offset the influence of the Republican judges appointed during the previous twelve years by presidents Reagan and Bush.
The tables were turned in 2001 when George W. Bush took office. Senate
Republicans had slowed action on Clinton nominees, enabling Bush to appoint Republicans to existing vacancies.

    Although the judiciary is subject to the influence of elected institutions,
the courts tend to see certain issues as questions of individual rights rather
than as matters to be settled by majority opinion. In such instances, the judiciary seldom lets the public or elected officials dictate its course of action. Despite continuing public support for school prayer, for instance, the Supreme
Court has not backed down from its basic position that prayer in the schools

is unconstitutional (see Chapter 4). The Court prizes its independence and its position as a coequal branch of government. The fact that judges are not popularly elected and that they hold their appointments indefinitely makes it possible for them to resist pressures from Congress and the president.

Inside Influences: The Justices' Own Political Beliefs

Although the judiciary symbolizes John Adams's characterization of the U.S. political system as "a government of laws, and not of men," judicial rulings are affected by the political beliefs of the men and women who sit on the courts.[33] Decisions of the Supreme Court, for example, often divide along political lines. During the 2001 Supreme Court term, for instance, twenty-six cases were decided by a 5-4 decision. In a substantial number of these cases, Chief Justice William Rehnquist and justices Antonin Scalia and Clarence Thomas, all of whom are Republican appointees, were opposed by justices Stephen Breyer and Ruth Bader Ginsburg, the two Democratic appointees on the Court.[34]

Arguably, partisanship was never more evident than in the Supreme Court's *Bush v. Gore* (2000) decision. The five justices in the majority were the same justices who in previous decisions had upheld states' rights and had opposed expansive applications of the Fourteenth Amendment's equal protection clause. Yet they invoked the equal protection clause to block the statewide manual recount that had been ordered by Florida's high court because no uniform standard for counting the ballots existed. When the Court issued a rare stay order to stop the recount, Justice Antonin Scalia claimed that it was justified because the recount could cast doubt on the legitimacy of Bush's election. The fact was, Bush had not yet been officially elected. Some observers suggested that if Bush had been trailing in the Florida vote, the Court's majority would have allowed the recount to continue. Justice John Paul Stevens, who thought the Florida high court had acted properly in ordering a manual count, accused the Court's majority of devising a ruling based on their partisan desires rather than on the law. Stevens noted that different standards for casting and counting ballots were found throughout the United States.[35]

Most Supreme Court justices do not change their views greatly during their tenure. As a result, major shifts in the Supreme Court's positions usually occur when its membership changes. Such shifts are related to political changes. When the Court in the 1980s moved away from the criminal justice rulings of the 1960s, for instance, it was largely because the more recently appointed justices, like the presidents who had nominated them, believed that government should have more leeway in its efforts to fight crime.

JUDICIAL POWER AND DEMOCRATIC GOVERNMENT

The issue of judicial power is heightened by the fact that federal judges are not elected. The principle of self-government asserts that lawmaking majorities have the power to decide society's policies. Because the United States has a constitutional system that places checks on the will of the majority, there is obviously an important role in the system for a counter-majoritarian institution such as the judiciary (see Table 14-2). Yet court decisions often reflect the political philosophy of the judges, who constitute a tiny political elite that wields significant power.[36] A critical question is how far unelected judges ought to go in substituting their policy judgments for those of legislative and executive officials who are elected by the people.

The judiciary's power is most evident when it declares executive or legislative action to be unconstitutional. The power of the courts to make such determinations is called **judicial review** and was first asserted in the landmark *Marbury v. Madison* case of 1803, when the Supreme Court rebuked both the president and Congress (see Chapter 2). Without judicial review, the federal courts would be unable to restrain an elected official or institution that had gone out of control.

Yet judicial review places the judgment of the courts above that of elected officials when interpretation of the Constitution is at issue, creating the possibility of conflict between the courts and the elected branches. The imposing nature of judicial review has led the judiciary to apply judicial review somewhat sparingly, although the Supreme Court alone has invoked it in more than one thousand cases—the large majority of which have involved action by state and local officials rather than the president or Congress. Many of these cases, as seen in Chapters 4 and 5, involved issues of civil liberties (e.g., free expression) and civil rights (e.g., racial discrimination).

Even in the area of statutory law, however, there is plenty of room for the exercise of judicial power. Most statutes (legislative acts) specify general goals, which judges then have to apply in particular situations. Often, a case reaches the courts precisely because the law in question is vague as to how it might apply to the case, which enables courts to make the determination.

The Debate over the Proper Role of the Judiciary

The question of judicial power centers on the basic issue of **legitimacy:** the proper authority of the judiciary in a political system based in part on the principle of majority rule. The judiciary's policymaking significance and discretion have been sources of controversy throughout the country's history, but the controversies have seldom been livelier than during recent decades.

| TABLE | 14-2 | Significant Supreme Court Cases |

Included are some of the most influential cases decided by the U.S. Supreme Court.

Case	Ruling
Marbury v. Madison (1803)	Established principle of judicial review (Chapter 2)
McCullough v. Maryland (1819)	Strengthened national power over states (Chapter 3)
Dred Scott v. Sanford (1857)	Decided that slaves were property and not citizens (Chapter 3)
Plessy v. Ferguson (1896)	Established the "separate but equal" doctrine (Chapter 5)
Gitlow v. New York (1925)	Protected free expression from state action by Fourteenth Amendment (Chapter 4)
National Labor Relations Board v. Jones and Laughlin Steel (1937)	Decided that Congress can apply its commerce powers broadly (Chapter 3)
Brown v. Topeka Board of Education (1954)	Abolished the "separate but equal" doctrine and banned segregation in public schools (Chapter 5)
Gideon v. Wainwright (1963)	Decided that states must provide an attorney for poor defendants accused of committing felonies (Chapter 4)
Miranda v. Arizona (1966)	Decided that the police must inform suspects of their rights when they are arrested (Chapter 4)
Roe v. Wade (1973)	Decided that women have full freedom to choose abortion during the first three months of pregnancy under the right of privacy (Chapter 4)
Bush v. Gore (2000)	Decided that a Florida manual recount would violate the Fourteenth amendment (Chapter 14)

The judiciary at times has acted almost legislatively by defining broad social policies, such as abortion, busing, affirmative action, church-state relations, and prison reform. In a recent year, for example, the prison systems in forty-two states were operating under court orders that mandated improvements in health care or overcrowding. School prayer is an older example. Until the Supreme Court in 1962 prohibited the reciting of prayer

LIBERTY, EQUALITY, AND SELF-GOVERNMENT
What's Your Opinion?

Judicial Review

Judicial review is the process by which a court invalidates legislature or executive action because it violates the Constitution. Judicial review is most dramatic in cases where the Supreme Court strikes down action taken by Congress or the president. However, most applications of judicial review take place in the context of action taken by state or local governments. The Supreme Court has struck down well over a thousand state laws and local ordinances, most of which involved issues of liberty and equality. Examples include *Near v. Minnesota* (freedom of the press), *Brown v. Board of Education* (racial segregation in the schools), and *Gideon v. Wainwright* (legal counsel for the poor).

Why have encroachments on people's liberties occurred more frequently at the hands of state and local governments? Is it simply because there are so many of them that, by chance alone, most constitutional cases will arise at these levels? Or do you accept James Madison's claim (*Federalist* No. 10) that the smaller the sphere of government, the more likely it is that a dominant faction will disregard the interests of a weaker one?

---

in public schools, the practice was governed by state legislatures and, in some cases, by local school districts. Through such actions the judiciary has restricted the policymaking authority of the states, has narrowed legislative discretion, and has made judicial action an effective alternative to election victory for certain interests.[37]

The judiciary has become more extensively involved in policymaking for many of the same reasons that Congress and the president have been thrust into new policy areas and become more deeply involved in old ones. Social and economic changes have required government to play a larger role in society, and this development has generated a seemingly endless series of new legal controversies.

Judicial action raises an important question. How far should the judiciary go in asserting its authority when that authority collides with or goes beyond the action of elected institutions? There are two general schools of thought on this question: one advocates judicial restraint and the other supports judicial activism. Although these terms are somewhat imprecise and often misused, they are helpful in efforts to clarify opposing philosophical positions on the Court's proper role.[38]

The Supreme Court resists pressure from the public and from elected officials on some issues, such as school prayer, that it considers to be questions of individual rights rather than of majority opinion.

The Doctrine of Judicial Restraint The doctrine of **judicial restraint** holds that the judiciary should be highly respectful of precedent and should defer to the judgment of legislatures. The restraint doctrine holds that public issues should be decided in nearly all cases by elected officials rather than judges. The judges' role is to determine how legislation and precedent apply in specific cases rather than to search for new principles that essentially change the meaning of the laws in question.

Advocates of judicial restraint support their position with two major arguments. First, they contend that when the judiciary assumes policy functions that traditionally belong to elected institutions, it undermines the fundamental premise of self-government: the right of the majority to choose society's policies.[39] Second, judicial self-restraint is admired because it preserves the public support that is essential to the long-term legitimacy of the courts.[40] The judiciary must be concerned with **compliance**—with whether its decisions will be respected and obeyed. If judges impose their own views on the law, public confidence in the judiciary will be undermined.[41]

Advocates of judicial restraint acknowledge that established law is never so precise as to provide exact answers to every question raised by every case and requires some degree of judicial discretion. And in rare circumstances, decisive judicial action may be both appropriate and necessary, as in the historic *Brown v. Board of Education* decision (1954). The contradiction between the Fourteenth Amendment's equal protection clause and government-created segregated schools is so blatant that even though the Constitution does not expressly prohibit racially segregated public schools, there is today no respectable jurist or legal scholar who would argue that such schools are constitutionally permissible.[42]

Yet advocates of judicial restraint see no constitutional justification for many of the Supreme Court's civil rights decisions. In *Romer v. Evans* (1996), for example, the Court's majority struck down an amendment to the Colorado constitution that was adopted by majority vote in a statewide referendum. The amendment had banned existing and future laws granting civil rights protections to homosexuals (see Chapter 5). Justice Antonin Scalia, who was in the Court's minority on the issue, said that the ruling was "an act not of judicial judgment but of political will." Scalia said that the statewide referendum was "the most democratic of procedures" and that the decision of Colorado voters should have been upheld.[43]

The Doctrine of Judicial Activism In contrast to the judicial restraint position is the idea that the courts should take a generous view of judicial power and involve themselves extensively in interpreting and enlarging upon the law. Although advocates of this doctrine, which is known as **judicial activism,** acknowledge the principles of precedent and majority rule, they claim that the courts should not be overly deferential to existing legal principles or to the judgments of elected officials.

Until recently, the doctrine of judicial activism was associated almost entirely with liberal activists who contend that courts should resort to general principles of fairness when existing law is inadequate. In areas in which social justice depends substantially on activist policies on behalf of the disadvantaged, liberal judicial activists argue that the courts have a responsibility to act positively and decisively.[44] These activists believe, for example, that busing was an appropriate remedy for achieving racial integration in public schools in communities where residential patterns and other legacies of racial discrimination kept black children from attending the same schools as white children. These activists find justification for their position in the U.S. Constitution's strong moral language and several of its provisions.[45] They view the Constitution as designed chiefly to protect individuals from unresponsive or repressive government, a goal that can be accomplished only by a judiciary that is willing to act when lawmaking majorities fail to correct injustice or perpetrate it. Judicial activists see the Constitution as a charter for protecting individuals who are weak or vulnerable, not as a set of narrow rules.

Judicial activism is not, however, confined to liberals. In the period from the 1860s to the 1930s, conservative activists on the Supreme Court struck down most legislative efforts to regulate economic activity (see Chapter 3). Judicial activism from the right recently became an issue again when the

How the United States Compares

Judicial Power

U.S. courts are highly political by comparison with the courts of most other democracies. First, U.S. courts operate within a common-law tradition, which makes judge-made law (through precedent) a part of the legal code. Many democracies have a civil-law tradition, in which nearly all law is defined by legislative statutes. Second, because U.S. courts operate in a constitutional system of divided power, they are required to rule on conflicts between state and nation or between the executive and legislative branches, which thrusts the judiciary into the middle of political conflicts. It should not be surprising, then, that federal judges and justices are appointed through an overtly political process in which partisan views and activities are major considerations. Many federal judges, particularly at the district level, have no significant prior judicial experience. In fact, the United States is one of the few countries that does not mandate formal training for judges.

The pattern is different in most European democracies. Judgeships there tend to be career positions. Individuals are appointed into the judiciary at an early age and then work their way up the judicial ladder largely on the basis of seniority. Partisan politics does not play a large role in appointment and promotion. By tradition, European judges see their job as the strict interpretation of statutes, not the creative application of them.

The power of U.S. courts is nowhere more evident than in the exercise of judicial review: the voiding of a legislative or executive action on the grounds that it violates the Constitution. Judicial review had its origins in European experience and thought, but it was first formally applied in the United States when, in *Marbury v. Madison* (1803), the Supreme Court declared an act of Congress unconstitutional. Some democracies, including Great Britain, still do not allow broadscale judicial review, but most democracies now provide for it.

Court overturned several precedents in the area of the rights of the accused. In 1990, Chief Justice William Rehnquist, in a rare action, asked Congress to restrict the right of those convicted in state courts to file habeas corpus appeals in federal courts. Congress rejected the proposal, and in 1991 a majority on the Rehnquist Court took action on its own to achieve the goal. In one ruling, the Court held that an inmate could not obtain a federal appeal simply because his or her lawyer had made a procedural mistake during the trial in a state court.[46]

Conservative activism is also evident in recent Supreme Court cases on the issue of federalism. Since the late 1930s, the Court had deferred almost completely to Congress, but it has recently struck down several acts of Congress (see Chapter 3). The Court's four most conservative justices (Rehnquist, Scalia, Thomas, and Kennedy), joined by Justice O'Connor, supported the major decisions, each of which was decided by a 5-4 margin. In one of these cases, *Kimel v. Florida Board of Regents* (2000), the Court ruled that Congress did not have the power to require states to comply with the federal age-discrimination law because age is not among the forms of discrimination expressly prohibited by the Fourteenth Amendment's equal protection clause. The various rulings reflected Chief Justice William Rehnquist's long-held goal of limiting Congress's authority over the states.[47] "[The Rehnquist Court] doesn't defer to government at any level," said Walter Dellinger, a former solicitor general. "The Court is confident it can come up with the right decisions, and it believes it is constitutionally charged with doing so."[48]

Whether from the right or the left, judicial activism is characterized by a willingness to pit the judgment and power of the courts against the judgment and power of elected representatives or their administrative agents. To a degree, all judges are activists in the sense that their decisions are necessarily

I was sentenced to the State Penitentiary by The Circuit Court of Bay County, State of Florida. The present proceeding was commenced on a writ petition for a Writ of Habeus Corpus To The Supreme Court of The State of Florida to vacate the sentence, on the grounds that I was made to stand Trial without the aid of counsel, and, at all times of my incarseretion. The said Court refused To appoint counsel and therefore deprived me of Due process of law, and violate my rights in The Bill of Rights and the constitution of the United states.

5th day of Jan 1962 Petitioner

Notary Public

Gideon's Letter to the Supreme Court
John F. Davis, Clerk, Supreme Court of the United States

The handwritten letter that Clarence Gideon (insert) sent to the Supreme Court in 1962. The letter led eventually to the *Gideon* decision in which the Court held that states must provide poor defendants with legal counsel (see Chapter 4). Seen by many people at the time as judicial activism, the ruling is now fully accepted.

creative ones. The law as expressed through the Constitution, statutes, and precedent is not precise enough to provide an automatic answer to every court case. Judges and justices have no choice but to exercise judgment when the text of the law is inexact. And, to a degree, all judges are restrained in the sense that their decisions must have roots in the law. Judges cannot simply make any decision they might choose; they are confined by the facts of a case and the laws that might reasonably be applied to it. But judges and justices vary in the degree to which they are willing to contest the judgment of other political institutions and the degree to which they are willing to depart from the wording of the law. These differences separate the judicial activists from the practitioners of judicial restraint.

The Judiciary's Proper Role: A Question of Competing Values

The dispute between advocates of judicial activism and advocates of judicial restraint is a philosophical one that involves opposing values. The debate is important because it addresses the normative question of what role the judiciary ought to play in American democracy. Should unelected judges involve themselves deeply in policy by adopting a broad conception of their power, or should they give wide discretion to elective institutions? Should judges defer to precedent, or should they be willing to change course, even at the risk of sending the law down uncharted paths? These questions cannot be answered simply on the basis of whether one personally agrees or disagrees with a particular judicial decision. The answer necessarily depends on a value judgment about the role of the judiciary in a governing system based on the often-conflicting concepts of majority rule and individual rights.

The United States is a constitutional democracy that recognizes both the power of the majority to rule and the claim of the minority to protection of its rights. The judiciary was not established as the nation's moral conscience and does not have a monopoly on the issue of minority interests and rights. Yet the judiciary was established as a coequal branch of government and was charged with the responsibility for protecting individual rights and minority interests. In short, the constitutional question of how far the courts should be allowed to go in substituting their judgment for that of elected institutions and established law is open to interpretation. The trade-off is significant on all issues: minority rights versus majority rule, states' rights versus federal power, legislative authority versus judicial authority.

SUMMARY

At the lowest level of the federal judicial system are the district courts, where most federal cases begin. Above them are the federal courts of appeals, which review cases appealed from the lower courts. The U.S. Supreme Court is the nation's highest court. Each state has its own court system, consisting of trial courts at the bottom and one or two appellate levels at the top. Cases originating in state courts ordinarily cannot be appealed to the federal courts unless a federal issue is involved, and then the federal courts can choose to rule only on the federal aspects of the case. Federal judges at all levels are nominated by the president, and if confirmed by the Senate, they are appointed by the president to the office. Once on the federal bench, they serve until they die, retire, or are removed by impeachment and conviction.

The Supreme Court is unquestionably the most important court in the country. The legal principles it establishes are binding on lower courts, and its capacity to define the law is enhanced by the control it exercises over the cases it hears. However, it is inaccurate to assume that lower courts are inconsequential (the upper-court myth). Lower courts have considerable discretion, and the great majority of their decisions are not reviewed by a higher court. It is also inaccurate to assume that federal courts are far more significant than state courts (the federal court myth).

The courts have less discretionary authority than elected institutions do. The judiciary's positions are constrained by the facts of a case and by the laws as defined through the Constitution, statutes and government regulations, and legal precedent. Yet existing legal guidelines are seldom so precise that judges have no choice in their decisions. As a result, political influences have a strong impact on the judiciary. It responds to national conditions, public opinion, interest groups, and elected officials, particularly the president and members of Congress. Another political influence on the judiciary is the personal beliefs of judges, who have individual preferences that are evident in the way they decide on issues that come before the courts. Not surprisingly, partisan politics plays a significant role in judicial appointments.

In recent decades, the Supreme Court has issued broad rulings on individual rights, some of which have required governments to take positive action on behalf of minority interests. As the Court has crossed into areas traditionally left to lawmaking majorities, the legitimacy of its policies has been questioned. Advocates of judicial restraint claim that the justices' personal values are inadequate justification for exceeding the proper judicial role. They argue that the Constitution entrusts broad issues of the public good to elective institutions and that judicial activism ultimately undermines public respect for the judiciary. Judicial activists counter that the courts were established as an independent branch and should not hesitate to promote new principles when they see a need, even if this action puts them into conflict with elected officials.

KEY TERMS

appellate jurisdiction

compliance

concurring opinion

decision

dissenting opinion

facts (of a court case)

judicial activism

judicial conference

judicial restraint

judicial review

jurisdiction (of a court)

laws (of a court case)

legitimacy (of judicial power)

majority opinion

opinion (of a court)

original jurisdiction

plurality opinion

precedent

senatorial courtesy

writ of certiorari

SUGGESTED READINGS

Carp, Robert A. *The Federal Courts*, 3d ed. Washington, D.C.:
Congressional Quarterly Press, 1998. An overview of the federal
judiciary system.

Gillman, Howard. *Votes That Counted: How the Court Decided the 2000
Presidential Election.* Chicago: University of Chicago Press, 2001. An
accounting of the *Bush v. Gore* ruling.

McGuire, Kevin T. *Understanding the Supreme Court: Cases and
Controversies.* New York: McGraw-Hill, 2002. An overview of Supreme
Court decisions and approaches to legal disputes.

O'Brien, David M. *Storm Center,* 5th ed. New York: Norton, 2000. An
analysis of the Supreme Court in the context of the controversy
surrounding the role of the judiciary in the U.S. political system.

Salokar, Rebecca Mae. *The Solicitor General: The Politics of Law.*
Philadelphia, Pa.: Temple University Press, 1992. A study of the
important and increasingly political role of the nation's top trial
lawyer.

Scalia, Antonin. *A Matter of Interpretation: Federal Courts and the Law.*
Princeton, N.J.: Princeton University Press, 1997. A critical assessment
of how the Supreme Court interprets law.

Schwartz, Bernard. *Decision: How the Supreme Court Decides Cases.* New
York: Oxford University Press, 1996. A behind-the-scenes look at
Supreme Court justices' decisions.

Watson, George L., and John Alan Stookey. *Shaping America: The Politics
of Supreme Court Appointments.* New York: Longman, 1995. An
examination of the process by which Supreme Court justices are
nominated and confirmed.

LIST OF WEBSITES

http://www.courttv.com/cases A website that allows you to take the facts of actual court cases, examine the law and the arguments, and then decide each case for yourself.

http://www.fjc.gov The home page of the Federal Judicial Center, an agency created by Congress to conduct research and provide education on the federal judicial system.

http://www.lib.umich.edu/libhome/Documents.center/_fedjudi.html A University of Michigan web page that provides detailed information on the federal judicial system.

http://www.rominger.com/supreme.htm A vast site that provides links to the Supreme Court, pending cases, the state court systems, and other subjects.

POLITICS IN THEORY AND PRACTICE

Thinking: Which philosophy—that of judicial restraint or judicial activism—comes closer to your own thinking about the proper role of the courts? Or, does your support for restraint or activism depend on whether a judicial decision conforms to your own preference on the issue in question?

Acting: The right to a fair and open trial decided by a jury is one of the oldest hallmarks of the American justice system. If you have never done so, you might want to attend a trial at your local courthouse to see how the process works. If you live in or near Washington, D.C., or a state capital, you might choose instead to observe a session of a supreme court. Such courts are appellate courts, so there is no jury, but you are more likely to hear arguments on cases of broad significance. Finally, if you have the opportunity to serve on a jury, you should welcome the chance to participate in a decision that is important to society as well as to the parties directly involved. Too many Americans today see jury duty as a responsibility to be shirked.

𝕿𝖍𝖊 𝕹𝖊𝖜 𝖄𝖔𝖗𝖐 𝕿𝖎𝖒𝖊𝖘   **reading 14**

Divining the Consequences of a Court Divided

by Linda Greenhouse

In the 1830s, Alexis de Tocqueveille wrote that, sooner or later, there is not a political issue in America that does not become also a judicial issue. This tendency stems in part from the judiciary's position as an independent and coequal branch of government. Yet, unlike Congress or the president, judicial officers are not elected by the people they govern. As a result, judicial action can be controversial, particularly when the courts intervene in policy disputes ordinarily settled by executive or legislative action. In this article, which appeared on December 17, 2000, New York Times correspondent Linda Greenhouse discusses the political dimensions of recent Supreme Court decisions.

WASHINGTON—Sixty years ago, Robert H. Jackson, President Franklin D. Roosevelt's attorney general, published a reflection on F.D.R.'s titanic battle with the Supreme Court that had reached its climax in the failed court-packing plan. In 1937, the president, enraged by the court's striking down of the New Deal's economic cornerstones, had proposed to expand its membership to as many as 15 justices by adding a new seat for each member who refused to retire at 70. Born in political desperation, the plan came under withering

attack as a threat to the separation of powers and died after the court began to uphold some New Deal programs.

The smoke had cleared by 1940, and Mr. Jackson, on the threshold of his own distinguished Supreme Court career, sought to extract some deeper meaning from the events. "So now, as always before, the struggle against judicial excess has ended by leaving it to the justices themselves to correct the errors of the court," he wrote in "The Struggle for Judicial Supremacy." And then he added: "Another generation may find itself fighting what is essentially the same conflict that we, under Roosevelt, and our fathers under Theodore Roosevelt and Wilson, and our grandfathers under Lincoln, and our great-grandfathers under Jackson, and our great-great-grandfathers under Jefferson fought before them. The truce between judicial authority and popular will may, or may not, ripen into a permanent peace."

Given the current court's activism on a variety of fronts—its attack on Congressional authority and its tilting of the federal-state balance toward the states—those long-ago words had acquired a strong resonance even before the justices' plunge into presidential politics last week. Now, in their invocation of profound political struggle over the appropriate boundaries of judicial power, Robert Jackson's words sound eerily prescient for a time when the dividing line between law and politics, however clear in theory, has been blurred in practice.

The same five justices who, in effect, decided the outcome of a presidential election Tuesday night—Chief Justice William H. Rehnquist and Associate Justices Sandra Day O'Connor, Antonin Scalia, Anthony M. Kennedy, and Clarence Thomas—have been allies in a series of decisions that have placed the court at the center of a fundamental, if until now largely unobserved, debate over the exercise of political power in America.

For the first time since the New Deal, the court has curbed the use of what Congress assumed to be its authority over interstate commerce; in two recent cases, the court found that neither a federal gun control law nor the Violence Against Women Act had a sufficient connection to interstate commerce to come under Congressional jurisdiction.

The 5-to-4 majority has endorsed sweeping new theories of sovereign immunity for the states against the reach of federal law, while at the same time overturning state legislatures' own political judgments on whether and how to take race into account in drawing lines for Congressional and legislative districts.

While on the surface, not all these rulings seem consistent, what unifies them is a kind of judicial triumphalism—an overriding of judgments made elsewhere in the political system, an insistence on having the last word—that is, in many respects, the opposite of what conservative politicians and judges said they wanted most as the Supreme Court emerged from the activist turmoil of midcentury.

"I'll use the adjective 'untethered,'" William E. Leuchtenburg, a leading historian of the New Deal period at the University of North Carolina at Chapel Hill and a longtime student of the court, said in

an interview last week. "These decisions are not tethered to any text. It's precisely the conservative objection to the Warren court, or to Roe v. Wade."

But until now, Professor Leuchtenburg said, the court's recent decisions have provoked nowhere near the public scrutiny or unease engendered by the court's rulings of the mid-1930's.

That was because while the New Deal decisions were direct obstacles to Roosevelt's economic recovery plans, grabbing the public's attention by threatening its welfare, the federalism revolution of the Rehnquist court has played out in highly technical decisions involving obscure, even elusive doctrinal areas like the 10th and 11th Amendments.

"There's not one person in 10,000 who ever heard of *Alden v. Maine,*" Professor Leuchtenburg said, referring to a 1999 decision that went far beyond the court's precedents to immunize states from suits in their own courts under federal labor law.

One effect of last week's events, he predicted, could be to bring about renewed, sustained scrutiny of the court's role in the country's political life.

While the court's intervention in the presidential election was unprecedented, the justices do, in fact, venture regularly into the thicket of electoral politics and are likely to do so more often as cases reach the court from the round of redistricting certain to follow the imminent release of population figures from the 2000 census.

As a taste of the cases to come, the court heard arguments several weeks ago on the validity of a North Carolina Congressional district that an earlier decision had found to be an unconstitutional race-based gerrymander. Following the court's opinion, the district has been redrawn and is no longer majority black. But the question remains whether the legislature drew the lines with race too much in mind, with the further question being, how much is too much?

During the argument last month in *Hunt v. Cromartie,* the lawyer for the plaintiffs accused the North Carolina legislature of hiding its racial motive by claiming as a "nice dodge" that it drew the lines simply to protect incumbents. Suddenly a voice from the bench interrupted. "Well, it isn't usually a dodge," Justice Sandra Day O'Connor, former majority leader of the Arizona State Senate, said firmly. "Legislators constantly are faced with drawing legislative districts, and my own experience is that the motive in most cases is political in drawing those boundaries."

It was surprising to see a justice stepping outside the judicial role to summon so overtly the directly relevant experience of an earlier, far different life.

Seen from the current context, that moment is a concrete reminder that for all the television-camera-free, cloistered atmosphere of the Supreme Court building, the justices are very much of the world. While Justice O'Connor is the only one of the current justices to have held elective office, David H. Souter was a state attorney general, Anthony M. Kennedy a lawyer-lobbyist in Sacramento, Stephen G. Breyer a senior Senate committee aide, Chief Justice Rehnquist a Republican poll-watcher in Phoenix and later a Justice Department official in the Nixon administration. Without political sophistication and sponsorship, no one is considered for a federal district judgeship, let alone the Supreme Court.

That justices embrace particular ideologies is neither surprising nor in any way illegitimate; it is part of how they came to be selected. In a culture where political differences are so often packaged as lawsuits, political sophistication is an asset to any judge.

But what has troubled many critics of the court's actions first to stop the Florida recount and then to prevent it from resuming is that the pair of 5-to-4 decisions appeared driven not by the high politics of

judicial philosophy but by naked partisanship. In fact, the majority's ideology, which includes deference to the states and a high threshold for getting into federal court with untested constitutional theories, would have predicted an opposite result.

One Republican law professor, a supporter of Gov. George W. Bush with ties to several justices, said the perception of rank politics was inaccurate but at the same time understandable. "I would have hoped they would have found a way not to be perceived as acting on their own political preferences," Professor Richard J. Pierce Jr. of George Washington University Law School said in an interview. "When very sophisticated, knowledgeable people, not rabid people, believe that's what happened, it's tragic. I am very, very concerned for the court."

Professor Pierce said he did not believe the members of the majority were motivated by a desire to install Mr. Bush as president. The dynamic was more nuanced.

"I assume every judge always tries to do the right thing, to act in a judgelike manner, to be fair and impartial," he said. "They struggle within themselves, with recognizing the political implications of cases but doing their best to put that knowledge aside. But the justices are human beings, and this case offered the worst environment to place a human being trying not to be a politician in robes."

First, he said, was the context; those who defend the court's ruling see it as a necessary corrective to a liberal, if not lawless, state court that twisted state law in an effort to change the election's outcome. "The perception of everything that happened is tremendously colored by individual preference," he said. "Every Republican I know was screaming bloody murder about the Florida Supreme Court, that it was engaged in an outrageous robbery and that its decision could not stand. It was not so much 'get my man in office' as 'keep the evil people from stealing the office from my man.'"

The final factor was speed. "It takes a while for the good part of a judge to conquer the powerful human instinct to make a decision in accord with his or her political preferences," he said. Once the justices decided to hear the Bush appeal, he added, "time became the enemy."

Given the mood with which the week ended, Robert Jackson's 60-year-old inquire about whether there might ever be "permanent peace" between judicial authority and popular will sounds almost quaint. The question is whether there can be anything that might resemble peace, even fleetingly. When the court reopens for business three weeks from tomorrow, nothing will appear to have changed, and yet nothing will be quite the same.

The debate over whether the justices acted out of partisanship or necessity will continue. But the possibility, however remote, that a Supreme Court decision can determine the presidency has now entered the public consciousness. The chance that a nominee as ideologically combative as Justice Scalia, whose confirmation vote 13 years ago was 98-0, would be confirmed today, at least without a major battle in a closely divided Senate, appears almost impossible.

Accountability is elusive for life-tenured judges, so it is their successors who may well be called, prospectively, to account. One result of the justices' remarkable exercise of power last week could be to raise the court's own political profile so high that any future vacancy might well produce a rancorous political struggle.

What's Your Opinion?

How partisan was the Supreme Court's opinion in *Bush v. Gore*? Does the opinion affect your view of the Supreme Court's impartiality and its role in the American political system?

CHAPTER 15

ECONOMIC AND ENVIRONMENTAL POLICY: CONTRIBUTING TO PROSPERITY

“We the people of the United States, in order to . . . insure domestic tranquility . . . **”**

PREAMBLE, U.S. CONSTITUTION

The stock market was downright scary. The Dow Jones and Nasdaq indexes had dropped sharply, knocking trillions of dollars off the value of stocks. Stocks that sold on the technology-heavy Nasdaq index were particularly hard hit. In a period of less than two years, they had fallen 75 percent—a steeper decline over the same length of time than had occurred at the onset of the Great Depression. Was history about to repeat itself? Was the U. S. economy on the verge of collapse?

In fact, Wall Street and the rest of America reacted rather calmly to the market downturn. Institutional and individual investors were unhappy with the drop in the value of their stocks, but they did not panic. Among the reasons was the fact that substantial government programs were in place to stabilize and stimulate the U.S. economy. When the Great Depression struck, no such programs existed. Moreover, the response to the 1929–1931 drop in stock prices made matters worse. Businesses cut back on production, investors fled the stock market, depositors withdrew their bank savings, and consumers slowed their spending. All these actions accelerated the downward spiral. In 2002, however, government programs were in place to protect

471

depositors' savings, to slow the drop in stock prices, and to steady the economy through adjustments in interest rates and spending programs.

This chapter examines the economic role of the government, focusing on its promotion and regulation of economic interests and its fiscal and monetary policies. Directly or indirectly, the federal government is a party to almost every economic transaction in which Americans engage. Although the private decisions of firms and individuals are the main force in the American economic system, these decisions are influenced by government policy. Washington seeks to maintain high productivity, employment, and purchasing power; regulates business practices that would otherwise harm the environment or result in economic inefficiencies and inequities; and promotes economic interests. The main ideas presented in this chapter are the following:

★ *Through regulation, the U.S. government imposes restraints on business activity that are designed to promote economic efficiency and equity.* This regulation is often the cause of political conflict, which is both ideological and group centered.

★ *Through regulatory and conservation policies, the U.S. government seeks to protect and preserve the environment from the effects of business firms and consumers.*

★ *Through promotion, the U.S. government helps private interests achieve their economic goals.* Business in particular benefits from the government's promotional efforts, which take place largely in the context of group politics.

★ *Through its taxing and spending decisions (fiscal policy), the U.S. government seeks to maintain a level of economic supply and demand that will keep the economy prosperous.* The condition of the economy is generally the leading issue in American electoral politics and has a major influence on each party's success.

★ *Through its money-supply decisions (monetary policy), the U.S. government— through the Fed—seeks to maintain a level of inflation consistent with sustained controllable economic growth.*

GOVERNMENT AS REGULATOR OF THE ECONOMY

An **economy** is a system of production and consumption of goods and services, which are allocated through exchange. When a shopper chooses groceries at a store and pays money for them, that transaction is one of the millions of economic exchanges that make up the economy. In *The Wealth*

The collapse in 2002 of the Enron Corporation, which had been American's seventh largest firm, cost investors and Enron employees (through the loss of retirement accounts) billions of dollars. The debacle brought calls for closer government regulation of corporations, accounting firms, and pension plans. Shown here is a scene from Senate Commerce Committee hearings into the role that Enron's top executive, Ken Lay, played in the collapse. Lay is in the center of the group seated just behind the empty chairs on the left side of the photo.

of Nations (1776), Adam Smith presented the case for the **laissez-faire doctrine,** which holds that private individuals and firms should be left alone to make their own production and distribution decisions. Smith reasoned that when there is a demand for a good (that is, when people are willing and able to buy a good), private entrepreneurs will respond by producing the good and distributing it to places where demand exists. Smith argued that the desire for profit is the "invisible hand" that guides the system of demand and supply toward the greatest benefit for all.

Smith acknowledged that the doctrine of laissez-faire capitalism had a few limits. Certain areas of the economy, such as roadways and postal services, were natural monopolies and were better run by government than by private firms. In addition, by regulating banking, currency, and contracts, government could give stability to private transactions. Otherwise, Smith argued, the economy was best left in private hands.

In contrast, Karl Marx proposed a worker-controlled economy. In *Das Kapital* (*Capital*, 1867) Marx argued that a free market system is exploitative because producers, through their control of markets, can compel workers to labor at a wage below the value they add to production and can force consumers to pay higher prices for goods than are justified by the cost of

| TABLE | 15-1 | THE MAIN OBJECTIVES OF REGULATORY POLICY |

The government intervenes in the economy to promote efficiency and equity.

Objective	Definition	Representative Actions by Government
Efficiency	Fulfillment of as many of society's needs as possible at the cost of as few of its resources as possible. The greater the output is for a given input, the more efficient is the process.	Preventing restraint of trade; requiring producers to pay the costs of damage to the environment, reducing restrictions on business that cannot be justified on a cost-benefit basis.
Equity	Fairness of the outcome of an economic transaction to each party	Requiring firms to bargain in good faith with labor; protecting consumers in their purchases; protecting workers' safety and health.

production. To end the exploitation of labor, Marx proposed a collective economy. When the workers owned the means of production, the economy would operate in the interest of all people.

Marx and Smith represent the extremes of economic theory. No country in the world has an economy that conforms fully to either the laissez-faire or the collectivist model. All national economies today are of "mixed" form in that they contain elements of both private and public control. However, the world's economies vary in their mix. Compared with European countries and much more so with China, the United States relies more heavily on private ownership and initiative.

Nevertheless, the U.S. government plays a substantial economic role through the **regulation** of privately owned businesses. U.S. firms are not free to act as they please but must operate within production and distribution rules set by federal regulations. Regulatory policy is generally intended to promote either economic *efficiency* or *equity* (see Table 15-1).

Efficiency Through Government Intervention

Economic efficiency results when firms fulfill as many of society's needs as possible while using as few of its resources as possible. **Efficiency** refers to the relationship of inputs (the labor and material that go into making a product or service) to outputs (the product or service itself). The greater the output for a given input, the more efficient the production process.

Adam Smith and other classical economists believed that the free market was the optimal means of achieving efficiency. Producers would try to use as few resources as possible in order to keep their prices low so that they could compete successfully for customers. Efficient producers would be able to underprice inefficient ones, who would thereby be driven out of business.

Preventing Restraint of Trade The assumption that the market always determines price is flawed. The same incentive—the profit motive—that drives producers to respond to demand can drive them to corner the market on a good. If a producer gains a monopoly on a good or colludes with other producers to fix its price, consumers are forced to pay an artificially high price. Rather than selling at a low price in order to attract customers, the producer will charge as high a price as the market will bear.

Restraint of trade was prevalent in the United States in the late nineteenth century when large trusts came to dominate many areas of the economy, including the oil, steel, railroad, and sugar markets. Railroad companies, for example, had no competition on short routes and charged such high rates that many farmers went broke because they could not afford to ship their crops to markets. In 1887, Congress took its first step toward regulating the trusts by enacting the Interstate Commerce Act. The legislation created the Interstate Commerce Commission (ICC), which was charged with regulating railroad practices and fares.

Business competition today is regulated by a wide range of federal agencies, including, for example, the Federal Trade Commission (FTC), the Food and Drug Administration (FDA), and the Antitrust Division of the Justice Department. The goal of regulatory activity is to protect customers while preserving the market incentives that create a dynamic economy. In some cases, the government has prohibited mergers or required divestments in order to increase competition. In 1999, for example, the Federal Communications Commission (FCC) voided a proposed merger of Bell Atlantic and GTE, ruling that the companies had failed to show that the merger would not hurt consumers. In other cases, the government has pressured companies whose marketing practices threaten competition. An example is the Justice Department's suit against Microsoft for using its Windows operating system to promote its Internet Explorer at the expense of other web browsers such as Netscape Navigator.

In most cases, however, the government tolerates business concentration, even permitting the merger of competing firms, such as Time Warner's merger with America Online (AOL) in 2001. Although such mergers reduce competition, the government tolerates concentrated ownership in the oil, automobile, and other industries in which high capital costs make it difficult for smaller firms to compete successfully.[1] Government acceptance of corporate giants also reflects a realization that market competition no longer involves just domestic firms. For example, the "Big Three" U.S. automakers (General Motors, Ford, and Chrysler) face stiff competition from imports, particularly those from Japan and Germany. The merger of Chrysler and Germany's Daimler-Benz is testimony to the increased globalization of market competition.

The U.S. government's general policy toward corporate giants that act in restraint of trade has been to penalize them financially. In 1993, for example, a number of air carriers (including American, Delta, United, Northwest, and US Air) were found to have engaged in price fixing and were ordered to award hundreds of millions of dollars in certificates to travelers who could prove they had flown on these carriers during the period in question. More than four million individuals, organizations, and businesses filed claims.

Making Business Pay for Indirect Costs Economic inefficiencies can result not only from restraint of trade but from the failure of businesses or consumers to pay the full costs of resources used in production. Classical economics assumed that market prices reflect all the costs of production, but this assumption is rarely warranted. Consider companies whose industrial wastes seep into nearby lakes and rivers. The price of these companies' products does not reflect the water pollution, and hence customers do not pay all the costs that society has incurred in the making of the products. Economists label such unpaid costs **externalities.**

Until the 1960s, the federal government did not require firms to pay such costs. The impetus to begin doing so came not only from lawmakers but also from the scientific community and environmental groups. The Clean Air Act of 1963 and the Water Quality Act of 1965 required industry to install antipollution devices to keep the discharge of air and water pollutants within specified limits. In 1970, Congress created the Environmental Protection Agency (EPA) to monitor firms to ensure their compliance with federal regulations governing air and water quality and the disposal of toxic wastes. (Environmental policy is discussed more fully later in the chapter.)

Overregulation Although government intervention is intended to increase economic efficiency, the effect can be the opposite. Government regulation raises the cost of doing business. Firms have to expend work hours to monitor and implement government regulations, which in some instances (for example, pollution control) also require companies to buy and install expensive equipment. These costs are efficient to the degree that they produce commensurate benefits.

Yet if government places needless or excessive regulatory burdens on firms, they waste resources in the process of complying. The result is higher-priced goods that are more expensive for consumers and less competitive in the domestic and global markets (see "How the United States Compares"). Overregulation can also be costly to governments. An example is a provision of the Safe Drinking Water Act that required communities to reduce contaminants in their water supply from the current level, whatever that level happened to be. In most communities, the effect was to improve the quality of the water supply. But in Anchorage, Alaska, the result was an absurd remedy. The city's water supply was so clean already that officials had to ask local fish-processing plants to dump their wastes into the sewer system so that Anchorage would have impurities to remove from its water.[2]

Situations of this kind have led to regulatory reform.[3] In 1995, Congress enacted legislation to tighten the regulatory process by requiring cost-benefit analysis and risk assessment (the severity of the problem) to be taken into account in certain regulatory decisions.

Deregulation Another response to regulatory excess is the policy of **deregulation**—the rescinding of regulations already in force for the purpose of improving efficiency. This process began in 1977 with passage of the Airlines Deregulation Act, which eliminated government-set airfares and, in some instances, government-mandated air routes. The change had the intended effect: airfares declined in price, and there was more competition between airlines on most routes. Congress followed airline deregulation with partial deregulation of the trucking, banking, energy, and communications industries, among others.

Reductions in regulation, however, can be carried too far. Underregulation can result in harmful business practices. The profit motive can lead firms and their executives to manipulate the market illegally. They are more likely to try unlawful schemes when weak regulation leads them to believe they can escape detection. Such was the case with top executives of the Enron Corporation. They had employed illegal maneuvers that falsely inflated the firm's earnings, which drove up the price of its stock. Only after the schemes failed and the firm went bankrupt in 2001 were their deceptions exposed. It was too late to help the stockholders who lost billions of dollars and the low-level Enron employees who lost their jobs and their company-based retirement savings.

The Enron scandal demonstrates that the issue of business regulation is not a simple question of whether or not to regulate. On the one hand, too

How the United States Compares

Global Economic Competitiveness

The United States ranks second only to Singapore in global economic competitiveness, according to a survey by the World Economic Forum, a private economic research organization in Switzerland.

The ranking is based on eight different factors: institutional openness, internationalization, government, management, finance, infrastructure, science and technology, and labor. The United States is strong on its technology, management, and finance. Its weakest point was the people factor, where it was downgraded on education programs and welfare services (for example, the United States, unlike other advanced industrialized countries, does not have government-provided health care).

The United States is ranked substantially higher than its major economic rivals, Japan and Germany. They trailed by a wide margin.

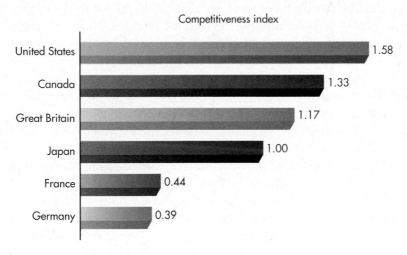

Competitiveness index

United States	1.58
Canada	1.33
Great Britain	1.17
Japan	1.00
France	0.44
Germany	0.39

much regulation can burden firms with bureaucratic red tape, costly implementation procedures, and limited options. On the other hand, too little regulation can give firms the leeway to exploit the public unfairly or recklessly. Either too little or too much regulation can result in economic inefficiency. The challenge for policymakers is to strike the proper balance between regulatory measures and free market mechanisms.

Deregulation: The Case of Your Phone Bill

Have you or your parents ever been sent an outlandish telephone bill that was hundreds or even thousands of dollars? Lots of Americans have, and their experiences reveal the pitfalls of deregulation.

In 1984, the U.S. government deregulated long-distance telephone service. AT&T was forced to compete with other carriers in a market in which carriers could set their own rates rather than having rates approved first by the Federal Communication Commission (FCC). The theory was that competition would drive rates downward, which would benefit consumers.

Rates have come down, but deregulation has also created a buyer-beware marketplace. The unscrupulous practices of MCI-Worldcom alone are enough to fill a book. One of MCI's schemes was an illegal practice called "slamming." Through deceptive telemarketing and direct mail advertising, MCI would trick people into changing to MCI as their carrier when they thought they were agreeing to something else, or in some cases not agreeing to anything at all. They found out the truth when a bill from MCI arrived in the mail. In 2000, the FCC fined MCI $3.5 million, the largest federal penalty ever for slamming.

MCI-Worldcom was also a leader in "cramming," which is the assessment of new rates and charges without informing customers of the change. MCI would attract customers with low advertised rates and later raise the rates. The first awareness that customers would have of the change would be when their bills arrived in the mail—too late for them to avoid paying the higher rate. In 2001, the FCC banned the practice.

For customers who call MCI-Worldcom to say they are switching to another carrier, MCI has a final surprise in store. In the interval during which the switch is taking place (which can be a week or more), MCI moves the customer to a higher rate category, charging as much as twenty to thirty times the original rate.

To protect consumers against such practices, *Consumer Reports* and other publications have suggested that people who are ordering new phone service or changing their existing one should read the fine print on any contract; ask a lot of questions—for example, some carriers charge only a few pennies more for calls to Canada, whereas others charge as much as $1.50 a minute for such calls; and if switching from one long-distance carrier to another, inform only the new carrier and the local service provider.

Equity Through Government Intervention

The government intervenes in the economy to bring equity as well as efficiency to the marketplace. **Equity** occurs when an economic transaction is fair to each party.[4] Equity is judged by *outcomes:* whether they are reasonable and mutually acceptable to the parties involved. A transaction can be considered fair if each party enters into it freely and is not unknowingly at a disadvantage (for example, if the seller knows a product is defective, equity requires that the buyer also know of the defect).

An early equity measure was the creation of the Food and Drug Administration (FDA) in 1907. Because consumers are often unable to tell whether foods and drugs are safe to use, the FDA works to keep adulterated foods and dangerous or ineffective drugs off the market. In the 1930s, financial reforms were among the equity measures enacted under the New Deal. The Securities and Exchange Act of 1934 and the Banking Act of 1934 were designed in part to protect investors and savers from dishonest or imprudent brokers and bankers. The New Deal also provided greater equity for organized labor, which previously had been in a weak position in its dealings with management. The Fair Labor Standards Act of 1938, for example, established minimum wages, maximum working hours, and constraints on the use of child labor.

The 1960s and 1970s produced the greatest number of equity reforms. From 1965 to 1977, ten federal agencies, such as the Consumer Product Safety Commission, were established to protect consumers, workers, and the public from harmful effects of business activity. Among the products declared to be unsafe in the 1960s and 1970s were the insecticide DDT, cigarettes, and leaded gasoline. The rule eliminating lead in gasoline, for example, has given society a major benefit; the average level of lead in children's blood has decreased by 75 percent since the measure went into effect.[5]

The Politics of Regulatory Policy

Economic regulation has come in waves, as changes in national conditions have produced intermittent bursts of social consciousness.

The Reforms of the Progressive and New Deal Eras The first wave of regulation came during the Progressive era, when reformers sought to break the power of the trusts by placing constraints on unfair business practices. The second wave came in the New Deal era, when reformers sought to stimulate economic recovery through regulatory policies that were designed as much to save business as to restrain it.

LIBERTY, EQUALITY, AND SELF-GOVERNMENT

What's Your Opinion?

Economic Freedom and Equity

The U.S. economy is based on free-market principles. Producers and consumers are more or less free to act as they please, subject of course to their financial resources.

Few Americans would trade their capitalist system for one of the alternatives, such as socialism or communism (see Chapter 1). In fact, Americans' conception of liberty is closely tied to their sense of economic freedom. Yet most Americans also prize a degree of economic equity. Consumer protection, the minimum wage, bargaining rights, and other such policies have broad public support. The challenge, as most Americans see it, is to find the proper balance between freedom and equity in the marketplace. In your view, is the current balance about right, or does it tilt too far in the direction of freedom or in the direction of equity?

Equity is an issue of whether economic transactions are fair to each party. A separate issue is economic equality: whether wealth is spread across society without too much of it at the top or too little of it at the bottom. In your opinion, is wealth distributed evenly enough that nearly all Americans are able to enjoy the type of liberty that the economic marketplace can provide?

Although business fought Progressive and New Deal reforms, long-term opposition was lessened by the fact that most of the resulting regulation applies to a particular industry rather than to firms of all types. This pattern makes it possible for an affected industry to gain influence with those officials who are responsible for regulating its activities. By cultivating close ties to the FCC, for example, the broadcast networks manage to obtain policies that protect their near monopoly on broadcasting and give them high and sustained profits.[6] Although not all industries have as much leverage with their regulators as broadcasting has, it is generally true that industries have not been greatly hampered by the older form of regulation and in many cases have substantially benefited from it.

The Era of New Social Regulation The third wave of regulatory reform, in the 1960s and 1970s, differed from the Progressive and New Deal phases in both its policies and its politics. The third wave has been called the era of "new social regulation" because of the social goals it addressed in its three major policy areas: environmental protection, consumer protection, and worker safety.

Most of the regulatory agencies established during the third wave have broader mandates than those created earlier. They have responsibility not for a single industry but for firms of all types, and their policy scope covers a wide range of activities. The EPA, for example, is charged with regulating environmental pollution of almost any kind by almost any firm. Unlike the older agencies that are run by a commission whose members serve for fixed terms, some of the newer agencies, including the EPA, are headed by a single director who is appointed by the president with Senate approval and is subject to immediate removal by the president.

Because newer agencies such as the EPA have a wide-ranging clientele, no one firm or industry can easily influence agency policy to a great extent. There is also strong group competition in some of the newer regulatory spheres. For example, business lobbies must compete with environmental groups such as the Sierra Club and Greenpeace for influence with the EPA.[7] The firms regulated by the older agencies, in contrast, face no powerful competition in their lobbying activities. Broadcasters, for example, are largely unopposed in their efforts to influence the FCC. Although television viewers and radio listeners have a stake in FCC decisions, they are not well enough organized to petition it effectively.

GOVERNMENT AS PROTECTOR OF THE ENVIRONMENT

Few changes in public opinion and policy during recent decades have been as dramatic as those relating to the environment. Most Americans today recycle some of their garbage, and nearly two-thirds say they are either an active environmentalist or sympathetic to environmental concerns. In the 1960s, few Americans bothered to sort their trash and few could have answered a polling question that asked them whether they were an "environmentalist." The term was not commonly used, and people would not have understood its meaning.

The environmental movement gained impetus with the publication in 1962 of Rachel Carson's *The Silent Spring*.[8] Written at a time when the author was dying of breast cancer, *Silent Spring* revealed the threat of harmful pesticides such as DDT and challenged the notion that scientific progress was an unqualified benefit to society. Carson's appearance at a Senate hearing contributed to legislative action that produced the 1963 Clean Air Act and the 1965 Water Quality Act. It was the first time in the nation's history that the federal government had taken major steps to protect the nation's air, water, and ground from pollution. Today, this protection extends to nearly two hundred harmful forms of emission.

Conservationism: The Older Wave

Although government policy aimed at protecting the air, water, and soil is relatively new, the government has been involved in land conservation for more than a century. The first national park was created at Yellowstone in 1872 and, like the later ones, was established to preserve the nation's natural heritage for generations to come. The national park system serves more than one hundred million visitors each year and covers a total of eighty million acres, an area larger than every state except Alaska, Texas, California, and Montana.

The national parks are run by the National Park Service, an agency within the Department of Interior. Another agency, the U.S. Forest Service, which is located within the Department of Agriculture, manages the national forests, which cover an area more than twice the size of the national parks. They too have been preserved in part to protect America's natural heritage.

However, the nation's parks and forests are subject to a "dual use" policy. They are nature preserves and recreation areas, but they are also rich in natural resources—minerals, forests, and grazing lands. The federal government sells permits to ranchers, timber companies, and mining firms that gives them the right to take some of these resources, a policy that can place their interests in conflict with those of conservationists. A case in point is the spotted owl controversy that erupted in the Pacific Northwest in the late 1980s. The spotted owl is an endangered species found in the region's virgin forests, which are also a mainstay of the region's timber industry. The issue of timber rights in the spotted owl's habitat pitted timber companies, loggers, and logging towns against conservationists in a bitter dispute that was waged through lawsuits, public demonstrations, and the lobbying of Congress and the White House. The timber industry eventually prevailed, although it got fewer logging rights than it was seeking.

Environmentalism: The Newer Wave

The 1960s was the pivotal decade in the federal government's realization that Americans needed protection from the harmful effects of air, water, and ground pollutants. The period was capped by the first Earth Day. Held in the spring of 1970, it was the brainchild of Senator Gaylord Nelson (D-Wis.), who had devoted nearly ten years to finding ways to draw the public's attention to environmental issues. With the first Earth Day, Nelson succeeded to a degree not even he could have imagined: ten thousand grade

Environmental regulations restricting the level of automobile pollution have greatly improved air quality in America's cities. Nevertheless, motor vehicles are the major source of emissions that contribute to global warming.

schools and high schools, two thousand colleges, and one thousand communities participated in the event, which included public rallies and environmental cleanup efforts. Earth Day has been held every year since and is now a worldwide event.

The year 1970 also marked the creation of the Environmental Protection Agency. Within a few months, the EPA was issuing new regulations at such a rapid pace that business firms had difficulty keeping track of all the mandates, much less complying fully with them. Corporations eventually found an ally in President Gerald Ford, who, in a 1975 speech to the National Federation of Industrial Business, claimed that business regulation was costing $150 billion annually, or $2,000 for every American family.[9] Although Ford's estimate exceeded that of economic analysts, his point was not lost on policymakers or the people. The economy was in a slump, and the costs of complying with the new regulations were impeding an economic recovery. Polls indicated a decline in public support for regulatory action.

Since then, environmental protection policy has not been greatly expanded but neither has it greatly contracted. The emphasis has been on administering and amending the laws put into effect in the 1960s and 1970s. Nevertheless, the EPA has a broad mandate to protect America's air and water. In a 2001 decision, the Supreme Court ruled unanimously that the

EPA is to consider only public health and not industry costs in setting air quality standards.[10]

Environmental regulation has had a dramatic effect on air and water quality. Pollution levels today are far below their levels of the 1960s when yellowish-gray fog ("smog") hung over cities like Los Angeles and New York and when bodies of water like the Potomac River and Lake Erie were open sewers.

Although environmental regulation has had positive effects, it remains an ongoing source of controversy. The debate over global warming is an example. The scientific community has concluded that carbon emissions are creating a "greenhouse effect" (the trapping of heat in the atmosphere) that is producing a gradual rise in the earth's temperature. Among the effects is a melting of the polar icecaps, which is raising sea levels and threatening coastal areas. Global warming can be retarded only by controls on emissions but that solution would entail costly technological innovations and cutbacks in economic development. The situation has resulted in heated debate between proponents of economic growth and proponents of environmental protection. So far, the pro-growth side has had the upper hand. The United States is the single largest source of worldwide carbon emissions, and U.S. policymakers have resisted demands at home and from abroad to enact substantial new restrictions on air pollution, fearing that any such policy would harm the U.S. economy.

GOVERNMENT AS PROMOTER OF ECONOMIC INTERESTS

The U.S. government has always made important contributions to the nation's economy. Congress in 1789 gave a boost to the nation's shipping industry by placing a tariff on imported goods carried by foreign ships. Since that first favor, the U.S. government has provided thousands of direct benefits to economic interests. The following sections provide brief examples of a few of these benefits.

Promoting Business

American business is not opposed to government regulation as such. It objects only to regulatory policies that hurt its interests. At various times and in differing ways, as in the case of the FCC and broadcasters, some regulatory agencies have promoted the interests of the very industries they are supposed to regulate in the public interest.

Loans and tax breaks are another way that government promotes business. Firms receive loan guarantees, direct loans, tax credits for capital investments, and tax deductions for capital depreciation. Over the past forty years, the burden of federal taxation has shifted dramatically, from corporations to individuals. A few decades ago, the revenues raised from taxes on corporate income were roughly the same as the revenues raised from taxes on individual income. Today, individual taxpayers carry the heavier burden by a five-to-one ratio. Some analysts do not regard the change as particularly significant, arguing that higher corporate taxes would be passed along to the public anyway in the form of higher prices for goods and services.

The most significant contribution that government makes to business is the traditional services it provides, such as education, transportation, and defense. Colleges and universities, which are funded primarily by governments, furnish business with most of its professional and technical work force and with much of the basic research that goes into product development. The nation's roadways, waterways, and airports are other public sector contributions without which business could not operate. In short, America's business has no bigger booster than government.

Promoting Labor

Laissez-faire thinking dominated government's approach to labor well into the twentieth century. The governing principle, developed by the courts in the early nineteenth century, held that workers had limited rights of collective action. Union activity was regarded as interference with the natural supply of labor and the free setting of wages. Government's hostility toward labor was evident, for example, in the use of U.S. Army troops during the late 1800s to break up strikes.

The 1930s brought significant changes. The key legislation was the National Labor Relations Act of 1935, which guaranteed workers the right to

Striking janitors parade in Beverly Hills, California. Although government provides support for labor through a variety of policies, U.S. workers have less power and fewer rights than their European counterparts, a reflection of America's individualistic culture.

bargain collectively and prohibited business from discriminating against union employees and from unreasonably interfering with union activities. Government has also aided labor over the years by legislating minimum wages and maximum work hours, unemployment benefits, safer and more healthful working conditions, and nondiscriminatory hiring practices.

Although government support for labor extends beyond these examples, it is not nearly as extensive as its assistance to business. America's culture of individualism has resulted in public policies that are less favorable to labor than are those in European countries.

Promoting Agriculture

Until well into the twentieth century, most Americans still lived on farms and in small rural communities. Agriculture was America's dominant business and was assisted by government's land policies. The Homestead Act of 1862, for example, opened government-owned lands to settlement, creating spectacular "land rushes" by offering 160 free acres of government land to each family that staked a claim, built a house, and farmed the land for five years.

Farm programs today provide assistance to small farmers and large commercial enterprises (agribusinesses) and cost the federal government billions of dollars annually. A major goal of this spending is to eliminate some of the risks associated with farming. Weather, world markets, and other factors can radically affect crop and livestock prices, and federal programs are designed to protect farmers from these adverse developments.

In 1996, Congress passed the Freedom to Farm Act. It trimmed the crop allocation and price subsidy programs that had previously characterized U.S. farm policy. The 1996 legislation was designed to let the market largely determine the prices that farmers would receive for their crops and to let farmers themselves decide on the crops they would plant. However, when the six-year expiration date of the 1996 bill was reached in 2002, Congress increased crop subsidies and expanded them to include more crops, thus abandoning the free-market principle that was the basis for the earlier legislation. The 2002 Farm Bill was a response to sluggish agricultural markets and depressed farm incomes, and it puts farmers in line for hundreds of billions of dollars in government assistance in the coming years. At present, federal subsidies account for more than a third of net farm income.

FISCAL POLICY: GOVERNMENT AS MANAGER OF ECONOMY, I

Until the 1930s, the U.S. government adhered to the prevailing free-market theory and made no attempt to maintain the stability of the economy as a

| TABLE | 15-2 | FISCAL POLICY: A SUMMARY |

Taxing and spending levels can be adjusted in order to affect economic conditions.

Problem	Fiscal Policy Actions
Low productivity and high unemployment	Demand side: increase spending Supply side: cut business taxes
Excess production and high inflation	Decrease spending Increase taxes

whole. The economy, which was regarded as largely self-regulating, was fairly prosperous, but it collapsed periodically, resulting in widespread joblessness and financial loss.

The greatest economic catastrophe in the nation's history—the Great Depression of the 1930s—finally brought an end to traditional economics. Franklin D. Roosevelt's emergency spending and job programs, designed to stimulate the economy and put Americans back to work, heralded the change. Roosevelt's efforts to stimulate the economy were controversial at the time, but today government is expected to have ongoing policies that will contribute to economic growth and stability.

Taxing and Spending Policy

The government's efforts to maintain a thriving economy are made mainly through its taxing and spending decisions, which together are referred to as its fiscal policy (see Table 15-2).

The annual federal budget is the foundation of fiscal policy. Thousands of pages in length, the budget allocates federal expenditures among government programs and identifies the revenues—taxes, social insurance receipts, and borrowed funds—that will be used to pay for these programs (see Figure 15-1). From one perspective, the budget is the national government's allocation of costs and benefits. Every federal program benefits some interest, whether it be farmers who get price supports, defense firms that obtain military contracts, or retirees who receive monthly social security checks. Not surprisingly, the process of enacting the annual federal budget is a highly political one. Agencies and interests compete for federal dollars.

From another standpoint, that of fiscal policy, the budget is a device for stimulating or dampening economic growth. Changes in overall levels of spending and taxing are a means of smoothing out the economy's normal ups and downs.

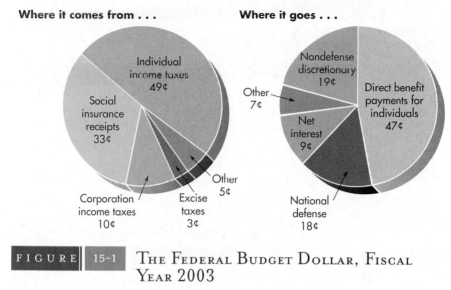

Where it comes from . . .   **Where it goes . . .**

FIGURE   15-1   THE FEDERAL BUDGET DOLLAR, FISCAL YEAR 2003

Source: Office of Management and Budget.

Fiscal policy has its origins in the economic theories of John Maynard Keynes. In *The General Theory of Employment, Interest, and Money* (1936), Keynes noted that employers become overly cautious during a depression and will not expand production, even as wages drop. Challenging the traditional idea that government should draw back during depressions, Keynes claimed that severe economic downturns can be shortened only by increased government spending. Keynes said that government should engage in **deficit spending**—spending more than it gets from taxes, which can be accomplished through the borrowing and printing of money. By placing additional money in the hands of consumers and investors, government can stimulate production, employment, and spending and thus promote recovery.[11]

According to Keynesian theory, the government's response should be commensurate with the severity of the problem. During an **economic depression**—an exceptionally steep and sustained downturn in the economy—the government should engage in massive new spending programs to hasten the recovery. During a less severe **economic recession**, new government spending should be less substantial.

Demand-Side Stimulation Keynes's theory focused on government's efforts to stimulate consumer spending. This **demand-side economics** emphasizes the consumer "demand" component of the supply-demand equation. When the economy is sluggish, the government can increase its spending, thus placing more money in consumers' hands. With additional money to spend, consumers buy more goods and services. This increased

John Maynard Keynes
(1883–1946)

Trained in mathematics and economics, John Maynard Keynes developed a theory of government spending and taxation that became the basis for government efforts to manage the economy through fiscal policy. His theory developed in part from his belief that there would be dire economic and hence dire political consequences from the heavy reparation levied on Germany after World War I. When the world economy then went into a slump in 1929, Keynes set about developing a theory of economic cycles. The result was *The General Theory of Employment, Interest, and Money*, published in 1936.

demand, in turn, stimulates businesses to produce more goods and hire more workers. In this way, government spending contributes to economic recovery.

Although heightened spending is a tool that government can employ during a severe economic crisis, it is not a sensible response to every economic dip. Its application is affected by government's overall financial situation. In the early 1990s, for example, the U.S. economy was in its longest downturn since World War II, but policymakers chose not to boost federal spending temporarily as a means of blunting the recession. The reason was simple enough. During the previous two decades, there had been a **budget deficit**—each year, the federal government had spent more than it had received in tax and other revenues. The result was a huge **national debt**, which is the total cumulative amount that the U.S. government owes to creditors. By the early 1990s, the debt had reached $4 trillion, and an enormous amount of money was required each year merely to pay the interest on the national debt. Interest payments were larger than the entire federal budget as recently as 1970 and were roughly the total of all federal income taxes paid by Americans who lived west of the Mississippi River. This drain on the government's resources made it politically difficult for policymakers to increase the level of government spending in order to boost the economy.

The situation changed dramatically in the late 1990s. In 1998, for the first time since 1969, the U.S. government had a **balanced budget**—revenues from taxes were equal to government expenditures. Thereafter, there was a **budget surplus**—the federal government received more in tax and other revenues than it spent. The surplus was attributable to a surging U.S. economy that was in the midst of its longest period of sustained growth in the country's history. With more people working and with the stock market moving ever higher, tax revenues had increased and government welfare expenditures had declined. The rosy budget picture also reflected the fiscal discipline of the Clinton administration and the Republican Congress, which had slowed the growth in federal expenditures.

However, the turnaround was short-lived. An economic downturn in 2001, which was accelerated by the terrorist bombings of the World Trade Center and the Pentagon on September 11 of that year, produced a budget deficit of substantial proportion that is expected to last for a number of years (see Figure 15-2). The severity of the deficit limited policymakers' willingness to apply demand-side measures to hasten an economic recovery. Nevertheless, some steps were taken, including an increase in the number of weeks that laid-off workers were eligible to receive unemployment payments from the government.

The importance of demand-side fiscal policy, however, cannot be measured only by its effect during economic downturns. Although the United States has had recessionary periods since the 1930s, none of these downturns has been anywhere near the severity of the Great Depression. One reason is that government spending is now at permanently high levels. Each month, for example, roughly forty million Americans receive a social security check from the government. In turn, they spend it on food, clothing, housing, entertainment, and other goods and services. They pump billions of dollars each month into the U.S. economy, which creates jobs and income for millions of other Americans. And social security is only one—albeit the largest—of the federal spending programs. Every day, the federal government spends about $4 billion, which is more than the typical large corporation pumps into the economy during an entire year. The U.S. economy thus has a constant demand-side stimulus: government spending on an ongoing and massive scale.

Supply-Side Stimulation A fiscal policy alternative to demand-side stimulation is **supply-side economics,** which emphasizes the business (supply) component of the supply-demand equation.[12] Supply-side theory was a cornerstone of President Reagan's economic program. He believed that economic growth could occur as easily from stimulation of the business sector as from stimulation of consumer demand. "Reaganomics" included substantial tax breaks for businesses and upper-income individuals.

The Reagan administration overestimated the stimulus effect of its tax-cuts policy. It had estimated that the increased tax revenues from increased

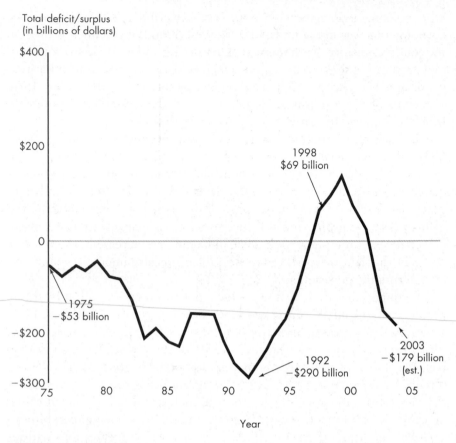

Total deficit/surplus
(in billions of dollars)

| FIGURE | 15-2 | **The Federal Budget Deficit/Surplus, 1975–2003** |

The federal government ran a budget deficit until 1998, at which time a surplus that was expected to last for years occurred. In 2001, however, the surplus quickly disappeared as a result of an economic downturn, costs associated with the war on terrorism, and a cut in federal taxes.
Source: U.S. Treasury Department, 2003

business activity would soon offset the loss of revenue from reducing the tax rate. However, the loss from the tax cuts was much greater than the gain in revenues from the economic growth that followed. As a result, the tax cuts contributed to the growing budget deficit.

Despite this discouraging aspect, Reagan's supply-side measures contributed to the economic growth that began in the United States during the 1980s. The Reagan tax cuts allowed business firms to spend more on capital investments and enabled higher-income Americans to place more money into the stock markets, which provided additional funds for business investment.

★ STATES IN THE NATION

Federal Taxing and Spending

Fiscal policy (the federal government's taxing and spending policies) varies in its effect on the states. The residents of some states pay a lot more in federal taxes than they receive in benefits from federal spending (the leader here is Connecticut, where the deficit is $2,820 per person on average). The residents of other states get more back from federal spending programs than they contribute in taxes (the leader here is New Mexico, where the gain is $3,944 per person on average).

Q. Why are most of the "winners" in the South?

A. The federal taxes that originate in a state reflect its wealth. In contrast, many federal assistance programs are designed to help poorer people and areas. The South is less affluent than other regions.

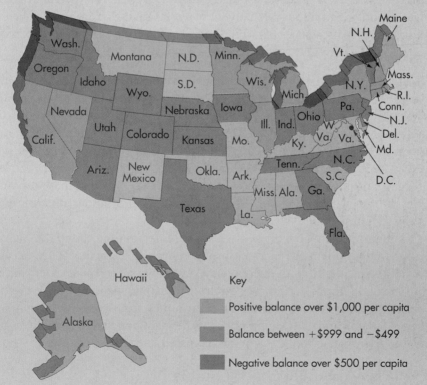

Key

Positive balance over $1,000 per capita

Balance between +$999 and −$499

Negative balance over $500 per capita

Source: Created by author from data provided by Taubman Center for State and Local Government, John F. Kennedy School of Government, Harvard University, December 2000.

Supply-side ideas also underpinned some economic policies of the 1990s. After the Republicans assumed control of Congress in 1995, for example, they reduced the **capital-gains tax,** which is the tax that individuals pay on gains in capital investments, such as property and stocks. A reduction in the capital-gains tax increases the incentive for individuals to invest their money in capital markets. Firms use this money to expand their operations and markets, thereby creating jobs and increasing the supply of goods, each of which can stimulate consumer demand, which contributes to economic growth.

Supply-side economics also defined several of George W. Bush's tax initiatives. The Economic Growth and Tax Relief Reconciliation Act of 2001 included both demand-side measures (for example, immediate cash rebates to taxpayers) and supply-side measures (for example, a phased-in reduction in the marginal tax rate on wealthy taxpayers). Then, in 2003, Bush proposed that the reduction in the top marginal rate be phased in more rapidly and that stock dividends not be taxed at all. The joint Urban Institute–Brookings Institution Tax Policy Center estimated that the wealthiest 1 percent of taxpayers would get more than 42 percent of the tax savings from these policies. Bush argued that the tax cuts would increase business investment, thereby contributing to economic growth.

Controlling Inflation High unemployment and low production are only two of the economic problems that government is called on to solve. Another is **inflation,** which is an increase in the average level of prices of goods and services. Before the late 1960s, inflation was a minor problem: prices rose by less than 4 percent annually. But inflation rose sharply during the last years of the Vietnam War and remained high throughout the 1970s, reaching a postwar record rate of 13 percent in 1979. Since then, the annual inflation rate has been about 4 percent, and concern about inflation has lessened significantly.

To fight inflation, government can apply remedies opposite to those used to fight unemployment and low productivity. Inflation normally occurs when jobs are plentiful and people have extra money to spend. Demand is high in such periods, and prices go up. By cutting spending or by raising personal income taxes, government takes money from consumers, thus reducing demand and dampening prices. (The main policy tool for addressing inflation is monetary policy, which is discussed later in the chapter.)

The Process and Politics of Fiscal Policy

The president and Congress jointly determine fiscal policy, mainly through the annual budgetary process. The Constitution grants Congress the power to tax and spend, but the president, as chief executive, has a major role in shaping the budget. The president's veto power also provides a strong tool when negotiating the budget with Congress. In reality, the budgetary process involves give-and-take between Congress and the president, as each tries to exert influence over the final budget.[13]

The Budgetary Process The budgetary process is a very elaborate one, as could be expected when billions of dollars in federal spending are at issue. From beginning to end, the process lasts a year and a half (see Figure 15-3).

The budgetary process begins in the executive branch when the president, in consultation with the Office of Management and Budget (OMB), establishes general budget guidelines. The OMB is part of the Executive Office of the President (see Chapter 12) and takes its directives from the president. Hundreds of agencies and thousands of programs are covered by the budget, and the OMB uses the president's decisions to determine the

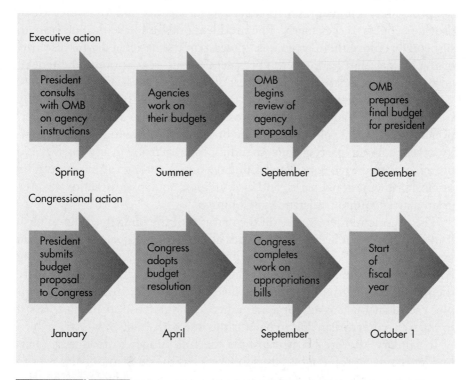

Executive action

President consults with OMB on agency instructions — Spring

Agencies work on their budgets — Summer

OMB begins review of agency proposals — September

OMB prepares final budget for president — December

Congressional action

President submits budget proposal to Congress — January

Congress adopts budget resolution — April

Congress completes work on appropriations bills — September

Start of fiscal year — October 1

FIGURE 15-3 FEDERAL BUDGETARY PROCESS

The budget begins with the president's instructions to the agencies and ends when Congress enacts the budget. The entire process spans about eighteen months.

instructions that will guide each agency's budget preparations. For example, each agency is assigned a budget ceiling within which it must work.

The agencies receive these instructions in the spring and then work through the summer to develop a detailed agency budget, taking into account their existing programs and any new or proposed ones. These agency budgets then go to the OMB in September for a full review that invariably includes further consultation with each agency. The agency budgets are then finalized and combined into the full budget. Throughout, the OMB is in close touch with the White House to ensure that the budget items conform to the president's objectives.

The OMB usually acts to restrain the agencies since they naturally tend to want more money whereas the OMB has the job of matching the budget to the president's priorities. In point of fact, however, the president does not have any real say over most of the budget. About two-thirds of the budget involves mandatory spending. This spending is authorized by current law, and the government must allocate and spend the money unless the law itself is rescinded, which is unlikely. Examples are social security and Medicare, which provide benefits to the elderly. The president does not have the authority to suspend or reduce these programs. Interest on the national debt is also part of the budget, and here too the president has no real option. The federal government is obligated to pay interest on the money it has borrowed.

The OMB focuses on the third of the budget that involves discretionary spending, which includes such areas as defense, foreign aid, education, national parks, space exploration, public broadcasting, and highways. In reality, even a large part of this spending is not truly discretionary. No president would even consider slashing defense spending to almost nothing or closing the national parks, and even modest cuts in a discretionary program may encounter resistance in Congress.

The president, then, works on the margins of the budget, trying to push it in directions that are consistent with administration goals. The effort in many policy areas consists of a modest increase or decrease in spending compared with the previous year. There are also always a few areas where the president will attempt a more dramatic adjustment. In 2003, for example, President Bush asked for a large increase in defense spending to assist in the war on terrorism and to pay for the war with Iraq.

In January, the president transmits the full budget to Congress. This budget is only a proposal because Congress has the constitutional power to appropriate funds. In reviewing the president's proposed budget, Congress relies heavily on the Congressional Budget Office (CBO), which, as was discussed in Chapter 11, is the congressional equivalent to the OMB. The CBO reviews the items in the budget and develops estimates of their costs.

If the CBO believes that an agency has misjudged the amount of money that is needed to meet its legislatively required programs, it will bring this information to the attention of the appropriate committees of Congress. Similarly, if the CBO concludes that the OMB has miscalculated how much the government can be expected to receive in taxes and other revenues, committees will be notified of the discrepency.

The key congressional committees in the budgetary process are the budget and the appropriations committees. The House and Senate Budget Committees are responsible for drafting a "budget resolution," which includes projections on total spending, total revenues, and allocations between the mandatory and discretionary spending categories. These guidelines are then submitted to the full House and Senate for approval. The budget ceilings that are part of the resolution place a tentative limit on how much money will be allocated for each spending area.

The House Appropriations Committee through its subcommittees then takes on the primary task of reviewing the budget items, which includes hearings with each federal agency. There are thirteen such subcommittees, and each has responsibility for a substantive area, such as defense or agriculture. Agency budgets are invariably changed at this stage. A subcommittee may cut an agency's budget because it believes that the agency's work is not very important or that the agency has asked for more funds than it needs for its programs. Or the subcommittee may decide to increase an agency's budget beyond what the president has requested. Whichever, each subcommittee leaves its own mark on each agency's budget. The subcommittees' recommendations are then submitted to the House Appropriations Committee for final review and submission to the full House for a vote. The Senate Appropriations Committee and its subcommittees conduct a similar process, but the Senate is a smaller body and its review of agency requests is normally less thorough. To some degree, the Senate committee and its subcommittees serve as a "court of appeals" for agencies that have had their budget requests reduced by the House.

During Congress's work on the budget, the president's recommendations undergo varying degrees of change. The priorities of a majority in Congress are never exactly those of the president, even when they are of the same party. When they are of opposite parties, their priorities may differ greatly.

After the work of the appropriations committees is completed and has been approved by the full House and Senate, differences in the Senate and House versions of the appropriations bills are reconciled in conference committee (see Chapter 11). The legislation is then sent to the president for approval or veto. The threat of a presidential veto is often enough to persuade Congress to accept many of the president's recommendations. In the end, the budget inevitably reflects both presidential and congressional priorities. Neither branch ever gets everything that it wants, but each branch always gets some of what it wants.

Once the budget has been passed by both the House and Senate and is signed by the president, it takes effect on October 1, which is the starting date of the federal government's fiscal year. If agreement on the budget has not been reached by October 1, temporary funding is required in order to maintain government operations. In late 1995, President Clinton and the Republican Congress deadlocked to such an extent on budgetary issues that they could not even agree on temporary funding. Their standoff twice forced a brief shutdown of nonessential government activities.

Partisan Differences Partisan politics is a significant part of fiscal policy. The Democratic coalition has traditionally included the majority of lower-income and working-class Americans. Accordingly, the party's leaders are sensitive to rising unemployment because blue-collar workers are often the first and most deeply affected. Democrats in Washington have usually responded to a sluggish economy with increased government spending (demand-side fiscal policy), which offers direct help to the unemployed and stimulates consumption. Virtually every increase in federal unemployment benefits during the past fifty years, for example, has been initiated by Democratic officeholders.

Republican leaders are more likely than Democrats to be concerned about inflation. It attacks the purchasing power of all Americans, including higher-income individuals who are less likely than lower-income persons to be affected by rising unemployment rates. Inflation also raises the cost of doing business, because firms must pay higher interest rates for the money they borrow. Since business and the middle class make up a significant chunk of its electoral base, the Republican party usually wants to hold government spending at a level where the inflationary effects are small.

Tax policy also has partisan dimensions. Democratic policymakers have typically sought tax policies that help working-class and lower-middle-class Americans. Democrats have favored a **graduated** (or progressive) **personal income tax,** in which the tax rate goes up substantially as income rises. Republicans have preferred to keep taxes on upper incomes at a relatively low level, contending that this policy encourages the savings and investment that foster economic growth (supply-side fiscal policy). These differences were evident, for example, in the battle over the Economic Growth and Tax Relief Reconciliation Act of 2001. Proposed by President Bush, the legislation contained the largest tax cut since 1981. The chief beneficiaries were upper-income taxpayers. In both the Senate and the House of Representatives, the bill had the overwhelming support of Republicans and very little support from Democrats. In the Senate, for example, only two Republicans voted against it whereas thirty-nine Democrats did so.[14] (Tax policy is discussed further in Chapter 16).

MONETARY POLICY: GOVERNMENT AS MANAGER OF ECONOMY, II

Fiscal policy is not the only instrument of economic management available to government; another is **monetary policy,** which is based on manipulation of the amount of money in circulation (see Table 15-3). Monetarists such as the economist Milton Friedman hold that control of the money supply is the key to sustaining a healthy economy. Too much money in circulation contributes to inflation because too many dollars are chasing too few goods, which drives up prices. Too little money in circulation results in a slowing economy and rising unemployment, because consumers lack the ready cash and easy credit required to push spending levels up. Monetarists believe in

TABLE 15-3 MONETARY POLICY: A SUMMARY	
The money supply can be adjusted in order to affect economic conditions.	
Problems	**Monetary Policy Action by Federal Reserve**
Low productivity and high unemployment (require an increase in the money supply)	Buys securities Lowers interest rate on loans to member banks Lowers cash reserve that member banks must deposit in Federal Reserve System
Excess productivity and high inflation (require a decrease in the money supply)	Sells securities Raises interest rate on loans to member banks Raises cash reserves that member banks must deposit in Federal Reserve System

tightening or loosening the money supply as a way of slowing or invigorating the economy.

The Fed

Control over the money supply rests not with the president or Congress but with the Federal Reserve System (known as the "Fed"), which was created by the Federal Reserve Act of 1913. The Fed has a board of governors whose seven members serve for fourteen years, except for the chair and vice chair, who serve for four years. All members are appointed by the president with the approval of the Senate. The Fed regulates the activities of all national banks and those state banks that choose to become members of the Federal Reserve System—about six thousand banks in all.

The Fed decides how much money to add or to subtract from the economy, seeking a balance that will permit steady growth without causing an unacceptable level of inflation. The most visible way that the Fed affects the money supply is by lowering or raising the interest rates charged on money borrowed from the Federal Reserve by its member banks. When the Fed raises the interest rate, banks also tend to raise the rate they charge for new loans, which discourages borrowing and thus reduces the amount of money entering the economy. Conversely, by lowering the interest rate, the Fed encourages firms and individuals to borrow from banks, which increases the money supply.

The Fed also affects the money supply by selling and buying government securities in the open market. By offering securities at an attractive price, the Fed encourages investors to exchange their cash for securities, thus taking money out of the economy. On the other hand, when the Fed buys securities that people hold, it puts cash into their hands, thus expanding the money supply.

The third and final way the Fed affects the money supply is by raising or lowering the cash reserve that member banks are required to deposit with the Federal Reserve. This reserve is a proportion of each member's total deposits. By increasing the reserve rate, the Fed takes money from member banks and thus takes it out of circulation. When the Fed lowers the reserve rate, banks have more money available and can make more loans to consumers and investors.

Economists debate the relative effectiveness of monetary policy and fiscal policy, but monetary policy has one obvious advantage: it can be implemented more quickly. The Fed can adjust interest and reserve rates on short notice, thus providing the economy a psychological boost to go along with the financial effect of a change in the money supply. In contrast, changes in fiscal policy usually take much longer to implement. Congress is normally a slow-acting institution, and new taxing and spending programs ordinarily require a substantial preparation period before they can be put into effect. Moreover, Republicans and Democrats are often divided over which fiscal policy tool to use—taxing or spending—and may not be able to reach agreement on how to respond to a faltering economy. In 2003, for example, economic-stimulus legislation was delayed because Republicans wanted it to be rooted in tax cuts while Democrats pushed for spending on jobs-related programs.

The Politics of the Fed

The greater flexibility of monetary policy has positioned the Fed as the institution with primary policy responsibility for keeping the U.S. economy on a steady course. The Fed's power can easily be exaggerated. The U.S. economy is subject to a lot of influences, and the Fed's impact is relatively modest. Nevertheless, the Fed is a vital component of U.S. economic policy and has become increasingly so.[15]

The power of the Fed raises important questions. One is the issue of representation: whose interests does the Fed serve—those of the public as a whole or those of the banking sector? The Fed is not a wholly impartial body. Although it makes decisions in the context of economic theories and projections, it is "the bankers' bank" and is protective of monied interests. The Fed is typically more concerned with rising inflation, which erodes the value of money, than with rising unemployment, which has its greatest impact on people at the bottom of the economic ladder. The Fed tends to hike interest rates when signs of rising inflation appear. Higher rates have the effect of slowing inflation but also slow job and income growth.

A related issue is one of accountability: should the Fed, an unelected body, have so much power? Although appointed by the president, members of the Federal Reserve Board are not subject to removal. They serve for fixed terms and are relatively insulated from political pressures, including the changes that take place through elections. Moreover, the Fed announces its decisions after closed-door meetings, although it has implemented a policy of signaling beforehand the policies it is likely to announce. Of course, the Fed, as a banking institution, has a vested interest in a healthy economy (too much inflation erodes banks' returns on loans, too much unemployment decreases demand for loans) and thus operates within its own system of checks and balances. Nevertheless, the restraints on the Fed are much weaker than are those on popularly elected institutions.

At the time the Fed was created in 1913, economists had not yet "invented" the theory of monetary policy, and the Fed had no role in the management of the nation's economy. If the Fed were being created today, it

Fed chairman Alan Greenspan testifies before a congressional committee. Greenspan has at times been called "the most powerful man in America."

would likely have a different structure, although there is general agreement among policymakers that some degree of independence is desirable.

The Fed is a preeminent example of *elitist* politics at work. Congress at some future point may decide that an overly independent Fed can no longer be tolerated and may bring monetary policy more closely under the control of elected institutions. Whether this move happens may hinge on the Fed's willingness to exercise power sparingly and in the broad interests of society. (The economic policies of the federal government in the areas of social welfare and national security are discussed in the next two chapters.)

Summary

Although private enterprise is the main force in the American economic system, the federal government plays a significant role through its policies to regulate, promote, and stimulate the economy.

Regulatory policy is designed to achieve efficiency and equity, which require government to intervene, for example, to maintain competitive trade practices (an efficiency goal) and to protect vulnerable parties in economic transactions (an equity goal). Many of the regulatory decisions of the federal government, particularly those of older agencies (such as the Federal Communication Commission), are made largely in the context of group politics. Business lobbies have an especially strong influence on the regulatory policies that affect them. In general, newer regulatory agencies (such as the Environmental Protection Agency) have policy responsibilities that are broader in scope and apply to a larger number of

/pattersonwtp5

firms than those of the older agencies. As a result, the policy decisions of newer agencies are more often made in the context of party politics. Republican administrations are less vigorous in their regulation of business than are Democratic administrations.

Business is the major beneficiary of the federal government's efforts to promote economic interests. A large number of programs, including those that provide loans and research grants, are designed to assist businesses, which are also protected from failure through such measures as tariffs and favorable tax laws. Labor, for its part, obtains government assistance through laws concerning such matters as worker safety, the minimum wage, and collective bargaining. Yet America's individualistic culture tends to put labor at a disadvantage, keeping it less powerful than business in its dealings with the government. Agriculture is another economic sector that depends substantially on government's help, particularly in the form of income stabilization programs, such as those that provide crop subsidies and price supports.

The U.S. government pursues policies that are designed to protect and conserve the environment. A few decades ago, the environment was not a policy priority. Today, there are many programs in this area, and the public has become an active participant in efforts to conserve resources and prevent exploitation of the environment.

Through its fiscal and monetary policies, Washington attempts to maintain a strong and stable economy—one that is characterized by high productivity, high employment, and low inflation. Fiscal policy is based on government decisions in regard to spending and taxing, which are aimed at either stimulating a weak economy or dampening an overheated (inflationary) economy. Fiscal policy is worked out through Congress and the president and is consequently responsive to political pressures. However, since it is difficult to raise taxes or cut programs, the government's ability to apply fiscal policy as an economic remedy is limited. Monetary policy is based on the money supply and works through the Federal Reserve System, which is headed by a board whose members hold office for fixed terms. The Fed is a relatively independent body, a fact that has given rise to questions as to whether it should have such a large role in national economic policy.

Key Terms

balanced budget	demand-side economics
budget deficit	deregulation
budget surplus	economic depression
capital-gains tax	economic recession
deficit spending	economy

efficiency
equity (in relation to economic
    policy)
externalities
fiscal policy
graduated personal income tax

inflation
laissez-faire doctrine
monetary policy
national debt
regulation
supply-side economics

SUGGESTED READINGS

Friedman, Milton, and Walter Heller. *Monetary Versus Fiscal Policy*. New
    York: Norton, 1969. Opposing arguments by a leading monetarist and
    a leading Keynesian.
Gonzalez, George A. *Corporate Power and the Environment: The Political
    Economy of U.S. Environmental Policy*. Lanham, Md.: Rowman and
    Littlefield, 2001. A study of the politics and policy of the
    environmental issue.
Harris, Richard A., and Sidney M. Milkis. *The Politics of Regulatory Change:
    A Tale of Two Agencies*, 2d ed. New York: Oxford University Press,
    1996. An analysis of the Reagan, Bush, and Clinton administrations'
    approaches to regulatory policy.
Mayer, Martin. *Fed: The Inside Story of How the World's Most Powerful
    Financial Institution Drives the Markets*. New York: Free Press, 2001. A
    look at the Fed's impact on the economy and politics.
Schick, Allen, with Felix Lostracco. *The Federal Budget: Politics, Policy,
    Process*, rev. ed. Washington, D.C.: Brookings Institution Press, 2000. A
    forward look at the federal budget.
Shaiko, Ronald G. *Voices and Echoes for the Environment*. New York:
    Columbia University Press, 1999. The representation and
    communication of environmental groups.
Young, H. Peyton. *Equity: In Theory and Practice*. Princeton, N.J.:
    Princeton University Press, 1995. A systematic assessment of what
    economic equity entails in theory and actual situations.

LIST OF WEBSITES

http://www.bog.frb.fed.us The Federal Reserve System's website; it
    describes the Fed, provides information about its current activities, and
    has links to some of the Fed's national and international information
    sources.

http://www.epa.gov The Environmental Protection Agency (EPA)
   website; it has information on environmental policy and regulations,
   EPA projects, and related subjects.

http://www.ftc.gov The Federal Trade Commission, one of the older
   regulatory agencies; its website describes the range of its activities.

http://www.whitehouse.gov/WH/EOP/OMB The home page of the
   Office of Management and Budget; it contains a summary of the annual
   federal budget and describes the OMB's operations and responsibilities.

POLITICS IN THEORY AND PRACTICE

Thinking: What are the tools of fiscal policy and monetary policy? What
are the advantages and disadvantages of these two approaches to
managing the economy?

Acting: In recent decades, Americans have become increasingly aware of
how their actions can harm the environment and what they might do to
lessen the effect. Consider taking a personal inventory of your impact on
the environment. Think about such things as your driving, eating, and
living habits. For example, do you habitually turn off the lights when you
leave a room? This simple practice conserves energy and reduces the
pollution associated with energy production. A number of websites
contain suggestions on what individuals can do to reduce harmful
environmental effects. The following site is one of them:
http://www.crd.bc.ca/rte/report/suggest.htm.

𝕿𝖍𝖊 𝕹𝖊𝖜 𝖄𝖔𝖗𝖐 𝕿𝖎𝖒𝖊𝖘   **reading 15**

Will Reforms with Few Teeth Be Able to Bite?

by Stephen Labation

When the stock market was booming in the 1990s, some corporations manipulated their earnings records in order to boost the price of their stock. This manipulation came to light in 2001 and 2002 when the stock market declined sharply and corporations such as Enron and Worldcom were no longer able to sustain their deceptive practices. These practices were ruinous to investors who bought the overvalued stock and to employees who lost their jobs and pensions when the corporations for which they worked were plunged into bankruptcy. In this September 22, 2002, article, New York Times *reporter Stephen Labaton describes the regulatory measures that Washington policymakers enacted in response to corporate abuses.*

WASHINGTON—Roughly three weeks from adjourning for the election campaign season, Congress has all but completed its response to the most scandalous corporate year in generations.

A few relatively minor hearings may yet be held, like one this week in the House on the complex swaps between Qwest Communications and Global Crossing that some investigators believe may be fraudulent. And Senate leaders vow to take up a bill to tighten rules on retirement plans, although the current versions are significantly watered down from those proposed shortly after disclosures of rampant problems with 401(k) plans at companies like Enron.

But the momentum on these issues is already fading as Congress focuses on the possibility of war with Iraq.

Moreover, the one major corporate corruption law completed by Congress, the Sarbanes-Oxley bill, requires the Securities and Exchange Commission to issue scores of regulations that will ultimately determine if the law is effective or toothless.

"We won't know for some time whether Washington overreacted or underreacted," said Roger B. Porter, a professor of business and government at Harvard who served as a senior White House official under the first President Bush and now serves on four corporate boards.

But some experts are already pointing out that lawmakers left a variety of significant issues unaddressed.

Congress refused, for instance, to require companies to account for stock options issued to executives as expenses on corporate balance sheets. That has led to a sharp divide between some companies, like Coca-Cola, that will now expense such options and others, like Intel, that will not.

Congress did not restore an old law that had held investment banks, lawyers and accountants liable in investor lawsuits as "aiders and abettors" of fraud. Its restoration could have given investors a major new way to go after advisers to companies.

The lawmakers did not change how directors are selected in a corporate voting system, which generally offers shareholders no choice of competing slates of candidates. And lawmakers left to regulators the task of addressing abuses in new stock offerings.

Moreover, investor groups view as weak the new rules intended to curtail conflicts of interests between stock analysts and investment bankers at the same companies. No efforts have been made to rein in huge compensation packages of executives, although the S.E.C. may require that they be disclosed more accurately. And Congress did not take any action that would reduce the conflicts of interest of directors.

But for all the unaddressed areas, many people who have urged change are pleased with what was accomplished this year.

"Washington has done a whole lot better than we ever would have dreamed, but it was only because we had a fraud a week for a few months," said Sarah Teslik, executive director of the Council of Institutional Investors, which represents many large shareholders like pension funds and labor unions. "It covered a lot of territory. It also didn't cover some key territory that we would have liked to have covered, but that is simply too controversial."

This summer, after the huge collapse of Worldcom, President Bush signed the Sarbanes-Oxley bill, which contained many provisions opposed by his allies in Congress. The measure creates a new regulatory body for accountants, imposes faster and tougher disclosure requirements for public companies and requires corporate lawyers to take a more active role in ferreting out fraud.

It requires members of audit committees to be independent, restricts the consulting activities of auditors and prohibits most corporate loans to senior executives. It creates a federal crime of securities fraud. And it lengthens the statute of limitations for civil securities fraud claims.

The legislation, written primarily by Senator Paul Sarbanes, Democrat of Maryland, and pushed through the House of Representatives by Michael G. Oxley, Republican of Ohio, is already beginning to change the way corporate boardrooms and management suites do business.

Senator Sarbanes, in an interview last week, said he was heartened to hear the story of one company director who described a presentation to his board.

"He went to a meeting that had a big chart with columns," Mr. Sarbanes said. "One column showed what was required by the Securities and Exchange Commission. Another showed what was required by the self-regulatory organizations and the exchanges. Another showed what the company was already doing and a fourth showed what needed to be done."

"You have a real process that is working around the country," he added.

While many provisions in the Sarbanes-Oxley bill impose new requirements on corporate managers and directors, they do not impose significant new liability on them. For instance, the requirement that chief executives and chief financial officers certify their financial statements does not change their exposure to criminal and civil prosecution. But it does seem likely to make them more careful. "The threat of liability is no different, but the awareness of the sense of right and wrong, the procedures to implement that, seem to be heightened," said Michael Klausner, a corporate law specialist at Stanford. "This is an interesting example, if it works, of the interaction of law and professional ethics."

But the lawmakers have also left one important issue, revisions in the laws governing worker retirement funds, to the very end of the session. Senator Tom Daschle, the majority leader, said in a recent interview that retirement funds and domestic security are the most important issues remaining for Capitol Hill. But it remains uncertain whether Congress will be able to adopt a bill on retirement funds, particularly because it presents a final legislative vehicle for Democrats and Republicans to add controversial new tax reductions and minimum-wage proposals that could sink the entire measure.

Congress has already signaled that it will not adopt some stringent pension protection proposals in the retirement funds bill, like a requirement that companies force workers to diversify their investments and another that employee representatives serve on trustee boards that manage 401(k) plans.

The bill would permit employees to sell company stock held in their 401(k)'s, however, in as little as three years after it is received. A similar bill that passed in the House last April would also make it easier for workers to sell company stock.

Lawmakers say that despite the huge sums of money lost by investors in their portfolios and retirement funds, voters are unlikely to make their decisions in November based on the failure of Washington to adopt broader reforms.

"I don't think it's an issue necessarily that either party could take a lot of advantage of," Mr. Daschle said. "Even though the president opposed us and fought us, at the end of the day, he was there and had a bill-signing ceremony, so I think he's been able to minimize whatever political exposure he and his party had on the issue."

Some experts, like Charles Bowsher, the former comptroller general and head of the General Accounting Office, have suggested that the government take broader steps to discourage market bubbles by reducing the amount of borrowing by investors and companies. They have proposed measures like reducing the margin—the amount of stock that can be bought with borrowed money—or more tightly regulating complicated derivative securities, which would make it harder to bet on a market's direction with borrowed money. But such measures are thought to have no chance of passage.

"Most people don't realize how much leverage you can put in a balance sheet if your friendly neighborhood banker shows you how to do it," Mr. Bowsher said. "That's what Enron and Dynegy and many other companies did."

"What the government has the ability to do is to try to prevent leverage that can contribute to a bubble getting out of control," he added. "But there are very formidable political forces on the other side of the issue. I remember when we were issuing reports on derivatives in the 1990's how much pressure we got from the banks in New York. Every time there is a scandal, they swoop into town with their lobbyists and they are able to convince people."

What's Your Opinion?

Do you think Congress should have enacted more substantial policy reforms? What might explain Congress's limited response to the recent corporate scandals?

CHAPTER 16

WELFARE AND EDUCATION POLICY: PROVIDING FOR PERSONAL SECURITY AND NEED

❝We the people of the United States, in order to . . . promote the general welfare . . .**❞**

PREAMBLE, CONSTITUTION OF THE UNITED STATES

It happened with surprising speed. In just five years, the number of people on the welfare rolls plummeted by 48 percent nationwide. Since 1994, the number of families on welfare had declined by more than 80 percent in Wisconsin, Idaho, and Wyoming, and by more than half in twenty-three other states. There were only three states—Hawaii, Rhode Island, and New Mexico—in which the drop was less than 20 percent (see "States in the Nation"). The trend defied what had been called welfare policy's "reverse gravity" law: welfare rolls that went up but never came down.

Two factors were driving the change. One was the booming national economy. Unemployment had steadily declined, and as more Americans went into the work force, the demand for welfare decreased. The second factor was the 1996 Welfare Reform Act, which had shortened welfare eligibility and required that able-bodied recipients find work or risk loss of benefits. The question on policymakers' minds was the proportion of the decline that was attributable to the change in the welfare system. Representative Clay Shaw Jr. (R-Fla.), who sponsored the reform law, declared that it was the primary reason for the dramatic drop: "It shows the faith we

★ | STATES IN THE NATION

The Declining Number of Families on Welfare

The welfare rolls in the United States peaked in March 1994. After that, the rolls dropped precipitously, due to the surge in the U.S. economy and to the 1996 welfare reform legislation that instituted new work rules. The biggest drop (89 percent) was in Wisconsin. The smallest (7 percent) was in Hawaii.

Q. What might explain the state-to-state variation in the decline in the welfare rolls?

A. States that had weaker economies in the early 1990s had bigger drops in their welfare rolls in the latter part of the 1990s. These states had more laid-off workers on welfare and, as the ecomony strengthened, many of these workers found another job.

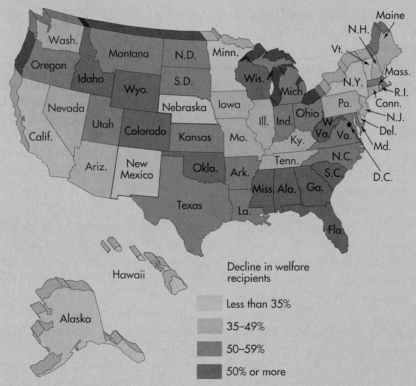

Decline in welfare recipients

- Less than 35%
- 35–49%
- 50–59%
- 50% or more

Source: Department of Health and Human Services, 2003. Period of change in January 1993 to March 1999.

had in [the legislation] was well placed." Senator Daniel Patrick Moynihan (D-N.Y.), who led the opposition to the bill, said: "It doesn't show anything yet." Moynihan claimed the real test would come when the economy turned downward, and he expressed doubt that the chronically unemployed would find jobs in that situation.[1]

These opposing views typify opinions about social welfare policy. It's an area in which opposing philosophies of government collide. Many people, like Moynihan, believe the government must provide substantial and sustained assistance to those Americans who are less equipped to compete effectively in the marketplace. Others, like Shaw, believe that welfare payments, except to those who are unmistakably unfit to work, discourage personal effort and create welfare dependency.

Another source of conflict over welfare policy is the country's federal system of government. Welfare was traditionally a responsibility of state and local governments. Only since the 1930s has the federal government also played a significant role. Some welfare programs are jointly run by the federal and state governments. They are funded at different levels from one state to the next but operate within guidelines set down by the national government and are partly funded by Washington. The strictness of federal guidelines and the amount that the federal government should contribute to the programs are sources of contention.

This chapter examines the social problems that federal welfare programs are designed to alleviate and describes how these programs operate. It also addresses public education policies. A goal of this chapter is to provide an informed basis for understanding issues of social welfare and education and to show why disagreements in these areas are so substantial. They involve hard choices that almost inevitably require trade-offs between federal and state power and between the values of individual self-reliance and egalitarian compassion. The main points of the chapter are these:

★ *Poverty is a large and persistent problem in America, deeply affecting about one in seven Americans, including many of the country's most vulnerable individuals—children, female-headed families, and minority group members.* Social welfare programs have been a major factor in reducing the extent of poverty in the United States.

★ *Welfare policy has been a partisan issue, with Democrats taking the lead on government programs to alleviate economic insecurity and Republicans acting to slow down or reverse these initiatives.* Major changes in social welfare have usually occurred in the context of majority support for the change.

★ *Social welfare programs are designed to reward and foster self-reliance or, when this is not possible, to provide benefits only to those individuals who are*

truly in need. U.S. welfare policy is not based on the assumption that
every citizen has a right to material security.

★ *Americans favor social insurance programs (such as social security) over public
assistance programs (such as food stamps).* As a result, most social welfare
expenditures are not targeted toward the nation's neediest citizens.

★ *A prevailing principle in the United States is equality of opportunity, which in
terms of policy is most evident in the area of public education.* America
invests heavily in its public schools and colleges.

POVERTY IN AMERICA: THE NATURE OF THE PROBLEM

In the broadest sense, social welfare policy includes any effort by government to improve social conditions. In a narrower sense, which is the way
the term will be used in most of this chapter, social welfare policy refers to
those efforts by government to help individuals meet basic human needs,
including food, clothing, and shelter.

The Poor: Who and How Many?

Americans' social welfare needs are substantial. Although Americans are far
better off economically than most of the world's peoples, poverty is a significant and persistent problem in the United States. The government defines the **poverty line** as the annual cost of a thrifty food budget for an
urban family of four, multiplied by three to include the cost of housing,
clothes, and other necessities. Families whose incomes fall below that line
are officially considered poor. In 2003, the poverty line was set at an annual
income of roughly $18,500 for a family of four. One in nine Americans,
roughly thirty million people, including more than ten million children,
live below the poverty line. If they could join hands, they would form a line
that stretched from New York to Los Angeles and back again.

America's poor include individuals of all ages, races, religions, and regions, but poverty is concentrated among certain groups. Children are one
of the largest groups of poor Americans. One in every five children lives in
poverty. Most poor children live in single-parent families, usually with the
mother. In fact, as can be seen from Figure 16-1, a high proportion of
Americans residing in families headed by divorced, separated, or unmarried
women live below the poverty line. These families are at a disadvantage because most women earn less than men for comparable work, especially in
nonprofessional fields. Women without higher education or special skills

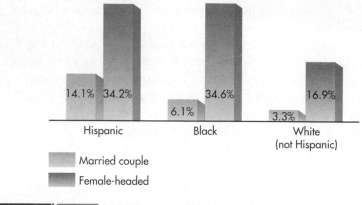

14.1% 34.2%   34.6%   16.9%

6.1%   3.3%

Hispanic   Black   White
                                      (not Hispanic)

■ Married couple
■ Female-headed

FIGURE | 16-1 | PERCENTAGE OF FAMILIES LIVING IN
POVERTY, BY FAMILY COMPOSITION AND
RACE/ETHNICITY

Poverty is far more prevalent among female-headed households and African American
and Hispanic households.
Source: U.S. Bureau of the Census, 2002.

often cannot find jobs that pay significantly more than the child care expenses they incur if they work outside the home. In recent years, single-
parent, female-headed families have been five times as likely as two-income
families to fall below the poverty line, a situation referred to as "the femi-
nization of poverty."

Poverty is also widespread among minority group members. More than
20 percent of African Americans and Hispanics live below the poverty line,
compared with 10 percent of whites.

Poverty is geographically concentrated. Although it is often portrayed as
an urban problem, it is somewhat more prevalent in rural areas. About one
in seven rural residents—as compared with one in nine urban residents—
live in families with incomes below the poverty line. The urban figure is
misleading, however, in that the poverty rate is very high in inner-city areas. Suburbs are the safe haven from poverty. Because suburbanites are removed from it, many of them have no sense of the impoverished condition
of what Michael Harrington called "the other America."[2]

The "invisibility" of poverty in America is evident in polls that show that
most Americans greatly underestimate the number of poor in their country.
There is certainly nothing in the daily lives of many Americans or what
they see on television that would lead them to think that poverty rates are
uncommonly high. Yet the United States has the highest level of poverty
among the advanced industrialized nations, and its rate of child poverty is

more than twice the average of the others (see "How the United States Compares").

Living in Poverty: By Choice or Chance?

Many Americans hold to the idea that poverty is largely a matter of choice—that most low-income Americans are unwilling to make the effort to hold a responsible job and get ahead in life. In his book *Losing Ground*, Charles Murray argued that America has a permanent underclass of unproductive citizens who prefer to live on welfare and whose children receive little educational encouragement at home and grow up to be copies of their parents.[3] There are, indeed, many such people in America. They number in the millions. They are the toughest challenge for policymakers because almost nothing about their lives equips them to escape from poverty and its attendant ills.

Yet most poor Americans are in their situation as a result of circumstance rather than of choice. A ten-year study of American families by a University of Michigan research team found that most of the poor are poor only for a while and that they are poor for temporary reasons such as the loss of a job or desertion by the father.[4] When the U.S. economy goes into a tailspin the impact devastates many families. In the recessionary period that began in 2001, several million Americans fell into poverty as a result of job loss.

It is also true that a full-time job does not guarantee that a family will rise above the poverty line. A family of four with one employed adult who works forty hours a week at six dollars an hour (which is roughly the minimum wage level) has an annual income of about twelve thousand dollars, which is well below the poverty line. Millions of Americans—mostly household workers, service workers, unskilled laborers, and farm workers—are in this position. The U.S. Bureau of Labor Statistics estimates that roughly 7 percent of full-time workers do not earn enough to lift their family above the poverty line.[5]

THE POLITICS AND POLICIES OF SOCIAL WELFARE

Welfare policy has generally been debated along partisan lines, a reflection of differences in the coalitions and philosophies of the Republican and Democratic parties. With its ties to labor, the poor, and minorities, the Democratic party has initiated nearly all major federal welfare programs. The key House of Representatives vote on the Social Security Act of 1935, for example, found 85 percent of Democrats voting for it and 99 percent of Republicans voting against it.[6]

▌HOW THE UNITED STATES COMPARES

Children Living in Poverty

The United States has the highest child poverty rate among industrialized nations. One in five American children live in poverty; in most other industrialized nations, fewer than one in ten does so.

One reason for the difference is that income in the United States is less evenly distributed. As a consequence, the United States has the highest percentage of both rich and poor children in the industrialized world. In addition, the United States spends less on government assistance for the poor. Without government help, for example, the child poverty rate in the United States and France would be about equal: 25 percent. Through its government programs, France reduces the ratio to less than 8 percent. Through its welfare programs, the United States cuts the rate only slightly.

Child poverty in the United States is made worse by the relatively large number of single-parent families, although Sweden, which has a similarly large number, has one of the world's lowest rates of child poverty.

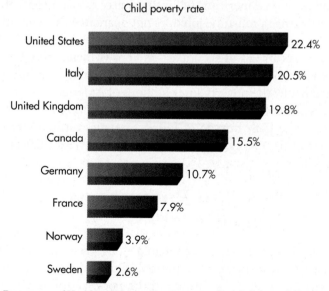

Child poverty rate

United States — 22.4%
Italy — 20.5%
United Kingdom — 19.8%
Canada — 15.5%
Germany — 10.7%
France — 7.9%
Norway — 3.9%
Sweden — 2.6%

Source: Department of Health and Human Services, 2003. Period of change is January 1993 to March 1999.

Republicans gradually came to accept the idea that the federal government has a role in social welfare but argued that the role should be kept as small as practicable. Thus, in the 1960s, Republican opposition to President Lyndon Johnson's Great Society was substantial. His programs included federal initiatives in health care, education, public housing, nutrition, and other areas traditionally dominated by state and local government. More than 70 percent of congressional Republicans voted against the 1965 Medicare and Medicaid programs, which provide government-paid medical assistance for the elderly and the poor. In contrast, the 1996 Welfare Reform Act, which was designed to cut welfare rolls and costs, had the overwhelming support of congressional Republicans. A majority of congressional Democrats voted against it.

Although the Republican and Democratic parties have been at odds on social welfare issues, they have also had reason to work together. There are millions of Americans who need help from government if they are to meet their basic subsistence needs. This help has taken various forms: job training efforts, special education programs, income redistribution measures, and individual-benefit policies.

/pattersonwtp5

Job Training

The government's social welfare effort has included attempts to provide jobs and job training. Employment policy and welfare policy have been loosely linked since the Great Depression, when Franklin D. Roosevelt combined public jobs programs with social security legislation. At one point during the depression, a fifth of the nation's entire work force was employed in public jobs.

Work-related programs are Americans' preferred answer to the problem of poverty. Work is believed to foster initiative and responsibility, whereas welfare payments are thought to create dependency and irresponsibility. In a Los Angeles Times poll, respondents were asked what action government should take to help the poor. Only 6 percent said that the government should provide money or services, whereas 20 percent preferred public works jobs and 72 percent favored job training.

The history of work and job training programs, however, is an uneven one. For example, an ambitious program that began in the early 1970s under Republican president Richard Nixon, and which at its peak provided employment for four million people, was terminated a decade later amid charges that it was too costly and had failed to place people in permanent jobs as opposed to subsidized temporary positions. Subsequent job-training programs were less ambitious and, if anything, even less successful in moving the unemployed into permanent jobs.

A New Beginning

Welfare to Work

President Clinton signs into law the 1996 welfare reform bill that ended the 61-year-old federal guarantee of aid to the poor. The legislation limits eligibility for federal welfare assistance to a period of five years.

The picture changed with passage of the 1996 Welfare Reform Act. The historic bill ended a six-decade federal guarantee of cash assistance to needy families and replaced it with a system of cash grants to the states, which were given the responsibility for caring for welfare recipients and getting them into jobs. The legislation's goal is to reduce long-term welfare dependency by limiting the time that recipients can receive welfare and by providing the states with incentives to prepare recipients for work. States may not let recipients receive federal welfare assistance for more than five years (although a fifth of recipients can be exempted from this requirement), and within two years on welfare, a recipient must find work or face the loss of benefits. States receive federal funds with which to provide benefits, community service jobs, and job training, but unless they meet the program's goals (for example, half of their welfare recipients had to be moved from welfare to work by the year 2002), their federal assistance is reduced.

The long-term effectiveness of the new program is yet to be determined. The trend so far is cause for optimism. The number of Americans on welfare has declined sharply since the 1996 Welfare Reform Act was passed. Nevertheless, there is the lingering question of whether the states can train welfare recipients who are severely lacking in job skills. Most of the welfare recipients who have found employment since 1996 had enough skills that they required little or, in most cases, no job training. Most of those who have been unable to find employment have limited education and few job-related skills.[7]

Welfare recipients are not the only targets of federal jobs programs. In 1998, Congress created the Workforce Investment Act, which is designed to help local communities place the unemployed in jobs. The legislation includes a significant role for local businesses; if they make job positions available, workers will be trained specifically for these positions. The program includes Youth Opportunities grants. Localities compete for these grants, which are designed to train difficult-to-employ fourteen- to twenty-one-year-old youths. The program has been so popular with local leaders that the U.S. Conference of Mayors protested loudly when the Bush administration in 2002 proposed to cut the program's funding from $225 million to $45 million. Local leaders recognized that some federal programs would have to be cut because of the economic downturn and the cost of funding the war on terrorism, but they argued that a large reduction in the Youth Opportunities program would be shortsighted.

Education Initiatives: Head Start

The social welfare effort also includes formal education programs, most notably Head Start. This program provides preschool education for poor children in order to give them a better chance to succeed when they enter school. Head Start was established in the 1960s as part of President Lyndon Johnson's war on poverty.

In the 1980s, Head Start's budget was dropped to a level that allowed only 10 percent of eligible children to participate. As evidence mounted of poverty's devastating impact on children's development, Congress concluded that Head Start was the kind of social investment that the country could hardly afford not to make, and its funding was increased substantially. Nevertheless, less than half of eligible children are enrolled in Head Start, and many who complete the program do not benefit in the long run because they get no educational support at home.

Income and Tax Measures

The United States has substantial income inequality (see Figure 16-2). The top fifth of Americans receive 49 percent of the total income, while the bottom fifth get a mere 4 percent. This twelve-to-one ratio is greater than that found in any other industrialized democracy, and the gap between rich and poor in the United States has widened in recent decades.

Income taxes in the United States are not the instrument of redistribution that they are in other democracies. As of 2003, the top tax rate in the United States was 38.6 percent, and it did not apply until taxable income reached the $250,000 level. An upper tax rate of 50 percent or more is common in Europe, and there are fewer loopholes, such as the deduction of home mortgage interest, that provide tax breaks for the more well-to-do. In addition, this country's other major tax on individuals—the social security tax—is nonprogressive. It is a flat rate of about 6 percent that begins with the first dollar earned each year and stops completely after about $85,000 in earnings. Thus, individuals earning less than this amount pay social security taxes on every dollar they make while those making more than $85,000 pay no social security taxes on dollars they make above this amount.

The net result is that the **effective tax rate** (the actual percentage of income that is spent to pay taxes) of high-income and middle-income Americans is not greatly different. When social security and personal income taxes are combined, the average family's effective tax rate is roughly 25 percent. For families with an income of a million dollars or more, the effective tax rate is only a few points higher.[8]

Although well-to-do Americans pay relatively low taxes, the fact that they make a lot of money means, in absolute terms, that they contribute a sizable share of tax revenues. The top 10 percent of taxpayers in terms of

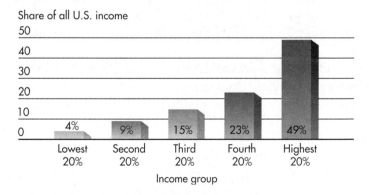

| FIGURE | 16-2 | INCOME INEQUALITY |

The United States has the highest degree of income inequality of any industrialized democracy. Citizens in the top fifth get nearly half of all income; those in the bottom fifth get less than one-twentieth of all income.
Source: U.S. Bureau of the Census, 2003.

income pay about half the personal income taxes received by the federal government. Some of this tax revenue is redistributed downward to lower-income groups through social welfare programs.

The United States also has a policy designed to reallocate income directly to lower-income persons. This policy is the Earned Income Tax Credit (EITC). Low-income families with at least one child are eligible for EITC. About ten million American families receive EITC payments; the maximum yearly payment to any one family is about $3,750. Eligibility for payment is determined when persons file their personal income taxes. Those with family incomes below a specified level receive the payment, which phases out as income rises.

The EITC is widely regarded as one of the country's most successful welfare programs. According to the U.S. Census Bureau, 6 percent of Americans are living above the poverty line because of the extra income from their EITC payments. Without EITC, the poverty rate in America would exceed 15 percent. Moreover, because EITC payments are based on income tax returns, the program does not require a large and costly administrative structure. EITC payments are processed in the same way as refunds for overpayment of withholding taxes.

INDIVIDUAL-BENEFIT PROGRAMS

EITC involves what is called a **transfer payment,** or a government benefit that is given directly to an individual. All spending to promote the general welfare is designed to help individuals, but much of it—such as federal funds for public school construction and hospital equipment—is not in the form of transfer payments. Many federal programs, however, do transfer benefits directly to individuals, such as the monthly social security checks that retired people receive.

Individual-benefit programs are designed to alleviate the personal hardships associated with such conditions as joblessness, poverty, and old age. For most of these programs, any individual who meets the established criteria of eligibility is entitled to the benefits. For this reason, such programs are termed **entitlement programs.** In this sense, they have the same force in law as taxes. Just as individuals are required by law to pay taxes to government on the income they earn, individuals are entitled by law to receive government benefits for which they qualify.

All told, individual-benefit programs are the major component of U.S. social welfare policy. Federal spending on such programs is roughly $1 trillion ($1,000 billion) annually, which is more money than is spent on all other government activity, including national defense.

At an earlier time in the nation's history, the federal government spent almost nothing on social welfare. Welfare policy was deemed to fall within the powers reserved to the states by the Tenth Amendment and to be adequately addressed by them, even though they did not offer substantial welfare services. Individuals were expected to fend for themselves, and those unable to do so were usually supported by relatives and friends. This approach reflected the idea of **negative government,** which holds that government governs best by staying out of people's lives, thus giving them as much freedom as possible to determine their own pursuits and encouraging them to become self-reliant.

The situation changed dramatically with the Great Depression. The unemployment level reached 25 percent, which prompted demands for help from the federal government. Franklin D. Roosevelt's New Deal brought economic relief in the form of public jobs and welfare programs and helped change opinions about the federal government's welfare role.[9] Americans came to look favorably on Washington's help. This attitude reflected a faith in **positive government:** the idea that government intervention is necessary in order to enhance personal liberty and security when individuals are buffeted by economic and social forces beyond their control.

Since the 1930s, the federal government's welfare role has increased substantially, and individuals now expect the federal government to provide benefits to ease the loss of income caused by retirement, disability, unemployment, and the like. Not all individual-benefit programs are alike, however, in their philosophy or level of public support. Individual-benefit programs fall into two general categories: *social insurance* and *public assistance.* Programs in the first category enjoy widespread public support and receive a higher level of funding; programs in the second category encounter substantial public opposition and receive less funding.

Social Insurance Programs

More than forty million Americans receive monthly benefits from social insurance programs—including social security, Medicare, unemployment insurance, and workers' compensation. The two major programs, social security and Medicare, cost the federal government more than $700 billion per year. Such programs are labeled **social insurance** because only those individuals who paid special payroll taxes when they were employed are eligible for these benefits. This self-financing feature of social insurance programs accounts for their strong public support.[10]

Social Security The leading social insurance program is social security for retirees. The program began with passage of the Social Security Act of

Franklin D. Roosevelt
(1882–1945)

Franklin D. Roosevelt won the presidency in 1932 during the depths of the Great Depression. FDR's job programs put Americans back to work, and his social programs met their immediate and long-term economic needs. His greatest domestic policy legacy is the Social Security Act of 1935, which for nearly eight decades has been the foundation of elderly Americans' financial security. Having been elected to an unprecedented third term in 1940, Roosevelt was in office when the Japanese attacked Pearl Harbor. His leadership during World War II was critical in the Allies' defeat of the Axis powers. FDR won a fourth term in 1944 but died in office of a cerebral hemorrhage as the war was coming to a close.

1935 and is funded through payroll taxes on employees and employers (currently set at 6.2 percent). Franklin D. Roosevelt emphasized that retiring workers would receive an insurance benefit that they had earned through their payroll taxes, not a handout from the government. Today, social security has Americans' full support. Public opinion polls indicate that upwards of 90 percent of Americans favor current or higher levels of social security benefits for the elderly. Social security is one of the few welfare programs run entirely by the federal government. Washington collects the payroll taxes that fund the program and sends monthly checks directly to the nearly forty million social security recipients, who each, on average, receive more than $650 a month.

Although people qualify for social security by paying payroll taxes during their working years, the money they receive upon retirement is paid out of the payroll taxes levied on current workers. This arrangement poses a long-term threat to the viability of the social security program because people live longer than they once did. Roughly one in five Americans will be over age sixty-five in the year 2030, and there will not be enough workers by then to pay for retirees' social security benefits. Some kind of adjustment in the current program will be required.

There are a number of ways of ensuring the solvency of social security, and there are proponents for nearly every possibility, from investing social security taxes in stocks, to raising the income level on which social security taxes are levied, to extending the retirement age. Many analysts believe that the plan most likely to be enacted is one that will preserve social security as a safety net for the elderly poor while creating limited opportunities for taxpayers to get a greater return on a portion of their social security payments through the stock market.

Unemployment Insurance The 1935 Social Security Act provides for unemployment benefits for workers who have lost their jobs involuntarily. Unemployment insurance is a joint federal-state program. The federal government collects the payroll taxes that fund unemployment benefits, but states have the option of deciding whether the taxes will be paid by both employees and employers or by employers only (most states use the latter option). Individual states also set the tax rate, conditions of eligibility, and benefit level, subject to minimum standards established by the federal government. Although unemployment benefits vary widely among states, they average about a third ($240 a week) of what an average worker makes while employed, and in most cases the benefits are terminated after twenty-six to thirty-nine weeks.

The unemployment program does not have the same high level of public support that social security does. The situation reflects in part a common belief that the loss of a job, or the failure to find a new one right away, is somehow a personal failing. Unemployment statistics suggest otherwise. For example, U.S. Bureau of Labor statistics indicate that of those workers who lost their jobs in 2001, only 13 percent had made the decision to quit working or were fired. The others became unemployed because of either a temporary layoff or the permanent elimination of a job position.

Medicare After World War II, most European democracies created government-paid health care systems, and President Harry Truman, a Democrat, proposed a similar program for Americans. The American Medical Association (AMA) called Truman's plan "un-American" and threatened to mobilize local physicians to campaign against members of Congress who supported "socialized medicine." Truman's proposal never came to a vote in Congress. In 1961, President John F. Kennedy, also a Democrat, proposed a health care program restricted to social security recipients, but the AMA, the insurance industry, and conservative members of Congress succeeded in blocking the plan.[11]

The 1964 elections swept a tide of liberal Democrats into Congress, and the result was Medicare. Enacted in 1965, the program provides medical assistance to retirees and is funded primarily through payroll taxes. Medicare is based on the insurance principle, and therefore it has gained nearly the same high level of public support that social security has.

Medicare provides for care in a hospital or nursing home, but the recipient pays part of the initial cost and pays most of the expenses after one hundred days. Medicare does not cover all physicians' fees, but enrollees in the program have the option of paying an insurance premium for fuller coverage of these fees. Enrollees who cannot afford the additional premium can apply to have the government pay it.

A major reform of the Medicare program may occur in the near future. The rising cost of medical care and the growing number of elderly have combined to threaten the solvency of the Medicare program; it is projected to run out of money within a decade unless new revenues and cost-cutting measures are devised. Among the options under consideration are increased payroll taxes, more cost sharing by recipients, more use of managed care options, and more substantial controls on government payments to doctors and hospitals. The solvency of the Medicare program will also be tested if, as some leaders within both political parties have proposed, prescription drugs become part of the benefits provided by Medicare.

Public Assistance Programs

Unlike social insurance programs, **public assistance** programs are funded through general tax revenues and are available only to the financially needy. Eligibility for such entitlement programs is established by a **means test;** applicants must prove they are poor enough to qualify for the benefit. Public assistance programs are commonly referred to as "welfare" and the recipients as "welfare cases." Opinion polls show that public assistance programs have less public support than do social insurance programs.

About twenty-five million Americans receive public assistance, typically through programs established by the federal government, administered mainly by the states, and funded jointly by the state and federal governments. Most Americans have the mistaken impression that public assistance programs account for the lion's share of federal welfare spending. A poll found that Americans believe welfare programs are the second-costliest federal program (foreign aid ranked first).[12] In fact, the federal government spends tens of billions more on its two major social insurance programs, social security and Medicare, than it does on all public assistance programs combined.

Supplemental Security Income A major public assistance program is Supplemental Security Income (SSI), which originated as federal assistance to the blind and elderly poor as part of the Social Security Act of 1935. By the 1930s, most states had begun or were considering such programs. Although the federal legislation was designed to replace their efforts, the

Supplemental Security Income (SSI) is a combined federal-state program that provides public assistance to blind and disabled people.

states have retained a measure of control over benefits and eligibility and are required to provide some of the funding. Because SSI recipients (who now include the disabled in addition to the blind and elderly poor) have obvious reasons for their inability to provide for themselves, this public assistance program is not widely criticized.

Aid to Needy Families Perhaps the most controversial of the major public assistance programs was Aid for Families with Dependent Children (AFDC). Partly funded by the federal government but administered by the states, the AFDC program was created in the 1930s as survivors' insurance to assist children whose fathers had died prematurely. Relatively small and noncontroversial at inception, AFDC was the target of severe criticism by the 1970s. Although some attacks on it were based on false claims (for example, that most of the recipients were unwed teenage mothers when in fact less than 10 percent were in this category),[13] AFDC was widely unpopular because it was linked in people's minds to welfare dependency and irresponsibility. It was an entitlement program, which meant that any single parent (and in some states, two parents) living in poverty could claim the benefit and keep it for as long as a dependent child was in the household. Some AFDC recipients were content to live indefinitely on this assistance, and in some cases, their children also grew to become AFDC recipients, thereby creating what was called "a vicious cycle of poverty." By 1995, AFDC was supporting fourteen million Americans at an annual cost of more than $15 billion.

In 1996, AFDC was terminated as part of the Welfare Reform Act. Funding for AFDC was replaced by the Temporary Assistance for Needy Families bloc grant (TANF), which gives each state an annual cash grant that it uses to design its own program for assisting needy families and moving welfare recipients into jobs. These programs must operate within tight federal guidelines, including the following:

- Americans' eligibility for federal cash assistance is limited to no more than five years in their lifetime.
- Within two years, the head of most families on welfare will have to find work or risk the loss of benefits.
- Unmarried teenage mothers are qualified for welfare benefits only if they remain in school and live with a parent or legal guardian.
- Single mothers will lose a portion of their benefits if they refuse to cooperate in identifying for child support purposes the father of their children.

Although states are allowed to make some exceptions to some of the rules (for example, an unmarried teenage mother who faces sexual abuse at home is permitted to live elsewhere), the exceptions are limited. States can choose in some areas to impose more restrictive rules. For example, a state can deny increased benefits to an unwed mother on assistance who gives birth to another child.

The biggest challenge facing the states, in addition to ensuring that the poor do not wind up in the streets, is the development of welfare-to-work programs that actually do free families from welfare dependency. Republicans and Democrats alike agree that the success of the program will ultimately be determined by whether the able-bodied unemployed are able to find meaningful, long-term work.

Food Stamps The food stamp program, which took its present form in 1961, is fully funded by the federal government. The program provides an **in-kind benefit**—not cash, but food stamps that can be spent only on grocery items.

Food stamps are available only to people who qualify on the basis of low income. The program is intended to improve the nutrition of poor families by enabling them to purchase qualified items, mainly foodstuffs, with food

Shown here is a supermarket customer paying for groceries with food stamps. They are available to qualified low-income individuals and can be used only to purchase certain items, mainly foodstuffs. Critics say food stamps at the checkout counter stigmatize the user as a "welfare case." Several states are experimenting with Benefit Security Cards, which are debit cards that can be used in place of food stamps. Because these cards look like any other credit or debit card, they are less obvious to onlookers than food stamps are.

stamps. Some critics say that food stamps stigmatize their users by making it obvious to onlookers in the checkout line that they are "welfare cases." More prevalent criticisms are that the program is too costly and that too many undeserving people receive food stamps. The 1996 welfare reform bill allows states to restrict to three months in any three-year period the food-stamp eligibility of able-bodied adults with no children.

Subsidized Housing Low-income persons are also eligible for subsidized housing. Most of the federal spending in this area is on housing vouchers, an in-kind benefit. Under the voucher system, the individual receives a monthly rent-payment voucher, which is given in lieu of cash to the land-lord, who then hands the voucher over to the government in exchange for cash. About five million households annually receive a federal housing subsidy.

The U.S. government spends much less on public housing than on tax breaks for homeowners, most of whom are middle- and upper-income Americans. Homeowners are allowed tax deductions for their mortgage in-terest payments and their local property tax payments. The total of these tax concessions is three times as much as is spent by the federal government on housing for low-income families.

Medicaid When it enacted Medicare in 1965, Congress also established Medicaid, which provides health care for poor people who are already on welfare. It is considered a public assistance program, rather than a social insurance program like Medicare, because it is based on need and funded by general tax revenues. Roughly 60 percent of Medicaid funding is provided by the federal government, and about 40 percent by the states. More than twenty million Americans receive Medicaid assistance.

Medicaid is controversial because of its costs. As health care costs have spiraled far ahead of the inflation rate, so have the costs of Medicaid. It absorbs more than half of all public assistance dollars spent by the U.S. government and has forced state and local governments to cut other services to meet the costs of their share. "It's killing us," was how one local official described the impact of Medicaid on his community's budget.[14] As is true of other public assistance programs, Medicaid has been criticized for supposedly serving too many people who could take care of themselves if they tried harder. The idea is contradicted, ironically, by the situation faced by many working Americans. There are nearly forty million Americans who make too much money to qualify for Medicaid but who cannot afford health insurance.

EDUCATION AS EQUALITY OF OPPORTUNITY: THE AMERICAN WAY

All democratic societies promote economic security, but they do so to different degrees. Economic security has a higher priority in European democracies than in the United States. European democracies have instituted such programs as government-paid health care for all citizens, compensation for all unemployed workers, and retirement benefits for all elderly citizens. As this chapter shows, the United States provides these benefits only to some citizens in each category. For example, not all elderly Americans are entitled to social security benefits. If they paid social security taxes for a long enough period when they were employed, they (including their spouses) receive benefits. Otherwise, they do not, even if they are in dire economic need.

Such policy differences between Europe and the United States stem from cultural and historical differences. Democracy developed in Europe in reaction to centuries of aristocratic rule, which brought the issue of human equality to the forefront. When strong labor and socialist parties then emerged as a consequence of industrialization, European democracies initiated sweeping social welfare programs that brought about greater economic equality. In contrast, American democracy emerged out of a tradition of limited government that emphasized personal freedom. Equality was a lesser issue, and class consciousness was weak. No major labor or socialist party emerged in America during industrialization to represent the working class, and there was no persistent and strong demand for welfare policies that would bring about the widespread sharing of wealth.

Americans look upon jobs and the personal income that comes from work as the proper basis of economic security. Rather than giving welfare payments to the poor, Americans would prefer that the poor be given training and education so that they can learn to help themselves. This attitude is consistent with Americans' preference for **equality of opportunity,** which is the idea that individuals should have an equal chance to succeed on their own. The concept embodies *equality* in its emphasis on giving everyone a fair chance to get ahead. Yet equality of opportunity also embodies *liberty* because it allows people to succeed or fail on their own as a result of what they do with their opportunities. The expectation is that people will end up differently—some rich, some poor. It is sometimes said that equality of opportunity offers individuals an equal chance to become unequal.

In practice, equality of opportunity works itself out primarily in the private sector, where Americans compete for jobs, promotions, and other advantages. However, a few public policies have the purpose of enhancing equality of opportunity. The most significant of these policies is public education.

Public Education: Leveling Through the Schools

During the nation's first century, the question of a free education to all children was a divisive issue. Wealthy interests feared that an educated public would challenge their power. The proponents of a more equal society wanted to use education as a means of enabling ordinary people to get ahead. This view won out. Public schools sprang up in nearly every community and were open free of charge to children who could attend.

Today, as was discussed in Chapter 1, the United States invests more heavily in public education at all levels than does any other country. The curriculum in American schools is also relatively standardized. Unlike those countries that divide children even at the grade school level into different tracks that lead ultimately to different occupations, the United States aims to educate all children in much the same way. Of course, public education is not a uniform experience for American children. The quality of education depends significantly on the wealth of the community in which a child resides.

Nevertheless, the United States through its public schools educates a broad segment of the population. Arguably, no country in the world has made an equivalent effort to give children, whatever their parents'

LIBERTY, EQUALITY, AND SELF-GOVERNMENT

What's Your Opinion?

Public Education

America's broad-based system of public education stems from a melding of its egalitarian and individualistic traditions. Leon Sampson, a nineteenth-century socialist, noted the stark difference between the philosophy of public education in the United States and that in Europe. "The European ruling classes," he wrote, "were open in their contempt for the proletariat. But in the United States equality, and even classlessness, the creation of wealth for all and political liberty were extolled in the public schools." Sampson concluded that American schools embodied a unique conception of equality; everyone was being trained in much the same way so that each person would have the opportunity to succeed. "It is," he said, "a socialist conception of capitalism."

From your experience with the U.S. system of public education, do you think Sampson's observation is true today? Would you describe "equality"—in the sense of providing an adequate education to everyone who truly wants it—as a contemporary goal of U.S. public schools? Why or why not?

background, an equal opportunity in life through education. Spending on public elementary and secondary schools averages roughly six thousand dollars per pupil, compared with less than three thousand dollars per pupil in western Europe. America's commitment to broad-based education extends to college. The United States is far and away the world leader in terms of the proportion of adults receiving a college education.[15]

The nation's education system preserves both the myth and reality of the American dream. The belief that success can be had by anyone who works for it could not be sustained if the education system were tailored for a privileged elite. And educational attainment is related to personal success, at least as measured by annual incomes. In fact, the gap in income between those with and without a college education is now greater than at any time in the country's history.

In part because the public schools have such a large role in creating an equal opportunity society, they have been heavily criticized in recent years. Violence in the schools is a major parental concern. So too is student performance on standardized tests. American students are not even in the top ten internationally by their test scores in science or math.[16]

Disgruntled parents have demanded changes, and these demands have led some communities to allow parents to choose the public school their children will attend. Under this policy, the schools compete for students, and those that attract the most students are rewarded with the largest budgets. Americans, by more than a two-to-one margin, say they favor such a policy. Advocates of the policy contend that it compels school administrators and teachers to do a better job and gives students the option of rejecting a school that is performing poorly.[17] Opponents of the policy say that it creates a few well-funded schools and a lot of poorly funded ones, yielding no net gain in educational quality. Critics also claim that the policy discriminates against poor and minority group children, whose parents are less likely to be in a position to steer them toward the better schools.[18]

A more contentious issue is a voucher system that would allow parents to use tax dollars to send their children even to private or parochial schools (see Figure 16-3). The recipient school would receive a voucher redeemable from the government, and the student would get a corresponding reduction in his or her tuition. Advocates claim that vouchers force failing schools to improve their instructional programs. Opponents argue that vouchers weaken the public schools by siphoning off revenue and students. They also note that vouchers are of little value to students from poor families because these vouchers pay only part of the cost of attending a private or parochial

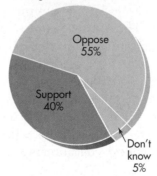

"In areas where schools are not improving, would you support or oppose the federal government giving parents money to send their children to private or religious schools instead?"

Oppose 55%

Support 40%

Don't know 5%

FIGURE　16-3　OPINIONS ON SCHOOL VOUCHERS

Americans are divided in their opinions on school vouchers.

Source: Washington Post/Kaiser Family Foundation/Harvard University survey, October, 2000.

school. In 2002 (*Zelman v. Simmons-Harris*), the Supreme Court declared that vouchers are constitutionally permissible.[19]

The issue of school choice reflects the tensions inherent in the concept of equal opportunity. On the one hand, competition between schools expands the number of alternatives available to students. On the other hand, not all students have the opportunity to choose from the alternatives.

The Federal Role in Education: Political Differences

Education has traditionally been a state and local responsibility. Most school policies—from length of the school year to teachers' qualifications—are set by state legislatures and local school boards. Over 90 percent of the funds spent on schools are provided through state and local tax revenues. Federal intervention in school policy has often been resisted by states and localities, as exemplified by their response to desegregation and busing directives (see Chapter 5). State and local governments have been less hesitant when it comes to federal education grants, but it is difficult to get congressional support for grant programs targeted only at the schools that are most in need. Few members of Congress are willing to support large appropriations for education that do not benefit their constituents, which has reduced Washington's contribution to a goal—quality education for every American child—that nearly every official endorses, at least in the abstract.

Indeed, it was not until 1965 that Congress enacted the first general federal aid to education legislation: the Higher Education Act, and the Elementary and Secondary Education Act. The former became the foundation for Pell Grants, federal loans to college students, and federally subsidized college work-study programs. The latter provided funding for such items as school construction, textbooks, special education, and teacher training.

These acts were not the very first federal programs in the education area. A century earlier, for example, Congress had passed the Morrill Act, which provided states with free tracts of land if the land was used to establish colleges. America's great "land grant" universities are the consequence. Another program was the G.I. bill enacted after World War II that enabled millions of service veterans to attend college. Yet a third program was the National Defense Education Act of 1958, which provided loans and special institutes for students in science and related fields. But not until the 1965 legislation did the federal government assume a broader, ongoing role in public education.

Since then, federal assistance to public schools and colleges has been an important part of their financing, albeit a small part relative to the overall amount that the nation spends on public education. Federal funds during

The Supreme Court has held that American children are entitled to an "adequate" education but do not have the right to an "equal" education. America's public schools differ greatly in quality primarily as a result of the differences in the wealth of the communities they serve. Some public schools are overcrowded and have few facilities and little equipment. Others are very well equipped, have spacious facilities, and have small class sizes.

the past two decades have been split almost equally between support for college and for public school education.

As education has become increasingly an issue of national debate, Washington officials have been drawn into it. President Clinton rejected the idea of unrestricted school choice, arguing that it would weaken the nation's public schools and make them a repository of America's poorest and most difficult-to-educate children. Then in 1998, Clinton persuaded reluctant congressional Republicans to accept, as part of a budget compromise, a multibillion-dollar grant that would allow the nation's overcrowded schools to hire tens of thousands of new teachers. GOP lawmakers are philosophically less inclined to federal solutions to public school problems and are politically less responsive than Democratic lawmakers to the interests of less-affluent constituents. In other words, many of the partisan and philosophical differences that affect federal welfare policy also affect federal education policy.

Nevertheless, education has become such a large political issue that national leaders of both parties have favored an expanded federal role. In his 2000 presidential campaign, Republican George W. Bush proposed more than $15 billion in new federal spending in areas such as reading programs for disadvantaged students, teacher training and recruitment, charter schools, and technology equipment. Once in office, Bush pursued his education agenda, working with Congress to create the Elementary and Secondary Education Act of 2001, which provided $8 billion in new funding for public education. The act also requires national testing in reading, math, and science. After a transition period, schools will be required to administer standardized tests annually in these subject areas. Schools that show no improvement in students' test scores during the first two years will be eligible for additional federal assistance. If there is no improvement by the end of the third year, however, students in these schools will be eligible to transfer elsewhere and the schools themselves will have their federal assistance reduced.

CULTURE, POLITICS, AND SOCIAL WELFARE

Surveys have repeatedly indicated that a majority of Americans are convinced that most people on welfare could get along without it if they tried. Because public assistance programs have limited public support, there is constant political pressure to reduce welfare expenditures and to weed out undeserving recipients. The unwritten principle of social welfare in America, reflecting the country's individualistic culture, is that the individual must somehow earn any social welfare benefit, or, barring that, demonstrate a convincing need for the benefit. The result is a welfare system that is both *inefficient*, in that much of the money spent on welfare never reaches the recipients, and *inequitable*, in that most of the money spent on social welfare never gets to the people who are most in need of help.

Inefficiency: The Welfare Web

The United States has the most complex system of social welfare in the world. Scores of separate programs have been established to address different, often overlapping needs. A single individual in need of public assistance may qualify for many, none, or one of these programs, and the eligibility criteria are sometimes bizarre. Consider the case of Gary Myers of Springfield, Missouri, who declared bankruptcy because he could not afford to pay $1,400 in hospital bills that his family had incurred. Had Myers made exactly $4 less than his $509 monthly wage as a security guard, he would have qualified for government payment of his medical expenses. Because of the extra $4 Myers received nothing.

Beyond the question of the fairness of such rules is the question of their efficiency. The unwritten principle that the individual must somehow earn or deserve a particular benefit makes the U.S. welfare system heavily bureaucratic. For example, the 1996 welfare reform bill—which limits eligibility to families with incomes below a certain level and, in most instances, to families with a single parent living in the home—requires that the eligibility

FIGURE 16-4 THE CUMBERSOME ADMINISTRATIVE
PROCESS BY WHICH WELFARE RECIPIENTS
GET THEIR BENEFITS

of each applicant be periodically checked by a caseworker. This procedure
makes such programs doubly expensive; in addition to payments to the recipients, the programs must pay caseworkers, supervisors, and support staffs
and must pay to process the extensive paperwork (see Figure 16-4).

The bureaucratic costs of welfare are substantially lower in Europe because eligibility is either universal, as in the case of health care, or less strin-
gently defined. There have been proposals to adopt a European-like system
in the United States; President Nixon's attempt to establish a guaranteed
annual income for every American family is an example. All these proposals
have failed to win broad support, mainly because they run counter to Americans' belief in individualism.

Inequity: The Middle-Class Advantage

Most Americans hold to the traditional belief in individualism and self-
reliance, which they generalize to other people. Although they recognize a
need for programs for the poor and disadvantaged, they tend to minimize
both the number of such individuals and the extent of their need. The situation means that less advantaged Americans cannot count on a great deal of
political support from other sectors of society. Even the much-heralded war
on poverty of the 1960s was less a war than a skirmish. Weak middle-class
support for the effort, reports that the programs were poorly administered
and were not reaching the target audience, and the fiscal pressures of the
Vietnam conflict combined to undermine the antipoverty effort. Congressional appropriations for the war on poverty programs never totaled so
much as $2 billion in a given year.

Social security and Medicare are another story entirely.[20] These two social insurance programs have broad public support, even though together
they cost the federal government much more than is spent on all major

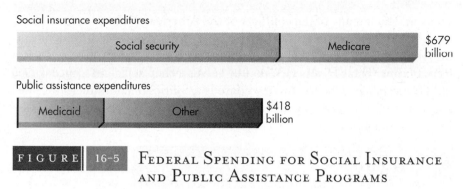

Social insurance spending far exceeds public assistance spending.
Source: Office of Management and Budget, FY 2003.

public assistance programs (see Figure 16-5). A reason for the difference in public funding and approval for social security is that it benefits the majority. Most Americans are either actual or potential social security recipients. It is good politics for elected officials to appeal to the forty million retired Americans who get a monthly social security check.

Social security recipients feel entitled to their benefits by virtue of their payroll tax contributions. However, most recipients receive far more in benefits than they have "earned" through their payroll taxes. So they are, in a sense, getting public assistance.

It is important to note, however, that the existence of social security substantially lessens the demand for other forms of public assistance. Monthly social security keeps millions of Americans, mostly widows, out of poverty. About a fourth of social security recipients have no other significant source of income. Without social security, they would be completely dependent on public assistance programs.

Nevertheless, many social security recipients, while legally entitled to the benefits they receive, have no actual financial need for them. Only a third of social security recipients are in the lowest fifth of the population in income. Families in the top fifth of the income population receive more in federal social insurance benefits than is spent on TANF, food stamps, and housing subsidies combined.

The contradictions and difficulties of social welfare in America come together in the contrasting cases of social insurance and public assistance. Although the latter is targeted toward the truly needy, it is less acceptable politically and culturally and receives much less funding. The situation testifies to the strength of traditional American values of individualism and self-reliance and to the power of money and votes. Social welfare is the arena in which many of the conflicts of the American political system come together: individualism versus equality, Congress versus the president, national authority versus local authority, public sector versus private sector, Republicans versus Democrats, poorer versus richer, social insurance versus public assistance. The politics of welfare is a politics of contradictory values and competing interests, which ensures that it will be a contentious issue for years to come.

SUMMARY

The United States has a complex social welfare system of multiple programs addressing specific welfare needs. Each program applies only to those individuals who qualify for benefits by meeting the specific eligibility criteria. In general, these criteria are designed to encourage self-reliance or, when help is necessary, to ensure that laziness is not rewarded or fostered. This approach to social welfare reflects Americans' traditional belief in individualism.

/pattersonwtp5

Poverty is a large and persistent problem in America. About one in nine people fall below the government-defined poverty line, and they include a disproportionate number of children, female-headed families, minority group members, and rural and inner-city dwellers. The ranks of the poor are increased by economic recessions and reduced through government welfare programs.

Welfare policy has been a partisan issue, with Democrats taking the lead on government programs to alleviate economic insecurity and Republicans acting to slow down or decentralize these initiatives. Changes in social welfare have usually occurred through presidential leadership in the context of majority support for the change. Welfare policy has been worked out through programs to provide jobs and job training, education programs, income measures, and especially transfer payments through individual-benefit programs.

Individual-benefit programs fall into two broad categories: social insurance and public assistance. The former includes such programs as social security for retired workers and Medicare for the elderly. Social insurance programs are funded by payroll taxes on potential recipients, who thus, in a sense, earn the benefits they later receive. Because of this arrangement, social insurance programs have broad public support. Public assistance programs, in contrast, are funded by general tax revenues and are targeted toward needy individuals and families. These programs are not controversial in principle: most Americans believe that government should assist the truly needy. However, because of a widespread belief that most welfare recipients could get along without assistance if they tried, these programs do not have universal public support, are only modestly funded, and are politically vulnerable.

The balance between economic equality and individualism tilts more heavily toward individualism in the United States than in other advanced industrialized democracies. Entitlement to social security, for example, is not a universal right of the elderly in the United States, whereas it is elsewhere. Compared to other democracies, however, the United States attempts to more equally educate its children, a policy consistent with its cultural emphasis on equality of opportunity.

Social welfare is a contentious issue. A major reason is that opposing sides disagree fundamentally on the nature of the problem. In one view, social welfare is too costly and assists too many people who could help themselves; another view holds that social welfare is not broad enough and that too many disadvantaged Americans live in poverty. Because of these irreconcilable differences and because of federalism and the widely shared view that welfare programs should target specific problems, the existing system of multiple programs, despite its administrative complexity and inefficiency, has been the only politically feasible alternative.

KEY TERMS

entitlement program
equality of opportunity
in-kind benefits
means test
negative government

positive government
poverty line
public assistance
social insurance
transfer payment

SUGGESTED READINGS

Day, Phyllis, J. *A New History of Social Welfare*. Boston: Allyn and Bacon, 1999. A comprehensive look at social welfare policy and traditions.

Henig, Jeffrey R. *Rethinking School Choice: Limits of the Market Metaphor*. Princeton, N.J.: Princeton University Press, 1995. An argument against parental choice as the basis of public school enrollment.

Melnick, R. Shep. *Between the Lines: Interpreting Welfare Rights*. Washington, D.C.: Brookings Institution Press, 1994. An analysis of the intricate relationship between social welfare legislation and its interpretation in the courts.

Newman, Katherine S. *No Shame in My Game*. New York: Alfred A. Knopf and Russell Sage Foundation, 1999. A careful study of America's working poor.

Patterson, James T. *America's Struggle Against Poverty in the Twentieth Century*. Cambridge, Mass.: Harvard University Press, 2000. A thorough analysis of poverty and its history.

Wagner, Tony, and Thomas Vander Ark. *Making the Grade: Reinventing America's Schools*. New York: Routledge, 2001. An assessment of the changing needs of American schoolchildren.

Wilson, William Julius. *When Work Disappears: The World of the New Urban Poor*. New York: Knopf, 1996. An important analysis of jobs and poverty in the inner city.

LIST OF WEBSITES

http://www.doleta.gov The U.S. Department of Labor's website on the status of the welfare-to-work program, including state-by-state assessments.

http://www.nea.org The home page of the National Education Association (NEA); it provides information on the organization's membership and policy goals.

http://www.os.dhhs.gov The website of the Department of Health and Human Services (HHS)—the agency that is responsible for most federal social welfare programs.

http://www.ssw.umich.edu/poverty/mission.html The website of the University of Michigan's Program on Poverty and Social Welfare Policy; the program seeks to stimulate interest in policy issues and to transmit research findings to policymakers.

POLITICS IN THEORY AND PRACTICE

Thinking: How has welfare and education policy been influenced by Americans' belief in individualism? By America's federal system of government?

Acting: Although conservatives and liberals disagree on the question of how far government should go in helping the poor, virtually all Americans—right and left—support private efforts to help the poor. Numerous local religious, civic, social, and economic groups have programs for the poor, such as food kitchens or clothing drives. Consider volunteering some of your time to such a group.

𝕿𝖍𝖊 𝕹𝖊𝖜 𝖄𝖔𝖗𝖐 𝕿𝖎𝖒𝖊𝖘   **reading 16**

Vouchers: A Shift, But Just How Big?

by Kate Zernike

The nation's public schools have been heavily criticized in recent years. Disorder and poor student performance have prompted parents to pressure officials to reform the schools. Vouchers have been proposed as one means of bringing about change. A voucher system allows parents to use tax dollars to send their children even to private or parochial schools. Critics have argued that vouchers will needlessly weaken the public schools and violate the First Amendment's separation of church and state. In Zelman v. Simmons-Harris *(2002), the U.S. Supreme Court upheld the constitutionality of Cleveland's school voucher program. In this June 30, 2002, article,* New York Times *reporter Kate Zernike explores the probable impact of the Court's ruling.*

WHEN the Supreme Court upheld Cleveland's school voucher program, voucher supporters exulted that the decision would be as important as *Brown v. Board of Education.* It would, they said, create a seismic wave of similar programs across the country, shifting students, money and attention from public to private schools.

But the voucher ruling may resemble Brown less because of what will happen than because of what won't. "It may very well be *Brown v. Board of Ed,* but guess what, Brown didn't do all that much to desegregate the schools because there was so much political opposition to it," said James E. Ryan, a professor of constitutional law at the University of Virginia who was co-author of an article on the politics of school choice in the most recent Yale Law Review.

In fact, despite the *Brown* decision, schools are still largely segregated, and most poor black children still receive a substandard education. Its real importance was spiritual, not practical; it raised the nation's consciousness about its obligation to provide blacks the same educational opportunities as whites. So, too, the main effect of the voucher decision may be to make people more open to different forms of public education, especially in poor cities.

"The doomsday idea is that somehow this is going to destroy the public school system," said Terry M. Moe, a Stanford professor whose book, "Politics, Markets, and America's Schools," written with John E. Chubb, helped push the voucher movement in the early 1990's. "I think it's just going to change people's idea of what a public school system is."

To begin with, there are not enough spaces in private or parochial schools to accommodate more than a relative handful of children. And the teachers' unions have successfully blocked vouchers in almost every instance. In addition, there are other, less visible obstacles to the spread of vouchers, like the fact that well-off suburban parents oppose them.

As first proposed by the economist Milton Friedman and embraced by the Reagan administration, vouchers were individual educational subsidies, taken from state and local education budgets, to be given to everyone. They were based on the free market notion that the way to improve public schools was to force them to compete.

But the argument that swayed the court last week was rooted in morality, not economics. In recent years, conservatives have talked little about the need for competition and instead aligned themselves with groups of black parents who argued that, unlike wealthy whites, they couldn't choose where to school their children. They were stuck with neighborhood schools, which were often dreadful. In Cleveland, for example, just 10 percent of students scored at acceptable levels at the worst schools.

"Parental school choice is widespread—unless you're poor," became the mantra of the Black Alliance for Educational Options, one of the largest pro-voucher groups. And these groups say they don't support vouchers for anyone but poor students.

"We didn't get into this to give resources to people who already have them," said Howard Fuller, the chairman of the Black Alliance and a former schools superintendent in Milwaukee, the site of the nation's first voucher program.

Even some voucher proponents who once argued for universal subsidies now say the programs should be focused on city schools. And that will likely be just fine with suburban parents who have opposed vouchers in polls and recent state referendums.

"The most compelling argument for vouchers is a moral argument, but there's a fit between the moral argument and the political reality," said Joseph P. Viteritti, a professor of public policy at New York University.

Suburban parents oppose vouchers, as they did busing, in part because they do not want to open up their schools to students from the cities. The Cleveland choice program allowed parents to use the vouchers in suburban schools, but only if suburban schools agreed, and none did.

These parents may also resist vouchers, as they have resisted charter schools, because their existence might suggest that the local schools aren't as good as advertised—which would be bad for property values.

In poll after poll, people are likely to say they think their own schools are doing a good job. The problem, they believe, is in other people's schools, especially when those other people are in the cities.

"That feeling may create sympathy for vouchers, but it's also going to limit vouchers," Mr. Viteritti said.

That could change if suburban parents begin to feel that their schools are faltering—which could happen if the results of a whole new battery of standardized tests begin to expose faults in the system.

There is also the possibility that a more well-to-do parent might go to court to challenge a program that gives vouchers to some but not to others, just as whites have fought minority preferences for minority students at elite public schools.

Still, there are other factors limiting the spread of voucher programs.

The original notion of vouchers would have left it to the market to determine the quality of the private schools where they were used. Now, proponents like Mr. Moe argue that the programs should include regulations requiring the private schools to use a lottery for admissions, so they don't take only the top students, and tests to make sure the curriculum is high quality.

"Will private schools agree? Not all of them," Mr. Moe said.

In the end, then, vouchers are likely to push the public school system to evolve, albeit slowly, into one that embraces more choices for more students. "The way to look at it is, this will encourage a movement toward a mixed system, where we have the regular public school system that serves more than half the kids, but where there are many kids in urban areas that use vouchers to go to public schools," Mr. Moe said.

It is a change that is already under way, with 1 in 4 parents using some kind of public school choice.

Opponents of vouchers may rue the court's decision as the demise of the democratic notion of the common school. In reality, Bruce Fuller, a professor of education at the University of California–Berkeley, said, "The idealism around common schooling has worn pretty thin in the minds of many parents."

What's Your Opinion?

Where do you stand on the issue of school vouchers? Are vouchers good public policy or bad public policy?

CHAPTER 17

FOREIGN AND DEFENSE POLICY: PROTECTING THE AMERICAN WAY

❝We the people of the United States, in order to . . . provide for the common defense . . .❞

PREAMBLE, U.S. CONSTITUTION

Just after dark on March 19, 2003, the first bombs fell on Baghdad, signaling the start of the U.S. attack on Iraq. But if the war was foremost in the minds of U.S. policymakers, they also had their eye on a second set of issues. They were concerned about the economic consequences of the conflict with Iraq. There were fears that the war could destabilize the world economy, particularly if the flow of Middle Eastern oil was disrupted. There were also concerns about the effect of the war on the U.S. economy. The war would cost tens of billions of dollars—this at a time when the U.S. budget was already deeply in the red. Then there was the issue of the reconstruction of Iraq, which also would cost tens of billions of dollars, yet was necessary if that nation was to become something other than a breeding ground for terrorists and an impediment to economic globalization. Securing an economically stable peace would be as daunting a task as waging a militarily successful war.

As America's war with Iraq illustrates, national security is an issue that ranges from military strength to economic vitality.[1] The primary goal of

537

U.S. foreign policy is protection of the American state. This objective requires military readiness in order to protect the territorial integrity of the United States, and it rises to the fore with every occurrence of an immediate threat, such as the terrorist attacks of September 11, 2001. But the American state also represents a society of more than 280 million people whose livelihood depends in significant part on the nation's position in the international economy.[2] Through participation in economic policies that foster economic growth and international stability, the United States can secure the jobs and trade that are essential to the maintenance of a high standard of living.

The national security policies of the United States include an extraordinary array of activities—so many, in fact, that they could not possibly be addressed adequately in an entire book, much less a single chapter. There are some 190 countries in the world, and the United States has relations of one kind or another—military, diplomatic, economic—with all of them. This chapter narrows the subject by focusing on a few main ideas:

★ *Since World War II, the United States has acted in the role of world leader, which has substantially affected its military, diplomatic, and economic policies.*

★ *The policy machinery for foreign and defense affairs is dominated by the president and includes military, intelligence, diplomatic, and economic agencies and organizations.*

★ *The United States maintains a high degree of defense preparedness, which mandates a substantial level of defense spending and a worldwide deployment of U.S. conventional and strategic forces.*

★ *Changes in the international marketplace have led to increased economic interdependence among nations, which has had a marked influence on the U.S. economy and on its security planning.*

THE ROOTS OF U.S. FOREIGN AND DEFENSE POLICY

For nearly half a century, U.S. defense policy was defined by conflict with the Soviet Union. From the Berlin airlift in 1948 to the Vietnam escalation in 1965 to the Star Wars initiative in 1983, the United States seemed willing to pay any price to halt the spread of communism. Then, in the late 1980s, the Soviet empire suddenly and dramatically began to fall apart. In December 1991, the Soviet Union itself ceased to exist. For decades, there had been two superpowers, the Soviet Union and the United States. Now there is only one.

President George W. Bush talks with firefighters and police on the site of the collapsed World Trade Center buildings. The terrorist attacks of September 11, 2001, produced a fundamental shift in U.S. foreign policy and public opinion.

Since the end of the cold war, the United States has redefined its foreign and defense policies. The country is still at the center of world politics, but its challenges have changed. The attacks on the World Trade Center and the Pentagon revealed to all what some analysts had been warning: the biggest threat to the physical security of the American people is not other nations but international terrorists who fight on behalf of causes. Developments in the previous decade had made another fact abundantly clear: a strong domestic base is the key to success in the increasingly important global economy.[3]

Although the age of superpower conflict is over, America's role in world affairs was shaped by that era. Accordingly, an understanding of the nation's foreign and defense policies and capabilities necessarily begins with an awareness of key developments during that period.

The United States as Global Superpower

Before World War II, the United States was an **isolationist** country, deliberately avoiding a large role in world affairs. A different America emerged from the war. It had more land, sea, and air power than any other country in the world, a huge military-industrial base, and several hundred overseas military bases. The United States had become an **internationalist** country, deeply involved in the affairs of other nations.

U.S. national security policy after World War II was built on a concern with the power and intentions of the Soviet Union.[4] At the Yalta Conference in 1945, U.S. president Franklin Roosevelt and Soviet leader Josef Stalin had agreed that Eastern European nations were entitled to self-determination within a Soviet zone of influence, but Stalin breached the agreement. After the war, Soviet occupation forces assisted the communist parties in Eastern Europe in capturing state power, usually by coercive means. In the words of Britain's wartime prime minister, Winston Churchill, an "iron curtain" had fallen across Europe.

The Soviet Union's aggressive action led U.S. policymakers to assess Soviet aims. Particularly noteworthy was the evaluation of George Kennan, a U.S. diplomat and expert on Soviet affairs. Kennan concluded that invasions from the West in World Wars I and II had made the Soviet Union (which had lost twenty-five million lives in World War II, compared with U.S. losses of five hundred thousand) almost paranoid in its concern for regional security. Although Kennan believed that the USSR would someday mature into a responsible world power, he contended that it was an immediate threat to neighboring countries.[5] Kennan's analysis contributed to the formulation of the doctrine of **containment,** which was based on the idea that the Soviet Union was an aggressor nation that had to be stopped from achieving its territorial ambitions.

Harry S Truman, who became president after Roosevelt's death in 1945, rejected Kennan's view that the USSR was motivated by a concern for *regional* security. Truman saw the Soviet Union as an aggressive ideological foe that was bent on *global* domination and that could be stopped only by the forceful use of U.S. power. Truman's view was based on assumptions derived from territorial concessions made to Germany's Adolf Hitler by Britain and France at a conference in Munich in 1938; rather than appeasing Hitler, these concessions convinced him that Germany could bully its way to further gains. The idea that appeasement only encourages further aggression was the *lesson of Munich,* and it became the dominant view of U.S. policymakers in the postwar period.

The Cold War and Vietnam

Developments in the late 1940s embroiled the United States in a **cold war** with the Soviet Union. The term refers to the fact that the two countries were not directly engaged in actual combat (a "hot war") but were locked into a deep-seated hostility that lasted forty-five years. From the United States's perspective, the cold war was an extension of containment policy and included support for governments threatened by communist takeovers. In China, the Nationalist government had the support of the United States, but it was defeated in 1949 by the Soviet-supplied communist forces of Mao Zedong. In June 1950, when the Soviet-backed North Koreans invaded

IS THIS TOMORROW

AMERICA UNDER COMMUNISM!

Cold war propaganda, like this poster warning of the danger of communism, contributed to a climate of opinion in the United States that led to public support of efforts to contain Soviet power.

South Korea, President Truman immediately committed U.S. troops to the conflict, which ended in stalemate and the loss of thirty-five thousand American lives.

For the United States, a major turning point in foreign policy was the Vietnam War. Responding to the threat of a communist takeover, the United States became ever more deeply involved in the civil war in Vietnam. By the late 1960s, 550,000 Americans were on station in South Vietnam. U.S. forces were technically superior in combat to the communist fighters, but they were fighting an enemy they could not easily identify in a society they did not fully understand.[6] Vietnam was a guerrilla war, with no front lines and few set battles. As the conflict dragged on, American public opinion, most visibly among the young, turned against the war, which contributed to President Lyndon Johnson's decision not to run for reelection in 1968. Public opinion forced Richard Nixon, who became president in 1969, to aim not for victory but for a gradual disengagement. U.S. combat troops left Vietnam in 1973, and two years later, North Vietnamese forces concluded their takeover of the country. Vietnam was the most painful and costly application of the containment doctrine: fifty-eight thousand American soldiers lost their lives in the fighting.[7]

Détente and Disintegration of the Evil Empire

America's defeat in Vietnam forced U.S. policymakers to reconsider the country's international role. The *lesson of Vietnam* was that there were limits to the country's ability to assert its will in the world. Nixon claimed that the United States could no longer act as the "Lone Ranger" for the free world and sought to reduce tensions with communist countries.[8] The new philosophy was reflected by the Helsinki Accords of 1971, in which the United States accepted the territorial boundaries of Eastern Europe. Then Nixon took a historic journey to the People's Republic of China in 1972, the first official contact with that country since the communists took power in 1949.

Another indication of a change in policy was the Strategic Arms Limitation Talks (SALT), which began in 1969. The SALT talks presumed that the United States and the Soviet Union each had an interest in retaining enough nuclear weapons to deter the other from an attack but that neither side had an interest in mutual destruction. Along with the lowering of east-west trade barriers, these efforts marked the start of a new era of communication and cooperation, or **détente** (a French word meaning "a relaxing"), between the United States and the Soviet Union.[9]

Although the period of détente during the 1970s marked a major shift in U.S.-Soviet relations, it did not last. The Soviet invasion of Afghanistan in 1979 convinced U.S. leaders that the USSR was still bent on expansion and threatened Western interests in the oil-rich Middle East. Ronald Reagan, elected president in 1980, called for a renewed hard line toward the Soviet Union, which he described as the "evil empire."

U.S. policymakers did not fully realize it at the time, but the Soviet Union was collapsing under its heavy defense expenditures, isolation from Western technology and markets, and inefficient centralized command economy. In March 1985, Mikhail Gorbachev became the Soviet leader and proclaimed a need to restructure Soviet society, an initiative known as *perestroika*. He also ordered the withdrawal of Soviet troops from Afghanistan (which had become his country's Vietnam) and sought to reduce tensions with the United States.

Gorbachev's efforts came too late to save the Soviet Union. In 1989, the withdrawal of Soviet troops from Eastern Europe accelerated a pro-democracy movement that was already under way in the region. Poland initiated major reforms. Hungary dismantled the "iron curtain" that had blocked free travel to Austria. Then, in November, the Berlin Wall between East and West Germany—the most visible symbol of the separation of East and West—came down. On December 8, 1991, the leaders of the Russian, Belarus, and Ukrainian republics declared that the Soviet Union no longer existed.

A New World Order

The end of the cold war prompted the first President Bush in 1990 to call for a "new world order." His formulation abandoned the assumption that world affairs are a zero-sum game, in which for one nation to gain something, another nation has to lose. Bush contended that nations can move forward together. The concept emphasized **multilateralism**—the idea that major nations should act together in response to problems and crises.[10]

Multilateralism characterized the U.S. response to Iraq's invasion of Kuwait in August 1990. President Bush worked through the United Nations, which demanded the unconditional withdrawal of Iraqi forces and imposed a trade embargo on Iraqi oil. The military force arrayed against Iraq was also nominally a UN force, although it was led by a U.S. commander and consisted mostly of U.S. troops. Several countries, including Germany and Japan, supported the effort with money instead of troops.

The Gulf operation was successful from a strictly military perspective. Despite the size and combat readiness of Iraq's army, the shooting war ended quickly, prompting President Bush to claim that the United States had "kicked the Vietnam syndrome [the legacy of America's defeat in Vietnam] once and for all." But the outcome of the Gulf War was much less successful from another perspective. Bush's decision to stop the war short of a march on Baghdad left Saddam Hussein in power, and he responded by repressing ethnic and religious minorities in Iraq and by defying UN directives that called for the dismantling of Iraq's weapons of mass destruction. The United States was forced to conduct periodic air strikes on Iraqi installations, which helped contain Hussein but did not dislodge him from power.

Multilateralism was also applied in the Balkans. In 1992, the Bosnian Serbs, supported by the Serb-dominated Yugoslav government, attacked Muslims and Croats in Bosnia. Forced evacuations and mass executions were part of the Serbs' effort to rid areas of Bosnia of rival ethnic and religious groups. Finally, in 1995, after UN economic sanctions and limited air strikes had failed to deter Serb aggression, planes of the United States and its Western allies undertook a bombing campaign that led to U.S.-negotiated peace talks (the Dayton Accords). The talks brought an end to hostilities and the deployment to Bosnia of sixty thousand peacekeeping troops (including twenty thousand from the United States). War in the Balkans flared again in 1999, after the Yugoslav Serbs began a campaign of "ethnic cleansing" in the Serbian province of Kosovo, which had a population that was 90 percent ethnic Albanian. After failed attempts at a negotiated settlement, planes from the NATO countries (North Atlantic Treaty Organization, discussed later in this chapter) attacked Serbia. (Yugoslavia is a federation that includes Serbia and Montenegro.) After weeks of intensive bombing, Yugoslav president Slobodan Milosevic (who was subsequently arrested and put on trial for war crimes) pulled his troops out of Kosovo. Ethnic Albanians moved back in and, despite the presence of UN peacekeeping troops, commenced revenge attacks on some of the Serbs who remained.

As these examples indicate, multilateralism has been only somewhat successful as a strategy for resolving international conflicts. With the deployment of enough resources, the world's major powers can intervene with some success in many parts of the developing world. However, these interventions offer no guarantee of long-term success. Regional and internal conflicts typically stem from enduring ethnic, religious, factional, or national hatreds or from chronic problems such as famine, overcrowding, or government corruption. Even if these hatreds or problems can be momentarily eased, they are often too deep-seated to be permanently resolved.

The War on Terrorism

When he took office in 2001, George W. Bush declared that the United States would have a less active role in international conflicts than it had been playing. That position abruptly changed when terrorists attacked the World Trade Center and the Pentagon, killing nearly three thousand people. The horror of the September 11 attacks prompted a massive international response that Bush called "the war on terrorism."

This war is unlike past wars because most of its targets are not nations but groups engaged in terrorism that is aimed at U.S. interests at home and abroad. A war without sharply defined battlefronts, it is being waged through a wide variety of instruments, including military force, intelligence gathering, law enforcement, foreign aid, international cooperation, and immigration control. The tactics are also unusual. The rooting out of terrorist cells in the United States and Europe, for example, will be entrusted more to law enforcement agencies than to military units. Bush declared that the goal of the war was the elimination of the international terrorist threat. This objective too has thrust the United States into uncharted territory. It is not clear when and if the goal can be accomplished. Bush promised only that it would be "a long war."

The first U.S. military operation of the war was an attack on Taliban and Al Qaeda forces in Afghanistan. By early 2002, the Taliban government had been toppled, even though Al Qaeda leader Osama bin Laden and most of his top lieutenants evaded capture. On the home front, the most visible signs of the war were long lines at airports, where heightened security measures had been put into effect.

A Gallup survey indicated that nine of ten Americans backed the war in Afghanistan and eight of ten supported its extension to other countries that harbored terrorists (see Figure 17-1). In a CBS News poll, most Americans also expressed confidence in the ability of the U.S. government to protect its citizens, although citizens also said they expected further attacks on the United States. Americans also supported the congressional action that gave the government broad powers to indefinitely detain legal immigrants suspected, even remotely, of having terrorist links. In a Newsweek poll, only 19 percent felt that this grant of authority was excessive.

In 2002, President Bush called Iraq, Iran, and North Korea an "axis of evil," thereby signaling a widening of the war. Attorney General John Ashcroft echoed Bush's words. Said Ashcroft: "A calculated, malignant, devastating evil has arisen in our world." The administration announced its

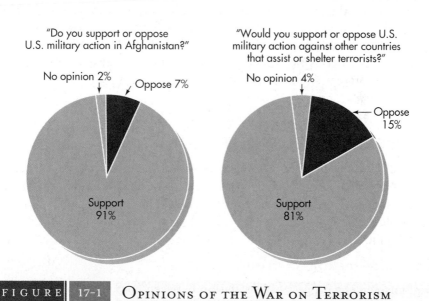

"Do you support or oppose U.S. military action in Afghanistan?"

No opinion 2%   Oppose 7%

Support 91%

"Would you support or oppose U.S. military action against other countries that assist or shelter terrorists?"

No opinion 4%

Oppose 15%

Support 81%

FIGURE 17-1 OPINIONS OF THE WAR ON TERRORISM

Americans were highly supportive of President Bush's decision to use military force in Afghanistan and also willing to back military action in other countries that pose a terrorist threat.

Source: Gallup survey, November 27, 2001.

determination to overthrow Iraq's Saddam Hussein by the use of U.S. military force if necessary. Bush said he was willing to engage in "preventive war"—one in which the United States would strike first and before a threat was immediate rather than striking only if it was attacked. This announcement troubled America's traditional allies, who worried that an unprovoked attack on Iraq would so thoroughly alienate the Arab world that the terrorists would have no trouble finding the money and volunteers to carry out their war against the West. America's allies urged the Bush administration to use the United Nations as the means of obtaining Iraqi disarmament. In late 2002, the UN passed a resolution that required Iraq to accept weapons inspections or face a use of force to ensure its compliance with previous resolutions requiring its elimination of all weapons of mass destruction. A two-track policy ensued. UN weapons inspectors entered Iraq while at the same time a buildup of U.S. combat forces took place in the region in case a military attack was deemed necessary by the Bush administration. And as those two events were taking place, tensions with North Korea intensified when that nation announced it had been pursuing a secret nuclear weapons program.

In March 2003, U.S. military forces launched an attack on Saddam Hussein's regime in Iraq, marking an end to the negotiation process. But it hardly marked the end of the war on terrorism, which will be a prolonged one, perhaps extending over several decades. The U.S. budget for fiscal year 2004 reflected the post-September 11 agenda. The budget included substantial increases in spending for military defense, intelligence-gathering, foreign assistance, and homeland security.

THE PROCESS OF FOREIGN AND MILITARY POLICYMAKING

National security is unlike other areas of government policy because it rests on relations with actors outside rather than inside a country. As a result, the chief instruments of national security policy—diplomacy, military force, economic exchange, and intelligence gathering—differ from those of domestic policy.

The Policymaking Instruments

Diplomacy is the process of negotiation between countries. In most cases, nations prefer to settle their differences by talking rather than by fighting. Through negotiation, countries can usually reach agreement on common (mutual) problems. By definition, acts of diplomacy involve negotiations between two (*bilateral*) or more (*multilateral*) nations.

Military power is a second instrument of foreign policy, and it can be used *unilaterally*—that is, by a single nation acting alone. Most countries use military power as a defensive measure; they maintain forces, or enter into military alliances with other countries, in order to protect themselves from potential aggressors. Throughout the history of nations, however, there have always been a few countries that use military force more actively. The United States is such a nation. In the nineteenth century, it used force to take territory from Native Americans and from Mexico and Spain. Although the United States has not pursued territorial goals since then, it has otherwise made frequent use of its military power. Recent examples include the unilateral invasions of Grenada in 1983, Panama in 1989, and Haiti in 1994; the multilateral war against Iraq in 1991 and the bombing of Serbs in 1995 and 1999; and the nominally multilateral but basically unilateral wars against the Afghan regime in 2002 and against Iraq in 2003.

Economic exchange is a third instrument of world politics. This tool of international relations usually takes one of two forms: trade or assistance. Trade among nations is the more important form. Nearly all countries aspire to a strong trading position so as to have access to outside products and markets for their products. Some countries, however, are so weak economically that they require assistance from more prosperous countries. This assistance is typically also designed to help the stronger partner by providing a market for its goods.

A fourth instrument of world politics is intelligence gathering, which is the process of monitoring other countries' activities. For many reasons, but primarily because all nations pursue their individual self-interest, each nation keeps a watchful eye on the others.

The Policymaking Machinery

In the United States, the lead actor in the application of these four instruments of foreign policy is the president. As was indicated in Chapter 12 and as discussed later in this chapter, the president shares power and responsibility for foreign and military policy with Congress, but the president has the stronger claim to leadership because of the constitutional roles of commander in chief, chief diplomat, and chief executive. For example, although President Bush briefed congressional leaders on his plan for the war in Afghanistan, they played no significant role in the plan's formulation or execution.

The National Security Council (NSC), which is part of the Executive Office of the President (see Chapter 12), coordinates advice on foreign and military issues. Chaired by the president, the NSC includes the vice president and the secretaries of state and defense as full members and the director of the Central Intelligence Agency (CIA) and the chair of the Joint Chiefs of Staff as advisory members. Since the State Department, the Defense Department, and the CIA often have conflicting and self-centered views of national security, the NSC acts to keep the president in charge by providing a more comprehensive perspective. The NSC's staff of experts is directed by the president's national security advisor, who, with an office in the White House and access to defense, diplomatic, and intelligence sources, has become influential in the formulation of foreign policy.

The complexity of international politics makes it impossible for the president or any government agency to fully control U.S. policy. Moreover, as a world power, the United States relies on outside institutions, such as the United Nations, to pursue some of its policy objectives. The key organizational units in the foreign policy area can be categorized according to their primary functions—defense, intelligence, diplomacy, and trade.

Defense Organizations The Department of Defense (DOD), which has roughly 1.1 million uniformed personnel and seven hundred thousand civilian employees, is responsible for the military security of the United States. DOD was created in 1947 when the three military services—the Army, Navy, and Air Force—were placed under the secretary of defense. Each service has its own secretary, but they report to the defense secretary, who represents all the services in relations with Congress and the president. Each service naturally regards its mission and budget as more important than those of the other services. The defense secretary is expected to reduce the adverse effects of these interservice rivalries.

The president also receives military advice from the Joint Chiefs of Staff (JCS). The JCS includes a chair, a vice chair, and a member from each of the uniformed services—the Army, Navy, Air Force, and Marine Corps. The JCS helps shape military strategy and evaluates the military's personnel and weapons needs.

In 2002, the Department of Homeland Security was created to coordinate domestic efforts to protect the United States from terrorist attacks and threats. The responsibilities of the homeland security agency include securing the nation's borders, enhancing defense against biological attacks, preparing emergency personnel (police, firefighters, and rescue workers) for their roles in responding to terrorist attacks, and coordinating efforts to stop domestic terrorism.

Of the country's military alliances, the North Atlantic Treaty Organization (NATO) is the most important. NATO was created after World War II as a "forward defense" against the possible Soviet invasion of Western Europe. After the demise of the Soviet Union, NATO was restructured as

National Security Advisor Condoleezza Rice is shown speaking at a White House gathering. The president's national security advisor is responsible for combining information provided by military, diplomatic, and intelligence agencies into advice on broad issues of foreign and defense policy.

a smaller, more flexible force that could deal with new risks, such as international terrorism and ethnic rivalries. The NATO forces, which now include troops from the United States, Canada, and most Western and Eastern European countries, conduct joint military exercises and engage in joint strategic and tactical military planning. NATO's attack on Serbia in 1999 was the first ever military campaign for the alliance. In 2003, NATO's future was thrown into doubt when several key members, including France, Germany, and Belgium, opposed America's war on Iraq, claiming that UN arms inspections were the better alternative.

Intelligence Organizations Foreign and military policy requires a high state of knowledge about what is happening in the world. Responsibility for the gathering of such information falls on specialized federal agencies, including the Central Intelligence Agency (CIA); the National Security Agency, which specializes in electronic communications analysis; and separate intelligence agencies within the Departments of State and Defense.[11] The federal government spends a vast amount annually on intelligence activities: $30 billion is roughly the figure for 2003.

With the decline of the Soviet threat, intelligence agencies have made increased efforts to stop international drug trafficking and terrorism. These efforts are a deterrent but cannot prevent all such activities. The U.S. embassies in Kenya and Tanzania, for example, had no advance warning when terrorist bombs blew them apart in 1998, killing several hundred people, including a dozen Americans. Intelligence agencies also failed to uncover the terrorist planning that culminated in the 2001 attacks on the World Trade Center and the Pentagon.

Diplomatic Organizations The Department of State conducts most of the country's day-to-day business with foreign countries through its embassies, headed by U.S. ambassadors. The secretary of state is one of the most visible and important members of the administration. The department's traditional duties include negotiating political agreements with other nations, protecting U.S. citizens and interests abroad, promoting U.S. economic interests, gathering foreign intelligence, and representing the United States abroad. For all its activities and prominence, the State Department is relatively small. Only about twenty-five thousand people—foreign service officers, policy analysts, administrators, and others—work in the State Department.

America's diplomatic efforts also take place through international organizations such as the Organization of American States (OAS) and the United Nations. The UN was established after the Second World War by the victorious allies.[12] It's security council, which included the United States, France, Britain, the Soviet Union, and the Republic of China, was to be an instrument of multilateral policymaking; the world's strongest powers would work together for global harmony and prosperity. When the United States and Soviet Union entered into the cold war, all hope of such cooperation vanished.

The breakdown of the Soviet bloc in 1989 renewed the possibility that the world's great powers could work together to achieve common goals. The first major opportunity came in the Persian Gulf conflict of 1990–91, when the United States led a UN force that first blocked Iraqi forces and then attacked them. Some analysts believe that the UN might someday be able to play the large role in international affairs that was envisioned for it when it was chartered. International terrorism, ethnic conflict, and drug trafficking are among the problems that the UN has recently addressed. Other analysts are skeptical about the UN's capacity to solve difficult international problems. UN operations are normally effective only to the degree that member nations agree on a course of action. In 2003, opposition from France, China, and Russia forced the United States and Britain to pursue the war against Iraq without UN Security Council approval.

Economic Organizations The increased importance of the global economy has brought to the fore a new set of government agencies, those representing economic sectors. The Agriculture, Commerce, Labor, and Treasury Departments are playing increasingly important roles in foreign affairs. In addition, some specialty agencies, such as the Federal Trade

Commission and the Export-Import Bank of the United States, are involved in international trade and finance.

The United States also works through major international organizations that promote goals, such as economic development and free trade, that are consistent with U.S. policy objectives. The newest of these international organizations is the World Trade Organization (WTO), which was created in 1995 and is the formal institution through which most nations negotiate general rules of international trade. The WTO also adjudicates disagreements over the meaning of these rules. In 1998, for example, the American film company Kodak lost a dispute with the Japanese film company Fuji. Kodak had charged that Fuji was involved in unfair marketing practices, which prevented Kodak from gaining a significant share of film sales in Japan. The WTO sided with Fuji's argument that its sales volume was a result of the quality of its film and customer preference.

The World Bank and the International Monetary Fund (IMF) are older institutions. Created at the 1944 Bretton Woods Conference by the United States and Great Britain, these organizations provide financial assistance to developing countries. The World Bank makes long-term loans to poor countries for capital investment projects—such as the construction of dams, power plants, highways, and factories—that will promote economic growth. In contrast, the IMF makes short-term loans so that countries experiencing temporary problems will not collapse economically or resort to ruinous practices, such as the imposition of high tariffs. In 1997 and 1998, for example, the IMF made multibillion-dollar loans to Korea, Thailand, and other Asian countries whose economies had gone into a tailspin from poor investment practices and currency devaluation.

THE MILITARY DIMENSION OF NATIONAL SECURITY POLICY

The launching of the war on terrorism brought about the first major increase—tens of billions of dollars—in U.S. defense spending since the 1980s. The United States spends far more on defense, in both relative and absolute terms, than its allies do. On a per capita basis, U.S. military spending is more than twice that of other nations in the NATO alliance (see "How the United States Compares"). The U.S. defense budget is second to none in the world, but so is the military power it buys. During the Gulf War, the Iraqi army, fourth largest in the world, was no match for the United States's superior military equipment and technology. The war lasted about six weeks, and incurred fewer than two hundred U.S. casualties, but it left an estimated fifty thousand to one hundred thousand Iraqi dead.

How the United States Compares

The Burden of Military Spending

The United States bears a disproportionate share of the defense costs on the NATO alliance. The U.S. military establishment is deployed across the globe, and American taxpayers provide roughly $300 billion annually to maintain it. This expenditure amounts to about $1,000 per year for every man, woman, and child in the United States. By comparison, American's allies annually spend less than $500 per capita on their military establishments.

The war on terrorism has resulted in an increase in U.S. military spending that so far has not been matched by increased spending by America's allies. However, some U.S. policymakers prefer the imbalance because it gives the United States more freedom to act on its own when it prefers to do so.

Annual spending on defense, per capita

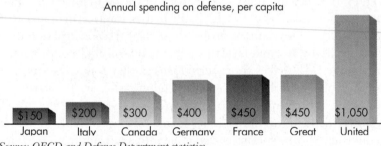

Japan	Italy	Canada	Germany	France	Great	United
$150	$200	$300	$400	$450	$450	$1,050

Source: OECD and Defense Department statistics.

Defense Capability

The United States owes its status as the world's only superpower in part to the strength of its conventional forces. The U.S. Navy has a dozen aircraft carriers, nearly one hundred attack submarines, and hundreds of other fighting and supply ships. The U.S. Air Force has thousands of high-performance aircraft. The U.S. Army has more than five hundred thousand troops on active duty, and they are amply supported by tanks, artillery pieces, armored personnel carriers, and attack helicopters.

Assessments of military power have traditionally been based on the number of planes, tanks, and other weapons that a nation has. But increasingly, these assessments must also account for the ability of a nation to connect these weapons to information. Surveillance devices (such as satellites), high-speed computers, and sophisticated software give military commanders the ability to gather, process, and disseminate information about tactical and strategic situations and thus to direct the use of their weaponry. In the war in Afghanistan, the United States was able to avoid the risk of committing large troop units to the fighting. Special forces soldiers, operating individually and in small groups, were deployed. Using their night-vision equipment and computer-assisted locators, they directed air strikes on Taliban and Al Qaeda positions. According to analysts, no other nation has anywhere near the advanced weapons systems that the United States possesses.[13]

Even though there is a "revolution in military power," older weapons systems are still a part of the American arsenal. The nuclear weapons that starkly defined the nation's cold war with the Soviet Union are an example. During the cold war, the United States followed a policy of **deterrence,** which included a nuclear arsenal capable of destroying the Soviet Union many times over. Deterrence was based on the notion that the Soviet Union would be deterred from launching a nuclear attack by the knowledge that even if it destroyed the United States, it too would be obliterated.

The Uses of Military Power

U.S. military forces have been trained for or called on for six types of military action.

Unlimited Nuclear Warfare The idea of an all-out nuclear war was always too horrible to imagine, but the fear of nuclear holocaust has diminished since the cold war ended. The United States and Russia have reduced their nuclear arsenals and have created monitoring systems that are designed to reduce the possibility that either side could launch a surprise attack. Nevertheless, both sides retain their capacity for a full-scale nuclear war. America's nuclear weapons are deployed in what is called the "nuclear triad," which refers to the three ways in which these weapons can be launched—by land-based missiles, submarine-based missiles, and bombers. The triad provides a "second-strike capability"—the ability to absorb a first-strike nuclear attack and survive with enough nuclear power for massive retaliation (second strike).

Limited Nuclear Warfare Some experts believe that although the risk of an all-out nuclear attack on the United States has diminished, the possibility that a single nuclear weapon might be used against the United States may have increased. A major concern arising from the breakup of the Soviet Union has been control of its nuclear weapons, strategic and tactical. In addition, terrorist groups and "outlaw" regimes, such as North Korea, are a threat because the technology and materials that are required to build nuclear weapons are more widely accessible than ever before. Accordingly, the United States, Russia, and other nuclear powers are cooperating to reduce the spread of nuclear weapons. One goal of the war on terrorism is the destruction of nuclear programs in countries such as North Korea.

Unlimited Conventional Warfare The end of the cold war has also reduced the prospect of an unlimited conventional war. A great part of U.S. military preparedness and strategy in the past half century was based on the scenario of an invasion of Western Europe by the Soviet Union and its allies. Even if the cold war should begin anew, Russia or any other part of the former Soviet Union would require years to build its military capacity to the point where it could pose a credible threat to the West. Since the end of the cold war, U.S. policy has aimed to prevent a resurgence of aggressive Russian nationalism. Through economic and other forms of encouragement, the United States and other industrialized nations have sought to assist Russia in a transition toward a more open and democratic political system.

Limited Conventional Warfare Recent conflicts in Iraq, the Balkans, and Afghanistan have demonstrated that the United States has the military capacity to punish a well-armed foe. These conflicts have not demonstrated, however, that limited conventional wars routinely produce satisfactory results over the longer term. The reason is simple enough. If a political problem can be easily resolved, there is almost never a reason to apply military force. Diplomatic, economic, and other forms of intervention are normally sufficient to achieve a resolution. Limited conventional warfare comes into play when other methods fail—that is, when the division between the contending parties is too deep to be resolved peacefully or when an aggressor is unrelenting. However, military force cannot always correct the problem that triggered the military response. Thus, in Iraq and Kosovo, intervention by the United States succeeded militarily but did not completely resolve the underlying problems.

Counterinsurgency The Vietnam conflict was an **insurgency,** an uprising by irregular forces against an established government. In most Third World countries, insurgencies originate in the grievances of people who are struggling against the monopoly of economic and political power by a ruling elite. In the past, the insurgents often received support in the form of military equipment from the Soviet Union. Most insurgencies were therefore seen by the United States as a threat to its political and economic interests.

U.S. involvement in Third World insurgencies dropped sharply after Vietnam and diminished even further with the end of the cold war. Neither the American public nor U.S. officials have wanted to involve the nation deeply in such wars, although more limited activities, such as the training and equipping of foreign troops, are a part of U.S. defense policy. Nearly a thousand U.S. troops were placed in an advisory role in the Philippines in

2002 as part of an effort to defeat a Muslim insurgent group there with loose ties to the Al Qaeda terrorist network. A 2002 Fox News poll indicated that 81 percent of Americans approved of the deployment.

Police-Type Action With the end of the cold war, U.S. policymakers began to pay closer attention to other global problems, including drug trafficking, political instability, population movement, and terrorism. The U.S. military has become increasingly involved with these problems. U.S. peacekeeping missions in Somalia, the Balkans, and Haiti are examples, as is the use of U.S. military advisers in drug-interdiction operations in Latin America. U.S. military personnel have also been used to stop boat people from Cuba, Haiti, and other Caribbean islands from entering the United States illegally.

U.S. military commanders have been reluctant to expand their mission to include police-type actions, such as immigration control, that traditionally have been a civilian responsibility. But given the high cost of keeping a large defense force, the absence of a highly visible and dangerous enemy such as the former Soviet Union, and the increase in the types of problems that require police-type action, it is likely that the pressure to use U.S. troops in unconventional ways will continue.

The Politics of National Defense

All Americans would agree that the physical security of the United States is of paramount concern. The consensus sometimes breaks down, however, on specific issues. The Vietnam conflict created deep and lasting divisions

U.S. Army troops in Afghanistan emerge from a small meeting room on the edge of the Kandahar Airport. The strategy session took place during the U.S. attack on Taliban and Al Qaeda forces, which was dubbed Operation Enduring Freedom.

of opinion over the proper uses of America's military capacity. In contrast, U.S. policy in the Afghanistan war had majority support from start to end.

Public Opinion and Elite Conflict Defense policy is a mix of *majoritarian* and *elite* politics. On issues of broad national concern, majority opinion is a vital component.[14] It was public opinion, for example, that ultimately forced U.S. policymakers to withdraw American troops from Vietnam and Somalia.

Debates over foreign and defense policy, however, typically take place among political elites.[15] Most citizens are not interested enough to contribute significantly to most of these debates. Few Americans, for example, can name even half the countries in Africa, much less speak knowledgeably about their politics. This situation gives officials and foreign policy specialists wide latitude in determining policy.

The Military-Industrial Complex Political disputes over defense policy are more than honest differences of opinion among people. They also involve billions of dollars in jobs and contracts.[16] In fiscal year 2003, the U.S. defense budget exceeded $300 billion, or roughly 5 percent of the gross national product. A high level of defense spending has been justified by reference to the nation's security needs. However, an alternative explanation for high defense spending points to the demands of the U.S. armed services and defense firms. In his 1961 farewell address, President Dwight D. Eisenhower warned against the "unwarranted influence" and "misplaced power" of what he termed "the military-industrial complex."[17]

The **military-industrial complex** has three components: the military establishment, the arms industry, and the members of Congress from states and districts that depend heavily on the arms industry. All three benefit from a high level of defense spending, regardless of whether these expenditures can be justified from the standpoint of national security. The economic impact of even a single weapon system can be substantial. The B-1 bomber, for example, was built with the help of 5,200 subcontractors located in forty-eight states and in all but a handful of congressional districts. "This geographic spread gives all sections of the country an important stake in the airplane," concluded one assessment of the B-1.[18] Without doubt, some proportion of U.S. defense spending reflects the workings of the military-industrial complex rather than the requirements of national security. The problem is that no one knows exactly what this proportion is, and the estimates vary widely.

THE ECONOMIC DIMENSION OF NATIONAL SECURITY POLICY

Economic considerations are a vital component of national security policy. In the simplest sense, economic strength is a prerequisite of military strength: a powerful defense establishment can be maintained only by a country that is economically well off. In a broader and more important sense, economic prosperity enables a people to "secure" their way of life. As President Eisenhower said, it is folly to weaken at home what one is trying to strengthen abroad.

A Changing World Economy

Some aspects of U.S. superpower policy have economic benefits. The clearest example is the European Recovery Plan, better known as the Marshall Plan. Proposed in 1947 and named after one of its chief architects, the widely respected General George Marshall, it is perhaps the boldest and most successful U.S. foreign policy initiative of the twentieth century. It called for $3 billion in immediate aid for the postwar rebuilding of Europe, with an additional $10 billion or so to follow. The Marshall Plan was unprecedented both in its scope (today, the equivalent cost would exceed $100 billion) and in its implications—for the first time, the United States had committed itself to an ongoing role in European affairs. The Marshall Plan enabled Western Europe to regain economic and political stability in a relatively short time.

Apart from enabling the countries of Western Europe to better confront the perceived Soviet threat, the Marshall Plan was also designed to meet the economic needs of the United States. Wartime production had lifted the country out of the Great Depression, but the end of the war in 1945 brought a recession and renewed fears of hard times. A rejuvenated Western Europe furnished a market for U.S. goods. In effect, Western Europe became a junior partner within a system of global trade that worked to the advantage of the United States.

Since then, major changes have taken place in the world economy. Germany and Japan have become economic rivals of the United States. Trade between these countries results in a deficit for the United States, particularly with Japan. The United States imports billions more annually in goods and services from Japan than it exports to that country. In addition, Western Europe, including Germany, has become a less-receptive market for U.S. goods. European countries are now each other's best customers, trading among themselves through the European Union (EU).

In economic terms, the world is tripolar—power is concentrated in three centers. One center is the United States, which produces roughly 20 percent of the world's goods and services. Another center is Japan, which accounts for 10 percent of the world's economy; China with its fast-growing economy is also part of this center. The third and largest center, with more than 25 percent of the world's economy product, is the EU, which includes Belgium, Denmark, France, Germany, Great Britain, Greece, Ireland, Italy,

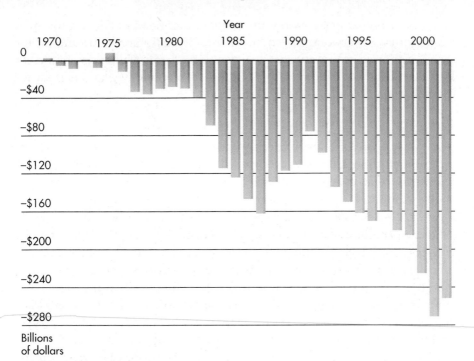

FIGURE   17-2   THE TRADE DEFICIT

Not since 1975 has the United States exported more goods and services than it
imports.
Source: U.S. Census Bureau, 2003.

Luxembourg, the Netherlands, Portugal, Spain, Sweden, Finland, and Austria. In 2004, the EU will expand to include ten new members—Cyprus,
the Czech Republic, Estonia, Hungary, Latvia, Lithuania, Malta, Poland,
Slovakia, and Slovenia.

By a few indicators, the United States is the weakest of the three economic centers. It has, for example, the worst trade imbalance. Although the
United States exports roughly $1 trillion annually in goods and services, the
country imports an even larger amount. The result is a huge trade deficit
that is easily the world's largest. The United States has not had a trade surplus since 1975 and in recent years has run deficits of more than $150 bil-
lion (see Figure 17-2).

In most ways, however, the United States is the strongest of the three
economic powers. The American economy is the best balanced. Like the
EU and Japan, the United States has a strong industrial base, but unlike
Japan, it also has a strong agricultural sector, and unlike both Japan and the

EU, it has abundant natural resources. Its vast fertile plains have made it the world's leading agricultural producer. The United States ranks among the top three countries worldwide in production of wheat, corn, potatoes, peanuts, cotton, eggs, cattle, and pigs. As for natural resources, the United States ranks among the top five nations in copper, uranium, lead, sulfur, zinc, coal, gold, iron ore, natural gas, silver, and magnesium.[19]

According to the Switzerland-based Institute for Management Development, the United States also is more economically competitive than are its trading rivals (see Chapter 15). The United States owes this position to such factors as the strength of its domestic economy and its technical know-how.[20]

This competitive advantage has been evident since the early 1990s. As Asia and parts of Europe have struggled with slow growth rates, the United States has enjoyed economic growth without the accelerated inflation that normally accompanies such a period. The slowdown in the U.S. economy that began in 2000 has tempered the belief that technical know-how had unleashed unstoppable growth. Nevertheless, other countries have looked to the United States, and particularly its technology sector, for policy and market innovations that could spark their own economic expansion.

America's Global Economic Goals

The United States depends on other countries for raw materials, finished goods, and capital to meet Americans' production and consumption demands. Meeting this objective requires the United States to have influence on world markets. The broad goals of the United States in the world economy include:

- Sustaining a stable and open system of trade that will promote prosperity at home
- Maintaining access to energy and other resources that are vital to the strength of the U.S. economy
- Keeping the widening gap between the rich and poor countries from destabilizing the world's economy[21]

Global Trade International commerce is more competitive and important than in the past. Nations' economies are increasingly interconnected as a result of the transportation and communication revolution. Because of it, **multinational corporations** (firms with major operations in more than one country) now find it easy to manage worldwide operations. From a headquarters in New York, a firm has no difficulty directing a production facility in Thailand that is filling orders for markets in Europe and South America. Money, goods, and services now flow freely and quickly across

Some U.S. firms are now as recognizable in other countries as they are in the United States. A Pepsi sign adorns the front of this small shop in Vietnam's Ho Chi Minh City (formerly Saigon).

national borders, and large firms increasingly think about markets in global rather than national terms.

Economic globalization is a term that describes the increased interdependence of nations' economies. This development is both an opportunity and a threat to U.S. economic interests. The opportunity rests with the possibility of increased demand abroad for U.S. goods and services as a result of open trade with other countries and economic growth within these countries. The threat lies in the fact that foreign firms also compete in the global marketplace and may use their competitive advantages, such as cheaper labor, to outposition U.S. firms. In addition, as nations' economies become more interdependent, instability in one market can spread quickly to others, causing a broad decline in the global economy.

The effect of interdependency was evident in the summer of 1998 when the U.S. stock market dropped sharply in response to adverse economic developments in Asia and Latin America. The economic downturn in these regions also affected the U.S. balance of trade. As their economies slowed, their demand for goods declined, and U.S. exports declined accordingly. In addition, as the value of currency in these regions dropped, U.S. firms had

★ STATES IN THE NATION

Exports and State Economies

All states are affected by the global economy, but some states are more dependent on it. Exports are a larger fraction of their economies. The state of Washington, with its aerospace, fishing, and logging industries, depends most heavily on trade with other countries. Exports account for nearly 20 percent of Washington State's economy.

Q. What do most of the states that rely heavily on exports have in common?

A. Most of the top exporting states are located on the nation's borders, which gives them easier access to other countries. For example, the state of Washington abuts Canada, and its seaports are a departure point for goods destined for Asia.

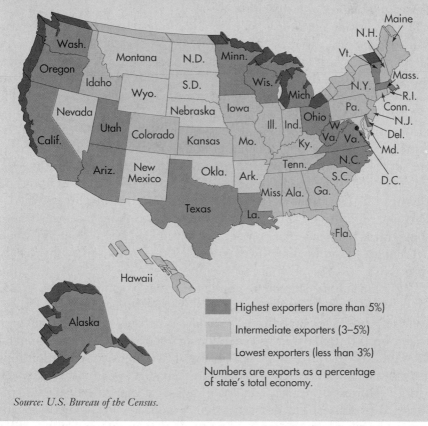

Highest exporters (more than 5%)

Intermediate exporters (3–5%)

Lowest exporters (less than 3%)

Numbers are exports as a percentage of state's total economy.

Source: U.S. Bureau of the Census.

to compete at home with foreign goods that were suddenly lower in price. The net effect was a then-record trade deficit of $180 billion.

Not surprisingly, global economic stability has been a high priority for U.S. officials. Working unilaterally and through international organizations such as the World Bank and IMF, the U.S. government has provided financial and other assistance when economic instability occurs elsewhere in the world. The United States has also pressured other nations to reform their economic policies to meet the demands of a global marketplace. Banking reforms in Japan, Thailand, and Argentina are examples of the type of changes the United States has sought.

If U.S. policymakers are generally in agreement on the need for stable international markets, they are divided over a second issue: free trade. Although the principle of free trade is widely embraced as a linchpin of the global economy, it is a contentious issue in specific contexts. In simple terms, the opposing sides on trade issues can be described as the protectionism and the free-trade positions.

The **free-trade** position assumes that the long-term economic interests of all countries are advanced when tariffs and other trade barriers are kept to a minimum. Most free-trade advocates couple their advocacy with fair-trade demands, but they are committed philosophically and in practice to the idea that free trade fuels economic growth and results in a net gain for U.S. business.

In contrast, **protectionism** emphasizes the immediate interests of domestic producers and includes measures designed to enable them to compete successfully in the domestic market with foreign competitors. For some protectionists, the issue is simply a matter of defending domestic firms against the actions of their foreign competitors. For others, the issue is one of fair trade. They are protectionists in those instances where foreign firms have an unfair competitive advantage, as, for example, when government subsidies allow them to market their goods at an artificially low price.

The political leadership on free trade has typically come from the White House. From a presidential perspective—that is, from a national perspective—free trade is good politics. Although some firms and workers are invariably hurt by it, free trade is generally regarded as good for the economy as a whole. Further, free trade is a means of building strong relationships with other countries, which presidents in their role as national leader seek to forge. (However, presidents do not always act as expected. In 2002, in response to pressure from domestic steel producers, President Bush announced he would impose tariffs of up to 30 percent on imported steel for a period of three years.)

From a congressional perspective, free trade often looks better in theory than in practice. Some members of Congress are unabashed advocates of free trade. Many of them, however, take a protectionist stance when it comes to important local economic interests that are threatened by foreign competition.

Opposing views on global trade clashed in 1993 over the issue of the North American Free Trade Agreement (NAFTA), which aims to create an EU-type market among the United States, Canada, and Mexico. Opponents of the agreement, who included organized labor, most environmental groups, and a majority of the Democrats in Congress, argued that it would result in the loss of countless jobs to Mexico. Its proponents, who included President Clinton, most large U.S. corporations, and most congressional Republicans, contended that the agreement would boost the economies of all three countries and was necessary if the United States was to maintain a leading position in global trade. The measure received majority support in Congress, but only after side agreements were worked out to protect some American producers from the adverse effects of open trade in North America.

NAFTA-like trading agreements with some South American countries can be expected in upcoming years. The United States is already in the process of negotiating these arrangements. The likelihood of their adoption increased when Congress in 2002 granted the president "fast-track authority" in trade negotiations. This authority allows the president to negotiate comprehensive trade agreements with other countries, which are then submitted to Congress for an up or down vote only. This restriction on Congress gives a country the assurance that if it makes concessions in return for concessions from the United States, Congress cannot selectively eliminate the provisions beneficial to that country.

In general, the free-trade position has prevailed during the past decade or so. A prime example is U.S. support for the WTO, which seeks to promote a global free market through reductions in tariffs, protections for intellectual property (copyrights and patents), and similar policies. WTO member nations (roughly 130 in number) have committed themselves to an open trade policy buttressed by regulations that are designed to ensure fair play among the participants. Trade disputes among WTO members are settled by arbitration panels consisting of representatives from the member nations.

The WTO has been criticized by Americans who are opposed in principle to any international organization with the power to establish policy that is binding on the United States. The WTO has also been criticized for placing trade ahead of environmental and labor interests, which sparked mass protests at the 1999 WTO Conference in Seattle. The Seattle protests, which drew activists from around the globe, were aimed at forcing the WTO to take environmental and labor practices (for example, child labor) into account in its trade agreements. The protests were but the first round in an ongoing dispute between economic interests and human-rights and environmental activists. At the World Economic Forum in New York City in 2002, for example, protesters were arrested for disorderly behavior after they attempted to disrupt the proceedings.

Access to Natural Resources Although the United States is rich in natural resources, it is not self-sufficient. The major deficiency is oil; domestic production provides for only about half the nation's use.

Outside the United States, most of the world's oil is found in the Middle East, Latin America, and Russia. Access to this oil has occurred mainly through the marketplace, but U.S. military force has also been a factor. The

Since the end of the cold war, U.S. national security policy has increasingly been defined in the context of America's position in the global economy. Pictured here is the Seattle harbor, one of the nation's busiest ports. Of the fifty states, Washington is the most economically dependent on international trade.

1990–91 war in the Persian Gulf is an example. Iraq's invasion of oil-rich Kuwait threatened Western supplies, and its defeat quelled the threat.

In general, however, military power is not an ideal means of preserving economic leverage. Economic interdependence has made military intervention risky. For example, when Iranian fundamentalists took over the U.S. embassy in Teheran in 1979, the United States refrained from attacking Iran's oil fields in part because the action would have sharply reduced the Middle East's oil-producing capacity.

Relations with the Developing World Political instability in the less developed countries, as in the case of Iraq's invasion of Kuwait, is disruptive to world markets. Less developed countries also offer marketplace opportunities. In order to develop, they need to acquire the goods and services that more industrialized countries can provide. To foster this demand, the United States and the other industrialized countries provide developmental assistance to poorer countries. These contributions include direct foreign aid and also indirect assistance through international organizations such as the IMF and the World Bank. Since World War II, the United States has been far and away the leading source of aid to the developing countries of the world. The United States is still a major contributor but is now far down the list in terms of its per capita annual contributions (see Figure 17-3). The primary recipient of U.S. foreign aid is Israel, which gets more than a third of the total.

Foreign aid is a prime target of politicians. Upon being named chair of the Senate Foreign Relations Committee in 1995, Jesse Helms (R-N.C.) said he would trim millions in aid "going down foreign ratholes."[22] Many Americans share the view that the United States ought not to be funding discretionary programs abroad when there are pressing needs at home. The unpopularity of foreign aid is also a consequence of the public's exaggerated notion of how much the United States spends in this area. In a 1994 poll that asked respondents to name the largest federal programs, foreign aid was at the top of the list (27 percent said it was the most expensive federal program). In fact, foreign aid is near the bottom, accounting for less than 1 percent of the total federal budget.[23]

Foreign aid accounts for only some of the funds that flow from the United States to developing countries: private investment is another source. U.S. firms invest more heavily abroad than do firms from any other country. Foreign investment by U.S.-based multinationals works to America's advantage in at least two important ways. First, it sends a flow of overseas profits back to the United States, which strengthens the country's financial base. Second, it makes other nations dependent on the prosperity of the United States; their economies are linked to U.S. businesses.[24]

Economic development and foreign aid were the focus of President Clinton's 1998 trip to sub-Saharan Africa, the first such trip by an American president. In Johannesburg, South Africa, Clinton said that economic development was the long-term goal, but it was not a substitute for short-term assistance. "Trade cannot replace aid when there is still so much poverty," the president said.[25] During the cold war, the United States had been willing to back almost any type of regime in Africa as long as it was aligned against the Soviet Union. Since then, the United States has had a different view of Africa, much as its view of Asia, Eastern Europe, and South America has changed. The emphasis has been on economic trade, human rights, and democratic institutions. These objectives, more clearly now than at any time since World War I, are the foundation of U.S. foreign policy.

Some critics suggest that the United States has placed too much emphasis on trade issues and not enough on issues of human rights and democracy. Trade with China, in particular, has been a point of contention. The

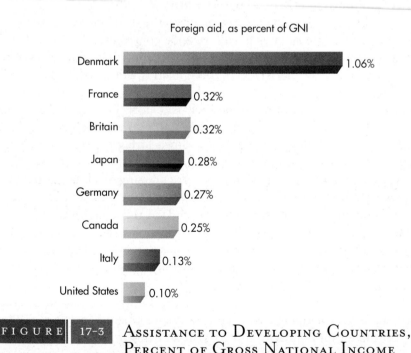

Foreign aid, as percent of GNI

Denmark	1.06%
France	0.32%
Britain	0.32%
Japan	0.28%
Germany	0.27%
Canada	0.25%
Italy	0.13%
United States	0.10%

FIGURE 17-3 ASSISTANCE TO DEVELOPING COUNTRIES, PERCENT OF GROSS NATIONAL INCOME

The United States ranks relatively high (though not the highest) in terms of total amount spent on foreign aid to developing countries but ranks low in terms of percentage of gross national income.

Source: OECD (Organization for Economic Cooperation and Development), 2002.

LIBERTY, EQUALITY, AND SELF-GOVERNMENT
What's Your Opinion?

American Values

During the 1950s, President Dwight Eisenhower warned against neglecting at home the values that the United States is trying to promote abroad. He worried that measures designed to protect freedom elsewhere in the world could shrink freedom in the United States. He thought that excessive governmental secrecy and limits on civil liberties—justified in the name of national security—were a threat to American liberty and self-government.

This argument has resurfaced in the context of the war on terrorism. Nearly all Americans agree that the terrorist threat cannot be met without some changes in how government operates. However, disagreement has arisen over specific policies, such as the prolonged detention of noncitizens and the secrecy surrounding U.S. security activities.

How much latitude do you think policymakers should have in their pursuit of the war on terrorism? If you had to take a risk one way or the other, would you err on the side of a lot of latitude or a little?

Chinese government's brutal crackdown on pro-democracy demonstrators in Beijing's Tiananmen Square in 1989 and subsequent treatment of political dissidents led some U.S. policymakers and activists to conclude that China's trade with the United States should be contingent on a dramatic improvement in its human-rights record. And in fact the United States has pressured China and other countries to improve their human-rights policies. On his 2002 trip to China, President Bush criticized that nation's restrictions on religious freedom. But U.S. pressure in such instances has stopped at the point where trade relations would be seriously jeopardized. In 2000, Congress voted to normalize trade with China on a continuing basis. Free trade has been seen as a key to political liberalization. According to this view, improved trade raises living standards, which gradually creates a demand for individual rights and democratic institutions. President Bush describes free trade as "a forward strategy for freedom."

The Politics of Global Economic Policy

The global economy has changed a great deal since America's halcyon days in the period immediately following World War II. It is greatly more competitive and less responsive to military power. The United States depends more heavily than in the past on the strength of its own economy to forge a favorable position in world trade. This situation has caused U.S. corporations in recent years to launch cost-cutting measures in order to make their products more competitive in the global market.[26] The changes have also led U.S. policymakers to alter their approaches to business regulation, public education, and many other policies that affect the country's competitive position. Another indicator of a new approach is the emphasis that the United States has placed on the WTO, whose member nations are committed to lowering trade barriers so as to promote the type of world trading system that can benefit all participating countries.

Public opinion in recent years has consistently supported the idea that the United States must be a leader in global trade. This opinion seems to reflect the lesson that American elites and officials have drawn from international experiences during the last half-century, particularly during the past decade or so. The consensus is broad enough to suggest that economic priorities will continue to be a driving factor in American foreign policy.

A NEW WORLD?

Nevertheless, global terrorism promises to be the driving force in American foreign policy in the near future. Within a day of the September 11 attack on the World Trade Center and the Pentagon, analysts were comparing it to the attack on Pearl Harbor, which had a transforming effect on the nation's security policies.

It is now clear that the events of September 11, 2001, were not of the magnitude of those of December 7, 1941. That earlier assault on America mobilized the entire nation in a worldwide war on fascism, brought a permanent end to U.S. isolationism, and thrust the United States into a global military and economic leadership role. Nevertheless, September 11 has had and will continue to have a profound effect on U.S. policy. Stopping terrorism has become the nation's most urgent policy goal, which has led to huge increases in spending to combat the threat at home and abroad. The nation's intelligence and law enforcement agencies have been reorganized to increase their capacity to blunt the threat. Shifts in policy toward the Middle East and South Asia have occurred. The U.S. attack on Iraq in 2003 was premised on the assumption that Iraq's chemical and biological weapons could be funneled into the hands of anti-American terrorists. And these are only a few examples of the changes brought about by the events of September 11. There is barely an area of U.S. foreign and defense policy that has been unaffected by the tragic events of that day.

One of the largest changes has been in a direction the terrorists had not predicted. They sought, through the September 11 attack as well as earlier ones on American installations overseas, to force the United States to reduce its presence in the Middle East and in the Arab world generally. The effect has been just the opposite. Just as Pearl Harbor ended isolationism, September 11 blunted a belief among some Washington policymakers that the United States had become too involved in regional conflicts and in the internal affairs of other nations. As the security analyst Philip Gordon noted: "The result of the September 11 attacks will not be an American return to isolationism, but a reinvigoration of engagement."[27]

SUMMARY

From 1945 to 1990, U.S. foreign and defense policies were dominated by a concern with the Soviet Union. During most of this period the United States pursued a policy of containment based on the premise that the Soviet Union was an aggressor nation bent on global conquest. Containment policy led the United States into wars in Korea and Vietnam and to maintain a large defense establishment. U.S. military forces are deployed around the globe, and the nation has a large nuclear arsenal. The end of the cold war, however, made some of this weaponry and much of the traditional military strategy less relevant to maintaining America's security. A redefinition of the military's role in meeting the nation's security needs is taking place.

/pattersonwtp5

The first response of the United States after the end of the cold war was multilateralism: the idea that nations should work together toward common goals, including efforts to address global problems such as drug trafficking, environmental pollution, and regional conflicts. The interventions in the Persian Gulf and the Balkans during the 1990s are examples of this multilateral approach to foreign affairs.

The terrorist attacks on the World Trade Center and the Pentagon resulted in a further adjustment in national security policy. The scope of the terrorist threat has led to large increases in spending on defense and homeland security. This expenditure has been coupled with a partial reorganization of intelligence, law enforcement, immigration, and other agencies as well as new laws affecting the scope of their activities. The terrorist threat also forced the Bush administration to abandon its intention to reduce U.S. involvement abroad. The September 11 attacks have deepened and broadened America's presence overseas while also producing changes at home, such as heightened airport security and intelligence gathering.

Economic considerations have also played a large role in defining national security policy. After World War II, the United States helped establish a global trading system within which it was the leading partner. The nation's international economic position gradually changed, however, owing to the emergence of strong economic competitors, particularly Europe and Japan, and then to economic globalization. Changes in communication, transportation, and computing have altered the way that large corporations operate, and as they have changed their practices, nations have changed their foreign policies. The United States has increasingly defined its national security in economic terms, which means, for example, that trade considerations now play a larger role in defining its relationships with other countries.

The chief instruments of national security policy are diplomacy, military force, economic exchange, and intelligence gathering. These are exercised through specialized agencies of the U.S. government, such as the Departments of State and Defense, which are largely responsive to presidential leadership. National security policy has also relied on international organizations, such as the UN and the World Trade Organization, which are responsive to the global concerns of major nations.

KEY TERMS

cold war	internationalism
containment	isolationism
détente	military-industrial complex
deterrence	multilateralism
economic globalization	multinational corporations
free trade	protectionism
insurgency	

SUGGESTED READINGS

Berger, Peter. *Holy War Inc.: Inside the Secret World of Osama Bin Laden*. New York: Free Press, 2001. A best-selling book on Osama Bin Laden's terrorist network and goals.

Dumbrell, John. *American Foreign Policy: Carter to Clinton*. New York: St. Martin's Press, 1996. A thorough history of United States foreign policy since the Vietnam War.

Greider, William. *One World, Ready or Not: The Manic Logic of Global Capitalism*. New York: Simon and Schuster, 1997. A critical analysis of the global economy and its effect on Americans' lives.

Holsti, Ole. *Public Opinion and American Foreign Policy*. Ann Arbor: University of Michigan Press, 1996. An analysis that concludes public opinion has had a significant and positive impact on U.S. foreign policy.

Johnson, Loch K. *Secret Agencies: U.S. Intelligence Agencies in a Hostile World.* New Haven, Conn.: Yale University Press, 1996. A nuanced assessment of the record of U.S. intelligence agencies.

Kirshner, Jonathan. *Currency and Coercion: The Political Economy of International Monetary Power.* Princeton, N.J.: Princeton University Press, 1997. A study of how states use currency and coercion to advance their security.

Pillar, Paul R., and Michael A. Armacost. *Terrorism and U.S. Foreign Policy.* Washington, D.C.: Brookings Institution, 2001. A look at U.S. foreign policy from the perspective of the global terrorist threat.

Rothgeb, John M. *U.S. Trade Policy: Balancing Economic Dreams and Political Realities.* Washington, D.C.: Congressional Quarterly Press, 2001. A look at the politics and policies of global trade.

LIST OF WEBSITES

http://www.defenselink.mil The U.S. Department of Defense's website; it provides information on each of the armed services, daily news from the American Forces Information Service, and other material.

http://www.foreignrelations.org A website that includes reports and assessments of the Council of Foreign Relations and transcripts of speeches by U.S. and world political leaders on topics of international interest.

http://www.igc.org/igc Website of the Institute for Global Communications (IGC); it provides information and services to organizations and activists on a broad range of international issues, including human rights.

http://www.wto.org The World Trade Organization (WTO) website; it contains information on the organization's activities and has links to related sites.

POLITICS IN THEORY AND PRACTICE

Thinking: What are the major objectives of U.S. foreign and defense policy? What are the mechanisms for pursuing those objectives?

Acting: International conflicts stem from real causes but also have roots in cultural misunderstandings. Americans are thought to be more prone than most peoples to such misunderstandings because they have not been forced by geography to take different cultures, languages, and national identities fully into account. The British social scientist Harold Lasswell remarked that Americans tend to think about the world through the lens of their own experiences. This perspective has become a greater handicap as trade and communication have made the countries of the world ever more interdependent. Even the war on terrorism will depend for its success on a greater sensitivity to the beliefs and aspirations of peoples elsewhere. Individual Americans can do their part by educating themselves about the world. Consider taking a college course in history, political science, language and culture, geography, religion, or any other subject that will introduce you to a part of the world you have not previously studied. Close attention to the foreign affairs coverage in a quality newspaper or periodical can also deepen your understanding of other peoples and cultures.

The New York Times   reading 17

People's Choice: It's Democracy, Like It or Not

by Todd S. Purdum

In 2003, U.S military forces attacked Iraq, seeking to overthrow the regime of Saddam Hussein. President George W. Bush promised the Iraqi people that Hussein's downfall would be followed by the creation of a popular government in Iraq. In this March 9, 2003 article, New York Times correspondent Todd Purdum discusses Americans' faith in democracy and the obstacles to establishing it elsewhere, including America's own unwillingness at times to accept the consequences of free elections.

Washington—For more than two centuries, no nation on earth has preached the healing powers of democracy more consistently than the United States. H. L. Mencken summed up the native faith as "the theory that the common people know what they want, and deserve to get it good and hard."

Now President Bush pledges that by ridding Iraq of Saddam Hussein, "free people will set the course of history, and free people will keep the peace of the world."

If only it were that easy.

Since its emergence as a world power at the beginning of the last century, the United States has often made cold-eyed compromises with the crosscurrents of democracy around the world. From Latin America to Asia, Africa and beyond, Republican and Democratic administrations alike have welcomed democracy when it serves American interests, and been far more ambivalent when it complicates American strategic goals or national security.

Mr. Bush may welcome the idea of an Iraq more democratic than Saddam Hussein's despotic regime, but his administration bemoaned the democratic vote of Turkey's Parliament to deny American troops access to Turkish soil, and the resistance of democracies in "old Europe" to a march to war. The president would doubtless blanch at plebiscites that installed Islamic fundamentalists in Saudi Arabia or Egypt, or a Palestinian democracy that kept Yasir Arafat in power. . . .

Such a gap between preachment and practice is common to all powerful democracies. Only tyrannies can be entirely consistent. But from its earliest days, the American ideal promised something more, and was held up as a global example.

Yet for most of the 19th century, the United States bought or won territory from foreign powers in war, avoided alliances and stood alone. And even though the United States helped found the United Nations and the post-World War II international security framework, it has faced varying degrees of anti-Americanism and charges of hypocrisy.

"It's something much deeper now," said James Chace, a professor of government and public law at Bard College. "What's happening is that the manner in which this administration has largely talked about the world, the kind of general arrogance and bullying tone, just reinforces the sense that we are now seen, and I think rightly, as an imperial power."

"The question," he added, "is whether it will be seen as relatively benevolent, or not."

Shibley Telhami, a Middle East expert at the University of Maryland, said: "It is not about not wanting democracy. I think that we underestimate the extent to which other priorities overtake democracy in our foreign policy."

In a famous speech in 1982 outlining his foreign policy to the British Parliament, Ronald Reagan declared, "The objective I propose is quite simple to state: to foster the infrastructures of democracy, the system of a free press, unions, political parties, universities, which allows a people to choose their own way to develop their own culture, to reconcile their own differences through peaceful means."

But President Reagan often settled for less. The first President Bush protested when a military coup overthrew the democratically elected leader of Haiti, the Rev. Jean-Bertrand Aristide, but was far less exercised around the same time when the Algerian Army canceled the second round of elections that seemed certain to put an Islamic fundamentalist regime in power.

"The romance of democracy is that somehow the results will come out the way you want, but everything we know about democracy is that the result comes out the way the people want," said John Mueller, a political scientist at Ohio State University. "It's a very creaky instrument."

Robert D. Kaplan, a foreign policy expert and author who has twice briefed President Bush, contends that there is no double standard to American ambitions abroad. He argues that the United States should promote democratic change where it can, but not do so irresponsibly in places unready to handle it, where the result could unleash anti-democratic forces.

"Anyone can hold an election," he said, "but building real democratic institutions—police, judges, a constitution—is much harder." He added: "There will always be places where the alternatives are bad, and without hypocrisy you will improve human rights dramatically by going for a more liberal-minded dictator over a Stalinist one. . . ."

Franklin D. Roosevelt established the pattern of choosing stability over freedom in 1945 when he overlooked the autocratic ways of the Saudis and assured King ibn Saud of American protection in exchange for guaranteed supplies of oil—helping make the world safe for Wahhabism. Harry S. Truman's swift recognition of Israel has complicated that compromise ever since, and Mr. Bush has been at pains for months to prove he is serious about making peace in the region.

"When it comes to the Middle East, we have to face the fact that the critical mobilizing issue is the Israeli-Palestinian conflict," said Zbigniew Brzezinski, who was President Jimmy Carter's national security adviser. "Democracy is a consequence of incremental hard work. It's not the consequence of either direct repression, a la Ariel Sharon, or bringing the entire Middle East structure tumbling down, a la Bush. It's an incremental process of building confidence, establishing relationships and pushing people in the direction of compromise."

"Grand-sounding rhetoric on the sidelines, followed by an intense war, which is likely to produce local resentments and further alienate the world, is not going to either produce democracy, or ultimately increase Israel's security," he added. "If we had democracy today in Egypt, we wouldn't have Mubarak but some members of the Muslim Brotherhood. If we're not careful, and pushed for a plebiscite in Saudi Arabia, Prince Abdullah might not do as well as Osama bin Laden."

Perhaps nowhere has the United States' support for democracy and its acceptance of dictatorships clashed more sharply than in Latin America, where one administration after another countenanced repressive regimes from Nicaragua to Chile in the name of hemispheric security.

But starting in the mid-1980's, "there began to emerge a bipartisan consensus about the value of supporting democracy,"

said Peter Hakim, president of the Inter-American Dialogue, a policy study group in Washington. "The Democrats came at it from a human-rights perspective, and the right came at it from an anti-Communist perspective, and there was a kind of merger of both."

No one defined democracy more famously than Winston Churchill, who in 1947 called it "the worst form of government, except all those other forms that have been tried from time to time." Perhaps no statesman knew more of what he spoke: after all, his own people had voted him out of office two years earlier, after he led them to the greatest military victory in their history.

What's Your Opinion?

What conditions are necessary for democracy to take root in countries that have little or no experience with this form of government? Should the United States accept the risk of supporting free elections in countries that do not have the kind of society or institutions conducive to the maintenance of a stable democratic government?

The Declaration of Independence

IN CONGRESS, JULY 4, 1776

The Unanimous Declaration of the Thirteen United States of America

When, in the course of human events, it becomes necessary for one people to dissolve the political bands which have connected them with another, and to assume, among the powers of the earth, the separate and equal station to which the laws of nature and of nature's God entitle them, a decent respect to the opinions of mankind requires that they should declare the causes which impel them to the separation.

We hold these truths to be self-evident, that all men are created equal; that they are endowed by their Creator with certain unalienable rights; that among these, are life, liberty, and the pursuit of happiness. That, to secure these rights, governments are instituted among men, deriving their just powers from the consent of the governed; that, whenever any form of government becomes destructive of these ends, it is the right of the people to alter or to abolish it, and to institute a new government, laying its foundation on such principles, and organizing its powers in such form, as to them shall seem most likely to effect their safety and happiness. Prudence, indeed, will dictate that governments long established, should not be changed for light and transient causes; and, accordingly, all experience hath shown, that mankind are more disposed to suffer, while evils are sufferable, than to right themselves by abolishing the forms to which they are accustomed. But, when a long train of abuses and usurpations, pursuing invariably the same object, evinces a design to reduce them under absolute despotism, it is their right, it is their duty, to throw off such government and to provide new guards for their future security. Such has been the patient sufferance of these colonies, and such is now the necessity which constrains them to alter their former systems of government. The history of the present King of Great Britain is a history of repeated injuries and usurpations, all having, in direct object, the establishment of an absolute tyranny over these States. To prove this, let facts be submitted to a candid world:

He has refused his assent to laws the most wholesome and necessary for the public good.

He has forbidden his governors to pass laws of immediate and pressing importance, unless suspended in their operation till his assent should be obtained; and, when so suspended, he has utterly neglected to attend to them.

He has refused to pass other laws for the accommodation of large districts of people, unless those people would relinquish the right of representation in the legislature; a right inestimable to them, and formidable to tyrants only.

He has called together legislative bodies at places unusual, uncomfortable, and distant from the depository of their public records, for the sole purpose of fatiguing them into compliance with his measures.

He has dissolved representative houses repeatedly for opposing, with manly firmness, his invasions on the rights of the people.

He has refused, for a long time after such dissolutions, to cause others to be elected; whereby the legislative powers, incapable of annihilation, have returned to the people at large for their exercise; the state remaining, in the meantime, exposed to all the danger of invasion from without, and convulsions within.

He has endeavored to prevent the population of these States; for that purpose, obstructing the laws for naturalization of foreigners, refusing to pass others to encourage their migration hither, and raising the conditions of new appropriations of lands.

He has obstructed the administration of justice, by refusing his assent to laws for establishing judiciary powers.

He has made judges dependent on his will alone, for the tenure of their offices, and the amount and payment of their salaries.

He has erected a multitude of new offices, and sent hither swarms of officers to harass our people, and eat out their substance.

He has kept among us, in time of peace, standing armies, without the consent of our legislatures.

He has affected to render the military independent of, and superior to, the civil power.

He has combined, with others, to subject us to a jurisdiction foreign to our Constitution, and unacknowledged by our laws; giving his assent to their acts of pretended legislation:

For quartering large bodies of armed troops among us:

For protecting them by a mock trial, from punishment, for any murders which they should commit on the inhabitants of these States:

For cutting off our trade with all parts of the world:

For imposing taxes on us without our consent:

For depriving us, in many cases, of the benefit of trial by jury:

For transporting us beyond seas to be tried for pretended offences:

For abolishing the free system of English laws in a neighboring province, establishing therein an arbitrary government, and enlarging its boundaries, so as to render it at once an example and fit instrument for introducing the same absolute rule into these colonies:

For taking away our charters, abolishing our most valuable laws, and altering, fundamentally, the powers of our governments:

For suspending our own legislatures, and declaring themselves invested with power to legislate for us in all cases whatsoever.

He has abdicated government here, by declaring us out of his protection, and waging war against us.

He has plundered our seas, ravaged our coasts, burnt our towns, and destroyed the lives of our people.

He is, at this time, transporting large armies of foreign mercenaries to complete the works of death, desolation, and tyranny, already begun, with circumstances of cruelty and perfidy scarcely paralleled in the most barbarous ages, and totally unworthy of the head of a civilized nation.

He has constrained our fellow citizens, taken captive on the high seas, to bear arms against their country, to become the executioners of their friends, and brethren, or to fall themselves by their hands.

He has excited domestic insurrections amongst us, and has endeavored to bring on the inhabitants of our frontiers, the merciless Indian savages, whose known rule of warfare is an undistinguished destruction of all ages, sexes, and conditions.

In every stage of these oppressions, we have petitioned for redress, in the most humble terms; our repeated petitions have been answered only by repeated injury. A prince, whose character is thus marked by every act which may define a tyrant, is unfit to be the ruler of a free people.

Nor have we been wanting in attention to our British brethren. We have warned them, from time to time, of attempts made by their legislature to extend an unwarrantable jurisdiction over us. We have reminded them of the circumstances of our emigration and settlement here. We have appealed to their native justice and magnanimity, and we have conjured them, by the ties of our common kindred, to disavow these usurpations, which would inevitably interrupt our connections and correspondence. They, too, have been deaf to the voice of justice and of consanguinity. We must, therefore, acquiesce in the necessity which denounces our separation, and hold them as we hold the rest of mankind, enemies in war, in peace, friends.

We, therefore, the representatives of the United States of America, in general Congress assembled, appealing to the Supreme Judge of the world for the rectitude of our intentions, do, in the name, and by the authority of the good people of these colonies, solemnly publish and declare, that these united colonies are, and of right ought to be, free and independent states: that they are absolved from all allegiance to the British Crown, and that all political connection between them and the state of Great Britain is, and ought to be, totally dissolved; and that, as free and independent states, they have full power to levy war, conclude peace, contract alliances, establish commerce, and to do all other acts and things which independent states may of right do. And, for the support of this declaration, with a firm reliance on the protection of Divine Providence, we mutually pledge to each other our lives, our fortunes, and our sacred honor.

The foregoing Declaration was, by order of Congress, engrossed, and signed by the following members:

JOHN HANCOCK

New Hampshire
Josiah Bartlett
William Whipple
Matthew Thornton

Massachusetts Bay
Samuel Adams
John Adams
Robert Treat Paine
Elbridge Gerry

Rhode Island
Stephen Hopkins
William Ellery

Connecticut
Roger Sherman
Samuel Huntington
William Williams
Oliver Wolcott

New York
William Floyd
Philip Livingston
Francis Lewis
Lewis Morris

New Jersey
Richard Stockton
John Witherspoon
Francis Hopkinson
John Hart
Abraham Clark

Pennsylvania
Robert Morris
Benjamin Rush
Benjamin Franklin
John Morton
George Clymer
James Smith
George Taylor
James Wilson
George Ross

Delaware
Caesar Rodney
George Reed
Thomas M'Kean

Maryland
Samuel Chase

William Paca
Thomas Stone
Charles Carroll, of
  Carrollton

Virginia
George Wythe
Richard Henry Lee
Thomas Jefferson
Benjamin Harrison
Thomas Nelson, Jr.
Francis Lightfoot Lee
Carter Braxton

North Carolina
William Hooper
Joseph Hewes
John Penn

South Carolina
Edward Rutledge
Thomas Heyward, Jr.
Thomas Lynch, Jr.
Arthur Middleton

Georgia
Button Gwinnett
Lyman Hall
George Walton

Resolved, That copies of the Declaration be sent to the several assemblies, conventions, and committees, or councils of safety, and to the several commanding officers of the continental troops; that it be proclaimed in each of the United States, at the head of the army.

The Constitution of The United States of America[1]

We the People of the United States, in Order to form a more perfect Union, establish Justice, insure domestic Tranquility, provide for the common defence, promote the general Welfare, and secure the Blessings of Liberty to ourselves and our Posterity, do ordain and establish this CONSTITUTION for the United States of America.

ARTICLE I

Section 1
All legislative Powers herein granted shall be vested in a Congress of the United States, which shall consist of a Senate and House of Representatives.

Section 2
The House of Representatives shall be composed of Members chosen every second Year by the People of the several States, and the Electors in each State shall have the Qualifications requisite for Electors of the most numerous Branch of the State Legislature.

No Person shall be a Representative who shall not have attained to the Age of twenty-five Years, and been seven Years a Citizen of the United States, and who shall not, when elected, be an Inhabitant of that State in which he shall be chosen.

[Representatives and direct Taxes[2] shall be apportioned among the several States which may be included within this Union, according to their respective Numbers, which shall be determined by adding to the whole Number of free Persons, including those bound to Service for a Term of Years, and excluding Indians not taxed, three fifths of all other Persons.][3] The actual Enumeration shall be made within three Years after the first Meeting of the Congress of the United States, and within every subsequent Term of ten Years, in such Manner as they shall by Law direct. The Number of Representatives shall not exceed one for every thirty Thousand, but each State shall have at Least one Representative; and until such

---

[1]This version, which follows the original Constitution in capitalization and spelling, was published by the United States Department of the Interior, Office of Education, in 1935.
[2]Altered by the Sixteenth Amendment.
[3]Negated by the Fourteenth Amendment.

enumeration shall be made, the State of New Hampshire shall be entitled to chuse three, Massachusetts eight, Rhode-Island and Providence Plantations one, Connecticut five, New York six, New Jersey four, Pennsylvania eight, Delaware one, Maryland six, Virginia ten, North Carolina five, South Carolina five, and Georgia three.

When vacancies happen in the Representation from any State, the Executive Authority thereof shall issue Writs of Election to fill such Vacancies.

The House of Representatives shall chuse their Speaker and other Officers; and shall have the sole Power of Impeachment.

Section 3

The Senate of the United States shall be composed of two Senators from each State, chosen by the Legislature thereof, for six Years; and each Senator shall have one Vote.

Immediately after they shall be assembled in Consequence of the first Election, they shall be divided as equally as may be into three Classes. The Seats of the Senators of the first Class shall be vacated at the Expiration of the second Year, of the second Class at the Expiration of the fourth Year, and of the third Class at the Expiration of the sixth Year, so that one-third may be chosen every second Year; and if Vacancies happen by Resignation, or otherwise, during the Recess of the Legislature of any State, the Executive thereof may make temporary Appointments until the next Meeting of the Legislature, which shall then fill such Vacancies.

No Person shall be a Senator who shall not have attained to the Age of thirty Years, and been nine Years a Citizen of the United States, and who shall not, when elected, be an Inhabitant of that State for which he shall be chosen.

The Vice President of the United States shall be President of the Senate, but shall have no vote, unless they be equally divided.

The Senate shall chuse their other Officers, and also a President pro tempore, in the absence of the Vice President, or when he shall exercise the Office of President of the United States.

The Senate shall have the sole Power to try all Impeachments. When sitting for that purpose they shall be on Oath or Affirmation. When the President of the United States is tried, the Chief Justice shall preside: And no person shall be convicted without the Concurrence of two thirds of the Members present.

Judgment in Cases of Impeachment shall not extend further than to removal from Office, and disqualification to hold and enjoy any Office of honor, Trust, or Profit under the United States: but the Party convicted shall nevertheless be liable and subject to Indictment, Trial, Judgment and Punishment, according to Law.

Section 4

The Times, Place and Manner of holding Elections for Senators and Representatives, shall be prescribed in each State by the Legislature thereof; but the Congress may at any time by Law make or alter such Regulations, except as to the Places of Chusing Senators.

The Congress shall assemble at least once in every Year, and such Meeting shall be on the first Monday in December, unless they shall by Law appoint a different Day.

Section 5

Each House shall be the Judge of the Elections, Returns and Qualifications of its own Members, and a Majority of each shall constitute a Quorum to do Business; but a smaller number may adjourn from day to day, and may be authorized to compel the Attendance of absent Members, in such Manner, and under such Penalties, as each House may provide.

Each House may determine the Rules of its Proceedings, punish its Members for disorderly Behaviour, and, with the Concurrence of two thirds, expel a Member.

Each House shall keep a Journal of its Proceedings, and from time to time publish the same, excepting such Parts as may in their Judgment require Secrecy; and the Yeas and Nays of the Members of either House on any question shall, at the Desire of one fifth of those Present, be entered on the Journal.

Neither House, during the Session of Congress, shall, without the Consent of the other, adjourn for more than three days, nor to any other Place than that in which the two Houses shall be sitting.

Section 6

The Senators and Representatives shall receive a Compensation for their Services, to be ascertained by Law, and paid out of the Treasury of the United States. They shall in all Cases, except Treason, Felony, and Breach of the Peace, be privileged from Arrest during their Attendance at the Session of their respective Houses, and in going to and returning from the same; and for any Speech or Debate in either House, they shall not be questioned in any other Place.

No Senator or Representative shall, during the Time for which he was elected, be appointed to any civil Office under the Authority of the United States, which shall have been created, or the Emoluments whereof shall have been increased, during such time; and no Person holding any Office under the United States shall be a Member of either House during his continuance in Office.

Section 7

All Bills for raising Revenue shall originate in the House of Representatives; but the Senate may propose or concur with Amendments as on other bills.

Every Bill which shall have passed the House of Representatives and the Senate, shall, before it becomes a Law, be presented to the President of the United States; if he approve he shall sign it, but if not he shall return it, with his Objections, to that House in which it shall have originated, who shall enter the Objections at large on their Journal, and proceed to reconsider it. If after such Reconsideration two thirds of that House shall agree to pass the bill, it shall be sent, together with the objections, to the other House, by which it shall likewise be reconsidered, and if approved by two thirds of that House, it shall become a Law. But in all such Cases the Votes of both Houses shall be determined by Yeas and Nays, and the Names of the Persons voting for and against the Bill shall be entered on the Journal of each House respectively. If any Bill shall not be returned by the President within ten Days (Sundays excepted) after it shall have been presented to him, the Same shall be a Law, in like Manner as if he had signed it, unless the Congress by their Adjournment prevent its Return, in which Case it shall not be a Law.

Every Order, Resolution, or Vote to which the Concurrence of the Senate and House of Representatives may be necessary (except on a question of Adjournment) shall be presented to the President of the United States; and before the Same shall take Effect, shall be approved by him, or being disapproved by him, shall be repassed by two thirds of the Senate and House of Representatives, according to the Rules and Limitations prescribed in the Case of a Bill.

Section 8

The Congress shall have Power To lay and collect Taxes, Duties, Imposts and Excises, to pay the Debts and provide for the common Defence and general Welfare of the United States; but all Duties, Imposts and Excises shall be uniform throughout the United States;

To borrow money on the credit of the United States;

To regulate Commerce with foreign Nations, and among the several States, and with the Indian Tribes;

To establish a uniform rule of Naturalization, and uniform Laws on the subject of Bankruptcies throughout the United States;

To coin Money, regulate the Value thereof, and of foreign Coin, and fix the Standard of Weights and Measures;

To provide for the Punishment of counterfeiting the Securities and current Coin of the United States;

To establish Post Offices and post Roads;

To promote the Progress of Science and useful Arts, by securing for limited Times to Authors and Inventors the exclusive Right to their respective Writings and Discoveries;

To constitute Tribunals inferior to the Supreme Court;

To define and punish Piracies and Felonies committed on the high Seas, and Offenses against the Law of Nations;

To declare War, grant Letters of Marque and Reprisal, and make Rules concerning Captures on Land and Water;

To raise and support Armies, but no Appropriation of Money to that Use shall be for a longer Term than two Years;

To provide and maintain a Navy;

To make Rules for the Government and Regulation of the land and naval forces;

To provide for calling forth the Militia to execute the Laws of the Union, suppress Insurrections and repel Invasions;

To provide for organizing, arming, and disciplining the Militia, and for governing such Part of them as may be employed in the Service of the United States, reserving to the States respectively, the Appointment of the Officers, and the Authority of training the Militia according to the discipline prescribed by Congress;

To exercise exclusive Legislation in all Cases whatsoever, over such District (not exceeding ten Miles square) as may, by Cession of particular States, and the acceptance of Congress, become the Seat of the Government of the United States, and to exercise like Authority over all Places purchased by the Consent of the Legislature of the State in which the Same shall be, for the Erection of Forts, Magazines, Arsenals, Dock-yards, and other needful Buildings;—And

To make all Laws which shall be necessary and proper for carrying into Execution the foregoing Powers, and all other Powers vested by this Constitution in the Government of the United States, or in any Department or Officer thereof.

Section 9

The Migration or Importation of such Persons as any of the States now existing shall think proper to admit, shall not be prohibited by the Congress prior to the Year one thousand eight hundred and eight, but a tax or duty may be imposed on such Importation, not exceeding ten dollars for each Person.

The privilege of the Writ of Habeas Corpus shall not be suspended, unless when in Cases of Rebellion or Invasion the public Safety may require it.

No bill of Attainder or ex post facto Law shall be passed.

No capitation, or other direct, Tax shall be laid unless in Proportion to the Census or Enumeration herein before directed to be taken.

No Tax or Duty shall be laid on Articles exported from any State.

No Preference shall be given by any Regulation of Commerce or Revenue to the Ports of one State over those of another: nor shall Vessels bound to, or from, one State, be obliged to enter, clear, or pay Duties in another.

No Money shall be drawn from the Treasury, but in Consequence of Appropriations made by Law; and a regular Statement and Account of the Receipts and Expenditures of all public Money shall be published from time to time.

No Title of Nobility shall be granted by the United States: And no Person holding any Office of Profit or Trust under them, shall, without the Consent of the Congress, accept of any present, Emolument, Office, or Title, of any kind whatever, from any King, Prince, or foreign State.

Section 10

No State shall enter into any Treaty, Alliance, or Confederation; grant Letters of Marque and Reprisal; coin Money; emit Bills of Credit; make any Thing but gold and silver Coin a Tender in Payment of Debts; pass any Bill of Attainder, ex post facto Law, or Law impairing the Obligation of Contracts, or grant any Title of Nobility.

No State shall, without the Consent of the Congress, lay any Imposts or Duties on Imports or Exports, except what may be absolutely necessary for executing its inspection Laws; and the net Produce of all Duties and Imposts, laid by any State on Imports or Exports, shall be for the use of the Treasury of the United States; and all such Laws shall be subject to the Revision and Control of the Congress.

No state shall, without the Consent of Congress, lay any duty of Tonnage, keep Troops, or Ships of War in time of Peace, enter into any Agreement or Compact with another State, or with a foreign Power, or engage in War, unless actually invaded, or in such imminent Danger as will not admit of delay.

ARTICLE II

Section 1

The executive Power shall be vested in a President of the United States of America. He shall hold his Office during the Term of four years, and, together with the Vice President, chosen for the same Term, be elected, as follows:

Each State shall appoint, in such Manner as the Legislature thereof may direct, a Number of Electors, equal to the whole Number of Senators and Representatives to which the State may be entitled in the Congress: but no Senator or Representative, or Person holding an Office of Trust or Profit under the United States, shall be appointed an Elector.

[The Electors shall meet in their respective States, and vote by Ballot for two persons, of whom one at least shall not be an Inhabitant of the same State with themselves. And they shall make a List of all the Persons voted for, and of the Number of Votes for each; which List they shall sign and certify, and transmit sealed to the Seat of the Government of the United States, directed to the President of the Senate. The President of the Senate shall, in the Presence of the Senate and House of Representatives, open all the Certificates, and the Votes shall then be counted. The Person having the greatest Number of Votes shall be the President, if such Number be a Majority of the whole Number of Electors appointed; and if there be more than one who have such Majority, and have an equal Number of Votes, then the House of Representatives shall immediately chuse by Ballot one of them for President; and if no Person have a Majority, then from the five highest on the List the said House shall in like Manner chuse the President. But in chusing the President, the Votes shall be taken by States, the Representation from each State having one Vote; a quorum for this Purpose shall consist of a Member or Members from two-thirds of the States, and a Majority of all the States shall be necessary to a Choice. In every Case, after the Choice of the President, the Person having the greatest Number of Votes of the Electors shall be the Vice President. But if there should remain two or more who have equal votes, the Senate shall chuse from them by Ballot the Vice President.]⁴

The Congress may determine the Time of chusing the Electors, and the Day on which they shall give their Votes; which Day shall be the same throughout the United States.

No person except a natural-born Citizen, or a Citizen of the United States, at the time of the Adoption of this Constitution, shall be eligible to the Office of President; neither shall any Person be eligible to that Office who shall not have attained to the Age of thirty-five years, and been fourteen Years a Resident within the United States.

In Case of the Removal of the President from Office, or of his Death, Resignation, or Inability to discharge the Powers and Duties of the said Office, the same shall devolve on the Vice President, and the Congress may by Law provide for the Case of Removal, Death, Resignation, or Inability,

---

⁴Revised by the Twelfth Amendment.

both of the President and Vice President, declaring what Officer shall then act as President, and such Officer shall act accordingly, until the disability be removed, or a President shall be elected.

The President shall, at stated Times, receive for his Services a Compensation, which shall neither be increased nor diminished during the Period for which he shall have been elected, and he shall not receive within that Period any other Emolument from the United States, or any of them.

Before he enter on the execution of his Office, he shall take the following Oath or Affirmation:—"I do solemnly swear (or affirm) that I will faithfully execute the Office of President of the United States, and will, to the best of my Ability, preserve, protect, and defend the Constitution of the United States."

Section 2

The President shall be Commander in Chief of the Army and Navy of the United States, and of the Militia of the several States, when called into the actual Service of the United States; he may require the Opinion, in writing, of the principal Officer in each of the executive Departments, upon any subject relating to the Duties of their respective Offices, and he shall have Power to Grant Reprieves and Pardons for Offenses against the United States, except in Cases of Impeachment.

He shall have Power, by and with the Advice and Consent of the Senate, to make Treaties, provided two-thirds of the Senators present concur; and he shall nominate, and by and with the Advice and Consent of the Senate, shall appoint Ambassadors, other public Ministers and Consuls, Judges of the supreme Court, and all other Officers of the United States, whose Appointments are not herein otherwise provided for, and which shall be established by Law: but the Congress may by Law vest the Appointment of such inferior Officers, as they think proper, in the President alone, in the Courts of Law, or in the Heads of Departments.

The President shall have Power to fill up all Vacancies that may happen during the Recess of the Senate, by granting Commissions which shall expire at the End of their next Session.

Section 3

He shall from time to time give to the Congress Information of the State of the Union, and recommend to their Consideration such Measures as he shall judge necessary and expedient; he may, on extraordinary occasions, convene both Houses, or either of them, and in Case of Disagreement between them, with respect to the Time of Adjournment, he may adjourn them to such Time as he shall think proper; he shall receive Ambassadors and other public Ministers; he shall take care that the Laws be faithfully executed, and shall Commission all the Officers of the United States.

Section 4

The President, Vice President and all civil Officers of the United States, shall be removed from Office on Impeachment for, and Conviction of, Treason, Bribery, or other high Crimes and Misdemeanors.

ARTICLE III

Section 1

The judicial Power of the United States, shall be vested in one supreme Court, and in such inferior Courts as the Congress may from time to time ordain and establish. The Judges, both of the supreme and inferior Courts, shall hold their Offices during good Behaviour, and shall, at stated Times, receive for their Services, a Compensation, which shall not be diminished during their Continuance in Office.

Section 2

The judicial Power shall extend to all Cases, in Law and Equity, arising under this Constitution, the Laws of the United States, and Treaties made, or which shall be made, under their Authority;—to all Cases affecting ambassadors, other public ministers and consuls;—to all cases of admiralty and maritime Jurisdiction;—to Controversies to which the United States shall be a Party;—to Controversies between two or more states;—between a State and Citizens of another State;[5]—between Citizens of different States—between Citizens of the same State claiming Lands under Grants of different States, and between a State, or the Citizens thereof, and foreign States, Citizens, or Subjects.

In all Cases affecting Ambassadors, other public Ministers and Consuls, and those in which a State shall be Party, the supreme Court shall have original Jurisdiction. In all the other Cases before mentioned, the supreme Court shall have appellate Jurisdiction, both as to Law and Fact, with such Exceptions, and under such Regulations as the Congress shall make.

---

[5]Qualified by the Eleventh Amendment.

The trial of all Crimes, except in Cases of Impeachment, shall be by Jury; and such Trial shall be held in the State where the said Crimes shall have been committed; but when not committed within any State, the Trial shall be at such Place or Places as the Congress may by Law have directed.

Section 3

Treason against the United States, shall consist only in levying War against them, or in adhering to their Enemies, giving them Aid and Comfort. No Person shall be convicted of Treason unless on the Testimony of two Witnesses to the same overt Act, or on Confession in open Court.

The Congress shall have power to declare the Punishment of Treason, but no Attainder of Treason shall work Corruption of Blood, or Forfeiture except during the Life of the Person attainted.

ARTICLE IV

Section 1

Full Faith and Credit shall be given in each State to the public Acts, Records, and judicial Proceedings of every other State. And the Congress may by general Laws prescribe the Manner in which such Acts, Records and Proceedings shall be proved, and the Effect thereof.

Section 2

The Citizens of each State shall be entitled to all Privileges and Immunities of Citizens in the several States.

A Person charged in any State with Treason, Felony, or other Crime, who shall flee from Justice, and be found in another State, shall on demand of the executive Authority of the State from which he fled, be delivered up, to be removed to the State having Jurisdiction of the crime.

No Person held to Service or Labour in one State, under the Laws thereof, escaping into another, shall, in Consequence of any Law or Regulation therein, be discharged from such Service or Labour, but shall be delivered up on Claim of the Party to whom such Service or Labour may be due.

Section 3

New States may be admitted by the Congress into this Union; but no new State shall be formed or erected within the Jurisdiction of any other State; nor any State be formed by the Junction of two or more States, or parts of

States, without the Consent of the Legislatures of the States concerned as well as of the Congress.

The Congress shall have Power to dispose of and make all needful Rules and Regulations respecting the Territory or other Property belonging to the United States; and nothing in this Constitution shall be so construed as to Prejudice any Claims of the United States, or of any particular State.

Section 4

The United States shall guarantee to every State in this Union a Republican Form of Government, and shall protect each of them against Invasion; and on Application of the Legislature, or of the Executive (when the Legislature cannot be convened) against domestic Violence.

ARTICLE V

The Congress, whenever two-thirds of both Houses shall deem it necessary, shall propose Amendments to this Constitution, or, on the Application of the Legislatures of two-thirds of the several States, shall call a Convention for proposing Amendments, which, in either Case, shall be valid to all Intents and Purposes, as part of this Constitution, when ratified by the Legislatures of three-fourths of the several States, or by Conventions in three-fourths thereof, as the one or the other Mode of Ratification may be proposed by the Congress; Provided that no Amendment which may be made prior to the Year One thousand eight hundred and eight shall in any Manner affect the first and fourth Clauses in the Ninth Section of the first Article; and that no State, without its Consent, shall be deprived of its equal Suffrage in the Senate.

ARTICLE VI

All Debts contracted and Engagements entered into, before the Adoption of this Constitution, shall be as valid against the United States under this Constitution, as under the Confederation.

This Constitution, and the Laws of the United States which shall be made in Pursuance thereof; and all Treaties made, or which shall be made, under the Authority of the United States, shall be the supreme Law of the Land; and the Judges in every State shall be bound thereby, any Thing in the Constitution or Laws of any State to the Contrary notwithstanding.

The Senators and Representatives before mentioned, and the Members of the several State Legislatures, and all executive and judicial Officers, both of the United States and of the several States, shall be bound by Oath or Affirmation to support this Constitution; but no religious Tests shall ever be required as a qualification to any Office or public Trust under the United States.

Article VII

The Ratification of the Conventions of nine States shall be sufficient for the Establishment of this Constitution between the States so ratifying the same.

Done in Convention by the Unanimous Consent of the States present the Seventeenth Day of September in the Year of our Lord one thousand seven hundred and Eighty seven, and of the Independence of the United States of America the Twelfth. In Witness whereof We have hereunto subscribed our Names.[6]

George Washington
President and deputy
from Virginia

New Hampshire
John Langdon
Nicholas Gilman

Massachusetts
Nathaniel Gorham
Rufus King

Connecticut
William Samuel
Johnson
Roger Sherman

New York
⋆ Alexander Hamilton
New Jersey
William Livingston
David Brearley
William Paterson
Jonathan Dayton

Pennsylvania
⋆Benjamin Franklin
Thomas Mifflin
Robert Morris
George Clymer
Thomas FitzSimmons
Jared Ingersoll
James Wilson
Gouverneur Morris

Delaware
George Read
Gunning Bedford, Jr.
John Dickinson
Richard Bassett
Jacob Broom

Maryland
James McHenry
Daniel of St. Thomas
Jenifer
Daniel Carroll

Virginia
John Blair
⋆ James Madison, Jr.

North Carolina
William Blount
Richard Dobbs
Spaight
Hugh Williamson

South Carolina
John Rutledge
Charles Cotesworth
Pinckney
Charles Pinckney
Pierce Butler

Georgia
William Few
Abraham Baldwin

------

[6]These are the full names of the signers, which in some cases are not the signatures on the document.

Articles in Addition to, and Amendment of, the Constitution of the United States of America, Proposed by Congress, and Ratified by the Legislatures of the Several States, Pursuant to the Fifth Article of the Original Constitution[7]

AMENDMENT I

Congress shall make no law respecting an establishment of religion, or prohibiting the free exercise thereof; or abridging the freedom of speech, or of the press; or the right of the people peaceably to assemble, and to petition the Government for a redress of grievances.

AMENDMENT II

A well regulated Militia, being necessary to the security of a free State, the right of the people to keep and bear Arms shall not be infringed.

AMENDMENT III

No Soldier shall, in time of peace, be quartered in any house, without the consent of the Owner, nor in time of war, but in a manner to be prescribed by law.

AMENDMENT IV

The right of the people to be secure in their persons, houses, papers, and effects, against unreasonable searches and seizures, shall not be violated, and no Warrants shall issue, but upon probable cause, supported by Oath or affirmation, and particularly describing the place to be searched, and the persons or things to be seized.

AMENDMENT V

No person shall be held to answer for a capital or otherwise infamous crime, unless on a presentment or indictment of a Grand Jury, except in cases arising in the land or naval forces, or in the Militia, when in actual

---

[7]This heading appears only in the joint resolution submitting the first ten amendments, which are collectively known as the Bill of Rights. They were ratified on December 15, 1791.

service in time of War or public danger; nor shall any person be subject for the same offence to be twice put in jeopardy of life or limb; nor shall be compelled in any criminal case to be a witness against himself, nor be deprived of life, liberty, or property, without due process of law; nor shall private property be taken for public use, without just compensation.

Amendment VI

In all criminal prosecutions, the accused shall enjoy the right to a speedy and public trial, by an impartial jury of the State and district wherein the crime shall have been committed, which district shall have been previously ascertained by law, and to be informed of the nature and cause of the accusation; to be confronted with the witnesses against him; to have compulsory process for obtaining witnesses in his favour, and to have the Assistance of Counsel for his defence.

Amendment VII

In suits at common law, where the value in controversy shall exceed twenty dollars, the right of trial by jury shall be preserved, and no fact tried by a jury, shall be otherwise reexamined in any Court of the United States, than according to the rules of the common law.

Amendment VIII

Excessive bail shall not be required, nor excessive fines imposed, nor cruel and unusual punishments inflicted.

Amendment IX

The enumeration of the Constitution, of certain rights, shall not be construed to deny or disparage others retained by the people.

Amendment X

The powers not delegated to the United States by the Constitution, nor prohibited by it to the States, are reserved to the States respectively, or to the people.

AMENDMENT XI [1798]

The Judicial power of the United States shall not be construed to extend to any suit in law or equity, commenced or prosecuted against one of the United States by Citizens of another State, or by Citizens or Subjects of any Foreign State.

AMENDMENT XII [1804]

The Electors shall meet in their respective States and vote by ballot for President and Vice-President, one of whom, at least, shall not be an inhabitant of the same State with themselves; they shall name in their ballots the person voted for as President, and in distinct ballots the person voted for as Vice-President, and they shall make distinct lists of all persons voted for as President, and of all persons voted for as Vice-President, and of the number of votes for each, which lists they shall sign and certify, and transmit sealed to the seat of the government of the United States, directed to the President of the Senate;—The President of the Senate shall, in the presence of the Senate and House of Representatives, open all the certificates and the votes shall then be counted;—The person having the greatest number of votes for President, shall be the President, if such number be a majority of the whole number of Electors appointed; and if no person have such majority, then from the persons having the highest numbers not exceeding three on the list of those voted for as President, the House of Representatives shall choose immediately, by ballot, the President. But in choosing the President, the votes shall be taken by states, the representation from each state having one vote; a quorum for this purpose shall consist of a member or members from two-thirds of the states, and a majority of all the states shall be necessary to a choice. And if the House of Representatives shall not choose a President whenever the right of choice shall devolve upon them, before the fourth day of March next following, then the Vice-President shall act as President, as in the case of the death or other constitutional disability of the President.—The person having the greatest number of votes as Vice-President, shall be the Vice-President, if such number be a majority of the whole number of Electors appointed, and if no person have a majority, then from the two highest numbers on the list, the Senate shall choose the Vice-President; a quorum for the purpose shall consist of two-thirds of the whole number of Senators, and a majority of the whole number shall be necessary to a choice. But no person constitutionally ineligible to the office of President shall be eligible to that of Vice-President of the United States.

AMENDMENT XIII [1865]

Section 1
Neither slavery nor involuntary servitude, except as a punishment for crime whereof the party shall have been duly convicted, shall exist within the United States, or any place subject to their jurisdiction.

Section 2
Congress shall have power to enforce this article by appropriate legislation.

AMENDMENT XIV [1868]

Section 1
All persons born or naturalized in the United States, and subject to the jurisdiction thereof, are citizens of the United States and of the State wherein they reside. No State shall abridge the privileges or immunities of citizens of the United States; nor shall any State deprive any person of life, liberty, or property, without due process of law; nor deny to any person within its jurisdiction the equal protection of the laws.

Section 2
Representatives shall be apportioned among the several States according to their respective numbers, counting the whole number of persons in each State, excluding Indians not taxed. But when the right to vote at any election for the choice of electors for President and Vice-President of the United States, Representatives in Congress, the Executive and Judicial officers of a State, or the members of the Legislature thereof, is denied to any of the male inhabitants of such State, being twenty-one years of age, and citizens of the United States, or in any way abridged, except for participation in rebellion, or other crime, the basis of representation therein shall be reduced in the proportion which the number of such male citizens shall bear to the whole number of male citizens twenty-one years of age in such State.

Section 3
No person shall be a Senator or Representative in Congress, or elector of President and Vice-President, or hold any office, civil or military, under the United States, or under any State, who, having previously taken an oath, as a member of Congress, or as an officer of the United States, or as a member of any State legislature, or as an executive or judicial officer of any State, to support the Constitution of the United States, shall have engaged in insurrection or rebellion against the same, or given aid or comfort to the

enemies thereof. But Congress may by a vote of two-thirds of each House, remove such disability.

Section 4
The validity of the public debt of the United States, authorized by law, including debts incurred for payment of pensions and bounties for services in suppressing insurrection or rebellion, shall not be questioned. But neither the United States nor any State shall assume or pay any debts or obligation incurred in aid of insurrection or rebellion against the United States, or any claim for the loss or emancipation of any slave; but all such debts, obligations, and claims shall be held illegal and void.

Section 5
The Congress shall have the power to enforce, by appropriate legislation, the provisions of this article.

AMENDMENT XV [1870]

Section 1
The right of citizens of the United States to vote shall not be denied or abridged by the United States or by any State on account of race, color, or previous condition of servitude—

Section 2
The Congress shall have power to enforce this article by appropriate legislation.

AMENDMENT XVI [1913]

The Congress shall have power to lay and collect taxes on incomes, from whatever source derived, without apportionment among the several States, and without regard to any census or enumeration.

AMENDMENT XVII [1913]

The Senate of the United States shall be composed of two Senators from each State, elected by the people thereof, for six years; and each Senator shall have one vote. The electors in each State shall have the qualifications requisite for electors of the most numerous branch of the State legislatures.

When vacancies happen in the representation of any State in the Senate, the executive authority of such State shall issue writs of election to fill such vacancies: Provided, That the legislature of any State may empower the executive thereof to make temporary appointments until the people fill the vacancies by election as the legislature may direct.

This amendment shall not be so construed as to affect the election or term of any Senator chosen before it becomes valid as part of the Constitution.

AMENDMENT XVIII [1919]

Section 1
After one year from the ratification of this article the manufacture, sale, or transportation of intoxicating liquors within, the importation thereof into, or the exportation thereof from the United States and all territory subject to the jurisdiction thereof for beverage purposes is hereby prohibited.

Section 2
The Congress and the several States shall have concurrent power to enforce this article by appropriate legislation.

Section 3
This article shall be inoperative unless it shall have been ratified as an amendment to the Constitution by the legislatures of the several States, as provided in the Constitution, within seven years from the date of the submission hereof to the States by the Congress.

AMENDMENT XIX [1920]

The right of citizens of the United States to vote shall not be denied or abridged by the United States or by any State on account of sex.

Congress shall have power to enforce this article by appropriate legislation.

AMENDMENT XX [1933]

Section 1
The terms of the President and Vice-President shall end at noon on the 20th day of January, and the terms of Senators and Representatives at noon

on the 3d day of January, of the years in which such terms would have ended if this article had not been ratified; and the terms of their successors shall then begin.

Section 2

The Congress shall assemble at least once in every year, and such meeting shall begin at noon on the 3d day of January, unless they shall by law appoint a different day.

Section 3

If, at the time fixed for the beginning of the term of the President, the President elect shall have died, the Vice-President elect shall become President. If a President shall not have been chosen before the time fixed for the beginning of his term or if the President elect shall have failed to qualify, then the Vice-President elect shall act as President until a President shall have qualified; and the Congress may by law provide for the case wherein neither a President elect nor a Vice President elect shall have qualified, declaring who shall then act as President, or the manner in which one who is to act shall be selected, and such person shall act accordingly until a President or Vice-President shall have qualified.

Section 4

The Congress may by law provide for the case of the death of any of the persons from whom the House of Representatives may choose a President whenever the right of choice shall have devolved upon them, and for the case of the death of any of the persons from whom the Senate may choose a Vice-President whenever the right of choice shall have devolved upon them.

Section 5

Sections 1 and 2 shall take effect on the 15th day of October following the ratification of this article.

Section 6

This article shall be inoperative unless it shall have been ratified as an amendment to the Constitution by the legislatures of three-fourths of the several States within seven years from the date of its submission.

AMENDMENT XXI [1933]

Section 1

The eighteenth article of amendment to the Constitution of the United States is hereby repealed.

Section 2
The transportation or importation into any State, Territory, or possession of the United States for delivery or use therein of intoxicating liquors, in violation of the laws thereof, is hereby prohibited.

Section 3
This article shall be inoperative unless it shall have been ratified as an amendment to the Constitution by conventions in the several States, as provided in the Constitution, within seven years from the date of the submission hereof to the States by the Congress.

AMENDMENT XXII [1951]

No person shall be elected to the office of the President more than twice, and no person who has held the office of President, or acted as President, for more than two years of a term to which some other person was elected President shall be elected to the office of the President more than once.

But this Article shall not apply to any person holding the office of President when this Article was proposed by the Congress, and shall not prevent any person who may be holding the office of President, or acting as President, during the term within which this Article becomes operative from holding the office of President or acting as President during the remainder of such term.

This article shall be inoperative unless it shall have been ratified as an amendment to the Constitution by the legislatures of three-fourths of the several states within seven years from the date of its submission to the states by the Congress.

AMENDMENT XXIII [1961]

Section 1
The District constituting the seat of Government of the United States shall appoint in such manner as the Congress may direct:

A number of electors of President and Vice-President equal to the whole number of Senators and Representatives in Congress to which the District would be entitled if it were a State, but in no event more than the least populous State; they shall be in addition to those appointed by the States, but they shall be considered, for the purposes of the election of President and

Vice-President, to be electors appointed by a State; and they shall meet in the District and perform such duties as provided by the twelfth article of amendment.

Section 2

The Congress shall have power to enforce this article by appropriate legislation.

AMENDMENT XXIV [1964]

Section 1

The right of citizens of the United States to vote in any primary or other election for President or Vice President, for electors for President or Vice President, or for Senator or Representative in Congress, shall not be denied or abridged by the United States or any state by reason of failure to pay any poll tax or other tax.

Section 2

The Congress shall have the power to enforce this article by appropriate legislation.

AMENDMENT XXV [1967]

Section 1

In case of the removal of the President from office or of his death or resignation, the Vice President shall become President.

Section 2

Whenever there is a vacancy in the office of the Vice President, the President shall nominate a Vice President who shall take office upon confirmation by a majority vote of both Houses of Congress.

Section 3

Whenever the President transmits to the President Pro Tempore of the Senate and the Speaker of the House of Representatives his written declaration that he is unable to discharge the powers and duties of his office, and until he transmits to them a written declaration to the contrary, such powers and duties shall be discharged by the Vice President as Acting President.

Section 4

Whenever the Vice President and a majority of either the principal officers of the executive departments or of such other body as Congress may by law provide, transmit to the President Pro Tempore of the Senate and the Speaker of the House of Representatives their written declaration that the President is unable to discharge the powers and duties of his office, the Vice President shall immediately assume the powers and duties of the office as Acting President.

Thereafter, when the President transmits to the President Pro Tempore of the Senate and the Speaker of the House of Representatives his written declaration that no inability exists, he shall resume the powers and duties of his office unless the Vice President and a majority of either the principal officers of the executive departments or of such other body as Congress may by law provide, transmit within four days to the President Pro Tempore of the Senate and the Speaker of the House of Representatives their written declaration that the President is unable to discharge the powers and duties of his office. Thereupon Congress shall decide the issue, assembling within forty-eight hours for that purpose if not in session. If the Congress, within twenty-one days after receipt of the latter written declaration, or, if Congress is not in session, within twenty-one days after Congress is required to assemble, determines by two-thirds vote of both Houses that the President is unable to discharge the powers and duties of his office, the Vice President shall continue to discharge the same as Acting President; otherwise, the President shall resume the powers and duties of his office.

AMENDMENT XXVI [1971]

Section 1

The right of citizens of the United States, who are eighteen years of age or older, to vote shall not be denied or abridged by the United States or by any State on account of age.

Section 2

The Congress shall have the power to enforce this article by appropriate legislation.

AMENDMENT XXVII [1992]

No law varying the compensation for the service of Senators and Representatives shall take effect until an election of Representatives shall have intervened.

Federalist No. 10
(James Madison)

Among the numerous advantages promised by a well-constructed union, none deserves to be more accurately developed than its tendency to break and control the violence of faction. The friend of popular governments never finds himself so much alarmed for their character and fate as when he contemplates their propensity to this dangerous vice. He will not fail, therefore, to set a due value on any plan which, without violating the principles to which he is attached, provides a proper cure for it. The instability, injustice, and confusion introduced into the public councils have, in truth, been the mortal diseases under which popular governments have everywhere perished, as they continue to be the favorite and fruitful topics from which the adversaries to liberty derive their most specious declamations. The valuable improvements made by the American constitutions on the popular models, both ancient and modern, cannot certainly be too much admired; but it would be an unwarrantable partiality to contend that they have as effectually obviated the danger on this side, as was wished and expected. Complaints are everywhere heard from our most considerate and virtuous citizens, equally the friends of public and private faith and of public and personal liberty, that our governments are too unstable, that the public good is disregarded in the conflicts of rival parties, and that measures are too often decided, not according to the rules of justice and the rights of the minor party, but by the superior force of an interested and overbearing majority. However anxiously we may wish that these complaints had no foundation, the evidence of known facts will not permit us to deny that they are in some degree true. It will be found, indeed, on a candid review of our situation, that some of the distresses under which we labor have been erroneously charged on the operation of our governments; but it will be found, at the same time, that other causes will not alone account for many of our heaviest misfortunes; and, particularly, for that prevailing and increasing distrust of public engagements and alarm for private rights which are echoed from one end of the continent to the other. There must be chiefly, if not wholly, effects of the unsteadiness and injustice with which a factious spirit has tainted our public administration.

By a faction I understand a number of citizens, whether amounting to a majority or minority of the whole, who are united and actuated by some common impulse of passion, or of interest, adverse to the rights of other citizens, or to the permanent and aggregate interests of the community.

There are two methods of curing the mischiefs of faction: the one, by removing its causes; the other, by controlling its effects.

There are again two methods of removing the causes of faction: the one, by destroying the liberty which is essential to its existence; the other, by giving to every citizen the same opinions, the same passions, and the same interests.

It could never be more truly said than of the first remedy that it was worse than the disease. Liberty is to faction what air is to fire, an ailment without which it instantly expires. But it could not be a less folly to abolish liberty, which is essential to political life, because it nourishes faction than it would be to wish the annihilation of air, which is essential to animal life, because it imparts to fire its destructive agency.

The second expedient is as impracticable as the first would be unwise. As long as the reason of man continues fallible, and he is at liberty to exercise it, different opinions will be formed. As long as the connection subsists between his reason and his self-love, his opinions and his passions will have a reciprocal influence on each other; and the former will be objects to which the latter will attach themselves. The diversity in the faculties of men, from which the rights of property originate, is not less an insuperable obstacle to a uniformity of interest. The protection of these faculties is the first object of government. From the protection of different and unequal faculties of acquiring property, the possession of different degrees and kinds of property immediately results; and from the influence of these on the sentiments and views of the respective proprietors ensues a division of the society into different interests and parties.

The latent causes of faction are thus sown in the nature of man; and we see them everywhere brought into different degrees of activity, according to the different circumstances of civil society. A zeal for different opinions concerning religion, concerning government, and many other points, as well of speculation as of practice; an attachment to different leaders ambitiously contending for pre-eminence and power; or to persons of other descriptions whose fortunes have been interesting to the human passions, have, in turn, divided mankind into parties, inflamed them with mutual animosity, and rendered them much more disposed to vex and oppress each other than to co-operate for their common good. So strong is this propensity of mankind to fall into mutual animosities that where no substantial occasion presents itself the most frivolous and fanciful distinctions have been sufficient to kindle their unfriendly passions and excite their most violent conflicts. But the most common and durable source of factions has been the various and unequal distribution of property. Those who hold and those who are without property have ever formed distinct interests in society.

Those who are creditors, and those who are debtors, fall under a like discrimination. A landed interest, a manufacturing interest, a mercantile interest, a moneyed interest, with many lesser interests, grow up of necessity in civilized nations, and divide them into different classes, actuated by different sentiments and views. The regulation of these various and interfering interests forms the principal task of modern legislation and involves the spirit of party and faction in the necessary and ordinary operations of government.

No man is allowed to be a judge in his own cause, because his interest would certainly bias his judgment, and, not improbably, corrupt his integrity. With equal, nay with greater reason, a body of men are unfit to be both judges and parties at the same time; yet what are many of the most important acts of legislation but so many judicial determinations, not indeed concerning the rights of single persons, but concerning the rights of large bodies of citizens? And what are the different classes of legislators but advocates and parties to the causes which they determine? Is a law proposed concerning private debts? It is a question to which the creditors are parties on one side and the debtors on the other. Justice ought to hold the balance between them. Yet the parties are, and must be, themselves the judges; and the most numerous party, or in other words, the most powerful faction must be expected to prevail. Shall domestic manufacturers be encouraged, and in what degree, by restrictions on foreign manufacturers? [These] are questions which would be differently decided by the landed and the manufacturing classes, and probably by neither with a sole regard to justice and the public good. The apportionment of taxes on the various descriptions of property is an act which seems to require the most exact impartiality; yet there is, perhaps, no legislative act in which greater opportunity and temptation are given to a predominant party to trample on the rules of justice. Every shilling with which they overburden the inferior number is a shilling saved to their own pockets.

It is in vain to say that enlightened statesmen will be able to adjust these clashing interests and render them all subservient to the public good. Enlightened statesmen will not always be at the helm. Nor, in many cases, can such an adjustment be made at all without taking into view indirect and remote considerations, which will rarely prevail over the immediate interest which one party may find in disregarding the rights of another or the good of the whole.

The inference to which we are brought is that the *causes* of faction cannot be removed and that relief is only to be sought in the means of controlling its *effects*.

If a faction consists of less than a majority, relief is supplied by the republican principle, which enables the majority to defeat its sinister views by regular vote. It may clog the administration, it may convulse the society; but it will be unable to execute and mask its violence under the forms of the Constitution. When a majority is included in a faction, the form of popular government, on the other hand, enables it to sacrifice to its ruling passion or interest both the public good and the rights of other citizens. To secure the public good and private rights against the danger of such a faction, and at the same time to preserve the spirit and the form of popular government, is then the great object to which our inquiries are directed. Let me add that it is the great desideratum by which alone this form of government can be rescued from the opprobrium under which it has so long labored and be recommended to the esteem and adoption of mankind.

By what means is this object attainable? Evidently by one of two only. Either the existence of the same passion or interest in a majority at the same time must be prevented, or the majority, having such coexistent passion or interest, must be rendered, by their number and local situation, unable to concert and carry into effect schemes of oppression. If the impulse and the opportunity be suffered to coincide, we well know that neither moral nor religious motives can be relied on as an adequate control. They are not found to be such on the injustice and violence of individuals, and lose their efficacy in proportion to the number combined together, that is, in proportion as their efficacy becomes needful.

From this view of the subject it may be concluded that a pure democracy, by which I mean a society consisting of a small number of citizens, who assemble and administer the government in person, can admit of no cure for the mischiefs of faction. A common passion or interest will, in almost every case, be felt by a majority of the whole, a communication and concert results from the form of government itself; and there is nothing to check the inducements to sacrifice the weaker party or an obnoxious individual. Hence it is that such democracies have ever been spectacles of turbulence and contention; have ever been found incompatible with personal security or the rights of property; and have in general been as short in their lives as they have been violent in their deaths. Theoretic politicians, who have patronized this species of government, have erroneously supposed that by reducing mankind to a perfect equality in their political rights, they would at the same time be perfectly equalized and assimilated in their possessions, their opinions, and their passions.

A republic, by which I mean a government in which the scheme of representation takes place, opens a different prospect and promises the cure for which we are seeking. Let us examine the points in which it varies from pure democracy, and we shall comprehend both the nature of the cure and the efficacy which it must derive from the Union.

The two great points of difference between a democracy and a republic are: first, the delegation of the government, in the latter, to a small number of citizens elected by the rest; secondly, the greater number of citizens and greater sphere of country over which the latter may be extended.

The effect of the first difference is, on the one hand, to refine and enlarge the public views by passing them through the medium of a chosen body of citizens, whose wisdom may best discern the true interest of their country and whose patriotism and love of justice will be least likely to sacrifice it to temporary or partial considerations. Under such a regulation it may well happen that the public voice, pronounced by the representatives of the people, will be more consonant to the public good than if pronounced by the people themselves, convened for the purpose. On the other hand, the effect may be inverted. Men of factious tempers, of local prejudices, or of sinister designs, may, by intrigue, by corruption, or by other means, first obtain the suffrages, and then betray the interests of the people. The question resulting is, whether small or extensive republics are most favorable to the election of proper guardians of the public weal; and it is clearly decided in favor of the latter by two obvious considerations.

In the first place it is to be remarked that however small the republic may be the representatives must be raised to a certain number in order to guard against the cabals of a few; and that however large it may be they must be limited to a certain number in order to guard against the confusion of a multitude. Hence, the number of representatives in the two cases not being in proportion to that of the constituents, and being proportionally greatest in the small republic, it follows that if the proportion of fit characters be not less in the large than in the small republic, the former will present a greater option, and consequently a greater probability of a fit choice.

In the next place, as each representative will be chosen by a greater number of citizens in the large than in the small republic, it will be more difficult for unworthy candidates to practice with success the vicious arts by which elections are too often carried; and the suffrages of the people being more free, will be more likely to center on men who possess the most attractive merit and the most diffusive and established characters.

It must be confessed that in this, as in most other cases, there is a mean, on both sides of which inconveniencies will be found to lie. By enlarging too much the number of electors, you render the representative too little acquainted with all their local circumstances and lesser interests; as by reducing it too much, you render him unduly attached to these, and too little fit to comprehend and pursue great and national objects. The federal Constitution forms a happy combination in this respect; the great and aggregate interests being referred to the national, the local and particular to the State legislatures.

The other point of difference is the greater number of citizens and extent of territory which may be brought within the compass of republican than of democratic government; and it is this circumstance principally which renders factious combinations less to be dreaded in the former than in the latter. The smaller the society, the fewer probably will be the distinct parties and interests composing it; the fewer the distinct parties and interests, the more frequently will a majority be found of the same party; and the smaller the number of individuals composing a majority, and the smaller the compass within which they are placed, the more easily will they concert and execute their plans of oppression. Extend the sphere and you take in a greater variety of parties and interests; you make it less probable that a majority of the whole will have a common motive to invade the rights of other citizens; or if such a common motive exists, it will be more difficult for all who feel it to discover their own strength and to act in unison with each other. Besides other impediments, it may be remarked that, where there is a consciousness of unjust or dishonorable purposes, communication is always checked by distrust in proportion to the number whose concurrence is necessary.

Hence, it clearly appears that the same advantage which a republic has over a democracy in controlling the effects of faction is enjoyed by a large over a small republic—is enjoyed by the Union over the States composing it. Does this advantage consist in the substitution of representatives whose enlightened views and virtuous sentiments render them superior to local prejudices and to schemes of injustice? It will not be denied that the representation of the Union will be most likely to possess these requisite endowments. Does it consist in the greater security afforded by a greater variety of parties, against the event of any one party being able to outnumber and oppress the rest? In an equal degree does the increased variety of parties comprised within the Union increase this security. Does it, in fine, consist in the greater obstacles opposed to the concert and accomplishment of the secret wishes of an unjust and interested majority? Here again the extent of the Union gives it the most palpable advantage.

The influence of factious leaders may kindle a flame within their particular States but will be unable to spread a general conflagration through the other States. A religious sect may degenerate into a political faction in a part of the Confederacy; but the variety of sects dispersed over the entire face of it must secure the national councils against any danger from that source. A rage for paper money, for an abolition of debts, for an equal division of property, or for any other improper or wicked project, will be less apt to pervade the whole body of the Union than a particular member of it, in the same proportion as such a malady is more likely to taint a particular county or district than an entire State.

In the extent and proper structure of the Union, therefore, we behold a republican remedy for the diseases most incident to republican government. And according to the degree of pleasure and pride we feel in being republicans ought to be our zeal in cherishing the spirit and supporting the character of federalists.

Federalist No. 51
(James Madison)

To what expedient, then, shall we finally resort, for maintaining in practice the necessary partition of power among the several departments as laid down in the constitution? The only answer that can be given is that as all these exterior provisions are found to be inadequate, the defect must be supplied, by so contriving the interior structure of the government as that its several constituent parts may, by their mutual relations, be the means of keeping each other in their proper places. Without presuming to undertake a full development of this important idea i will hazard few general observations which may perhaps place it in a clearer light, and enable us to form a more correct judgment of the principles and structure of the government planned by the convention.

In order to lay a due foundation for that separate and distinct exercise of the different powers of government, which to a certain extent is admitted on all hands to be essential to the preservation of liberty, it is evident that each department should have a will of its own; and consequently should be so constituted that the members of each should have as little agency as possible in the appointment of the members of the others. Were this principle rigorously adhered to, it would require that all the appointments for the supreme executive, legislative, and judiciary magistracies should be drawn from the same fountain of authority, the people, through channels having no communication whatever with one another. Perhaps such a plan of constructing the several departments would be less difficult in practice than it may be in contemplation appear. Some difficulties, however, and some additional expense would attend the execution of it. Some deviations, therefore, from the principle must be admitted. In the constitution of the judiciary department in particular, it might be inexpedient to insist rigorously on the principle; first, because peculiar qualifications being essential in the members, the primary consideration ought to be to select that mode of choice which best secures these qualifications; second, because the permanent tenure by which the appointments are held in that department must soon destroy all sense of dependence on the authority conferring them.

It is equally evident that the members of each department should be as little dependent as possible on those of the others for the emoluments annexed to their offices. Were the executive magistrate, or the judges, not independent of the legislature in this particular, their independence in every other would be merely nominal.

But the great security against a gradual concentration of the several powers in the same department consists in giving to those who administer each department the necessary constitutional means and personal motives to resist encroachments of the others. The provision for defense must in this, as in all other cases, be made commensurate to the danger of attack. Ambition must be made to counteract ambition. The interest of the man must be connected with the constitutional rights of the place. It may be a reflection on human nature that such devices should be necessary to control the abuses of government. But what is government itself but the greatest of all reflections on human nature? If men were angels no government would be necessary. If angels were to govern men, neither external nor internal controls on government would be necessary. In framing a government which is to be administered by men over men, the great difficulty lies in this: you must first enable the government to control the governed; and in the next place oblige it to control itself. A dependence on the people is, no doubt, the primary control on the government; but experience has taught mankind the necessity of auxiliary precautions.

This policy of supplying, by opposite and rival interests, the defect of better motives, might be traced through the whole system of human affairs, private as well as public. We see it particularly displayed in all the subordinate distributions of power, where the constant aim is to divide and arrange the several offices in such a manner as that each may be a check on the other—that the private interest of every individual may be a sentinel over the public rights. These inventions of prudence cannot be less requisite in the distribution of the supreme powers of the State.

But it is not possible to give to each department an equal power of self-defense. In republican government, the legislative authority necessarily predominates. The remedy for this inconveniency is to divide the legislature into different branches; and to render them, by different modes of election and different principles of action, as little connected with each other as the nature of their common functions and their common dependence on the society will admit. It may even be necessary to guard against dangerous encroachments by still further precautions. As the weight of the legislative authority requires that it should be thus divided, the weakness of the executive may require, on the other hand, that it should be fortified. An absolute negative on the legislature appears, at first view, to be the natural defense with which the executive magistrate should be armed. But perhaps it would be neither altogether safe nor alone sufficient. On ordinary occasions it might not be exerted with the requisite firmness, and on extraordinary occasions it might be perfidiously abused. May not this defect of an absolute negative be supplied by some qualified connection between this weaker department and the weaker branch of the stronger department, by which the latter may be led to support the constitutional rights of the former, without being too much detached from the rights of its own department?

If the principles on which these observations are founded be just, as I persuade myself they are, and they be applied as a criterion to the several State constitutions, and to the federal Constitution, it will be found that if the latter does not perfectly correspond with them, the former are infinitely less able to bear such a test.

There are, moreover, two considerations particularly applicable to the federal system of America, which place that system in a very interesting point of view.

First. In a single republic, all the power surrendered by the people is submitted to the administration of a single government; and the usurpations are guarded against by a division of the government into distinct and separate departments. In the compound republic of America, the power surrendered by the people is first divided between two distinct governments, and then the portion allotted to each subdivided among distinct and separate departments. Hence a double security arises to the rights of the people. The different governments will control each other, at the same time that each will be controlled by itself.

Second. It is of great importance in a republic not only to guard the society against the oppression of its rulers, but to guard one part of the society against the injustice of the other part. Different interests necessarily exist in different classes of citizens. If a majority be united by a common interest, the rights of the minority will be insecure. There are but two methods of providing against this evil: the one by creating a will in the community independent of the majority—that is, of the society itself; the other, by comprehending in the society so many separate descriptions of citizens as will render an unjust combination of a majority of the whole very improbable, if not impracticable. The first method prevails in all governments possessing an hereditary or self-appointed authority. This, at best, is but a precarious security; because a power independent of the society may as well espouse the unjust views of the major as the rightful interests of the minor party, and may possibly be turned against both parties. The second method will be exemplified in the federal republic of the United States. Whilst all authority in it will be derived from and dependent on the society, the society itself will be broken into so many parts, interests and classes of citizens, that the rights of individuals, or of the minority, will be in little danger from interested combinations of the majority. In a free government the security for civil rights must be the same as that for religious rights. It consists in the one case in the multiplicity of interests, and in the other in the multiplicity of sects. The degree of security in both cases will depend on the number of interests and sects; and this may be presumed to depend on the extent of country and number of people comprehended under the same government. This view of the subject must particularly recommend a proper federal system to all the sincere and considerate friends of republican government, since it shows that in exact proportion as the territory of the Union may be formed into more circumscribed Confederacies, or States, oppressive combinations of a majority will be facilitated; the best security, under the republican forms, for the rights of every class of citizen, will be diminished; and consequently the stability and independence of some member of the government, the only other security, must be proportionately increased. Justice is the end of government. It is the end of civil society. It ever has been and ever will be pursued until it be obtained, or until liberty be lost in the pursuit. In a society under the forms of which the stronger faction can readily unite and oppress the weaker, anarchy may as truly be said to reign as in a state of nature, where the weaker individual is not secured against the violence of the stronger; and as, in the latter state, even the stronger individuals are prompted, by the uncertainty of their condition, to submit to a government which may protect the weak as well as themselves; so, in the former state, will the more powerful factions or parties be gradually induced, by a like motive, to wish for a government which will protect all parties, the weaker as well as the more powerful. It can be little doubted that if the State of Rhode Island was separated from the Confederacy and left to itself, the insecurity of rights under the popular form of government within such narrow limits would be displayed by such reiterated oppressions of factious majorities that some power altogether independent of the people would soon be called for by the voice of the very factions whose misrule had proved the necessity of it. In the extended republic of the United States, and among the great variety of interests, parties, and sects which it embraces, a coalition of a majority of the whole society could seldom take place on any other principles than those of justice and the general good; whilst there being thus less danger to a minor from the will of a major party, there must be less pretext, also, to provide for the security of the former, by introducing into the government a will not dependent on the latter, or, in other words, a will independent of the society itself. It is no less certain than it is important, notwithstanding the contrary opinions which have been entertained, that the larger the society, provided it lie within a practicable sphere, the more duly capable it will be of self-government. And happily for the republican cause, the practicable sphere may be carried to a very great extent by a judicious modification and mixture of the federal principle.

NOTES

CHAPTER ONE

[1]Alexis de Tocqueville, *Democracy in America (1835–1840)*, ed. J. P. Mayer and A. P. Kerr (Garden City, N.Y.: Doubleday/Anchor, 1969), 640.

[2]John Harmon McElroy, *American Beliefs: What Keeps a Big Country and a Diverse People United* (Chicago: I. R. Dee, 1999).

[3]Clinton Rossiter, *Conservatism in America* (New York: Vintage, 1962), 67.

[4]Tocqueville, *Democracy in America*, 310.

[5]James Bryce, *The American Commonwealth*, vol. 2 (New York: Macmillan, 1960), 247–54. First published in 1900.

[6]Ralph Barton Perry, *Puritanism and Democracy* (New York: Vanguard, 1944), 124–25; see also Peter D. Salins, *Assimilation, American Style* (New York: Basic Books, 1996); Philip L. Fetzer, *The Ethnic Moment* (Armonk, N.Y.: M. E. Sharpe, 1996).

[7]See Gabriel Almond and Sidney Verba, *The Civic Culture* (Boston: Little, Brown, 1965); Richard Merelman, *Making Something of Ourselves: On Culture and Politics in the United States* (Berkeley: University of California Press, 1984).

[8]Paul Gagnon, "Why Study History?" *Atlantic Monthly*, November 1988, 47.

[9]Louis Hartz, *The Liberal Tradition in America* (New York: Harcourt, Brace, 1953), 12.

[10]James Bryce, *The American Commonwealth*, vol. 2 (Indianapolis, Ind.: Liberty Fund, 1995), 1419.

[11]Times Mirror Center for the People and the Press survey, 1990–1991.

[12]See Douglas Muzzio and Richard Behn, "Thinking About Welfare," *The Public Perspective*, February/March 1995, 35–38; Stanley Feldman and John Zaller, "The Political Culture of Ambivalence: Ideological Responses to the Welfare State," *American Journal of Political Science*, 36 (1992): 268–307.

[13]See Seymour Martin Lipset, *American Exceptionalism: A Double-Edged Sword* (New York: Norton, 1996); Claude Levi-Strauss, *Structural Anthropology* (Chicago: University of Chicago Press, 1983); Clifford Geertz, Myth, Symbol, and Culture (New York: Norton, 1974).

[14]U.S. Census Bureau figures.

[15]Quoted in Ralph Volney Harlow, *The Growth of the United States*, vol. 2 (New York: Henry Holt, 1943), 497.

[16]Survey of American Political Culture, James Davison Hunter and Carol Bowman, directors, University of Virginia, 1996; Debra L. DeLaet, *U.S. Immigration Policy in an Age of Rights* (Westport, Conn.: Praeger Publishers, 2000).

[17]Harold D. Lasswell, *Politics: Who Gets What, When, How* (New York: McGraw-Hill, 1938).

[18]Theodore Lowi and Benjamin Ginsberg, *American Government: Freedom and Power* (New York: Norton, 1990), 8.

[19]Harold D. Lasswell and Abraham Kaplan, *Power and Society* (New Haven, Conn.: Yale University Press, 1950), 75–77.

[20]See Charles H. McIlwain, *Constitutionalism: Ancient and Modern* (Ithaca, N.Y.: Cornell University Press, 1983).

[21]Alan S. Rosenbaum, ed., *Constitutionalism: The Philosophical Dimension* (Westport, Conn.: Greenwood, 1988), 4.

[22]Tocqueville, *Democracy in America*, ch. 6.

[23]Benjamin I. Page and Robert Shapiro, "Effects of Public Opinion on Policy," *American Political Science Review* 77 (March, 1983): 178; see also Urie Bronfenbrenner, Peter McClelland, Stephen Leci, Phyllis Moen, and Elaine Wethington, *The State of Americans* (New York: Free Press, 1996).

[24]See Robert Dahl, *Democracy and Its Critics* (New Haven, Conn.: Yale University Press, 1989).

[25]C. Wright Mills, *The Power Elite* (New York: Oxford University Press, 1965).

[26]G. William Domhoff, *Who Rules America?* (Mountain View, Calif.: Mayfield Publishing, 1998).

[27]See, for example, Robert Dahl, *On Democracy* (New Haven, Conn.: Yale University Press, 1998).

[28]See H. H. Gerth and C. Wright Mills, eds., *From Max Weber: Essays in Sociology* (New York: Oxford University Press, 1958).

[29]Roberto Michels, *Political Parties* (New York: Collier Books, 1962). First published in 1911.

[30]David Easton, *The Political System* (New York: Knopf, 1965), 97.

[31]E. E. Schattschneider, *Two Hundred Million Americans in Search of a Government* (New York: Holt, Rinehart & Winston, 1969), 42.

CHAPTER TWO

[1]Quoted in Charles S. Hyneman, "Republican Government in America," in George J. Graham Jr. and Scarlett G. Graham, eds., *Founding Principles*

of American Government, rev. ed. (Chatham, N.J.: Chatham House, 1984), 19.

[2]John Locke, *The Two Treatises of Government*, ed. Thomas I. Cook (New York: Hafner, 1947), 159–86, 228–47; see also A. John Simmons, *The Lockean Theory of Rights* (Princeton, N.J.: Princeton University Press, 1994).

[3]See Russell Hardin, *Liberalism, Constitutionalism, and Democracy* (New York: Oxford University Press, 1999).

[4]George Bancroft, *History of the Formation of the Constitution of the United States of America*, 3d ed., vol. 1 (New York: D. Appleton, 1883), 166.

[5]Catherine Drinker Bowen, *Miracle at Philadelphia* (Boston: Little, Brown, 1986), 10.

[6]Alfred H. Kelly, Winifred A. Harbison, and Herman Belz, *The American Constitution*, 7th ed. (New York: Norton, 1991), 122.

[7]Max Weber, "Politics as a Vocation," in Hans H. Gerth and C. Wright Mills, eds., *From Max Weber: Essays in Sociology* (New York: Oxford University Press, 1958), 78.

[8]Gaillard Hunt, ed., *The Writings of James Madison* (New York: Putnam, 1904), 274; Garret Ward Sheldon, *The Political Philosophy of James Madison* (Baltimore: Johns Hopkins University Press, 2000).

[9]*Federalist* No. 47.

[10]See *Federalist* Nos. 47 and 48.

[11]Richard Neustadt, *Presidential Power* (New York: Macmillan, 1986), 33.

[12]Henry J. Abraham, *The Judicial Process*, 6th ed. (New York: Oxford University Press, 1993), 320–22.

[13]*Marbury v. Madison*, 1 Cranch 137 (1803).

[14]Martin Diamond, *The Founding of the Democratic Republic* (Itasca, Ill.: Peacock, 1981), 62–71.

[15]*Federalist* No. 10.

[16]Leslie F. Goldstein, "Judicial Review and Democratic Theory: Guardian Democracy vs. Representative Democracy," *Western Political Quarterly* 40 (1987): 391–412.

[17]Benjamin Ginsberg, *The Consequences of Consent* (New York: Random House, 1982), 22.

[18]Robert Dahl, *Pluralist Democracy in the United States* (Chicago: Rand McNally, 1967), 92.

[19]This interpretation is taken from Walter Lippmann, *Public Opinion* (New York: Free Press, 1965), 178–79; for a general discussion of the uncertain meaning of the Constitution, see Lawrence H. Tribe and Michael C. Dorf, *On Reading the Constitution* (Cambridge, Mass.: Harvard University Press, 1991).

[20]Charles S. Beard, *An Economic Interpretation of the Constitution* (New York, Macmillan, 1941). First published in 1913.

CHAPTER THREE

[1]Woodrow Wilson, *Constitutional Government in the United States* (New York: Columbia University Press, 1908), 173.

[2]See Samuel Beer, *To Make a Nation: The Rediscovery of American Federalism* (Cambridge, Mass.: The Belknap Press of Harvard University, 1993).

[3]*Federalist* No. 2; for the Anti-Federalist view, see Saul Cornell, *The Other Founders* (Chapel Hill: University of North Carolina Press, 1999).

[4]*McCulloch v. Maryland,* 4 Wheaton 316 (1819).

[5]*Gibbons v. Ogden,* 22 Wheaton 1 (1824).

[6]Oliver Wendell Holmes Jr., *Collected Legal Papers* (New York: Harcourt, Brace, 1920), 295–96.

[7]John C. Calhoun, *The Works of John C. Calhoun* (New York: Russell & Russell, 1968).

[8]See *Cooley v. Board of Wardens of the Port of Philadelphia,* 53 Howard 299 (1851).

[9]*Dred Scott v. Sanford,* 19 Howard 393 (1857).

[10]*U.S. v. Cruikshank,* 92 U.S. 452 (1876).

[11]Edward S. Corwin, *The Constitution and What It Means Today,* 12th ed. (Princeton, N.J.: Princeton University Press, 1958), 248.

[12]*Slaughter-House Cases,* 16 Wallace 36 (1873); *Civil Rights Cases,* 109 U.S. 3 (1883).

[13]*Plessy v. Ferguson,* 163 U.S. 537 (1896).

[14]*Santa Clara County v. Southern Pacific Railroad Co.,* 118 U.S. 394 (1886).

[15]*U.S. v. E. C. Knight Co.,* 156 U.S. 1 (1895).

[16]*Hammer v. Dagenhart,* 247 U.S. 251 (1918).

[17]*Lochner v. New York,* 198 U.S. 25 (1905).

[18]Alfred H. Kelly, Winifred A. Harbison, and Herman Belz, *The American Constitution,* 7th ed. (New York: Norton, 1991), 529.

[19]James E. Anderson, *The Emergence of the Modern Regulatory State* (Washington, D.C.: Public Affairs Press, 1962), 2–3.

[20]*Schechter Poultry Co. v. United States,* 295 U.S. 495 (1935).

[21]*NLRB v. Jones and Laughlin Steel,* 301 U.S. 1 (1937).

[22]*American Power and Light v. Securities and Exchange Commission,* 329 U.S. 90 (1946); see also Richard A. Maidment, *The Judicial Response to the New Deal: The U.S. Supreme Court and Economic Regulation* (New York: Manchester University Press, 1992).

[23]Louis Fisher, *American Constitutional Law* (New York: McGraw-Hill, 1990), 384.

[24]Maidment, *Judicial Response to the New Deal.*

[25]*Brown v. Board of Education,* 347 U.S. 483 (1954).

[26]*Miranda v. Arizona,* 384 U.S. 436 (1966).

[27]*Garcia v. San Antonio Transit Authority*, 469 U.S. 528 (1985).

[28]See Thomas Anton, *American Federalism and Public Policy* (Philadelphia: Temple University Press, 1989).

[29]Morton Grodzins, *The American System: A New View of Government in the United States* (Chicago: Rand McNally, 1966).

[30]See Paul A. Peterson, *The Price of Federalism* (Washington, D.C.: The Brookings Institution, 1995).

[31]Rosella Levaggi, *Fiscal Federalism and Grants-in-Aid* (Brookfield, Vt.: Avebury, 1991).

[32]See David L. Shapiro, *Federalism: A Dialogue* (Evanston, Ill.: Northwestern University Press, 1995). See also Douglas D. Rose, "National and Local Forces in State Politics," *American Political Science Review* 67 (December 1973): 1162–63.

[33]Charles Schultze, "Federal Spending: Past, Present and Future," in Henry Owen and Charles Schultze, eds., *Setting National Priorities: The Next Ten Years* (Washington, D.C.: Brookings Institution, 1976), 323–69.

[34]Richard Nathan and Fred Doolittle, *Reagan and the States* (Princeton, N.J.: Princeton University Press, 1987); Timothy J. Conlan, *From New Federalism to Devolution* (Washington, D.C.: Brookings Institution, 1998).

[35]*Garcia v. San Antonio Authority*, 469 U.S. 528 (1985).

[36]*United States v. Lopez*, 514 U.S. 549 (1995).

[37]*Printz v. United States*, 117 S. Ct. 2157 (1997).

[38]*Kimel v. Florida Board of Regents*, No. 98-791 (2000).

[39]*Board of Trustees of the University of Alabama v. Garrett*, No. 99-1240 (2002).

[40]*Reno v. Condon*, No. 98-1464 (2000).

[41]Andrew W. Dobelstein, *Politics, Economics, and Public Welfare* (Englewood Cliffs, N.J.: Prentice-Hall, 1980), 5.

[42]Lloyd A. Free and Hadley Cantril, *The Political Beliefs of Americans* (New York: Simon & Schuster, 1968), 21; see also William Lunch, *The Nationalization of American Politics* (Berkeley: University of California Press, 1987).

[43]Survey for the Times Mirror Center for the People and the Press by Princeton Survey Research Associates, July 12–27, 1994; see also Tommy Thompson, *Power to the People* (New York: HarperCollins, 1996).

[44]Daniel J. Boorstin, *The Americans: The Democratic Experience* (New York: Vintage Books, 1974).

CHAPTER FOUR

[1]Julian P. Boyd, ed., *The Papers of Thomas Jefferson*, vol. 12 (Princeton, N.J.: Princeton University Press, 1955), 440.

[2]*Anderson v. Creighton*, 483 U.S. 635 (1987).

[3]*Bose Corp. v. Consumers Union of the United States*, 466 U.S. 485 (1984).

[4]*Schenck v. United States*, 249 U.S. 47 (1919).

[5]*Dennis v. United States*, 341 U.S. 494 (1951).

[6]See, for example, *Yates v. United States*, 354 U.S. 298 (1957); *Noto v. United States*, 367 U.S. 290 (1961); *Scales v. United States*, 367 U.S. 203 (1961).

[7]*United States v. Carolene Products Co.*, 304 U.S. 144 (1938).

[8]*United States v. O'Brien*, 391 U.S. 367 (1968).

[9]*Texas v. Johnson*, 109 S. Ct. 2544 (1989).

[10]*United States v. Eichman*, 496 U.S. 310 (1990).

[11]*New York Times Co. v. United States*, 403 U.S. 713 (1971).

[12]*Nebraska Press Assn. v. Stuart*, 427 U.S. 539 (1976).

[13]*Barron v. Baltimore*, 7 Peters 243 (1833).

[14]*Gitlow v. New York*, 268 U.S. 652 (1925).

[15]*Fiske v. Kansas*, 274 U.S. 30 (1927); *Near v. Minnesota*, 283 U.S. 697 (1931); *Hamilton v. Regents, U. of California*, 293 U.S. 245 (1934); *DeJonge v. Oregon*, 299 U.S. 253 (1937).

[16]*Near v. Minnesota*, 283 U.S. 697 (1931).

[17]*Brandenburg v. Ohio*, 395 U.S. 444 (1969).

[18]*R.A.V. v. St. Paul*, No. 90-7675 (1992).

[19]*Wisconsin v. Mitchell*, No. 92-515 (1993).

[20]*National Socialist Party v. Skokie*, 432 U.S. 43 (1977).

[21]*Forsyth County v. Nationalist Movement*, No. 91-538 (1992).

[22]*New York Times Co. v. Sullivan*, 376 U.S. 254 (1964).

[23]*Milkovich v. Lorain Journal*, 497 U.S. 1 (1990); see also *Masson v. The New Yorker*, No. 89-1799 (1991).

[24]*Roth v. U.S.*, 354 U.S. 476 (1957).

[25]*Miller v. California*, 413 U.S. 15 (1973).

[26]*Barnes v. Glen Theatre*, No. 90-26 (1991).

[27]*Stanley v. Georgia*, 394 U.S. 557 (1969).

[28]*Osborne v. Ohio*, 495 U.S. 103 (1990).

[29]*Ashcroft v. Free Speech Coalition*, No. 00-795 (2002).

[30]*Denver Area Consortium v. Federal Communications Commission*, No. 95-124 (1996).

[31]*Reno v. American Civil Liberties Union*, No. 96-511 (1997).

[32]*Ashcroft v. American Civil Liberties Union*, No. 00-1293 (2002).

[33]See Michael J. Perry, *Religion in Politics* (New York: Oxford University Press, 1997).

[34]*Board of Regents v. Allen*, 392 U.S. 236 (1968).

[35]*Lemon v. Kurtzman*, 403 U.S. 602 (1971).

[36]Ibid.

[37]*Mitchell v. Helms*, No. 98-1648 (2000).

[38]*Zelman v. Simmons-Harris*, No. 00-1751 (2002).

[39]*Engel v. Vitale*, 370 U.S. 421 (1962).

[40]*Abington School District v. Schempp*, 374 U.S. 203 (1963).

[41]*Wallace v. Jaffree*, 472 U.S. 38 (1985).

[42]*Santa Fe Independent School District v. Does*, No. 99-62 (2000).

[43]*Wisconsin v. Yoder*, 406 U.S. 295 (1972); see also *Church of the Lukumi Babalu Aye v. City of Hialeah*, No. 91-948 (1993).

[44]*Edwards v. Aguillard*, 487 U.S. 578 (1987).

[45]*Griswold v. Connecticut*, 381 U.S. 479 (1965).

[46]*Roe v. Wade*, 401 U.S. 113 (1973).

[47]*Webster v. Reproductive Health Services*, 492 U.S. 490 (1989); see also *Rust v. Sullivan*, No. 89-1391 (1991).

[48]*Planned Parenthood v. Casey*, No. 91-744 (1992).

[49]*Stenberg v. Carhart*, No. 99-830 (2000).

[50]*Bowers v. Hardwick*, 478 U.S. 186 (1986).

[51]*Vacco v. Quill*, 117 S.C. 36 (1996); *Washington v. Glucksberg*, No. 96-110 (1997).

[52]*Gregg v. United States*, No. 00-939 (2001).

[53]*Powell v. Alabama*, 287 U.S. 45 (1932).

[54]*Palko v. Connecticut*, 302 U.S. 319 (1937).

[55]*Mapp v. Ohio*, 367 U.S. 643 (1961).

[56]*Gideon v. Wainwright*, 372 U.S. 335 (1963).

[57]*Malloy v. Hogan*, 378 U.S. 1 (1964).

[58]*Miranda v. Arizona*, 384 U.S. 436 (1966); see also *Escobedo v. Illinois*, 378 U.S. 478 (1964).

[59]*Pointer v. Texas*, 380 U.S. 400 (1965).

[60]*Klopfer v. North Carolina*, 386 U.S. 213 (1967).

[61]*Duncan v. Louisiana*, 391 U.S. 145 (1968).

[62]*Benton v. Maryland*, 395 U.S. 784 (1969).

[63]*Dickerson v. United States*, No. 99-5525 (2000).

[64]*Michigan v. Sitz*, No. 88-1897 (1990).

[65]*Indianapolis v. Edmund*, No. 99-1030 (2001).

[66]*Kyllo v. United States*, No. 99-8508 (2001).

[67]*Ferguson v. Charleston*, No. 99-936 (2001).

[68]*Board of Education of Independent School District, No. 9 of Pottowatomie County v. Earls*, No. 01-332 (2002).

[69]*Weeks v. United States*, 232 U.S. 383 (1914).

[70]*Nix v. Williams*, 467 U.S. 431 (1984); see also *United States v. Leon*, 468 U.S. 897 (1984).

[71]*Whren v. United States*, 517 U.S. 806 (1996).

[72]*U.S. v. Drayton et al.*, No. 01-631 (2002).

[73]*Townsend v. Sain*, 372 U.S. 293 (1963).

[74]*Keeney v. Tamaya-Reyes*, No. 90-1859 (1992); see also *Coleman v. Thompson*, No. 89-7662 (1991).

[75]*Brecht v. Abrahamson*, No. 91-7358 (1993); see also *McCleskey v. Zant*, No. 89-7024 (1991).

[76]*Felker v. Turpin*, No. 95-8836 (1996); but see *Stewart v. Martinez-Villareal*, No. 97-300 (1998).

[77]*Williams v. Taylor*, No. 99-6615 (2000).

[78]Quoted in "Feds Get Wide Wiretap Authority," CBSNEWS.com, November 18, 2002.

[79]Kurt Heine, "Philadelphia Cops Beat One of Their Own," *Syracuse Herald-American*, January 15, 1995, A13.

[80]Richard Sobel, "Anti-Terror Campaign Has Wide Support, Even at Expense of Cherished Rights," *Chicago Tribune*, November 4, 2001, Internet copy.

[81]*Wilson v. Seiter*, No. 89-7376 (1991).

[82]*Harmelin v. Michigan*, No. 89-7272 (1991).

[83]*Atkins v. Virginia*, No. 01-8452 (2002).

[84]*Ring v. Arizona*, No. 01-488 (2002).

[85]Sobel, "Anti-Terror Campaign."

[86]See Alpheus T. Mason, *The Supreme Court: Palladium of Freedom* (Ann Arbor: University of Michigan Press, 1962); see also Henry J. Abraham, *Freedom and the Court* (New York: Oxford University Press, 1998).

CHAPTER FIVE

[1]Speech of Martin Luther King Jr. in Washington, D.C., August 2, 1963.

[2]*Washington Post* wire story, May 14, 1991.

[3]Reported on *CBS Evening News*, January 16, 1989.

[4]Robert Nisbet, "Public Opinion Versus Popular Opinion," *Public Interest* 41 (1975): 171.

[5]See, for example, John R. Howard, *The Shifting Wind* (Albany: State University of New York Press, 1999).

[6]The classic analysis of this system of legalized segregation is C. Vann Woodward, *The Strange Career of Jim Crow*, 3d rev. ed. (New York: Oxford University Press, 1974).

[7]*Plessy v. Ferguson*, 163 U.S. 537 (1896).

[8]See, for example, *Missouri ex rel. Gaines v. Canada*, 305 U.S. 57 (1938).

[9]*Brown v. Board of Education of Topeka*, 347 U.S. 483 (1954).

[10]See Francis M. Wilhoit, *The Politics of Massive Resistance* (New York: Braziller, 1973).

[11]See Steven A. Shull, *The President and Civil Rights Policy: Leadership and Change* (Westport, Conn.: Greenwood, 1989).

[12]See Sar Levitan, William Johnson, and Robert Taggert, *Still a Dream* (Cambridge, Mass.: Harvard University Press, 1975).

[13]See Derrick Bell, *And We Are Not Saved: The Elusive Quest for Racial Justice* (New York: Basic Books, 1987); Robert C. Smith and Richard S. Hzer, *Race, Class, and Culture* (Albany: State University of New York Press, 1992).

[14]Data from National Office of Drug Control Policy, 1997.

[15]See Keith Reeves, *Voting Hopes or Fears?* (New York: Oxford University Press, 1997).

[16]See Glenna Matthews, *The Rise of Public Women* (New York: Oxford University Press, 1994).

[17]*Tinker v. Colwell*, 193 U.S. 473 (1904).

[18]For a history of the women's voting rights movement, see Eleanor Flexner, *Century of Struggle*, rev. ed. (Cambridge, Mass.: Harvard University Press, 1975).

[19]See Ellen Carol DuBois, *Feminism and Suffrage: The Emergence of an Independent Women's Movement in America, 1848–1869* (Ithaca, N.Y.: Cornell University Press, 1978).

[20]See Jane Mansbridge, *Why We Lost the ERA* (Chicago: University of Chicago Press, 1986).

[21]See Kathleen Hall Jamieson, *Beyond the Double Bind* (New York: Oxford University Press, 1995).

[22]Linda Witt, Karen M. Paget, and Glenna Matthews, *Running as a Woman* (New York: Free Press, 1994).

[23]Mary Lou Kendrigan, *Political Equality in a Democratic Society: Women in the United States* (Westport, Conn.: Greenwood, 1984); Timothy Bledsoe and Mary Herring, "Victims of Circumstance: Women in Pursuit of Political Office," *American Political Science Review* 84 (1990): 213–24.

[24]*County of Washington v. Gunther*, No. 80-429 (1981).

[25]See, however, Sara M. Evans and Barbara Nelson, *Wage Justice* (Chicago: University of Chicago Press, 1989).

[26]*Faragher v. City of Boca Raton*, No. 97-282 (1998); *Burlington Industries v. Ellerth*, No. 97-569 (1998).

[27]See Joane Nagel, *American Indian Ethnic Renewal* (New York: Oxford University Press, 1996).

[28]See Rudulfo O. de la Garza, Louis DeSipio, F. Chris Garcia, John Garcia, and Angelo Falcon, *Latino Voices* (Boulder, Colo.: Westview Press, 1992).

[29]*De Canas v. Bica*, 424 U.S. 351 (1976).

[30]James Truslow Adams, *The March of Democracy*, vol. 4 (New York: Scribner's, 1933), 284–85; see also Charles McClain, *In Search of Equality* (Berkeley: University of California Press, 1994).

[31]*Lau v. Nichols*, 414 U.S. 563 (1974).

[32]*Bowers v. Hardwick*, 478 U.S. 186 (1986).

[33]*Boy Scouts of America v. Dale*, No. 99-699 (2000).

[34]*Romer v. Evans*, 517 U.S. 620 (1996).

[35]*Craig v. Boren*, 429 U.S. 190 (1976).

[36]*Rostker v. Goldberg*, 453 U.S. 57 (1980).

[37]*United States v. Virginia*, No. 94-1941 (1996).

[38]Survey by Federal Financial Institutions Examination Council, 1998.

[39]U.S. Conference of Mayors Report, 1998.

[40]See J. Morgan Kousser, *The Shaping of Southern Politics: Suffrage Restriction and the Establishment of the One-Party South, 1880–1910* (New Haven, Conn.: Yale University Press, 1974).

[41]V. O. Key Jr., *Southern Politics* (New York: Knopf, 1949), 495.

[42]*Smith v. Allwright*, 321 U.S. 649 (1944).

[43]See Bernard Grofman, Lisa Handley, and Richard Niemi, *Minority Representation and the Quest for Voting Equality* (New York: Cambridge University Press, 1992); David Lublin, *The Paradox of Representation* (Princeton, N.J.: Princeton University Press, 1997).

[44]*Bush v. Verg*, No. 94-805 (1996); *Shaw v. Hunt*, No. 94-923 (1996); *Muller v. Johnson*, No. 94-631 (1995).

[45]*Easley v. Cromartie*, No. 99-1864 (2001).

[46]See Terry Eastland, *Ending Affirmative Action* (New York: Basic Books, 1997); but see also Barbara A. Bergmann, *In Defense of Affirmative Action* (New York: Basic Books, 1997).

[47]*University of California Regents v. Bakke*, 438 U.S. 265 (1978).

[48]*Steelworkers v. Weber*, 443 U.S. 193 (1979); *Fullilove v. Klutnick*, 448 U.S. 448 (1980).

[49]*Local No. 28, Sheet Metal Workers v. Equal Employment Opportunity Commission*, 478 U.S. 421 (1986); see also *Local No. 93, International Association of Firefighters v. Cleveland*, 478 U.S. 501 (1986); *Firefighters v. Stotts*, 459 U.S. 969 (1984); *Wygant v. Jackson*, 476 U.S. 238 (1986).

[50]See *Wards Cove Packing v. Antonio*, 490 U.S. 642 (1989).

[51]*Adarand v. Pena*, No. 94-310 (1995).

[52]Jodi Wilgoren, "New Law in Texas Preserves Racial Mix in State's Colleges," *The New York Times*, November 24, 1999, A1.

[53]*Swann v. Charlotte-Mecklenburg County Board of Education*, 402 U.S. 1 (1971).

[54]See Jennifer Hochschild, *The New American Dilemma* (New Haven, Conn.: Yale University Press, 1984); Michael W. Giles and Thomas G. Walker, "Judicial Policy-Making and Southern School Segregation," *Journal of Politics* 37 (1975): 936.

[55]*Milliken v. Bradley*, 418 U.S. 717 (1974).

[56]Christopher Jencks and Meredith Phillips, eds., *The Black-White Test Score Gap* (Washington, D.C.: Brookings Institution Press, 1998).

[57]Quoted in Megan Twohey, "Desegregation Is Dead," *National Journal* 31, no. 38 (September 18, 1999), 2614.

[58]*Board of Education of Oklahoma City v. Dowell*, 498 U.S. 237 (1991).

[59]*Sheff v. O'Neill*, No. 95-2071 (1996).

[60]Quoted in Twohey, "Desegregation Is Dead." See also David J. Armor, *Forced Justice: School Desegregation and the Law* (New York: Oxford University Press, 1995).

[61]Linda Darling-Hammond, "Black America: Progress and Prospects," Brookings Institution, 1998.

[62]Gunnar Myrdal, *An American Dilemma: The Negro Problem and Modern Democracy* (New York: Harper, 1944).

CHAPTER SIX

[1]V. O. Key Jr., *Public Opinion and American Democracy* (New York: Knopf, 1961), 8.

[2]See Benjamin I. Page and Robert Shapiro, *The Rational Public* (Chicago: University of Chicago Press, 1992), 285–88.

[3]Jerry L. Yeric and John R. Todd, *Public Opinion*, 3rd ed. (Itasca, Ill.: Peacock, 1996), 3.

[4]Elisabeth Noelle-Neumann, *The Spiral of Silence*, 2d ed. (Chicago: University of Chicago Press, 1993), ch. 1.

[5]Survey of students of the eight Ivy League schools by Luntz & Weber Research and Strategic Services, for the University of Pennsylvania's Ivy League Study, November 13–December 1, 1992.

[6]Sidney Verba and Norman H. Nie, *Participation in America: Political Democracy and Social Equality* (New York: Harper & Row, 1972), 281–84.

[7]Steven A. Peterson, *Political Behavior: Patterns in Everyday Life* (Newbury Park, Calif.: Sage Publications, 1990), 28–29.

[8]Ibid.

[9]M. Kent Jennings and Richard G. Niemi, *Generations and Politics* (Princeton, N.J.: Princeton University Press, 1981); David Easton and Jack Dennis, *Children in the Political System* (New York: McGraw-Hill, 1969).

[10]See Robert D. Hess and Judith V. Torney, *The Development of Political Attitudes in Children* (Chicago: Aldine, 1967), 219; Orit Ichilov, *Political Socialization, Citizenship Education, and Democracy* (New York: Teachers College Press, 1990).

[11]Thomas E. Patterson, *Out of Order* (New York: Vintage, 1994), ch. 2.

[12]Noelle-Neumann, *Spiral of Silence.*

[13]See E. J. Dionne, *Why Americans Hate Politics* (New York: Simon & Schuster, 1992); E. J. Dionne, *They Only Look Dead* (New York: Simon & Schuster, 1996); David Frum, *What's Right?* (New York: Basic Books, 1996).

[14]John L. Sullivan, James E. Pierson, and George E. Marcus, "Ideological Constraint in the Mass Public," *American Journal of Political Science* 22 (May 1978): 233–49.

[15]CNN/USA Today poll conducted by the Gallup Organization, 1997.

[16]Philip Converse, "The Nature of Belief Systems in Mass Publics," in David Apter, ed., *Ideology and Discontent* (New York: Free Press, 1965), 206.

[17]"The Gender Story," *The Public Perspective*, August/September 1996, 1–33; Sue Tolleson Rinehart, *Gender Consciousness and Politics* (New York: Routledge, 1992).

[18]Susan A. MacManus, *Young v. Old: Generational Combat in the Twenty-first Century* (Boulder, Colo.: Westview Press, 1996).

[19]See Angus Campbell, Philip Converse, Warren Miller, and Donald Stokes, *The American Voter* (New York: Wiley, 1960), chs. 3 and 4.

[20]Martin P. Wattenberg, *The Decline of American Political Parties, 1952–1996* (Cambridge, Mass.: Harvard University Press, 1998).

[21]See E. E. Schattschneider, *The Semisovereign People* (New York: Holt, Rinehart & Winston, 1980), ch. 8.

[22]See William Domhoff, *The Power Elite and the State* (New York: Aldine de Gruyter, 1990).

[23]Benjamin I. Page and Robert Y. Shapiro, "Effects of Public Opinion on Policy," *American Political Science Review* 77 (March 1983): 178; see also Richard Sobel, *The Impact of Public Opinion on U.S. Foreign Policy* (New York: Oxford University Press, 2001).

[24]See Benjamin Ginsberg, *The Consequences of Consent* (New York: Random House, 1982); but also see Samuel L. Popkin, *The Reasoning Voter: Communication and Persuasion in Presidential Campaigns* (Chicago: University of Chicago Press, 1991).

[25]See Paul Brace and Barbara Hinckley, *Follow the Leader: Opinion Polls and Modern Presidents* (New York: Basic Books, 1992).

CHAPTER SEVEN

[1]Walter Lippmann, *Public Opinion* (New York: Free Press, 1965), 36.

[2]Quoted in Ralph Volney Harlow, *The Growth of the United States* (New York: Henry Holt, 1943), 312.

[3]See William H. Flanigan and Nancy Zingale, *The Political Behavior of the American Electorate*, 10th ed. (Washington, D.C.: Congressional Quarterly Press, 2002), 24–26.

[4]Example from Gus Tyler, "One Cheer for the Democrats," *New Leader*, November 3, 1986, 6.

[5]Turnout figures provided by Washington, D.C., embassies of the respective countries, 2000.

[6]See Stanley Kelley Jr., Richard E. Ayres, and William G. Bowen, "Registration and Voting: Putting First Things First," *American Political Science Review* 61 (June 1967): 359–79.

[7]Ivor Crewe, "Electoral Participation," in David Butler, Howard R. Penniman, and Austin Ranney, eds., *Democracy at the Polls* (Washington, D.C.: American Enterprise Institute, 1981), 249.

[8]Vanishing Voter Project, Joan Shorenstein Center on Press, Politics, and Public Policy, Harvard University, May 2000.

[9]Crewe, "Electoral Participation," 251–53.

[10]Malcom Jewell and David Olson, *American State Politics and Elections* (Homewood, Ill.: Irwin Press, 1978), 50.

[11]A. Karnig and B. Walter, "Municipal Elections," in *Municipal Yearbook, 1977* (Washington, D.C.: International City Management Assn., 1977).

[12]Richard Boyd, "Decline of U.S. Voter Turnout," *American Politics Quarterly* 9 (April 1981): 142.

[13]Ruy A. Teixeira, *The Disappearing American Voter* (Washington, D.C.: Brookings Institution, 1992).

[14]Crewe, "Electoral Participation," 251–53.

[15]G. Bingham Powell, "Voting Turnout in Thirty Democracies," in Richard Rose, ed., *Electoral Participation: A Comparative Analysis* (Beverly Hills, Calif.: Sage, 1980), 6.

[16]See, for example, Norman H. Nie, G. Bingham Powell, and Kenneth Prewitt, "Social Structure and Political Participation," *American Political Science Review* 63 (September 1969).

[17]See Joseph Nye, David King, and Philip Zelikow, *Why People Don't Trust Government* (Cambridge, Mass.: Harvard University Press, 1997).

[18]Ibid.

[19]John M. Strate, Charles J. Parrish, Charles D. Elder, and Coit Ford III, "Life Span Civic Development and Voting Participation," *American Political Science Review* 83 (June 1989): 443–65.

[20]M. Margaret Conway, *Political Participation in the United States*, 3d ed. (Washington, D.C.: Congressional Quarterly Press, 2000), 23–25.

[21]Sidney Verba, Kay Schlozman, and Henry Brady, *Voice and Equality* (Cambridge, Mass.: Harvard University Press, 1995); Jan Leighley, *Strength in Numbers* (Princeton, N.J.: Princeton University Press, 2001).

[22]Sidney Verba and Norman Nie, *Participation in America* (New York: Harper & Row, 1972), 340.

[23]But see Jeffrey Stonecash, *Class and Party in American Politics* (Boulder, Colo.: Westview Press, 2000).

[24]Vanishing Voter Survey, 2000.

[25]Michael Delli Carpini and Scott Keeter, *What Americans Know About Politics* (New Haven, Conn.: Yale University Press, 1996).

[26]Thomas E. Patterson, *The Mass Media Election* (New York: Praeger, 1980), chs. 7–10.

[27]Thomas E. Patterson, *The Vanishing Voter* (New York: Knopf, 2002), ch. 4.

[28]Gallup Reports, 1936–2000.

[29]V. O. Key Jr., *The Responsible Electorate* (Cambridge, Mass.: Belknap Press of Harvard University Press, 1966), ch. 1.

[30]See Verba, Schlozman, and Brady, *Voice and Equality*.

[31]Joseph Schumpeter, *Capitalism, Socialism, and Democracy* (New York: Harper Torchbooks, 1950), 269.

[32]W. Russell Neuman, *The Paradox of Mass Politics* (Cambridge, Mass.: Harvard University Press, 1986), 176.

[33]Samuel H. Barnes et al., eds., *Political Action* (Beverly Hills, Calif.: Sage, 1979), 541–42.

[34]Russell J. Dalton, *Citizen Politics in Western Democracies*, 3d ed. (Chatham, N.J.: Chatham House, 1996), 43.

[35]Robert Putnam, *Bowling Alone* (New York: Simon & Schuster, 2000).

[36]For example, interest group membership has risen.

[37]Patterson, *Vanishing Voter*, chs. 1, 4.

[38]Survey of Pew Center for People and the Press, 1990.

[39]See Benjamin Ginsberg, *The Consequences of Consent* (New York: Random House, 1982), ch. 2.

[40]See Laura R. Woliver, *From Outrage to Action* (Urbana: University of Illinois Press, 1993).

[41]Lee Bruce Stokes, "New Players in the Trade Game," *National Journal*, December 18, 1999, 3630.

[42]Dalton, *Citizen Politics in Western Democracies*, 38.

[43]Ibid., 68.

[44]Ronald Inglehart, "Post-Materialism in an Environment of Insecurity," *American Political Science Review* 75 (1981): 880–900; Edward N. Mueller and Mitchell A. Seligson, "Inequality and Insurgency," *American Political Science Review* 81 (1987): 425–51.

[45]William Watts and Lloyd A. Free, eds., *The State of the Nation* (New York: University Books, Potomac Associates, 1967), 97.

[46]Harry Holloway with John George, *Public Opinion*, 2d ed. (New York: St. Martin's Press, 1986), 157.

[47]Robert E. Lane, "Market Justice, Political Justice," *American Political Science Review* 80 (1986): 383; see also Jennifer Nedelsky, *Private Property and the Limits of American Constitutionalism* (New York: Oxford University Press, 1990).

[48]Verba and Nie, *Participation in America*, 131.

[49]See Verba and Nie, *Participation in America*, 332; V. O. Key Jr., *Southern Politics* (New York: Vintage Books, 1949), 527; Lawrence Jacobs and Robert Shapiro, *Politicians Don't Pander* (Chicago: University of Chicago Press, 2000).

CHAPTER EIGHT

[1]E. E. Schattschneider, *Party Government* (New York: Rinehart, 1942), 1.

[2]E. E. Schattschneider, *The Semisovereign People: A Realist's View of Democracy in America* (New York: Holt, Rinehart & Winston, 1961), 140.

[3]See John Aldrich, *Why Parties? The Origin and Transformation of Political Parties in America* (Chicago: University of Chicago Press, 1995).

[4]L. Sandy Maisel, *Parties and Elections in America*, 3d ed. (Latham, Md.: Rowman and Littlefield, 1999), 27.

[5]Thomas E. Patterson, *The Vanishing Voter* (New York: Knopf, 2002), ch. 2.

[6]Aldrich, *Why Parties?*

[7]See Richard P. McCormick, *The Second American Party System: Party Formation in the Jacksonian Era* (Chapel Hill: University of North Carolina Press, 1966).

[8]Alexis de Tocqueville, *Democracy in America (1835–1840)*, ed. J. P. Mayer and A. P. Kerr (Garden City, N.Y.: Doubleday/Anchor, 1969), 60.

[9]Aldrich, *Why Parties?* 151.

[10]See Kristi Andersen, *The Creation of a Democratic Majority, 1928–1936* (Chicago: University of Chicago Press, 1979).

[11]See Kevin Phillips, *The Emerging Republican Majority* (New Rochelle, N.Y.: Arlington House, 1969).

[12] See Harold W. Stanley, "Southern Partisan Changes: Dealignment, Realignment or Both?" *Journal of Politics* 50 (1988): 64–88; Earl Black and Merle Black, *Politics and Society in the South* (Cambridge, Mass.: Harvard University Press, 1987); Robert H. Swansbrough and David M. Brodsky, eds., *The South's New Politics: Realignment and Dealignment* (Columbia: University of South Carolina Press, 1988); Dewey L. Grantham, *The Life and Death of the Solid South* (Lexington: University of Kentucky Press, 1988).

[13] William H. Flanigan and Nancy Zingale, *Political Behavior of the American Electorate*, 9th ed. (Washington, D.C.: Congressional Quarterly Press, 1998), 58–63.

[14] Frederick G. Dutton, *Changing Sources of Power* (New York: McGraw-Hill, 1971), ch. 6.

[15] See E. J. Dionne Jr., *Why Americans Hate Politics* (New York: Simon & Schuster, 1992).

[16] The classic account of the relationship of electoral and party systems is Maurice Duverger, *Political Parties* (New York: Wiley, 1954), bk. 2, ch. 1; see also Arend Lijphardt, *Electoral Systems and Party Systems* (New York: Oxford University Press, 1994).

[17] Clinton Rossiter, *Parties and Politics in America* (Ithaca, N.Y.: Cornell University Press, 1960), 11.

[18] Nancy Gibbs and Michael Duffy, "Fall of the House of Newt," *Time*, November 16, 1998, 47.

[19] Gerald M. Pomper, *Passions and Interests: Political Party Concepts of American Democracy* (Lawrence: University of Kansas Press , 1992), ch. 1.

[20] Ibid.

[21] John F. Bibby, *Politics, Parties, and Elections in America*, 5th ed. (Belmont, Calif.: Wadsworth, 2002), 275–83.

[22] Steven J. Rosenstone, Roy L. Behr, and Edward H. Lazarus, *Third Parties in America*, 2d ed. (Princeton, N.J.: Princeton University Press, 1996).

[23] Daniel A. Mazmanian, *Third Parties in Presidential Elections* (Washington, D.C.: Brookings Institution, 1984), 143–44.

[24] See Lawrence Goodwyn, *The Populist Movement* (New York: Oxford University Press, 1978).

[25] Anthony King, *Running Scared* (New York: Free Press, 1997).

[26] See Alan Ehrenhalt, *The United States of Ambition* (New York: Times Books, 1991).

[27] See Paul S. Herrnson and John C. Green, eds., *Responsible Partisanship* (Lawrence: University Press of Kansas, 2003).

[28]See James L. Gibson, John P. Frendreis, and Laura L. Vertz, "Party Dynamics in the 1980s: Change in County Party Organizational Strength, 1980–1984" *American Journal of Political Science* 33 (1989): 67–90.

[29]James L. Gibson, Cornelius Cotter, John Bibby, and Robert Huckshorn, "Assessing Party Organizational Strength," *American Journal of Political Science* 27 (May 1983): 200.

[30]See Sarah McCally Morehouse, "Money Versus Party Effort," *American Journal of Political Science* 34 (1990): 706–24.

[31]David Adamany, "Political Parties in the 1980s," in Michael J. Malbin, ed., *Money and Politics in the United States* (Chatham, N.J.: Chatham House, 1984), 114.

[32]Joseph Napolitan, *The Election Game and How to Win It* (New York: Doubleday, 1972).

[33]David B. Magleby and Candice J. Nelson, *The Money Chase: Congressional Campaign Finance Reform* (Washington, D.C.: Brookings Institution, 1990).

[34]Bibby, *Politics, Parties, and Elections in America*, 207.

[35]Federal Elections Commission data, 2002.

[36]David Chagall, *The New King-Makers* (New York: Harcourt Brace Jovanovich, 1981).

[37]Michael W. Traugott and Paul J. Lavrakas, *The Voters' Guide to Election Polls* (Chatham, N.J.: Chatham House, 1996).

[38]Kiku Adatto, "Sound Bite Democracy," Joan Shorenstein Center on the Press, Politics, and Public Policy, Research Paper R-2, Harvard University, Cambridge, Mass., June 1990.

[39]Darrell M. West, *Air Wars: Television Advertising in Election Campaigns, 1952–2000* (Washington, D.C.: Congressional Quarterly Press, 2001), 140–46.

[40]Ibid.

[41]Stephen Ansolabehere and Shanto Iyengar, *Going Negative* (New York: Free Press, 1995), ch. 5.

[42]West, *Air Wars*, 12.

[43]Ibid., 143.

[44]David E. Price, *Bringing Back the Parties* (Washington, D.C.: Congressional Quarterly Press, 1984), 116.

CHAPTER NINE

[1]E. E. Schattschneider, *The Semisovereign People: A Realist's View of Democracy in America* (New York: Holt, Rinehart & Winston, 1960), 35.

[2]Alexis de Tocqueville, *Democracy in America (1835–1840)*, ed. J. P. Mayer and A. P. Kerr (Garden City, N.Y.: Doubleday/Anchor, 1969), bk. 2, ch. 4.

[3]Mancur Olson, *The Logic of Collective Action*, rev. ed. (Cambridge, Mass.: Harvard University Press, 1971), 147.

[4]See Jack L. Walker, *Mobilizing Interest Groups in America* (Ann Arbor: University of Michigan Press, 1991).

[5]See Lawrence Rothenberg, *Linking Citizens to Government: Interest Group Politics at Common Cause* (New York: Cambridge University Press, 1992); Jeffrey M. Berry, *The New Liberalism: The Rising Power of Citizen Groups* (Washington, D.C.: Brookings Institution Press, 1999).

[6]Olson, *Logic of Collective Action*, 64.

[7]Christopher J. Bosso, "The Color of Money: Environmental Groups and the Pathologies of Fund Raising," in Allan J. Cigler and Burdett Loomis, *Interest Group Politics*, 4th ed. (Washington, D.C.: Congressional Quarterly Press, 1995), 101–3.

[8]Kay Lehman Schlozman and John T. Tierney, *Organized Interests and American Democracy* (New York: Harper & Row, 1986), 54; see also Ronald J. Hrebenar and Ruth K. Scott, *Interest Group Politics in America* (Englewood Cliffs, N.J.: Prentice-Hall, 1990), 167.

[9]See Beverly A. Cigler, "Not Just Another Special Interest: Intergovernmental Representation," in Cigler and Loomis, *Interest Group Politics*, 4th ed., 131–53.

[10]Norman J. Ornstein and Shirley Elder, *Interest Groups, Lobbying, and Policymaking*, (Washington, D.C.: Congressional Quarterly Press, 1978); 82–86.

[11]See John Mark Hansen, *Gaining Access* (Chicago: Chicago University Press, 1991).

[12]Robert H. Salisbury and Paul Johnson, "Who You Know Versus What You Know," *American Journal of Political Science* 33 (February 1989): 175–95; see also William P. Browne, *Cultivating Congress* (Lawrence: University Press of Kansas, 1995).

[13]Ornstein and Elder, *Interest Groups, Lobbying, and Policymaking*, 70.

[14]Quoted in ibid., 77.

[15]See Marver Bernstein, *Regulating Business by Independent Commission* (Princeton, N.J.: Princeton University Press, 1955).

[16]Paul J. Quirk, *Industry Influence in Federal Regulatory Agencies* (Princeton, N.J.: Princeton University Press, 1981).

[17]John E. Chubb, *Interest Groups and the Bureaucracy: The Politics of Energy* (Stanford, Calif.: Stanford University Press, 1983), 200–201.

[18]Charles T. Goodsell, *The Case for Bureaucracy*, 3rd ed. (Chatham, N.J.: Chatham House, 1994), 55–60.

[19]Lee Epstein and C. K. Rowland, "Interest Groups in the Courts," *American Political Science Review* 85 (1991): 205–17.

[20]See Hansen, *Gaining Access*; but, see Browne, *Cultivating Congress*.

[21]Hugh Heclo, "Issue Networks and the Executive Establishment," in Anthony King, ed., *The New American Political System* (Washington, D.C.: American Enterprise Institute, 1978), 87–124.

[22]Ornstein and Elder, *Interest Groups, Lobbying, and Policymaking*, 88–93.

[23]Ernest Wittenberg and Elisabeth Wittenberg, *How to Win in Washington* (Cambridge, Mass.: Blackwell, 1989), 81.

[24]Quoted in Mark Green, "Political PAC-Man," *The New Republic*, December 13, 1982, 20; see also Frank J. Sorauf, *Inside Campaign Finance* (New Haven, Conn.: Yale University Press, 1992).

[25]Quoted in Larry Sabato, *PAC Power: Inside the World of Political Action Committees* (New York: Norton, 1984), 72.

[26]Federal Elections Commission, 2002.

[27]See Michael J. Malbin, "Of Mountains and Molehills," in Michael J. Malbin, *Parties, Interest Groups, and Campaign Finance Laws* (Washington, D.C.: American Enterprise Institute, 1981), 157–77.

[28]See Dan Clawson, Alan Neustadtl, and Denise Scott, *Money Talks* (New York: Basic Books, 1992); Thomas L. Gatz, *Improper Influence* (Ann Arbor: University of Michigan Press, 1996).

[29]V. O. Key Jr., *Public Opinion and American Democracy* (New York: Knopf, 1961), 428; Gene M. Grossman and Elhanan Helpman, *Interest Groups and Trade Policy* (Princeton, N.J.: Princeton University Press, 2002).

[30]See Robert Dahl, *Who Governs?* (New Haven, Conn.: Yale University Press, 1961).

[31]Walker, *Mobilizing Interest Groups in America*, 112.

[32]Theodore J. Lowi, *The End of Liberalism: The Second Republic of the United States* (New York: Norton, 1979).

[33]See William Domhoff, *The Power Elite and the State* (New York: Aldine de Gruyter, 1990).

[34]See Rothenberg, *Linking Citizens to Government*.

[35]Benjamin Ginsberg, *The Consequences of Consent* (New York: Random House, 1982), 214.

CHAPTER TEN

[1]Theodore H. White, *The Making of the President, 1972* (New York: Bantam Books, 1973), 327.

[2]See Richard Davis, *The Press and American Politics*, 2d ed. (Upper Saddle River, N.J.: Prentice-Hall, 1996), 24–27.

[3]Comment at the annual meeting of the American Association of Political Consultants, Washington, D.C., 1977.

[4]Frank Luther Mott, *American Journalism, a History: 1690–1960* (New York: Macmillan, 1962), 114–15.

[5]Culver H. Smith, *The Press, Politics, and Patronage* (Athens: University of Georgia Press, 1977), 163–68.

[6]Doris A. Graber, *Mass Media and American Politics*, 5th ed. (Washington, D.C.: Congressional Quarterly Press, 1997), 36; Mark Wahlgren Summers, *The Press Gang* (Chapel Hill: University of North Carolina Press, 1994).

[7]See Michael Schudson, *Discovering the News* (New York: Basic Books, 1978).

[8]Mott, *American Journalism*, 122–23, 220–27.

[9]Commission on Freedom of the Press, *A Free and Responsible Press* (Chicago: University of Chicago Press, 1974), 62–63.

[10]Mott, *American Journalism*, 220–27, 241, 243.

[11]Edwin Emery, *The Press and America: An Interpretive History of the Mass Media* (Englewood Cliffs, N.J.: Prentice-Hall, 1977), 350.

[12]Quoted in Mott, *American Journalism*, 529.

[13]See Dean Alger, *The Media and Politics*, 2d ed. (Belmont, Calif.: Wadsworth, 1996), 122–23.

[14]Quoted in David Halberstam, *The Powers That Be* (New York: Knopf, 1979), 208–9.

[15]Theodore H. White, *America in Search of Itself: The Making of the President, 1956–1980* (New York: Harper & Row, 1982), 172–73.

[16]Quoted in Michael Robinson and Margaret Sheehan, *Over the Wire and on TV* (New York: Russell Sage Foundation, 1983), 226.

[17]William Cole, ed. *The Most of A. J. Liebling* (New York: Simon, 1963), 7.

[18]Figures from *Standard Rate and Data Service and Electronic Media*, various dates.

[19]Ibid.

[20]Graber, *Mass Media and American Politics*, 36.

[21]See Ben Bagdikian, *The Media Monopoly*, 6th ed. (Boston: Beacon, 2000).

[22]Edward J. Epstein, *News from Nowhere: Television and the News* (New York: Random House, 1973), 37.

[23]White, *The Making of the President*, 1972, 346–48.

[24]See John Chancellor and Walter R. Mears, *The News Business* (New York: Harper & Row, 1983).

[25]David L. Paletz and Robert M. Entman, *Media Power Politics* (New York: Free Press, 1981), 16.

[26]James David Barber, "Characters in the Campaign: The Literary Problem," in James David Barber, ed., *Race for the Presidency* (Englewood Cliffs, N.J.: Prentice-Hall, 1978), 114–15.

[27]See Timothy E. Cook, *Governing with the News* (Chicago: University of Chicago Press, 1997); Bartholomew Sparrow, *Uncertain Guardians* (Baltimore: Johns Hopkins University Press, 1999).

[28]Dean Alger, *Megamedia* (Lanham, Md.: Rowman & Littlefield, 1998).

[29]Ibid., 13–14; see also Leonard Downie Jr. and Robert G. Kaiser, *The News About the News: American Journalism in Peril* (New York: Knopf, 2002).

[30]Study for Committee of Concerned Journalists, 2000.

[31]Walter Lippmann, *Public Opinion* (New York: Free Press, 1965), 214. First published in 1922.

[32]See Kenneth T. Walsh, *Feeding the Beast* (New York: Free Press, 1996).

[33]Donald Shaw and Maxwell McCombs, *The Emergence of American Political Issues: The Agenda-Setting Function of the Press* (St. Paul, Minn.: West Publishing, 1977).

[34]See, for example, F. Cook, T. Tyler, E. Goetz, M. Gordon, D. Protess, D. Leff, and H. Molotch, "Media and Agenda Setting: Effects on the Public, Interest Group Leaders, Policy Makers, and Policy," *Public Opinion Quarterly* 47 (1983): 16–35.

[35]Bernard C. Cohen, *The Press and Foreign Policy* (Princeton, N.J.: Princeton University Press, 1963), 13.

[36]Kiku Adatto, "Sound Bite Democracy," Joan Shorenstein Center on the Press, Politics, and Public Policy, Research Paper R-2, Harvard University, Cambridge, Mass., June 1990.

[37]See James Fallows, *Breaking the News* (New York: Pantheon, 1996).

[38]Thomas E. Patterson, *Out of Order* (New York: Vintage, 1994), ch. 3.

[39]Thomas E. Patterson, "Bad News, Bad Governance," *ANNALS* 546 (July 1996): 97–108; Larry J. Sabato, Mark Stencel, and S. Robert Lichter, *Peep Show: Media and Politics in the Age of Scandal* (Latham, Md.: Rowman and Littlefield, 2000).

[40]Data from Center for Media and Public Affairs, Washington, D.C., 1996.

[41]Quoted in Doreen Carvajal, "For News Media, Some Introspection," *The New York Times*, April 5, 1998, 28.

[42]Quoted in Max Kampelman, "The Power of the Press," *Policy Review* 6 (1978): 19.

[43]Ibid.

[44]James Reston, "End of the Tunnel," *The New York Times*, April 30, 1975, 41.

[45]Quoted in Epstein, *News from Nowhere*, ix.
[46]Lippmann, *Public Opinion*, 221.
[47]Bill Kovach and Tom Rosensteil, *Warp Speed* (New York: The Century Foundation Press, 1999).

CHAPTER ELEVEN

[1]Roger H. Davidson and Walter J. Oleszek, *Congress and Its Members*, 2d ed. (Washington, D.C.: Congressional Quarterly Press, 1985), 7.
[2]See Paul S. Herrnson, *Congressional Elections: Campaigning at Home and in Washington* (Washington, D.C.: Congressional Quarterly Press, 1995).
[3]See Gary C. Jacobson, *The Politics of Congressional Elections*, 5th ed. (New York: Longman, 2001).
[4]See Jonathan S. Krasno, *Challenges, Competition, and Reelection* (New Haven, Conn.: Yale University Press, 1995).
[5]*Congressional Quarterly Weekly Report*, various dates.
[6]Lawrence C. Dodd, "A Theory of Congressional Cycles," in Gerald Wright, Leroy Rieselbach, and Lawrence C. Dodd, *Congress and Policy Change* (New York: Agathon, 1986).
[7]Bruce Cain, John Ferejohn, and Morris P. Fiorina, *The Personal Vote* (Cambridge, Mass.: Harvard University Press, 1987).
[8]See Diana Evans Yiannakis, "House Members' Communication Styles," *Journal of Politics* 44 (November 1982): 1049–73.
[9]Information provided by Clerk of the House.
[10]Harold W. Stanley and Richard G. Niemi, *Vital Statistics on American Politics*, 5th ed. (Washington, D.C.: Congressional Quarterly Press, 1995), 217.
[11]*Congressional Quarterly Guide to Congress*, 3d ed. (Washington, D.C.: Congressional Quarterly Press, 1982), 666; see also Frank J. Sorauf, *Inside Campaign Finance* (New Haven, Conn.: Yale University Press, 1992), 67, 86.
[12]Federal Elections Commission data, 2002.
[13]Federal Elections Commission, 2002.
[14]Jennifer Babson and Kelly St. John, "Momentum Helps GOP Collect Record Amounts from PACs," *Congressional Quarterly Weekly Report*, December 3, 1994, 3456.
[15]Gary C. Jacobson, *The Electoral Origins of Divided Government* (Boulder, Colo.: Westview Press, 1990).
[16]Quoted in "A Tale of Myths and Measures: Who Is Truly Vulnerable?" *Congressional Quarterly Weekly Report*, December 4, 1993, 7; see also

Dennis F. Thompson, *Ethics in Congress* (Washington, D.C.: Brookings Institution Press, 1995).

[17]James E. Campbell, *The Presidential Pulse of Congressional Elections* (Lexington: University Press of Kentucky, 1993).

[18]Linda L. Fowler and Robert D. McClure, *Political Ambition* (New Haven, Conn.: Yale University Press, 1989); see also Jonathan S. Krasno and Donald Philip Green, "Preempting Quality Challengers in House Elections," *Journal of Politics* 50 (November 1988): 878.

[19]Thomas Kazee, "Recruiting Challengers in U.S. House Elections," *Legislative Studies Quarterly* (August 1983): 469–80.

[20]Keith R. Poole and Howard Rosenthal, "Patterns of Congressional Voting," *American Journal of Political Science*, 35 (February 1991): 228.

[21]See Linda L. Fowler, Candidates, *Congress, and the American Democracy* (Ann Arbor: University of Michigan Press, 1994).

[22]*Congressional Quarterly Weekly Report*, various dates.

[23]Linda Witt, Karen M. Paget, and Glenna Matthews, *Running as a Woman: Gender and Power in American Politics* (New York: Free Press, 1993); see also Sue Thomas, *How Women Legislate* (New York: Oxford University Press, 1994).

[24]See Barbara Sinclair, *Legislators, Leaders, and Lawmaking* (Baltimore, Md.: Johns Hopkins University Press, 1995).

[25]Ronald M. Peters Jr., *The American Speakership* (Baltimore: Johns Hopkins University Press, 1990).

[26]Fred R. Harris, *Deadlock or Decision: The U.S. Senate and the Rise of National Politics* (New York: Oxford University Press, 1993), 182.

[27]See, for example, Donald Matthews, *U.S. Senators and Their World* (Chapel Hill: University of North Carolina Press, 1960).

[28]See Barbara Sinclair, *Transformation of the U.S. Senate* (Baltimore, Md.: Johns Hopkins University Press, 1989).

[29]See Sinclair, *Legislators, Leaders, and Lawmaking*.

[30]See David W. Rohde, *Parties and Leaders in the Postreform House* (Chicago: University of Chicago Press, 1991).

[31]Jonathan D. Salant, "New Chairman Swing to Right: Freshmen Get Choice Posts," *Congressional Quarterly Weekly Report*, December 10, 1994, 3493.

[32]See Steven H. Haeberle, "The Institutionalization of the Subcommittee in the United States House of Representatives," *Journal of Politics* 40 (November 1978): 1054–65.

[33]Ibid.

[34]David W. Rhode and Kenneth A. Shepsle, "Domestic Committee Assignments in the House of Representatives," *American Political Science Review*, September 1973, 889–905.

[35]Steven S. Smith, *The American Congress* (Boston: Houghton Mifflin, 1995), 189–98.

[36]See Stephen E. Frantzich and Steven E. Schier, *Congress: Games and Strategies* (Dubuque, Iowa: Brown & Benchmark, 1995), 127.

[37]See Gerald S. Strom, *The Logic of Lawmaking* (Baltimore: Johns Hopkins University Press, 1990).

[38]See Barbara Sinclair, *Unorthodox Lawmaking: New Legislative Processes in the U.S. Congress* (Washington, D.C.: Congressional Quarterly Press, 1997).

[39]See Robert Spitzer, *President and Congress* (New York: McGraw-Hill, 1993).

[40]See Paul C. Light, *The President's Agenda*, rev. ed. (Baltimore: Johns Hopkins University Press, 1991).

[41]Walter J. Oleszek, *Congressional Procedures and the Policy Process*, 4th ed. (Washington, D.C.: Congressional Quarterly Press, 1995), ch. 10.

[42]See Gary Orfield, *Congressional Power: Congress and Social Change* (New York: Harcourt Brace Jovanovich, 1975).

[43]James L. Sundquist, "Congress and the President: Enemies or Partners?" in Lawrence C. Dodd and Bruce I. Oppenheimer, eds., *Congress Reconsidered* (New York: Praeger, 1977), 240.

[44]See Paul C. Light, *Forging Legislation* (New York: Norton, 1992).

[45]Steven S. Smith and Christopher J. Deering, *Committees in Congress*, 3d ed. (Washington, D.C.: Congressional Quarterly Press, 1997), 74.

[46]Keith Krehbiel, "Are Congressional Committees Composed of Preference Outliers?" *American Political Science Review* 84 (1990): 149–64; Richard L. Hall and Bernard Grofman, "The Committee Assignment Process and the Conditional Nature of Committee Bias," *American Political Science Review* 84 (1990): 1149–66.

[47]See Gary W. Cox and Mathew D. McCubbins, *Legislative Leviathan* (Berkeley: University of California Press, 1993).

[48]Eric M. Uslaner, *The Decline of Comity in Congress* (Ann Arbor: University of Michigan Press, 1994).

[49]Joel A. Aberbach, *Keeping a Watchful Eye* (Washington, D.C.: Brookings Institution, 1990); William T. Gormley, *Taming the Bureaucracy* (Princeton, N.J.: Princeton University Press, 1989).

[50]Mathew D. McCubbins and Thomas Schwartz, "Congressional Oversight Overlooked," *American Journal of Political Science* 2 (February 1984): 165–79.

[51]Davidson and Oleszek, *Congress and Its Members*, 2d ed., 7.

CHAPTER TWELVE

[1]Woodrow Wilson, *Constitutional Government in the United States* (New York: Columbia University Press, 1908), 67.

[2]Charles O. Jones, *Separate But Equal Branches* (New York: Chatham House, 1999).

[3]James W. Davis, *The American Presidency* (New York: Harper & Row, 1987), 13.

[4]See Barry M. Blechman and Stephen S. Kaplan, *Force Without War* (Washington, D.C.: Brookings Institution, 1978).

[5]*United States v. Belmont*, 57 U.S. 758 (1937).

[6]Robert DiClerico, *The American President*, 4th ed. (Englewood Cliffs, N.J.: Prentice-Hall, 1995), 47.

[7]Quoted in Wilfred E. Binkley, *President and Congress*, 3d ed. (New York: Vintage, 1962), 142.

[8]Theodore Roosevelt, *An Autobiography* (New York: Scribner's, 1931), 383.

[9]See Richard M. Pious, *The American Presidency* (New York: Basic Books, 1979), 83.

[10]Harry S Truman, 1946–1952: *Years of Trial and Hope* (New York: Signet, 1956), 535.

[11]Robert J. Spitzer, *President and Congress* (New York: McGraw-Hill, 1993), 35–37; Raymond Tatalovich and Byron W. Daynes, *Presidential Power in the United States* (Monterey, Calif.: Brooks/Cole, 1984), 322–23.

[12]Kenneth A. Oye, Robert J. Lieber, and Donald Rothchild, *Eagle in a New World* (New York: HarperCollins, 1992).

[13]Spitzer, *President and Congress*, 137–232.

[14]James Bryce, *The American Commonwealth* (New York: Commonwealth Edition, 1908), 230.

[15]Davis, *The American Presidency*, 20.

[16]Hugh Heclo, "Introduction: The Presidential Illusion," in Hugh Heclo and Lester M. Salamon, eds., *The Illusion of Presidential Government* (Boulder, Colo.: Westview Press, 1981), 6.

[17]Thomas R. Marshall, *Presidential Nominations in a Reform Age* (New York: Praeger, 1981); James W. Ceaser, *Presidential Selection: Theory and Development* (Princeton, N.J.: Princeton University Press, 1979).

[18]Thomas E. Patterson, *Out of Order* (New York: Vintage, 1994); John S. Jackson and William J. Crotty, *The Politics of Presidential Selection* (New York: Longman, 2001).

[19]See Hugh Winebrenner, *The Iowa Precinct Caucuses* (Ames: Iowa State University Press, 1987); Gary R. Orren and Nelson W. Polsby, eds., *Media*

and Momentum: The New Hampshire Primary and Nomination Politics (Chatham, N.J.: Chatham House, 1987).

[20]Myron A. Levine, *Presidential Campaigns and Elections* (Itasca, Ill.: Peacock, 1995), 30.

[21]Kiku Adatto, "Sound Bite Democracy," Joan Shorenstein Center on the Press, Politics, and Public Policy, Research Paper R-2, Harvard University, Cambridge, Mass., June 1990.

[22]Sidney Kraus, ed., *The Great Debates* (Bloomington: Indiana University Press, 1962), 190.

[23]John P. Burke, *The Institutionalized Presidency* (Baltimore: Johns Hopkins University Press, 1992); Charles E. Walcott and Karen M. Hult, *Governing the White House* (Lawrence: University Press of Kansas, 1995).

[24]Davis, *The American Presidency*, 240; see also Bradley Patterson, *The Ring of Power* (New York: Basic Books, 1988), 90–91.

[25]James Pfiffner, *The Modern Presidency* (New York: St. Martin's Press, 1994), 91–96.

[26]Quoted in Stephen J. Wayne, *Road to the White House, 1992* (New York: St. Martin's Press, 1992), 143; see also Timothy Welch, ed., *At the President's Side* (Columbia: University of Missouri Press, 1997).

[27]See Shirley Anne Warshaw, *Powersharing: White House–Cabinet Relations in the Modern Presidency* (Albany: State University of New York Press, 1995).

[28]See Jeffrey E. Cohen, *The Politics of the United States Cabinet* (Pittsburgh: University of Pittsburgh Press, 1988).

[29]Pfiffner, *The Modern Presidency*, 123.

[30]Quoted in James MacGregor Burns, "Our Super-Government—Can We Control It?" *The New York Times*, April 24, 1949, 32.

[31]See Paul C. Light, *Thickening Government: Federal Hierarchy and the Diffusion of Accountability* (Washington, D.C.: Brookings Institution, 1995).

[32]James Pfiffner, "The President's Chief of Staff: Lessons Learned," *Presidential Studies Quarterly* 22 (Winter 1993): 77–102.

[33]Pfiffner, *The Modern Presidency*, 117–22.

[34]Erwin Hargrove, *The Power of the Modern Presidency* (New York: Knopf, 1974); see also John H. Kessel, *Presidents, the Presidency, and the Political Environment* (Washington, D.C.: Congressional Quarterly Press, 2001).

[35]James P. Pfiffner, *The Strategic Presidency: Hitting the Ground Running*, 2d ed. (Chicago: Dorsey Press, 1996).

[36]Aaron Wildavsky, "The Two Presidencies," *Trans-Action*, December 1966, 7.

[37]See Lance T. LeLoup and Steven A. Shull, "Congress Versus the Executive: The Two Presidencies Reconsidered," *Social Science Quarterly*, March 1979, 707.

[38]Pfiffner, *The Modern Presidency*, ch. 6.

[39]Thomas P. (Tip) O'Neill, with William Novak, *Man of the House: The Life and Political Memoirs of Speaker Tip O'Neill* (New York: Random House, 1987), 297.

[40]Fred I. Greenstein, ed., *Leadership in the Modern Presidency* (Cambridge, Mass.: Harvard University Press, 1988), ch. 10.

[41]Robert J. Spitzer, *The Presidential Veto: Touchstone of the American Presidency* (Albany: State University of New York Press, 1988).

[42]Richard E. Neustadt, *Presidential Power and the Modern Presidents* (New York: Free Press, 1990), 71–72.

[43]Ibid., 33.

[44]Ibid.

[45]*Congressional Quarterly Weekly Report*, December 11, 1999.

[46]Mary E. Stuckey, *The President as Interpreter-in-Chief* (Chatham, N.J.: Chatham House, 1991).

[47]Harvey G. Zeidenstein, "Presidents' Popularity and Their Wins and Losses on Major Issues: Does One Have a Greater Influence over the Other?" *Presidential Studies Quarterly*, Spring 1985, 287–300; see also Richard Brody, *Assessing the President* (Stanford, Calif.: Stanford University Press, 1991).

[48]Gallup Polls, November 2–5, 1979, and November 30–December 3, 1979.

[49]John E. Mueller, "Presidential Popularity from Truman to Johnson," *American Political Science Review* 64 (March 1970): 18–34; Kathleen Frankovic, "Public Opinion in the 1992 Campaign," in Gerald M. Pomper, ed., *The Election of 1992* (Chatham, N.J.: Chatham House, 1993).

[50]See John Anthony Maltese, *Spin Control* (Chapel Hill: University of North Carolina Press, 1994); Howard Kurtz, *Spin Cycle* (New York: Basic Books, 1998).

[51]Samuel Kernell, *Going Public: New Strategies of Presidential Leadership*, 3d ed. (Washington, D.C.: Congressional Quarterly Press, 1997), 1.

[52]Jeffrey Tulis, *The Rhetorical Presidency* (Princeton, N.J.: Princeton University Press, 1987); Craig Allen Smith, *The White House Speaks* (Westport, Conn.: Greenwood, 1994); but also see Kenneth Walsh, *Feeding the Beast* (New York: Random House, 1996).

[53]Stuckey, *The President as Interpreter-in-Chief*.

[54]Heclo, "Introduction: The Presidential Illusion," 2.

[55]Theodore J. Lowi, *The "Personal" Presidency: Power Invested, Promise Unfulfilled* (Ithaca, N.Y.: Cornell University Press, 1985); see also Jeffrey E. Cohen, *Presidential Responsiveness and Public Policymaking* (Ann Arbor: University of Michigan Press, 1997).

CHAPTER THIRTEEN

[1]Norman Thomas, *Rule 9: Politics, Administration, and Civil Rights* (New York: Random House, 1966), 6.

[2]Quoted in Albert Gore Jr., *From Red Tape to Results: Creating a Government That Works Better and Costs Less* (Washington, D.C.: U.S. Superintendent of Documents, 1993), 1.

[3]James P. Pfiffner, "The National Performance Review in Perspective," working paper 94-4, Institute of Public Policy, George Mason University, 1994, 2.

[4]Ibid., 12.

[5]Max Weber, *Economy and Society*, trans. Guenther Roth and Claus Wittich (New York: Bedminster Press, 1968), 23.

[6]See John J. DiIulio, ed., *Deregulating the Public Service* (Washington, D.C.: Brookings Institution, 1994).

[7]See Cornelius M. Kerwin, *Rulemaking* (Washington, D.C.: Congressional Quarterly Press, 1994).

[8]Michael Lipsky, *Street-Level Bureaucracy* (New York: Russell Sage Foundation, 1980); see also George Serra, "Citizen-Initiated Contact and Satisfaction with Bureaucracy," *Journal of Public Administration* 5 (April 1995): 175–88.

[9]Paul Van Riper, *History of the United States Civil Service* (Evanston, Ill.: Peterson, 1958), 36.

[10]Jay M. Shafritz, *Personnel Management in Government* (New York: Marcel Dekker, 1981), 9–13; Herbert Kaufman, "Emerging Conflicts in the Doctrine of Public Administration," *American Political Science Review* 50 (December 1956): 1060.

[11]James Q. Wilson, "The Rise of the Bureaucratic State," *Public Interest* 41 (Fall 1975): 77–103.

[12]U.S. Bureau of the Census, *Historical Statistics of the United States: Colonial Times to 1970*, pt. 2 (Washington, D.C.: U.S. Government Printing Office, 1975), 1102.

[13]David H. Rosenbloom, *Federal Service and the Constitution* (Ithaca, N.Y.: Cornell University Press, 1971), 83.

[14]Kaufman, "Emerging Conflicts in the Doctrine of Public Administration," 1060.

[15]Ibid., 1062.

[16]See Richard W. Waterman, *Presidential Influence and the Administrative State* (Knoxville: University of Tennessee Press, 1989).

[17]Quoted in Hugh Heclo, *A Government of Strangers* (Washington, D.C.: Brookings Institution, 1977), 225.

[18]Norton E. Long, "Power and Administration," *Public Administration Review* 10 (Autumn 1949): 269; Joel D. Aberbach and Bert A. Rockman, *In the Web of Politics* (Washington, D.C.: Brookings Institution Press, 2000).

[19]See Herbert Kaufman, *The Administrative Behavior of Federal Bureaucrats* (Washington, D.C.: Brookings Institution, 1981), 4.

[20]See Heclo, *A Government of Strangers*, 117–18.

[21]Quoted in Aaron Wildavsky, *The Politics of the Budgetary Process*, 4th ed. (Boston: Little, Brown, 1984), 19.

[22]Joel D. Aberbach and Bert A. Rockman, "Clashing Beliefs Within the Executive Branch," *American Political Science Review* 70 (June 1976): 461.

[23]See B. Dan Wood and Richard W. Waterman, *Bureaucratic Dynamics* (Boulder, Colo.: Westview Press, 1994).

[24]See John Brehm and Scott Gates, *Working, Shirking, and Sabotage* (Ann Arbor: University of Michigan Press, 1996).

[25]Long, "Power and Administration," 269; see also John Mark Hansen, *Gaining Access* (Chicago: University of Chicago Press, 1991).

[26]See B. Guy Peters, *The Politics of Bureaucracy*, 4th ed. (New York: Longman, 1995).

[27]See Martin Laffin, "Reinventing the Federal Government," in Christopher Peele, Christopher J. Bailey, Bruce Cain, and B. Guy Peters, eds., *Developments in American Politics* 2 (Chatham, N.J.: Chatham House, 1995), 172–76.

[28]See Paul Light, *Thickening Government* (Washington, D.C.: Brookings Institution, 1995).

[29]James G. March and Johan P. Olson, "Organizing Political Life: What Administrative Reorganization Tells Us About Government," *American Political Science Review* 77 (June 1983): 281–96.

[30]Kenneth J. Meier, *Regulation* (New York: St. Martin's Press, 1985), 110–11.

[31]See Heclo, *A Government of Strangers*.

[32]See William F. West, *Controlling the Bureaucracy* (Armonk, N.Y.: Sharp, 1995).

[33]See Donald Kettl, *Deficit Politics* (New York: Macmillan, 1992).

[34]See Joel D. Aberbach, *Keeping a Watchful Eye* (Washington, D.C.: Brookings Institution, 1990).

[35]B. Dan Wood and Richard W. Waterman, "Political Control of the Bureaucracy," *American Political Science Review* 85 (September 1991): 820–21; see also Cathy Marie Johnson, *The Dynamics of Conflict Between Bureaucrats and Legislators* (Armonk, N.Y.: Sharpe, 1992).

[36]David Rosenbloom, "The Evolution of the Administrative State, and Transformations of Administrative Law," in David Rosenbloom and

Richard Schwartz, eds., *Handbook of Regulation and Administrative Law* (New York: Marcel Dekker, 1994), 3–36.

[37]See *Vermont Yankee Nuclear Power Corp. v. National Resources Defense Council, Inc.*, 435 U.S. 519 (1978); *Chevron v. National Resources Defense Council*, 467 U.S. 837 (1984); *Heckler v. Chaney*, 470 U.S. 821 (1985); but see *FDA v. Brown & Williamson Tobacco Co.* (2000).

[38]Roberta Ann Johnson and Michael E. Kraft, "Bureaucratic Whistleblowing and Policy Change," *Western Political Quarterly* 43 (December 1990): 849–74.

[39]"FBI Whistleblower to Speak," *CNN.com*, June 6, 2002.

[40]See Brian J. Cook, *Bureaucracy and Self-Government* (Baltimore, Md.: Johns Hopkins University Press, 1996).

[41]Ibid.

[42]See Wood and Waterman, *Bureaucratic Dynamics*.

[43]David Osborne and Ted Gaebler, *Reinventing Government: How the Entrepreneurial Spirit Is Transforming the Public Sector* (New York: Addison-Wesley, 1992); see also Michael Barzelay and Babak J. Armajani, *Breaking Through Bureaucracy* (Berkeley: University of California Press, 1992); Robert D. Behn, *Leadership Counts* (Cambridge, Mass.: Harvard University Press, 1991).

[44]Pfiffner, "The National Performance Review in Perspective," 7.

[45]Ronald C. Moe, "The 'Reinventing Government' Exercise: Misinterpreting the Problem, Misjudging the Results," *Public Administration Review* (March/April 1994): 125–36.

CHAPTER FOURTEEN

[1]*Marbury v. Madison*, 1 Cranch 137 (1803).

[2]*Bush v. Gore*, No. 00-949 (2000).

[3]Rebecca Mae Salokar, *The Solicitor General: The Politics of Law* (Philadelphia: Temple University Press, 1992); see also Cornell W. Clayton, *The Politics of Justice: The Attorney General and the Making of Legal Policy* (Armonk, N.Y.: Sharpe, 1992).

[4]See Bernard Schwartz, *Decision: How the Supreme Court Decides Cases* (New York: Oxford University Press, 1996).

[5]Henry Glick, *Courts, Politics, and Justice*, 3d ed. (New York: McGraw-Hill, 1993), 214.

[6]Lawrence Baum, *The Supreme Court*, 4th ed. (Washington, D.C.: Congressional Quarterly Press, 1996), 117.

[7]*Brown v. Board of Education of Topeka*, 347 U.S. 483 (1954).

[8]*Gideon v. Wainwright*, 372 U.S. 335 (1963).

[9]From a letter to the author by Frank Schwartz of Beaver College. This section reflects substantially Professor Schwartz's recommendations to the author, as does the later section that addresses the federal court myth. See also Robert A. Carp, *The Federal Courts*, 3d ed. (Washington, D.C.: Congressional Quarterly Press, 1998).

[10]*Hutto v. Davis*, 370 U.S. 256 (1982).

[11]*Roe v. Wade*, 401 U.S. 113 (1973).

[12]See George L. Watson and John Alan Stookey, *Shaping America: The Politics of Supreme Court Appointments* (New York: Longman, 1995).

[13]See Carp, *The Federal Courts*.

[14]Stephen L. Wasby, *The Supreme Court in the Federal Judicial System*, 4th ed. (Chicago: Nelson-Hall, 1993), 75.

[15]Henry J. Abraham, *The Judicial Process*, 7th ed. (New York: Oxford University Press, 1998), 24–26.

[16]Robert Scigliano, *The Supreme Court and the Presidency* (New York: Free Press, 1971), 146; see also David Savage, *Turning Right: The Making of the Rehnquist Supreme Court* (New York: Wiley, 1992).

[17]Quoted in Baum, *The Supreme Court*, 37.

[18]See John C. Hughes, *The Federal Courts, Politics, and the Rule of Law* (New York: Longman, 1995).

[19]John Gottschall, "Reagan's Appointments to the U.S. Courts of Appeals," 70 *Judicature* 48 (1986): 54.

[20]Carp, *The Federal Courts*.

[21]Joseph B. Harris, *The Advice and Consent of the Senate* (Berkeley: University of California Press, 1953), 313.

[22]People for the American Way data, 1998.

[23]Quoted in Louis Fisher, *American Constitutional Law* (New York: McGraw-Hill, 1990), 5.

[24]Baum, *The Supreme Court*, 117.

[25]Quoted in Charles P. Curtis, *Law and Large as Life* (New York: Simon & Schuster, 1959), 156–57.

[26]See Joan Biskupic and Elder Witt, *The Supreme Court and the Powers of the American Government* (Washington, D.C.: Congressional Quarterly Press, 1996), ch. 1.

[27]See Lee Epstein and Jack Knight, *The Choices Justices Make* (New York: Longman, 1995).

[28]*Faragher v. City of Boca Raton*, No. 97-282 (1998).

[29]Wasby, *The Supreme Court in the Federal Judicial System*, 53.

[30]See Lee Epstein, *Conservatives in Court* (Knoxville: University of Tennessee Press, 1985), 80–88.

[31]Linda Greenhouse, "Sure Justices Legislate. They Have To," *The New York Times*, July 5, 1998, sect. 4, p. 1.

[32]See Watson and Stookey, *Shaping America*.

[33]John Schmidhauser, *The Supreme Court* (New York: Holt, Rinehart & Winston, 1964), 6.

[34]Linda Greenhouse, "In Year of Florida Vote, Supreme Court Also Did Much Other Work," *The New York Times*, July 2, 2001, p. A12.

[35]*Bush v. Gore*, No. 00-949 (2000).

[36]David M. O'Brien, *Storm Center: The Supreme Court in American Politics*, 5th ed. (New York: Norton, 2000), 14–15.

[37]Ibid., 59–61.

[38]Some of the references cited in the following sections are taken from Henry J. Abraham, "The Judicial Function Under the Constitution," *News for Teachers of Political Science* 41 (Spring 1984): 12–14; see also Harry H. Wellington, *Interpreting the Constitution* (New Haven, Conn.: Yale University Press, 1990).

[39]Abraham, "The Judicial Function," 14.

[40]Alexander M. Bickel, *The Supreme Court and the Idea of Progress* (New Haven, Conn.: Yale University Press, 1978), 173–81.

[41]See Antonin Scalia, *A Matter of Interpretation* (Princeton, N.J.: Princeton University Press, 1997).

[42]Louis Lusky, *By What Right? A Commentary on the Supreme Court's Power to Revise the Constitution* (Charlottesville, Va.: Michie, 1975), 214–16.

[43]*Romer v. Evans*, No. 94-1039 (1996).

[44]Abraham, "The Judicial Function," 13.

[45]See Larry W. Yackle, *Reclaiming the Federal Courts* (Cambridge, Mass.: Harvard University Press, 1994).

[46]"Good for the Left, Now Good for the Right," *Newsweek*, July 8, 1991, 22.

[47]Linda Greenhouse, "The Justices Decide Who's in Charge," *The New York Times*, June 27, 1999, sect. 4, p. 1.

[48]Quoted in ibid.

CHAPTER FIFTEEN

The section titled "Efficiency Through Government Intervention" relies substantially on Alan Stone, *Regulation and Its Alternatives* (Washington, D.C.: Congressional Quarterly Press, 1982).

[1]See Marc Allen Eisner, *Regulatory Politics in Transition* (Baltimore: Johns Hopkins University Press, 1993).

[2]Paul Portney, "Beware of the Killer Clauses Inside the GOP's 'Contract,'" *The Washington Post National Weekly Edition*, January 23–29, 1995, 21.
[3]See Richard A. Harris and Sidney M. Milkis, *The Politics of Regulatory Change* (New York: Oxford University Press, 1996).
[4]H. Peyton Young, *Equity: In Theory and Practice* (Princeton, N.J.: Princeton University Press, 1995).
[5]"Hill Foes of New Clean Air Rules Unite Behind Moratorium Bill," *Congressional Quarterly Weekly Report*, Spring 1998 (Washington, D.C.: Congressional Quarterly Press, 1998), 61.
[6]See Thomas Streeter, *Selling the Air* (Chicago: University of Chicago Press, 1996).
[7]See Kenneth Gould, Allan Schnaiberg, and Adam Weinberg, *Local Environmental Struggles* (New York: Cambridge University Press, 1996).
[8]Rachel Carson, *The Silent Spring* (Boston: Houghton Mifflin, 1962).
[9]*U.S. News & World Report*, June 30, 1975, 25.
[10]*Whitman v. American Trucking Association*, No. 99-1257 (2001).
[11]See Robert Lekachman, *The Age of Keynes* (New York: Random House, 1966).
[12]See Bruce Bartlett, *Reaganomics: Supply-Side Economics* (Westport, Conn.: Arlington House, 1981); Kenneth Hoover and Raymond Plant, *Conservative Capitalism in Britain and the United States* (New York: Routledge, 1989).
[13]Aaron Wildavsky, *The New Politics of the Budgetary Process* (New York: Harper-Collins, 1992); Allen Schick, rev. ed. *The Federal Budget* (Washington, D.C.: Brookings Institution Press, 2000).
[14]U.S. Senate clerk, 2002.
[15]Martin Mayer, *FED: The Inside Story of How the World's Most Powerful Financial Institution Drives the Markets* (New York: Free Press, 2001).

CHAPTER SIXTEEN

[1]Jason DeParle, "Welfare Reform, One Year Later," *Syracuse Herald American*, January 4, 1998, D1.
[2]Michael Harrington, *The Other America: Poverty in the United States* (New York: Macmillan, 1962); see also Sheldon H. Danziger, Gary D. Sandefur, and Daniel H. Weinberg, eds., *Confronting Poverty* (Cambridge, Mass.: Harvard University Press, 1994); James T. Patterson, *America's Struggle Against Poverty in the Twentieth Century* (Cambridge, Mass.: Harvard University Press, 2000).
[3]Charles Murray, *Losing Ground: American Social Policy, 1950–1980* (New York: Basic Books, 1984).

[4]*Five Thousand American Families* (Ann Arbor: University of Michigan Institute for Social Research, 1977); also see William Julius Wilson, *When Work Disappears* (New York: Knopf, 1996).

[5]See Katherine S. Newman, *No Shame in My Game* (New York: Alfred A. Knopf and Russell Sage Foundation, 1999), 41.

[6]Everett Carll Ladd, *American Political Parties* (New York: Norton, 1970), 205.

[7]DeParle, "Welfare Reform, One Year Later," D4.

[8]Kevin Phillips, *Boiling Point* (New York: Random House, 1993), 109–11.

[9]V. O. Key Jr., *The Responsible Electorate* (Cambridge, Mass.: Belknap Press of Harvard University, 1966), 43.

[10]Fay Lomax Cook and Edith J. Barrett, *Support for the American Welfare State* (New York: Columbia University Press, 1992).

[11]For a general overview of 1950s and 1960s policy disputes, see James Sundquist, *Politics and Policy* (Washington, D.C.: Brookings Institution, 1968).

[12]Hobart Rowan, "The Budget: Fact and Fiction," *The Washington Post National Weekly Edition*, January 16–22, 1995, 5.

[13]"Welfare: Myths, Reality," Knight-Ridder News Service story, *Syracuse Post-Standard*, December 5, 1994, A1, A6.

[14]Quoted in Malcolm Gladwell, "The Medicaid Muddle," *The Washington Post National Weekly Edition*, January 16–22, 1995, 31.

[15]Based on Organization for Economic Cooperation and Development (OECD) data, 2000.

[16]Laurel Shaper Walters, "World Educators Compare Notes," *Christian Science Monitor*, September 7, 1994, 8.

[17]See John E. Chubb and Terry M. Moe, *Politics, Markets, and America's Schools* (Washington, D.C.: Brookings Institution, 1990); Tony Wagner and Thomas Vander Ark, *Making the Grade* (New York: Routledge, 2001).

[18]See Jeffrey R. Henig, *Rethinking School Choice* (Princeton, N.J.: Princeton University Press, 1995).

[19]*Zelman v. Simmons-Harris*, No. 00-1751 (2002).

[20]See Phillip Longman, *Return of Thrift: How the Collapse of the Middle Class Welfare System in the United States Will Reawaken Values in America* (New York: Free Press, 1996).

CHAPTER SEVENTEEN

[1]John Dumbrell, *American Foreign Policy* (New York: St. Martin's Press, 1996).

[2]See Peter B. Kenen, ed., *Understanding Interdependence: The Macroeconomics of the Open Economy* (Princeton, N.J.: Princeton University Press, 1995).

[3]American Assembly Report (cosponsored by the Council on Foreign Relations), *Rethinking America's Security* (New York: Harriman, 1991), 8.

[4]For an overview of Soviet policy, see Alvin Z. Rubenstein, *Soviet Foreign Policy Since World War II*, 4th ed. (New York: HarperCollins, 1992); for an assessment of U.S. policy, see Robert Dallek, *The American Style of Foreign Policy* (New York: Oxford University Press, 1990).

[5]Mr. X. (George Kennan), "The Sources of Soviet Conduct," *Foreign Affairs* 25 (July 1947): 566–82.

[6]David M. Barrett, *Uncertain Warriors: Lyndon Johnson and His Vietnam Advisors* (Lawrence: University Press of Kansas, 1993).

[7]See Stanley Karnow, *Vietnam: A History* (New York: Penguin, 1983).

[8]Charles Kegley and Eugene Wittkopf, *American Foreign Policy*, 2d ed. (New York: St. Martin's Press, 1982), 48.

[9]See Keith L. Nelson, *The Making of Détente* (Baltimore, Md.: Johns Hopkins University Press, 1995).

[10]For a general view of America's new world role, see Kenneth A. Oye, Robert J. Lieber, and Donald Rothchild, *Eagle in a New World: American Grand Strategy in the Post–Cold War Era* (New York: HarperCollins, 1992).

[11]Loch K. Johnson, *Secret Agencies* (New Haven, Conn.: Yale University Press, 1996).

[12]Adam Roberts and Benedict Kingsbury, *United Nations, Divided World*, 2d ed. (New York: Oxford University Press, 1993).

[13]John Barry, "The Battle over Warfare," *Newsweek*, December 5, 1994, 27–28.

[14]Ole Holsti, *Public Opinion and American Foreign Policy* (Ann Arbor: University of Michigan Press, 1996).

[15]See James M. Lindsay, *Congress and the Politics of U.S. Foreign Policy* (Baltimore, Md.: Johns Hopkins University Press, 1994); William Conrad Gibbons, *The U.S. Government and the Vietnam War* (Washington, D.C.: U.S. Government Printing Office, 1994).

[16]Murray L. Weidenbaum, *Small Wars, Big Defense* (New York: Oxford University Press, 1992).

[16]Quoted in Steve Rosen, *Testing Theories of the Military-Industrial Complex* (Lexington, Mass.: Lexington Books, 1973), 1.

[18]"The B-1: A Flight Through Adversity," *Los Angeles Times*, reprinted in *Syracuse Post-Standard*, July 29, 1983, A7.

[19]U.S. government data, various agencies, 2000.

[20]*The World Competitiveness Yearbook* (Lausanne, Switzerland: International Institute for Management Development, 1999).

[21]American Assembly Report, *Rethinking America's Security*, 9; see also Robert O. Keohane, Joseph S. Nye, and Stanley Hoffmann, eds., *After the Cold War* (Cambridge, Mass.: Harvard University Press, 1993).

[22]Tom Masland, "Going Down the Aid 'Rathole'?" *Newsweek*, December 5, 1994, 39.

[23]Hobart Rowen, "The Budget: Fact and Fiction," *The Washington Post National Weekly Edition*, January 16–22, 1995, 5.

[24]See Jonathan Kirshner, *Currency and Coercion* (Princeton, N.J.: Princeton University Press, 1997).

[25]Associated Press, "Clinton Remembers Those Who Fought Apartheid," *Syracuse Herald American*, March 29, 1998, A5.

[26]See Richard J. Barnet and John Cavanagh, *Global Dreams* (New York: Simon & Schuster, 1994).

[27]Philip Gordon, "September 11 and American Foreign Policy," Website of the Brookings Institution, downloaded on June 21, 2002. The chapter's last section is based substantially on Gordon's observations.

GLOSSARY

accountability The ability of the public to hold government officials responsible for their actions.

affirmative action A term that refers to programs designed to ensure that women, minorities, and other traditionally disadvantaged groups have full and equal opportunities in employment, education, and other areas of life.

age-cohort tendency The tendency for a significant break in the pattern of political socialization to occur among younger citizens, usually as the result of a major event or development that disrupts preexisting beliefs.

agency point of view The tendency of bureaucrats to place the interests of their agency ahead of other interests and ahead of the priorities sought by the president or Congress.

agenda setting The power of the media through news coverage to focus the public's attention and concern on particular events, problems, issues, personalities, and so on.

agents of socialization Those agents, such as the family and the media, that have significant impact on citizens' political socialization.

air wars A term that refers to the fact that modern campaigns are often a battle of opposing televised advertising campaigns.

alienation A feeling of personal powerlessness that includes the notion that government does not care about the opinions of people like oneself.

Anti-Federalists A term used to describe opponents of the Constitution during the debate over ratification.

apathy A feeling of personal noninterest or unconcern with politics.

appellate jurisdiction The authority of a given court to review cases that have already been tried in lower courts and are appealed to it by the losing party; such a court is called an appeals court or appellate court. (See also **original jurisdiction.**)

authority The recognized right of an individual or institution to exercise power. (See also **power.**)

balanced budget When the government's tax revenues for

G-1

the year are roughly equal to its expenditures.

bill A proposed law (legislative act) within Congress or another legislature. (See also **law.**)

Bill of Rights The first ten amendments to the Constitution. They include such rights as freedom of speech and trial by jury.

block grants Federal grants-in-aid that permit state and local officials to decide how the money will be spent within a general area, such as education or health. (See also **categorical grants.**)

budget deficit When the government's expenditures exceed its tax revenues.

budget surplus When the government's tax and other revenues exceed its expenditures.

bureaucracy A system of organization and control based on the principles of hierarchical authority, job specialization, and formalized rules. (See also **formalized rules; hierarchical authority; job specialization.**)

bureaucratic rule The tendency of large-scale organizations to develop into the bureaucratic form, with the effect that administrators make key policy decisions.

cabinet A group consisting of the heads of the (cabinet) executive departments, who are appointed by the president, subject to

confirmation by the Senate. The cabinet was once the main advisory body to the president but no longer plays this role. (See also **cabinet departments.**)

cabinet (executive) departments The major administrative organizations within the federal executive bureaucracy, each of which is headed by a secretary (cabinet officer) and has responsibility for a major function of the federal government, such as defense, agriculture, or justice. (See also **cabinet; independent agencies.**)

candidate-centered politics Election campaigns and other political processes in which candidates, not political parties, have most of the initiative and influence. (See also **party-centered politics.**)

capital-gains tax Tax that individuals pay on money gained from the sale of a capital asset, such as property or stocks.

capitalism An economic system based on the idea that government should interfere with economic transactions as little as possible. Free enterprise and self-reliance are the collective and individual principles that underpin capitalism.

categorical grants Federal grants-in-aid to states and localities that can be used only for designated projects. (See also **block grants.**)

checks and balances The elaborate system of divided spheres of authority provided by the U.S. Constitution as a means of controlling the power of government. The separation of powers among the branches of the national government, federalism, and the different methods of selecting national officers are all part of this system.

citizens' (noneconomic) groups Organized interests formed by individuals drawn together by opportunities to promote a cause in which they believe but that does not provide them significant individual economic benefits. (See also **economic groups; interest group.**)

civic duty The belief of an individual that civic and political participation is a responsibility of citizenship.

civil liberties The fundamental individual rights of a free society, such as freedom of speech and the right to a jury trial, which in the United States are protected by the Bill of Rights.

civil rights (equal rights) The right of every person to equal protection under the laws and equal access to society's opportunities and public facilities.

civil service system See merit system.

clear-and-present-danger test A test devised by the Supreme Court in 1919 to define the limits of free speech in the context of national security. According to the test, government cannot abridge political expression unless it presents a clear and present danger to the nation's security.

clientele groups Special-interest groups that benefit directly from the activities of a particular bureaucratic agency and are therefore strong advocates of the agency.

cloture A parliamentary maneuver that, if a three-fifths majority votes for it, limits Senate debate to thirty hours and has the effect of defeating a filibuster. (See also **filibuster.**)

cold war The lengthy period after World War II when the United States and the USSR were not engaged in actual combat (a "hot war") but were nonetheless locked in a state of deep-seated hostility.

collective (public) goods Benefits that are offered by groups (usually citizens' groups) as an incentive for membership but that are nondivisible (e.g., a clean environment) and therefore are available to nonmembers as well as members of the particular group. (See also **free-rider problem; private goods.**)

commerce clause The clause of the Constitution (Article I, Section 8) that empowers the federal government to regulate commerce among the states and with other nations.

common-carrier role The media's function as an open channel through which political leaders can communicate with the public. (See also **public representative role; signaler role; watchdog role.**)

comparable worth The idea that women should get pay equal to men for work that is of similar difficulty and responsibility and that requires similar levels of education and training.

compliance The issue of whether a court's decisions will be respected and obeyed.

concurring opinion A separate opinion written by a Supreme Court justice who votes with the majority in the decision on a case but who disagrees with their reasoning. (See also **dissenting opinion; majority opinion; plurality opinion.**)

confederacy A governmental system in which sovereignty is vested entirely in subnational (state) governments. (See also **federalism; unitary system.**)

conference committee A temporary committee that is formed to bargain over the differences in the House and Senate versions of a bill. The committee's members are usually appointed from the House and Senate standing committees that originally worked on the bill.

conservatives Those who emphasize the marketplace as the means of distributing economic benefits but look to government to uphold traditional social values. (See also **liberals; libertarians; populists.**)

constituency The individuals who live within the geographical area represented by an elected official. More narrowly, the body of citizens eligible to vote for a particular representative.

constitution The fundamental law that defines how a government will legitimately operate.

constitutional democracy A government that is democratic in its provisions for majority influence through elections and constitutional in its provisions for minority rights and rule by law.

constitutionalism The idea that there are definable limits on the rightful power of a government over its citizens.

containment A doctrine, developed after World War II, based on the assumptions that the Soviet Union was an aggressor nation and that only a determined United States could block Soviet territorial ambitions.

cooperative federalism The situation in which the national, state, and local levels work together to solve problems.

de facto discrimination
Discrimination on the basis of race, sex, religion, ethnicity, and the like that results from social, economic, and cultural biases and conditions. (See also **de jure discrimination**.)

de jure discrimination
Discrimination on the basis of race, sex, religion, ethnicity, and the like that results from a law. (See also **de facto discrimination**.)

dealignment A situation in which voters' partisan loyalties have been substantially and permanently weakened. (See also **party identification; party realignment**.)

decision A vote of the Supreme Court in a particular case that indicates which party the justices side with and by how large a margin.

deficit spending When the government spends more than it collects in taxes and other revenues.

delegates Elected representatives whose obligation is to act in accordance with the expressed wishes of the people whom they represent. (See also **trustees**.)

demand-side economics A form of fiscal policy that emphasizes "demand" (consumer spending). Government can use increased spending or tax cuts to place more money in consumers' hands and thereby increase demand. (See also **fiscal policy; supply-side economics**.)

democracy A form of government in which the people govern, either directly or through elected representatives.

demographic representativeness The idea that the bureaucracy will be more responsive to the public if its employees at all levels are demographically representative of the population as a whole.

denials of power A constitutional means of limiting governmental action by listing those powers that government is expressly prohibited from using.

deregulation The rescinding of excessive government regulations for the purpose of improving economic efficiency.

descriptive reporting The style of reporting that aims to describe what is taking place or has occurred.

détente A French word meaning "a relaxing" and used to refer to an era of improved relations between the United States and the Soviet Union that began in the early 1970s.

deterrence The idea that nuclear war can be discouraged if each side in a conflict has the capacity to destroy the other with nuclear weapons.

devolution The passing down of authority from the national government to states and localities.

direct primary See **primary election.**

dissenting opinion The opinion of a justice in a Supreme Court case that explains his or her reasons for disagreeing with the majority's decision. (See also **concurring opinion; majority opinion; plurality opinion.**)

diversity The principle that individual and group differences should be respected and are a source of national strength.

dual federalism A doctrine based on the idea that a precise separation of national power and state power is both possible and desirable.

due process clause (of the Fourteenth Amendment) The clause of the Constitution that has been used by the judiciary to apply the Bill of Rights to the actions of state governments.

economic depression A very severe and sustained economic downturn. Depressions are rare in the United States: the last one was in the 1930s.

economic globalization The increased interdependence of nations' economies. The change is a result of technological, transportation, and communication advances that have enabled firms to deploy their resources across the globe.

economic groups Interest groups that are organized primarily for economic reasons but that engage in political activity in order to seek favorable policies from government. (See also **citizens' groups; interest group.**)

economic recession A moderate but sustained downturn in the economy. Recessions are part of the economy's normal cycle of ups and downs.

economy A system of production and consumption of goods and services that are allocated through exchange among producers and consumers.

efficiency An economic principle that holds that firms should fulfill as many of society's needs as possible while using as few of its resources as possible. The greater the output (production) for a given input (for example, an hour of labor), the more efficient the process.

elastic clause See **"necessary and proper" clause.**

Electoral College An unofficial term that refers to the electors who cast the states' electoral votes.

electoral votes The method of voting that is used to choose the U.S. president. Each state has the same number of electoral votes as it has members in Congress (House and Senate combined). By tradition, electoral voting is tied to a state's popular voting; thus, the presidential candidate with the most popular votes overall has usually also had the most electoral votes.

elitism The view that the United States is essentially run by a tiny elite (composed of wealthy or well-connected individuals) who control public policy through both direct and indirect means.

entitlement program Any of a number of individual benefit programs, such as social security, that require government to provide a designated benefit to any person who meets the legally defined criteria for eligibility.

enumerated (expressed) powers The seventeen powers granted to the national government under Article I, Section 8 of the Constitution. These powers include taxation and the regulation of commerce as well as the authority to provide for the national defense.

equal-protection clause A clause of the Fourteenth Amendment that forbids any state to deny equal protection of the laws to any individual within its jurisdiction.

equal rights See **civil rights.**

equality The notion that all individuals are equal in their moral worth, in their treatment under the law, and in their political voice.

equality of opportunity The idea that all individuals should be given an equal chance to succeed on their own.

equality of result The objective of policies intended to reduce or eliminate the effects of discrimination so that members of traditionally disadvantaged groups will have the same benefits of society as do members of advantaged groups.

equity (in relation to economic policy) The situation in which the outcome of an economic transaction is fair to each party. An outcome can usually be considered fair if each party enters into a transaction freely and is not knowingly at a disadvantage.

establishment clause The First Amendment provision that government may not favor one religion over another or favor religion over no religion, and that prohibits Congress from passing laws respecting the establishment of religion.

exclusionary rule The legal principle that government is prohibited from using in trials any evidence that was obtained by unconstitutional means (for example, illegal search and seizure).

executive departments See **cabinet departments.**

executive leadership system An approach to managing the bureaucracy that is based on presidential leadership and presidential management tools, such as the president's annual budget proposal. (See also **merit system; patronage system.**)

expressed powers See **enumerated powers.**

externalities Burdens that society incurs when firms fail to pay the full cost of resources used in production. An example of an externality is the pollution that results when corporations dump industrial wastes into lakes and rivers.

facts (of a court case) The relevant circumstances of a legal dispute or offense as determined by a trial court. The facts of a case are crucial because they help determine which law or laws are applicable in the case.

federalism A governmental system in which authority is divided between two sovereign levels of government: national and regional. (See also **confederacy; unitary system.**)

Federalists A term used to describe supporters of the Constitution during the debate over ratification.

filibuster A procedural tactic in the U.S. Senate whereby a minority of legislators prevents a bill from coming to a vote by holding the floor and talking until the majority gives in and the bill is withdrawn from consideration. (See also **cloture.**)

fiscal federalism A term that refers to the expenditure of

federal funds on programs run in part through states and localities.

fiscal policy A tool of economic management by which government attempts to maintain a stable economy through its taxing and spending decisions. (See also **demand-side economics; monetary policy; supply-side economics.**)

formalized rules A basic principle of bureaucracy that refers to the standardized procedures and established regulations by which a bureaucracy conducts its operations. (See also **bureaucracy.**)

free-exercise clause A First Amendment provision that prohibits the government from interfering with the practice of religion or prohibiting the free exercise of religion.

free-rider problem The situation in which the benefits offered by a group to its members are also available to nonmembers. The incentive to join the group and to promote its cause is reduced because nonmembers (free riders) receive the benefits (e.g., a cleaner environment) without having to pay any of the group's costs. (See also **collective goods.**)

free trade The view that the long-term economic interests of all countries are advanced when tariffs and other trade barriers are kept to a minimum. (See also **protectionism.**)

freedom of expression Americans' freedom to communicate their views, the foundation of which is the First Amendment rights of freedom of conscience, speech, press, assembly, and petition.

gender gap The tendency of women and men to differ in their political attitudes and voting preferences.

gerrymandering The process by which the party in power draws election district boundaries in a way that advantages its candidates.

government The institutions, processes, and rules that facilitate control of a particular area and its inhabitants.

government corporations Bodies, such as the U.S. Postal Service and Amtrak, that are similar to private corporations in that they charge for their services, but different in that they receive federal funding to help defray expenses. Their directors are appointed by the president with Senate approval.

graduated personal income tax A tax on personal income in which the tax rate increases as income increases; in other words, the tax rate is higher for higher income levels.

grants-in-aid Federal cash payments to states and localities for programs they administer.

grants of power The method of limiting the U.S. government by confining its scope of authority to those powers expressly granted in the Constitution.

grassroots lobbying A form of lobbying designed to persuade officials that a group's policy position has strong constituent support.

grassroots party A political party organized at the level of the voters and dependent on their support for its strength.

Great Compromise The agreement of the constitutional convention to create a two-chamber Congress with the House apportioned by population and the Senate apportioned equally by state.

hard money Campaign funds given directly to candidates to spend as they choose.

hierarchical authority A basic principle of bureaucracy that refers to the chain of command within an organization whereby officials and units have control over those below them. (See also **bureaucracy.**)

hired guns The professional consultants who run campaigns for high office.

honeymoon period The president's first months in office, a time when Congress, the press, and the public are more inclined than usual to support presidential initiatives.

ideology A consistent pattern of opinion on particular issues that stems from a core belief or set of beliefs.

imminent-lawless-action test A legal test that says government cannot lawfully suppress advocacy that promotes lawless action unless such advocacy is aimed at producing, and is likely to produce, imminent lawless action.

implied powers The federal government's constitutional authority (through the "necessary and proper" clause) to take action that is not expressly authorized by the Constitution but that supports actions that are so authorized. (See also **"necessary and proper" clause.**)

in-kind benefits Government benefits that are cash equivalents, such as food stamps or rent vouchers. This form of benefit ensures that recipients will use public assistance in a specified way.

inalienable (natural) rights Those rights that persons theoretically possessed in the state of nature, prior to the formation of governments. These rights, including those of life, liberty, and property, are considered inherent and as such are inalienable. Since government is established by people, government has the responsibility to preserve these rights.

independent agencies Bureaucratic agencies that are similar to cabinet departments but usually have a narrower area of responsibility. Each such agency is headed by a presidential appointee who is not a cabinet member. An example is the National Aeronautics and Space Administration. (See also **cabinet departments.**)

individual goods See **private goods.**

individualism The idea that people should take the initiative, be self-sufficient, and accumulate the material advantages necessary for their well-being.

inflation A general increase in the average level of prices of goods and services.

initiative The process by which citizens can place a legislative measure on the ballot through signature petitions, and if the measure receives a majority vote, it becomes law.

inside lobbying Direct communication between organized interests and policymakers, which is based on the assumed value of close ("inside") contacts with policymakers.

insurgency A type of military conflict in which irregular soldiers rise up against an established regime.

interest group A set of individuals who are organized to promote a shared political interest. (See also **citizens' groups; economic groups.**)

interest-group liberalism The tendency of public officials to support the policy demands of self-interested groups (as opposed to judging policy demands according to whether they serve a larger conception of "the public interest").

intermediate-scrutiny test A test applied by courts to laws that attempt a gender classification. In effect, the test eliminates gender as a legal classification unless it serves an important objective and is substantially related to the objective's achievement.

internationalism The view that the country should involve itself deeply in world affairs. (See also **isolationism.**)

interpretive reporting The style of reporting that aims to explain why something is taking place or has occurred.

iron triangle A small and informal but relatively stable group of well-positioned legislators, executives, and lobbyists who seek to promote policies beneficial to a particular interest. (See also **issue network.**)

isolationism The view that the country should deliberately avoid a large role in world affairs and instead concentrate on domestic concerns. (See also **internationalism.**)

issue network An informal network of public officials and lobbyists who have a common interest and expertise in a given area and who are brought together temporarily by a proposed policy in that area. (See also **iron triangle.**)

job specialization A basic principle of bureaucracy that holds that the responsibilities of each job position should be explicitly defined and that a precise division of labor within the organization should be maintained. (See also **bureaucracy.**)

judicial activism The doctrine that the courts should develop new legal principles when judges see a compelling need, even if this action places them in conflict with the policy decisions of elected officials. (See also **judicial restraint.**)

judicial conference A closed meeting of the justices of the U.S. Supreme Court to discuss and vote on the cases before them; the justices are not supposed to discuss conference proceedings with outsiders.

judicial restraint The doctrine that the judiciary should be highly respectful of precedent and should defer to the judgment of legislatures. The doctrine claims that the job of judges is to work within the confines of laws set down by tradition and lawmaking majorities. (See also **judicial activism.**)

judicial review The power of courts to decide whether a governmental institution has acted within its constitutional powers and, if not, to declare its action null and void.

jurisdiction (of a congressional committee) The policy area in which a particular congressional committee is authorized to act.

jurisdiction (of a court) A given court's authority to hear cases of a particular kind. Jurisdiction may be original or appellate.

laissez-faire doctrine A classic economic philosophy that holds that owners of businesses should be allowed to make their own production and distribution decisions without government regulation or control.

law (as enacted by Congress) A legislative proposal, or bill, that is passed by both the House and Senate and is either signed or not vetoed by the president. (See also bill.)

lawmaking function The authority (of a legislature) to make the laws necessary to carry out the government's powers. (See also **oversight function; representation function.**)

laws (of a court case) The con-stitutional provisions, legislative statutes, or judicial precedents that apply to a court case.

legitimacy (of election) The idea that the selection of officeholders should be based on the will of the people as reflected through their votes.

legitimacy (of judicial power) The issue of the proper limits of judicial authority in a political system based in part on the principle of majority rule.

libel Publication of material that falsely damages a person's reputation.

liberals Those who favor activist government as an instrument of economic security and redistribution but reject the notion that government should favor a particular set of social values. (See also **conservatives; libertarians; populists.**)

libertarians Those who oppose government as an instrument of traditional values and of economic security. (See also **conservatives; liberals; populists.**)

liberty The principle that individuals should be free to act and think as they choose, provided they do not infringe unreasonably on the rights and freedoms of others.

limited government A government that is subject to strict limits on its lawful uses of powers and hence on its ability to deprive people of their liberty.

lobbying The process by which interest-group members or lobbyists attempt to influence public policy through contacts with public officials.

logrolling The trading of votes between legislators so that each gets what he or she most wants.

majoritarianism The idea that the majority prevails not only in elections but also in determining policy.

majority opinion A Supreme Court opinion that results when a majority of the justices are in agreement on the legal basis of the decision. (See also **concurring opinion; dissenting opinion; plurality opinion.**)

material incentive An economic or other tangible benefit that is used to attract group members.

means test The requirement that applicants for public assistance must demonstrate they are poor in order to be eligible for the assistance. (See also **public assistance.**)

merit (civil service) system An approach to managing the bureaucracy whereby people are appointed to government positions on the basis of either competitive examinations or special qualifications, such as professional training. (See also **executive leadership system; patronage system.**)

military-industrial complex The three components (the military establishment, the industries that manufacture weapons, and the members of Congress from states and districts that depend heavily on the arms industry) that mutually benefit from a high level of defense spending.

momentum A strong showing by a candidate in early presidential nominating contests, which leads to a buildup of public support for the candidate.

monetary policy A tool of economic management, available to government, based on manipulation of the amount of money in circulation. (See also **fiscal policy.**)

money chase A term used to describe the fact that U.S. campaigns are very expensive and that candidates must spend a great amount of time raising funds in order to compete successfully.

multilateralism The situation in which nations act together in response to problems and crises.

multinational corporations Business firms with major operations in more than one country.

multiparty system A system in which three or more political parties have the capacity to gain control of government separately or in coalition.

national debt The total cumulative amount that the U.S. government owes to creditors.

natural rights See **inalienable rights.**

"necessary and proper" clause (elastic clause) The authority granted Congress in Article I, Section 8 of the Constitution "to make all laws which shall be necessary and proper" for the implementation of its enumerated powers. (See also **implied powers.**)

negative government The philosophical belief that government governs best by staying out of people's lives, thus giving individuals as much freedom as possible to determine their own pursuits. (See also **positive government.**)

neutral competence The administrative objective of a merit-based bureaucracy. Such a bureaucracy should be "competent" in the sense that its employees are hired and retained on the basis of their expertise and "neutral" in the sense that it operates by objective standards rather than partisan ones.

New Jersey (small-state) Plan A constitutional proposal for a strengthened Congress but one in which each state would have a single vote, thus granting a small state the same legislative power as a larger state.

news The news media's version of reality, usually with an emphasis on timely, dramatic, and compelling events and developments.

news media See **press.**

nomination The designation of a particular individual to run as a political party's candidate (its "nominee") in the general election.

noneconomic groups See **citizens' groups.**

North-South Compromise The agreement over economic and slavery issues that enabled northern and southern states to settle differences that threatened to defeat the effort to draft a new constitution.

objective journalism A model of news reporting that is based on the communication of "facts" rather than opinions and that is "fair" in that it presents all sides of partisan debate. (See also **partisan press.**)

open party caucuses Meetings at which a party's candidates for nomination are voted on and that are open to all the party's rank-and-file voters who want to attend.

open-seat election An election in which there is no incumbent in the race.

opinion (of a court) A court's written explanation of its decision, which serves to inform others of the legal basis for the decision. Supreme Court opinions are expected to guide the decisions of other courts. (See also **concurring opinion; dissenting opinion; majority opinion; plurality opinion.**)

original jurisdiction The authority of a given court to be the first court to hear a case. (See also **appellate jurisdiction.**)

outside lobbying A form of lobbying in which an interest group seeks to use public pressure as a means of influencing officials.

oversight function A supervisory activity of Congress that centers on its constitutional responsibility to see that the executive carries out the laws faithfully and spends appropriations properly. (See also **lawmaking function; representation function.**)

packaging (of a candidate) A term of modern campaigning that refers to the process of recasting a candidate's record into an appealing image.

partisan press Newspapers and other communication media that openly support a political party and whose news in significant part follows the party line. (See also **objective journalism.**)

party caucus A group that consists of a party's members in the House or Senate and that serves to elect the party's leadership, set policy goals, and determine party strategy.

party-centered politics Election campaigns and other political processes in which political parties, not individual candidates, hold most of the initiative and influence. (See also **candidate-centered politics.**)

party coalition The groups and interests that support a political party.

party competition A process in which conflict over society's goals is transformed by political parties into electoral competition in which the winner gains the power to govern.

party discipline The willingness of a party's House or Senate members to act together as a cohesive group and thus exert collective control over legislative action.

party identification The personal sense of loyalty that an individual may feel toward a particular political party. (See also **dealignment; party realignment.**)

party leaders Members of the House and Senate who are chosen by the Democratic or Republican caucus in each chamber to represent the party's interests in that chamber and who give some central direction to the chamber's deliberations.

party organizations The party organizational units at national, state, and local levels; their influence has decreased over time because of many factors. (See also **candidate-centered politics; party-centered politics; primary election.**)

party realignment An election or set of elections in which the electorate responds strongly to an extraordinarily powerful issue that has disrupted the established political order. A realignment has a lasting impact on public policy, popular support for the parties, and the composition of the party coalitions. (See also **dealignment; party identification.**)

patronage system An approach to managing the bureaucracy whereby people are appointed to important government positions as a reward for political services they have rendered and because of their partisan loyalty. (See also **executive leadership system; merit system; spoils system.**)

pluralism A theory of American politics that holds that society's interests are substantially represented through the activities of groups.

plurality opinion A court opinion that results when a majority of justices agree on a decision in a case but do not agree on the legal basis for the decision. In this instance, the legal position held by most of the justices on the winning side is called a plurality opinion. (See also **concurring opinion; dissenting opinion; majority opinion.**)

policy Generally, any broad course of governmental action; more narrowly, a specific government program or initiative.

policy implementation The primary function of the bureaucracy; it refers to the process of carrying out the authoritative decisions of Congress, the president, and the courts.

political action committee (PAC) The organization through which an interest group raises and distributes funds for election purposes. By law, the funds must be raised through voluntary contributions.

political culture The characteristic and deep-seated beliefs of a particular people.

political movements See **social movements.**

political participation A sharing in activities designed to influence public policy and leadership, such as voting, joining political parties and interest groups, writing to elected officials, demonstrating for political causes, and giving money to political candidates.

political party An ongoing coalition of interests joined together to try to get their candidates for public office elected under a common label.

political socialization The learning process by which people acquire their political opinions, beliefs, and values.

political system The various components of American government. The parts are separate, but they connect with each other, affecting how each performs.

politics The process through which society makes its governing decisions.

population In a public opinion poll, the people (for example, the citizens of a nation) whose opinions are being estimated through interviews with a sample of these people.

populists Those who favor activist government as a means of promoting both economic security and traditional values. (See also **conservatives; liberals; libertarians.**)

pork barrel projects Legislative acts whose tangible benefits are targeted at a particular legislator's constituency.

positive government The philosophical belief that government intervention is necessary in order to enhance personal liberty when individuals are buffeted by economic and social forces beyond their control. (See also **negative government.**)

poverty line As defined by the federal government, the annual cost of a thrifty food budget for an urban family of four, multiplied by three to allow also for the cost of housing, clothes, and other expenses. Families below the poverty line are considered poor and are eligible for certain forms of public assistance.

power The ability of persons or institutions to control policy. (See also **authority.**)

precedent A judicial decision in a given case that serves as a rule of thumb for settling subsequent cases of a similar nature; courts are generally expected to follow precedent.

presidential approval rating A measure of the degree to which the public approves or disapproves of the president's performance in office.

presidential commissions Organizations within the bureaucracy that are headed by commissioners appointed by the president. An example is the Commission on Civil Rights.

press (news media) Those print and broadcast organizations that are in the news-reporting business.

primacy tendency The tendency for early learning to become deeply embedded in one's mind.

primary election A form of election in which voters choose a party's nominees for public office. In most states, eligibility to vote in a primary election is limited to voters who designated themselves as party members when they registered to vote. A primary is direct when it results directly in the choice of a nominee; it is indirect (as in the case of presidential primaries) when it results in the selection of delegates who then choose the nominee.

prior restraint Government prohibition of speech or publication before the fact, which is presumed by the courts to be unconstitutional unless the justification for it is overwhelming.

private (individual) goods Benefits that a group (most often an economic group) can grant directly and exclusively to the individual members of the group. (See also **collective goods.**)

probability sample A sample for a poll in which each individual in the population has a known probability of being selected randomly for inclusion in the sample. (See also **public opinion poll.**)

procedural due process The constitutional requirement that government must follow proper legal procedures before a person can be legitimately punished for an alleged offense.

proportional representation A form of representation in which seats in the legislature are allocated proportionally according to each political party's share of the popular vote. This system enables smaller parties to compete successfully for seats. (See also **single-member districts.**)

prospective voting A form of electoral judgment in which voters choose the candidate whose policy promises most closely match their own preferences. (See also **retrospective voting.**)

protectionism The view that the immediate interests of domestic producers should have a higher priority (through, for example, protective tariffs) than should free trade between nations. (See also **free trade.**)

public assistance A term that refers to social welfare programs funded through general tax revenues and available only to the financially needy. Eligibility for such a program is established by a means test. (See also **means test; social insurance.**)

public goods See **collective goods.**

public opinion Those opinions held by ordinary citizens that they express openly.

public opinion poll A device for measuring public opinion whereby a relatively small number of individuals (the sample) is interviewed for the purpose of estimating the opinions of a whole community (the population). (See also **probability sample.**)

public policy A decision of government to pursue a course of action designed to produce an intended outcome.

public-representative role A role whereby the media attempt to act as the public's representatives. (See also **common-carrier role; signaler role; watchdog role.**)

purposive incentive An incentive to group participation based on the cause (purpose) that the group seeks to promote.

realignment See **party realignment.**

reapportionment The reallocation of House seats among states after each census as a result of population changes.

reasonable-basis test A test applied by courts to laws that treat individuals unequally. Such a law may be deemed constitutional if its purpose is held to be "reasonably" related to a legitimate government interest.

recall The process by which citizens can petition for the removal from office of an elected official before the scheduled completion of his or her term.

redistricting The process of altering election districts in order to make them as nearly equal in population as possible. Redistricting takes place every ten years, after each population census.

referendum The process through which the legislature may submit proposals to the voters for approval or rejection.

registration The practice of placing citizens' names on an official list of voters before they are eligible to exercise their right to vote.

regulation Government restrictions on the economic practices of private firms.

regulatory agencies Administrative units, such as the Federal Communications Commission and the Environmental Protection Agency, that have responsibility for the monitoring and regulation of ongoing economic activities.

representation function The responsibility of a legislature to represent various interests in society. (See also **lawmaking function; oversight function.**)

representative democracy A system in which the people participate in the decision-making process of government not directly but indirectly, through the election of officials to represent their interests.

republic Historically, the form of government in which representative officials met to decide on policy issues. These representatives were expected to serve the public interest but were not subject to the people's immediate control. Today, the term republic is often used interchangeably with democracy.

reserved powers The powers granted to the states under the Tenth Amendment to the Constitution.

retrospective voting A form of electoral judgment in which voters support the incumbent candidate or party when their policies are judged to have succeeded and oppose the candidate or party when their policies are judged to have failed. (See also **prospective voting**.)

rider An amendment to a bill that deals with an issue unrelated to the content of the bill. Riders are permitted in the Senate but not in the House.

sample In a public opinion poll, the relatively small number of individuals interviewed for the purpose of estimating the opinions of an entire population. (See also **public opinion poll**.)

sampling error A measure of the accuracy of a public opinion poll. It is mainly a function of sample size and is usually expressed in percentage terms. (See also **probability sample**.)

selective incorporation The absorption of certain provisions of the Bill of Rights (for example, freedom of speech) into the Fourteenth Amendment so that these rights are protected from infringement by the states.

self-government The principle that the people are the ultimate source and proper beneficiary of governing authority; in practice, a government based on majority rule.

senatorial courtesy The tradition that a U.S. senator from the state

in which a federal judicial vacancy has arisen should have a say in the president's nomination of the new judge if the senator is of the same party as the president.

seniority A member of Congress's consecutive years of service on a particular committee.

separated institutions sharing power The principle that, as a way to limit government, its powers should be divided among separate branches, each of which also shares in the power of the others as a means of checking and balancing them. The result is that no one branch can exercise power decisively without the support or acquiescence of the others.

separation of powers The division of the powers of government among separate institutions or branches.

service relationship The situation in which party organizations assist candidates for office but have no power to require them to accept or campaign on the party's main policy positions.

service strategy Use of personal staff by members of Congress to perform services for constituents in order to gain their support in future elections.

signaler role The accepted responsibility of the media to alert the public to important developments as soon as possible after they happen or are discovered. (See also **common-carrier role; public representative role; watchdog role.**)

single-issue politics The situation in which separate groups are organized around nearly every conceivable policy issue and press their demands and influence to the utmost.

single-member districts The form of representation in which only the candidate who gets the most votes in a district wins office. (See also **proportional representation.**)

slander Spoken words that falsely damage a person's reputation.

social capital The sum of face-to-face interactions among citizens in a society.

social insurance Social welfare programs based on the "insurance" concept, so that individuals must pay into the program in order to be eligible to receive funds from it. An example is social security for retired people. (See also **public assistance.**)

social (political) movements Active and sustained efforts to achieve social and political change by groups of people who feel that government has not been properly responsive to their concerns.

soft money Campaign contributions that are not subject to legal limits and are given to parties rather than directly to candidates.

sovereignty The ultimate authority to govern within a certain geographical area.

split-ticket voting The pattern of voting in which the individual voter in a given election casts a ballot for one or more candidates of each major party. (See also **straight-ticket voting.**)

spoils system The practice of granting public office to individuals in return for political favors they have rendered. (See also **patronage system.**)

standing committee A permanent congressional committee with responsibility for a particular area of public policy. An example is the Senate Foreign Relations Committee.

stewardship theory A theory that argues for a strong, assertive presidential role, with presidential authority limited only at points specifically prohibited by law. (See also **Whig theory.**)

straight-ticket voting The pattern of voting in which the individual voter in a given election supports only candidates of one party. (See also **split-ticket voting.**)

strict-scrutiny test A test applied by courts to laws that attempt a racial or ethnic classification. In effect, the strict scrutiny test eliminates race or ethnicity as legal classification when it places minority group members at a disadvantage. (See also **suspect classifications.**)

structuring tendency The tendency of earlier political learning to structure (influence) later learning.

suffrage The right to vote.

sunset law A law containing a provision that fixes a date on which a program will end unless the program's life is extended by Congress.

supply-side economics A form of fiscal policy that emphasizes "supply" (production). An example of supply-side economics would be a tax cut for business. (See also **demand-side economics; fiscal policy.**)

supremacy clause Article VI of the Constitution, which makes national law supreme over state law when the national government is acting within its constitutional limits.

suspect classifications Legal classifications, such as race and national origin, that have invidious discrimination as their purpose and are therefore unconstitutional. (See also **strict scrutiny test.**)

symbolic speech Action (for example, the waving or burning of a flag) for the purpose of expressing a political opinion.

transfer payment A government benefit that is given directly to

an individual, as in the case of social security payments to a retiree.

trustees Elected representatives whose obligation is to act in accordance with their own consciences as to what policies are in the best interests of the public. (See also **delegates.**)

two-party system A system in which only two political parties have a real chance of acquiring control of the government.

tyranny of the majority The potential of a majority to monopolize power for its own gain and to the detriment of minority rights and interests.

unitary system A governmental system in which the national government alone has sovereign (ultimate) authority. (See also **confederacy; federalism.**)

unit rule The rule that grants all of a state's electoral votes to the candidate who receives most of the popular votes in the state.

unity The principle that Americans are one people and form an indivisible union.

veto When the president refuses to sign a bill, thereby keeping it from becoming law unless Congress overrides the veto.

Virginia (large-state) Plan A constitutional proposal for a strong Congress with two chambers, both of which would be based on numerical representation, thus granting more power to the larger states.

voter turnout The proportion of persons of voting age who actually vote in a given election.

watchdog role The accepted responsibility of the media to protect the public from deceitful, careless, incompetent, and corrupt officials by standing ready to expose any official who violates accepted legal, ethical, or performance standards. (See also **common-carrier role; public representative role; signaler role.**)

Whig theory A theory that prevailed in the nineteenth century and held that the presidency was a limited or restrained office whose occupant was confined to expressly granted constitutional authority. (See also **stewardship theory.**)

whistle-blowing An internal check on the bureaucracy whereby individual bureaucrats report instances of mismanagement that they observe.

writ of certiorari Permission granted by a higher court to allow a losing party in a legal case to bring the case before it for a ruling; when such a writ is requested of the U.S. Supreme Court, four of the Court's nine justices must agree to accept the case before it is granted certiorari.

CREDITS

TEXT

Chapter 1 p. 16, Table 1.1: From James Davison Hunter and Carol Bowman, **Survey of American Political Culture,** 1996. Reprinted by permission of Gallup Polls, Inc.; p. 25, Table 1.2: From Thomas E. Patterson, **The American Democracy,** 6/e. Copyright © The McGraw-Hill Companies, Inc. Reproduced by permission of The McGraw-Hill Companies, Inc.; p. 29, Figure 1.4: From Thomas E. Patterson, **The American Democracy,** 6/e. Copyright © The McGraw-Hill Companies, Inc. Reproduced by permission of The McGraw-Hill Companies, Inc.

Chapter 2 p. 49, Box: From Thomas E. Patterson, **The American Democracy,** 6/e. Copyright © The McGraw-Hill Companies, Inc. Reproduced by permission of The McGraw-Hill Companies, Inc.; p. 62, Box: From Thomas E. Patterson, **The American Democracy,** 6/e. Copyright © The McGraw-Hill Companies, Inc. Reproduced by permission of The McGraw-Hill Companies, Inc.

Chapter 3 p. 71, Box: From Thomas E. Patterson, **The American Democracy,** 6/e. Copyright © The McGraw-Hill Companies, Inc. Reproduced by permission of The McGraw-Hill Companies, Inc.

Chapter 5 p. 157, Box: From Thomas E. Patterson, **The American Democracy,** 6/e. Copyright © The McGraw-Hill Companies, Inc. Reproduced by permission of The McGraw-Hill Companies, Inc.

Chapter 6 p. 185, Figure 6.2: From Gallup Poll, December 2001. Used by permission of Gallup Inc.; p. 187, Box: From Thomas E. Patterson, **The American Democracy,** 6/e. Copyright © The McGraw-Hill Companies, Inc. Reproduced by permission of The McGraw-Hill Companies, Inc.; p. 194, Fig. 6.4: From Gallup Poll, September 21-22, 2001. Used by permission of Gallup Inc.

Chapter 7 p. 203, Table 7.1: From James Davison Hunter and Carol Bowman, **Survey of American Political Culture,** 1996. Reprinted by permission of Gallup Polls, Inc.; p. 226, Box: From Thomas E. Patterson, **The American Democracy,** 6/e. Copyright © The McGraw-Hill Companies, Inc. Reproduced by permission of The McGraw-Hill Companies, Inc.

Chapter 8 p. 234, Fig. 8.1: From Thomas E. Patterson, **The American Democracy,** 6/e. Copyright © The McGraw-Hill Companies, Inc. Reproduced by permission of The McGraw-Hill Companies, Inc.; p. 259, Box: From Thomas E. Patterson, **The American Democracy,** 6/e. Copyright © The McGraw-Hill Companies, Inc. Reproduced by permission of The McGraw-Hill Companies, Inc.; p. 264, Box: From Thomas E. Patterson, **The American Democracy,** 6/e. Copyright © The McGraw-Hill Companies, Inc. Reproduced by permission of The McGraw-Hill Companies, Inc.; p. 292, Box: From Thomas E. Patterson, **The American Democracy,** 6/e. Copyright © The McGraw-Hill Companies, Inc. Reproduced by permission of The McGraw-Hill Companies, Inc.; p. 295, Box: From Thomas E. Patterson, **The American Democracy,** 6/e. Copyright © The McGraw-Hill Companies, Inc. Reproduced by permission of The McGraw-Hill Companies, Inc.

C

Chapter 9 p. 306, Box: From Thomas E. Patterson, **The American Democracy,** 6/e. Copyright © The McGraw-Hill Companies, Inc. Reproduced by permission of The McGraw-Hill Companies, Inc.; p. 310, Box: From Thomas E. Patterson, **The American Democracy,** 6/e. Copyright © The McGraw-Hill Companies, Inc. Reproduced by permission of The McGraw-Hill Companies, Inc.

Chapter 11 p. 335, Box: From Thomas E. Patterson, **The American Democracy,** 6/e. Copyright © The McGraw-Hill Companies, Inc. Reproduced by permission of The McGraw-Hill Companies, Inc.; p. 337, Table 11.1: From Thomas E. Patterson, **The American Democracy,** 6/e. Copyright © The McGraw-Hill Companies, Inc. Reproduced by permission of The McGraw-Hill Companies, Inc.; p. 355, Box: From Thomas E. Patterson, **The American Democracy,** 6/e. Copyright © The McGraw-Hill Companies, Inc. Reproduced by permission of The McGraw-Hill Companies, Inc.

Chapter 12 p. 370, Box: From Thomas E. Patterson, **The American Democracy,** 6/e. Copyright © The McGraw-Hill Companies, Inc. Reproduced by permission of The McGraw-Hill Companies, Inc.; p. 379, Table 12.2: From Thomas E. Patterson, **The American Democracy,** 6/e. Copyright © The McGraw-Hill Companies, Inc. Reproduced by permission of The McGraw-Hill Companies, Inc.

Chapter 13 p. 425, Fig. 13.3: From Thomas E. Patterson, **The American Democracy,** 6/e. Copyright © The McGraw-Hill Companies, Inc. Reproduced by permission of The McGraw-Hill Companies, Inc.; p. 426, Box: From Thomas E. Patterson, **The American Democracy,** 6/e. Copyright © The McGraw-Hill Companies, Inc. Reproduced by permission of The McGraw-Hill Companies, Inc.; p. 432, Table 13.3: From Thomas E. Patterson, **The American Democracy,** 6/e. Copyright © The McGraw-Hill Companies, Inc. Reproduced by permission of The McGraw-Hill Companies, Inc.

Chapter 15 p. 479, Box: From Thomas E. Patterson, **The American Democracy,** 6/e. Copyright © The McGraw-Hill Companies, Inc. Reproduced by permission of The McGraw-Hill Companies, Inc.; p. 481, Box: From Thomas E. Patterson, **The American Democracy,** 6/e. Copyright © The McGraw-Hill Companies, Inc. Reproduced by permission of The McGraw-Hill Companies, Inc.; p. 492, Figure 15.2: From Thomas E. Patterson, **The American Democracy,** 6/e. Copyright © The McGraw-Hill Companies, Inc. Reproduced by permission of The McGraw-Hill Companies.

Chapter 16 p. 527, Box: From Thomas E. Patterson, **The American Democracy,** 6/e. Copyright © The McGraw-Hill Companies, Inc. Reproduced by permission of The McGraw-Hill Companies, Inc.; p. 528, Figure 16-3: From Thomas E. Patterson, **The American Democracy,** 6/e. Copyright © The McGraw-Hill Companies, Inc. Reproduced by permission of The McGraw-Hill Companies.

Chapter 17 p. 545, Figure 17-1: From Gallup survey, November 27, 2001. Used by permission of Gallup Inc.; p. 567, Box: From Thomas E. Patterson, **The American Democracy,** 6/e. Copyright © The McGraw-Hill Companies, Inc. Reproduced by permission of The McGraw-Hill Companies, Inc.

PHOTO

Chapter 1 p. 2, © AP/Wide World Photos; p. 4, © Joseph Sohm/Stock Boston; p. 7, Library of Congress, Prints and Photographs Division (LC-USZC4-2474); p. 14, © Newshouse News Services; p. 18, © Peter Beck/CORBIS; p. 23, © Najlah Feany/SABA; p. 28, © Bob Daemmrich/The Image Works.

Chapter 2 p. 35, © Jim Wells/Archive Photos; p. 39, © The Granger Collection; p. 42, © The Granger Collection; p. 46, Library of Congress, Prints and Photographs Division (LC-USZ62-13004); p. 59, Architect of the Capitol.

Chapter 3 p. 71, © The Granger Collection; p. 79, Library of Congress, Prints and Photographs Division (LC-USZ62-54940); p. 81, "Home Sweet Home" by Winslow Homer/Christie's Images; p. 83, Library of Congress; p. 94, © AP/Wide World Photos.
Chapter 4 p. 104, © David Paul Morris/Getty Images: p. 107, © AP/Wide World Photos; p. 114, © Bonnie Kamin/PhotoEdit; p. 115, © AP/Wide World Photos; p. 125, © John Cadge/Getty Images; p. 130, © Paul Conklin/PhotoEdit.
Chapter 5 p. 140, © Charles Moore/Black Star; p. 107, Library of Congress, Prints and Photographs Division, US News and World Report Division (LC-USZ62-47-8171); p. 147, © Peter Bryon/PhotoEdit; p. 150, © AP/Wide World Photos; p. 153, © Frank Siteman/Stock Boston/PictureQuest; p. 156, © Ann States/CORBIS/SABA; p. 164, © Kim Kulish/SABA.
Chapter 6 p. 174, Department of Defense, photo by Petty Officer First Class Greg Messier US Navy; p. 182, © Charles Gupton/CORBIS Stock Market; p. 186, © Paul Conklin/PhotoEdit; p. 191, © Charles E. Rotkin/CORBIS; p.197, © Charles Gupton/CORBIS.
Chapter 7 p. 204, © Culver Pictures; p. 211, © Jonathan Nourok/Getty Images; p. 218, © Paul Warner/AP Wide World Photos; p. 219, © Michael Newman/PhotoEdit; p. 222, © David Young Wolff/PhotoEdit; p. 224, © Steve Rubin/The Image Works.
Chapter 8 p. 235, Library of Congress, Prints and Photograph Divisions (LC-USZ62-1171201); p. 238, © Bettmann/CORBIS; p. 248, © AFP/CORBIS; p. 254, Republican National Committee; p. 261, © AP/Wide World Photos.
Chapter 9 p. 271, Courtesy of AARP; p. 277, © Reuters/Getty Images; p. 280, © Wally McNamee/CORBIS; p. 283, © Tom Mcarty/PhotoEdit; p. 289, © Greg Smith/CORBIS; p. 294, © Davis Barber/PhotoEdit.
Chapter 10 p. 301, © AP/Wide World Photos; p. 308, US Senate; p. 316, © AP Photo/Gino Domenico; p. 320, © Jeff Greenberg/PhotoEdit.
Chapter 11 p. 331, © AP/Wide World Photos; p. 336, © Vanessa Vick/PhotoResearchers; p. 352, © AP/Wide World Photos; p. 358, © US Senate/AP Wide World Photos.
Chapter 12 p. 367, © AP/Wide World Photos; p. 372, © James P. Blair/Getty Images; p. 383, © UPI/Corbis/Bettmann; p. 396, Library of Congress, Prints and Photograph Divisions (LC-USZ62-130371); p. 400, © AP/Wide World Photos.
Chapter 13 p. 406, © AP/Wide World Photos; p. 415, © Bob Daemmrich/Stock Boston; p. 424, © Don Perdue; p. 428, © Wally McNamee/Woordfin Camp and Associates. p. 431, © Mark Mackowiak US Coast Guard.
Chapter 14 p. 439, © AP/Wide World Photos; p. 439, © AP/Wide World Photos; p. 450, © Ken Heinen/AP Wide World Photos; p. 457, © Corbis; p. 463, © Bruce Flynn; p. 466, © AP/Wide World Photos.
Chapter 15 p. 473, © AP/Wide World Photos; p. 484, © PhotoDisc/Getty Images; p. 486, © Damin Dovarganes/AP Wide World Photos; p. 490, © Hulton -Deutsch CORBIS Collection; p. 502, © Karin Cooper/Getty Images.
Chapter 16 p. 514, © Stepphen-Jaffe/Reuters/Archive; p. 519, Library of Congress, Prints and Photographs Division, (LC-USZ62 117121); p. 522, © Bob Daemmrich/The Image Works; p. 524, © Mary Steinbacker/PhotoEdit; p. 530, © Bob Daemmrich/The Image Works.
Chapter 17 p. 539, © AP/Wide World Photos; p. 541, © Michael Barson Collection/Past Perfect; p. 549, © AP/Wide World Photos; p. 555, Staff Sgt. Jeremy T. Lock, US Air Force; p. 560, © Wolfgang Kaehler; p. 564, © Craig J. Brown/Getty.

INDEX